Public Children Law

A Case Law Compendium

Public Children Law
A Case Law Compendium

William Seagrim

LLB (Hons), Barrister, of Gray's Inn,
of 9 Park Place Chambers,
and of the Wales and Chester Circuit,
Senior Lecturer, Swansea University

Bloomsbury Professional

LONDON • DUBLIN • EDINBURGH • NEW YORK • NEW DELHI • SYDNEY

BLOOMSBURY PROFESSIONAL
Bloomsbury Publishing Plc

50 Bedford Square, London, WC1B 3DP, UK
1385 Broadway, New York, NY 10018, USA
29 Earlsfort Terrace, Dublin 2, Ireland

First published in Great Britain 2022

British Library Cataloguing-in-Publication Data

A catalogue record for this book is available from the British Library.

ISBN: PB: 978-1-52651-870-5
Epub: 978-1-52651-871-2
Epdf: 978-1-52651-872-9

Typeset by Evolution Design & Digital Ltd (Kent)

Preface

> 'In a free society, it is a serious thing indeed for the state compulsorily to remove a child from his family of birth. Interference with the right to respect for family life, protected by art 8 of the European Convention for the Protection of Human Rights and Fundamental Freedoms 1950 (as set out in Pt I of Sch 1 to the Human Rights Act 1998) (the Convention), can only be justified by a pressing social need. Yet it is also a serious thing for the state to fail to safeguard its children from the neglect and ill-treatment which they may suffer in their own homes. This may even amount to a violation of their right not to be subjected to inhuman or degrading treatment, protected by art 3 of the Convention. How then is the law to protect the family from unwarranted intrusion while at the same time protecting children from harm?'[1]

Lady Hale SCJ

Public children law proceedings are of the utmost importance to those involved. Within a society that simultaneously safeguards the welfare of children and tolerates a diverse standard of parenting, care cases require anxious scrutiny. They involve heavy burdens and high stakes. Compulsory state interference with the upbringing of children inevitably proliferates a wealth of case law. The aim of this text is to create a comprehensive compendium of cases in the field of public children law. It therefore concentrates exclusively on case law.

Public Children Law: A Case Law Compendium presents principles and guidance from cases on an issue-by-issue basis. Subheadings are used for each issue. They are organised to be intuitive. Their arrangement inevitably involves an element of subjectivity on the part of the author. The objective is for the compendium to be navigable by those subheadings (or by the Contents, Chapter Contents, Table of Cases or Index). Under each subheading the most useful case is referenced. More than one case may be presented on an issue. If different principles or guidance arise from one case it may appear in multiple sections of the *Compendium*.

The critical application of cases referenced within the *Compendium* depends on numerous factors. They are well known. Three are highlighted. First, the principle of stare decisis operates in the hierarchical structure of the courts of England and Wales[2]. Second, within the principle of precedent, cases are only binding

1 *Re J (children) (non-accidental injury: past possible perpetrator in new family)* [2013] UKSC 9, [2013] 2 FCR 149, [1] (Lady Hale).

2 D Kelly, *Slapper and Kelly's The English Legal System* (19th edn, Routledge 2020) 147; J Bell, 'Sources of Law' in A Burrows (ed), *English Private Law* (2nd edn, OUP 2007) 29–30.

authority for what they actually decide[3]. Third, judicial dicta may become highly persuasive; sometimes as important as ratio[4]. To borrow from Sir James Munby, 'there are obiter dicta and obiter dicta'[5]. Relevant considerations include any case's material facts; the level of court and / or judiciary; and the context of any judicial pronouncement, such as whether full argument was heard, the presence or absence of full judicial reasoning and the judge's intentions when making any statement. Of primary importance to the application of case law is the ability to locate it. It is hoped that the *Compendium* assists practitioners in these endeavours.

In the *Compendium*, cases are referenced as follows:

1. A case's name appears as reported in the Family Court Reports (FCR). If unreported therein, the name appears as in any official transcript;
2. Neutral citation is provided for all judgments determined following its implementation. Only in the absence of neutral citation is level of court indicated. If needed, the following terms are used: '(FD)' for Family Division; '(QBD)' for Queen's Bench Division; '(CA)' for Court of Appeal; '(HL)' for House of Lords; '(ECrtHR)' for European Court of Human Rights; and '(CJEU)' for Court of Justice of the European Union;
3. One report citation is always provided, unless unreported. FCR citation is preferred. In the online edition of the *Compendium* a hyperlink to any FCR report is provided.
4. If unreported in the FCR, another series of law reporting is cited. This is chosen in accordance with the Practice Direction: Citation of Authorities (2012)[6], ie therefore preferring the Official Law Reports (AC, Fam, QB, Ch, etc), then the Weekly Law Reports (WLR) or All England Law Reports (All ER), and finally other specialist reports, eg the Family Law Reports (FLR) or European Human Rights Reports (EHRR);
5. The relevant paragraph(s) from any judgment are identified using square brackets. In the absence of paragraph numbers, page numbers from any law report are identified unbracketed;
6. Judicial identity is indicated showing judicial level at the time of the decision. The term 'as (s)he then was' is not used;

3 *Quinn v Leatham* [1901] AC 495 (HL), 506 (Earl of Halsbury LC).

4 R Cross and JW Harris, *Precedent in English Law* (4th edn, Clarendon Press 1991) 77. The exceptional treatment of obiter as strictly binding is illustrated by the criminal case of *R v Barton and another* [2020] EWCA Crim 575, [2020] 3 WLR 1333, [1], [104]–[105] (Lord Burnett CJ). The Lord Chief Justice confirmed that the dictum of Lord Hughes in the civil case of *Ivey v Genting Casinos (UK) Ltd (trading as Crockfords Club)* [2017] UKSC 67, [2018] AC 391 had changed the 35 year old approach to dishonesty in criminal law established by the Court of Appeal (Criminal Division) in *R v Ghosh* [1982] QB 1053, modifying the ordinary rules of precedent to a limited extent.

5 *Re X (a child) (no 2)* [2021] EWHC 65 (Fam), [2021] 4 WLR 11, [59]–[60] (Sir James Munby, sitting as a judge of the High Court).

6 [2012] 1 WLR 780, [6]–[9] (Lord Judge CJ).

7. If a referenced decision has a subsequent appellate history it is identified using the term '*affd*' (for affirmed) or '*revd*' (for reversed) and the appellate decision is then referenced. Any appealed decision will only be referenced if the quoted part of its reasoning is considered to have survived the appeal;

8. The identified section is then quoted. Quotations are taken from either the FCR report or a case's official transcript. For reasons of space, quotation is sometimes further limited to the most important aspect of the identified section. If so, the words '*quotation limited to*' are used, identifying the limited quotation;

9. '…' appears between paragraphs in order to signify the omission of paragraphs. '…' appears within a paragraph to signify the omission of part of a paragraph;

10. If the term 'See Chapter' appears, the reader is directed to another section of the *Compendium*; and

11. If the term 'See also' appears, another noteworthy case will be identified, absent quotation. The purpose of referencing additional cases is identified as one of the following:
    a. 'considering [a referenced case]';
    b. 'addressing the same point';
    c. 'addressing a related point' (the related point will be identified in brackets); or
    d. 'providing an overview of the law on this point / a related point'.

    If the additional decision has a noteworthy context such is identified in brackets.

In the printed edition of the *Compendium* the law is up to date as at 9 November 2021. Any mistakes or omissions are entirely those of the author.

William Seagrim
9 November 2021

Acknowledgments

I would like to express my gratitude to Bloomsbury Publishing, especially to Mrs Kiran Goss, publisher at Bloomsbury Professional. I am indebted to numerous fellow members of 9 Park Place Chambers. I am always grateful to Mr Owen Thomas QC and Mr Owen Prys Lewis for their support. For their consideration of draft chapters, Miss Kate Hughes QC, Mr Paul Hopkins QC, Mr Owen Thomas QC, Mr Matthew Barry, Miss Cadi Dewi, Mr David Gareth Evans, and Mr James Lewis. I wish to thank Ms Alison Perry and Professor Ruth Costigan of Swansea University for inspiring me as a law student and for supporting me as a colleague. Finally, my thanks go to my loved ones, especially to my partner, Cadi.

Contents

Abbreviations

This list contains abbreviations used within Public Children Law: A Case Law Compendium. Abbreviations are explained in a footnote when first used in any chapter.

ABE	Achieving Best Evidence in Criminal Proceedings: Guidance on interviewing victims and witnesses, and guidance on using special measures (2011) Ministry of Justice
ACA 2002	Adoption and Children Act 2002
ADM	Agency decision maker
BIIa	Council Regulation (EC) No 2201/2003 Matrimonial and parental judgments: jurisdiction, recognition and enforcement of matrimonial and parental judgments
CMH	Case management hearing
DoL	Deprivation of liberty
ECHR	Convention for the Protection of Human Rights and Fundamental Freedoms (1950) CETS 5
EPO	Emergency protection order
FGM	Female genital mutilation
FII	Fabricated or induced illness
FPR	Family Procedure Rules 2010, SI 2010/2955
Hague Convention	1980 Convention on the Civil Aspects of International Child Abduction (1980) HCCH 28
HRA	Human Rights Act 1998
ICO	Interim care order
ISO	Interim supervision order
LA	Local authority
LAA	Legal Aid Agency
LIP	Litigants in person
Oxfordshire	*A County Council v DP and others* [2005] EWHC 1593 (Fam), [2005] 2 FLR 1031
PR	Parental responsibility
Re B-S	*Re B-S (children) (adoption: leave to oppose)* [2013] EWCA Civ 1146, [2013] 3 FCR 481
Re L-A	*Re L-A (children)* [2009] EWCA Civ 822, [2010] 1 FLR 80
Re W	*Re W (children) (abuse: oral evidence)* [2010] UKSC 12, [2010] 1 FCR 615
s 1	Children Act 1989, s 1
s 10(9)	Children Act 1989, s 10(9)
s 20	Children Act 1989, s 20, including references to s 20(11)
s 25	Children Act 1989, s 25, including references to s 25(1)

s 31	Children Act 1989, s 31
s 33	Children Act 1989, s 33
s 34	Children Act 1989, s 34, including references to s 34(4)
s 38	Children Act 1989, s 38, including references to s 38(6), (7A) and (7B)
s 37	Children Act 1989, s 37
s 47	Children Act 1989, s 47
s 76	Social Services and Well-being (Wales) Act 2014, s 76
SGO	Special guardianship order
Storck	*Storck v Germany* (61603/00) (ECrtHR), (2006) 43 EHRR 6
Vienna Convention	Vienna Convention on Consular Relations (1963) 596 UNTS 261
UNCRC	United Nations Convention on the Rights of the Child (1989) 1577 UNTS 3
1996 Convention	1996 Convention on Jurisdiction, Applicable Law, Recognition, Enforcement and Co-operation in Respect of Parental Responsibility and Measures for the Protection of Children (1996) HCCH 34

Table of Statutes

[All references are to heading number]

Table of Statutory Instruments

[All references are to heading number]

Table of Other Material

[All references are to heading number]

Table of Cases

[All references are to heading number]

B

C

D

E

H

I

J

M

N

O

P

Q

R

S

T

CHAPTER 1

s 20/s 76 accommodation

Chapter contents

CHAPTER 1

s 20/s 76 Accommodation

1.1 S 20[1]/S 76[2] ACCOMMODATION:[3] VOLUNTARY NATURE

1.1.1 s 20/s 76 accommodation: voluntary nature: leading guidance

Williams and another v London Borough of Hackney [2018] UKSC 37, [2019] AC 421, [21], [38]–[49] (Lady Hale P)

21. Section 20 contains no express requirement of parental consent to a child being accommodated. Indeed, it envisages circumstances in which no such consent could be obtained, such as where the child is abandoned or lost or appears to have no person with parental responsibility for him. However, the judge had before him several authorities which not only held that informed consent to section 20 accommodation was required but also gave detailed guidance about how it should be obtained.

...

1 Children Act 1989 (CA 1989), s 20 (applicable in England).

2 Social Services and Well-being (Wales) Act 2014 (SSW(W)A 2014), s 76. In 2016, the CA 1989, s 20 was repealed in Wales and replaced by the SSW(W)A 2014, s 76. The Welsh statute effectively restates the duty under the CA 1989, s 20, albeit with several slight differences. It is submitted that jurisprudence concerning the CA 1989, s 20 and SSW(W)A 2014, s 76 should be applicable to each other except in the unlikely event that any dissimilarity is material. The differences appear to include the following. First, the CA 1989, s 20(6) requires, so far as practicable and consistent with the child's welfare, the child's wishes and feelings to be ascertained and provided due consideration (having regard to their age and understanding). This is not directly replicated within the SSW(W)A 2014, s 76. An effectively similar but overarching duty acts on those exercising functions under the SSW(W)A 2014, under s 6(1) and (2) (expressed in similar terms). Section 7(2) of the SSW(W)A 2014 requires those exercising functions under the SSW(W)A 2014 in respect of children to have due regard to Part I of the United Nations Convention on the Rights of the Child (1989) 1577 UNTS 3 (UNCRC), thereby including UNCRC, Art 12 (children's rights to express views and for those to be provide due weight). See also the related and specific duty arising regarding looked after children under the SSW(W)A 2014, s 78(3) (local authorities shall have regard to the views, wishes and feelings of any person they consider relevant) (similar to the duty under the CA 1989, s 22(4)). Secondly, the CA 1989, s 20(4) does not have a corresponding Welsh provision. Thirdly, CA 1989, s 20(9)(a), which limits parental objection to accommodation, refers to a 'lives with' child arrangements order, whereas the SSW(W)A 2014, s 76(6)(a) refers more widely (and possibly problematically) to a 'child arrangements order'.

3 It is submitted that any authorities pre-dating March 2021 may need reading in light of the President's Public Law Working Group report *Recommendations to achieve best practice in the child protection and family justice systems* (March 2021), which includes *Best practice guidance: Section 20/section 76 accommodation*. The report is not law but was endorsed by the President of the Family Division, Sir Andrew McFarlane. Available at www.judiciary.uk/publications/message-from-the-president-of-the-family-division-publication-of-the-presidents-public-law-working-group-report/, accessed 18 December 2021.

38. The starting point must be parental responsibility. All mothers and (now) most fathers have it automatically. It encompasses all the rights of a parent. The most obvious and fundamental of these is the right to look after and bring up one's own children. A person with parental responsibility may arrange, of his or her own accord, for some or all of his or her parental responsibility to be met by others acting on his or her behalf (section 2(9), para 18 above) and the exercise of parental responsibility may be circumscribed by court order. But a local authority cannot interfere with a person's exercise of their parental responsibility, against their will, unless they have first obtained a court order. Accordingly, no local authority have the right or the power to remove a child from a parent who is looking after the child and wants to go on doing so without a court order. Only the police can do that under section 46 of the 1989 Act. It follows that the decision in *R (G) v Nottingham City Council* (paras 22–23 above) was absolutely right. The mother had just given birth. She wanted to look after her baby. The local authority had no power to prevent her and neither did the hospital. Helpless submission to asserted power does not amount to a delegation of parental responsibility or its exercise.

39. Secondly, it may be confusing to talk of parental 'consent' to the removal (or accommodation) of her child. If a parent does agree to this, she is simply delegating the exercise of her parental responsibility for the time being to the local authority. Any such delegation must be real and voluntary. Otherwise the local authority have no power to interfere with her parental responsibility by taking the child away. At the very least, therefore, it should not occur in the sort of circumstances in which 'consent' was obtained in *Coventry City Council v C, B, CA and CH* (para 24 above); nor should any impression be given that the parent has no choice in the matter, as happened in *In re W (Parental Agreement with Local Authority)* (para 26 above). Obviously, the best way to avoid this is by informing the parent fully of her rights under section 20, but a delegation can be 'real and voluntary' without being fully 'informed'.

40. Thirdly, removing a child from the care of a parent is very different from stepping into the breach when a parent is not looking after the child. That is what happened in *In re AS, London Borough of Brent v MS, RS and AS* (para 30 above) and section 20 is designed to give the local authority the power, and indeed the duty, to do that. The active consent or delegation of a parent who is not in fact looking after or offering to look after the child is not required, any more than it is when there is no-one with parental responsibility or the child is abandoned or lost. But the local authority's duty and power are subject to the later provisions of the section, in particular, to subsections (7) to (11). In such cases, as a matter of good practice, local authorities should give parents clear information about what they have done and what the parents' rights are. This should include, not only their rights under subsections (7) and (8), but also their rights under other provisions of the 1989 Act, such as that in paragraph 15 of Schedule 2 to know the whereabouts of their child. Parents should also

be informed of the local authority's own responsibilities. In appropriate cases, this may include information about the local authority's power (and duty) to bring proceedings if they have reasonable grounds to believe that the child is at risk of significant harm if they do not.

41. Fourthly, parents may ask the local authority to accommodate a child, as part of the services they provide for children in need. If the circumstances fall within section 20(1), there is a duty to accommodate the child. If they fall within section 20(4), there is power to do so. Once again, this operates as a delegation of the exercise of parental responsibility for the time being. The section does not expressly require that such delegation be with 'informed' consent, but the duty and the power are subject to subsections (7) to (11). Once again, as a matter of good practice, parents should be given clear information about their rights and the local authority's responsibilities.

42. Fifthly, subsection (7) operates as a restriction on the powers and duties of the local authority under subsections (1) to (5). The authority cannot accommodate a child if a parent with parental responsibility who is willing and able either to accommodate the child herself or to arrange for someone else to do so objects to the local authority doing so. It says nothing about the suitability of the parent or of the accommodation which the parent wishes to arrange. As Black LJ explained in *In re B (Looked after Child)* [2013] EWCA Civ 964; [2014] 1 FLR 277, para 34:

> 'I raised the question during the appeal hearing as to whether a parent who is inadequate is in fact "willing and able to … provide accommodation" but it did not excite much argument. That is explained, I think, by there being a common understanding that where parents in fact object to a local authority providing accommodation, a local authority will have to have recourse to care proceedings if they seek to accommodate a child and any debate as to whether the parents are "able" to provide accommodation is to be had in that context, not in the context of section 20.'

43. I agree. The words interpolated by amendment into subsection (7) (see para 19 above) serve a different purpose. Thus, for example, a father who is separated from the mother and is not offering the child a home or offering to arrange an alternative, cannot object to the local authority accommodating the child at the mother's request; or, for example, the mothers in *In re AS* (para 30 above) or in *Medway Council v M and T* (para 31 above) who were compulsorily detained in hospital could not object to the local authority accommodating the child unless they were able to arrange alternative accommodation. But that is all that subsection (7) does. It means that the local authority have neither the power nor the duty to accommodate the child if a parent with parental responsibility proposes to accommodate the child herself or to arrange for someone else to do so. If the local authority consider the proposed arrangements, not merely unsuitable, but likely to cause the child significant harm, they should apply for an emergency protection order.

44. Sixthly, subsection (8) makes it absolutely clear that a parent with parental responsibility may remove the child from accommodation provided or arranged by a local authority at any time. There is no need to give notice, in writing or otherwise. The only caveat, as Munby J said in *R (G) v Nottingham City Council* (para 22 above), is the right of anyone to take necessary steps to protect a person, including a child, from being physically harmed by another: for example, if a parent turned up drunk demanding to drive the child home. In such circumstances the people caring for the child would have the power (under section 3(5) of the 1989 Act) to do what is reasonable in all the circumstances for the purpose of safeguarding or promoting the child's welfare (see para 18 above).

45. It follows that, if a parent unequivocally requires the return of the child, the local authority have neither the power nor the duty to continue to accommodate the child and must either return the child in accordance with that requirement or obtain the power to continue to look after the child, either by way of police protection or an emergency protection order. These can, of course, only be obtained if there is reasonable cause to believe that the child will otherwise suffer significant harm. Thus, in *Herefordshire Council v AB and CD* (para 33 above), the Council should have acted upon the mother's formal withdrawal of her consent to CD's being accommodated – which would be better framed in terms of a request for the immediate (or timed) return of the child – rather than advising her to seek legal advice.

46. A parent whose unequivocal request for the immediate (or timed) return of an accommodated child is refused could take a variety of steps to enforce her rights. The simplest step would be to remove the child. At common law there were torts of depriving a parent of the services of a child and harbouring a child, but these were abolished by section 5 of the Law Reform (Miscellaneous Provisions) Act 1970 (and see *F v Wirral Metropolitan Borough Council* [1991] Fam 69). The traditional method of securing the release of a child through habeas corpus proceedings remains, subject of course to any court orders to the contrary. It is also an offence for a person, without lawful authority or excuse, to take or detain a child under the age of 16 so as to remove him from the lawful control of any person having lawful control of the child or so as to keep him out of the lawful control of any person entitled to lawful control of the child: Child Abduction Act 1984, section 2. But far preferable to any of these is for the local authority promptly to honour an unequivocal request from the parent for the child's immediate (or timed) return.

47. Seventhly, the right to object in subsection (7) and the right to remove in subsection (8) are qualified by subsections (9) and (10). These cater for court orders which have determined with whom a child is to live. Thus if there is a child arrangements order under section 8 of the 1989 Act or an order under the inherent jurisdiction of the High Court, providing for the child to live with a particular person or persons, or if there is a special guardianship order, then that parent cannot object or remove the child if the person or persons with whom the child is to live, or the special

guardian or guardians, agree to the child being accommodated. These orders restrict that parents' exercise of parental responsibility; but without such an order it is not restricted.

48. Eighthly, section 20 makes special provision for children who have reached 16. In addition to the general duty in subsection (1), there is a duty in subsection (3) to provide accommodation for any child in need who has reached 16 and whose welfare will be seriously prejudiced if this is not done; and in addition to the general power in subsection (4), there is power in subsection (5) to accommodate anyone who has reached 16 but is under 21 in a community home which caters for over 16-year-olds. Subsection (11) makes it clear that once an accommodated child reaches 16, a parent has no right to object or to remove the child if she is willing to be accommodated by the local authority.

49. Finally, there is nothing in section 20 to place a limit on the length of time for which a child may be accommodated. However, local authorities have a variety of duties towards the children whom they are accommodating. Their general duties towards looked after children in section 22 of the 1989 Act include a duty to safeguard and promote their welfare, in consultation with both the children and their parents. This is reinforced by the Care Planning, Placement and Case Review (England) Regulations 2010, SI 2010/959, which require local authorities to assess a child's 'needs for services to achieve or maintain a reasonable standard of health or development' and prepare a care plan for her, to be agreed with the parents if practicable (regulation 4(1), (4)). The care plan has to record, inter alia, the arrangements made to meet the child's needs and the long term plan for her upbringing ('the plan for permanence') (regulation 5(a) and (b)).

1.1.2 s 20/s 76 accommodation: voluntary nature: good practice

Coventry City Council v C and others [2012] EWHC 2190 (Fam), [2013] 1 FCR 54, [45]–[46] (Hedley J)

[45] In the light of all this can the court offer any guidance to social workers in respect of obtaining consent under s 20 from a parent to the removal of a child immediately or soon after birth? The court can but must be astute to avoid excessive prescription as no such guidance can prevail against human capacity to produce wholly unforeseen situations.

[46] The following can perhaps be offered as the more important aspects—

(i) Every parent has the right, if capacitous, to exercise their parental responsibility to consent under s 20 to have their child accommodated by the local authority and every local authority has power under s 20(4) so to accommodate provided that it is consistent with the welfare of the child.

(ii) Every social worker obtaining such a consent is under a personal duty (the outcome of which may not be dictated to them by others) to be satisfied that the person giving the consent does not lack the capacity to do so.

(iii) In taking any such consent the social worker must actively address the issue of capacity and take into account all the circumstances prevailing at the time and consider the questions raised by s 3 of the 2005 Act, and in particular the mother's capacity at that time to use and weigh all the relevant information.

(iv) If the social worker has doubts about capacity no further attempt should be made to obtain consent on that occasion and advice should be sought from the social work team leader or management.

(v) If the social worker is satisfied that the person whose consent is sought does not lack capacity, the social worker must be satisfied that the consent is fully informed:

   (a) Does the parent fully understand the consequences of giving such a consent?

   (b) Does the parent fully appreciate the range of choice available and the consequences of refusal as well as giving consent?

   (c) Is the parent in possession of all the facts and issues material to the giving of consent?

(vi) If not satisfied that the answers to (a)–(c) above are all 'yes', no further attempt should be made to obtain consent on that occasion and advice should be sought as above and the social work team should further consider taking legal advice if thought necessary.

(vii) If the social worker is satisfied that the consent is fully informed then it is necessary to be further satisfied that the giving of such consent and the subsequent removal is both fair and proportionate.

(viii) In considering that it may be necessary to ask:

   (a) What is the current physical and psychological state of the parent?

   (b) If they have a solicitor, have they been encouraged to seek legal advice and/or advice from family or friends?

   (c) Is it necessary for the safety of the child for her to be removed at this time?

   (d) Would it be fairer in this case for this matter to be the subject of a court order rather than an agreement?

(ix) If having done all this and, if necessary, having taken further advice (as above and including where necessary legal advice), the social worker then considers that a fully informed consent has been received from a capacitous mother in circumstances where removal is necessary and proportionate, consent may be acted upon.

(x) In the light of the foregoing, local authorities may want to approach with great care the obtaining of s 20 agreements from mothers in the aftermath of birth, especially where there is no immediate danger to the child and where probably no order would be made.

Re N (children) (adoption: jurisdiction) [2015] EWCA Civ 1112, [2016] 1 FCR 217, [170] (Sir James Munby P) *revd Re N (children) (adoption: jurisdiction)* [2016] UKSC 15, [2016] 3 FCR 394

[170] It follows, in my judgment, that for the future good practice requires the following, in addition to proper compliance with the guidance given by Hedley J which I have set out above:

(i) Wherever possible the agreement of a parent to the accommodation of their child under s 20 should be properly recorded in writing and evidenced by the parent's signature.
(ii) The written document should be clear and precise as to its terms, drafted in simple and straightforward language that the particular parent can readily understand.
(iii) The written document should spell out, following the language of s 20(8), that the parent can 'remove the child' from the local authority accommodation 'at any time'.
(iv) The written document should not seek to impose any fetters on the exercise of the parent's right under s 20(8).
(v) Where the parent is not fluent in English, the written document should be translated into the parent's own language and the parent should sign the foreign language text, adding, in the parent's language, words to the effect that 'I have read this document and I agree to its terms'.

See also *London Borough of Hackney v Williams and another* [2017] EWCA Civ 26, [2017] 3 WLR 59, [77] (Sir Brian Leveson P) *affd Williams and another v London Borough of Hackney* [2018] UKSC 37, [2019] AC 421 addressing the same point

See also *R (on the application of G) v Nottingham City Council* [2008] EWHC 400, [2008] 3 FCR 568 (Admin), [53] (Munby J) addressing a related point (it being prudent to record consent in writing, signed), see Chapter 1.1.3 s 20/s 76 accommodation: voluntary nature: absence of objection may not suffice

1.1.3 s 20/s 76 accommodation: voluntary nature: absence of objection may not suffice

R (on the application of G) v Nottingham City Council [2008] EWHC 400 (Admin), [2008] 3 FCR 568, [53]–[55] (Munby J)

[53] I do not wish to be misunderstood. I am not suggesting that consent to the accommodation of a child in accordance with s 20 is required by law to be in writing—though, that said, a prudent local authority would surely always wish to ensure that an alleged parental consent in such a case is properly recorded in writing and evidenced by the parent's signature. Nor am I disputing that there may be cases where a child has in fact, and without parental objection, been accommodated by a local authority for such a period as might entitle a court to infer that the parent had in fact consented.

[54] But the local authority here seemed to be going far beyond this. It seemed to be conflating absence of objection with actual consent—a doctrine which at least in this context is, in my judgment, entirely contrary to principle and which, moreover, contains within it the potential for the most pernicious consequences, not least because there are probably many mothers who believe, quite erroneously, that a local authority has power, without any court order, to do what the local authority did in this case.

[55] To equate helpless acquiescence with consent when a parent is confronted in circumstances such as this with the misuse (or perhaps on another occasion the misrepresentation) of non-existent authority by an agent of the state is, in my judgment, both unprincipled and, indeed, fraught with potential danger.

See also *Coventry City Council v C and others* [2012] EWHC 2190 (Fam), [2013] 1 FCR 54, [25]–[28] (Hedley J) addressing a related point (use of s 20 not being 'compulsion in disguise')

See also *Re W (children)* [2014] EWCA Civ 1065, [2015] 1 FLR 949, [31]–[34] (Sir James Munby P), [40]–[41] (Tomlinson LJ) considering *Coventry City Council v C and others* [2012] EWHC 2190 (Fam), [2013] 1 FCR 54

1.1.4 s 20/s 76 accommodation: voluntary nature: doubts as to capacity

Coventry City Council v C and others [2012] EWHC 2190 (Fam), [2013] 1 FCR 54, [27], [37]–[39], [45]–[46] (Hedley J) quotation limited to [27], [37]–[39]

[27] However, the use of s 20 is not unrestricted and must not be compulsion in disguise. In order for such an agreement to be lawful, the parent must have the requisite capacity to make that agreement. All consents given under s 20 must be considered in the light of ss 1–3 of the Mental Capacity Act 2005 (the 2005 Act).

...

[37] However, and whatever the context, s 20 agreements are not valid unless the parent giving consent has capacity so to do. It is important to note that by s 1(2) of the 2005 Act a person is to be presumed to have capacity unless it is established that he lacks it. Moreover, the effect of s 1(4) is to prevent inferences of incapacity from the making of unwise decisions. Incapacity must be due to an 'impairment of, or disturbance in the functioning of, the mind or brain' (see s 2(1)). Capacity is issue and situation specific. It follows that not only may a person have capacity to make one decision but not another but also may have capacity at one time to make the very decision in respect of which he lacks capacity at another.

[38] That can be seen in the context of this case. The fact that the mother could make decisions about surgery and pain relief does not indicate that she could make decisions about the removal of her child. Again the fact that before the birth or sometime after the birth she could make decisions about removal does not mean she could on the day of birth. This latter factor (the impact of the birth itself) is the basis on which Parliament enacted for example s 52(3) of the 2002 Act in respect of adoption and s 54(7) of the Human Fertilisation Act 2008 in respect of surrogacy.

[39] Capacity is not always an easy judgment to make, and it is usually to be made by the person seeking to rely on the decision so obtained. Sometimes it will be necessary to seek advice from carers and family;

occasionally a formal medical assessment may be required; always it will be necessary to have regard to Ch 4 of the code of practice under the 2005 Act. Assistance is, however, to be found in s 3 of the 2005 Act which provides by sub-s (1) that a person is unable to make a decision if he is unable—

'(a) to understand the information relevant to the decision,
(b) to retain that information,
(c) to use or weigh that information as part of the process of making the decision, or
(d) to communicate his decision …
(4) The information relevant to a decision includes information about the reasonably foreseeable consequence of—
(a) deciding one way or the other, or
(b) failing to make the decision.'

See also Chapter 1.1.2 s 20/s 76 accommodation: voluntary nature: good practice

1.1.5 s 20/s 76 accommodation: voluntary nature: doubts as to capacity: child-parents

Re S (child as parent: adoption: consent) [2017] EWHC 2729 (Fam), [2018] 1 FCR 74, [15]–[16], [62] (Cobb J) *quotation limited to* [62]

[62] By way of summary and conclusion, I distil the following principles from my analysis above:

(i) The test of competence for decision-making of a young person is that set out in the House of Lords decision of *Gillick v West Norfolk and Wisbech Area Health Authority* [1985] 3 WLR 830, [1986] 1 AC 112 (*Gillick*) ('a sufficient understanding and intelligence to enable him or her to understand fully what is proposed'); in this regard, the child should be able to:
  (a) Understand the nature and implications of the decision and the process of implementing that decision;
  (b) Understand the implications of not pursuing the decision;
  (c) Retain the information long enough for the decision-making process to take place;
  (d) Be of sufficient intelligence and maturity to weigh up the information and arrive at a decision;
  (e) Be able to communicate that decision.

(ii) The determination of a child's competence must be decision-specific and child-specific; It is necessary to consider the specific factual context when evaluating competence;

(iii) Just because a child lacks litigation competence in (for example) care or placement order proceedings does not mean that she lacks subject matter competence in relation to consent to s 20 CA 1989 accommodation of her baby, or indeed to the adoption of the baby;

(iv) The assessment of competence must be made on the evidence available;

(v) When considering the issue of *Gillick* competence of a child parent, an important distinction must be drawn between the *determination* of competence to make the decision, and the *exercise* by that young person of their competent decision making;

(vi) The relevant information that a child under 16 would need to be able to understand, retain and weigh up in order to have competency to consent to the s 20 accommodation of a child would be:

  (a) That the child will be staying with someone chosen by the local authority, probably a foster carer;

  (b) That the parent can change her mind about the arrangements, and request the child back from accommodation at any time;

  (c) That the parent will be able to see the child; …

See also *Herefordshire Council v AB, CD; Herefordshire Council v EF, GH* [2018] EWFC 10, [2018] 2 FCR 142, [47] (Keehan J) addressing the same point (providing an example of it being a 'serious omission' not to consider a 14 year old's competence)

1.1.6 s 20/s 76 accommodation: voluntary nature: use with newborns

R (on the application of G) v Nottingham City Council [2008] EWHC 400 (Admin), [2008] 3 FCR 568, [56]–[61] (Munby J)

[56] What the local authority and the NHS trust did to G and K was unlawful absent consent by G. Let it be assumed that G did not object (though her account of these events would, I was told, be very different). As I observed during the hearing, the fact that she did not object does not mean that she consented. Even on the local authority's own case the fact is that G did not consent.

[57] Least of all could it sensibly be said that G was consenting because she did not, as the local authority puts it, 'raise objection' at the point when her baby was actually removed. This happened at 5.10am, following his birth less than three hours before, at 2.11am. The hospital notes record that at 1.10am during labour G had been 'getting distressed' and that at 1.30am she was 'very distressed'. The notes record her later that morning at 11.30am as being 'very tearful and upset at situation with baby'. The idea that this mother in this situation—physically and emotionally weakened and distressed by events—can sensibly be said to have given consent to the removal of her baby verges, in my judgment, on the unreal: consider, for example, the discussion in *Re T (an adult: medical treatment)* [1992] 2 FCR 861, [1992] 4 All ER 649.

[58] I accept that there can of course be cases where a woman is able to give a valid consent to the accommodation of her newly-born baby by the local authority immediately after birth. *Re L (a child) (adoption: disclosure)* [2007] EWHC 1771 (Fam), [2008] 1 FLR 1079 is a recent example, where a woman who had entered a labour ward with a settled intention to

hand over her baby for adoption immediately after birth left the hospital within two hours of her daughter's birth without seeing her and requesting that she be adopted. But the present case is far removed indeed from the rather unusual circumstances in *Re L*.

[59] The contention that G consented to the removal of her baby in the circumstances in which she found herself at 5.10am on 30 January 2008 is, if I may borrow a phrase of Frankfurter J (see *US v Dege* (1960) 364 US 51 at 53, adopted by Oliver J, as he then was, in *Midland Bank Trust Co Ltd v Green (No 3)* [1979] 2 All ER 193 at 219, [1979] Ch 496 at 526), 'unnourished by sense.'

[60] I referred during the course of the hearing on 18 February 2008 to the principle, frequently reiterated by the European Court of Human Rights at Strasbourg (see for example *HL v UK* (2004) 81 BMLR 131, 17 BHRC 418 at para 90, and *Storck v Germany* (2006) 43 EHRR 96, [2005] ECHR 61603/00 at para 75), that although consent may render lawful what would otherwise be an unlawful deprivation of liberty 'the right to liberty is too important in a democratic society for a person to lose the benefit of Convention protection for the single reason that he may have given himself up to be taken into detention.'

[61] Now that, of course, was said with reference to art 5 of the Convention, which protects the right to liberty, whereas I am here concerned with art 8, which protects and enjoins respect for family life, in particular a mother's right not to be separated from her baby without her consent (and her baby's corresponding right not to be separated from his mother without her consent) except in circumstances, permitted by law, where the interests of the child necessitate the intervention of state authorities. But it might be thought that the underlying point is the same, whether what is in issue is the removal of one's liberty or the removal of one's child. Submission in the face of asserted state authority is not the same as consent. In this context, as in that, nothing short of consent will suffice.

See also *Coventry City Council v C and others* [2012] EWHC 2190 (Fam), [2013] 1 FCR 54, [46 (x)] (Hedley J) addressing the same point (in the context of concerns regarding capacity), see Chapter 1.1.2 s 20/s 76 accommodation: voluntary nature: good practice

1.2 S 20/S 76 ACCOMMODATION: OVERALL APPROACH

1.2.1 s 20 /s 76 accommodation: overall approach: judgment about a series of matters

R (on the application of A) v Croydon London Borough Council; R (on the application of M) v Lambeth London Borough Council [2008] EWCA Civ 1445, [2009] 1 FCR 317, [75] (Ward LJ) *revd R (on the application of A) v Croydon London Borough Council; R (on the application of M) v Lambeth London Borough Council* [2009] UKSC 8, [2009] 3 FCR 607

[75] To answer the question whether decisions under s 20 of the 1989 Act should be entrusted to social workers, one must consider the legislative scheme as a whole. Confining myself for a moment to s 20 alone, it is immediately obvious that the decision involves a judgment being formed about a range of facts and matters such as:

(1) Is the applicant a child?
(2) Is the applicant a child in need?
(3) Is he within the local authority's area?
(4) Does he appear to the local authority to require accommodation?
(5) Is that need the result of:
    (a) there being no person who has parental responsibility for him;
    (b) his being lost or having been abandoned; or
    (c) the person who has been caring for him being prevented from providing him with suitable accommodation or care?
(6) What are the child's wishes regarding the provision of accommodation for him?
(7) What consideration (having regard to his age and understanding) is duly to be given to those wishes?
(8) Does any person with parental responsibility who is willing to provide accommodation for him object to the local authority's intervention?
(9) If there is objection, does the person in whose favour a residence order is in force agree to the child being looked after by the local authority?

See also *R (on the application of G) v Southwark London Borough Council* [2009] UKHL 26, [2009] 2 FCR 459, [28] (Baroness Hale) considering *R (on the application of A) v Croydon London Borough Council; R (on the application of M) v Lambeth London Borough Council* [2008] EWCA Civ 1445, [2009] 1 FCR 317

See also *R (on the application of A) v Croydon London Borough Council; R (on the application of M) v Lambeth London Borough Council* [2009] UKSC 8, [2009] 3 FCR 607, [35] (Lady Hale DP) addressing a related point (meeting the criteria is a matter of judgment, not discretion)

1.2.2 s 20/s 76 accommodation: overall approach: 'prevented … from providing him with suitable accommodation or care': wide scope

R (on the application of M) v Hammersmith and Fulham London Borough Council [2008] UKHL 14, [2008] 3 FCR 688, [43] (Baroness Hale)

[43] For what it is worth, it will be obvious from what has gone before that I agree with the broad approach to the interpretation of when a parent is 'prevented' from providing suitable accommodation or care under s 20(1)(c), which was favoured by Michael Burton J in the *Nottinghamshire* case and by Stanley Burnton J at first instance in the *Sutton* case [2007] EWCA 1196 (Admin), [2007] 2 FLR 849, rather than with the narrow approach favoured by Lloyd LJ in this case. This mother may not have been prevented from providing her daughter with any accommodation or care but she was surely prevented from providing her with suitable accommodation or care. …

R (on the application of A) v Lambeth London Borough Council; R (on the application of G) v Barnet London Borough Council; R (on the application of W) v Lambeth London Borough Council [2003] UKHL 57, [2003] 3 FCR 419, [100] (Lord Hope)

[100] The appellants must show, in the second place, that the respondents were under a duty to provide their children with accommodation. Local social services authorities are under a duty to provide accommodation for a child in need within their area who appears to them to require accommodation as a result, among other things, of the person who has been caring from him being prevented (whether or not permanently, and for whatever reason) from providing him with suitable accommodation or care: s 20(1)(c). This provision must be read in the light of the general duties set out in s 17(1). Among these duties there is the duty to safeguard and promote the welfare of the child. At first sight the concept of the carer being prevented from providing the child with suitable accommodation or care does not sit easily with the situation where the carer has chosen to refuse offers of accommodation or other forms of assistance by the relevant local authority. But the words 'for whatever reason' indicate that the widest possible scope must be given to this provision. The guiding principle is the need to safeguard and promote the child's welfare. So it makes no difference whether the reason is one which the carer has brought about by her own act or is one which she was resisting to the best of her ability. On the facts, it is plain that the respondents were under a duty to provide accommodation for the appellants' children under s 20(1).

1.2.3 s 20/s 76 accommodation: overall approach: current problems not future risk in s 20(1)

R (on the application of JL) v London Borough of Islington and others [2009] EWHC 458 (Admin), [2009] 2 FLR 515, [96] (Black J)

96. It seems to me that the problems with which section 20(1) aims to deal are current problems. The subsection has throughout an appearance of the present tense. The child has to appear to the local authority to require accommodation. This does not look, to me, like the sort of wording that would be used were the draftsman contemplating a duty arising if it appeared to the local authority that the child would be likely to require accommodation tomorrow, for example, or would be likely to require accommodation if forthcoming possession proceedings in relation to its home were successful. If one looks at the condition of 'having been abandoned' (section 20(1)(b)), it is plain that that condition must be in place at the time of the local authority's consideration. It does not permit of possible abandonment that might be about to happen. If one turns to section 20(1)(c) itself, one might see a significance also in the use of the words 'the person who *has* been caring for him'; does this perhaps indicate an assumption that by the time the child presents to the local authority, that person is no longer caring for the child at all or is no longer delivering 'suitable care'? The draftsman of the Children Act 1989 spells out elsewhere in the Act situations where action can or must be taken on the basis of something that will or may happen in the future. The obvious example is section 31 which provides that a court may make a care order where 'the child concerned is suffering, *or is likely to suffer*, significant harm'. There is no acknowledgment of future risks in section 20(1). Reinforced by the stringent duty that it imposes, I have concluded that this section is designed to cope with actual crises and not with possible or prospective ones. The local authority has other powers (and duties) to act in relation to these matters, not least by providing for a child under section 20(4), but in my judgment, no duty under section 20(1) arises where the most that can be said is that without assistance, even assistance by way of temporary accommodation, a parent may (or possibly, even, will) be prevented from providing the child with suitable accommodation or care.

1.2.4 s 20/s 76 accommodation: overall approach: wishes and feelings: relevance

R (on the application of Liverpool City Council) v Hillingdon London Borough Council [2009] EWCA Civ 43, [2009] 3 FCR 46, [23]–[34] (Dyson LJ) *quotation limited to* [31]–[34]

[31] It is clear that in some cases, there will be issues which can be resolved at an early stage of the s 20 process whose resolution may prove to be decisive. For example, if there is an issue as to whether the putative child

is indeed a child, it makes sense to resolve that issue first. If he or she is not a child, then s 20 does not apply at all. Further examples are where there is an issue as to whether the child is within the local authority's area, or whether he or she appears to be in need of accommodation as a result of any of the matters listed in s 20(1)(a), (b) or (c). A yet further example is where there is an issue as to whether s 20(7) applies. If a person who has parental responsibility for the child objects and sub-s (7)(i) or (ii) is satisfied, then the authority *may not* provide accommodation under s 20. The resolution of these issues may determine the matter so that the authority is not required to go on to consider whether the child is in need of accommodation.

[32] But the position in relation to sub-s (6) is different. It does not provide that the child's wishes and feelings are determinative. In view of the emphasis of the 1989 Act on a child's welfare (replicated in sub-s (6) itself), this is hardly surprising. Children are often not good judges of what is in their best interests. Subsection (6) is carefully drafted. The local authority is required 'so far as is reasonably practicable and consistent with the child's welfare' to ascertain the child's wishes and feelings regarding the provision of accommodation and 'give *due* consideration (having regard to his age and understanding) to such wishes and feelings … as they have been able to ascertain' (emphasis added). The child's wishes are to be given 'due' consideration in the assessment process, no more and no less.

[33] There may be cases where the child's wishes are decisive. But in my view a local authority should reach the conclusion that the child's wishes are decisive only as part of its overall judgment including an assessment of the child's welfare needs and the type and location of accommodation that will meet those needs. That is what, in effect, Arden LJ was saying in the *Sutton* case. It is also clear that this is what Ward LJ was contemplating in the *Croydon* case. He said that the s 20 decision involves a judgment being made about a range of facts and matters such as the nine that he listed, which included the sub-s (6) questions.

[34] Where the child is mature, articulate and intelligent and has strong and reasoned views as to why he or she wants to have a certain type of accommodation in a certain place, it may be that the local authority will be able swiftly and easily to form the view that it ought to accommodate the child in accordance with his or her wishes. I believe that this is what Baroness Hale (in the *Hammersmith and Fulham* case) and Bennett J (in the *Lambeth* and *Croydon* case) had in mind. But an assessment of needs will always be required. Otherwise, the authority will not be able to give due consideration to the question whether it is consistent with the child's welfare needs to accede to his or her wishes. I do not believe that Baroness Hale or Bennett J were contemplating a short-cut which would obviate the need for that consideration.

See also *R (on the application of M) v Hammersmith and Fulham London BC* [2008] UKHL 14, [2008] 3 FCR 688, [17] (Baroness Hale) addressing the same point (within a short outline of the s 20 scheme)

See also *R (on the application of H) v Wandsworth London Borough Council; R (on the application of Barhanu) v Hackney London Borough Council; R (on the application of B) v Islington London Borough Council* [2007] EWHC 1082 (Admin), [2007] 2 FCR 378, [55]–[56] (Holman J) addressing the same point (including touching on the proper effect of s 20(11))

1.2.5 s 20/s 76 accommodation: overall approach: wishes and feelings: relevance: older children

R (on the application of G) v Southwark London Borough Council [2009] UKHL 26, [2009] 2 FCR 459, [28] (Baroness Hale)

[28] Section 20(1) entails a series of judgments, helpfully set out by Ward LJ in *R (on the application of A) v London Borough of Croydon, R (on the application of M) v London Borough of Lambeth* [2008] EWCA Civ 1445 at [75], [2009] 1 FCR 317 at [75], [2009] 1 FLR 1324. I take that list and apply it to this case. …

(6) What are the child's wishes and feelings regarding the provision of accommodation for him? This is a reference to the requirement in s 20(6) of the 1989 Act, as amended by s 53(2) of the Children Act 2004:

> 'Before providing accommodation under this section, a local authority shall, so far as is reasonably practicable and consistent with the child's welfare—
>
> (a) ascertain the child's wishes and feelings regarding the provision of accommodation; and
>
> (b) give due consideration (having regard to his age and understanding) to such wishes and feelings of the child as they have been able to ascertain.'

Some have taken the view that this refers only to the child's views about the sort of accommodation he should have, rather than about whether he should be accommodated at all: see *R (on the application of S) v Sutton London BC* [2007] EWHC 1196 (Admin) at [51], [2007] 2 FLR 849 at [51]. This is supported by the opening words, which are 'before providing' rather than 'before deciding whether to provide'; contrast the equivalent provision in s 17(4A), '[b]efore determining what (if any) service to provide'. On the other hand, as explained in *R (on the application of M) v Hammersmith and Fulham London BC*, it is unlikely that Parliament intended that local authorities should be able to oblige a competent 16- or 17-year-old to accept a service which he does not want. This is supported by s 20(11), which provides that a child who has reached 16 may agree to be accommodated even if his parent objects or wishes to remove him. It is a service, not a coercive intervention. Whether one reaches the same result via a broader construction of s 20(6) or via the more direct route, that there is nothing in s 20 which allows the local authority to force their services upon older and competent children who do not want them, may not matter very much. It is not

> an issue in this case, because A wanted to be accommodated under s 20. But a homeless 16- or 17-year-old who did not want to be accommodated under s 20 would be another example of a child in priority need under the 2002 Order.

See also *R (on the application of M) v Hammersmith and Fulham London Borough Council* [2008] UKHL 14, [2008] 3 FCR 688, [43] (Baroness Hale) addressing the same point

See also *R (on the application of Liverpool City Council) v Hillingdon London Borough Council* [2009] EWCA Civ 43, [2009] 3 FCR 46, [34] (Dyson LJ) addressing the same point, see Chapter 1.2.4 s 20/s 76 accommodation: wishes and feelings: relevance

See also *R (on the application of H) v Wandsworth London Borough Council; R (on the application of Barhanu) v Hackney London Borough Council; R (on the application of B) v Islington London Borough Council* [2007] EWHC 1082 (Admin), [2007] 2 FCR 378, [55]–[56] (Holman J) addressing the same point (including considering a 16 year old's views and s 20(11))

See also *Re W (a child)* [2016] EWCA Civ 804, [2016] 4 WLR 159, [11]–[14] (Macur LJ) considering *R (on the application of M) v Hammersmith and Fulham London Borough Council* [2008] UKHL 14, [2008] 3 FCR 688, considering *R (on the application of G) v Southwark London Borough Council* [2009] UKHL 26, [2009] 2 FCR 459 (in the context of an appeal against a s 25 order)

1.2.6 s 20/s 76 accommodation: overall approach: relationship with other duties: LAs[4] cannot 'finesse' away specific duties

R (on the application of H) v Wandsworth London Borough Council; R (on the application of Barhanu) v Hackney London Borough Council; R (on the application of B) v Islington London Borough Council [2007] EWHC 1082 (Admin), [2007] 2 FCR 378, [57]–[58] (Holman J)

> [57] In my view, the approach of the majority of the House of Lords in the *Barnet* case in the various passages which I have already quoted does require and have the effect that, if a local authority do provide accommodation for a child in need, and if on the facts a duty to do so did arise under s 20, then the local authority must be regarded as providing that accommodation under s 20 and not under s 17. This seems to me necessarily to follow from Lord Hope saying at [85] that s 17 contains a general duty owed to all children who are in need within their area 'and not to each child individually', and from his agreement at [91] with Auld J's distinction between duties which are general and duties 'which are particular' and 'governed by individual circumstances'. It follows, too, from the distinction drawn by Lord Scott of Foscote at [114] between overarching or framework duties and specific duties owed to specific children.

4 Local authorities.

[58] As in the case of *R v London Borough of Bexley, ex p B*, a local authority cannot finesse away their specific or particular duty by claiming merely to act under a general one. Still less, in my view, can a local authority, when they are under a duty, finesse the duty away by claiming merely to exercise a power.

See also *R (on the application of G) v Southwark London Borough Council* [2009] UKHL 26, [2009] 2 FCR 459, [9]–[10] (Baroness Hale) considering *R (on the application of H) v Wandsworth London Borough Council; R (on the application of Barhanu) v Hackney London Borough Council; R (on the application of B) v Islington London Borough Council* [2007] EWHC 1082 (Admin), [2007] 2 FCR 378 (highlighting that LAs cannot 'side-step' the s 20 duty)

1.2.7 s 20/s 76 accommodation: overall approach: private fostering arrangements

D v London Borough of Southwark [2007] EWCA Civ 182, [2007] 1 FCR 788, [48]–[51] (Smith LJ) *quotation limited to* [48]–[49]

[48] We turn to the substance of appeal. Was Southwark ever under a s 20(1) duty to provide accommodation for S? As we have said, before this court, Southwark accepted not only that S was a child in need but also that her father, who had been caring for her, was, for the foreseeable future, prevented from providing such care. Southwark contended that its s 20(1) duty was on the verge of arising but never crystallised, because it did not appear to the authority that S required accommodation; ED was willing to provide it.

[49] We are prepared to accept that, in some circumstances, a private fostering arrangement might become available in such a way as to permit a local authority, which is on the verge of having to provide accommodation for a child, to 'side-step' that duty by helping to make a private fostering arrangement. However, it will be a question of fact as to whether that happens in any particular case. Usually, a private fostering arrangement will come about as the result of discussions between the proposed foster parent and either the child's parent(s) or a person with parental responsibility. But we accept that there might be occasions when a private arrangement is made without such direct contact. We accept that there might be cases in which the local authority plays a part in bringing about such an arrangement. However, where a local authority takes a major role in making arrangements for a child to be fostered, it is more likely to be concluded that, in doing so, it is exercising its powers and duties as a public authority pursuant to ss 20 and 23. If an authority wishes to play some role in making a private arrangement, it must make the nature of the arrangement plain to those involved. If the authority is facilitating a private arrangement, it must make it plain to the proposed foster parent that s/he must look to the parents or person with parental responsibility for financial support. The authority must explain that any financial assistance from public funds would be entirely a matter for the discretion

of the local authority for the area in which the foster parent is living. Only on receipt of such information could the foster parent give informed consent to acceptance of the child under a private fostering agreement. If such matters are left unclear, there is a danger that the foster parent (and subsequently the court) will conclude that the local authority was acting under its statutory powers and duties and that the arrangement was not a private one at all.

1.2.8 s 20/s 76 accommodation: overall approach: age disputes

R (on the application of A) v Croydon London Borough Council; R (on the application of M) v Lambeth London Borough Council [2009] UKSC 8, [2009] 3 FCR 607, [1], [26]–[28], [32]–[33] (Lady Hale), [51], [54] (Lord Hope)

[1] So much depends upon how one frames the question. Put simply, when disputes arise about the age of someone who is asking a local children's services authority to provide him with accommodation under s 20(1) of the Children Act 1989 (the 1989 Act), who decides whether he is a child or not?

…

[26] … The 1989 Act draws a clear and sensible distinction between different kinds of question. The question whether a child is 'in need' requires a number of different value judgments. What would be a reasonable standard of health or development for this particular child? How likely is he to achieve it? What services might bring that standard up to a reasonable level? What amounts to a significant impairment of health or development? How likely is that? What services might avoid it? Questions like this are sometimes decided by the courts in the course of care or other proceedings under the 1989 Act. Courts are quite used to deciding them upon the evidence for the purpose of deciding what order, if any, to make. But where the issue is not, what order should the court make, but what service should the local authority provide, it is entirely reasonable to assume that Parliament intended such evaluative questions to be determined by the public authority, subject to the control of the courts on the ordinary principles of judicial review. Within the limits of fair process and 'Wednesbury reasonableness' there are no clear cut right or wrong answers.

[27] But the question whether a person is a 'child' is a different kind of question. There is a right or a wrong answer. It may be difficult to determine what that answer is. The decision-makers may have to do their best on the basis of less than perfect or conclusive evidence. But that is true of many questions of fact which regularly come before the courts. That does not prevent them from being questions for the courts rather than for other kinds of decision-makers.

[28] The arguments advanced by Mr Béar might have to provide an answer in cases where Parliament has not made its intentions plain. But in this case it appears to me that Parliament has done just that. In s 20(1) a clear distinction is drawn between the question whether there is a 'child in need within their area' and the question whether it appears to the local authority that the child requires accommodation for one of the listed reasons. In s 17(10) a clear distinction is drawn between whether the person is a 'child' and whether that child is to be 'taken to be' in need within the meaning of the Act. 'Taken to be' imports an element of judgment, even an element of deeming in the case of a disabled child, which Parliament may well have intended to be left to the local authority rather than the courts.

...

[32] However, as already explained, the 1989 Act does draw a distinction between a 'child' and a 'child in need' and even does so in terms which suggest that they are two different kinds of question. The word 'child' is undoubtedly defined in wholly objective terms (however hard it may be to decide upon the facts of the particular case). With a few limited extensions, it defines the outer boundaries of the jurisdiction of both courts and local authorities under the 1989 Act. This is an Act for and about children. If ever there were a jurisdictional fact, it might be thought, this is it.

[33] The final arguments raised against such a conclusion are of a practical kind. The only remedy available is judicial review and this is not well-suited to the determination of disputed questions of fact. This is true but it can be so adapted if the need arises: see *R (on the application of Wilkinson) v Responsible Medical Officer Broadmoor Hospital* [2001] EWCA Civ 1545, [2002] 1 WLR 419. That the remedy is judicial review does not dictate the issue for the court to decide or the way in which it should do so, as the cases on jurisdictional fact illustrate. Clearly, as those cases also illustrate, the public authority, whether the children's services authority or the UK Border Agency, has to make its own determination in the first instance and it is only if this remains disputed that the court may have to intervene. But the better the quality of the initial decision-making, the less likely it is that the court will come to any different decision upon the evidence. If the other members of the court agree with my approach to the determination of age, it does not mean that all the other judgments involved in the decision whether or not to provide services to children or to other client groups must be subject to determination by the courts. They remain governed by conventional principles.

...

[51] It seems to me that the question whether or not a person is a child for the purposes of s 20 of the 1989 Act is a question of fact which must ultimately be decided by the court. There is no denying the difficulties that the social worker is likely to face in carrying out an assessment of the question whether an unaccompanied asylum seeker is or is not under the age of 18. Reliable documentary evidence is almost always lacking in such cases. So the process has to be one of assessment. This involves the application of

judgment on a variety of factors, as Stanley Burnton J recognised in *R (on the application of B) v Merton London BC* [2003] EWHC 1689 (Admin) at [37], [2005] 3 FCR 69 at [37], [2003] 4 All ER 280. But the question is not whether the person can properly be described as a child. Section 105(1) of the 1989 Act provides:

> 'In this Act …
>
> "child" means, subject to paragraph 16 of Schedule 1, a person under the age of eighteen.'

The question is whether the person is, or is not, under the age of 18. However difficult it may be to resolve the issue, it admits of only one answer. As it is a question of fact, ultimately this must be a matter for the court.

…

[54] As for the practical consequences, the process begins with the carrying out of an assessment of the person's age by the social worker. Resort to the court will only be necessary in the event of a challenge to that assessment. So I do not accept that our conclusion will inevitably result in an inappropriate judicialisation of the process. It may, of course, require a judicial decision in some cases. But I would hope that the fact that the final decision rests with the court will assist in reducing the number of challenges. The initial decision-taker must appreciate that no margin of discretion is enjoyed by the local authority on this issue. But the issue is not to be determined by a consideration of issues of policy or by a view as to whether resort to a decision by the court in such cases is inappropriate. It depends entirely on the meaning of the statute. We must construe the 1989 Act as we find it. As I have said, when the subsection is properly construed in the light of what s 105(1) provides, the question admits of only one answer.

See also *R (on the application of F) v Lewisham London Borough Council and related claims* [2009] EWHC 3542 (Admin), [2010] 2 FCR 292, [5] (Holman J) considering *R (on the application of A) v Croydon London Borough Council; R (on the application of M) v Lambeth London Borough Council* [2009] UKSC 8 (identifying the process as being an assessment by the LA; then a challenge via judicial review; and that on judicial review it is an issue of pure fact)

See also *R (on the application of F) v Lewisham London Borough Council and related claims* [2009] EWHC 3542 (Admin), [2010] 2 FCR 292, [16] (Holman J) addressing a related point (the standard is the ordinary civil standard but the burden in age disputes is more problematic and depends on the case)

See also *R (on the application of CJ) v Cardiff County Council* [2011] EWHC 23 (Admin), [126]–[131] (Ouseley J) addressing a related point (suggesting LAs may bear the burden regarding s 20 and age disputes, in obiter)

1.3 S 20/S 76 ACCOMMODATION: LIMITS

1.3.1 s 20/s 76 accommodation: limits: misuses of s 20

Re N (children) (adoption: jurisdiction) [2015] EWCA Civ 1112, [2016] 1 FCR 217, [157]–[169], [171] (Sir James Munby P) *revd Re N (children) (adoption: jurisdiction)* [2016] UKSC 15, [2016] 3 FCR 394

[157] The first relates to the use by the local authority—in my judgment the misuse by the local authority—of the procedure under s 20 of the 1989 Act. As we have seen, the children were placed in accordance with s 20 in May 2013, yet it was not until January 2014, over eight months later, that the local authority eventually issued care proceedings. Section 20 may, in an appropriate case, have a proper role to play as a *short-term* measure pending the commencement of care proceedings, but the use of s 20 as a prelude to care proceedings for a period as long as here is wholly unacceptable. It is, in my judgment, and I use the phrase advisedly and deliberately, a misuse by the local authority of its statutory powers.

[158] As I said in *Re A (a child), Darlington BC v M* [2015] EWFC 11, [2016] 1 FLR 1, [2015] All ER (D) 234 (Feb) (at [100]):

> 'There is, I fear, far too much misuse and abuse of section 20 and this can no longer be tolerated.'

I drew attention there, and I draw attention again, to the extremely critical comments of the Court of Appeal in *Re W (parental agreement with local authority)* [2014] EWCA Civ 1065, [2015] 1 FLR 949, as also to the decision of Keehan J in *Northamptonshire CC v AS* [2015] EWHC 199 (Fam), [2015] All ER (D) 52 (Feb). As Keehan J pointed out in the latter case (para [37]), the accommodation of a child under a s 20 agreement deprives the child of the benefit of having an independent children's guardian to represent and safeguard his interests and deprives the court of the ability to control the planning for the child and prevent or reduce unnecessary and avoidable delay. In that case the local authority ended up having to pay substantial damages.

[159] Then there was the decision of Cobb J in *Newcastle City Council v WM* [2015] EWFC 42. He described the local authority (paras [46], [49]) as having acted unlawfully and in dereliction of its duty. We had occasion to return to the problem very recently in *Re CB (a child)* [2015] EWCA Civ 888, (2015) Times, 24 September (at [86]), a case involving the London Borough of Merton. Even more recent is the searing judgment of Sir Robert Francis QC, sitting as a Deputy High Court Judge in the Queen's Bench Division in *Williams v Hackney London BC* [2015] EWHC 2629 (QB), [2015] All ER (D) 99 (Sep), another case in which the local authority had to pay damages.

[160] Moreover, there has in recent months been a litany of judgments in which experienced judges of the Family Court have had occasion to condemn local authorities, often in necessarily strong, on occasions withering, language, for misuse, and in some cases plain abuse, of s 20: see, for example, *Re*

P (A Child: Use of s 20 CA 1989) [2014] EWFC 775, a case involving the London Borough of Redbridge, *Re N (children)* [2015] EWFC 37, [2015] All ER (D) 131 (May), a case involving South Tyneside Metropolitan Borough Council, *Medway Council v A* [2015] EWFC B66, *Gloucestershire CC v M* [2015] EWFC B147, *Gloucestershire CC v S* [2015] EWFC B149, *Re AS (a child)* [2015] EWFC B150, a case where damages were awarded against the London Borough of Brent, and *Medway Council v M* [2015] EWFC B164, another case where substantial damages were awarded against a local authority. I need not yet further lengthen this judgment with an analysis of this melancholy litany but, if I may say so, Directors of Social Services and Local Authority Heads of Legal Services might be well advised to study all these cases, and all the other cases I have mentioned on the point, with a view to considering whether their authority's current practices and procedures are satisfactory.

[161] The misuse of s 20 in a case, like this, with an international element, is particularly serious. I have already drawn attention (paras [50]–[51], above) to the consequences of the delay in this case. In *Leicester City Council v S* [2014] EWHC 1575 (Fam), [2015] 1 FLR 1182, a Hungarian child born in this country on 26 March 2013 was accommodated by the local authority under s 20 on 12 April 2013 but the care proceedings were not commenced until 10 October 2013. Moylan J was extremely critical of the local authority. I have already set out (para [115], above) his observations on the wider picture.

[162] What the recent case law illustrates to an alarming degree are four separate problems, all too often seen in combination.

[163] The first relates to the failure of the local authority to obtain informed consent from the parent(s) at the outset. A local authority cannot use its powers under s 20 if a parent 'objects': see s 20(7). So where, as here, the child's parent is known and in contact with the local authority, the local authority requires the consent of the parent. We dealt with the point in *Re W (parental agreement with local authority)* [2014] EWCA Civ 1065, [2015] 1 FLR 949 (at [34]):

> '… as Hedley J put it in *Coventry City Council v C, B, CA and CH* [2012] EWHC 2190 (Fam), [2013] 2 FLR 987, para 27, the use of section 20 "must not be compulsion in disguise". And any such agreement requires genuine consent, not mere "submission in the face of asserted State authority": *R (G) v Nottingham City Council and Nottingham University Hospital* [2008] EWHC 400 (Admin), [2008] 1 FLR 1668, para 61, and *Coventry City Council v C, B, CA and CH* [2012] EWHC 2190 (Fam), [2013] 2 FLR 987, para 44.'

[164] In this connection local authorities and their employees *must* heed the guidance set out by Hedley J in *Coventry City Council v C* [2012] EWHC 2190 (Fam), [2013] 1 FCR 54, [2013] 2 FLR 987 (at [46]):

[165] I add that in cases where the parent is not fluent in English it is vital to ensure that the parent has a proper understanding of what precisely they are being asked to agree to.

[166] The second problem relates to the *form* in which the consent of the parent(s) is recorded. There is, in law, no requirement for the agreement to be in or evidenced by writing: *R (on the application of G) v Nottingham City Council* [2008] EWHC 400 (Admin), [2008] 3 FCR 568, [2008] 1 FLR 1668 (at [53]). But a prudent local authority will surely always wish to ensure that an alleged parental consent in such a case is properly recorded in writing and evidenced by the parent's signature.

[167] A feature of recent cases has been the serious deficiencies apparent in the drafting of too many s 20 agreements. In *Re W (parental agreement with local authority)* [2014] EWCA Civ 1065, [2015] 1 FLR 949, we expressed some pungent observations about the form of an agreement which in places was barely literate. Tomlinson LJ (para [41]) described the agreement as 'almost comical in the manner in which it apparently proclaims that it has been entered into under something approaching duress'. In *Williams v Hackney London BC* [2015] EWHC 2629 (QB), [2015] All ER (D) 99 (Sep), the Deputy Judge was exceedingly critical (para [65]) both of the terms of the agreement and of the circumstances in which the parents' 'consent' had been obtained. There had, he said, been 'compulsion in disguise' and 'such agreement or acquiescence as took place was not fairly obtained'.

[168] The third problem relates to the fact that, far too often, the arrangements under s 20 are allowed to continue for far too long. This needs no elaboration.

[169] This is related to the fourth problem, the seeming reluctance of local authorities to return the child to the parent(s) immediately upon a withdrawal of parental consent. It is important for local authorities to recognise that, as s 20(8) of the 1989 Act provides:

> 'Any person who has parental responsibility for a child may at any time remove the child from accommodation provided by or on behalf of the local authority under this section.'

This means what it says. A local authority which fails to permit a parent to remove a child in circumstances within s 20(8) acts unlawfully, exposes itself to proceedings at the suit of the parent and may even be guilty of a criminal offence. A parent in that position could bring a claim against the local authority for judicial review or, indeed, seek an immediate writ of habeas corpus against the local authority. I should add that I am exceedingly sceptical as to whether a parent can lawfully contract out of s 20(8) in advance, as by agreeing with the local authority to give a specified period of notice before exercising their s 20(8) right.

…

[171] The misuse and abuse of s 20 in this context is not just a matter of bad practice. It is wrong; it is a denial of the fundamental rights of both the parent and the child; it will no longer be tolerated; and it must stop. Judges will and must be alert to the problem and proactive in putting an end to it. From now on, local authorities which use s 20 as a prelude to care

proceedings for lengthy periods or which fail to follow the good practice I have identified, can expect to be subjected to probing questioning by the court. If the answers are not satisfactory, the local authority can expect stringent criticism and possible exposure to successful claims for damages.

See also *Herefordshire Council v AB, CD; Herefordshire Council v EF, GH* [2018] EWFC 10, [2018] 2 FCR 142, [15]–[16] (Keehan J) addressing a related point (examples of appropriate uses of s 20)

See also *Worcestershire County Council v AA* [2019] EWHC 1855 (Fam), [12]–[13] (Keehan J) addressing a related point (examples of appropriate uses of s 20)

1.3.2 s 20/s 76 accommodation: limits: care or s 20: advantages of care

Williams and another v London Borough of Hackney [2018] UKSC 37, [2019] AC 421, [49]–[52] (Lady Hale P)

49. Finally, there is nothing in section 20 to place a limit on the length of time for which a child may be accommodated. However, local authorities have a variety of duties towards the children whom they are accommodating. Their general duties towards looked after children in section 22 of the 1989 Act include a duty to safeguard and promote their welfare, in consultation with both the children and their parents. This is reinforced by the Care Planning, Placement and Case Review (England) Regulations 2010, SI 2010/959, which require local authorities to assess a child's 'needs for services to achieve or maintain a reasonable standard of health or development' and prepare a care plan for her, to be agreed with the parents if practicable (regulation 4(1), (4)). The care plan has to record, inter alia, the arrangements made to meet the child's needs and the long term plan for her upbringing ('the plan for permanence') (regulation 5(a) and (b)).

50. Thus, although the object of section 20 accommodation is partnership with the parents, the local authority have also to be thinking of the longer term. There are bound to be cases where that should include consideration of whether or not the authority should seek to take parental responsibility for an accommodated child by applying for a care order. Good examples are *Medway Council v M and T* (para 31 above), where the mother suffered from long term mental health problems and was not meeting her parental responsibility, so it was necessary for someone to do so; and *Herefordshire Council v EF and GH* (above, para 33), where it was recognised as soon as the mother and baby foster placement of GH and his 14-year-old mother broke down that care proceedings should be brought, but this did not happen until he was nine years old.

51. Care proceedings have obvious advantages for the child. They involve a rigorous scrutiny of the risk of harm to her health and development if an order is not made, of the assessment of her needs and of the plans for her

future. Her interests are safeguarded by an expert children's guardian. If an order is made, it means that the local authority have parental responsibility for her and can put their plans into effect. But, as pointed out by Judge Rowe QC in *In re AS* (para 30 above) there are also advantages for the parents and for the wider family. The parents are entitled to legal aid. Their rights are safeguarded in the proceedings. Even if a care order is made, the court may make orders about their continued contact with the child. Hence it is scarcely surprising that the President and other judges have deplored the delay in bringing care proceedings in cases where it was obvious that they should have been brought. Section 20 must not be used in a coercive way: if the state is to intervene compulsorily in family life, it must seek legal authority to do so.

52. Thus although it is not a breach of section 20 to keep a child in accommodation for a long period without bringing care proceedings, it may well be a breach of other duties under the Act and Regulations or unreasonable in public law terms to do so. In some cases there may also be breaches of the child's or the parents' rights under article 8 of ECHR.

See also *Re J (child refugees)* [2017] EWFC 44, [2017] 4 WLR 192, [18]–[25] (Peter Jackson J) addressing a related point (the relative advantages and disadvantages of s 20 and care in respect of unaccompanied refugees)

1.3.3 s 20/s 76 accommodation: limits: s 20 does not grant PR: extent of powers

R v Tameside Metropolitan Borough Council, ex p J [2000] 1 FCR 173 (QBD), 179H–180F (Scott Baker J)

The definition of parental responsibility in s 3(1) includes, says Mr Pleming QC, and I agree, the right to decide where a child shall live. The applicants put their case in this way. The present accommodation of J at C Avenue is pursuant to an agreement between her parents and the respondent. The respondent's proposed move of her to foster parents would be without the parent's consent and its effect would negative their parental responsibility as outlined in the 1989 Act. The local authority would be acting as if they were the beneficiary of a care order in respect of the child. This is essentially a parental act that the local authority have no power to perform without the parents' consent. Their rights to dictate the future of the child never extended beyond Pt III of the 1989 Act. A care order would have given them parental responsibility (see s 33(3)), and the situation would have been different. Furthermore, the provisions of s 20 make it clear that parental responsibility continues even after a local authority have made arrangements to accommodate a child. A local authority are not empowered to accommodate a child when a person with responsibility objects and is willing and able to provide accommodation for him (see s 20(7)). And a person with parental responsibility may at any time remove a child from accommodation provided by the local authority (see s 20(8)).

> Of course, that sanction is of little practical benefit to the parents in the present case because they cannot themselves accommodate J and, in practice, are dependent on the local authority for doing so. Put shortly, Mr Pleming poses the question, By what power can the local authority override the views of the parents and place J with foster parents?
>
> Of course, a local authority that accommodates a child pursuant to s 20 are able to exercise mundane day-to-day powers of management; but a move of the kind envisaged in this case goes much further and trespasses into the kind of decision-making that is ultimately exercised by those with parental responsibility. A mere power of management cannot override the wishes of the parent with parental responsibility. And the answer to the question is that nowhere in the 1989 Act does one find the necessary power for the local authority to override the views of the parents and place J with foster parents. The unspoken word in Pt III of the 1989 Act is co-operation—co-operation between the parents and the local authority to work together in the best interests of the child.

See also *R (on the application of M) v Hammersmith and Fulham London BC* [2008] UKHL 14, [2008] 3 FCR 688, [20] (Baroness Hale) addressing a related point (that although LAs do not have PR[5] under s 20, to some extent they replace the parental role)

1.3.4 s 20/s 76 accommodation: limits: s 20 does not preclude wardship

Re E (a child) [2012] EWCA Civ 1773, [2013] 2 FLR 63, [1], [16]–[17] (Thorpe LJ)

1. This appeal raises a short point of construction. It is this. Where a minor is accommodated voluntarily under Section 20 of the Children Act 1989, is the court prevented by Section 100 of the same Act from making the child a ward of court? The question arises from the judgment of HHJ Bellamy sitting in a difficult and exceptional case on its facts in the Coventry County Court as a deputy judge of the division.

...

16. So in the end it seems to me that this is a simple point. Plainly the intention and effect of Section 100 is to prevent the court in wardship making any order which has the effect of requiring a child to be placed in care or under the supervision of a local authority. That end can only be achieved by going through the proper route of threshold finding opening the court's discretionary jurisdiction to make either a care or a supervision order. The same result cannot be achieved under the court's inherent jurisdiction. But there is nothing in Section 100 that either explicitly or implicitly

5 Parental responsibility.

precludes the court from making an order in wardship where the child is not required to be accommodated, but is voluntarily accommodated.

17. Of course, if the accommodation agreement is terminated by either or both of the parties to the agreement, then obviously the court is not in a position to then require the local authority to accommodate or to supervise, but, so long as the Section 20 placement remains there, in my judgment the judge was not prevented from making the order which he clearly found to be the order most likely to promote the welfare of the child.

1.4 S 20/S 76 ACCOMMODATION: CHALLENGING LA DECISIONS

1.4.1 s 20/s 76 accommodation: challenging LA decisions: procedure: judicial review

Re J (a minor) (specific issue order) [1995] 3 FCR 799 (FD), 801G–802C, 803F, 805A–B (Wall J)

It is in my judgment significant that in sharp distinction to Part IV, the only section in Part III of the Act in which there is any reference to 'the court' is s 25, which deals with secure accommodation, and which empowers the court to authorize the retention of a child for limited periods of time in secure accommodation. It is thus plain that Part III of the Act deals with the duties imposed on local authorities by Parliament and that the only court intervention envisaged is the power to regulate the use of secure accommodation. No power is given by Parliament to the court in Part III to regulate, for example, the selection of children in need or the enforcement of the duty to accommodate such children. To the contrary, s 20(1) of the Act leaves the selection of children requiring accommodation to the local authority. That section begins:

> 'Every local authority shall provide accommodation for any child in need within their area *who appears to them* (the emphasis is mine) to require accommodation …'

…

It therefore seems very clear to me that it was the intention of Parliament that the exercise of the local authority's powers and duties under Part III should not be the subject of judicial scrutiny or control except by means of judicial review. It follows, in my judgment, that Miss Mayer is correct when she submits that a specific issue order is inapposite to determine the question of whether or not J is a child in need.

…

This case provides a further reminder that s 7 of the Family Law Act 1989 has been repealed. The court does not have the power directly to determine the issue which J has attempted to bring before it for decision. There is no doubt at all in my mind that it was the intention of Parliament not to make

> the issue justiciable by way of specific issue order: my only regret is that in order to challenge the decision, J must now take separate proceedings in a different Division of the High Court.

See also *Re T (Accommodation of Child by Local Authority)* [1995] 1 FCR 517 (QBD), 519F–G (Johnson J) addressing the same point

1.4.2 s 20/s 76 accommodation: challenging LA decisions: human rights claims

Williams and another v London Borough of Hackney [2018] UKSC 37, [2019] AC 421, [3], [52] (Lady Hale P)

[3] Also relevant are the rights of both parents and children under article 8 of the European Convention on Human Rights ('ECHR'):

> '(1) Everyone has the right to respect for his private and family life, his home and his correspondence.
>
> (2) There shall be no interference by a public authority with the exercise of this right except such as is in accordance with the law and is necessary in a democratic society in the interests of national security, public safety or the economic well-being of the country, for the prevention of disorder or crime, for the protection of health or morals, or for the protection of the rights and freedoms of others.'

If the use of section 20 amounts to an interference with a parent's or a child's exercise of their right to respect for their family life, it will violate article 8 unless it is 'in accordance with the law' and a proportionate means of achieving one of the legitimate aims listed in article 8(2). In that event, it will be unlawful under section 6(1) of the Human Rights Act 1998 and the parent or child may seek a remedy, which could be an award of damages, under section 7(1) of that Act.

…

[52] Thus although it is not a breach of section 20 to keep a child in accommodation for a long period without bringing care proceedings, it may well be a breach of other duties under the Act and Regulations or unreasonable in public law terms to do so. In some cases there may also be breaches of the child's or the parents' rights under article 8 of ECHR.

CHAPTER 2

Emergencies and investigations

Chapter contents

CHAPTER 2

Emergencies and investigations

2.1 EMERGENCIES AND INVESTIGATIONS: POLICE POWERS OF PROTECTION

2.1.1 Emergencies and investigations: police powers of protection: only when executing EPOs[1] is impracticable

Langley and others v Liverpool City Council and another [2005] EWCA Civ 1173, [2005] 3 FCR 303, [38]–[42] (Dyson LJ), [76] (Thorpe LJ)

[38] In my judgment, the statutory scheme clearly accords primacy to s 44. Removal under s 44 is sanctioned by the court and it involves a more elaborate, sophisticated and complete process than removal under s 46. The primacy accorded to s 44 is further reinforced by s 46(7) and 47(3)(c). The significance of these provisions is that they show that it was contemplated by Parliament that an EPO may well not be in force when a removal is effected under s 46, and that removal under s 46 is but the first step in a process which may later include an application for an EPO.

[39] It is also relevant to point out that children who require emergency protection and have to be removed are often already well known to the social services department within whose area the children are ordinarily resident. It is obviously preferable for the removal of a child to be effected if possible by, or at least with the assistance of, social workers who are known to the child, rather than by uniformed police officers who will almost certainly be strangers to the child. Whether known to the child or not, a social worker has skills in dealing with the removal of children from their homes which the most sensitive police officer cannot be expected to match.

[40] I would, therefore, hold that (i) removal of children should usually be effected pursuant to an EPO, and (ii) s 46 should be invoked only where it is not practicable to execute an EPO. In deciding whether it is practicable to execute an EPO, the police must always have regard to the paramount need to protect children from significant harm.

[41] We were shown Home Office Circular 44/2003 on the duties and powers of the police under the Act. This came into force on 9 August 2003. It was not in force at the time of the events with which this appeal is concerned. It does not have any statutory force. Nevertheless, I find what it says about s 46 instructive, viz:

1 Emergency protection orders.

'When to use police protection

14. Police protection powers should only be used when necessary, the principle being that wherever possible the decision to remove a child from a parent or carer should be made by a court.

15. All local authorities should have in place arrangements (through their local chief Executive and Clerks to the Justices) whereby out of hours applications for Emergency Protection Orders (EPOs—see paras 49 to 54 below) may be made speedily and without an excess of bureaucracy. Police protection powers should only be used when this is not possible.'

[42] The circular that was in force in September 2001 was Circular No 54/1991. Paragraph 13 states: '*Section 46* provides for the taking of a child into police protection in cases of emergency when there is no time to apply for an order.' Both circulars are consistent with my interpretation of the Act.

...

[76] In the first place it is Pts IV and V of the Children Act 1989 that provides the state, through the agency of the local authority, with power to intervene in the life of a family. Practitioners, whether in the legal department or the social services department of the local authority, will naturally consider the powers provided by Pts IV and V, and the limitations on those powers, when considering how and to what degree they should invade the territory of the family in order to protect its children. If there is no imminent danger the appropriate application is for an interim care order. If there is greater urgency the appropriate remedy is an emergency protection order. It is to be emphasised that even in an emergency the local authority must apply in the family proceedings court for the order and prove the need for the order to the satisfaction of the court. This is a potent check on the local authority's powers of intervention in emergency. In the present case I emphasise that the family proceedings court was satisfied that the local authority's proposed intervention by way of an emergency protection order was appropriate and proportionate.

See also *A v East Sussex County Council and another* [2010] EWCA Civ 743, [2011] 1 FCR 116 [8], [10], [23]–[25] (Hedley J) considering *Langley and others v Liverpool City Council and another* [2005] EWCA Civ 1173, [2005] 3 FCR 303 (including emphasising the need, where possible, for LAs[2] to work with parents)

See also *Surrey County Council v M and others* [2013] EWHC 2400 (Fam), [2014] 1 FCR 429 [76] (Theis J) addressing the same point (emphasising that police powers should only be used in exceptional circumstances, eg where there is insufficient time to seek an EPO)

See also *Re A and Others (minors) (child abuse: guidelines)* [1991] 1 WLR 1026, 1030B–E (Hollings J) addressing a related point (early morning police-removals only where clear grounds for significant harm or to obtain vital evidence)

2 Local authorities.

2.1.2 Emergencies and investigations: police powers of protection: use when EPOs are in force

Langley and others v Liverpool City Council and another [2005] EWCA Civ 1173, [2005] 3 FCR 303, [24]–[37] (Dyson LJ) quotation limited to [30]–[36]

[30] In my judgment, therefore, there is nothing in the language of the Act which compels the conclusion that s 46 cannot be invoked where an EPO is in force. As Mr Wells points out, it would be most unfortunate if the position were otherwise. Two examples will suffice to demonstrate this. Let us suppose that an EPO is in force, but a constable is unaware of it. He comes across a child who he has reasonable cause to believe would be likely to suffer significant harm if not removed (ie the s 46(1) criteria are satisfied). If the judge is right, the removal of the child, otherwise unimpeachable, is unlawful because, unknown to the officer, an EPO is in force in respect of the child. In my view, the jurisdiction to remove a child under s 46 where an EPO is in force cannot depend on whether the constable is aware of its existence. There is nothing in the Act which suggests that the officer's knowledge is relevant. On the judge's interpretation, the existence of the EPO is fatal: of itself it renders the officer's removal unlawful. If this is right, its implications for the protection of children at risk of significant harm are serious. Since police officers cannot have a comprehensive knowledge of all the EPOs that are in force, they would be at risk of acting unlawfully every time they remove a child under s 46. Such an interpretation would be likely to discourage the police from invoking s 46. In this way, there would be a real danger that one of the important powers provided by Parliament for the protection of children at risk would be emasculated.

[31] In the second example, an EPO has been made in respect of a child on the application of the local authority in Liverpool, and the constable comes across the child in Cornwall. Let us suppose that the officer is aware of the EPO, and he considers that the child is in real danger. He considers that it is necessary to act urgently to remove the child to suitable accommodation in order to protect him or her, and it will take some time to contact the Social Services of Liverpool City Council to alert them to the need to execute the EPO. It would be most unfortunate if in such circumstances the constable were unable to invoke s 46 to protect the child.

[32] The relevant provisions of the Act should be construed so as to further the manifest object of securing the protection of children who are at risk of significant harm. A construction of the Act which prohibits a constable from removing a child under s 46 where he has reasonable cause to believe that the child would otherwise be likely to suffer significant harm would frustrate that object. I would, therefore, reject the judge's interpretation of the Act. The s 46 power to remove a child can be exercised even where an EPO is in force in respect of the child.

[33] The next question is whether, on the assumption that the criteria in s 46(1) are met, there are any limitations on the power of the police to remove

a child under s 46 where an EPO is in existence. No such limitations are expressed in the Act. But it is trite law that discretionary statutory powers must be exercised to promote the policy and objects of the statute: see *Padfield v Minister of Agriculture Fisheries and Food* [1968] 1 All ER 694 at 699, [1968] AC 997 at 1030. The broad policy and objects of Pt V of the Act are not in doubt: they are to provide for the protection of children in circumstances where there is reasonable cause to believe that they are suffering or likely to suffer significant harm. But in enacting Pt V, Parliament has provided a detailed and carefully structured scheme for the removal of children in such circumstances.

[34] The first point to make about s 44 is that an EPO is a court order, which cannot be made unless the court is satisfied that the conditions prescribed by s 44(1) (a), (b) or (c) are met. An EPO gives an applicant parental responsibility for the child, but it does not of itself require the applicant to remove the child. The applicant may only remove the child 'in order to safeguard the welfare of the child' and 'shall take only such action in meeting his parental responsibility for the child as is reasonably required to safeguard or promote the welfare of the child' (sub-s (5)). The court may give such directions (if any) as it considers appropriate 'with respect to (a) the contact which is, or is not, to be allowed between the child and any named person; (b) the medical or psychiatric examination or other assessment of the child' (sub-s (6)). Where an EPO is in force, the applicant shall, subject to any direction given under sub-s (6) allow the child reasonable contact with the persons specified in sub-s (13).

[35] The s 46 regime is quite different. The court is not involved. A police constable is authorised to remove a child if he has reasonable cause to believe that the child would otherwise be likely to suffer significant harm. As we have already seen, as soon as is reasonably practicable after taking the child into police protection, the constable must inform the local authority within whose area the child was found of the steps that have been, and are proposed to be, taken and the reasons for taking them, and give details to the appropriate authority of the place at which the child is being accommodated. The designated officer may apply on behalf of the appropriate authority for an EPO.

[36] For the reasons which follow, I would hold that, where a police officer knows that an EPO is in force, he should not exercise the power of removing a child under s 46, unless there are compelling reasons to do so. The statutory scheme shows that Parliament intended that, if practicable, the removal of a child from where he or she is living should be authorised by a court order and effected under s 44. Parliament could have provided simply that specified persons could remove children if the statutory criteria are satisfied without any court involvement at all. But the removal of children, usually from their families, is a very serious matter. It is, therefore, not at all surprising that Parliament decided that the court should play an important part in the process. This is a valuable safeguard. The court must be satisfied that the statutory criteria for removal exist.

See also *Lumba (Congo) v Secretary of State for the Home Department; Mighty (Jamaica) v Secretary of State for the Home Department* [2011] UKSC 12, [2012] 1 AC 245, [80]–[82] (Lord Dyson) considering *Langley and others v Liverpool City Council and another* [2005] EWCA Civ 1173, [2005] 3 FCR 303

2.2 EMERGENCIES AND INVESTIGATIONS: EMERGENCY PROTECTION ORDERS

2.2.1 Emergencies and investigations: EPOs: factors to consider

X Council v B and others (emergency protection orders) [2004] EWHC 2015 (Fam), [2007] 1 FCR 512, [57] (Munby J)

[57] The matters I have just been considering are so important that it may be convenient if I here summarise the most important points:

(i) An EPO, summarily removing a child from his parents, is a 'draconian' and 'extremely harsh' measure, requiring 'exceptional justification' and 'extraordinarily compelling reasons'. Such an order should not be made unless the FPC is satisfied that it is both necessary and proportionate and that no other less radical form of order will achieve the essential end of promoting the welfare of the child. Separation is only to be contemplated if immediate separation is essential to secure the child's safety; 'imminent danger' must be 'actually established'.

(ii) Both the local authority which seeks and the FPC which makes an EPO assume a heavy burden of responsibility. It is important that both the local authority and the FPC approach every application for an EPO with an anxious awareness of the extreme gravity of the relief being sought and a scrupulous regard for the Convention rights of both the child and the parents.

(iii) Any order must provide for the least interventionist solution consistent with the preservation of the child's immediate safety.

(iv) If the real purpose of the local authority's application is to enable it to have the child assessed then consideration should be given to whether that objective cannot equally effectively, and more proportionately, be achieved by an application for, or by the making of, a CAO under s 43 of the Act.

(v) No EPO should be made for any longer than is absolutely necessary to protect the child. Where the EPO is made on an ex parte (without notice) application very careful consideration should be given to the need to ensure that the initial order is made for the shortest possible period commensurate with the preservation of the child's immediate safety.

(vi) The evidence in support of the application for an EPO must be full, detailed, precise and compelling. Unparticularised generalities will not suffice. The sources of hearsay evidence must be identified. Expressions of opinion must be supported by detailed evidence and properly articulated reasoning.

(vii) Save in wholly exceptional cases, parents must be given adequate prior notice of the date, time and place of any application by a local authority for an EPO. They must also be given proper notice of the evidence the local authority is relying upon.

(viii) Where the application for an EPO is made ex parte the local authority must make out a compelling case for applying without first giving the parents notice. An ex parte application will normally be appropriate only if the case is genuinely one of emergency or other great urgency—and even then it should normally be possible to give some kind of albeit informal notice to the parents—or if there are compelling reasons to believe that the child's welfare will be compromised if the parents are alerted in advance to what is going on.

(ix) The evidential burden on the local authority is even heavier if the application is made ex parte. Those who seek relief ex parte are under a duty to make the fullest and most candid and frank disclosure of all the relevant circumstances known to them. This duty is not confined to the material facts: it extends to all relevant matters, whether of fact or of law.

(x) Section 45(7)(b) permits the FPC to hear oral evidence. But it is important that those who are not present should nonetheless be able to know what oral evidence and other materials have been put before the FPC. It is therefore particularly important that the FPC complies meticulously with the mandatory requirements of rr 20, 21(5) and 21(6) of the Family Proceedings Courts (Children Act 1989) Rules 1991. The FPC must 'keep a note of the substance of the oral evidence' and must also record in writing not merely its reasons but also any findings of fact.

(xi) The mere fact that the FPC is under the obligations imposed by rr 21(5), 21(6) and 21(8), is no reason why the local authority should not immediately, on request, inform the parents of exactly what has gone on in their absence. Parents against whom an EPO is made ex parte are entitled to be given, if they ask, proper information as to what happened at the hearing and to be told, if they ask, (i) exactly what documents, bundles or other evidential materials were lodged with the FPC either before or during the course of the hearing and (ii) what legal authorities were cited to the FPC. The local authority's legal representatives should respond forthwith to any reasonable request from the parents or their legal representatives either for copies of the materials read by the FPC or for information about what took place at the hearing. It will therefore be prudent for those acting for the local authority in such a case to keep a proper note of the proceedings, lest they otherwise find themselves embarrassed by a proper request for information which they are unable to provide.

(xii) Section 44(5)(b) provides that the local authority may exercise its parental responsibility only in such manner 'as is reasonably required to safeguard or promote the welfare of the child'. Section 44(5)(a) provides that the local authority shall exercise its power of removal under s 44(4)(b)(i) 'only … in order to safeguard the welfare of the child.' The local authority must apply its mind very carefully to whether removal is essential in order to secure the child's immediate safety. The mere fact that the local authority has obtained an EPO is not of itself enough. The FPC decides whether to make an EPO. But the local authority decides whether to remove. The local authority, even after it has obtained an EPO, is under an obligation to consider less drastic alternatives to emergency removal. Section 44(5) requires a process within the local authority whereby there is a further consideration of the action to be taken after the EPO has been obtained. Though no procedure is specified, it will obviously be prudent for local authorities to have in place procedures to ensure both that the required decision making actually takes place and that it is appropriately documented.

(xiii) Consistently with the local authority's positive obligation under art 8 to take appropriate action to reunite parent and child, ss 44(10)(a) and 44(11)(a) impose on the local authority a mandatory obligation to return a child who it has removed under s 44(4)(b)(i) to the parent from whom the child was removed if 'it appears to [the local authority] that it is safe for the child to be returned.' This imposes on the local authority a continuing duty to keep the case under review day by day so as to ensure that parent and child are separated for no longer than is necessary to secure the child's safety. In this, as in other respects, the local authority is under a duty to exercise exceptional diligence.

(xiv) Section 44(13) requires the local authority, subject only to any direction given by the FPC under s 44(6), to allow a child who is subject to an EPO 'reasonable contact' with his parents. Arrangements for contact must be driven by the needs of the family, not stunted by lack of resources.

Re X (emergency protection orders) [2006] EWHC 510 (Fam), [2007] 1 FCR 551, [51], [61]–[65] (McFarlane J) *quotation limited to* [51], [65]

[51] As a matter of future guidance, in all EPO applications the court should be furnished at the very least with copies of the minutes of the most recent case conference (if there has been one), unless there are very pressing reasons to the contrary.

...

[65] Many of the matters described by Munby J in *X Council v B* are clearly applicable to the present case. I agree with each and every one of his observations. I regard this list of 14 factors to be 'required reading' for every magistrate and justices clerk involved in any EPO application. The list should be copied and placed before the court on every occasion that an application is made for an EPO, so that the bench may consider its applicability to the case that is before them. Applicants for an EPO and their legal advisers should consider themselves under a duty to the court to ensure that this list is expressly and in terms drawn to the attention of the bench.

See also *A v East Sussex County Council and another* [2010] EWCA Civ 743, [2011] 1 FCR 116, [11]–[12] (Hedley J) considering *X Council v B and others (emergency protection orders)* [2004] EWHC 2015 (Fam), [2007] 1 FCR 512, considering *Re X (emergency protection orders)* [2006] EWHC 510 (Fam), [2007] 1 FCR 551

See also *Re C and B (children) (care order: future harm)* [2000] 2 FCR 614 (CA), [18]–[19] (Hale LJ) addressing a related point (EPOs are intended for emergencies)

2.2.2 Emergencies and investigations: EPOs: factors to consider: Additional factors when applying without notice

Re X (emergency protection orders) [2006] EWHC 510 (Fam), [2007] 1 FCR 551, [66] (McFarlane J)

[66] The only development of the *X Council v B* guidelines that I would offer is in relation to the record of the hearing. It seems to me that the following two steps should be undertaken whenever an application is made without notice for an EPO:

(a) The hearing ought to be tape recorded. Most magistrates' courts are not wired up for regular recording, but in my view resources ought to be made for the introduction of a small portable tape recorder (or even a dictation recorder). In the absence of such provision then a dedicated note taker, in addition to the clerk, should attend the hearing with the task of compiling a verbatim note;

(b) Paragraph (xi) of the *B Council* guidance limits the requirement to provide information to parents, where the hearing has taken place without notice, to cases where the parents ask for the information. I would go further and say that unless there is very good reason to the contrary, the parents should always be given a full account of the material submitted to the court, the evidence given at the hearing, the submissions made to support the application and the justices reasons whether they ask for this information or not.

2.2.3 Emergencies and investigations: EPOs: human rights considerations

See Chapter 4.1.4 Interim care and supervision orders: test for ICOs[3]: interim removals: human rights considerations

2.2.4 Emergencies and investigations: EPOs: no appeal

Re BC (a child) [2016] EWCA Civ 970, [17] (McFarlane LJ), [27]–[28] (King LJ)

17. As is well known, the Children Act 1989 section 45(10) provides that no appeal lies from the making of, or in this case the refusal to make, an emergency protection order. So a Local Authority who are concerned at

3 Interim care orders.

> the outcome of a case where an EPO is refused have no remedy in terms of appeal against the judge's determination. That that is so may well be because the Local Authority always have, if they consider it to be justified, the ability to apply for an interim care order from which of course there is an avenue of appeal, and that is what the Local Authority did.

…

27. I would agree and simply add that as my Lord has said, emergency protection orders do not carry with them a right of appeal, for reasons which we all understand. In the event that an emergency protection order is not granted, local authorities may if appropriate seek an interim care order which often is accompanied by more extensive evidence, or, more commonly these days, is the first port of call to the court.

28. Parents are protected, rightly, by the very high test that is applied by judges before a child is removed following the making of either an emergency protection order or an interim care order. Equally, however, where a Local Authority has a real concern that a judge may have fallen into error in failing to grant a protective order following a child having been injured, it is in my judgment imperative that that Local Authority, to meet its statutory duties, is able to bring the matter before this court or another court by way of appeal in order to allow the failure to grant a protective order to be reviewed.

See also *Essex County Council v F* [1993] 2 FCR 289 (FD), 294E–295G (Douglas Brown J) addressing the same point

2.3 EMERGENCIES AND INVESTIGATIONS: S 37[4] INVESTIGATIONS

2.3.1 Emergencies and investigations: s 37 investigations: criteria: 'child's circumstances' to be construed widely

Re H (child's circumstances: direction to investigate) [1993] 2 FCR 277 (FD), 287E–F (Scott Baker J)

> In my judgment, the child's circumstances, as referred to in s 37(1), should be widely construed and include any situation which may have a bearing on the child being likely to suffer significant harm in the future, which is of course the critical factor as regards making a care order.
>
> The purposive construction of s 37(1) leads me to this conclusion.

4 Children Act 1989, s 37.

2.3.2 Emergencies and investigations: s 37 investigations: jurisdiction to order multiple investigations

Re K (children) (private law proceedings: direction to investigate child's circumstances) [2012] EWCA Civ 1549, [2013] 1 FCR 87, [23]–[26], [31]–[32] (McFarlane LJ) *quotation limited to* [31]–[32]

[31] In an appropriate case the jurisdiction in private law proceedings for the court to make a s 37 direction is an important and useful facility under which a local authority is required to investigate a child's circumstances and required to consider issuing care proceedings. A private law case may last for a significant time and the circumstances of a child who is the subject of the proceedings may change. It would be wholly artificial to limit the court's ability to utilise the s 37 jurisdiction to 'one shot' in each case. Nothing in the statutory language suggests that there is to be such a limitation on use. To the contrary, by s 37(1) the jurisdiction exists '[w] here, in any family proceedings in which a question arises with respect to the welfare of any child, it appears to the court that it may be appropriate for a care or supervision order to be made'. Circumstances sufficient to justify it appearing to the court that a public order may be appropriate may occur for a variety of reasons and at different stages during a single set of proceedings.

[32] In the present case, the judge made a series of s 37 directions arising out of the same factual context on the basis that the investigation conducted by the local authority was, on each occasion, unsatisfactory. As a matter of principle, and before turning to the facts of this case and the justification for the judge's exercise of the jurisdiction in this case, it must be the case that where a judge is satisfied that the local authority has either simply not complied with an initial s 37 direction, or has conducted an investigation which fails to a significant degree to engage with the court's concerns, the court has jurisdiction to extend or renew its s 37 direction. It will be a question in each case to determine whether such a course is justified. In approaching that question it will be necessary to bear very much in mind that the statutory structure is firmly weighted in favour of the local authority, which, alone, has the power to issue a public law application under s 31 of the 1989 Act. In *Re M (Intractable Contact Dispute: Interim Care Order)* [2003] EWHC 1024 (Fam) at [123], [2003] 2 FLR 636 at [123], Wall J underlined the statutory structure thus: '[The court] cannot require the local authority to take proceedings. The limit of [the court's power] is to direct the authority to undertake an investigation of the children's circumstances.'

2.3.3 Emergencies and investigations: s 37 investigations: no power to compel LAs to bring proceedings

See Chapter 2.3.2 Emergencies and investigations: s 37 investigations: jurisdiction to order multiple investigations

2.3.4 Emergencies and investigations: s 37 investigations: dispute over 'child's' age: court determination

Lambeth London Borough Council v TK and another [2008] EWCA Civ 103, [2009] 1 FCR 285, [26]–[28] (Wilson LJ)

[26] So we must turn to the terms of s 37, set out at [18], above. The power under s 37 arises in any family proceedings in which a question arises with respect to the welfare of any 'child'. Where in such proceedings it appears to it that it may be appropriate for a care (or supervision) order to be made with respect to her, the court may direct an investigation of 'the child's' circumstances.

[27] If their appeal is to succeed, Lambeth need to establish that any issue whether a person is a 'child' within the meaning of s 37 is to be determined by the local authority to whom the direction thereunder is made. I do not agree. I consider that it is to be determined by the court which is minded to make—or has on a presumptive basis made—the direction.

[28] Apart from the need for it to appear to the court to be appropriate for a care order to be made, the terms of s 37 set three threshold requirements for the exercise of the power which it confers, namely that:

(a) there is a 'child';
(b) there are family proceedings; and
(c) a question arises therein with respect to her welfare.

A local authority are entitled to submit to the court that there is no 'child'; or that there are no 'family proceedings'; or even, I suppose, that no question arises therein with respect to the child's welfare; and thus that, by reason of any of such three alleged circumstances, there is no power to make—or on a presumptive basis to have made—the direction. But I am unable to subscribe to any such construction of the section as confers upon a local authority the right to determine whether such circumstances exist. The reference in the section is to a 'child', not to any person whom the local authority consider to be a child. Unless its terms make clear to the contrary, it is for the court to determine whether the threshold requirements set by statute for the exercise of a judicial power are satisfied.

2.4 EMERGENCIES AND INVESTIGATIONS: S 47[5] INVESTIGATIONS

2.4.1 Emergencies and investigations: s 47 investigations: purpose

R (on the application of AB and CD) v The London Borough of Haringey [2013] EWHC 416 (Admin), [2014] 2 FLR 63, [7]–[10] (HHJ Anthony Thornton QC)

7. Section 47 enquiries are one of the principal measures available to a local authority to enable it to exercise its child protection functions to

5 Children Act 1989, s 47.

protect children who are at risk of suffering or are suffering significant harm whether it be physical, emotional or psychological harm. Such harm and such risks are often very difficult to ascertain and root out and the purpose of section 47 is to provide a readily available means whereby a local authority can ascertain the facts and risks that a child is running and then to identify and implement necessary protective, supportive and developmental measures to safeguard and to promote that child's welfare. The objective of a section 47 enquiry is to protect children who are suffering from or are threatened with significant harm and the threshold for its operation in any given case is the need for the local authority concerned to have reasonable cause to suspect that that child is suffering or is likely to suffer significant harm.

8. The use of section 47 and the measures that may be taken by a local authority following its use are predominantly aimed at securing the best interests of children. Its use is intended to be child-focused and to take account of the child's views and wishes without unduly and unfairly disrupting her family life. The use of section 47 should also take account of the personal and family rights of a child's parents or carers so long as that does not interfere with the overriding duty of child protection and development.

9. Section 47 enquiries are multi-agency in their scope and they will usually include such agencies as the child's school, medical practitioner, social workers and the police. The police have an important role to play given the likelihood that in most cases where a child is suffering or is at risk of suffering significant harm, the perpetrator or perpetrators of that risk or that harm will have committed or will still be committing serious criminal offences whose victim is a child.

10. A section 47 enquiry involves an in-depth child-centred assessment of a child's developmental needs, of the harm she is suffering or may suffer, of the capacity of the child's parents or carers to respond to the child's needs and of the family and environmental factors that are playing a role in the harm she is suffering or may suffer. This intrusive assessment should take account of the views of the different agencies involved with and the external influences on the child and it must also directly involve both the parents and the child unless this will endanger the child. The necessary fact-gathering should include sessions with the child without her parents or carers present and it should ascertain that child's wishes and aspirations wherever possible. The assessment, known as a core assessment, must be concluded so that a holistic view may be taken of the child's needs, of the significant harm that the child is being or is at risk of being subjected to and the steps that can be implemented for the eradication of negative influences on the child and the promotion of favourable ones on her.

See also *Re I (Children: Child Assessment Order)* [2020] EWCA Civ 281, [2020] Fam 390, [9]–[14] (Peter Jackson LJ) addressing a related point (the purpose and scheme of child assessment orders)

2.4.2 Emergencies and investigations: s 47 investigations: 'reasonable cause to suspect': a low threshold

R (on the application of S) v Swindon Borough Council and another
[2001] EWHC 334 (Admin), [2001] 3 FCR 702, [34]–[36] (Scott Baker J)

[34] In my judgment the need to establish facts on the balance of probability has no place in the exercise by a local authority of its various protective responsibilities under the 1989 Act. *Re H* was concerned with the court's power to make care or supervision orders under s 31 of the 1989 Act. It is at this point in the child protection process that evidence has to be weighed and evaluated and decisions made as to what is proved and what is not. Decisions made earlier in the process have to be made in accordance with the power conferred by the section under which the authority is acting, and in the present case the critical question is whether the authority *have reasonable cause to suspect* a child is likely to suffer significant harm.

[35] It should be noted that if *Re H* governed the approach in cases such as the present the result would be to prevent local authorities from carrying out effective and timely risk assessments. They would be forced to take care proceedings to identify whether grounds for intervention were present. This would be completely contrary to the principle of non-intervention in children cases. I do not accept that a local authority has to be satisfied on balance of probability that a person is an abuser before intervention is justified.

[36] What triggers the local authority's duty under s 47 is having reasonable cause *to suspect,* not reasonable cause to believe, which is the test in a number of other sections. Accordingly the threshold is quite low. This is hardly surprising as their obligation is to investigate ie make enquiries with a view to deciding whether to take any action to safeguard or promote the child's welfare. If the enquiries lead the local authority to the conclusion that action is necessary it is required by sub-s (8) to take it. Mr McCarthy points out that the whole structure of the Act is quite alien to the notion of establishing facts on the balance of probability before action can be taken in cases such as the present. He refers, for example, to s 17(10) where the definition of child in need does not require any previous finding that a child has been caused significant harm, but merely that it is likely the child will not achieve the appropriate standard of health and development without provision of the necessary services.

Gogay v Hertfordshire County Council [2001] 1 FCR 455 (CA), [48]–[50] (Hale LJ)

48. There is a real distinction between those cases and this, in that the constable must have 'reasonable cause to believe', whereas the authority need only have 'reasonable cause to suspect'. Suspicion is obviously a lower threshold than belief. The distinction is clearly deliberate: the power of a police officer to take a child into police protection under s 46 of the 1989 Act requires him to have 'reasonable cause to believe that a child

would otherwise suffer significant harm'; the court's power to make an emergency protection order under s 44 of the 1989 Act requires that there be 'reasonable cause to believe that the child is likely to suffer significant harm'; the court's power to make an interim care order under s 38 of the 1989 Act requires it to be satisfied that 'there are reasonable grounds for believing that' the necessary criteria are made out.

49. This is just as one would expect. These powers involve a compulsory intervention in the lives of both the child and those looking after him, usually his parents (they are clearly an interference with family life for the purpose of art 8 of the European Convention for the Protection of Human Rights and Fundamental Freedoms (Rome, 4 November 1950; TS 71 (1953); Cmd 8969) (the European Convention on Human Rights)). In contrast, a s 47 investigation does not generally infringe the legal rights of anyone involved. It merely imposes upon the local authority a duty to carry the investigation far enough to enable it to reach a conclusion. It also imposes upon certain other authorities (not including the police) a duty to help if asked.

50. In my view, the courts should be slow indeed to hold that a local authority does not have reasonable grounds such as will justify it in making further inquiries in a case such as this. Given that no infringement of legal rights is generally involved, the decision to hold such an investigation would normally only be challenged through judicial review. The court would be reluctant to grant such a remedy save in the most blatant case of arbitrary and unjustified inquiry. (It should not be forgotten that the European Convention may also impose positive obligations upon states to protect people from inhuman or degrading treatment or from serious invasions of their personal integrity: the immunity given to local authorities who fail to protect children from abuse, in the case of *X (minors) v Bedfordshire CC, M (a minor) v Newham London BC, E (a minor) v Dorest CC* [1995] 3 FCR 337, [1995] 2 AC 633, is currently under challenge before the European Court of Human Rights: see the European Commission on Human Rights' opinion, reported as *Z v UK* [2000] 2 FCR 245, and its earlier decision on admissibility, reported as *KL v UK* [2000] 2 FCR 274.)

2.4.3 Emergencies and investigations: s 47 investigations: outcome: challenging LA decisions to initiate proceedings

Re M (care proceedings: judicial review) [2003] EWHC 850 (Admin), [2004] 1 FCR 302, [29]–[41] (Munby J) *quotation limited to* [29], [41]

[29] The point is put very clearly by the local authority and by Miss Rowsell on its behalf. It says that it has ongoing duties in respect of child protection. It should not be barred from making an application under Pt IV or Pt V of the 1989 Act where it considers it necessary in order to safeguard a child's welfare. The parents' correct remedy if the local authority commences either emergency protection or care proceedings is through the court of application (the family proceedings court or, if the case is transferred up,

the county court or the Family Division) and by defending the proceedings commenced by the local authority. I wholeheartedly agree.

…

[41] I indicated above my very firm view that judicial review proceedings of the type which have been commenced here can only ever be appropriate, if at all, in wholly exceptional circumstances. By definition, exceptional circumstances defy definition. Indeed, I have difficulty envisaging any situation in which it could be appropriate to make the kind of application that was made in this case. But it would at the very least, I think, be necessary to demonstrate, and to demonstrate very clearly indeed, that it would be vexatious or an abuse of the process of the court for the local authority to commence the threatened emergency protection or care proceedings. Be that as it may, there is plainly nothing remotely out of the ordinary to justify recourse to the Administrative Court in the circumstances of the present case.

CHAPTER 3

Threshold criteria

Chapter contents

CHAPTER 3

Threshold criteria

3.1 THRESHOLD CRITERIA: BURDEN AND STANDARD OF PROOF

3.1.1 Threshold criteria: burden and standard of proof: establishing the s 31[1] criteria

Re H and R (minors) (sexual abuse: standard of proof) [1996] 1 FCR 509 (HL), 524G–525B (Lord Nicholls)

> The power of the court to make a care or supervision order only arises if the court is 'satisfied' that the criteria stated in s 31(2) exist. The expression 'if the court is satisfied', here and elsewhere in the Act, envisages that the court must be judicially satisfied on proper material. There is also inherent in the expression an indication of the need for the subject-matter to be affirmatively proved. If the court is left in a state of indecision the matter has not been established to the level, or standard, needed for the court to be 'satisfied'. Thus in s 31(2), in order for the threshold to be crossed, the conditions set out in paras (a) and (b) must be affirmatively established to the satisfaction of the court.
>
> The legal burden of establishing the existence of these conditions rests on the applicant for a care order. The general principle is that he who asserts must prove. Generally, although there are exceptions, a plaintiff or applicant must establish the existence of all the pre-conditions and other facts entitling him to the order he seeks. There is nothing in the language or context of s 31(2) to suggest that the normal principle should not apply to the threshold conditions.

3.1.2 Threshold criteria: findings: burden and standard of proof: proving a 'fact in issue'

Re B (children) (sexual abuse: standard of proof) [2008] UKHL 35, [2008] 2 FCR 339, [2]–[3] (Lord Hoffmann)

> [2] If a legal rule requires a fact to be proved (a 'fact in issue'), a judge or jury must decide whether or not it happened. There is no room for a finding that it might have happened. The law operates a binary system in which the only values are 0 and 1. The fact either happened or it did not. If the tribunal is left in doubt, the doubt is resolved by a rule that one party or the other carries the burden of proof. If the party who bears the burden of

1 Children Act 1989, s 31.

proof fails to discharge it, a value of 0 is returned and the fact is treated as not having happened. If he does discharge it, a value of 1 is returned and the fact is treated as having happened.

[3] The effect of the decision of the House in *Re H and R (minors) (sexual abuse: standard of proof)* [1996] 1 FCR 509, [1996] 1 All ER 1 is that s 31(2)(a) of the Children Act 1989 requires any facts used as the basis of a prediction that a child is 'likely to suffer significant harm' to be proved to have happened. Every such fact is to be treated as a fact in issue. The majority of the House rejected the analogy with facts which merely form part of the material from which a fact in issue may be inferred, which need not each be proved to have happened. There is of course no conceptual reason for rejecting this analogy, which in the context of some predictions (such as Lord Browne-Wilkinson's example of air raid warnings) might be prudent and appropriate. But the House decided that it was inappropriate for the purposes of s 31(2)(a). It is this rule which the House reaffirms today.

See also *Shagang Shipping Co Ltd (in liquidation) v HNA Group Co Ltd* [2020] UKSC 34, [2020] 1 WLR 3549, [99] (Lord Hamblen and Lord Leggatt) addressing the same point (emphasising the difference between 'facts in issue' and facts which make a fact in issue more or less probable)

3.1.3 Threshold criteria: burden and standard of proof: balance of probability

Re H and R (minors) (sexual abuse: standard of proof) [1996] 1 FCR 509 (HL), 525C–H (Lord Nicholls)

Where the matters in issue are facts the standard of proof required in non-criminal proceedings is the preponderance of probability, usually referred to as the balance of probability. This is the established general principle. There are exceptions such as contempt of court applications, but I can see no reason for thinking that family proceedings are, or should be, an exception. By family proceedings I mean proceedings so described in the Act of 1989, ss 105 and 8(3). Despite their special features, family proceedings remain essentially a form of civil proceedings. Family proceedings often raise very serious issues, but so do other forms of civil proceedings.

The balance of probability standard means that a court is satisfied an event occurred if the court considers that, on the evidence, the occurrence of the event was more likely than not. When assessing the probabilities the court will have in mind as a factor, to whatever extent is appropriate in the particular case, that the more serious the allegation the less likely it is that the event occurred and, hence, the stronger should be the evidence before the court concludes that the allegation is established on the balance of probability. Fraud is usually less likely than negligence. Deliberate physical injury is usually less likely than accidental physical injury. A step-father is usually less likely to have repeatedly raped and had non-consensual oral sex with his under age step-daughter than on some occasion to have lost his temper and slapped her. Built into the preponderance of probability standard is a generous degree of flexibility in respect of the seriousness of the allegation.

Although the result is much the same, this does not mean that where a serious allegation is in issue the standard of proof required is higher. It means only that the inherent probability or improbability of an event is itself a matter to be taken into account when weighing the probabilities and deciding whether, on balance, the event occurred. The more improbable the event, the stronger must be the evidence that it did occur before, on the balance of probability, its occurrence will be established. Ungoed-Thomas, J expressed this neatly in *Re Dellow's Will Trusts* [1964] 1 WLR 451, 455:

> 'the more serious the allegation the more cogent is the evidence required to overcome the unlikelihood of what is alleged and thus to prove it.'

Re B (children) (sexual abuse: standard of proof) [2008] UKHL 35, [2008] 2 FCR 339, [13] (Lord Hoffmann), [70]–[73] (Baroness Hale)

[13] My Lords, I would invite your Lordships fully to approve these observations. I think that the time has come to say, once and for all, that there is only one civil standard of proof and that is proof that the fact in issue more probably occurred than not …

…

[70] My Lords, for that reason I would go further and announce loud and clear that the standard of proof in finding the facts necessary to establish the threshold under s 31(2) or the welfare considerations in s 1 of the 1989 Act is the simple balance of probabilities, neither more nor less. Neither the seriousness of the allegation nor the seriousness of the consequences should make any difference to the standard of proof to be applied in determining the facts. The inherent probabilities are simply something to be taken into account, where relevant, in deciding where the truth lies.

[71] As to the seriousness of the consequences, they are serious either way. A child may find her relationship with her family seriously disrupted; or she may find herself still at risk of suffering serious harm. A parent may find his relationship with his child seriously disrupted; or he may find himself still at liberty to maltreat this or other children in the future.

[72] As to the seriousness of the allegation, there is no logical or necessary connection between seriousness and probability. Some seriously harmful behaviour, such as murder, is sufficiently rare to be inherently improbable in most circumstances. Even then there are circumstances, such as a body with its throat cut and no weapon to hand, where it is not at all improbable. Other seriously harmful behaviour, such as alcohol or drug abuse, is regrettably all too common and not at all improbable. Nor are serious allegations made in a vacuum. Consider the famous example of the animal seen in Regent's Park. If it is seen outside the zoo on a stretch of greensward

regularly used for walking dogs, then of course it is more likely to be a dog than a lion. If it is seen in the zoo next to the lions' enclosure when the door is open, then it may well be more likely to be a lion than a dog.

[73] In the context of care proceedings, this point applies with particular force to the identification of the perpetrator. It may be unlikely that any person looking after a baby would take him by the wrist and swing him against the wall, causing multiple fractures and other injuries. But once the evidence is clear that that is indeed what has happened to the child, it ceases to be improbable. Some-one looking after the child at the relevant time must have done it. The inherent improbability of the event has no relevance to deciding who that was. The simple balance of probabilities test should be applied.

See also *Re S-B (children) (non-accidental injury)* [2009] UKSC 17, [2010] 1 FCR 321, [8]–[13] (Lady Hale) considering *Re H and R (minors) (sexual abuse: standard of proof)* [1996] 1 FCR 509, considering *Re B (children) (sexual abuse: standard of proof)* [2008] UKHL 35, [2008] 2 FCR 339

See also *Re BR (proof of facts)* [2015] EWFC 41, [7] (Peter Jackson J) addressing the same point

3.1.4 Threshold criteria: burden and standard of proof: not reversing the burden

Re M (a child) [2012] EWCA Civ 1580, [2013] 2 FLR 874, [6] (Ward LJ)

6. ... The burden of proof lies on the local authority to prove the case against the parents. The standard of proof is the balance of probabilities, and that means the same in this kind of case as in every other, a simply balance of probability. Suspicion is not proof, and the burden must always remain on the local authority and should not be reversed.

See also *A Local Authority v PT and others (Re-Hearing of Fact-Finding)* [2018] EWHC 2670 (Fam), [16] (Williams J) addressing the same point (highlighting that parents have nothing to prove)

See also *Re M-B (children)* [2015] EWCA Civ 1027, [15] (Macur LJ) considering *Re M (a child)* [2012] EWCA Civ 1580, [2013] 2 FLR 874 (indicating that reliance on lack of satisfactory explanation is not necessarily reversal of the burden)

3.1.5 Threshold criteria: burden and standard of proof: reliance on the burden

Re A (children) [2018] EWCA Civ 1718, [2018] 3 FCR 207, [58] (King LJ)

[58] In my judgment what one draws from *Popi M* and *Nulty Deceased* is that:

i) Judges will decide a case on the burden of proof alone only when driven to it and where no other course is open to him given the unsatisfactory state of the evidence.

ii) Consideration of such a case necessarily involves looking at the whole picture, including what gaps there are in the evidence, whether the individual factors relied upon are in themselves properly established, what factors may point away from the suggested explanation and what other explanation might fit the circumstances.

iii) The court arrives at its conclusion by considering whether on an overall assessment of the evidence (i.e. on a preponderance of the evidence) the case for believing that the suggested event happened is more compelling than the case for not reaching that belief (which is not necessarily the same as believing positively that it did not happen) and not by reference to percentage possibilities or probabilities.

See also *Re B (children) (sexual abuse: standard of proof)* [2008] UKHL 35, [2008] 2 FCR 339, [32] (Baroness Hale) addressing the same point (noting that generally courts can determine the truth without relying on the burden)

3.1.6 Threshold criteria: burden and standard of proof: avoiding aggregation

Re A (children) [2018] EWCA Civ 1718, [2018] 3 FCR 207, [51]–[54] (King LJ)

[51] With respect to the judge I cannot agree that the use of percentages and or 'aggregation' is the proper approach to the judicial function in respect of the simple application of the balance of probabilities.

[52] The starting point remains the test as articulated by Baroness Hale of Richmond in *Re B (minors)* [2009] 1 AC 11, [2008] 2 FCR 339, [2008] 3 WLR 1, HL: …

[53] In *A County Council v M & F,* upon which the judge relied, Mostyn J having set out passages from *Re B* (and Baroness Hale's confirmation of *Re B* found in *Re S-B* [2009] UKSC 17, [2010] 1 AC 678, [2010] 1 FCR 321) went on:

> '[16] Thus the law sets a simple probability standard of 51/49, but the more serious or improbable the allegation the greater the need, generally speaking, for evidential 'cogency'. In *AA v NA and Others* [2010] 2 FLR 1173, FD, I attempted to summarise these principles at para [24]:
>
> > "[24] Thus, it is clear that in all civil proceedings P cannot be set higher than a scintilla above 0.5. The various judicial statements that a more serious charge requires more clear evidence is not an elevation of P > 0.5. The requirement of evidential clarity is quite distinct from an elevation of the probability standard. Were it otherwise, and, say, an allegation of rape or murder of a child made in civil proceedings required P to be set at > 0.6 then one could end up in the position where a court considered that P in such a case was, say 0.51 but still had to find that it did not happen;

when, as a matter of probability, is was more likely that not that it did. This would be absurd and perverse. P must always be set at > 0.5 in civil proceedings, but subject to the proviso that the more serious the allegation so the evidence must be clearer."'

[54] With the greatest respect to the erudition of Mostyn J's arithmetical approach to the application of the 'simple balance of probabilities', I do not agree that it represents the appropriate approach, and it seems to me that this passage had, in part, led the judge to decide that, in order to determine whether the local authority had discharged the burden of proof to the necessary standard, he had to adopt the same approach. As a consequence, the judge mistakenly attached a percentage to each of the possibilities and thereafter, added together the percentages which he attributed to an innocent explanation and before concluding that, only if the resulting sum was 49 per cent or less, could the court make a finding of inflicted injury.

3.2 THRESHOLD CRITERIA: GENERAL APPROACH TO THRESHOLD

3.2.1 Threshold criteria: general approach to threshold: matters to bear in mind if threshold is disputed

Re B (a child) (care order: proportionality: criterion for review) [2013] UKSC 33, [2013] 2 FCR 525, [193] (Lady Hale)

[193] I agree entirely that it is the statute and the statute alone that the courts have to apply, and that judicial explanation or expansion is at best an imperfect guide. I agree also that parents, children and families are so infinitely various that the law must be flexible enough to cater for frailties as yet unimagined even by the most experienced family judge. Nevertheless, where the threshold is in dispute, courts might find it helpful to bear the following in mind:

(1) The court's task is not to improve on nature or even to secure that every child has a happy and fulfilled life, but to be satisfied that the statutory threshold has been crossed.

(2) When deciding whether the threshold is crossed the court should identify, as precisely as possible, the nature of the harm which the child is suffering or is likely to suffer. This is particularly important where the child has not yet suffered any, or any significant, harm and where the harm which is feared is the impairment of intellectual, emotional, social or behavioural development.

(3) Significant harm is harm which is 'considerable, noteworthy or important'. The court should identify why and in what respects the harm is significant. Again, this may be particularly important where the harm in question is the impairment of intellectual, emotional, social or behavioural development which has not yet happened.

(4) The harm has to be attributable to a lack, or likely lack, of reasonable parental care, not simply to the characters and personalities of both the child and her parents. So once again, the court should identify

the respects in which parental care is falling, or is likely to fall, short of what it would be reasonable to expect.

(5) Finally, where harm has not yet been suffered, the court must consider the degree of likelihood that it will be suffered in the future. This will entail considering the degree of likelihood that the parents' future behaviour will amount to a lack of reasonable parental care. It will also entail considering the relationship between the significance of the harmed feared and the likelihood that it will occur. Simply to state that there is a 'risk' is not enough. The court has to be satisfied, by relevant and sufficient evidence, that the harm is likely: see *Re J (children) (non-accidental injury: past possible perpetrator in new family)* [2013] 2 FCR 149, [2013] 3 All ER 1.

3.2.2 Threshold criteria: general approach to threshold: approach to fact-finding

Re A (no 2) (children: findings of fact) [2019] EWCA Civ 1947, [2020] 1 FCR 313, [100] (Peter Jackson LJ)

[100] The questions for every fact-finder are *What, When, Where, Who, How and Why?* Their significance and difficulty varies from case to case. Some answers will be obvious while other questions can be extremely hard or even unanswerable. Sometimes a question may not need answering at all. At all events the questions come in no set order and each inquiry will suggest its own starting point. It will no doubt find apparently solid ground and progress from there, but conclusions can only ever be provisional until they have been checked against each other so as to arrive at a coherent outcome. At each stage, regard is had to the inherent probabilities and improbabilities surrounding what are inevitably abnormal circumstances.

See Chapter 7.3 Evidence: approach when fact-finding

3.2.3 Threshold criteria: general approach to threshold: case management

See Chapter 3.3 Threshold criteria: fact-finding: case management

3.2.4 Threshold criteria: general approach to threshold: formulating threshold allegations

Re A (a child) [2015] EWFC 11, [2016] 1 FLR 1, [7]–[12] (Sir James Munby P)

7. In the light of the way in which this case has been presented and some of the submissions I heard, it is important always to bear in mind in these cases, and too often, I fear, they are overlooked, three fundamentally important points. The present case is an object lesson in, almost a textbook example of, how not to embark upon and pursue a care case.

8. The first fundamentally important point relates to the matter of fact-finding and proof. I emphasise, as I have already said, that it is for the local authority to prove, on a balance of probabilities, the facts upon which it seeks to rely. I draw attention to what, in *Re A (A Child) (No 2)* [2011] EWCA Civ 12, [2011] 1 FCR 141, para 26, I described as:

> 'the elementary proposition that findings of fact must be based on evidence (including inferences that can properly be drawn from the evidence) and not on suspicion or speculation.'

This carries with it two important practical and procedural consequences.

9. The first is that the local authority, if its case is challenged on some factual point, must adduce proper evidence to establish what it seeks to prove. Much material to be found in local authority case records or social work chronologies is hearsay, often second- or third-hand hearsay. Hearsay evidence is, of course, admissible in family proceedings. But, and as the present case so vividly demonstrates, a local authority which is unwilling or unable to produce the witnesses who can speak of such matters first-hand, may find itself in great, or indeed insuperable, difficulties if a parent not merely puts the matter in issue but goes into the witness-box to deny it. As I remarked in my second *View from the President's Chambers*, [2013] Fam Law 680:

> 'Of course the court can act on the basis of evidence that is hearsay. But direct evidence from those who can speak to what they have themselves seen and heard is more compelling and less open to cross-examination. Too often far too much time is taken up by cross-examination directed to little more than demonstrating that no-one giving evidence in court is able to speak of their own knowledge, and that all are dependent on the assumed accuracy of what is recorded, sometimes at third or fourth hand, in the local authority's files.'

It is a common feature of care cases that a local authority asserts that a parent does not admit, recognise or acknowledge something or does not recognise or acknowledge the local authority's concern about something. If the 'thing' is put in issue, the local authority must both prove the 'thing' and establish that it has the significance attributed to it by the local authority.

10. The second practical and procedural point goes to the formulation of threshold and proposed findings of fact. The schedule of findings in the present case contains, as we shall see, allegations in relation to the father that 'he appears to have' lied or colluded, that various people have 'stated' or 'reported' things, and that 'there is an allegation'. With all respect to counsel, this form of allegation, which one sees far too often in such documents, is wrong and should never be used. It confuses the crucial distinction, once upon a time, though no longer, spelt out in the rules of pleading and well understood, between an assertion of fact and the evidence needed to prove the assertion. What do the words 'he appears to have lied' or 'X reports that he did Y' mean? More important, where does

it take one? The relevant allegation is not that 'he appears to have lied' or 'X reports'; the relevant allegation, if there is evidence to support it, is surely that 'he lied' or 'he did Y'.

11. Failure to understand these principles and to analyse the case accordingly can lead, as here, to the unwelcome realisation that a seemingly impressive case is, in truth, a tottering edifice built on inadequate foundations.

12. The second fundamentally important point is the need to link the facts relied upon by the local authority with its case on threshold, the need to demonstrate *why*, as the local authority asserts, facts A + B + C justify the conclusion that the child has suffered, or is at risk of suffering, significant harm of types X, Y or Z. Sometimes the linkage will be obvious, as where the facts proved establish physical harm. But the linkage may be very much less obvious where the allegation is only that the child is at risk of suffering emotional harm or, as in the present case, at risk of suffering neglect. In the present case, as we shall see, an important element of the local authority's case was that the father 'lacks honesty with professionals', 'minimises matters of importance' and 'is immature and lacks insight of issues of importance'. May be. But how does this feed through into a conclusion that A is at risk of neglect? The conclusion does not follow naturally from the premise. The local authority's evidence and submissions must set out the argument and explain explicitly why it is said that, in the particular case, the conclusion indeed follows from the facts. Here, as we shall see, the local authority conspicuously failed to do so.

Re J (a child) [2015] EWCA Civ 222, [56] (Aikens LJ)

56. The fundamental principles underlined by the President in *Re A*, which, as I say, are not new and are based on statute or the highest authority or both, can, I think, be summarised thus:

i) In an adoption case, it is for the local authority to prove, on a balance of probabilities, the facts on which it relies and, if adoption is to be ordered, to demonstrate that 'nothing else will do', when having regard to the overriding requirements of the child's welfare.

ii) If the local authority's case on a factual issue is challenged, the local authority must adduce proper evidence to establish the fact it seeks to prove. If a local authority asserts that a parent 'does not admit, recognise or acknowledge' that a matter of concern to the authority is the case, then if that matter of concern is put in issue, it is for the local authority to prove it is the case and, furthermore, that the matter of concern 'has the significance attributed to it by the local authority'.

iii) Hearsay evidence about issues that appear in reports produced on behalf of the local authority, although admissible, has strict limitations if a parent challenges that hearsay evidence by giving contrary oral evidence at a hearing. If the local authority is unwilling or unable to produce a witness who can speak to the relevant matter by first hand evidence, it may find itself in 'great, or indeed insuperable' difficulties in proving the fact or matter alleged by the local authority but which is challenged.

iv) The formulation of 'Threshold' issues and proposed findings of fact must be done with the utmost care and precision. The distinction between a fact and evidence alleged to prove a fact is fundamental and must be recognised. The document must identify the relevant facts which are sought to be proved. It can be cross-referenced to evidence relied on to prove the facts asserted but should not contain mere allegations ('he appears to have lied' etc.)

v) It is for the local authority to prove that there is the necessary link between the facts upon which it relies and its case on Threshold. The local authority must demonstrate *why* certain facts, if proved, 'justify the conclusion that the child has suffered or is at the risk of suffering significant harm' of the type asserted by the local authority. 'The local authority's evidence and submissions must set out the arguments and explain explicitly why it is said that, in the particular case, the conclusion [that the child has suffered or is at the risk of suffering significant harm] indeed follows from the facts [proved]'.

vi) It is vital that local authorities, and, even more importantly, judges, bear in mind that nearly all parents will be imperfect in some way or other. The State will not take away the children of 'those who commit crimes, abuse alcohol or drugs or suffer from physical or mental illness or disability, or who espouse antisocial, political or religious beliefs' simply because those facts are established. It must be demonstrated by the local authority, in the first place, that by reason of one or more of those facts, the child has suffered or is at risk of suffering significant harm. Even if that is demonstrated, adoption will not be ordered unless it is demonstrated by the local authority that 'nothing else will do' when having regard to the overriding requirements of the child's welfare. The court must guard against 'social engineering'.

vii) When a judge considers the evidence, he must take all of it into account and consider each piece of evidence in the context of all the other evidence, and, to use a metaphor, examine the canvas overall.

viii) In considering a local authority's application for a care order for adoption the judge must have regard to the 'welfare checklist' in *section1(3)* of the *Children Act 1989* and that in *section 1(4)* of the *Adoption and Children Act 2002*. The judge must also treat, as a paramount consideration, the child's welfare 'throughout his life' in accordance with *section 1(2)* of the *2002 Act*. In dispensing with the parents' consent, the judge must apply *section 52(1)(b)* as explained in *Re P (Placement Orders, parental consent) [2008] 2 RLR 625*.

3.2.5 Threshold criteria: general approach to threshold: adducing proper evidence if allegations are disputed

See Chapter 3.2.4 Threshold criteria: general approach to threshold: formulating threshold allegations

See also *Re BR (proof of facts)* [2015] EWFC 41, [4]–[7] (Peter Jackson J) addressing the same point

3.2.6 Threshold criteria: general approach to threshold: putting adverse cases

Re B (a child) [2018] EWCA Civ 2127, [2019] 1 FCR 120, [15]–[18] (Peter Jackson LJ)

The law: putting an adverse case

[15] It is an elementary feature of a fair hearing that an adverse finding can only be made where the person in question knows of the allegation and the substance of the supporting evidence and has had a reasonable opportunity to respond. With effective case-management, the definition of the issues will make clear what findings are being sought and the opportunity to respond will arise in the course of the evidence, both written and oral.

[16] The obligation to put relevant matters in cross-examination has been stated in a number of authorities from *Browne v Dunn* [1894] 6 R 67 (HL) to *Re W (a child)* [2016] EWCA Civ 1140, [2017] 1 FCR 349, [2017] 1 WLR 2415 at [88]–[89]. Still more recently, the Privy Council considered the matter in *Chen v Ng* [2017] UKPC 27, where the Board's judgment, given by Lords Neuberger and Mance, includes these passages:

> '[52] In a perfect world, any ground for doubting the evidence of a witness ought to be put to him, and a judge should only rely on a ground for disbelieving a witness which that witness has had an opportunity of explaining. However, the world is not perfect, and, while both points remain ideals which should always be in the minds of cross-examiners and trial judges, they cannot be absolute requirements in every case. Even in a very full trial, it may often be disproportionate and unrealistic to expect a cross-examiner to put every possible reason for disbelieving a witness to that witness, especially in a complex case, and it may be particularly difficult to do so in a case such as this, where the Judge sensibly rationed the time for cross-examination and the witness concerned needed an interpreter. Once it is accepted that not every point may be put, it is inevitable that there will be cases where a point which strikes the judge as a significant reason for disbelieving some evidence when he comes to give judgment, has not been put to the witness who gave it.
>
> [53] Mr Parker relies on a general rule, namely that 'it will not do to impeach the credibility of a witness upon a matter on which

he has not had any opportunity of giving an explanation by reason of there having been no suggestion whatever in the course of the case that his story is not accepted', as Lord Herschell LC put it in *Browne v Dunn* (1893) 6 R 67, 71. In other words, where it is not made clear during (or before) a trial that the evidence, or a significant aspect of the evidence, of a witness (especially if he is a party in the proceedings) is challenged as inaccurate, it is not appropriate, at least in the absence of further relevant facts, for the evidence then to be challenged in closing speeches or in the subsequent judgment. A relatively recent example of the application of this rule by the English Court of Appeal can be found in *Markem Corpn v Zipher Ltd* [2005] RPC 31 …'

[17] In *Chen*, the process had been unfair because the two grounds given by the judge for disbelieving a party had not been put to him in evidence. *Re W* was a very different situation where completely unheralded findings were made against professional witnesses. Those findings were described by Mr Geekie, who also appeared in that case, as being outside the four corners of the case.

[18] In assessing fairness, what is important is substance not form. The question of whether an adverse case has been sufficiently put to a witness is likely to be informed by the five factors set out in *Chen* at [55]. It is case-specific and rooted in the real world of litigation in which overall fairness can be achieved in a range of ways. In general a party is required to challenge in cross-examination the evidence of any witness of the opposing party if he wishes to submit to the court that the evidence should not be accepted on that point; if a party has decided not to cross-examine on a particular important point, he will be in difficulty in submitting the evidence should be rejected: see *Phipson on Evidence* (Sweet & Maxwell, 19th edn, 2017) 12.12. However, the rule is not an absolute one, and there will be cases in which it will be pointless to put formal challenges to a witness who knows perfectly well that his or her evidence is disputed, and where the challenge could in reality go no further than 'I put it to you that you are lying'. As my lord, Lord Justice Newey, put it in *Howlett v Davies* [2017] EWCA Civ 1696, [2018] 1 WLR 948, [2017] 6 Costs LO 761 at [39]:

> 'where a witness' honesty is to be challenged, it will always be best if that is explicitly put to the witness. There can then be no doubt that honesty is in issue. But what ultimately matters is that the witness has had fair notice of a challenge to his or her honesty and an opportunity to deal with it. It may be that in a particular context a cross-examination which does not use the words "dishonest" or "lying" will give a witness fair warning. That will be a matter for the trial judge to decide.'

3.2.7 Threshold criteria: general approach to threshold: departing from LA[2] allegations

Re A (no 2) (children: findings of fact) [2019] EWCA Civ 1947, [2020] 1 FCR 313, [96] (Peter Jackson LJ)

[96] The court is not bound by the cases put forward by the parties, but may adopt an alternative solution of its own: *Re S (a child)* [2015] UKSC 20, [2015] 1 FCR 549, [2015] 1 WLR 1631 at [20]. Judges are entitled, where the evidence justifies it, to make findings of fact that have not been sought by the parties, but they should be cautious when considering doing so: *Re G and B (fact-finding hearing)* [2009] EWCA Civ 10, [2010] 1 FCR 73, [2009] 1 FLR 1145, where Wall LJ said this:

> '[15] I am the first to acknowledge that a judge … is entitled to take a proactive, quasi investigative role in care proceedings. Equally, she will make findings of fact on all the evidence available to her, including her assessment of the parents' credibility; she is not limited to the expert evidence. I am also content to decide the question in this appeal on the basis that a judge … is not required slavishly to adhere to a schedule of proposed findings placed before her by a local authority. To take an obvious example: care proceedings are frequently dynamic and issues emerge in the oral evidence which had not hitherto been known to exist. It would be absurd if such matters had to be ignored.
>
> [16] All that said, however, the following propositions seem to me to be equally valid. Where, as here, the local authority had prepared its Schedule of proposed findings with some care, and where the fact finding hearing had itself been the subject of a directions appointment at which the parents had agreed not to apply for various witnesses to attend for cross-examination, it requires very good reasons, in my judgment, for the judge to depart from the schedule of proposed findings. Furthermore, if the judge is, as it were, to go "off piste", and to make findings of fact which are not sought by the local authority or not contained in its Schedule, then he or she must be astute to ensure; (a) that any additional or different findings made are securely founded in the evidence; and (b) that the fairness of the fact-finding process is not compromised.'

3.2.8 Threshold criteria: general approach to threshold: non-applicability of criminal law concepts

Re R (children) [2018] EWCA Civ 198, [2018] 3 FCR 26, [61]–[67], [81]–[91] (McFarlane LJ), [103]–[106] (Hickinbottom LJ) *quotation limited to* [81]–[84], [86], [90]–[91]

[81] Moving beyond the circumstances of the present appeal, and building upon what is said at paragraphs [61] to [67] above, the following general

2 Local authority.

observations as to the approach of a family court when trying, or re-trying, factual issues which could also be framed as a criminal charge are intended to be of assistance to all levels within the Family Court, where the need to undertake such a fact-finding exercise is by no means unusual.

[82] By way of summary, the following points are, in my judgment, clear:

(a) The focus and purpose of a fact-finding investigation in the context of a case concerning the future welfare of children in the Family Court are wholly different to those applicable to the prosecution by the State of an individual before a criminal court [paragraph [62] above],

(b) The primary purpose of the family process is to determine what has gone on in the past, so that those findings may inform the ultimate welfare evaluation as to the child's future with the court's eyes open to such risks as the factual determination may have established [paragraph [62]],

(c) Criminal law concepts, such as the elements needed to establish guilt of a particular crime or a defence, have neither relevance nor function within a process of fact-finding in the Family Court [paragraph [65]],

(d) As a matter of principle, it is fundamentally wrong for the Family Court to be drawn into an analysis of factual evidence in proceedings relating to the welfare of children based upon criminal law principles and concepts [paragraph [67]].

[83] Where there has been, or may be, a criminal prosecution in relation to the actions of a parent or other person connected with a child whose future welfare is the subject of public or private law proceedings before the Family Court, the question of whether the factual matters that may support such a prosecution should also be litigated within the family proceedings falls to be determined by the Family Court on a case-by-case basis.

[84] The Family Court should only embark upon a fact-finding process where it is necessary to do so. The recently updated Practice Direction FPR 2010, PD 12J 'Child Arrangements and Contact Orders: Domestic Abuse and Harm', relating to private law proceedings includes the following guidance which is of more general application to all proceedings relating to the welfare of children where 'domestic abuse' or other potentially criminal activity is alleged …

…

[86] On the basis of the guidance in PD 12J, and on the basis of general principles, a family court should only embark upon a fact-finding investigation where it is both necessary and proportionate to do so, having regard to the overarching purpose of public law proceedings of (a) establishing whether the CA 1989, s 31 threshold criteria are satisfied and (b) determining the future plan for the child's care by affording paramount consideration to his or her welfare.

...

[90] Lastly, I would mention the specific matter of the use of language. The potential for the court to become drawn into reliance upon criminal law principles is demonstrated by the present appeal. Even where the family court succeeds in avoiding direct reference to the criminal law, it is important that, so far as it is possible to do so, the language of the judgment (and in particular any findings) is expressed in terms which avoid specific words or phrases which may have a bespoke meaning in the context of the criminal jurisdiction, for example 'self-defence', 'reasonable force' or 'the loss of self-control'. Phrases such as 'inappropriate force' or 'proportionate force' may reflect the judge's findings in a particular case, and avoid the risk that the judge's words may be misunderstood as expressing a finding based directly upon criminal law principles.

[91] At the end of the day, the often very difficult role of a judge once it has been determined that a finding of fact hearing is necessary can be reduced to the short statement that the family judge's task in such cases is simply to find the facts. Once any facts are found, they will then form the basis of a more wide-ranging assessment of any consequent risks to the child whose future welfare needs will then fall to be determined.

See also *Re H-N and others (children) (domestic abuse: finding of fact hearings)* [2021] EWCA Civ 448, [60]–[74] (Sir Andrew McFarlane P) considering *Re R (children)* [2018] EWCA Civ 198, [2018] 3 FCR 26 (highlighting that it is findings of fact that matter, and that using criminal law expressions is acceptable but courts should not analyse the evidence of behaviour by direct application of criminal law to determine if allegations are proved)

3.2.9 Threshold criteria: general approach to threshold: precisely ascertaining the meaning of 'non-accidental injury'

Re S (a child) (split hearings: fact finding); Cambridgeshire County Council v PS and others [2014] EWCA Civ 25, [2014] 1 FCR 477, [19]–[22] (Ryder LJ) *quotation limited to* [19]–[21]

[19] The term 'non-accidental injury' may be a term of art used by clinicians as a shorthand and I make no criticism of its use but it is a 'catch-all' for everything that is not an accident. It is also a tautology: the true distinction is between an accident which is unexpected and unintentional and an injury which involves an element of wrong. That element of wrong may involve a lack of care and/or an intent of a greater or lesser degree that may amount to negligence, recklessness or deliberate infliction. While an analysis of that kind may be helpful to distinguish deliberate infliction from, say, negligence, it is unnecessary in any consideration of whether the threshold criteria are satisfied because what the statute requires is something different namely, findings of fact that at least satisfy the significant harm, attributability and objective standard of care elements of s 31(2).

[20] The court's function is to make the findings of fact that it is able on the evidence and then analyse those findings against the statutory formulation. The gloss imported by the use of unexplained legal, clinical or colloquial terms is not helpful to that exercise nor is it necessary for the purposes of s 31(2) to characterise the fact of what happened as negligence, recklessness or in any other way. Just as non-accidental injury is a tautology, 'accidental injury' is an oxymoron that is unhelpful as a description. If the term was used during the discussion after the judgment had been given as a description of one of the possibilities of how the harm had been caused, then it should not have been; it being a contradiction in terms. If, as is often the case when a clinical expert describes harm as being a 'non-accidental injury', there is a range of factual possibilities, those possibilities should be explored with the expert and the witnesses so that the court can understand which, if any, described mechanism is compatible with the presentation of harm.

[21] The threshold is not concerned with intent or blame; it is concerned with whether the objective standard of care which it would be reasonable to expect for the child in question has not been provided so that the harm suffered is attributable to the care actually provided. The judge is not limited to the way the case is put by the local authority but if options are not adequately explored a judge may find a vital piece of the jigsaw missing when s/he comes to look at all the evidence in the round.

3.3 THRESHOLD CRITERIA: FACT-FINDING: CASE MANAGEMENT

3.3.1 Threshold criteria: fact-finding: case management: need for fact-finding

A County Council v DP and others [2005] EWHC 1593 (Fam), [2005] 2 FLR 1031, [21]–[25] (McFarlane J)

(3) Exercise of discretion

21. If it is lawful for the court to conduct a fact finding exercise despite the fact that at this stage no party is seeking a public law order, it is common ground that the court has a discretion whether, on the individual facts of each case, it is right and necessary to do so.

22. The relevant case law is to be found in the following decisions:
Re G (A Minor) (Care Proceedings) [1994] 2 FLR 69 [Wall J]
Stockport Metropolitan BC v D [1995] 1 FLR 873 [Thorpe J]
Re B (Agreed Findings of Fact) [1998] 2 FLR 968 [Butler-Sloss + Thorpe LJJ]
Re M (Threshold Criteria: Parental Concessions) [1999] 2 FLR 728 [Butler-Sloss LJ and Wall J]
Re D (A Child) (9 August 2000) [Schiemann, Thorpe and Mummery LJJ]

23. It is not necessary to read substantial parts of this case law into this judgment. Indeed I note that, in a former life, I was myself rightly

discouraged in *Re M* from taking the Court of Appeal through the authorities because the law on this point is not in any particular doubt [see p 731B].

24. The authorities make it plain that, amongst other factors, the following are likely to be relevant and need to be borne in mind before deciding whether or not to conduct a particular fact finding exercise:
    a) The interests of the child (which are relevant but not paramount)
    b) The time that the investigation will take;
    c) The likely cost to public funds;
    d) The evidential result;
    e) The necessity or otherwise of the investigation;
    f) The relevance of the potential result of the investigation to the future care plans for the child;
    g) The impact of any fact finding process upon the other parties;
    h) The prospects of a fair trial on the issue;
    i) The justice of the case.

25. I am well familiar with the concept of 'necessity', arising as it does from ECHR Art 8 and, indeed, from the pre Human Rights Act 1998 case law to which I have been referred. It is rightly at the core of Mr Tolson's submissions in this case and, without overtly labouring the issue by including substantial descriptive text in this judgment, it is at the forefront of my consideration of the point. Amongst the pertinent questions are: Is there a pressing need for such a hearing? Is the proposed fact finding hearing solely, as Mr Tolson puts it, 'to seek findings against the father on criminal matters for their own sake'? Is the process, which will be costly and time consuming, with potentially serious consequences for the father if it goes against him, proportionate to any identified need?

See also *Re K (children) (adoption: freeing order)* [2004] EWCA Civ 1181, [2004] 3 FCR 123, [57]–[58] (Wall LJ) addressing a related point (identifying a public interest in identifying those who cause children serious inflicted injuries)

3.3.2 Threshold criteria: fact-finding: case management: need for fact-finding: approach to the *Oxfordshire*[3] factors

Re H-D-H (children); Re C (a child) [2021] EWCA Civ 1192, [2021] 4 WLR 106, [1], [3]–[24] (Peter Jackson LJ) *quotation limited to* [1], [3], [20]–[24]

1. On 1 July 2021, we heard these two appeals from the Family Court one after the other. In each case a judge hearing care proceedings made a case management decision that the court would not investigate and make findings of fact about a serious allegation and in each case the local authority appealed. The appeals raise the same question of principle and we now give our judgments on them together. They provide an opportunity for this court to review the long-standing guidance contained

3 *A County Council v DP and others* [2005] EWHC 1593 (Fam), [2005] 2 FLR 1031.

in *Oxfordshire County Council v DP, RS and BS* [2005] EWHC 1593 (Fam); [2005] 2 FLR 1031 in the light of the current pressures on the Family Court.

…

The scope of fact-finding

3. Decisions about the scope of fact-finding are core case management decisions with particular consequences for the length and cost of proceedings, the impact of the litigation on parties and others, and the allocation of court time. They arise in private law proceedings, including when a court is considering whether there should be a fact-finding hearing in relation to any disputed allegation of domestic abuse under PD12J, and in public law proceedings when the court is considering whether it should investigate a fact alleged as forming part of the threshold or as being relevant to the welfare decision. I will outline the statutory framework, administrative guidance, and the caselaw.

…

20. It is unnecessary to cite other authority. Although the approach outlined in *Oxfordshire* predates the incorporation of the overriding objective into the Family Procedure Rules and the 26-week requirement, in my judgement it remains valid when read alongside the statutory framework. It helps judges to reach well-reasoned decisions and counsel appearing in the present appeals were content to frame their submissions by reference to it. As Mr Rowley QC put it, the decision, properly applied, has stood the test of time.

21. Many of the factors identified in *Oxfordshire* overlap with each other and the weight to be given to them will vary from case to case. Clearly, *the necessity or otherwise of the investigation* will always be a key issue, particularly in current circumstances. Every fact-finding hearing must produce something of importance for the welfare decision. But the shorthand of necessity does not translate into an obligation to conclude every case as quickly as possible, regardless of other factors, and that is clearly not the intention of the administrative guidance. There will be cases in which the welfare outcome for the child is not confined to the resulting order. Not infrequently, a finding in relation to one child will have implications for the welfare of other children. Sometimes, findings that cross the threshold at a minimum level will not reflect the reality. The court's broad obligation is to deal with the case justly, having regard to the welfare issues involved. McFarlane J put it well in paragraph 21 of *Oxfordshire* when he identified the question as being whether, on the individual facts of each case, it is 'right and necessary' to conduct a fact-finding exercise.

22. The factors identified in *Oxfordshire* should therefore be approached flexibly in the light of the overriding objective in order to do justice efficiently in the individual case. For example:

(i) When considering *the welfare of the child*, the significance to the individual child of knowing the truth can be considered, as can the effect on the child's welfare of an allegation being investigated or not.

(ii) *The likely cost to public funds* can extend to the expenditure of court resources and their diversion from other cases.

(iii) *The time that the investigation will take* allows the court to take account of the nature of the evidence. For example, an incident that has been recorded electronically may be swifter to prove than one that relies on contested witness evidence or circumstantial argument.

(iv) *The evidential result* may relate not only to the case before the court but also to other existing or likely future cases in which a finding one way or the other is likely to be of importance. The public interest in the identification of perpetrators of child abuse can also be considered.

(v) *The relevance of the potential result of the investigation to the future care plans for the child* should be seen in the light of the s. 31(3B) obligation on the court to consider the impact of harm on the child and the way in which his or her resulting needs are to be met.

(vi) *The impact of any fact finding process upon the other parties* can also take account of the opportunity costs for the local authority, even if it is the party seeking the investigation, in terms of resources and professional time that might be devoted to other children.

(vii) *The prospects of a fair trial* may also encompass the advantages of a trial now over a trial at a possibly distant and unpredictable future date.

(viii) *The justice of the case* gives the court the opportunity to stand back and ensure that all matters relevant to the overriding objective have been taken into account. One such matter is whether the contested allegation may be investigated within criminal proceedings. Another is the extent of any gulf between the factual basis for the court's decision with or without a fact-finding hearing. The level of seriousness of the disputed allegation may inform this assessment. As I have said, the court must ask itself whether its process will do justice to the reality of the case.

23. These are not always easy decisions and the factors typically do not all point the same way: most decisions will have their downsides. However, the court should be able to make its ruling quite concisely by referring to the main factors that bear on the individual case, and identifying where the balance falls and why. The reasoned case management choice of a judge who approaches the law correctly and takes all relevant factors into account will be upheld on appeal unless it has been shown that something has gone badly wrong with the balancing exercise.

24. It is important for us to affirm that fundamental legal principles do not change in response to workload. At various points in the cases under appeal it has been said that there needs to be 'a culture shift' on the part of professionals away from the 'leave no stone unturned philosophy'.

But the proper approach has never been to leave no stone unturned. The desired shift in professional practice can be achieved by paying fresh attention to the fundamental principles of good case management.

See also *K County Council v W and others* [2010] EWHC 3342 (Fam), [2011] 2 FLR 199, [21] (Hedley J) considering *A County Council v DP and others* [2005] EWHC 1593 (Fam), [2005] 2 FLR 1031

See also *Re R (children)* [2018] EWCA Civ 198, [2018] 3 FCR 26, [87]–[89] (McFarlane LJ) addressing a related point (investigating the death of one parent during an altercation with the other)

See also *Re F-H (children) (fact-finding hearing)* [2008] EWCA Civ 1249, [2009] 1 FCR 749, [1], [26] (Wilson LJ) considering *A County Council v DP and others* [2005] EWHC 1593 (Fam), [2005] 2 FLR 1031 (in the context of aborting pre-arranged fact-finding exercises, and identifying additional factors to consider regarding such decisions)

3.3.3 Threshold criteria: fact-finding: case management: split hearings

Re S (a child) (split hearings: fact finding); Cambridgeshire County Council v PS and others [2014] EWCA Civ 25, [2014] 1 FCR 477, [27]–[31] (Ryder LJ)

[27] It is by no means clear why it was thought appropriate to have a 'split hearing' where discrete facts are severed off from their welfare context. Unless the basis for such a decision is reasoned so that the inevitable delay is justified it will be wrong in principle in public law children proceedings. Even where it is asserted that delay will not be occasioned, the use of split hearings must be confined to those cases where there is a stark or discrete issue to be determined and an early conclusion on that issue will enable the substantive determination (ie whether a statutory order is necessary) to be made more expeditiously. The reasons for this are obvious: to remove consideration by the court of the background and contextual circumstances including factors that are relevant to the credibility of witnesses, the reliability of evidence and the s 1(3) 1989 Act welfare factors such as capability and risk, deprives the court of the very material (ie secondary facts) upon which findings as to primary fact and social welfare context are often based and tends to undermine the safety of the findings thereby made. It may also adversely impinge on the subsequent welfare and proportionality evaluations by the court as circumstances change and memories fade of the detail and nuances of the evidence that was given weeks or months before.

[28] I ought to emphasise for the avoidance of doubt that although parallels can be drawn between the use of fact-finding hearings in public and private law children proceedings, the appropriate and measured use of fact-finding hearings in private law proceedings which are often safety cases, for example involving recent domestic abuse between parents, are not the subject of this court's consideration in this judgment. An example

of this court's guidance in relation to those proceedings can be found in *Re C (Domestic Violence: Fact-Finding Hearing)* [2009] EWCA Civ 994, [2010] 1 FLR 1728, [2009] All ER (D) 252 (Oct). In private law proceedings it is the court that is defining an aspect of parental responsibility in its determination of the arrangements that are put in place for the child and findings of fact are appropriate, where necessary, to inform that process by reference to the factors in s 1(3) of the 1989 Act and in particular where safety issues have arisen which justify the court's interference with the art 8 rights of the family members (European Convention for the Protection of Human Rights and Fundamental Freedoms 1950 (as set out in Pt I of Sch 1 to the Human Rights Act 1998)). In public law children cases where a care order is in issue, the court is being asked to sanction an agency of the state, namely the local authority, being permitted to exercise parental responsibility for a child. The jurisdiction in the court to undertake that task has to be based upon the existence of facts (primary and/or secondary) that satisfy the threshold in s 31 of the 1989 Act. Accordingly, concessions or findings of fact relevant to the threshold question will always be necessary in public law cases alongside such further findings of fact as are necessary to inform the welfare evaluation.

[29] It ought to be recollected that split hearings became fashionable as a means of expediting the most simple cases where there was only one factual issue to be decided and where the threshold for jurisdiction in s 31 of the 1989 Act would not be satisfied if a finding could not be made thereby concluding the proceedings (see *Re S (Care Order: Split Hearing)* [1996] 3 FCR 578n at 580, [1996] 2 FLR 773 at 775 per Bracewell J). Over time, they also came to be used for the most complex medical causation cases where death or very serious medical issues had arisen and where an accurate medical diagnosis was integral to the future care of the child concerned. For almost all other cases, the procedure is inappropriate. The oft repeated but erroneous justification for them that a split hearing enables a social care assessment to be undertaken is simply poor social work and forensic practice. The justification comes from an era before the present Rules and Practice Directions came into force and can safely be discounted in public law children proceedings save in the most exceptional case.

[30] Social work assessments are not contingent on facts being identified and found to the civil standard (see, for example *Oldham Metropolitan BC v GW* [2007] EWHC 136 (Fam), [2008] 1 FCR 331, [2007] 2 FLR 597 and *R (on the application of S) v Swindon BC* [2001] EWHC Admin 334, [2001] 3 FCR 702, [2001] 2 FLR 776 per Scott Baker J at [34] and [35]). That is the function of the court not a social worker (*Dingley v Chief Constable of Strathclyde Police* [2000] UKHL 14 per Lord Hope of Craighead). Social work assessments are based upon their own professional methodology like any other form of professional risk assessment. In care cases, an appropriate social work assessment and a CAFCASS analysis should be undertaken at the earliest possible opportunity to identify relevant background circumstances and context. In so far as it is

necessary to express a risk formulation as a precursor to an analysis or a recommendation to the court, that can be done by basing the same on each of the alternative factual scenarios that the court is being asked to consider (see, for example, *Re SW v Portsmouth City Council, Re W (children) (concurrent care and criminal proceedings)* [2009] EWCA Civ 644 at [33], [2009] 3 FCR 1 at [33], [2009] 2 FLR 1106).

[31] It may be helpful to highlight the fact that a decision to undertake a split hearing is a case management decision to which Pt 1 of the Family Procedure Rules 2010, SI 2010/2955 (FPR 2010) and Pilot Practice Direction 12A 'Care, Supervision and Other Pt 4 Proceedings: Guide to Case Management (the PLO)' apply. A split hearing is only justifiable where the delay occasioned is in furtherance of the overriding objective in r 1 of the FPR 2010, that is:

- (i) as a consequence of active case management by the court which includes in accordance with r 1.4:
  - '(a) setting timetables …
  - (b) identifying at an early stage … the issues,
  - (c) deciding promptly—
    - (i) which issues need full investigation and hearing and which do not; and
    - (ii) the procedure to be followed in the case;
  - (d) deciding the order in which issues are to be resolved …
  - (i) considering whether the likely benefits of taking a particular step justify the cost of taking it;
  - (j) dealing with as many aspects of the case as it can on the same occasion … and
  - (m) giving directions to ensure that the case proceeds quickly and efficiently.'
- (ii) in accordance with the child's welfare having regard to the timetable for the child within the meaning of that concept in para [5] of pilot PD12A; and
- (iii) in accordance with the timetable for proceedings within the meaning of that concept in para [5] pilot PD12A.

See also *Re P (children) (care proceedings: split hearing)* [2007] EWCA Civ 1265, [2008] 1 FCR 74, [50]–[56] (Wilson LJ) addressing a related point (the need for clarity regarding purpose, and clarity as to when threshold will be determined)

See also *Re A (children)* [2006] EWCA Civ 714, [2007] 1 FLR 905, [33]–[36] (Wall LJ) addressing a related point (the need to clearly define what will be decided in the first limb of the hearings and when threshold will be determined)

See also *Re G (a child) (care order: threshold criteria)* [2001] 1 FCR 165 (CA), [3] (Dame Elizabeth Butler-Sloss P) addressing a related point (in principle, split hearings should be heard by the same judge)

3.4 THRESHOLD CRITERIA: RELEVANT DATE

3.4.1 Threshold criteria: relevant date: protective arrangements continuously in place

Re M (a minor) (care order: threshold conditions) [1994] 2 FCR 871 (HL), 878H–879E (Lord Mackay LC)

> In my opinion the opening words of s 31 link the making of an order by the court very closely with the application to the court by a local authority or authorised person. Section 31(2) then goes on to specify the conditions which are necessary to be satisfied before the court can make a care order or supervision order, but it is plain from this and the statute as a whole that even if these conditions are satisfied the court is not bound to make an order but must go through the full procedure particularly set out in s 1 of the statute. It is also clear that Parliament expected these cases to proceed with reasonable expedition and in particular I refer to s 32 in which the hearing by the court is not regarded only as taking place at the time when the applications are disposed of. Indeed, I think there is much to be said for the view that the hearing that Parliament contemplated was one which extended from the time the jurisdiction of the court is first invoked until the case is disposed of and that was required to be done in the light of the general principle that any delay in determining the question is likely to prejudice the welfare of the child. There is nothing in s 31(2) which in my opinion requires that the conditions to be satisfied are disassociated from the time of the making of the application by the local authority. I would conclude that the natural construction of the conditions in s 31(2) is that where, at the time the application is to be disposed of, there are in place arrangements for the protection of the child by the local authority on an interim basis which protection has been continuously in place for some time, the relevant date with respect to which the court must be satisfied is the date at which the local authority initiated the procedure for protection under the Act from which these arrangements followed. If after a local authority had initiated protective arrangements the need for these had terminated, because the child's welfare had been satisfactorily provided for otherwise, in any subsequent proceedings, it would not be possible to found jurisdiction on the situation at the time of initiation of these arrangements. It is permissible only to look back from the date of disposal to the date of initiation of protection as a result of which local authority arrangements had been continuously in place thereafter to the date of disposal.

See also *Southwark London Borough Council v B* [1999] 1 FCR 550 (FD) 565B–G (Charles J) considering *Re M (a minor) (care order: threshold conditions)* [1994] 2 FCR 871

3.4.2 Threshold criteria: relevant date: subsequent events may be relevant

Re G (children) (care order: evidence) [2001] EWCA Civ 968, [2001] 2 FCR 757, [11]–[15] (Hale LJ)

[11] *Re M* was concerned with both the actual and likely harm limbs of s 31(2)(a). Although much of the discussion was directed at when the condition that the child 'is suffering' significant harm must be met, the case also raised the problem of likely harm: by the time of the hearing his father was serving his sentence but alternative loving homes were available with the foster mother or with his mother's cousin. It would be odd indeed if actual and likely harm had to be judged at different dates. Further, the policy considerations are equally strong in each case. Just as it would be odd if the local authority were precluded from obtaining a care order on the ground of actual harm because their own intervention had cured the problem, it would be odd if a court could make an order based on the likelihood of harm from an immediate return home even though the factual basis for the interim removal had not been proved and the proceedings had taken so long to be heard that a return home would be unsettling for the child. Obviously, if the initial likelihood of harm has been removed or reduced by later events (such as the separation of the mother from an abusive partner) the court may decline to make a care order because it will not be best for the child. By contrast, a local authority may launch proceedings on the basis that a child in local authority accommodation is likely to suffer harm if returned home, because that would be so at the date when the application was made.

[12] However, real life is not quite as simple as this. Care cases, like all children cases; look to the future and not the past. Things are changing all the time while the case progresses. The local authority are not required to plead their case at the outset or indeed at all. It is now the practice in many courts to require the local authority before the final hearing to make a clear statement of the facts they wish the court to find and the basis upon which they allege that the threshold is crossed. In my view this should be routine, so that the parents can know the case they have to meet and have a fair opportunity to meet it. The judge lamented the lack of such a statement in this case.

[13] But it is often the case that measures are taken to protect a child, often in something of an emergency, before anything approaching a full picture has emerged. The question then is the extent to which the local authority can rely upon matters, which have come to light or taken place since the proceedings began. At one end of the spectrum, there will often be information discovered after the relevant date, which throws light on what the facts were at the relevant date. The most obvious examples are further medical evidence about the injuries which promoted removal, new complaints by the child about other forms of abuse within the home or admissions made by the parents. Often these will emerge in the course of

expert assessments conducted partly for the purpose of establishing the threshold and partly for the purpose of considering the way forward.

[14] At the other end of spectrum, there may be entirely new events which introduce a completely different risk which did not exist at the relevant date. Examples of this are not so easy to devise: it could be that proceedings are begun because a baby has suffered injuries which turn out to be completely accidental; unfortunately, the stress and strain of the proceedings has led to one parent leaving home and the complete collapse of the other. More commonly, the removal of the child on the basis of suspicions, which turn out to be unwarranted, may make it harder for the child to return home.

[15] In the middle are new events, which may, or may not, be capable of proving that there was a risk of significant harm at the relevant time. Acts of violence occurring while the proceedings are pending might be capable of showing that a risk of such violence existed when the proceedings began. Subsequent neglect or abuse might be capable of showing that such neglect or abuse was likely when the proceedings were brought. This raises more difficult questions because there are obvious dangers of retrospectively validating a concern which was not in fact justified at the time: there may, after all, be other reasons for things to go badly wrong after proceedings are started.

3.5 THRESHOLD CRITERIA: SIGNIFICANT HARM

3.5.1 Threshold criteria: significant harm: meaning of 'significant harm'

Re B (a child) (care order: proportionality: criterion for review) [2013] UKSC 33, [2013] 2 FCR 525, [24]–[28] (Lord Wilson), [143], [181]–[185], [192] (Lady Hale)

[24] … Beyond this, however, the debate surrounds two matters.

[25] The first matter is the meaning of the word 'significant' In this regard Parliament chose to help the court to a limited extent by providing in s 31(10) as follows:

> 'Where the question of whether harm suffered by a child is significant turns on the child's health or development, his health or development shall be compared with that which could reasonably be expected of a similar child.'

When we read this subsection together with the definition of 'harm' in the preceding subsection, we conclude that, whereas the concept of 'ill-treatment' is absolute, the concept of 'impairment of health or development' is relative to the health or development which could reasonably be expected of a similar child. This is helpful but little more than common sense.

[26] In my view this court should avoid attempting to explain the word 'significant'. It would be a gloss; attention might then turn to the meaning of the gloss and, albeit with the best of intentions, the courts might find in due course that they had travelled far from the word itself. Nevertheless it might be worthwhile to note that in the White Paper which preceded the 1989 Act, namely *The Law on Child Care and Family Services* (Cm 62), January 1987, the government stated, at para 60:

> 'It is intended that 'likely harm' should cover all cases of unacceptable risk in which it may be necessary to balance the chance of the harm occurring against the magnitude of that harm if it does occur.'

It follows that when, in *Re C and B (children) (care order: future harm)* [2000] 2 FCR 614, [2001] 1 FLR 611, Hale LJ (as my Lady then was) said, at [28], that 'a comparatively small risk of really serious harm can justify action, while even the virtual certainty of slight harm might not', she was faithfully expressing the intention behind the subsection. But the other interesting feature of the sentence in the White Paper is the word 'unacceptable'. I suggest that it was later realised that whether the risk was 'unacceptable' was a judgement which fell to be made at the welfare stage of the inquiry; and so a different adjective was chosen.

[27] In *Re L (children) (care proceedings)* [2006] EWCA Civ 1282, [2006] 3 FCR 301, [2007] 1 FLR 1068, the Court of Appeal allowed an appeal by parents against a judge's conclusion that their children had suffered and were likely to suffer significant harm and it remitted the issue for re-hearing. The professional evidence had been that the parents' deficiencies had had 'subtle and ambiguous consequences' for the children; and it was not difficult for me, at [31](a) of my judgment in that court, to conclude that such consequences could not amount to significant harm. The rehearing was conducted by Hedley J and, by his judgment reported as *Re L (Care: Threshold Criteria)* [2007] 1 FLR 2050, he declined to hold that the threshold was crossed. He observed, at [50], that 'society must be willing to tolerate very diverse standards of parenting, including the eccentric, the barely adequate and the inconsistent'; and, at [51], that '[s]ignificant harm is fact-specific and must retain the breadth of meaning that human fallibility may require of it' but that 'it is clear that it must be something unusual; at least something more than the commonplace human failure or inadequacy.'

[28] In the present case Mr Feehan seeks to develop Hedley J's point. He submits that:

> 'many parents are hypochondriacs, many parents are criminals or benefit cheats, many parents discriminate against ethnic or sexual minorities, many parents support vile political parties or belong to unusual or militant religions. All of these follies are visited upon their children, who may well adopt or 'model' them in their own lives but those children could not be removed for those reasons.'

I agree with Mr Feehan's submission; but the question arises whether, in the light of the judge's key conclusion, it misses the point.

...

[143] This case raises some profound questions about the scope of courts' powers to take away children from their birth families when what is feared is, not physical abuse or neglect, but emotional or psychological harm. We are all frail human beings, with our fair share of unattractive character traits, which sometimes manifest themselves in bad behaviours which may be copied by our children. But the state does not and cannot take away the children of all the people who commit crimes, who abuse alcohol or drugs, who suffer from physical or mental illnesses or disabilities, or who espouse anti-social political or religious beliefs. Indeed, in *Dickson v UK* [2007] 3 FCR 877, [2008] 1 FLR 1315, the Strasbourg court held that the refusal of artificial insemination facilities to a convicted murderer and the wife whom he had met while they were both in prison was a breach of their rights under art 8 of the European Convention for the Protection of Human Rights and Fundamental Freedoms 1950 (as set out in Pt I of Sch 1 to the Human Rights Act 1998). How is the law to distinguish between emotional or psychological harm, which warrants the compulsory intervention of the state, and the normal and natural tendency of children to grow up to be and behave like their parents?

...

[181] *Re L* is an important case because it concerned parents with learning difficulties, very considerable in the case of the mother. The judge had found significant harm on the basis of the report of a psychologist who had not been asked to assess this. She had acknowledged that there was no obvious harm, no explicit malicious abuse or extreme abuse: 'On the contrary my concern in this family relates to the more subtle and ambiguous consequences on the children flowing from parental deficiencies'. Wilson LJ commented (at [31]): 'So which was it? 'Significant harm' or 'subtle and ambiguous consequences'? Speaking for myself, I regard the two concepts as mutually exclusive'. For these and many other concerns about the report, the case was sent back to be re-heard in the High Court. In *Re L (Care: Threshold Criteria)* [2007] 1 FLR 2050 at [50], Hedley J, having quoted Lord Templeman, continued:

> 'It follows inexorably from that, that society must be willing to tolerate very diverse standards of parenting, including the eccentric, the barely adequate and the inconsistent. It follows too that children will inevitably have both very different experiences of parenting and very unequal consequences flowing from it. It means that some children will experience disadvantage and harm, while others flourish in atmospheres of loving security and emotional stability. These are the consequences of our fallible humanity and it is not the provenance [semble: province] of the state to spare children all the consequences of defective parenting.'

[182] But clearly we do remove *some* of those children. The difficulty is to identify what it is that tips the case over the threshold. Although every parent, every child, every family is different, and, as Hedley J put it (at

[51]), 'significant harm is fact specific and must retain the breadth of meaning that human fallibility may require of it', there must be some consistency in the approach of both local authorities and the courts. Hedley J went on say that 'it must be something unusual; at least something more than the commonplace human failure or inadequacy'. It does appear that he considered that the children were suffering, and likely to suffer, some harm to their intellectual development as a result of their parents' inadequacies, but that it was not of a character or significance to justify the compulsory intervention of the state.

[183] The Court of Appeal wrestled with the problem of separating 'harm' from 'significant harm' in *Re MA (children) (care order: likelihood of significant harm)* [2009] EWCA Civ 853, [2010] 1 FCR 456, [2010] 1 FLR 431. The trial judge had found that although the parents had ill-treated another child, whose presence in their household remained something of a mystery, their own children were well cared-for, healthy, well-nourished and had strong bonds with their parents. The eldest child had been slapped, kicked and hit on the head by one or other of her parents. But that was not significant harm. Wilson LJ, at [29], quoted Booth J in *B v Humberside CC* [1993] 1 FCR 613 at 619, [1993] 1 FLR 257 at 263:

> 'Significant harm was defined by Miss Black, in accordance with the dictionary definition, first as being harm that the court should consider was either considerable or noteworthy or important. Then she expressed it as harm which the court should take into account in considering a child's future.'

Wilson LJ went on to comment that while 'I might not have expressed myself in quite such broad terms, they certainly foreshadow the view of Lord Nicholls, expressed three years later, that, in relation to a likelihood of harm, the threshold is set at a comparatively low level.'

[184] At [51], Ward LJ emphasised, correctly in my view, that Lord Nicholls' remark, in *Re H and R (minors) (sexual abuse: standard of proof)* [1996] 1 FCR 509, [1996] 1 All ER 1, was directed, not at the threshold as a whole, nor at the threshold of significant harm, but at the threshold of likelihood of harm in the future. Lord Nicholls said nothing in that case, or in any later case, to suggest that the threshold of significance was comparatively low. Ward LJ went on, at [54], to express the difference between 'harm' and 'significant harm' thus:

> 'Given the underlying philosophy of the Act, the harm must, in my judgment, be significant enough to justify the intervention of the State and disturb the autonomy of the parents to bring up their children by themselves in the way they choose.'

[185] The point can fairly be made, both of this definition and of the second of the two definitions suggested by Miss Black to Booth J (see [183], above), that they are somewhat circular: the state is justified in intervening if the harm is sufficient to justify the state's intervening. But it serves to make the point that not all harm which children may suffer as a result of their

parents' care falling short of what it is reasonable to expect is significant for this purpose. The dictionary definition, 'considerable, noteworthy or important', is to my mind more helpful. It chimes with the Guidance given by the Department of Health and Social Security when the 1989 Act first came into force: 'It is additionally necessary to show that the ill-treatment is significant, which given its dictionary definition means considerable, noteworthy or important' (para 3.19). There would be no point in the threshold if it could be crossed by trivial or unimportant harm.

...

[192] Allied to this is the definition of 'harm' itself (see [178], above). It is wide, but it is not infinite. The focus is upon the child *suffering* that harm, so upon the child suffering ill-treatment or suffering the impairment of her health or development. Ill-treatment will generally involve some active conduct, whether physical or sexual abuse, bullying or other forms of active emotional abuse. Impairment may also be the result of active conduct towards the child, but it could also be the result of neglecting the child's needs, for food, for warmth, for shelter, for love, for education, for health care. Generally speaking, however, the harm is likely to be the result of some abusive or neglectful behaviour towards the child. But this is not invariably the case, as is shown by the inclusion, by way of example, 'impairment suffered from seeing or hearing the ill-treatment of another'. We now know that serious harm may be done to the development of children who see or hear domestic violence between their parents.

3.5.2 Threshold criteria: significant harm: FGM[4]/male circumcision

Re B and G (children) (no 2) [2015] EWFC 3, [2015] 1 FLR 905, [55]–[70] (Sir James Munby P) *quotation limited to* [54]–[55], [67]–[70]

54. In the light of finding on issue (1), this point falls away, but given its obvious importance and the fact that I have heard argument on it, it is appropriate that I deal with it.

55. I do not want there to be any doubt. FGM is a criminal offence under the Female Genital Mutilation Act 2003. It is an abuse of human rights. It has no basis in any religion. I repeat what I first said as long ago as 2004 in *Singh v Entry Clearance Officer, New Delhi* [2004] EWCA Civ 1075, [2005] 1 FLR 308, para 68: it is a 'barbarous' practice which is 'beyond the pale.'

...

67. Mr Hayes submits, by reference in particular to what Baroness Hale of Richmond said in *Re B (Care Proceedings: Appeal)* [2013] UKSC 33, [2013] 2 FLR 1075, para 185, that any form of FGM, including FGM

4 Female genital mutilation.

WHO Type IV, amounts to 'significant harm'. To use Lady Hale's language, no form of FGM can, he says, be characterised as trivial or unimportant, having regard not merely to its purely physical characteristics but also to its associated trauma and potential emotional or psychological consequences. Mr Hayes also makes an exceedingly important practical point. Unless FGM in all its forms is treated as constituting significant harm, local authorities and other agencies, and indeed family courts, may be very significantly hampered in their ability to protect vulnerable children, given that 'significant harm' is the jurisdictional hurdle that has to be overcome not merely under section 31(2) but also under section 100(4)(b) of the Children Act 1989.

68. I agree with Mr Hayes. In my judgment, any form of FGM constitutes 'significant harm' within the meaning of sections 31 and 100. What then of male circumcision?

69. Mr Hayes points to the recognition, both by Wall J, as he then was, and by the Court of Appeal in *Re J (Specific Issue Orders: Muslim Upbringing and Circumcision)* [1999] 2 FLR 678, 693, on appeal *Re J (Specific Issue Orders: Child's Religious Upbringing and Circumcision)* [2000] 1 FLR 571, 573, 576, that male circumcision does involve harm, or the risk of harm. Given the comparison between what is involved in male circumcision and FGM WHO Type IV, to dispute that the more invasive procedure involves the significant harm involved in the less invasive procedure would seem almost irrational. In my judgment, if FGM Type IV amounts to significant harm, as in my judgment it does, then the same must be so of male circumcision.

70. I should add that my conclusions in relation to whether FGM, including FGM Type IV, constitutes 'significant harm' for the purposes of family law, is quite separate from the question of whether particular examples of FGM Type IV involve the commission of criminal offences under the Female Genital Mutilation Act 2003. As I have already pointed out, FGM Type IV comes within the ambit of the criminal law only if it involves 'mutilation'. The question of whether a particular case of FGM Type IV – for example, the case as presented here by the local authority in relation to G – involves mutilation is, in my judgment, not a matter for determination by the family court, and certainly not a matter I need to determine in the present case. It is a matter properly for determination by a criminal court as and when the point arises for decision in a particular case.

See Chapter 3.7.8 Threshold criteria: attributability: care given or likely to be given: FGM/male circumcision

3.6 THRESHOLD CRITERIA: LIKELY TO SUFFER

3.6.1 Threshold criteria: likely to suffer: meaning of 'likely to suffer'

Re H and R (minors) (sexual abuse: standard of proof) [1996] 1 FCR 509 (HL), 524F–G (Lord Nicholls)

> In my view, therefore, the context shows that in s 31(2)(a) likely is being used in the sense of a real possibility, a possibility that cannot sensibly be ignored having regard to the nature and gravity of the feared harm in the particular case. By parity of reasoning the expression likely to suffer significant harm bears the same meaning elsewhere in the Act; for instance, in ss 43, 44 and 46. Likely also bears a similar meaning, for a similar reason, in the requirement in s 31(2)(b) that the harm or likelihood of harm must be attributable to the care given to the child or 'likely' to be given him if the order were not made.

Re B (a child) (care order: proportionality: criterion for review) [2013] UKSC 33, [2013] 2 FCR 525, [187]–[190] (Lady Hale)

[187] Added to the difficult question of identifying significant harm is the question of identifying the degree of likelihood that such harm will be suffered in the future which is necessary to take the case over the threshold. It was held, albeit strictly obiter, in *Re H and R (minors) (sexual abuse: standard of proof)* [1996] 1 FCR 509, [1996] 1 All ER 1 that 'likely' does not mean 'probable' or 'more likely than not'. It means, in Lord Nicholls' well-known words, 'a real possibility, a possibility that cannot sensibly be ignored having regard to the nature and gravity of the feared harm in the particular case' ([1996] 1 FCR 509 at 524, [1996] 1 All ER 1 at 15–16). That standard has been adopted or approved in numerous later cases, including recently in this court in *Re J (children) (non-accidental injury: past possible perpetrator in new family)* [2013] UKSC 9, [2013] 2 FCR 149, [2013] 3 All ER 1. It is in this respect, and this respect alone, that Lord Nicholls observed that the threshold is 'comparatively low'.

[188] The reason for adopting a comparatively low threshold of likelihood is clear: some harm is so catastrophic that even a relatively small degree of likelihood should be sufficient to justify the state in intervening to protect the child before it happens, for example from death or serious injury or sexual abuse. But it is clear that Lord Nicholls did not contemplate that a relatively small degree of likelihood would be sufficient in all cases. The corollary of 'the more serious the harm, the less likely it has to be' is that 'the less serious the harm, the more likely it has to be'.

[189] Of course, another reason for adopting a test of 'real possibility', rather than 'more likely than not', is that it is extremely difficult to predict the future and to do so with the sort of accuracy which would enable a court to say that it was more likely than not that a parent would harm a child in the future. Once again, this is a particular problem with emotional or

psychological harm, which may take many years to manifest itself. The 1989 Act does not set limits upon when the harm may be likely to occur and clearly the court is entitled to look to the medium and longer term as well as to the child's immediate future.

[190] However, the longer term the prospect of harm, the greater the degree of uncertainty about whether it will actually happen. The child's resilience or resistance, and the many protective influences at work in the community, whether from the wider family, their friends, their neighbourhoods, the health and social services and, perhaps above all, their schools, mean that it may never happen. The degree of likelihood must be such as to justify compulsory intervention *now*, for there is always the possibility of compulsory intervention later, should the 'real possibility' solidify.

See also *Re S-B (children) (non-accidental injury)* [2009] UKSC 17, [2010] 1 FCR 321, [8]–[9] (Lady Hale) considering *Re H and R (minors) (sexual abuse: standard of proof)* [1996] 1 FCR 509

3.6.2 Threshold criteria: likely to suffer: risk of harm must be based on proved fact

Re H and R (minors) (sexual abuse: standard of proof) [1996] 1 FCR 509 (HL), 528C–529B (Lord Nicholls)

The starting point here is that courts act on evidence. They reach their decisions on the basis of the evidence before them. When considering whether an applicant for a care order has shown that the child is suffering harm or likely to do so, a court will have regard to the undisputed evidence. The Judge will attach to that evidence such weight, or importance, as he considers appropriate. Likewise with regard to disputed evidence which the Judge accepts as reliable. None of that is controversial. But the rejection of a disputed allegation as not proved on the balance of probability leaves scope for the possibility that the non-proven allegation may be true after all. There remains room for the Judge to have doubts and suspicions on this score. This is the area of controversy.

In my view these unresolved judicial doubts and suspicions can no more form the basis of a conclusion that the second threshold condition in s 31(2)(a) has been established than they can form the basis of a conclusion that the first has been established. My reasons are as follows.

Evidence is the means whereby relevant facts are proved in court. What the evidence is required to establish depends upon the issue the court has to decide. At some interlocutory hearings, for instance, the issue will be whether the plaintiff has a good arguable case. The plaintiff may assert he is at risk of the defendant trespassing on his land or committing a breach of contract and that, in consequence, he will suffer serious damage. When deciding whether to grant an interlocutory injunction this court will not be concerned to resolve disputes raised by the parties' conflicting affidavit evidence.

> At trials, however, the court normally has to resolve undisputed issues of relevant fact before it can reach its conclusion on the issue it has to decide. This is a commonplace exercise, carried out daily by courts and tribunals throughout the country. This exercise applies as much where the issue is whether an event may happen in the future as where the issue is whether an event did or did not happen in the past. To decide whether a car was being driven negligently, the court will have to decide what was happening immediately before the accident and how the car was being driven and why. Its findings on these facts form the essential basis for its conclusion on the issue of whether the car was being driven with reasonable care. Likewise, if the issue before the court concerns the possibility of something happening in the future, such as whether the name or get-up under which goods are being sold is likely to deceive future buyers. To decide that issue the court must identify and, when disputed, decide the relevant facts about the way the goods are being sold and to whom and in what circumstances. Then, but only then, can the court reach a conclusion on the crucial issue. A decision by a court on the likelihood of a future happening must be founded on a basis of present facts and the inferences fairly to be drawn therefrom.

See also *Re B (children) (care proceedings: standard of proof)* [2008] UKHL 35, [2008] 2 FCR 339, [3] (Lord Hoffmann) considering *Re H and R (minors) (sexual abuse: standard of proof)* [1996] 1 FCR 509 (reaffirming that likelihood of harm is required to be based on proved fact)

See also *Re J (children) (non-accidental injury: past possible perpetrator in new family)* [2013] UKSC 9, [2013] 2 FCR 149, [44], [47]–[50] (Lady Hale), [75] (Lord Wilson), [84] (Lord Hope) addressing the same point (including it being described as a 'bulwark against too ready an interference with family life on the part of the state', [75])

See also *Re S-B (children) (non-accidental injury)* [2009] UKSC 17, [2010] 1 FCR 321, [8] (Lady Hale) addressing the same point

3.6.3 Threshold criteria: likely to suffer: past uncertain perpetrator findings: value in later cases

See Chapter 3.8.5 Threshold criteria: 'whodunnit' cases: uncertain perpetrator findings: relevance in later cases

3.6.4 Threshold criteria: likely to suffer: failure to vaccinate

Re H (a child) (parental responsibility: vaccination) [2020] EWCA Civ 664, [2020] 2 FCR 683, [21] (King LJ)

> [21] It goes without saying that the giving of consent to having one's child vaccinated is an exercise of parental responsibility. Whilst, for the reasons rehearsed in the report of Dr Douglas and referred to below, it cannot be doubted that it is both reasonable and responsible parental behaviour to arrange for one's child to be vaccinated in accordance with the Public Health England guidelines, there is at present no legal requirement in this

country for a child to be vaccinated. It follows that, *taken in isolation*, a failure to arrange for an otherwise healthy child to be vaccinated would be unlikely to amount to 'significant harm or the likelihood of significant harm' such as to satisfy the threshold criteria necessary in order for a care order to be made pursuant to s 31 CA 1989. By contrast, a failure by parents to obtain vaccinations for their children may feature as one of a series of wider threshold allegations in support of a more generalised case of neglect.

3.7 THRESHOLD CRITERIA: ATTRIBUTABILITY

3.7.1 Threshold criteria: attributability: a contributory causal connection

Lancashire County Council v A [2000] 1 FCR 509 (HL), 511H–512A (Lord Nicholls)

> Before identifying the issue I should mention two preliminary points which attracted little, if any, controversy between the parties. First, the phrase 'attributable to' in s 31(2)(b) connotes a causal connection between the harm or likelihood of harm on the one hand and the care or likely care or the child's being beyond parental control on the other hand. Echoing the language of Donaldson J in a different context (in *Walsh v Rother DC* [1978] 1 All ER 510 at 514), the connection need not be that of a sole or dominant or direct cause and effect; a contributory causal connection suffices. For instance, if a parent entrusts a child to a third party without taking the precautionary steps a reasonable parent would take to check the suitability of the third party, and subsequently the third party injures or sexually abuses the child, the harm suffered by the child may be regarded as attributable to the inadequate care of the parent as well as the third party.

3.7.2 Threshold criteria: attributability: care given or likely to be given: an objective standard

Lancashire County Council v A [2000] 1 FCR 509 (HL), 512A–B (Lord Nicholls)

> The second preliminary point is that to be within s 31(2)(b)(i) the care given or likely to be given must fall below an objectively acceptable level. That level is the care a reasonable parent would provide for the child concerned. Thus an absence of a reasonable standard of parental care need not imply that the parents are at fault. It may be, for instance, that for reasons beyond their control the parents are not able to provide a reasonable standard of care for the child.

Re B (a child) (care order: proportionality: criterion for review) [2013] UKSC 33, [2013] 2 FCR 525, [30]–[31] (Lord Wilson)

> [30] The second matter relates to Mr Feehan's submission that the threshold set by section 31(2) is not crossed if the deficits relate only to the character

of the parents rather than to the quality of their parenting. His alternative submission is that harm suffered or likely to be suffered by a child as a result of parental action or inaction may cross the threshold only if, in so acting or failing to act, the parent or parents were deliberately or intentionally to have caused or to be likely to cause such harm. M is, of course, not responsible for her personality traits nor for her psychiatric disorders; and in effect the submission is that the dishonesty, animosities and obstructionism of the parents represent deficits only of character and that, if and insofar as they might cause harm to Amelia, whom they love, the harm is neither deliberate nor intentional.

[31] The first of these alternative submissions represents a false dichotomy: for the character of the parents is relevant to each stage of the inquiry whether to make a care order only to the extent that it affects the quality of their parenting. The second of them is misconceived: for there is no requisite mental element to accompany the actions or inactions which have caused, or are likely to cause, significant harm to the child. Section 31 (2)(b)(i) requires only that the harm or likelihood of harm should be 'attributable' to the care given or likely to be given to the child not being what it would be reasonable to expect a parent to give to him. Such is a requirement only of causation as between the care and the harm. The provision was prefigured in the White Paper, Cm 62, cited above, also at para 60:

> 'The court will also have to make a decision as to whether the harm was caused or will in future be caused by the child not receiving a reasonable standard of care or by the absence of adequate parental control. This is not intended to imply a judgment on the parent who may be doing his best but is still unable to provide a reasonable standard of care.'

See also *Re D (a child) (care proceedings: expert evidence)* [2010] EWCA Civ 1000, [2010] 3 FCR 244, [35] (Hughes LJ) addressing the same point, see Chapter 3.7.4 Threshold criteria: attributability: care given or likely to be given: parents with learning disabilities

See also *Re V (a minor) (care or supervision order)* [1996] 2 FCR 555 (CA), 563B–D (Waite LJ) addressing a related point (parents beyond criticism regarding devotion and affection but falling short on the standard reasonably expected)

3.7.3 Threshold criteria: attributability: care given or likely to be given: an objective standard: reasonableness evaluated by reference to particular circumstances

Lancashire County Council v M and others [2021] EWHC 2844 (Fam), [19]–[20] (Hayden J)

19. It is important to emphasise that the provision *'not being what it would be reasonable to expect a parent to give'* is not to be regarded as an abstract or

hypothetical test but must be evaluated by reference to the circumstances the parent is confronting i.e. what would it be reasonable to expect of a parent in these particular circumstances, recognising that in a challenging situation many of us may behave in a way which might not objectively be viewed as reasonable. The test is not to be construed in a vacuum nor applied judgementally by reference to some gold standard of parenting which few (if any) could achieve. On the contrary, it contemplates a range of behaviour, incorporating inevitable human frailty. The reasonableness of the care given requires to be evaluated strictly by reference to the particular circumstances and the individual child.

20. I would add that a similar dynamic and frequently for the same reasons identified here, arises in the Court of Protection when dealing with incapacitated adults. This is a particularly common situation in the context of young adults in their late teenage years and early twenties, but by no means confined to it.

See also *Re K* [2005] EWHC 2956 (Fam), [2007] 1 FLR 399, [26] (Munby J) addressing a related point (possible sensitivity to cultural differences)

See also *Re B (a child) (care order: proportionality: criterion for review)* [2013] UKSC 33, [2013] 2 FCR 525, [178] (Lady Hale) considering *Re K* [2005] EWHC 2956 (Fam), [2007] 1 FLR 399

3.7.4 Threshold criteria: attributability: care given or likely to be given: an objective standard: parents with learning disabilities

Re D (a child) (care proceedings: expert evidence) [2010] EWCA Civ 1000, [2010] 3 FCR 244, [32]–[38] (Hughes LJ)

Disability

[32] There is a second ground raised which needs to be dealt with. In the course of his judgment the judge observed that mother's learning difficulties could be described as a disability, and at two points in his judgment he posed questions relating such a disability in some manner to the threshold test contained in s 31(2) of the Children Act 1989. At para [26](ii) of his judgment, referring to s 31(2), he said this:

> 'The use of the indefinite article when referring to 'parent' signifies that the comparator is that elusive creature the hypothetical reasonable parent. An interesting question is whether the hypothetical reasonable parent is to be taken as possessing the same social, intellectual and psychological profile as the actual parent under consideration'.

[33] At the end of his judgment (see para [178](ii)) he said this in relation to the question of whether there was a likelihood of future significant harm to L and F:

> 'In making this assessment the standard of hypothetical reasonable care to be applied must have regard to the psychological profiles of these particular parents. Any other approach would be discriminatory'.

[34] Unsurprisingly that prompted the applicants present to raise with the judge after his judgment the question whether he had misdirected himself as to the threshold test. He responded by a short supplemental judgment, in the course of which he said this:

> 'By way of clarification I would say this … I did not state that a hypothetical reasonable parent must be endowed with the psychological profiles of the parents in question. Rather, at [178](ii) I stated … [and then he quoted the relevant paragraph]'.

[35] I will accept that this does demonstrate that the judge has not made what would have been a fundamental and most elementary error; indeed it would have been astonishing if he had, not least because he had been helpfully presented by counsel on all sides with an impeccable statement of law which made the objective nature of the test under s 31(2) entirely clear. For the avoidance of doubt, the test under s 31(2) is and has to be an objective one. If it were otherwise, and the 'care which it is reasonable to expect a parent to give' were to be judged by the standards of the parent with the characteristics of the particular parent in question, the protection afforded to children would be very limited indeed, if not entirely illusory. It would in effect then be limited to protection against the parent who was fully able to provide proper care but either chose not to do so or neglected through fault to do so. That is not the meaning of s 31(2). It is abundantly clear that a parent may unhappily fail to provide reasonable care even though he is doing his incompetent best.

[36] Quite what the judge did mean by para [178](ii) remains to me at least obscure, and the judge did not say. He may have meant that in deciding a care case the judge should examine the reasons why a parent is not living up to expectations. That I would agree a judge should do because once one knows the reasons one may be able to do something to cure the problem. He may have meant that in handling a parent with a handicap those who are dealing with him or her must remember who they are dealing with and adapt their approach accordingly. That must certainly be true of social workers, as of many others. It may be that that is what the judge had in mind because at the point in his judgment when he referred to the definition of disability at [134] and [135], he went on to refer to a Department of Health and Department for Education and Skills document summarising good practice guidance on working with parents with a learning disability. However that may be in fact, in this case I agree with Mr Macdonald that the question of the correct construction of s 31(2)(b) was not reached by the judge because he did not find that there was any likelihood of significant harm—that is to say, s 31(2)(a) was not satisfied. That said, this court should I think make it abundantly clear the nature of the test under s 31(2), which is and has to be an objective one.

[37] The judge's reference to discrimination is in any event generally puzzling. It may of course be that for the purposes of s 1 of the Disability Discrimination Act 1995 (the 1995 Act) , mother's learning disabilities might amount to a disability if they were a mental impairment having

a substantial and long-term effect on her ability to carry out normal day to day activities; but whether they were or they were not, the 1995 Act has nothing whatever to say about care proceedings. It does contain a general duty upon public authorities not to discriminate in carrying out their functions (see s 21B(1)) but that does not apply to judicial acts (see s 21C(1)). It may be, as I have said, the judge was making no more than general reference to the proposition that those such as the local authority or social workers dealing with anybody with any kind of handicap must tailor their approach to the person they are dealing with, but that is a mile away from bringing either the disability or the concept of discrimination into the exercise of deciding whether the threshold conditions for the making of a care order are satisfied. No one has suggested that that should be done in this case. I want to make it completely clear that it should not. When the judge is addressing the threshold conditions it is absolutely clear that concepts of discrimination in relation to the parents are simply not helpful and should not be permitted to intrude.

[38] There is, however, for the reasons that I have already set out, nothing in those slightly unclear remarks which vitiate the principal decision which the judge arrived at in this case.

3.7.5 Threshold criteria: attributability: care given or likely to be given: care given by whom?

Re S-B (children) (non-accidental injury) [2009] UKSC 17, [2010] 1 FCR 321, [20]–[22] (Lady Hale)

[20] So far the position is plain. But the threshold criteria do not in terms require that the person whose parental responsibility for the child is to be interfered with or even taken away by the order be responsible for the harm which the child has suffered or is likely to suffer in the future. It requires simply that 'the harm, or likelihood of harm, is attributable to … the care given to the child, or likely to be given to him if the order were not made, not being what it would be reasonable to expect a parent to give to him'. Clearly, the object is to limit intervention to certain kinds of harm—harm which should not happen if a child is being looked after properly. But is it also intended to limit intervention to cases where the person whose rights are to be interfered with bears some responsibility for the harm?

[21] It cannot have been intended that a parent whose child has been harmed as a result of a lack of proper care in a hospital or at school should be at risk of losing her child. The problem could be approached through the welfare test, because removal from home would not be in the best interests of such a child. However, because of the risk of social engineering, the threshold criteria were meant to screen out those cases where the family should not be put at any risk of intervention. Hence attention has focused on the attributability criterion. In the case confusingly reported in the Law Reports as *Lancashire CC v B* [2000]

2 AC 147, but in the All England Law Reports as *Lancashire CC v A* [2000] 2 All ER 97, the House of Lords considered what is meant by 'the care given to the child'. Does it mean only the care given by the parents or primary carers or does it mean the care given by anyone who plays a part in the child's care? Lord Nicholls, with whom Lord Slynn of Hadley, Lord Nolan and Lord Hoffmann agreed, found that it referred primarily to the former. But if, as in that case, the care of the child was shared between two households and the judge could not decide which was responsible for the harm suffered by the child, the phrase 'is apt to embrace not merely the care given by the parents or other primary carers; it is apt to embrace the care given by any of the carers' ([2000] 1 FCR 509 at 516, [2000] 2 All ER 97 at 103). Thus the criteria were satisfied in respect of a child, A, who had been injured, even though this might have been attributable to the care she had received from her childminder rather than from her parents.

[22] Lord Clyde put the test in this helpful way with the same result ([2000] 1 FCR 509 at 518, [2000] 2 All ER 97 at 106):

> 'That the harm must be attributable to the care given to the child requires that the harm must be attributable to the acts or omissions of someone who has the care of the child and the acts or omissions must occur in the course of the exercise of that care. To have the care of a child comprises more than being in a position where a duty of care towards the child may exist. It involves the undertaking of the task of looking after the child.'

See also *Lancashire County Council v A* [2000] 1 FCR 509 (HL) 513I–516G (Lord Nicholls) addressing the same point, see Chapter 3.8.4 Threshold criteria: 'whodunnit' cases: uncertain perpetrator findings: relevance in present cases

3.7.6 Threshold criteria: attributability: care given or likely to be given: uncertain perpetrator findings in present cases

See Chapter 3.8.4 Threshold criteria: 'whodunnit' cases: uncertain perpetrator findings: relevance in present cases

3.7.7 Threshold criteria: attributability: care given or likely to be given: blameless, accidental injuries

Re L (a child) (care proceedings: responsibility for child's injury) [2006] EWCA Civ 49, [2006] 1 FCR 285, [50]–[55] (Wall LJ)

[50] The inevitable consequences of the abandonment of the allegation of shaking were, in my judgment, twofold. The first was, as the local authority acknowledged, that it was unable to prove that the injuries were non-accidental: the second was that the occurrence of the injuries, by itself, was not sufficient to satisfy the threshold criteria under s 31.

[51] The wording of s 31(2) requires the local authority to prove that the significant harm suffered by the child (in this case the injuries) was attributable to the care given to BL by his parents 'not being what it would be reasonable to expect a parent to give to him'. A child may receive serious accidental injuries whilst in the care of his or her parents, even where those parents are both conscientious and competent. Such injuries plainly do not fall within s 31(2).

[52] The words of s 31(2) of the Children Act 1989, translated into everyday language and experience mean that in order to satisfy the threshold criteria, the local authority must prove that an injury is non-accidental. Once that finding can properly be made, the question of perpetrator arises. In many cases, where the injuries are pathognomonic of abuse, the medical evidence points overwhelmingly to non-accidental injury, and the judge is able to find on the medical evidence that non-accidental injury occurred. In such cases, if the judge cannot identify the perpetrator, it is often sufficient to satisfy the threshold criteria for the judge to find that the child was non-accidentally injured in the care of his parents and that either or both is/are responsible. To put the same point a different way, a finding of non-accidental injury to a child whilst in the care of his or her parents plainly satisfied the language of s 31(2) of the Children Act 1989.

[53] In my judgment, however, such considerations do not apply when, as here, the local authority cannot satisfy the court that the injuries were inflicted non-accidentally. Thus it is not open to the local authority, on the facts of the instant case, to use the fact of the injuries to BL as a basis for submitting that the threshold criteria are established in relation to the injuries, and that one of both of the parents is/are responsible.

[54] Accordingly, in my judgment, in so far as the judge found that the threshold criteria were satisfied because 'either the mother or the father was responsible for them' (the injuries), she was wrong to do so. The injuries simply did not satisfy the threshold criteria, and it was not open to the judge to allocate responsibility or guilt or to say that one or other of the parents had caused them.

[55] This does not, of course, mean that the injuries are irrelevant or have to be left out of account. The local authority is entitled to rely, where appropriate, on the behaviour of a child's parents in relation to an unexplained or even to an accidental injury. The failure to call the ambulance and the collusion over what was plainly an untrue account of the injuries are both relevant to the threshold criteria. Thus in the language of s 31(2), the judge was entitled to find that the failure to call the ambulance could legitimately constitute a proper basis for the proposition that BL was likely to suffer significant harm due to the parents' failure to ensure that he received immediate treatment. Similarly, parents who lie about their child's injuries may be behaving in a manner which, once again, falls fair and square within s 31(2), even if those injuries are accidental.

3.7.8 Threshold criteria: attributability: care given or likely to be given: FGM/male circumcision

Re B and G (children) (no 2) [2015] EWFC 3, [2015] 1 FLR 905, [71]–[73] (Sir James Munby P)

71. Moving on to the second limb of the statutory test, Mr Hayes submits that in assessing whether the infliction of any form of FGM can ever be an aspect of 'reasonable' parenting, it is vital to bear in mind that FGM involves physical harm which, it is common ground, has (except in the very narrow circumstances defined in section 1(2)(a) of the Female Genital Mutilation Act 2003, not relevant in a case such as this) *no* medical justification and confers *no* health benefits. The fact that it may be a 'cultural' practice does not make FGM reasonable; indeed, the proposition is specifically negatived by section 1(5) of the 2003 Act. And, as I have already pointed out, FGM has no religious justification. So, he submits, it can never be reasonable parenting to inflict any form of FGM on a child. I agree.

72. It is at this point in the analysis, as it seems to me, that the clear distinction between FGM and male circumcision appears. Whereas it can never be reasonable parenting to inflict *any* form of FGM on a child, the position is quite different with male circumcision. Society and the law, including family law, are prepared to tolerate non-therapeutic male circumcision performed for religious or even for purely cultural or conventional reasons, while no longer being willing to tolerate FGM in any of its forms. There are, after all, at least two important distinctions between the two. (In saying this I do not overlook the other important distinctions identified in the authorities I referred to in para 64 above.) FGM has no basis in any religion; male circumcision is often performed for religious reasons. FGM has no medical justification and confers no health benefits; male circumcision is seen by some (although opinions are divided) as providing hygienic or prophylactic benefits. Be that as it may, 'reasonable' parenting is treated as permitting male circumcision.

73. I conclude therefore that although both involve significant harm, there is a very clear distinction in family law between FGM and male circumcision. FGM in any form will suffice to establish 'threshold' in accordance with section 31 of the Children Act 1989; male circumcision without more will not.

3.7.9 Threshold criteria: attributability: beyond parental care: not a finding of blame

Re K (a child: post adoption placement breakdown) [2012] EWHC 4148 (Fam), [2013] 1 FLR 1, [148]–[153] (HHJ Clifford Bellamy sitting as a judge of the High Court) *revd Re E (a child)* [2012] EWCA Civ 1773, [2013] 2 FLR 63

148. The clearest statement concerning what the 'attributable' condition is to be found in *Lancashire County Council v B* [2000] 1 FLR 583. Lord Nicholls said that,

> '5. ...the phrase "attributable to" in section 31(2)(b) connotes a causal connection between the harm or likelihood of harm on the one hand and the care or likely care or the child's being beyond parental control on the other...the connection need not be that of a sole or dominant or direct cause and effect; a contributory causal connection suffices.'

149. In my judgment it is clear from that explanation that even if a child is likely to suffer significant harm as a direct result of a disorder which affects that child's behaviour, if the consequent behaviour is such that a parent is unable to control the child then the child's being beyond parental control is, at the very least, a contributory cause of the likelihood of future harm.

'the child's being beyond parental control'

150. That leads on to consideration of the expression *'the child's being beyond parental control'*. There is little authority on the meaning of this expression. It is an expression that appeared in earlier child protection legislation. Section 1(2)(d) of the Children and Young Persons Act 1969 provided that proof that a child 'is beyond the control of his parent or guardian' was sufficient of itself to empower the court to make a care order. The Children Act 1989 makes two important changes to that wording. First, the expression *'he is beyond parental control'* is replaced by *'the child's being beyond parental control'*. Second, proof of 'the child's being beyond parental control' is not of itself sufficient to empower the court to make a care order. The court must be satisfied that the child 'is suffering or is likely to suffer significant harm... attributable... to the child's being beyond parental control'.

151. The first reported authority is *M v Birmingham City Council* [1994] 2 FLR 141. Stuart-White J there said.

> '...Subsection (2)(a) contains a verb, in what is unquestionably the present tense...whereas subs (2)(b)(ii) contains no verb in the present or any other tense. It must be read together with the opening words of subs (2)(b) as follows: '...that the harm, or likelihood of harm, is attributable to – (ii) the child's being beyond parental control.' The expression contained in subs (2)(b)(ii) is, it seems to me, plainly a substantival expression capable of describing a state of affairs in the past, in the present or in the future according to the context in which it falls to be applied. No doubt this is why the concept of likelihood finds no place at this point in the subsection.
>
> Two other matters in relation to subs (2)(b)(ii) have been canvassed in argument. In relation to those I am prepared to assume for the purpose of this appeal, without deciding the point. That 'parental control' refers to the parent of the child in question and not to parents, or reasonable parents, in general...'

152. The only Court of Appeal authority addressing the concept of *'being beyond parental control'* is *L (A Minor)* 18 March 1997 (unreported). Butler-Sloss LJ says,

'It is suggested most attractively by Mr Jubb in a long, careful, comprehensive skeleton argument and short, succinct oral argument to us that in order to show that a child is beyond parental control you must show some misfeasance by the parents. There is almost no authority on the phrase 'beyond parental control' and certainly no authority to support the proposition, bold proposition as Mr Jubb is prepared to accept it as, that he makes to us today. We are asked to look at the useful guidance to the Children Act , Volume 1, under Court Orders, which says at paragraph 3.25:

> '...the second limb is that the child is beyond parental control...It provides for cases where, whatever the standard of care available to the child, he is not benefiting from it because of lack of parental control. It is immaterial whether this is the fault of the parents or the child. Such behaviour frequently stems from distorted or stressed relationships between parent and child.'

That seems to me to be a useful summary of how those who put the Act together saw the use of what is a long-standing part of the previous child legislation of 'beyond parental control'. I consider that we should be very careful not to look at the words of the Children Act other than broadly, sensibly and realistically...Quite simply this child is beyond the control of his parents. It is extremely sad. It is not a case of apportioning blame. It is a case of recognising a very worrying situation and one would have hoped, trying to work together, to make something of this child.'

153. *The Children Act 1989 Guidance and Regulations*, to which Butler-Sloss LJ referred, was updated in 2008. The text and tone of the latest guidance is noticeably different from the earlier version. The guidance now states:

> '3.41 If the child is determined by the court as being beyond parental control, this means that, whatever the standard of care provided by the parents, the child is suffering or is likely to suffer significant harm because of lack of parental control. This requires the court to determine whether as a matter of fact, the child is beyond control: it is immaterial who, if anyone, is to blame. In such cases, the local authority will need to demonstrate how the child's situation will improve if the court makes an order – how his behaviour can be brought under control, and why an order is necessary to achieve this.'

See also *Re T (a child: care order: beyond parental control: deprivation of liberty: authority to administer medication)* [2017] EWFC B1, [74]–[90] (Mr Recorder Darren Howe CQ sitting as a Judge of the High Court) addressing the same point

3.7.10 Threshold criteria: attributability: beyond parental care: 'parental' refers to the child's parent(s), not reasonable parents

M v Birmingham City Council [1995] 1 FCR 50 (FD), 57C–E (Stuart-White J)

Two other matters in relation to subs (2)(b)(ii) have been canvassed in argument. In relation to those I am prepared to assume for the purpose of this appeal, without deciding the point, that 'parental control' refers to the parent of the child in question and not to parents, or reasonable parents, in general. Moreover, in construing the word 'parental' in relation to this subsection I am prepared to hold that the control in question is that exercised, or to be exercised, not simply by the other but by the mother in conjunction with her cohabitant, Mr P.

In reaching this conclusion I am assisted by making reference to s 1(3)(f) and to s 2(9) and by the fact that many parents share *de facto* though not legal parental responsibility with cohabitants who are not related to the children and in respect of whom there is no parental responsibility order nor formal parental responsibility agreement.

3.8 THRESHOLD CRITERIA: 'WHODUNNIT' CASES

3.8.1 Threshold criteria: 'whodunnit' cases: general approach to the uncertain perpetrator issue

Re B (children: uncertain perpetrator) (rev 1) [2019] EWCA Civ 575, [2019] 2 FCR 685, [46]–[52] (Peter Jackson LJ)

[46] Drawing matters together, it can be seen that the concept of a pool of perpetrators seeks to strike a fair balance between the rights of the individual, including those of the child, and the importance of child protection. It is a means of satisfying the attributable threshold condition that only arises where the court is satisfied that there has been significant harm arising from (in shorthand) ill-treatment and where the only 'unknown' is which of a number of persons is responsible. So, to state the obvious, the concept of the pool does not arise at all in the normal run of cases where the relevant allegation can be proved to the civil standard against an individual or individuals in the normal way. Nor does it arise where only one person could possibly be responsible. In that event, the allegation is either proved or it is not. There is no room for a finding of fact on the basis of 'real possibility', still less on the basis of suspicion. There is no such thing as a pool of one.

[47] It should also be emphasised that a decision to place a person within the pool of perpetrators is not a finding of fact in the conventional sense. As is made clear in *Lancashire* at [19], *O and N* at [27]–[28] and *S-B* at [43], the person is not a proven perpetrator but a possible perpetrator. That conclusion is then carried forward to the welfare stage, when the court will, as was said in *S-B*, 'consider the strength of the possibility' that the person was involved as part of the overall circumstances of the case. At the same time it will, as Lord Nicholls put it in *Lancashire*, 'keep firmly in mind that the parents have not been shown to be responsible for the child's injuries'. In saying this, he recognised that a conclusion of this kind presents the court with a particularly difficult problem. Experience bears this out, particularly where a child has suffered very grave harm from someone within a pool of perpetrators.

[48] The concept of the pool of perpetrators should therefore, as was said in *Lancashire*, encroach only to the minimum extent necessary upon the general principles underpinning s 31(2). Centrally, it does not alter the general rule on the burden of proof. Where there are a number of people who might have caused the harm, it is for the local authority to show that in relation to each of them there is a real possibility that they did. No one can be placed into the pool unless that has been shown. This is why it is always misleading to refer to 'exclusion from the pool': see *Re S-B* at [43]. Approaching matters in that way risks, as Baroness Hale said, reversing the burden of proof.

[49] To guard against that risk, I would suggest that a change of language may be helpful. The court should first consider whether there is a 'list' of people who had the opportunity to cause the injury. It should then consider whether it can identify the actual perpetrator on the balance of probability and should seek, but not strain, to do so: *Re D (children)* [2009] EWCA Civ 472, [2009] 2 FCR 555, [2009] 2 FLR 668 at [12]. Only if it cannot identify the perpetrator to the civil standard of proof should it go on to ask in respect of those on the list: 'Is there a likelihood or real possibility that A or B or C was the perpetrator or a perpetrator of the inflicted injuries?' Only if there is should A or B or C be placed into the 'pool'.

[50] Likewise, it can be seen that the concept of a pool of perpetrators as a permissible means of satisfying the threshold was forged in cases concerning individuals who were 'carers'. In *Lancashire*, the condition was interpreted to include non-parent carers. It was somewhat widened in *North Yorkshire* at [26] to include 'people with access to the child' who might have caused injury. If that was an extension, it was a principled one. But at all events, the extension does not stretch to 'anyone who had even a fleeting contact with the child in circumstances where there was the opportunity to cause injuries': *North Yorkshire* at [25]. Nor does it extend to harm caused by someone outside the home or family unless it would have been reasonable to expect a parent to have prevented it: *S-B* at [40].

[51] It should also be noted that in the leading cases there were two, three or four known individuals from whom any risk to the child must have come. The position of each individual was then investigated and compared. That is as it should be. To assess the likelihood of harm having been caused by A or B or C, one needs as much information as possible about each of them in order to make the decision about which if any of them should be placed in the pool. So, where there is an imbalance of information about some individuals in comparison to others, particular care may need to be taken to ensure that the imbalance does not distort the assessment of the possibilities. The same may be said where the list of individuals has been whittled down to a pool of one named individual alongside others who are not similarly identified. This may be unlikely, but the present case shows that it is not impossible. Here it must be shown that there genuinely is a pool of perpetrators and not just a pool of one by default.

[52] Lastly, as part of the court's normal case-management responsibilities it should at the outset of proceedings of this kind ensure (i) that a list of possible perpetrators is created, and (ii) that directions are given for the local authority to gather (either itself or through other agencies) all relevant information about and from those individuals, and (iii) that those against whom allegations are made are given the opportunity to be heard. By these means some of the complications that can arise in these difficult cases may be avoided.

See also *Re S-B (children) (non-accidental injury)* [2009] UKSC 17, [2010] 1 FCR 321 [39]–[44] (Lady Hale) addressing the same point (including dispelling the notion of 'ruling out' a particular person, [43])

3.8.2 Threshold criteria: 'whodunnit' cases: not straining to identify perpetrators

NH v A County Council and others; Re D (children) (non-accidental injury) [2009] EWCA Civ 472, [2009] 2 FCR 555, [9]–[12] (Wall LJ) *quotation limited to* [12]

[12] … Nothing in *Re B*, in our judgment, requires the court to identify an individual as the perpetrator of non-accidental injuries to a child, simply because the standard of proof for such an identification is the balance of probabilities. If such an identification is not possible—because, for example, a judge remains genuinely uncertain at the end of a fact finding hearing, and cannot find on the balance of probabilities that A rather than B caused the injuries to the child, but that neither A nor B can be excluded as a perpetrator—it is the duty of the judge to state that as his or her conclusion. To put the matter another way, judges should not, as a result of the decision in *Re B*, and the fact that it supersedes *Re H*, strain to identify the perpetrator of non-accidental injuries to children. If an individual perpetrator can be properly identified on the balance of probabilities, then for the reasons given in *Re K* it is the judge's duty to identify him or her. But the judge should not start from the premise that it will only be in an exceptional case that it will not be possible to make such an identification. There will inevitably be cases—of which this, in our judgment, is one—where the only conclusion which the court can properly reach is that one of the two parents—or both—must have inflicted theinjuries, and that neither can be excluded.

3.8.3 Threshold criteria: 'whodunnit' cases: approach in binary cases

Re B (a child) [2018] EWCA Civ 2127, [2019] 1 FCR 120, [19]–[21] (Peter Jackson LJ)

[19] The proper approach to cases where injury has undoubtedly been inflicted and where there are several possible perpetrators is clear and applies as much to those cases where there are only two possible candidates as to those

where there are more. The court first considers whether there is sufficient evidence to identify a perpetrator on the balance of probabilities; if there is not, it goes on to consider in relation to each candidate whether there is a real possibility that they might have caused the injury and excludes those of which this cannot be said: *North Yorkshire County Council v SA* [2003] EWCA Civ 839, [2003] 3 FCR 118, [2003] 2 FLR 849, per Dame Elizabeth Butler-Sloss P at [26].

[20] Even where there are only two possible perpetrators, there will be cases where a judge remains genuinely uncertain at the end of a fact-finding hearing and cannot identify the person responsible on the balance of probabilities. The court should not strain to identify a perpetrator in such circumstances: *Re D (care proceedings: preliminary hearing)* [2009] EWCA Civ 472 at [12].

[21] In what Mr Geekie described as a simple binary case like the present one, the identification of one person as the perpetrator on the balance of probabilities carries the logical corollary that the second person must be excluded. However, the correct legal approach is to survey the evidence as a whole as it relates to each individual in order to arrive at a conclusion about whether the allegation has been made out in relation to one or other on a balance of probability. Evidentially, this will involve considering the individuals separately and together, and no doubt comparing the probabilities in respect of each of them. However, in the end the court must still ask itself the right question, which is not 'who is the more likely?' but 'does the evidence establish that this individual probably caused this injury?' In a case where there are more than two possible perpetrators, there are clear dangers in identifying an individual simply because they are the likeliest candidate, as this could lead to an identification on evidence that fell short of a probability. Although the danger does not arise in this form where there are only two possible perpetrators, the correct question is the same, if only to avoid the risk of an incorrect identification being made by a linear process of exclusion.

See also *Re A-C (a child); Re A (a child)* [2013] EWCA Civ 1321, [37]–[38] (McFarlane LJ) addressing a related point (deciding between possible perpetrators requires something in the 'evidential balance')

3.8.4 Threshold criteria: 'whodunnit' cases: uncertain perpetrator findings: relevance in present cases

Re O and N (children) (non-accidental injury) [2003] UKHL 18, [2003] 1 FCR 673, [19]–[32] (Lord Nicholls) *quotation limited to* [26]–[28]

[26] The first area concerns cases of the type involved in the present appeals, where the judge finds a child has suffered significant physical harm at the hands of his parents but is unable to say which. I stress one feature of this type of case. These are cases where it has been proved, to the requisite standard of proof, that the child is suffering significant harm or is likely to do so.

[27] Here, as a matter of legal policy, the position seems to me straightforward. Quite simply, it would be grotesque if such a case had to proceed at the welfare stage on the footing that, because neither parent, considered individually, has been proved to be the perpetrator, therefore the child is not at risk from either of them. This would be grotesque because it would mean the court would proceed on the footing that neither parent represents a risk even though one or other of them was the perpetrator of the harm in question.

[28] That would be a self-defeating interpretation of the legislation. It would mean that, in 'uncertain perpetrator' cases, the court decides that the threshold criteria are satisfied but then lacks the ability to proceed in a sensible way in the best interests of the child. The preferable interpretation of the legislation is that in such cases the court is able to proceed at the welfare stage on the footing that each of the possible perpetrators is, indeed, just that: a possible perpetrator. As Hale LJ said in *Re G (a child) (care order: threshold criteria)* [2001] 1 FCR 165 at 176:

> 'the fact that a judge cannot always decide means that when one gets to the later hearing, the later hearing has to proceed on the basis that each is a possible perpetrator'

This approach accords with the basic principle that in considering the requirements of the child's welfare the court will have regard to all the circumstances of the case.

Lancashire County Council v A [2000] 1 FCR 509 (HL), 511E–512A, 513I–516G (Lord Nicholls) *quotation limited to* 513I–516G

I can now identify the issue of interpretation arising on this appeal. In a case based on present harm ('is suffering … significant harm') the attributable condition requires the court to be satisfied that the harm is attributable to the care given to the child or, which is not this case, to the child's being beyond parental control. That nexus must be established on the basis of proved facts. But that prompts the question: care by whom? The contention of A's parents is that, having regard to the statutory context and the legislative policy behind Pt IV of the Children Act, 'the care given to the child' in s 31(2)(b)(i) means the care given to the child by the parents or other primary carers. The contrary contention, advanced by the local authority and A's guardian, is that no such limiting words are to be read into the statute: the relevant phrase means the care given by anyone who plays a part in the care arrangements for the child.

Stated more fully, the submission made by Mr Harris QC on behalf of A's parents was that at the heart of the Children Act is the belief that the welfare and development of children are in general best secured if they are brought up within the family by both parents playing a full part in their upbringing. The same philosophy applies, correspondingly, where substitute primary carers are bringing up a child in a settled home. The state, acting through a local authority, should only be permitted to intervene in the family life of the child by means of a care order if it can demonstrate that intervention is necessary for the child's protection by reason of some serious deficiency in care on the part of the parents or other primary carers, as the case may be, and that no other course is appropriate. Counsel submitted that a strictly literal interpretation of the phrase under consideration would lead to an absurdity. Parliament cannot have intended that a child should be at risk of being removed from his family, and the parents at risk of losing their child, because of an unforeseeable failure of care by a third party to whom the parents, wholly unexceptionably, had temporarily entrusted the child.

Counsel further submitted that the statutory phrase is ambiguous, and invited your Lordships' attention to observations made by Lord Mackay of Clashfern LC in this House when promoting the Children Bill. Two instances will suffice. On the second reading of the Bill, Lord Mackay LC stated (502 HL Official Series (5th series) col 493):

> '... as a matter of principle it is important for the law in a free society expressly to protect the integrity and independence of families save where there is at least likelihood of significant harm to the child from within the family.'

At the committee stage Lord Mackay LC said (503 HL Official Series (5th series) cols 349–350):

> 'I entirely agree that I have often said that where discretion is given it is wise to make it as flexible as possible. However, I do not think that that is an appropriate approach where the discretion will allow one of the most serious possible interventions in family life. Therefore, I think it is necessary to specify the grounds with reasonable particularity. That is what we seek to do in the Bill ... The purpose of this care order is to substitute the local authority for the parent in the sense of the local authority having parental responsibility for the child. That should only happen where something concerning the parent has gone wrong. That appears to me to be essential.'

This is a forceful argument, up to a point. I accept that the interpretation of the attributable condition urged on behalf of the respondents and upheld by the Court of Appeal is too wide and loose. For this one needs to look no further than Mr Harris QC's example of the one-off temporary entrustment of the child to a person reasonably believed by the parents to be suitable. Injury inflicted by the temporary carer would satisfy the threshold conditions. But the appellants' argument goes too far in the other direction. The interpretation urged on behalf of the appellants is too rigid. As with the respondents' submission, so also with the appellants' submission: the conclusion to which it leads cannot be right. As the present case exemplifies, the appellants' argument, if accepted, produces the result that where a child has repeatedly sustained non-accidental injuries the court may nevertheless be unable to intervene to protect the child by making a care order or, even, a supervision order. In the present case the child is proved to have sustained significant harm at the hands of one or both of her parents or at the hands of a daytime carer. But, according to this argument, if the court is unable to identify which of the child's carers was responsible for inflicting the injuries, the child remains outside the threshold prescribed by Parliament as the threshold which must be crossed before the court can proceed to consider whether it is in the best interests of the child to make a care order or supervision order. The child must, for the time being, remain unprotected, since s 31 of the Children Act and its associated emergency and interim provisions now provide the only court mechanism available to a local authority to protect a child from risk of further harm.

I cannot believe Parliament intended that the attributable condition in s 31(2)(b) should operate in this way. Such an interpretation would mean that the child's future health, or even her life, would have to be hazarded on the chance that, after all, the non-parental carer rather than one of the parents inflicted the injuries. Self-evidently, to proceed in such a way when a child is proved to have suffered serious injury on more than one occasion could be dangerously irresponsible.

There is a further factor which weighs with me. Sadly, the unhappy facts of the present case are far from being exceptional. As the Court of Appeal observed, the task of caring for children is often shared nowadays between parents and others. When questions of non-accidental injury or abuse arise, the court is frequently unable to discover precisely what happened. This is not surprising. And yet, on the appellants' construction of the attributable condition, in this common form situation of shared caring the court is powerless to make even a supervision order if the judge is unable to penetrate the fog of denials, evasions, lies and half-truths which all too often descends in court at fact finding hearings. Indeed, in the present case the judge observed, regarding the evidence of one witness, that it was impossible to identify what was or might have been fact and what was or might have been fiction.

Against this background, I consider that a permissible and preferable interpretation of s 31(2)(b)(i), between the two extremes, is as follows. The phrase 'care given to the child' refers primarily to the care given to the child by a parent or parents or other primary carers. That is the norm. The matter stands differently in a case such as the present one, where care is shared and the court is unable to distinguish in a crucial respect between the care given by the parents or primary carers and the care given by other carers. Different considerations from the norm apply in a case of shared caring where the care given by one or other of the carers is proved to have been deficient, with the child suffering harm in consequence, but the court is unable to identify which of the carers provided the deficient care. In such a case, the phrase 'care given to the child' is apt to embrace not merely the care given by the parents or other primary carers; it is apt to embrace the care given by any of the carers. Some such meaning has to be given to the phrase if the unacceptable consequences already mentioned are to be avoided. This interpretation achieves that necessary result while, at the same time, encroaching to the minimum extent on the general principles underpinning s 31(2). Parliament seems not to have foreseen this particular problem. The courts must therefore apply the statutory language to the unforeseen situation in the manner which best gives effect to the purposes the legislation was enacted to achieve.

I recognise that the effect of this construction is that the attributable condition may be satisfied when there is no more than a possibility that the parents were responsible for inflicting the injuries which the child has undoubtedly suffered. That is a consequence which flows from giving the phrase, in the limited circumstances mentioned above, the wider meaning those circumstances require. I appreciate also that in such circumstances, when the court proceeds to the next stage and considers whether to exercise its discretionary power to make a care order or supervision order, the judge may be faced with a particularly difficult problem. The judge will not know which individual was responsible for inflicting the injuries. The child may suffer harm if left in a situation of risk with his parents. The child may also suffer harm if removed from parental care where, if the truth were known, the parents present no risk. Above all, I recognise that this interpretation of the attributable condition means that parents who may be wholly innocent, and whose care may not have fallen below that of a reasonable parent, will face the possibility of losing their child, with all the pain and distress this involves. That is a possibility, once the threshold conditions are satisfied, although by no means a certainty. It by no means follows that because the threshold conditions are satisfied the court will go on to make a care order. And it goes without saying that when considering how to exercise their discretionary powers in this type of case judges will keep firmly in mind that the parents have not been shown to be responsible for the child's injuries.

I recognise all these difficulties. This is indeed a most unfortunate situation for everyone involved: the child, the parents, the child-minder, the local authority and the court. But, so far as the threshold conditions are concerned, the factor which seems to me to outweigh all others is the prospect that an unidentified, and unidentifiable, carer may inflict further injury on a child he or she has already severely damaged.

3.8.5 Threshold criteria: 'whodunnit' cases: uncertain perpetrator findings: relevance in later cases

Re J (children) (non-accidental injury: past possible perpetrator in new family) [2013] UKSC 9, [2013] 2 FCR 149, [48]–[54] (Lady Hale), [88]–[90] (Lord Hope DP) *quotation limited to* [48]–[54]

[48] Since *Re H and R*, a clear distinction has been drawn between the degree of likelihood required by the second limb and the basis upon which the court can be satisfied of that likelihood. It was held in *Re H and R* that 'likely' did not mean 'more likely than not', but a 'real possibility', the degree of possibility required depending upon the seriousness of the harm which was feared. The House might have held that 'likely' meant 'probable', but it adopted a more flexible test. It is worth noting that Lord Nicholls did not think that adopting this more flexible test would significantly prejudice the parents' interests: 'so far as the parents are

concerned, there is no particular magic in a threshold test based on a probability of significant harm as distinct from a real possibility' ([1996] 1 FCR 509 at 524, [1996] 1 All ER 1 at 15).

[49] Having adopted a flexible test of likelihood, it became all the more important to hold that an objective factual basis was required from which to draw the inference that future harm was likely. This was controversial in *Re H and R* but has been firmly established ever since and for very good reasons. Care courts are often told that the best predictor of the future is the past. But prediction is only possible where the past facts are proved. A real possibility that something has happened in the past is not enough to predict that it will happen in the future. It may be the fact that a judge has found that there is a real possibility that something has happened. But that is not sufficient for this purpose. A finding of a real possibility that a child has suffered harm does not establish that he has. A finding of a real possibility that the harm which a child has suffered is 'non-accidental' does not establish that it was. A finding of a real possibility that this parent harmed a child does not establish that she did. Only a finding that he has, it was, or she did, as the case may be, can be sufficient to found a prediction that because it has happened in the past the same is likely to happen in the future. Care courts need to hear this message loud and clear.

[50] In *Re S-B*, the 'real possibility' that the mother had harmed J was the *only* basis upon which the judge concluded that it was likely that W would suffer harm in the future. There was nothing else. J had suffered bruises, and all bruising to a tiny baby must be taken seriously. But they had probably been caused on one occasion by one parent. It could not be suggested that the other parent had failed to protect him. What was impermissible, as stated in para [49], was to make this, and this alone, the basis for predicting that the mother was likely to harm W in the future. It may well be that when the case was re-heard, facts emerged from which it was possible to make such a prediction.

[51] Cases such as *Re S-B* are vanishingly rare. As McFarlane LJ pointed out in the Court of Appeal ([2012] 2 FCR 1 at [109], [2012] 3 WLR 952), the *Lancashire* case [2000] 1 FCR 509, [2000] 2 All ER 97, in respect of the child-minder, was 'truly a one point case. There were no other adverse findings made against the child-minder' (he says 'other' but he must mean no adverse findings) (para [108]). Likewise, *Re S-B* 'was [a case] of a one-off ('whodunit') injury, there was no question of failure to protect and no finding of collusion' (para [111]). Even in *Re F* [2011] 2 FLR 856, there were no adverse findings against the father (para [112]). Most care cases are not 'one-off whodunit' cases. They come with a multitude of facts.

[52] It is, of course, a fact that a previous child has been injured or even killed while in the same household as this parent. No one has ever suggested that that fact should be ignored. Such a fact normally comes associated with innumerable other facts which may be relevant to the prediction of future harm to another child. How many injuries were there? When and how were they caused? On how many occasions were they inflicted?

How obvious will they have been? Was the child in pain or unable to use his limbs? Would any ordinary parent have noticed this? Was there a delay in seeking medical attention? Was there concealment from or active deception of the authorities? What do those facts tell us about the child care capacities of the parent with whom we are concerned?

[53] Then, of course, those facts must be set alongside other facts. What were the household circumstances at the time? Did drink and/or drugs feature? Was there violence between the adults? How have things changed since? Has this parent left the old relationship? Has she entered a new one? Is it different? What does this combination of facts tell us about the likelihood of harm to any of the individual children with whom the court is now concerned? Does what happened several years ago to a tiny baby in very different circumstances enable us to predict the likelihood of significant harm to much older children in a completely new household?

[54] Hence I agree entirely with McFarlane LJ when he said that *Re S-B* is not authority for the proposition that 'if you cannot identify the past perpetrator, you cannot establish future likelihood' (para [111]). There may, or may not, be a multitude of established facts from which such a likelihood can be established. There is no substitute for a careful, individualised assessment of where those facts take one. But *Re S-B* is authority for the proposition that a real possibility that this parent has harmed a child in the past is not, by itself, sufficient to establish the likelihood that she will cause harm to another child in the future.

3.9 THRESHOLD CRITERIA: CHILDREN'S ALLEGATIONS

3.9.1 Threshold criteria: children's allegations: ABE[5] interviews

See Chapter 7.4 Evidence: children

3.9.2 Threshold criteria: children's allegations: should children give evidence?

See Chapter 7.4 Evidence: children

3.9.3 Threshold criteria: children's allegations: avoiding the term 'disclosure'

Re P (sexual abuse: finding of fact hearing) [2019] EWFC 27 (Fam), [21] (MacDonald J)

21. Finally, by way of introduction, it is necessary to highlight an issue of terminology that has, once again, arisen in this case (see *AS v TH (False*

5 Achieving Best Evidence in Criminal Proceedings: Guidance on interviewing victims and witnesses and guidance on using special measures (Ministry of Justice, 2011).

Allegations of Abuse) [2016] EWHC 532 (Fam) at [33]). Despite the fact that the use of the term 'disclosure' to describe a statement or allegation of sexual abuse made by a child has been deprecated since the publication of the Cleveland Report in 1987 (see Paragraph 12.34(1) of that report), due to it precluding the notion that the abuse might *not* have occurred, nearly every professional who gave evidence in this case, including the investigating police officers, used the term 'disclosure' to describe what the children had said […], or to describe what they understood the children to have said to others. Within this context, where a witness has used the word 'disclosure' that word is used in this judgment when quoting passages of documentary or oral evidence from that witness. Otherwise, this judgment uses the term 'allegation'. Before too much approbation is heaped on those witnesses, I note that both Government guidance and publications from the NSPCC now use the word 'disclosure' even when speaking of matters that have not yet been the subject of proof to the requisite standard.

See also *AS v TH (false allegations of abuse)* [2016] EWHC 532 (Fam), [2016] 3 FCR 327, [33] (MacDonald J) addressing the same point

3.9.4 Threshold criteria: children's allegations: initial contact with children alleging abuse

AS v TH (false allegations of abuse) [2016] EWHC 532 (Fam), [2016] 3 FCR 327, [35]–[40] (MacDonald J)

[35] Where a child makes an allegation of abuse to a professional, the relevant guidance for professionals to whom allegations of abuse are reported makes clear the following principles with respect to the initial contact with the child.

[36] In the departmental advice *What to do if you're worried a child is being abused* (HM Government, March 2015) (replacing previous guidance published in 2006) states that before referring to children's services or the Police an attempt should be made to establish the basic facts. Within this context, the following is said at [28]:

> 'The signs of child abuse might not always be obvious and a child might not tell anyone what is happening to them. You should therefore question behaviours if something seems unusual and try to speak to the child, alone, if appropriate, to seek further information'

And at [29]:

> 'If a child reports, following a conversation you have initiated or otherwise, that they are being abused and neglected, you should listen to them, take their allegation seriously, and reassure them that you will take action to keep them safe.'

[37] The statutory guidance *Achieving Best Evidence in Criminal Proceedings* (March 2011) (hereafter the *ABE Guidelines*) makes clear at [2.4] that the

need to consider a video recorded interview in respect of the allegations may not be immediately apparent to professionals involved prior to the police being informed. Within this context the *ABE Guidelines* state at [2.5] that:

> 'Any initial questioning should be intended to elicit a brief account of what is alleged to have taken place; a more detailed account should not be pursued at this stage but should be left until the formal interview takes place. Such a brief account should include where and when the alleged incident took place and who was involved or otherwise present.'

[38] The *ABE Guidelines* goes on to state at [2.6] under the heading 'Initial Contact with Victims and Witnesses' that a person engaged in early discussion with an alleged victim or witness should, as far as possible, (a) listen, (b) not stop a free recall of events and (c) where it is necessary to ask questions, ask open-ended or specific closed questions rather than forced-choice, leading or multiple questions and ask no more questions than are necessary to take immediate action.

[39] Within this context, having examined the *ABE Guidelines*, in *Re S (a child)* [2013] EWCA Civ 1254 at [16] the Court of Appeal held that, with respect to initial contact with alleged victims, discussions about the facts in issue in respect of an allegation *as distinct* from whether and what allegation is being made and against whom, should be rare and should not be a standard practice.

[40] Again within the foregoing context, when social workers are speaking to children who have made allegations they must be very careful to consider the purpose of the exchange and whether it is being conducted with a view to taking proceedings to protect the child or for separate therapeutic purposes where the restrictions upon prompting would not apply but the interview would not be for the purposes of court proceedings (*Re D (minors) (child abuse: interviews)* [1998] 2 FCR 419, [1998] 2 FLR 10).

See also *AS v TH (false allegations of abuse)* [2016] EWHC 532 (Fam), [2016] 3 FCR 327, [41]–[44] (MacDonald J) addressing a related point (the need for proper professional recordings)

See Chapter 3.10.2 Threshold criteria: further specific guidance: cardinal principles for sexual abuse investigations

3.9.5 Threshold criteria: children's allegations: social work assessments

AS v TH (false allegations of abuse) [2016] EWHC 532 (Fam), [2016] 3 FCR 327, [45]–[47] (MacDonald J)

[45] Following the allegations being made in this case assessments were carried out by the London Borough of Hackney, including an investigation pursuant to s 47 of the Children Act 1989. The London Borough of

Westminster and the local authority in whose area the mother and children now reside have also been involved with the children.

[46] The Cleveland Report provides extensive guidance on proper social work practice in the context of allegations of sexual abuse. The salient points are as follows (emphasis added):

i) Whatever the nature of presentation, whether the response is immediate, prompt or deferred, the response should be planned and conducted with professional skill. Children's best interests are rarely served by precipitate action. *Initial action in securing the widest possible information about the child's circumstances and family background is an essential pre-requisite to careful judgment and purposeful intervention* (para 13.9);

ii) It is necessary to assess the family by looking at the parents individually, the parents' relationship, the vulnerability of the child, the child's situation in the family, the family's social situation, their contacts with extended family etc as well as considering and recording the family's perspective of events which set the referral in motion (para 13.13);

iii) The principle aim of the social worker's contact with the family at this stage should be to compile a social history, *obtaining as comprehensive a picture of relationships and pattern of family life as possible*. The quality of the marital relationship and parental skills should be carefully assessed (para 13.19);

iv) Social workers should seek a broadly based assessment of the child. *An outline of the child's social development together with information about the important relationships in the child's life is vital information*. Where a child is attending playgroup, childminders or school it will be helpful to record the views of those responsible for the child's day to day care (para 13.23);

v) Intervention should proceed as part of a planned and co-ordinated activity between agencies. *Children and families should not be subject to multiple examinations and interviews simply because agencies and their staff have failed to plan their work together* (para 13.10);

vi) The social worker will need to establish a clear understanding with the Police about how their respective roles are to be co-ordinated (para 13.12);

vii) Throughout the phase of the initial assessment and preliminary decision making, social workers should be conscious of the fact that *the presumption that abuse has taken place can have damaging repercussions for the child and the family*. Equally, *an abnormally low level of alertness to the possibility of child sexual abuse may deter children* from subsequently trusting adults sufficiently to reveal the fact of abuse to them (para 13.22).

[47] Within this context, and echoing this approach, the statutory guidance *Working Together to Safeguard Children* (HM Government March 2015) reiterates at [35] the principles and parameters of good assessment.

These principles and parameters include the need for such assessments to be rooted in child development and informed by evidence, to involve children and families, to adopt an integrated approach, to be a continuing process and not an event and to be transparent and open to challenge. The three domains of the assessment specified at [36] should be the child's developmental needs, the parents' or carers' capacity to respond to those needs and the impact and influence of wider family, community and environmental circumstances. At [37] the guidance makes clear that the interaction of these domains requires careful investigation during the assessment and that it is important that (a) information is gathered and recorded systematically, (b) information is checked and discussed with the child and their parents/carers where appropriate, (c) differences in views about information are recorded and (d) the impact of what is happening to the child is clearly identified.

3.10 THRESHOLD CRITERIA: FURTHER SPECIFIC GUIDANCE

3.10.1 Threshold criteria: further specific guidance: failure to protect

Re L-W (children) [2019] EWCA Civ 159, [2019] 2 FCR 76, [62]–[64] (King LJ)

[62] Failure to protect comes in innumerable guises. It often relates to a mother who has covered up for a partner who has physically or sexually abused her child or, one who has failed to get medical help for her child in order to protect a partner, sometimes with tragic results. It is also a finding made in cases where continuing to live with a person (often in a toxic atmosphere, frequently marked with domestic violence) is having a serious and obvious deleterious effect on the children in the household. The harm, emotional rather than physical, can be equally significant and damaging to a child.

[63] Such findings, where made in respect of a carer, often the mother, are of the utmost importance when it comes to assessments and future welfare considerations. A finding of failing to protect can lead a court to conclude that the children's best interests will not be served by remaining with, or returning to, the care of that parent, even though that parent may have been wholly exonerated from having caused any physical injuries.

[64] Any court conducting a finding of fact hearing should be alert to the danger of such a serious finding becoming 'a bolt on' to the central issue of perpetration or of falling into the trap of assuming too easily that, if a person was living in the same household as the perpetrator, such a finding is almost inevitable. As Aikens LJ observed in *Re J*, 'nearly all parents will be imperfect in some way or another'. Many households operate under considerable stress and men go to prison for serious crimes, including crimes of violence, and are allowed to return home by their long-suffering partners upon their release. That does not mean that for that reason alone, that parent has failed to protect her children in allowing her errant partner

home, unless, by reason of one of the facts connected with his offending, or some other relevant behaviour on his part, those children are put at risk of suffering significant harm.

See also *Re G-L-T (children)* [2019] EWCA Civ 717, [2019] 3 FCR 538, [68]–[74] (King LJ) considering *Re L-W (children)* [2019] EWCA Civ 159, [2019] 2 FCR 76 (including the exhortation to approach 'failure to protect' with 'assiduous care', [72])

3.10.2 Threshold criteria: further specific guidance: cardinal principles for sexual abuse investigations

Re P (sexual abuse: finding of fact hearing) [2019] EWFC 27 (Fam), [1245] (MacDonald J) *quotation limited to* [1245]

1245. In circumstances where there is a wealth of guidance for professionals and the police, it is not appropriate for this court to reinvent the wheel or burden those tasked with dealing with this fraught area with further detailed instructions. […] That said, it does appear that the following 'lessons' bear repeating as the foundation of rigorous forensic investigation by professionals and police of allegations of child sexual abuse. I venture to suggest that *whenever* a referral is received in a case that raises allegations of sexual abuse the social worker or police officer allocated to the case should, *before* they do anything else, pause and remind themselves of the following checklist of ten cardinal principles:

i) The investigation of child sexual abuse is a demanding, complex and sensitive task and should be undertaken by those who have received the requisite training.

ii) Very great professional care is required when dealing with allegations of child sexual abuse, both in the initial phases and at the ABE interview stage.

iii) Whatever the nature of the child's presentation, and whether the response is immediate, prompt or deferred, the response of professionals and the police must be planned. Children's best interests are rarely served by precipitate action.

iv) The primary principles governing, and the procedures for the investigation and assessment of alleged child sexual abuse are those set out in *Achieving Best Evidence 2011* and *Working Together 2018* and must be followed in all cases.

v) Any investigation into child sexual abuse that focuses attention on the statements of the child runs the risk of producing a false result if what the child says is unreliable, or if the child's primary caretaker is unreliable.

vi) All interactions with a child who is making or appears to be making an allegation of child sexual abuse have the potential to influence that child's memory.

vii) Accounts given by children are susceptible to influence as the result of bias or preconceived ideas on the part of professionals and police.

Those speaking to children who have made allegations of sexual abuse *must* keep an open mind with respect to the allegations made and *must* guard against the development of bias or preconceived ideas. A professional who loses their objectivity ceases, by definition, to act professionally.

viii) Questioning the child should ordinarily be left to a formal ABE interview. If any initial questioning is necessary, it should be limited to eliciting a brief account of what is alleged to have taken place; a more detailed account should not be pursued at that stage.

ix) Anything the child says must be recorded in a note that must detail (a) the timing, setting and people present, (b) what the child says in the words used by the *child* (avoiding summaries of the account in the interests of neatness or comprehensibility and avoiding recordings of the adult's interpretation of what the child said), (c) a full note of the actual *questions* asked (if any) and (d) what was said by anybody else present.

x) Overall, the proper methodology is one that combines listening to the child and taking them seriously with an open-minded approach that takes account of both sides of the story, is open to new evidence that disconfirms original ideas, that reasons dispassionately, that demands that claims be backed by evidence and that deduces and infers conclusions only from available facts.

3.10.3 Threshold criteria: further specific guidance: shaken babies: clinical symptoms

Henderson (Keran Louise) v R; Butler (Ben) v R; Oyediran (Oladapo) v R [2010] EWCA Crim 1269, [2011] 1 FLR 547, [1], [6] (Moses LJ)

1. There are few types of case which arouse greater anxiety and controversy than those in which it is alleged that a baby has died as a result of being shaken. It is of note that when the Attorney General undertook a review of 297 cases over a ten year period following the case of *R v Cannings* [2004] 2 Cr App R 63, 97 were cases of what is known as 'shaken baby syndrome'. The controversy to which such cases gives rise should come as no surprise. A young baby dies whilst under the sole care of a parent or childminder. That child can give no clue to clinicians as to what has happened. Experts, prosecuting authorities and juries must reconstruct as best they can what has happened. There remains a temptation to believe that it is always possible to identify the cause of injury to a child. Where the prosecution is able, by advancing an array of experts, to identify a non-accidental injury and the defence can identify no alternative cause, it is tempting to conclude that the prosecution has proved its case. Such a temptation must be resisted. In this, as in so many fields of medicine, the evidence may be insufficient to exclude, beyond reasonable doubt, an unknown cause. As *Cannings* [177] teaches, even where on examination of all the evidence, every possible known cause has been excluded, the cause may still remain unknown.

...

6. There is a further problem to which we should draw attention. Cases such as *R v Harris and Others* [2006] 1 Cr App R 5 contain detailed analysis of medical evidence and the conclusions of this court on that evidence. In particular, in that case, the court commented upon the cogency of the 'triad': widespread bilateral retinal haemorrhages, thin film subdural haemorrhage and encephalopathy [63] and [69]. The court rejected the unified hypothesis that the same triad of injuries could be caused by lack of oxygen in the tissues leading to brain swelling, a hypothesis which Dr Geddes herself accepted could no longer credibly be put forward [66-68]. These conclusions have inevitably informed the basis of the approach taken by the police and prosecution and have been relied on in argument either at trial or before this court. But it is trite to observe that the conclusion of any court as to the medical evidence, whether at first instance or on appeal, is dependent upon the evidence before that court. No appellate jurisprudence could provide authority for a medical proposition. The strength of a proposition in medicine depends upon the strength of the medical evidence on which it is based. The quality and extent of the evidence will inevitably vary from case to case. Whilst it is now commonly accepted that the triad is strong prima facie evidence of shaking, that depends upon the common acceptance of experts in the field and not upon the conclusion of courts which are only able to weigh the evidence presented before them. Previous legal authority cannot determine whether the conclusion of a medical report should be accepted or rejected. The most legal authority can do is present an accurate record of what was or was not accepted or propounded.

See also *Re A and D (non-accidental injury: subdural haematomas)* [2001] EWHC 9 (Fam), [2002] 1 FLR 337, [41] (Dame Elizabeth Butler-Sloss P) addressing a related point (discussing subdural haematomas and expert evidence)

See also *Re A (a minor) (retinal haemorrhages: non-accidental injury)* [2001] 3 FCR 262, [54] (Bracewell J) addressing a related point (discussing retinal haemorrhages)

3.10.4 Threshold criteria: further specific guidance: fabricated or induced illness

Re X, Y and Z (children) [2010] EWHC B12 (Fam), [2011] 1 FLR 1045, [79]–[90] (HHJ Clifford Bellamy sitting as a judge of the High Court)

79. In February 2002 the Royal College of Paediatrics and Child Health published the report of a Working Party under the title 'Fabricated or Induced Illness by Carers' ('the RCPCH guidance'). The Foreword to this report refers to forthcoming guidance from the Department of Health and states that 'The Department of Health document sets out policy and guidelines for all professionals, whereas the College document discusses clinical issues in more detail and provides practical advice for paediatricians.'

80. The report makes the point that

> 'The initial role for the Paediatrician is to find out whether a child's illness and individual symptoms and signs have an unequivocal explanation as a natural illness. If this is not clear the possibility of fabricated or illness induction and the effect of this on the child has to be considered as part of the range of possibilities'.

The report also makes the point that

> 'In comparison with other forms of child abuse, Fabricated or Induced Illness is unique in that health professionals have key involvement from the early stages of emerging concerns through to the completion of enquiries and investigations.'

81. The report provides practical guidance for paediatricians on evaluating signs and symptoms. It advises that

> 'If there is actual evidence that symptoms are being fabricated or induced child protection agencies should be informed immediately. More often medical evaluation takes time before it is clear that there are factors operating other than natural disorders...At some point in the process it will be clear to the paediatrician that the concerns are not being allayed. When there are PERSISTING CONCERNS there should be a wider assessment by social services department. The criterion for referral is that the paediatrician has continuing concerns about the child's welfare and not that fabrication or illness induction or harm has been proved.'

82. In 2002 the Department of Health published 'Safeguarding Children in Whom Illness is Fabricated or Induced' ('the 2002 guidance'). This guidance, which is supplementary to the guidance given in 'Working Together', was issued under Section 7 of the Local Authority Social Services Act 1970 and as such it 'should be complied with unless local circumstances indicate exceptional reasons which justify a variation'. In 2008 that guidance was updated by the publication by the Department for Children, Schools and Families ('DCSF') of 'Safeguarding Children in whom illness is fabricated or induced – Supplementary guidance to Working Together to Safeguard Children.' ('the 2008 guidance)

83. Like the RCPCH guidance, the 2008 guidance emphasises the point that 'Good practice calls for effective co-operation between different agencies and professionals...and the careful exercise of professional judgement, based on thorough assessment and critical analysis of the available information.' It goes on to say that 'Safeguarding and promoting the welfare of children depends crucially upon effective information sharing, collaboration and understanding between agencies and professionals.'

84. The 2008 guidance states that 'A key professional task is to distinguish between the very anxious carer who may be responding in a reasonable way to a very sick child and those who exhibit abnormal behaviour.'

85. In the context of the three children with whom I am concerned, it is interesting to note that the 2008 guidance states that

> 'A significant number of children in whom illness is fabricated or induced will have been well known to health professionals from birth…The medical histories of this group of children are likely to have started early and in many instances will have become extensive by the time the suspected abuse is identified. Some children may have been referred to a tertiary paediatric centre because they were thought to have a serious or rare illness requiring expert diagnosis and treatment. They may have been seen at many hospitals in different geographical areas and by a number of professionals. They may also have been seen in centres for alternative medicine or by private practitioners.'

86. Like the RCPCH guidance, the 2008 guidance states that when FII is suspected there should be a referral to Children's Social Care. It says:

> 'Children's social care should decide and record, within one working day what response is necessary. From the point of referral, all professionals involved with the child and children's social care should work together. Lead responsibility for action to safeguard and promote the child's welfare lies with [children's social care]
>
> 'Referrals…may lead to no further action or to an initial assessment of the needs and circumstances of the child, and the provision of services or other help. If children's social care decides to take no further action at this stage, feedback should be provided to the referrer.'

87. The 2008 guidance gives advice on the action children's social care should take if there is reasonable cause to suspect the child is suffering, or is likely to suffer significant harm. It says

> 'If there is reasonable cause to suspect the child is suffering, or is likely to suffer significant harm, children's social care should convene and chair a strategy discussion which involves all the key professionals responsible for the child's welfare…'

88. The 2008 guidance also notes that

> 'The GP and all members of the Primary Health Care Team (PHCT), particularly midwives, health visitors and practice nurses, are all well placed to recognise the early signs and symptoms of fabricated or induced illness in a child…. Professionals in PHCTs may have unique knowledge of uncorroborated, odd or unusual presentations.'

89. With respect to the particular duties of Children's Social Care, the 2008 guidance goes on to say that

> 'Children's social care also has lead responsibility for any core assessment and will co-ordinate the process of systematic information gathering to build up a medical, psychiatric and social history and an

understanding of the child's needs and the parents' capacities to meet the child's developmental needs. Children's social care should ensure that a comprehensive chronology of the child's history is compiled.

'Children's social care should work collaboratively with all other agencies currently involved with the child and family. In addition, it is likely to be necessary to contact agencies with past involvement in order to prepare a full history of the child's health and family situation.'

90. The importance of this guidance was underlined by McFarlane J in *Re X: Emergency Protection Orders* [2006] EWHC 510 (Fam) …

See also *A County Council v A Mother and others* [2005] EWHC 31 (Fam), [2005] 2 FLR 129, [175]–[178] (Ryder J) addressing a related point (cautioning against the use of the FII[6] label as a substitute for factual analysis and risk assessment)

3.11 THRESHOLD CRITERIA: THE COURT'S FINDINGS

3.11.1 Threshold criteria: the court's findings: reciting threshold findings

Re S and H-S (children) [2018] EWCA Civ 1282, [2018] 3 FCR 186, [55]–[61] (McFarlane LJ)

[55] Before leaving this case, and with Lady Hale's more detailed judgment in *Re B* in mind, I hope it is helpful to make the following observations as to how the difficulties that have led to this appeal could have been avoided in practice.

[56] In the course of a necessarily long judgment covering a range of issues and a substantial body of evidence, where the threshold criteria are in issue, it is good practice to distil the findings that may have been made in previous paragraphs into one or two short and carefully structured paragraphs which spell out the court's finding on threshold identifying whether the finding is that the child 'is suffering' and/or 'is likely to suffer' significant harm, specifying the category of harm and the basic finding(s) as to causation.

[57] When making a finding of harm, it is important to identify whether the finding is of 'significant harm' or simply 'harm'.

[58] A finding that the child 'has suffered significant harm' is not a relevant finding for s 31, which looks to the 'relevant date' and the need to determine whether the child 'is suffering' or 'is likely to suffer' significant harm.

[59] Where findings have been made in previous proceedings, either before the same judge or a different tribunal, a judgment in subsequent proceedings should make reference to any relevant earlier findings and identify which,

6 Fabricated or induced illness.

if any, are specifically relied upon in support of a finding that the threshold criteria are satisfied in the later proceedings as at the 'relevant date'.

[60] At the conclusion of the hearing, after judgment has been given, there is a duty on counsel for the local authority and for the child, together with the judge, to ensure that any findings as to the threshold criteria are sufficiently clear.

[61] The court order that records the making of a care order should include within it, or have annexed to it, a clear statement of the basis upon which the s 31 threshold criteria have been established. In the present case, during the oral appeal hearing, counsel for the guardian explained that, following the judgment, she had submitted a detailed draft order to the court by email for the judge's approval. We were shown the draft which, whilst in need of fine tuning, does provide a template account of the court's threshold findings. It is most unfortunate that counsel's email, which may not have been seen by the judge, did not result in further consideration of the form of the order and statement of threshold findings. Had it done so, the need for the present appeal may not have arisen.

See also *Re S (a child: adequacy of reasoning)* [2019] EWCA Civ 1845, [2020] 1 FCR 396, [38] (Peter Jackson LJ) addressing the same point (identifying an expectation that threshold findings should be recited in an order)

See also *Re W-P (children)* [2019] EWCA Civ 1120, [34] (Peter Jackson LJ) considering *Re S and H-S (children)* [2018] EWCA Civ 1282, [2018] 3 FCR 186

3.11.2 Threshold criteria: the court's findings: adequacy of reasons

See Chapter 15.2 Appeals: adequacy of reasons

3.11.3 Threshold criteria: the court's findings: failure to prove allegations

Re M (children) [2013] EWCA Civ 388, [17] (Ryder J)

17. Finally, and outside the grounds of appeal, is the allegation that father was forcing his son to watch Jihadist DVDs in order to radicalise him. The judge rejected the allegation; hence, no appeal is brought upon the same. But counsel for father asserts that the judge should have gone further, and declared the allegation to be false, thereby allowing the credibility issue arising to be taken into account in respect of all other matters. It is worth remembering that an alleged fact not proven is not a fact in English law. That is the effect of the binary system of proof: if a negative is to be proved, that has to be proved with cogent evidence, just as if the positive is to be proved. It is not a correct proposition of law that a rejection of evidence mandates a judge to find that something is false; that is misconceived. The judge made no error of law in the way she dealt with this allegation, and it is not asserted on any other basis that she was plainly wrong.

See also *Shagang Shipping Company Ltd (in liquidation) v HNA Group Company Ltd* [2020] UKSC 34, [2020] 1 WLR 3549, [92]–[94] (Lord Hamblen and Lord Leggatt) addressing the same point

See also *VBC v AGM and others* [2019] EWFC 64, [263]–[270] (Sir Mark Hedley) addressing a related point (exoneration, and suggesting that a party seeking exoneration assumes an evidential burden, albeit the legal consequences of exoneration are no different from a failure to prove allegations)

3.11.4 Threshold criteria: the court's findings: reopening findings: three stages

Re CDT (a child: rehearing) [2020] EWCA Civ 1316, [2021] 1 FCR 139, [2]–[13] (Jackson LJ) *quotation limited to* [2]–[9], [12]–[13]

Rehearings in family cases

[2] When an application is made to reopen findings of fact in a family case the court proceeds in three stages:

(1) It asks whether the applicant has shown that there are solid grounds for believing that the previous findings require revisiting.

(2) If that hurdle is overcome, it decides how the rehearing is to be conducted.

(3) It rehears the matter and determines the issues.

This appeal is an opportunity to draw together and in one respect to simplify the approach to be taken at each of these stages, which I now consider in turn.

The first stage

[3] In *Re E (children: reopening findings of fact)* [2019] EWCA Civ 1447, [2019] 3 FCR 334, [2019] 1 WLR 6765 at [28]–[34] I sought to set out the proper approach at the first stage. I recalled that there is no strict rule of issue estoppel in children cases, but that a decision to allow past findings to be relitigated must be a reasoned one and that the considerations identified by Hale J in *Re B (Children Act Proceedings: issue estoppel)* [1997] Fam 117, 128; [1997] 1 FCR 477, 488–489 provide a useful framework:

> '(1) The court will wish to balance the underlying considerations of public policy, (a) that there is a public interest in an end to litigation – the resources of the court and everyone involved in these proceedings are already severely stretched and should not be employed in deciding the same matter twice unless there is good reason to do so; (b) that any delay in determining the outcome of the case is likely to be prejudicial to the welfare of the individual child; but (c) that the welfare of any child is unlikely to be served by relying upon determinations of fact which turn out to have been erroneous; and (d) the court's discretion, like the rules of issue estoppel, as pointed out by Lord Upjohn in *Carl Zeiss Stiftung v Rayner & Keeler Ltd (No 2)* [1967] 1 AC 853, 947, "must be applied so as to work justice and not injustice."

(2) The court may well wish to consider the importance of the previous findings in the context of the current proceedings. If they are so important that they are bound to affect the outcome one way or another, the court may be more willing to consider a rehearing than if they are of lesser or peripheral significance.

(3) Above all, the court is bound to want to consider whether there is any reason to think that a rehearing of the issue will result in any different finding from that in the earlier trial. By this I mean something more than the mere fact that different judges might on occasions reach different conclusion upon the same evidence. No doubt we would all be reluctant to allow a matter to be relitigated on that basis alone. The court will want to know (a) whether the previous findings were the result of a full hearing in which the person concerned took part and the evidence was tested in the usual way; (b) if so, whether there is any ground upon which the accuracy of the previous finding could have been attacked at the time, and why therefore there was no appeal at the time; and (c) whether there is any new evidence or information casting doubt upon the accuracy of the original findings.'

Hale J observed that there may be other factors to be borne in mind. In *Re E* at [34] I noted that the court will need to be satisfied that the challenged finding has actual or potential legal significance: is it likely to make a significant legal or practical difference to the arrangements that are to be made for these or other children?

[4] The decision in *Re B* was taken forward in a number of decisions, of which three are significant: *Birmingham City Council v H (no 1)* [2005] EWHC 2885 (Fam) (Charles J); *Birmingham City Council v H (no 2)* [2006] EWHC 3062 (Fam) (McFarlane J); and *Re ZZ* [2014] EWFC 9, [2015] 1 WLR 95 (Sir James Munby P). These establish that at the first stage the applicant must show that there are solid grounds for believing that a rehearing will result in a different finding. Mere speculation and hope are not enough. I will refer to the latter two decisions again in more detail when considering the third stage.

The second stage

[5] At the second stage the court makes case management decisions governing the arrangements for the rehearing. This is also an important discipline to ensure that the hearing does not become a free-for-all in which evidence is repeated and issues reopened without good reason. Sometimes (the present case is an example) the court may need to rehear all aspects of the evidence, but in other cases a particular aspect of the case will need to be reheard while leaving the rest of the evidence undisturbed. An example *is F v Cumbria County Council & M (fact-finding no 2)* [2016] EWHC 14 (Fam) where I reheard only the medical evidence and then placed it together with unaffected lay evidence: see paragraphs [109] and [110] for a description of the process. A similar approach was taken by Cobb J in *Re AD and AM (fact-finding: rehearing)* [2016] EWHC 2912 (Fam),

[2017] 4 WLR 23 and by me in *St Helens Council v M and F (baby with multiple fractures: rehearing)* [2018] EWFC 1, [2018] 2 FLR 371.

[6] A methodical approach to the tests at the first and second stages will provide important protection against unmeritorious attempts to relitigate settled findings while allowing cases that genuinely require reconsideration to be identified and revisited in a proportionate way that uses the resources of the court sensibly and is fair to all the parties.

[7] The importance of framing the rehearing correctly at the second stage can be seen in the decision of this court in *D (a child) (fact-finding appeal)* [2019] EWCA Civ 2302, [2020] 2 FCR 15. The court found that a child had been injured by her mother's boyfriend. The injury was of a kind that was not inevitably the result of abuse, though the medical evidence pointed that way. The boyfriend later produced a solid alibi and at a rehearing limited to the issue of the identity of the perpetrator the judge made an amended finding that the child had been injured by an unidentified man known to the mother. The mother's appeal was allowed on the basis that the judge was wrong to have confined the ambit of the rehearing when the fresh evidence was relevant not only to the identification of a possible perpetrator but also whether the injuries had been inflicted at all. Similarly, an appeal was allowed in the related field of child abduction where a judge had refused an application to set aside a return order without carrying out a full reconsideration of all the evidence: *Re B (a child) (abduction: article 13(b))* [2020] EWCA Civ 1057, at [96].

The third stage

[8] The third stage is the rehearing itself. At this stage the issues are determined afresh on the basis of the whole of the evidence. The description of the event as a rehearing rather than a review is deliberate: once a decision has been taken to reopen the case the court approaches the task of fact-finding in the conventional way and reaches its own conclusions. It does not give presumptive weight to the earlier findings, as that would risk depriving the exercise of its fundamental purpose of doing justice and achieving the right outcome for the child. The burden of proof remains throughout on a party seeking findings of fact to prove them to the civil standard in the normal way. The court assesses the evidence on its merits, without privileging earlier evidence over later evidence, oral evidence over written evidence, or contentious evidence over uncontentious evidence. At all events, a rehearing is quite distinct from an appeal, in which findings stand unless they are shown to be wrong.

[9] This description of the nature of a rehearing is substantially in accordance with the statements in *Birmingham (no 2)* and *Re ZZ*, but omits some of the more peripheral observations found in those decisions. In *Re ZZ* at [35], Sir James Munby P aptly described the process of rehearing in this way:

> 'The judge has to consider the fresh evidence alongside the earlier material before coming to a conclusion in the light of the totality of the material before the court.'

However, that description was preceded by a sentence that needs further consideration:

> 'There is an evidential burden on those who seek to displace an earlier finding – in that sense they have to "make the running" – but the legal burden of proof remains throughout where it was at the outset.'

…

[12] In my view the concepts of 'a starting point', 'strong' evidence, 'making the running' and 'an evidential burden' which have ebbed and flowed in the distinguished judgments that developed the ground rules in this area, can now be laid aside as adding nothing and as being a possible source of misunderstanding. Of course the product of the rehearing will be that the earlier finding should or should not to be changed, but it is only in that very limited sense that the original finding is the starting point. Likewise, the original evidence was clearly strong enough to justify the original findings, but to describe evidence as strong before it is reconsidered is to beg the question that has to be decided. Lastly, concepts of 'making the running' and of an 'evidential burden' apply at the first stage (when securing a rehearing) and may do at the second stage (when persuading the court that a particular issue needs to be revisited). By the time of the rehearing itself the applicant will already have made the running by successfully adducing evidence to persuade the court to carry out an appropriate kind of rehearing and there is no need for further safeguards against unwarranted challenges to settled findings.

[13] Accordingly, the simple position is that when it carries out a rehearing the court looks at all the evidence afresh and reaches its own conclusions, requiring the party seeking the relevant findings to prove them to the civil standard in the normal way. The practical arrangements for the hearing may well be influenced by what occurred in the earlier proceedings, but insofar as the concepts mentioned in the previous paragraph might suggest that a rehearing is in principle a different process to an ordinary fact-finding hearing, that would be wrong. In saying this, I am reassured that there is no indication that any of the concepts have played any noticeable part in the decision-making in the reported cases. To take an example, in *Re Q (fact-finding rehearing)* [2019] EWFC 60, Baker LJ (sitting as a judge of the High Court) carried out a rehearing of findings that he had made in relation to a father's responsibility for injuries to a child in respect of which the mother was subsequently convicted at a criminal trial. He referred to the above authorities, assessed the evidence and stated his conclusion:

> '[104] Drawing all the various threads together and considering the evidence from the criminal trial alongside the earlier material, I conclude on the totality of the evidence that my findings of fact remain unchanged. Having conducted what I hope has been a thorough and comprehensive analysis of the individual areas where it is asserted that there was a

> change of evidence, and having evaluated that alongside the fact and circumstances of the conviction in the context of the totality of the evidence, I adhere to my original findings as to the perpetrator of the head injuries and my findings that I cannot identify the perpetrator of the rib fractures.'

In carrying out that rehearing, Baker LJ did not ascribe any evidential burden to the father. Instead, he identified the new material in the context of the evidence on which the original findings were based and he synthesised all of the evidence in order to reach his conclusion.

See also *Re E (children: reopening findings of fact)* [2019] EWCA Civ 1447, [2019] 3 FCR 334, [1], [45], [47]–[54] (Peter Jackson LJ) addressing the same point (including highlighting that, all other things being equal, further evidence is more suitably considered by trial courts than on appeal)

See also *Re W (children: re-opening: recusal)* [2020] EWCA Civ 1685, [2021] 2 FCR 793, [26]–[28] (Peter Jackson LJ) addressing the same point (emphasising that aggrieved parties should normally appeal)

See also *Re C (children: fact-finding)* [2018] EWCA Civ 801, [27] (Peter Jackson LJ) addressing a related point (findings are not generally under review)

See also *Re H-M (children)* [2021] EWCA Civ 748, [2021] 3 FCR 218, [25]–[26] (Peter Jackson LJ) addressing a related point (decisions concerning reopening are highly case-sensitive and an appeal court will be slow to interfere)

3.11.5 Threshold criteria: the court's findings: reopening findings: subsequent criminal convictions or acquittals

Re T and J (children) [2020] EWCA Civ 1344, [2021] 1 FCR 189, [35]–[38] (Baker LJ) *quotation limited to* [37]

[37] In my judgment, neither the fact that a jury has reached a verdict on criminal charges that is inconsistent with earlier findings in care proceedings nor the simple fact (if it be true) that the evidence heard by the jury was different from, or more comprehensive than, that adduced before the judge in the family proceedings is sufficient by itself to justify the conclusion that the findings in the family proceedings were wrong so as to require an appellate court to overturn the findings. It may, however, be sufficient to justify a reopening of all or part of the fact-finding hearing. I shall return to this point of the end of this judgment.

Re Q (a child) (fact-finding rehearing) [2019] EWFC 60, [43]–[46], [97]–[106] (Baker LJ) *quotation limited to* [46], [97]–[103]

46. In this case, when considering the weight to be attached to the conviction and to the evidence on which the mother relies to prove it is wrong, it is important to note the following features

(1) The criminal proceedings came after the civil proceedings. The issue of the weight to be attached to the conviction only arises in the context of the father's application for the court to set aside its earlier findings.

(2) Although the mother was convicted after trial, the father was acquitted of the offence on the direction of the judge after the prosecution decided not to proceed against him;

(3) This court had already conducted a comprehensive analysis of the evidence and reached its finding before the criminal trial;

(4) A significant point in the criminal proceedings was the prosecution's decision based on its assessment of the evidence. I will return to this point below, but it is clearly relevant to the weight to be attached to the conviction in these proceedings;

(5) This court is engaged in an inquisitorial process to determine findings of fact in order to facilitate future decision making for Q's welfare. It seems to me therefore that rules of court must be interpreted in the light of the paramountcy of the child's welfare.

…

97. Before reaching a final decision on the father's application, however, I must draw all the threads together and in particular return to the question as to the weight which should be attached to the outcome of the criminal trial and the conviction of the mother and the acquittal of the father in the light of Section 11 of the Civil Evidence Act 1968.

98. I have reached the clear conclusion that in the circumstances of this case, notwithstanding the terms of section 11, the mother's conviction carries no significant weight for the following reasons.

99. First, it seems to me that the purpose of section 11 is principally to establish a rule to be applied in circumstances in which the criminal trial and conviction occur before the civil fact-finding process. I accept Mr Storey's submission that it cannot have been the intention of Parliament that a subsequent conviction would lead to a presumption that a prior contrary finding in civil proceedings would be overturned on appeal. As discussed above, the proper interpretation of section 11 is that the weight to be attached to a conviction in these circumstances will vary depending on all the circumstances. The proper approach in the circumstances of this case is not to rely on this conviction alone but rather to look behind the conviction at the evidence as we have done at this hearing.

100. Secondly, the outcome of the criminal case was heavily influenced by the course taken by the prosecution. The prosecution withdrew counts 2 to 3 against the father and the jury was directed by the judge to acquit the father on those counts. I accept of course that it was still open to the jury, notwithstanding its verdict on those counts, to have acquitted the mother on counts 4 and 5 if they were not sure of her guilt but, when considering at this hearing the evidential weight to be attached to the mother's conviction itself, it is to my mind plainly relevant that the conviction was

entered in circumstances where (a) the case had originally been opened by the prosecution on the basis that Q's head injuries were inflicted either by the father or by the mother; (b) at the end of the evidence the prosecution indicated that they no longer contended that the father was responsible, and (c) the judge directed the jury to acquit the father of those charges.

101. Thirdly, it is relevant when assessing the weight to be attached by this court to the conviction itself to consider the reasons why the prosecution withdrew counts 2 and 3 from the jury …

102. There are a number of comments which could perhaps be made about that passage, but suffice it to say it is immediately apparent that the principal reason for the prosecution decision was that they accepted the father's account of having conflated a description of Q's condition between 4 am and the visit to the GP. In other words, the prosecution accepted the very account which I found particularly unconvincing. The weight to be attached by the court at this review hearing to the prosecution's assessment of that evidence is in my view very limited. In saying that, I stress that I am not criticising the prosecution for the course they took in the Crown Court proceedings, nor indeed am I criticising anybody else involved in the criminal process.

103. There is in my view considerable force in the observation by Ms Flexman on behalf of the guardian in closing submissions when she observed that there was no new evidence of any relevance adduced in the criminal trial that would in itself merit a review of the family court findings. 'Rather that the prosecution ran a narrative that was directly contradictory to the findings of the family court and the father joined in with that narrative.' That narrative resulted in a conviction which has created the conflict between the two jurisdictions and driven the need for this review. Central to that narrative is a different assessment of the father's credibility. It is regrettable that he did not allow that issue to be further examined by finishing his oral evidence.

CHAPTER 4

Interim care and supervision orders

Chapter contents

CHAPTER 4

Interim care and supervision orders

4.1 INTERIM CARE AND SUPERVISION ORDERS: TEST FOR ICO'S[1]

4.1.1 Interim care and supervision orders: test for ICOs: two stages

A Local Authority v KAB and others [2010] EWCA Civ 871, [2010] 3 FCR 1, [33]–[35] (Black LJ)

[33] It may nevertheless be of assistance to look briefly at the proper approach to the granting of interim care orders. It is trite law that the question must be approached in two stages. The first stage is encapsulated in s 38(2) of the 1989 Act and is sometimes referred to as the threshold for an interim care order. Section 38(2) provides:

> 'A court shall not make an interim care order or interim supervision order under this section unless it is satisfied that there are reasonable grounds for believing that circumstances with respect to the child are as mentioned in section 31(2).'

[34] Section 31(2) provides:

> 'A court may only make a care order or supervision order if it is satisfied—
>
> (a) that the child concerned is suffering, or is likely to suffer, significant harm; and
>
> (b) that the harm, or likelihood of harm, is attributable to—
> (i) the care given to the child, or likely to be given to him if the order were not made, not being what it would be reasonable to expect a parent to give to him; or
> (ii) the child's being beyond parental control.'

[35] If the court is satisfied as required by s 38(2), it must then go on to consider, as a discrete issue, whether or not to grant an interim care order. This is a question with respect to the upbringing of the child, so, in accordance with s 1 of the 1989 Act, the child's welfare is the court's paramount consideration. The delay principle (s 1(2)) applies, as does the no order principle in s 1(5). As the court is considering whether to make a Pt IV order, it is also to have regard to the welfare checklist set out in s 1(3). There are existing authorities in relation to interim care orders

1 Interim care order.

which serve as a guide as to how to approach this second stage of the court's determination, the purpose of which is, of course, to establish a holding position pending a full hearing.

See also *Re C (a child) (interim care: threshold)* [2011] EWCA Civ 918, [2011] 3 FCR 369, [1]–[3] (Ward LJ) addressing the same point

See also *Re A (children) (interim care order)* [2001] 3 FCR 402 (FD), 406E–407A (Hughes J) addressing the same point (highlighting that ICOs do not automatically follow the satisfaction of s 38[2])

4.1.2 Interim care and supervision orders: test for ICOs: interim removals: general propositions

Re C (a child) (interim separation) [2019] EWCA Civ 1998, [2020] 1 FCR 553, [1]–[2] (Peter Jackson LJ)

[1] The question that arises on this appeal is whether an interim order for the separation of a child aged four months from his young mother was justified.

[2] The ability to make interim care orders under s 38 Children Act 1989 is one of the family court's most significant powers and it is not surprising that it has been considered by this court on many occasions. A consistent series of propositions can be found in these decisions:

(1) An interim order is inevitably made at a stage when the evidence is incomplete. It should therefore only be made in order to regulate matters that cannot await the final hearing and it is not intended to place any party to the proceedings at an advantage or a disadvantage.

(2) The removal of a child from a parent is an interference with their right to respect for family life under art 8. Removal at an interim stage is a particularly sharp interference, which is compounded in the case of a baby when removal will affect the formation and development of the parent–child bond.

(3) Accordingly, in all cases an order for separation under an interim care order will only be justified where it is both necessary and proportionate. The lower ('reasonable grounds') threshold for an interim care order is not an invitation to make an order that does not satisfy these exacting criteria.

(4) A plan for immediate separation is therefore only to be sanctioned by the court where the child's physical safety or psychological or emotional welfare demands it and where the length and likely consequences of the separation are a proportionate response to the risks that would arise if it did not occur.

(5) The high standard of justification that must be shown by a local authority seeking an order for separation requires it to inform the court of all available resources that might remove the need for separation.

2 Children Act 1989, s 38.

4.1.3 Interim care and supervision orders: test for ICOs: interim removals: safety demands immediate separation

Re L-A (children) [2009] EWCA Civ 822, [2010] 1 FLR 80, [5]–[8] (Thorpe LJ) *quotation limited to* [7]–[8]

7. ... What is it then that the three authorities in this court seem to establish? In the first, the case of Re H, the crucial paragraphs are 38 and 39, from which can be extracted two propositions, the first that the decision taken by the court on an interim care order application must necessarily be limited to issues that cannot await the fixture and must not extend to issues that are being prepared for determination at that fixture. The second proposition which appears from the final sentence of paragraph 39 is that separation is only to be ordered if the child's safety demands immediate separation. In the subsequent case of Re N in paragraph 27 I described that a local authority in seeking to justify the continuing removal of a child from home necessarily must meet a very high standard. In the final authority, K and H, the key paragraph is paragraph 16 in which I described the court's approach thus:

> '...at an interim stage the removal of children from their parents is not to be sanctioned unless the child's safety requires interim protection.'

8. In his review of these authorities Ryder J coined a phrase which according to Mr Baker has given rise to considerable problems. The phrase is to be found in the first line of paragraph 10(a), namely: 'an imminent risk of really serious harm'. Mr Baker says that it has been the experience of practitioners and local authorities that this is the phrase within all these reported cases that is being emphasised as the key phrase, the key definition of the standard that must be achieved to justify the making of an interim care order. So for me the question today is: did HHJ Cleary construe these paragraphs in the judgment of Ryder J as simply restating the test defined in the appellate cases, or as the definition of the new standard to be applied to future cases? As a matter of principle it is transparent to me that a judge as experienced as Ryder J would not have been seeking to break fresh ground that was not for him. He was bound by the authorities in the Court of Appeal. He plainly recognised that and so expressed himself.

See also *Re L (a child) (interim care order: mother's imprisonment)* [2013] EWCA Civ 489, [2013] 3 FCR 90, [33]–[42] (Black LJ) providing an overview of the law on this point (including addressing proportionality)

See also *A Local Authority v KAB and others* [2010] EWCA Civ 871, [2010] 3 FCR 1, [35]–[42] (Black LJ) providing an overview of the law on this point (including outlining that safety includes emotional or psychological welfare, [41]–[42])

See also *MG and another v A Local Authority and others* [2011] EWCA Civ 745, [2011] 2 FLR 955, [22] (Sir Nicholas Wall P) addressing a related point (safety includes emotional or psychological welfare)

See also *Re O (a child: interim care order)* [2019] EWCA Civ 583, [2019] 2 FCR 995, [19]–[21] (Peter Jackson LJ) addressing a related point (an approach taken in a continued removal case)

See also *Re J (children)* [2019] EWCA Civ 2300, [2020] 1 FCR 572, [31]–[34] (Baker LJ) addressing a related point (the *Re L-A*[3] test is probably inappropriate at the end of proceedings)

4.1.4 Interim care and supervision orders: test for ICOs: interim removals: human rights considerations

Haase v Germany (app no 11057/02) [2004] 2 FCR 1 (ECtHR), [82]–[95] (Third Section) *quotation limited to* [90]–[95]

90. The margin of appreciation so to be accorded to the competent national authorities will vary in the light of the nature of the issues and the seriousness of the interests at stake. While the authorities enjoy a wide margin of appreciation in assessing the necessity of taking a child into care, in particular where an emergency situation arises, the court must still be satisfied in the particular case that there existed circumstances justifying the removal of the child, and it is for the respondent state to establish that a careful assessment of the impact of the proposed care measure on the parents and the child, as well as of the possible alternatives to taking the child into public care, was carried out prior to implementation of such a measure (see *K and T v Finland* [2001] 2 FCR 673 at 704 (para 166), *Kutzner v Germany* [2003] 1 FCR 249 at 261 (para 67), and *P, C and S v UK* [2002] 3 FCR 1 at 29 (para 116)).

91. Furthermore, the taking of a new-born baby into public care at the moment of its birth is an extremely harsh measure. There must be extraordinarily compelling reasons before a baby can be physically removed from its mother, against her will, immediately after birth as a consequence of a procedure in which neither she nor her partner has been involved (see *K and T v Finland* [2001] 2 FCR 673 at 705 (para 168)).

92. Following any removal into care, a stricter scrutiny is called for in respect of any further limitations by the authorities, for example on restrictions on parental rights and access, and on any legal safeguards designed to secure the effective protection of the right of parents and children to respect for their family life. Such further limitations entail the danger that the family relations between the parents and a young child are effectively curtailed (see *Elsholz v Germany* [2000] 3 FCR 385 at 397 (para 49)); *Kutzner v Germany* [2003] 1 FCR 249 at 261(para 67)); and *Sahin v Germany* [2003] 2 FCR 619 at 633 (para 65)).

93. The taking into care of a child should normally be regarded as a temporary measure to be discontinued as soon as circumstances permit, and any measures of implementation of temporary care should be

3 *Re L-A (children)* [2009] EWCA Civ 822, [2010] 1 FLR 80.

consistent with the ultimate aim of reuniting the natural parent and child (see *Johansen v Norway* (1996) 23 EHRR 33 at para 78, and *EP v Italy* [1999] ECHR 31127/96 at para 69). In this regard a fair balance has to be struck between the interests of the child remaining in care and those of the parent in being reunited with the child (see and *Hokkanen v Finland* [1995] 2 FCR 320 at 330–331 (para 55)). In carrying out this balancing exercise, the court will attach particular importance to the best interests of the child which, depending on their nature and seriousness, may override those of the parent (see *Johansen v Norway* (1996) 23 EHRR 33 at para 78). In particular, a parent cannot be entitled under art 8 to have such measures taken as would harm the child's health and development (see *Elsholz v Germany* [2000] 3 FCR 385 at 397 (para 50); and *Sahin v Germany* [2003] 2 FCR 619 at 633 (para 66)).

94. Whilst art 8 contains no explicit procedural requirements, the decision-making process involved in measures of interference must be fair and such as to ensure due respect of the interests safeguarded by art 8. The court must therefore determine whether, having regard to the circumstances of the case and notably the importance of the decisions to be taken, the applicants have been involved in the decision-making process, seen as a whole, to a degree sufficient to provide them with the requisite protection of their interests (see *W v UK* (1987) 10 EHRR 29 at para 64, *Elsholz v Germany* [2000] 3 FCR 385 at 397–398 (para 52), and *TP and KM v UK* [2001] 2 FCR 289 at 311 (para 72)).

95. The court accepts that when action has to be taken to protect a child in an emergency, it may not always be possible, because of the urgency of the situation, to associate in the decision-making process those having custody of the child. Nor may it even be desirable, even if possible, to do so if those having custody of the child are seen as the source of an immediate threat to the child, since giving them prior warning would be liable to deprive the measure of its effectiveness. The court must however be satisfied that the national authorities were entitled to consider that there existed circumstances justifying the abrupt removal of the child from the care of its parents without any prior contact or consultation. In particular, it is for the respondent state to establish that a careful assessment of the impact of the proposed care measure on the parents and the child, as well as of the possible alternatives to the removal of the child from its family, was carried out prior to the implementation of a care measure (see *K and T v Finland* [2001] 2 FCR 673 at 704 (para 166)). The fact that a child could be placed in a more beneficial environment for his or her upbringing will not on its own justify a compulsory measure of removal from the care of the biological parents; there must exist other circumstances pointing to the 'necessity' for such an interference with the parents' right under art 8 to enjoy a family life with their child (see *KA v Finland* [2003] 1 FCR 201 at 221 (para 92)).

See also *Venema v Netherlands* (app no 35731/97) [2003] 1 FCR 153 (ECtHR), [90]–[93] (Second Section) addressing the same point

4.1.5 Interim care and supervision orders: test for ICOs: interim removals: chronic cases

A Local Authority v KAB and others [2010] EWCA Civ 871, [2010] 3 FCR 1, [61] (Black LJ)

[61] The discretionary exercise that had to be carried out in this case was a delicate and difficult one. That is often so where an application is made for an interim care order, and not least when the application comes when care proceedings are finally launched after a very long history of difficulties. Into the balance must come not only the harm that may befall children in their home but also the harm that may be occasioned to them by removal from home. The recorder was acutely conscious that his decision was an interim decision and may not reflect the final outcome; he stressed this during the judgment. He had the benefit of studying the evidence in detail and heard a considerable amount of oral evidence. He is criticised for appearing to blame the older boys for the problems of the family and commenting that they are an obvious source of tension and violence in the home whereas the local authority submit that it was the father who was responsible for the risk. He is criticised for concluding, without proper foundation, that C would go to school if returned home and would keep up her personal hygiene. The reality was, however, that he had to do the best he could, looking not just at the detail but also at the matter as a whole, in a complex and as yet uncertain situation. This is not, in my view, a case in which it can validly be said, as the local authority and guardian do, that there was only one possible outcome. The catalogue of problems set out in the chronology ebb and flow over the years, with allegations of physical abuse being made periodically and incidents of domestic violence reported without this always, or even often, leading to the children being taken into foster care. It is notoriously difficult for a local authority to determine when, in a long history of neglect and alleged physical and emotional abuse, to take the step of seeking to remove children from home. A very fine balance has to be struck and this can be particularly sensitive and difficult when considering what is appropriate for the interim period pending the conclusion of care proceedings. The recorder's decision was one which was within the ambit of decisions that were open to him and I am not persuaded that his decision is flawed in such a way as to lead to it being overturned.

See also *Re L (Children)* [2016] EWCA Civ 1110, [2017] 2 FLR 547, [20]–[23] (King LJ) considering *A Local Authority v KAB and others* [2010] EWCA Civ 871, [2010] 3 FCR 1

4.1.6 Interim care and supervision orders: test for ICOs: interim removals: risk of harm is a two-sided coin

Re M (children) (interim care order) [2005] EWCA Civ 1594, [2006] 1 FCR 303 (Thorpe LJ), [23]–[25], [27] *quotation limited to* [23]

[23] Miss Reardon's separate and powerful attack on the judge is that although he has had regard to what everybody agrees to be the relevant authority,

the case of *Re H (a child) (interim care order)* [2002] EWCA Civ 1932, [2003] 1 FCR 350, he has failed to deliver a balanced judgment. He has simply regarded the risk of harm as a one-sided coin: what is the risk to R of returning her? He has not seen it as a two-sided coin, the other side being, what is the risk of short-term emotional harm to R in continuing her deprivation from parents, siblings and home.

4.2 INTERIM CARE AND SUPERVISION ORDERS: NEWBORNS

4.2.1 Interim care and supervision orders: newborns: proceedings only upon birth

Re F (in utero) [1988] FCR 529 (CA), 530H–534B (May LJ), 536F–538F (Balcombe LJ), 539D–G (Staughton LJ) *quotation limited to* 538D–F

> Approaching the question as one of principle, in my judgment there is no jurisdiction to make an unborn child a ward of court. Since an unborn child has, *ex hypothesi*, no existence independent of its mother, the only purpose of extending the jurisdiction to include a foetus is to enable the mother's actions to be controlled. Indeed, that is the purpose of the present application. In the articles already cited Lowe gives examples of how this might operate in practice:
>
> > 'It would mean, for example, that the mother would be unable to leave the jurisdiction without the court's consent. The court being charged to protect the foetus's welfare would surely have to order the mother to stop smoking, imbibing alcohol and indeed any activity which might be hazardous to the child. Taking it to the extreme were the court to be faced with saving the baby's life or the mother's it would surely have to protect the baby's.'

4.2.2 Interim care and supervision orders: newborns: contested LA removals require judicial sanction

R (on the application of G) v Nottingham City Council [2008] EWHC 152 (Admin), [2008] 1 FLR 1660, [15]–[21], [23]–[26] (Munby J)

15. The law is perfectly clear but perhaps requires re-emphasis. Whatever the impression a casual reader might gain from reading some newspaper reports, no local authority and no social worker has any power to remove a child from its parent or, without the agreement of the parent, to take a child into care, unless they have first obtained an order from a family court authorising that step: either an emergency protection order in accordance with section 44 of the Children Act 1989 or an interim care order in accordance with section 38 of the Act or perhaps, in an exceptional case (and subject to section 100 of the Act), a wardship order made by a judge of the Family Division of the High Court.

16. Section 46 of the Children Act 1989 permits a police constable to remove a child where he has reasonable cause to believe that the child would otherwise be likely to suffer significant harm, and that power can be exercised without prior judicial authority. But the powers conferred on the police by section 46 are *not* given to either local authorities or social workers.

17. Local authorities and social workers have no power to remove children from their parents unless they have first obtained judicial sanction for what they are proposing to do. Only a court can make a care order. Only if a court has authorised that step, whether by making an emergency protection order or by making a care order or an interim care order or in some other way, can a local authority or a social worker remove a child from a parent. And the same goes, of course, for a hospital and its medical staff.

18. As I said during the course of the hearing, no baby, no child, can be removed simply 'as the result of a decision taken by officials in some room.'

19. This is all elementary. It is well known to all family lawyers. And it is, or ought to be, well known to all social workers. That is why, as the media accurately reported, I made the comment during the course of the hearing that 'The professionals involved in this case should have known better.' I went on to point out, however, that the midwives and doctors in a delivery room in the small hours could not have been expected to understand this. No doubt they acted as they did in accordance with the 'Birth Plan' that had been given to them by their superiors.

20. Lest this judgment be misunderstood, I should make clear that what I have said is subject to two qualifications.

21. In the first place, a social worker or a nurse is of course entitled to intervene if that is necessary to protect a baby from immediate violence at the hands of a parent. That is not, however, because they have any special power or privilege entitling them to intervene. It is merely an application of the wider principle that anyone who happens to be present is entitled, whether by restraining the assailant or by removing the defenceless victim from his assailant's reach, to intervene in order to prevent an actual or threatened criminal assault taking place before his very eyes. Hence the observation I made that 'You cannot remove children, short of immediate murderous intent, except by lawful means, which means either by a police officer or court order.' There is, of course, no need to show murderous intent. Any threat of immediate significant violence is enough, particularly if it involves a young child.

…

23. The other qualification arises out of section 3(5) of the Children Act 1989, which provides that:

'A person who –

(a) does not have parental responsibility for a particular child; but

(b) has care of the child,

may (subject to the provisions of this Act) do what is reasonable in all the circumstances of the case for the purpose of safeguarding or promoting the child's welfare.'

24. Now section 3(5) could not avail the local authority, because it did not have the 'care' of G's son. But there might be circumstances in which a hospital could rely upon section 3(5) as justifying action taken in relation to a child in its medical care, despite the absence of parental consent and the absence of any court order.

25. For instance, medical intervention might be required in order to preserve the child's life or to protect a child from irreversible harm in circumstances of such urgency that there is not even time to make an urgent telephone application to a judge. In such a situation of emergency a doctor can act without parental or judicial consent and, if parents are acting unreasonably or contrary to the child's best interests, even despite a parental refusal of consent: see Grubb, *Principles of Medical Law*, ed 2, para 4.21.

26. Doctors, midwives and nurses do not have to stand idly by waiting for a court order if, for example, a premature baby desperately needs to be put in a special unit or placed on a ventilator. They are of course entitled to separate the child from the mother if medical necessity dictates, and even if she objects. Law, medical ethics and common sense march hand in hand.

4.2.3 Interim care and supervision orders: newborns: good practice for planned removals upon birth

Nottingham City Council v LM and others [2016] EWHC 11 (Fam), [2016] 1 WLR 2995, [29]–[34], [41]–[42] (Keehan J)

29. In my experience the errors made in this case are not an isolated example nor is the factual matrix of this case either unique nor even exceptional: on the contrary this case is fairly typical of the type of case in which local authorities propose or plan to seek the removal of a baby at birth. Thus, what principally concerns me is that such fundamental and egregious errors should be made in, what may colloquially be termed, 'a run of the mill case'. In paragraph33 below, I consider what steps should be taken by a local authority when it plans to seek the removal of an unborn child immediately or shortly after his/her birth.

30. Before I do so, I wish to make certain observations on the flawed approach apparently endorsed by both the senior children's services manager and the local authority's senior lawyer in this case. First, both made reference to the willingness of the hospital to keep the baby as an in-patient pending the issue of care proceedings. Plainly the period of time for which a hospital is prepared to keep a new born baby as an in-patient, either on medical or welfare grounds, maybe a material consideration for a local authority on the timing of the making of an application for an interim care order, but must not place too great a reliance on these indications or assurances. The fact that a hospital is prepared to keep a baby as an

in-patient is not a reason to delay making an application for an interim care order. The following should always be borne in mind:

a) a hospital may not detain a baby in hospital against the wishes of the mother or a father with parental responsibility;
b) the capability of a maternity unit or a hospital to accommodate a healthy new born child may change within hours, whatever the good intentions of the unit or hospital, depending upon the challenging demands it may be presented with;
c) the ability to invite the police to exercise a Police Protection Order, pursuant to s.46 of the 1989 Act or for a local authority to apply for an Emergency Protection Order, pursuant to s.44 of the 1989, are, of course, available as emergency remedies,
d) but such procedures do not afford the parents nor, most importantly, the child, with the degree of participation, representation and protection as an on notice interim care order application;
e) the indication of a maternity unit as to the date of discharge of a new born baby should never, save in the most extraordinary of circumstances, set or lead the time for an application for an interim care order in respect of a new born child.

31. Second, where the pre-birth plan provides for an application to be made for the removal of a child at or shortly after birth, it is neither 'usual' nor 'ideal' practice for an application for an interim care order to be made on the day of the child's birth, rather it is essential and best practice for this to occur.

32. Third, once it is determined by a local authority that sufficient evidence is available to make an application for an interim care order, on the basis of the removal of a new born child, the availability of additional evidence from the maternity unit or elsewhere, must not then cause a delay in the issue of care proceedings; the provision of additional evidence may be envisaged in the application and/or provided subsequently.

33. The local authority should have adopted good practice and the following basic, but fundamental, steps should have been taken:

a) The birth plan should have been rigorously adhered to by all social work practitioners and managers and by the local authority's legal department;
b) A risk assessment of the mother and the father should have been commenced immediately upon the social workers being made aware of the mother's pregnancy. The assessment should have been completed at least 4 weeks before the mother's expected date for delivery. The assessment should then have been updated to take account of relevant events immediately pre and post-delivery which could potentially affect the initial conclusions on risk and care planning for the unborn child;
c) The assessment should have been disclosed, forthwith upon initial completion, to the parents and, if instructed, to their solicitors to give them an opportunity, if necessary, to challenge the assessment of risk and the proposed care plan;

d) The social work team should have provided all relevant documentation, necessary for the legal department to issue care proceedings and the application for an interim care order, no less than 7 days before the expected date of delivery. The legal department must issue the application on the day of birth and, in any event, no later than 24 hours after birth (or as the case may be, the date on which the local authority is notified of the birth);

e) Immediately upon issue, if not before, the local authority's solicitors should have served the applications and supporting documents on the parents and, if instructed, upon their respective solicitors.

f) Immediately upon issue, the local authority should have sought from the court an initial hearing date, on the best time estimate that its solicitors could have provided.

34. If these steps had been followed in this case, unnecessary delay and procedural unfairness would have been avoided.

...

41. The message must go out loud and clear that, save in the most exceptional and unusual of circumstances, local authorities must make applications for public law proceedings in respect of new born babies timeously and especially, where the circumstances arguably require the removal of the child from its parent(s), within at most 5 days of the child's birth.

42. Given that in the vast majority of cases a local authority will be actively involved with the family and/or aware of the pregnancy and the estimated date of delivery, I cannot conceive how such a requirement places an unreasonable and/or disproportionate duty upon a local authority. Further it is likely that a local authority's failure to act fairly and/or timeously will be condemned in an order for costs.

See also *Bury Metropolitan Borough Council v D; Re D (unborn baby) (birth plan: future harm)* [2009] EWHC 446 (Fam), [2009] 2 FCR 93, [3]–[25] (Munby J) addressing a related point (the circumstances justifying birth plans encompassing without notice removals)

4.3 INTERIM CARE AND SUPERVISION ORDERS: EFFECT OF ICOS

4.3.1 Interim care and supervision orders: effect of ICOs: impartial steps

Re G (minors) (interim care order) [1993] 2 FCR 557 (CA), 562E–563D (Waite LJ)

... I am, for myself, persuaded, however, despite Mr Brasse's impressive argument, that the Judge fell into error in regarding an interim care order as being a step which involved any advance judgment on the part of the court. Given the acceptance of all parties that this was a case in which the threshold requirements of s 31 of the Act are satisfied, the making of an interim care order, far from inhibiting the *status quo*, was a neutral and arguably the most effective, way of preserving it. The regime of interim care orders laid down by s 38 of the Act (with its limitation to maximum periods of 8 weeks in the first instance and 4 weeks thereafter) is designed to leave the court with the ability to maintain strict control of any steps taken or proposed by a local authority in the exercise of powers that are by their nature temporary and subject to continuous review. The making of an interim care order is an essentially impartial step, favouring neither one side or the other, and affording to no one, least of all the local authority in whose favour it is made, an opportunity for tactical or adventitious advantage. The failure of the Judge to appreciate that quality was an error of principle which justifies intervention by this court and entitles us to take our own view of a matter which was within the ambit of a judicial discretion with the exercise of which the court would not normally be prepared to interfere on appeal.

The question is one that has to be regarded in the light of the general and specific requirements of the welfare of these boys as laid down by s 1 of the Act. When so regarded, the persuasive factors seems to me to be the following. The next few weeks and months between now and the main hearing are likely to be crucial in ensuring that the court is placed in a position to make an informed choice as between the various options that will be presented to the final hearing. In that process the assessment on which the authority will be engaged is bound to be of prime importance. An authoritative hand will be needed to ensure that the assessment proceeds fairly and swiftly. Matters of contact with the natural family, for example, will need to be regulated in tune with the requirements of the medical and other advice which the assessment will involve. That is not a process which it will be within the competence of the court to supervise on a day to day basis. It is something that could only be achieved by the authority, armed with the powers conferred by an interim care order. This does not mean that the powers of the court are abandoned or foreshortened in the meantime. On the contrary, the temporary nature of any interim care order ensures that no steps could be undertaken by the authority without an early opportunity being afforded to the court for its review and if necessary its cancellation or recall.

See also *Re L (a minor) (interim care order)* [1996] 2 FCR 706 (CA), 710G–711B (Ward LJ) addressing the same point

See also *Re B (a child) (interim care order)* [2009] EWCA Civ 1254, [2010] 1 FCR 114, [52]–[53] (Wall LJ) considering *Re G (minors) (interim care order)* [1993] 2 FCR 557

See also *Re L (a child) (interim care order: mother's imprisonment)* [2013] EWCA Civ 489, [2013] 3 FCR 90, [53] (Black LJ) considering *Re G (minors) (interim care order)* [1993] 2 FCR 557

4.3.2 Interim orders: effect of ICOs: s 33[4] applies to ICOs

Re H (a child) (parental responsibility: vaccination) [2020] EWCA Civ 664, [2020] 2 FCR 683, [25] (King LJ)

[25] It should be noted that s 33 applies equally to interim care orders as it does to final care orders: s 31(11) …

See Chapter 10.2 Care and supervision orders: care orders

4.3.3 Interim orders: effect of ICOs: disputed male circumcisions

Re P (circumcision: child in care) [2021] EWHC 1616 (Fam), [2021] 3 FCR 235, [22]–[30] (Cobb J) *quotation limited to* [22], [27]–[30]

The law

[22] I have been referred to a number of authorities relevant to this issue, though all previous decisions referred to me have been taken in the context of private law. Counsel have surprisingly not been able to locate any High Court or Court of Appeal authority in which the court has been required to consider circumcision of a child in interim care, as a contested issue, in public law proceedings.

…

[27] From the legislation and authorities cited to me, the following important guiding principles can be collected:

General

(i) While it can never be reasonable parenting to inflict any form of FGM on a child, the position is different with male circumcision; 'Society and the law, including family law, are prepared to tolerate non-therapeutic male circumcision performed for religious or even for purely cultural or conventional reasons, while no longer being willing to tolerate FGM in any of its forms' 1

Welfare

(ii) The welfare of the child, both in the immediate and long-term, is the paramount consideration in reaching a decision about circumcision for a male child (the law in its current form is in s 1(1) Children Act 1989); this is uncontroversial in the instant case, and has been the starting point of all previous decisions;

(iii) The welfare checklist (s 1(3) CA 1989) is engaged;

(iv) Religious upbringing of a child in care may be a matter of great importance; the significance of the issue will vary from case to case depending on the strength of the religious beliefs and observance of the child's parents; on any account, this factor will need to be incorporated within (and not in place of) the wider welfare review;

4 Children Act 1989, s 33.

Local authority duty

(v) A local authority is under a duty to ensure that a child in their care is not brought up in any different religious persuasion from that followed by his parents prior to the care order. If the local authority breaches that duty, it will be exceeding the limitation imposed on its exercise of parental responsibility by s 33(6)(a) CA 1989;

Medical issues

(vi) That the circumcision procedure is irreversible is a matter of significance when looking at the short and longer-term implications for the child;

(vii) The court must review the medical risks and benefits of such a procedure, particularly where it is proposed for a non-therapeutic purpose;

Views of parents and others

(viii) The religious views and wishes of both parents carry significant weight (they may of course as between themselves have different views/wishes); the court should pay these views 'serious heed'. The court will be slow to conclude that a parent faithfully striving to follow the teachings of their religion is acting unreasonably;

(ix) The court is not bound to give effect to the wishes of the parents about religious upbringing 'when satisfied that the child's welfare requires otherwise, and in giving effect to them the court has power to do so in such a manner as it may consider to be best in the child's interests';

(x) The views of the primary carers of the child (if not the parents) also carry significant weight; it is a strong thing to impose a medically unnecessary surgical intervention on a residential carer/parent who is opposed to it;

(xi) The particular environment in which the child is going to be raised is an important factor; if the environment is one in which circumcision is not a part of family life, or in which it is not in conformity with the religion practised by his primary carer, this would be a relevant factor; I would add this:

(xii) That where a disputed issue of non-therapeutic circumcision arises again in relation to a child in care, it is appropriate for the matter to be referred promptly to the court for resolution. In this instance, the mother has done so; it may be more appropriate for the Local Authority to take the initiative in such circumstances.

Conclusion

[28] As I indicated to counsel during the hearing, I regard this as a finely balanced decision, in which there are potent arguments on both sides of the debate.

[29] As a matter of law, no party holds the 'trump card' before the court. Had there been no interim care order in place, these two parents acting in agreement, and exercising their shared parental responsibility, would have

been able to provide consent for P's circumcision for either therapeutic or non-therapeutic reasons. But P is currently subject to an interim care order; the Local Authority currently has senior parental responsibility, and presently opposes the procedure. I am satisfied that s 33(3)(b)/(4) CA 1989 does not give the Local Authority absolute authority to oppose the procedure; I am equally satisfied that in opposing the procedure the authority is not offending against the statutory proscription on causing P 'to be brought up in any religious persuasion other than that in which he would have been brought up if the order had not been made' (s 33(6)) – P remains a Muslim boy being raised broadly in accordance with Muslim tenets.

[30] The issue for determination requires me to exercise a pure welfare-based jurisdiction. The authorities referred to above are of some assistance in shaping that welfare judgement; the principles extracted from those authorities it seems to me apply as much in public law as in private law.

4.3.4 Interim orders: effect of ICOs: duty to consult PR[5] holders

R (on the application of H) v Kingston upon Hull City Council (KS and others, interested parties) [2013] EWHC 388 (Admin), [2014] 2 FCR 433, [50]–[52] (HHJ Jeremy Richardson QC sitting as a judge of the High Court) *quotation limited to* [52]

[52] When an ICO is made the local authority and the parent share parental responsibility for the child—albeit the local authority is usually the one in the driving seat particularly when removal has been sanctioned. This plainly does not mean the parents or others are of little or no consequence. Although the local authority may be driving the vehicle, on a journey approved by the court, it does not mean it is able to ignore the views of the passengers as to the route to follow. There needs to be consultation; and concurrence (if possible). The consultation must be genuine and not merely a process whereby decisions are merely the subject of information to parents. I repeat a parent with parental responsibility does not surrender that when an ICO is made, nor when removal is permitted by the court. The weight to be attached to the views of parents and others is a different question. A local authority must always work in a carefully calibrated manner and act in a proportionate way commensurate with the issues involved and those involved. Calibration and proportionality are highly fact-specific. The level and manner of consultation with one family will inevitably differ to that of another family depending on the issues and circumstances. The weight to be attached to the views of a father who murdered the mother of his child is likely to be rather less (if any) to be attached to the views of grandparents who are looking after a child in a difficult family situation. A sense of reality and a sense of proportion are key to the concept of consultation; however, consultation there must be,

5 Parental responsibility.

save in exceptional circumstances where child safety or other pressing reasons are present. I should also add that proper records are an essential aspect of consultation and decision-making.

4.3.5 Interim care and supervision orders: effect of ICOs: ICOs do not endure beyond 17 or marriage if 16

Re Q (a child: interim care order: jurisdiction) [2019] EWHC 512 (Fam), [2019] 2 FCR 268, [18]–[32] (Knowles J) *quotation limited to* [27]–[28], [31]

[27] I endorse Mr Barnes' submissions that Parliament chose in passing the Act to demarcate 17 or 16 (if married) as the age after which a child could not be placed in the care or supervision of a local authority without a full disposal of the case having been achieved. That was a recognition of the growing autonomy of the individual child. Likewise, the ability of a final care order to persist until the age of 18 is a recognition of the obligations placed on a local authority, once parenting has been established to fall below the reasonable standard expected, to ensure a child is not left without appropriate care before becoming an adult. Those matters support my analysis of s 38(4) as amended.

[28] All the above brings me to the conclusion that no interim care or supervision order will endure beyond the date of a child's seventeenth birthday or the date of a child's marriage if aged 16. To be clear, interim care and supervision orders made for a period during which the child turns either 17 or gets married (if aged 16) are impermissible. If, prior to the 2014 amendments, interim public law orders were being made which extended beyond the child's seventeenth birthday, they should not have been given (a) the absence of an explicit power to continue such orders beyond a child's seventeenth birthday and (b) the age thresholds set out in the Act. The dicta of McFarlane LJ in *Re W* [see above] support this proposition.

...

[31] In my view, there is a distinction between the making of interim public law orders on an adjournment where a child has turned 17 and the continuation of the s 31 proceedings themselves. I remind myself that no court seised of public law proceedings is required to make either interim or final public law orders. It may decide that a section 8 order or indeed no order is an appropriate disposal at either an interim or final stage. Whilst no interim or final public law order would, on my analysis of s 38(4), be available in respect of a 17-year-old child (or 16 if married), I am not persuaded that these welfare-driven proceedings themselves would necessarily lack purpose and must fall away once the jurisdiction to make either interim or final public law orders is lost. In some cases, it may be crucial to establish whether the threshold criteria have been met because this might determine the basis for future decision making by a local authority, for example, as to the type of support available to the child or family concerned. Whether

that exercise is necessary and proportionate will be a matter for the good sense of the judge managing/determining the proceedings. For example, it might not be where a child of 17 wishes to be accommodated against the wishes of those with parental responsibility. Additionally, although final public law orders would not be available to the court, the court might conclude the proceedings before the child is 18 by making other orders available to it such as a s 8 order (assuming exceptional circumstances applied) or by making orders under the inherent jurisdiction. Whilst the latter could not operate to require a child to be placed in either the care or supervision of a local authority or to require a child to be accommodated by a local authority, other orders under the inherent jurisdiction may be entirely suitable in the circumstances of the individual case. I conclude that, when the jurisdiction to make interim and final public law orders is no longer available, careful scrutiny of the circumstances of each case is required by the court in order to discern whether the proceedings themselves lack merit and whether it is proportionate and in the child's welfare interests for them to continue. Discontinuance of the proceedings is likely to be the proportionate, welfare-driven outcome in many such cases and, if that is so, the local authority should be permitted to withdraw its application. There will, however, be some cases where a useful forensic and welfare-driven purpose might be served by the continuation of public law proceedings albeit without the structure provided by interim public law orders.

See also *A City Council v A Mother and others* [2019] EWHC 3076 (Fam), [2020] 1 FLR 515, [1], [2], [41]–[43] (Knowles J) considering *Re Q (a child: interim care order: jurisdiction)* [2019] EWHC 512 (Fam), [2019] 2 FCR 268 (this is a later determination in the same case)

4.3.6 Interim care and supervision orders: effect of ICOs: interim contact

See Chapter 10.3 Care and supervision orders: contact with children in care

4.4 INTERIM CARE AND SUPERVISION ORDERS: PROCEDURE

4.4.1 Interim care and supervision orders: procedure: format of evidence

Re N (children: interim order/stay) [2020] EWCA Civ 1070, [2020] 4 WLR 119, [28]–[31] (Peter Jackson LJ) *quotation limited to* [30]–[31]

30. A court considering an interim application in proceedings concerning children is required to undertake a level of investigation that is appropriate to the issues that need to be decided and sufficient to enable it to make a fair and effective evaluation of the advantages and disadvantages for the children of making or not making the interim order. Acting within the framework of the relevant substantive and procedural law, the court has

a wide and flexible discretion as to how its investigation and evaluation should be conducted at the interim stage. Depending upon the case and the issues to be decided, the decision may well be properly taken without hearing any oral evidence: the question will be whether it is necessary to hear some, probably limited, oral evidence to enable a fair and effective evaluation to be made.

31. It is understandable that the judge did not feel able to deal with the issue before her on submissions only and that she needed to hear some evidence. However, once she had decided to do that, fairness required that in this situation she should hear from both the accuser and the accused. There will be cases, for example where the court needs to hear and evaluate professional opinion, where it will be proper to hear from witnesses from one side only. This was not such a case. The investigation was a factual one into events where the parents were primary witnesses. It is no answer to say that the court would not have been helped by hearing their denials. They were not making bare denials but giving possible explanations for much of the evidence brought against them and, at least on paper, those explanations were not self-evidently implausible and deserved proper consideration. However, instead of taking them at face value (whatever that might be taken to mean), the judge largely left them out of account. The investigation that was carried out was therefore not fair and effective.

See also *Re W (a child)* [2012] EWCA Civ 106, [2012] 2 FLR 240, [13], [20]–[31] (McFarlane LJ) addressing a related point (where hearing no oral evidence was not unfair)

See also *Re Z (interim care order) (rev 1)* [2020] EWCA Civ 1755, [2021] 2 FCR 689, [33], [49] (Baker LJ) considering *Re N (children: interim order/stay)* [2020] EWCA Civ 1070, [2020] 4 WLR 119

See also *S v Merton London Borough* [1994] 1 FCR 186 (FD), 188G–190H (Ward J) addressing a related point (that there must be some evidence)

4.4.2 Interim care and supervision orders: procedure: care plans are not strictly required

Re L (children) [2016] EWCA Civ 1110, [2017] 2 FLR 547, [24]–[27] (King LJ)

24. The parents also have permission to appeal in relation to their ground that the judge had erred in making the order sanctioning removal in the absence of any viable care plan being before the court.

25. The local authority in their skeleton argument rightly draw the court's attention to the statutory provisions in relation to care plans. By section 31A of the Children Act 1989 provision is made at 31A(1):

> 'Where an application is made on which a care order might be made with respect to a child, the appropriate local authority must, within such time as the court may direct, prepare a plan ('a care plan') for the future care of the child.'

26. Subsections (2), (3) and (4) have no relevance to this case, but subsection (5) provides:

> 'In section 31(3A) and this section, references to a care order do not include an interim care order.'

27. It follows, therefore, that there is no statutory requirement for a care plan to be put before the court in an application for an interim care order. With respect to the local authority, to rely on that provision for justification for the making of the order made by this judge might be regarded as somewhat disingenuous. In considering the making of an interim care order, PL's welfare is paramount. Whilst there is no statutory requirement, and it would undoubtedly be premature in many cases to file a care plan which complies with the stringent conditions now found in section 31A and the Family Procedure Rules 2010, nevertheless, in order for the court to conduct its welfare analysis it is essential that the judge has adequate information in relation to the local authority's proposals for placement, particularly where, as here, a child has particular difficulties or presents particular challenges. A judge must be aware of the viability of and timescales for identifying such a placement.

4.4.3 Interim care and supervision orders: procedure: rare to make threshold findings at interim hearings

Re G (children: fair hearing) [2019] EWCA Civ 126, [2019] 2 FCR 115, [32]–[35] (Moor J)

[32] During the course of the hearing, we were told that it was commonplace in certain courts to warn parents that, if the application for an interim care order was opposed, the court may have to make findings as to facts in dispute. The implication was that these findings would then stand for all time. Indeed, Ms Ford, on behalf of the Local Authority told us that this would be done 'to prevent the need to go over the same ground again' later in the proceedings.

[33] It is important to remember that there is a fundamental difference between ss 31 and 38 of the Children Act 1989. Section 31 sets out what needs to be established before a court can make a full care order. Section 38(2) is in very different terms:

> 'A court shall not make an interim care order or supervision order under this section unless it is satisfied that there are reasonable grounds for believing that the circumstances with respect to the child are as mentioned in section 31(2)'.

[34] Section 38(2) does not require the court to make findings of fact to the civil standard, nor to be satisfied that the main threshold document is proved. Instead, the section requires the court to be satisfied that 'there are reasonable grounds' for believing that the threshold in s 31 is made out. It follows that, at an interim hearing, rarely, if ever, will findings of

fact be made that will have the effect of establishing the threshold at a final hearing. Accordingly, we consider that courts, if they do it at all, should be very cautious before making reference to the significance of conclusions drawn at the interim stage as such comments may appear to the parents to be a form of pressure.

[35] If the court is satisfied that there are 'reasonable grounds' for believing the threshold is made out, it will say so, but, in doing so, the court is not making final findings pursuant to s 31 on matters that must be proved to the requisite standard in due course.

4.4.4 Interim care and supervision orders: procedure: reviewing continuation of interim measures

Re H-B-S (children: discharge of interim care order) [2020] EWCA Civ 1027, [2020] 3 FCR 439, [16] (Peter Jackson LJ)

[16] At the end of the hearing we informed the parties that the appeal would be allowed. These are my reasons for agreeing with that decision:

(1) There is no doubt that the court has the power to review the continuation of interim measures that it has put in place and that it may decide to exercise that power where the balance of the evidence significantly changes during the proceedings. This may lead to the removal of children previously at home or the return of children previously in foster care. If the court considers it appropriate to revisit its previous decision, the essential question is likely to be whether the further information changes its original assessment of risk. Delay in making a decision is presumed to be detrimental to children but where children have been removed from home for their own protection it is not on its own likely to affect the risk assessment …

4.5 INTERIM CARE AND SUPERVISION ORDERS: S 38(6)[6] ASSESSMENTS

4.5.1 Interim care and supervision orders: s 38(6) assessments: broad construction of 'assessment of the child'

Re C (a minor) (interim care order: residential assessment) [1997] 1 FCR 149 (HL), 154F–156D, 157E–F (Lord Browne-Wilkinson)

Against that background, I turn to consider the construction of s 38(6) which I have already quoted. It is important also to refer to s 38(7) which provides as follows:

> 'A direction under subs-s (6) may be to the effect that there is to be –
>
> (a) no such examination or assessment; or

6 Children Act 1989, s 38(6).

(b) no such examination or assessment unless the court directs otherwise.'

There are two possible constructions of sub-ss (6) and (7), one narrow, the other purposive and broader. The Court of Appeal in *Re M (Minors) (Interim Care Order: Directions)* [1996] 3 FCR 137 adopted the narrow view. They held that the words 'other assessment of the child' had to be construed as *ejusdem generis* with the words 'medical or psychiatric examination'. They attached decisive importance to the fact that the subsection only refers to the examination or assessment 'of the child' and makes no reference to the examination or assessment of any other person in relation to the child. They further held that for the court to order a residential assessment of the parents and child together at a specified place would involve the court in an unwarranted usurpation by the court of the local authority's power (as the authority having parental responsibility under the interim care order) to regulate where the child is to reside. In addition to supporting the arguments of the Court of Appeal in *Re M* (above), Mr Harris, for the local authority in the present appeal, submitted that Parliament cannot have intended the court to have power to require the local authority against its own judgment to expend scarce resources: he submitted that the local authority is the only body which can properly assess how such resources are to be allocated as between the social services and the other services it has to provide and as between the various calls on its social services budget.

My Lords, I cannot accept this narrow construction of the subsection. The Act should be construed purposively so as to give effect to the underlying intentions of Parliament. As I have sought to demonstrate, the dividing line between the functions of the court on the one hand and the local authority on the other is that a child in interim care is subject to control of the local authority, the court having no power to interfere with the local authority's decisions save in specified cases. The cases where, despite that overall control, the court is to have power to intervene are set out, *inter alia*, in sub-s (6) and (7). The purpose of sub-s (6) is to enable the court to obtain the information necessary for its own decision, notwithstanding the control over the child which in all other respects rests with the local authority. I therefore approach the subsection on the basis that the court is to have such powers to override the views of the local authority as are necessary to enable the court to discharge properly its function of deciding whether or not to accede to the local authority's application to take the child away from its parents by obtaining a care order. To allow the local authority to decide what evidence is to go before the court at the final hearing would be in many cases, including the present, to allow the local authority by administrative decision to preempt the court's judicial decision.

This broad approach is supported by consideration of sub-s (7) which does not appear to have been drawn to the attention of the Court of Appeal either in *Re M* (above) or in the present case. Subsection (7) confers on the court the power to prohibit an examination or assessment which the local authority is proposing to make. It is manifestly directed to the type of conduct by social services revealed by the Cleveland Inquiry (Report of the Inquiry into Child Abuse in Cleveland in 1987 (1988) Cm 412), ie repeated interviews and assessments of the child and his parents which are detrimental to the child. This negative control by the court cannot have been intended to be limited to cases where the child, and only the child, is to be assessed. If it is to be fully effective to prevent damage to the child, the power under sub-s (7) must also extend to cases where it is proposed to assess the relationship between the parents and the child.

I am not convinced by the reasons which persuaded the Court of Appeal in *Re M* (above) to adopt the narrow construction limiting the ambit of the section to assessments of the child alone, such assessments to be of the same type as medical or psychiatric examinations. First, I can see no reason for the application of the *ejusdem generis* principle. What is the *genus*? Subsection (6) refer not to the 'medical psychiatric or other *examination*' of the child but to 'other *assessment*' of the child. Some assessments, even if confined to the child itself, may not involve any examination of that child, yet plainly such an assessment is authorized by the subsection. I can find no *genus* to which the principle can apply.

Next, it is true that sub-s (6) and (7) only refer to the assessment 'of the child' and not, as is proposed in the present case, a joint assessment of the child and the parents, including the parents' attitude and behaviour towards the child. But it is impossible to assess a young child divorced from his environment. The interaction between the child and his parents or other persons looking after him is an essential element in making any assessment of the child. This is shown particularly clearly by cases in which the courts have to decide whether the threshold requirements of s 31 are satisfied because of the harm to the child that is likely to be suffered because the child is beyond parental control. How can the court determine that issue without considering the relationship between the child and the parents? The court has no power to order the parents to take part in any assessment against their wishes, any more than, as the final words of sub-s (6) show, the court can order the child to do so if the child is capable of making an informed decision. But what the interests of justice require is not a power to compel the parent to take part in such assessment but a power in the court to override the powers over the child which the local authority would otherwise enjoy under the interim care order. If the narrow construction were to be adopted the local authority could simply refuse to allow the child to take part in any assessment with his parents.

...

In my judgment, therefore, sub-ss (6) and (7) of s 38 of the Act are to be broadly construed. They confer jurisdiction on the court to order or prohibit any assessment which involves the participation of the child and is directed to providing the court with the material which, in the view of the court, is required to enable it to reach a proper decision at the final hearing of the application for a full care order. In exercising its discretion whether to order any particular examination or assessment, the court will take into account the cost of the proposed assessment and the fact that local authorities' resources are notoriously limited.

See also *Re G (a child) (inter care order: residential assessment)* [2005] UKHL 68, [2005] 3 FCR 621, [27] (Lord Clyde), [43], [61]–[69] (Baroness Hale) addressing the same point, see Chapter 4.5.2 interim care and supervision orders: s 38(6) assessments: purpose

4.5.2 Interim care and supervision orders: s 38(6) assessments: purpose

Re G (a child) (inter care order: residential assessment) [2005] UKHL 68, [2005] 3 FCR 621, [4], [6]–[13] (Lord Scott), [26]–[31] (Lord Clyde), [61]–[71] (Baroness Hale) *quotation limited to* [27]–[31], [64]–[69]

[27] Plainly a broad and purposive construction is appropriate for s 38(6) of the Children's Act 1989. Thus the phrase 'of the child' is to be understood as meaning the child in the context of his or her family, so that the investigation may extend to considering the capacity of a parent to care for the child. But whatever the range of the investigation it must still qualify as a 'medical or psychiatric examination or other assessment' of the child.

[28] The purpose of the subsection is to enable the court to receive guidance for the making of a decision on the application for a care order. That includes the matters on which it has to be satisfied under s 31(2). The investigation with regard to which the court may give directions appears from the statute to be focused on the current state of affairs. That can be seen in the use of the present tense in s 1(3) (e) and (f). It may include an understanding of the present capacity of the parent to overcome any present deficiency. So to an extent it may look to the future, but only as a matter of a current forecast. What does not seem to be envisaged is any continuing assessment over a period of months to follow the progress, if any, of the parent in improving his or her capacity to give proper care to the child or in reducing the risk to the child which led to the interim care order being sought at the outset.

[29] That point is in my view supported by the intention of the statute that the process of examination or assessment should extend only over a relatively short period. The general approach is stated in s 1(2). The life of an interim assessment order under s 38 is only eight weeks with extensions of only four weeks. Under s 32(1) the court must draw up a timetable with a view to disposing of the case without delay. Correspondingly relatively short periods are envisaged for investigations in s 37(4) and for child assessment orders under s 43(5). It seems from the statute as if the process for obtaining care orders was intended to be rapid and usually to extend over no longer than some two or three months.

[30] It may be tempting to suppose that the court should remain in control of the future management of the child. But while the regime introduced by Pt IV of the Act gives the court power to make care orders and supervision orders it leaves the management of a child who is in care to the local

authority. On the grant of a care order, whether interim or final, the local authority not only has a duty under s 33(1) to receive the child into its care but it also under s 33(3) assumes parental responsibility for the child. The court may not assume the mantle of responsibility which by its own order has been laid upon the shoulders of the local authority. In the present case the decision whether the course of treatment should be carried out in the Cassel or in the community was a matter for the parental responsibility of the local authority.

[31] Plainly a distinction can be made as matter of language between what constitutes an assessment and what constitutes treatment. Moreover the two may co-exist. An institution directed to make an assessment may incidentally commence some form of treatment, if only to assess whether the case is susceptible to treatment. Treatment will often be accompanied by some form of assessment of the degree of success or failure as the treatment progresses. But without engaging in the terminological distinction it should be enough to recognise that the jurisdiction of the court is confined to obtaining information about the current state of affairs, including perhaps a forecast of what future progress might be possible, and does not extend to a continuing survey of the effects of treatment. Such a continuing oversight might, if the treatment is successful, lead to the termination of a care order, but it does not form part of the court's responsibility in deciding whether or not to impose such an order

...

[64] The purpose of these provisions is, therefore, not only to enable the court to obtain the information it needs, but also to enable the court to control the information-gathering activities of others. But the emphasis is always on obtaining information. This is clear from the use of the words 'examination' and 'other assessment'. If the framers of the Act had meant the court to be in charge, not only of the examination and assessment of the child, but also of the medical or psychiatric treatment to be provided for her, let alone for her parents, it would have said so. Instead, it deliberately left that in the hands of the local authority.

[65] A fortiori, the purpose of s 38(6) cannot be to ensure the provision of services either for the child or his family. There is nothing in the 1989 Act which empowers the court hearing care proceedings to order the provision of specific services for anyone. To imply such a power into s 38(6) would be quite contrary to the division of responsibility which was the 'cardinal principle' of the 1989 Act. (This is reinforced by the position in judicial review proceedings, recently considered by the House in *R (on the application of G) v Barnet London BC* [2003] UKHL 57, [2003] 3 FCR 419.)

[66] I appreciate, of course, that it is not always possible to draw a hard and fast line between information-gathering and service-providing. Some information can only be gathered through the provision of services. It may be necessary to observe the parents looking after the child at close

quarters for a short period in order to assess the quality of the child's attachment to the parents, the degree to which the parents have bonded with the child, the current parenting skills of the parents, and their capacity to learn and develop. That is the sort of assessment which was involved in *Re C (a minor) (interim care order: residential assessment)* [1997] 1 FCR 149, [1996] 4 All ER 871.

[67] But the court only has power to insist where this is relevant to the questions which the court has to answer. Where the threshold criteria are in issue, it must be recalled that these are phrased (in s 31(2)) in the present tense: that the child 'is suffering or is likely to suffer significant harm'; and 'that the harm or likelihood of harm is attributable to' the quality of actual or likely parental care or to the child's being beyond parental control. Where the threshold is found or conceded but the proper order is in issue, the welfare checklist is likewise focussed on the present, for example, in s 1(3)(f): 'how capable each of his parents is of meeting his needs'. The capacity to change, to learn and to develop may well be part of that. But it is still the present capacity with which the court is concerned. It cannot be a proper use of the court's powers under s 38(6) to seek to bring about change.

[68] These conclusions are reinforced by the Act's emphasis on reaching decisions without delay. It cannot have been contemplated that the examination or assessment ordered under s 38(6) would take many months to complete. It would be surprising if it were to last more than two or three months at most. The important decision for the court is whether or not to make a care order, with all that that entails. But the care order is not the end of the story. The court retains jurisdiction over the contact between the child and his family (see s 34). The local authority has a duty to place the child with parents or other members of the family unless this is impracticable or inconsistent with the child's welfare (see s 23(6)). The court may sometimes have to accept that it is not possible to know all that is to be known before a final choice is made, because that choice will depend upon how the family and the child respond and develop in the future.

Conclusion

[69] In short, what is directed under s 38(6) must clearly be an examination or assessment of the child, including where appropriate her relationship with her parents, the risk that her parents may present to her, and the ways in which those risks may be avoided or managed, all with a view to enabling the court to make the decisions which it has to make under the Act with the minimum of delay. Any services which are provided for the child and his family must be ancillary to that end. They must not be an end in themselves. In this case, the judge was clearly entitled to reach the conclusion that any further in-patient treatment in the Cassel had gone beyond what fell within his power to order under s 38(6). I would allow this appeal.

See also *TL v Hammersmith and Fulham London Borough Council and others* [2011] EWCA Civ 812, [2011] 3 FCR 343, [68]–[95] (Black LJ) providing an overview of the law on this point

4.5.3 Interim care and supervision orders: s 38(6) assessments: questions to ask

Re Y (a child) (s 38(6) assessment) [2018] EWCA Civ 992, [2018] 2 FLR 1085, [10]–[18] (Peter Jackson LJ) *quotation limited to* [11]–[15], [18]

11. Section 38(6) was twice considered by the House of Lords. Since then, subsections (7A) and (7B) have been added by amendment, but the two decisions remain determinative of the interpretation of sub-section (6).

12. The first decision is Re C (Interim Care Order: Residential Assessment) [1997] 1 FLR 1. In that case the issue concerned the breadth of section 38(6), and in particular whether it covered only an assessment of the child or, on a wider interpretation, an assessment of the child with the parent. The House of Lords favoured the latter interpretation: see Lord Browne-Wilkinson at [6-7]. At the end of paragraph 7, he stated:

> 'But to come within section 38(6) the proposed assessment must, in my opinion be an assessment of the child. The main focus must be on the child.'

He then considered the situation in that case and continued:

> 'What was to be assessed was the mother's capacity for beneficial response to the psychotherapeutic treatment that she was to receive. Such an assessment, no matter how valuable the information might be for the purposes of the eventual final care order decision could not, in my opinion, be brought within section 38(6).'

13. The second decision is Re G (Interim Care Order: Residential Assessment) [2006] 1 FLR 601. There Lord Scott said at [14]:

> 'It seems to me clear that the main purpose of the proposed programme was therapy for the mother in order to give her the opportunity of change so as to become a safe and acceptable carer... This purpose in my opinion does not come within section 38(6), notwithstanding that the results of the programme would be valuable and influential in enabling the court to decide whether a care order ... should be made and that if the purpose were to be achieved, it would very greatly benefit the [child].'

14. Baroness Hale summarised matters at [64-71]. At paragraph 64 she said this:

> 'The purpose of these provisions is, therefore, not only to enable the court to obtain the information it needs but also to enable the court to control the information gathering activities of others. But the emphasis is always on obtaining the information. This is clear from the use of the words 'examination' and 'other assessment.' If the framers of the 1989 Act had meant the court to be in charge, not only of the examination and assessment of the child, but also of the medical or psychiatric treatment to be provided for her, let alone for

her parents, it would have said so. Instead, it deliberately left that in the hands of the local authority.'

At paragraph 66:

> 'I appreciate, of course, that it is not always possible to draw a hard and fast line between information-gathering and service-providing. Some information can only be gathered through the provision of services. It may be necessary to observe the parents looking after the child at close quarters for a short period in order to assess the quality of the child's attachment to the parents, the degree to which the parents have bonded with the child, the current parenting skills of the parents and their capacity to learn and develop…'

At paragraph 69:

> 'In short, what is directed under section 38(6) must clearly be an examination or assessment of the child, including where appropriate her relationship with her parents, the risk that her parents may present to her, and the ways in which those risks may be avoided or managed, all with a view to enabling the court to make the decisions which it has to make under the 1989 Act with the minimum of delay. Any services which are provided for the child and his family must be ancillary to that end. They must not be an end in themselves.'

And finally, at paragraph 71:

> 'Further or other assessments should only be commissioned if they can bring something important to the case which neither the local authority nor the guardian is able to bring.'

15. The approach taken in these two cases remains authoritative, with only the substitution of the word 'necessary' for the word 'important' in the last citation.

…

18. In my view, a judge deciding an application under s.38(6) must address two questions:
    (1) Is this a proposal for an assessment that falls within the terms of section 38(6)?
    (2) If so, is the assessment necessary to assist the court to resolve the proceedings justly, as required by ss. 7A, having regard to the matters in ss. 7B?

    Both questions must be approached in a manner that upholds the right to a fair trial under Article 6 and the right to respect for family life under Article 8. Only if both are answered affirmatively can the court make the direction requested.

See also *Re G (a child: s 38(6) assessment)* [2020] EWCA Civ 282, [2020] 2 FCR 673, [15]–[18], [23] (Peter Jackson LJ) addressing the same point (considering 'necessary' in this context)

4.6 INTERIM CARE AND SUPERVISION ORDERS: ISO[7]S

4.6.1 Interim care and supervision orders: ISOs: ICOs only if ISOs are insufficient

Re W (a minor) (care proceedings: interim orders) [1994] 3 FCR 102 (CA), 109D–F (Glidewell LJ)

> I have said that the joint effect of s 38 and s 31 of the Act is that before making an interim order, the court must be satisfied that there are reasonable grounds for believing that the criteria set out in s 31(2) are satisfied, which are the same criteria for care orders and for supervision orders. However, if the court is so satisfied, it must then go on to decide, firstly, whether it is necessary to make any order at all. That obligation is placed on the court by s 1(5) of the Act. If it decides that an order is necessary, the court must then decide whether to make a supervision order or a care order. If it appears to the court that the risk of harm is such that it can probably be met or obviated by a supervision order, then that is the appropriate order to be made.
>
> It is only if the supervision order appears unlikely to be sufficient to obviate the risk that the court should go on to make a care order.

4.6.2 Interim care and supervision orders: ISOs: no interim orders on applications to extend supervision orders

Re A (a minor) (supervision order: extension) [1995] 2 FCR 114 (CA), 117D–117G (Butler-Sloss LJ), 118G–119D (Hoffmann LJ)

> The s 38 provision for interim orders has, in my view, no application to extension orders. If the application to extend the supervision order is within time and opposed but the hearing date is after the original supervision order has expired, the court can make one or more short extension orders pending the determination of the opposed application. It is not permissible to make an interim order under s 38. That section is designed to make holding orders pending an original or fresh application under s 31.
>
> A technical but important consequence of not importing the provisions of s 31 into an application to extend a supervision order is lack of jurisdiction in the court to make a care order on an extension application, whereas by s 31(5) the court may:
>
> ‘(b) on an application for a supervision order, make a care order.’
>
> I am satisfied that the view of the Judge that this was a section 31 application and that he had jurisdiction to make a care order was wrong. In the absence of a specific application by the local authority under s 31 there was no

7 Interim supervision order.

jurisdiction to make an interim care order.

I would allow this appeal and set aside the interim care order and extend the supervision order to a period to be discussed with counsel.

...

Finally I should say something about the short-term extensions of the supervision order which the magistrates granted before the final hearing on 7 February 1994. The Judge described this as a rather curious situation: the magistrates appeared to be making a series of final orders pending a hearing to decide whether a final order should be granted. The correct procedure, he thought, would have been to make interim orders under s 38(1)(a), which says that:

> 'Where ... in any proceedings on an application for a care order or supervision order, the proceedings are adjourned ... the court may make an interim care order or an interim supervision order with respect to the child concerned.'

It will be apparent from what I have said earlier that I disagree. An application to extend is not an 'application for a supervision order' within the meaning of s 38(1)(a). In my judgment the justices acted perfectly correctly. Paragraph 6(3) says nothing about the period for which the order may be extended and I see no reason why magistrates should not grant a succession of extensions to cover adjournments of the application if they think that the interests of the child and the principle of no delay so requires. The distinction between a final and an interim order makes sense in relation to the initial care or supervision order. The former will operate indefinitely and the latter will potentially operate for three years. Furthermore, neither order can be made at all unless the s 31(2) conditions are satisfied and the investigation of this question may cause delay. A power to make an interim order is therefore necessary. But the distinction between an 'interim' and 'final' order is meaningless in relation to an extension which can be granted for such period as the court thinks fit on the basis of the principles in s 1.

CHAPTER 5

Case management

Chapter contents

CHAPTER 5

Case management

5.1 CASE MANAGEMENT[1]: ACTIVE CASE MANAGEMENT

5.1.1 Case management: active case management: generally

Re TG (a child) (care proceedings: biomechanical engineering evidence) [2013] EWCA Civ 5, [2013] 1 FCR 229, [23]–[37] (Sir James Munby P), [82]–[85] (Sir Mark Hedley) *quotation limited to* [23]–[28], [35]–[37]

[23] As will be appreciated the appeal is against a case-management decision. Before turning to the issues specific to this particular case, it may be of assistance if I rehearse some basic principles.

[24] (1) First, active judicial case management has for some years now been an integral and essential part of practice in family cases, as it is for all other civil and criminal cases. The obligation of the court to further the overriding objective, as set out in r 1.1 of the 2010 Rules, is now enshrined in rr 1.2 and 1.4. The overriding objective as defined in r 1.1(1) is that the court should 'deal with cases justly, having regard to any welfare issues involved'. Rule 1.1(2) provides that this includes, so far as is practicable:

'(a) ensuring that [the case] is dealt with expeditiously and fairly;

(b) dealing with the case in ways which are proportionate to the nature, importance and complexity of the issues;

(c) ensuring that the parties are on an equal footing;

(d) saving expense; and

(e) allotting to it an appropriate share of the court's resources, while taking into account the need to allot resources to other cases.'

[25] Essential aspects of case management are set out in r 1.4(2). Of particular relevance for present purposes, this provides that active case management includes:

1 It is submitted that any authorities pre-dating March 2021 may need reading in light of the President's Public Law Working Group report *Recommendations to achieve best practice in the child protection and family justice systems* (March, 2021), which includes *Best practice guidance: The application and case management.* The report is not law but was endorsed by the President of the Family Division, Sir Andrew McFarlane. Available at www.judiciary.uk/publications/message-from-the-president-of-the-family-division-publication-of-the-presidents-public-law-working-group-report/, accessed 18 December 2021.

'(b) identifying at an early stage—
 (i) the issues …

(c) deciding promptly—
 (i) which issues need full investigation and hearing and which do not; and
 (ii) the procedure to be followed in the case …

(g) fixing timetables or otherwise controlling the progress of the case;

(h) considering whether the likely benefits of taking a particular step justify the cost of taking it …

(l) giving directions to ensure that the case proceeds quickly and efficiently.'

[26] (2) Second, an essential part of appropriate case management is the power of the court to control evidence. Rule 22.1 provides that:

'(1) The court may control the evidence by giving directions as to—
 (a) the issues on which it requires evidence;
 (b) the nature of the evidence which it requires to decide those issues; and
 (c) the way in which the evidence is to be placed before the court.

(2) The court may use its power under this rule to exclude evidence that would otherwise be admissible …

(4) The court may limit cross-examination.'

[27] In this connection I venture to repeat what I recently said in *Re C (children) (residence order: application being dismissed at fact-finding stage)* [2012] EWCA Civ 1489 at [14]–[15], [2012] All ER (D) 223 (Nov) at [14]–[15]:

'[14] … these are not ordinary civil proceedings, they are family proceedings, where it is fundamental that the judge has an essentially inquisitorial role, his duty being to further the welfare of the children which is, by statute, his paramount consideration. It has long been recognised—and authority need not be quoted for this proposition—that for this reason a judge exercising the family jurisdiction has a much broader discretion than he would in the civil jurisdiction to determine the way in which an application … should be pursued. In an appropriate case he can summarily dismiss the application as being, if not groundless, lacking enough merit to justify pursuing the matter. He may determine that the matter is one to be dealt with on the basis of written evidence and oral submissions without the need for oral evidence. He may … decide to hear the evidence of the applicant and then take stock of where the matter stands at the end of the evidence.

> [15] The judge in such a situation will always be concerned to ask himself: is there some solid reason in the interests of the children why I should embark upon, or, having embarked upon, why I should continue exploring the matters which one or other of the parents seeks to raise. If there is or may be solid advantage to the children in doing so, then the inquiry will proceed, albeit it may be on the basis of submissions rather than oral evidence. But if the judge is satisfied that no advantage to the children is going to be obtained by continuing the investigation further, then it is perfectly within his case-management powers and the proper exercises of his discretion so to decide and to determine that the proceedings should go no further.'

[28] I returned to the same theme in *Re B (a child)* [2012] EWCA Civ 1545 at [19]:

> 'even in family cases the days are long past when a litigant was entitled to call however many witnesses he or she wanted. The court as part of its case-management powers has undoubted jurisdiction to determine the way in which the case is to be argued, whether the case is to be argued on paper, whether the case is to be argued with witnesses giving oral evidence, who those witnesses should be, what issues they should give evidence on, and so on and so forth. Plainly, this being a final hearing, it was appropriate for the judge to contemplate that the witnesses would give oral evidence, but the mere fact that she limited the number of witnesses in the way in which she did does not of itself demonstrate any error on the part of Judge Robertshaw; it was in principle within the scope of her case-management powers to determine that the witnesses she had identified were the witnesses who the court required to hear in order to determine the issues raised before it.'

…

[35] (4) Fourth, the Court of Appeal has recently re-emphasised the importance of supporting first-instance judges who make robust but fair case-management decisions: *Cherney v Deripaska* [2012] EWCA Civ 1235 at [17], [30], [2012] All ER (D) 43 (Oct) at [17], [30], and *Stokors SA v IG Markets Ltd* [2012] EWCA Civ 1706 at [25], [45], [46], [2012] All ER (D) 31 (Nov) at [25], [45], [46]. Of course, the Court of Appeal must and will intervene when it is proper to do so. However, it must be understood that in the case of appeals from case-management decisions the circumstances in which it can interfere are limited. The Court of Appeal can interfere only if satisfied that the judge erred in principle, took into account irrelevant matters, failed to take into account relevant matters, or came to a decision so plainly wrong that it must be regarded as outside the generous ambit of the discretion entrusted to the judge: *Royal & Sun Alliance Insurance plc v T & N Ltd* [2002] EWCA Civ 1964 at [37]–[38], [47], [2003] PIQR P26 at [37]–[38], [47], *Fattal v Walbrook Trustee (Jersey) Ltd* [2008] EWCA Civ 427 at [33], and *Stokors SA v*

IG Markets Ltd at [46]. This is not a question of judicial comity; there are sound pragmatic reasons for this approach. First, as Arden LJ pointed out in *Royal & Sun Alliance Insurance plc v T & N Ltd* at [47]: 'Case management should not be interrupted by interim appeals as this will lead to satellite litigation and delays in the litigation process.' Second, as she went on to observe: 'the judge dealing with case management is often better equipped to deal with case management issues.' The judge well acquainted with the proceedings because he or she has dealt with previous interlocutory applications will have a knowledge of and 'feel' for the case superior to that of the Court of Appeal.

[36] Exactly the same applies in family cases. Thus in *Re C (children) (residence order: application being dismissed at fact-finding stage)* [2012] All ER (D) 223 (Nov) Thorpe LJ and I dismissed the appeal notwithstanding what I said was the 'robust view' Judge Cliffe had formed when deciding to stop the hearing. And in *Re B (a child)* [2012] EWCA Civ 1545 I refused permission to appeal from an order of Judge Miranda Robertshaw involving what I described (para [16]) as 'appropriately vigorous and robust case management'. I said (para [17]):

> 'The circumstances in which this court can or should interfere at the interlocutory stage with case-management decisions are limited. Part of the process of family litigation in the modern era is vigorous case management by allocated judges who have responsibility for the case which they are managing. This court can intervene only if there has been serious error, if the case-management judge has gone plainly wrong; otherwise the entire purpose of case management, which is to move cases forward as quickly as possible, will be frustrated, because cases are liable to be derailed by interlocutory appeals.'

As Black LJ very recently observed in *Re B (a child) (interim residence order)* [2012] EWCA Civ 1742 at [35], [2013] All ER (D) 16 (Jan) at [35]: 'a judge making case-management decisions has a very wide discretion and anyone seeking to appeal against such a decision has an uphill task.'

[37] None of this, of course, is intended to encourage excess on the part of case-management judges or inappropriate deference on the part of the Court of Appeal. There is, as always, a balance to be struck. As Black LJ went on to observe in *Re B (a child) (interim residence order)* at [48]: 'Robust case management ... very much has its place in family proceedings but it also has its limits.' I respectfully agree. The task of the case-management judge is to arrange a trial that is fair; fair, that is, judged both by domestic standards and by the standards mandated by arts 6 and 8 of the European Convention for the Protection of Human Rights and Fundamental Freedoms 1950 (as set out in Sch 1 to the Human Rights Act 1998) (the Convention). The objective is that spelt out in r 1.1 of the 2010 Rules, namely a trial conducted 'justly', 'expeditiously and fairly' and in a way which is 'proportionate to the nature, importance and complexity of the issues', but never losing sight of the need to have regard to the welfare issues involved.

See also *Re C (A Child)* [2015] EWCA Civ 539, [2016] 3 FCR 177, [30]–[31] (Ryder LJ) considering *Re TG (a child) (care proceedings: biomechanical engineering evidence)* [2013] EWCA Civ 5, [2013] 1 FCR 229

5.1.2 Case management: active case management: robust and fair case management

Re S-W (children) (care proceedings: summary disposal at Case Management Hearing) [2015] EWCA Civ 27, [2015] 2 FCR 173, [24]–[29], [39]–[41] (King LJ), [43]–[45] (Lewison LJ), [55]–[61] (Sir James Munby P) *quotation limited to* [24]–[25], [47]–[48]

[24] A key feature of the family justice reforms now found in the CA 1989 as amended and FPR 2010 Pt 12 and Practice Direction 12A, has been the use by the courts 'vigorous and robust case management' as a tool for ensuring that, wherever possible, delay is minimised and the statutory 26 week requirement found at s 32 of the CA 1989, is achieved. It is undoubtedly the case that, as a result of the reforms, there has been a significant change in culture, driven through by dedicated judges and specialist counsel and solicitors up and down the country. Many care cases are now concluded at either the IRH or well within 26 weeks, to the considerable benefit of the children involved. The Liverpool area has been notable in its successful implementation of the reforms and its early achievement of the routine disposal of care cases within 26 weeks.

[25] Part of the way in which effective case management is achieved is by virtue of the judge allocated to the case retaining considerable flexibility in the manner in which he manages the particular case before him; FPR 2010; PD12A has at para 2, 'Flexible powers of the court'. Provision is made for:

(i) steps which ordinarily take place at various stages in the proceedings, to be taken at another step (PD12A para 2.2);
(ii) the paragraph anticipates cases in which the IRH will be the final hearing (PD12A para 2.3);
(iii) for oral evidence to be heard at CMH or IRH although PD12A, para 2.3 specifies that the court must be notified in advance of such an intention and directions sought for the conduct of the hearing at which it is intended evidence will be heard (PD12A para 2.5), thereby ensuring that no party can be caught unawares.

...

[47] In both civil and family cases the Court of Appeal has said on more than one occasion that it will uphold robust but fair case management decisions by first instance judges: *Cherney v Deripaska* [2012] EWCA Civ 1235, [2012] All ER (D) 43 (Oct) (at [17], [30]); *Re TG (a child) (care proceedings: biomechanical engineering evidence)* [2013] EWCA Civ 5, [2013] 1 FCR 229, [2013] 1 FLR 1250 (at [35], [36]). Both adjectives are important. Robustness cannot trump fairness.

[48] Family cases, however inquisitorial and streamlined they may be, are not exempt from these basic principles. As the President put it in *Re TG* at [37]:

> 'The task of the case-management judge is to arrange a trial that is fair; fair, that is, judged both by domestic standards and by the standards mandated by arts 6 and 8 of the European Convention for the Protection of Human Rights and Fundamental Freedoms 1950 (as set out in Sch 1 to the Human Rights Act 1998) (the Convention).'

See also *Re R-B (a child)* [2019] EWCA Civ 1560, [25]–[26], [35]–[37] (Baker LJ) considering *Re S-W (children) (care proceedings: summary disposal at Case Management Hearing)* [2015] EWCA Civ 27, [2015] 2 FCR 173

See also *Re P (a child) (adoption: placement with non-UK resident family)* [2014] EWCA Civ 888, [2014] 3 FCR 349, [56]–[57] (McCombe LJ) addressing the same point

See also *Re B (a child) (interim residence order)* [2012] EWCA Civ 1742, [2013] 1 FCR 344, [35]–[36], [48] (Black LJ) addressing the same point

5.1.3 Case management: active case management: summarily determining issues

Re S-W (children) (care proceedings: summary disposal at Case Management Hearing) [2015] EWCA Civ 27, [2015] 2 FCR 173, [24]–[29], [39]–[41] (King LJ), [43]–[45] (Lewison LJ), [55]–[61] (Sir James Munby P) *quotation limited to* [41], [51]–[61]

[41] It follows that whilst one can conceive of cases where a final order will be made at the case management hearing (the application for permission to appeal of *Re R* referred to above was one such case), in reality it is likely that such a course will be appropriate only occasionally and in any event:

(i) Where there remains any significant issue as to threshold, assessment, further assessment or placement, it will not be appropriate to dispose of the case at CMH.

(ii) It can never be appropriate to dispose of the case where the children's guardian has not at least had an opportunity of seeing the child or children in question and to prepare a case analysis in which he/she considers the s 31A care plan of the local authority.

(iii) Where, unusually a case is to be disposed of at CMH, adequate notice must be given to the representatives of the parents and guardian; reluctance on their part will ordinarily be fatal to the proposed course. Having said that, where all that is required is for the parties to have a little more time or for the local authority to prepare a s 31A care plan one can envisage cases where the matter is adjourned for a further CMH with the intention that final orders will be made at the adjourned hearing. Another example where in exceptional circumstances it may be appropriate to make final orders at the CMH could be where the outcome is inevitable and the child's need for an immediate resolution to the proceedings is critical to his or her welfare.

(iv) A care order should not be made without some reasons or a judgment no matter how concise. It is not enough to proceed on the basis that the reasons for making a care order, and still more a placement order, can be distilled from the transcript of discussion between the judge and the parties at court. Whilst appreciating the ever increasing burden on family court judges in the preparing and giving of judgments there must at least be a short judgment/ reasons noting the available options, the positions of the parties and confirming that the outcome for the child is in his or her best interests and is proportionate and therefore Convention compliant.

…

[51] My Lord has drawn attention to the famous words of Lord Hewart CJ in *R v Sussex Justices, ex p McCarthy* [1924] 1 KB 256 at 259, [1923] All ER Rep 233 at 234. In the present case it is unhappily all too apparent that no dispassionate observer of the proceedings or reader of the transcript could think that justice was done, let alone that it was seen to be done. It was not.

[52] Vigorous and robust case management has a vital role to play in all family cases, but as r 1.1 of the Family Procedure Rules 2010, SI 2010/2955 makes clear, the duty of the court is to 'deal with cases justly, having regard to any welfare issues involved'. So, as my Lord has emphasised, robustness cannot trump fairness.

[53] In the context of case management, fairness has two aspects: first, the case management hearing itself must be conducted fairly; secondly, as I observed in the passage in *Re TG (a child) (care proceedings: biomechanical engineering evidence)* [2013] EWCA Civ 5, [2013] 1 FCR 229, [2013] 1 FLR 1250 to which my Lord has referred, the task of the case management judge is to arrange a trial that is fair. Here, there was a failure in both respects.

[54] We are all familiar with the aphorism that 'justice delayed is justice denied'. But justice can equally be denied if inappropriately accelerated. An unseemly rush to judgment can too easily lead to injustice. As Pauffley J warned in *Re NL (a child) (appeal: interim care order: facts and reasons)* [2014] EWHC 270 (Fam), [2014] 3 FCR 464, [2014] 1 WLR 2795 (at [40]), 'Justice must never be sacrificed upon the altar of speed'.

[55] Rule 22.1 gives the case management judge extensive powers to control the evidence in a children case: see *Re TG* [2013] 1 FCR 229, [2013] 1 FLR 1250 at [27]–[28]. But these powers must always be exercised, especially in care cases where the stakes are so high, in a way which pays due regard to two fundamental principles which apply as much to family cases as to any other type of case.

[56] First, a parent facing the removal of their child must be entitled to put their case to the court, however seemingly forlorn. It is one of the oldest principles of our law—it goes back over 400 years, to the earliest years

of the seventeenth century—that no one is to be condemned unheard: see *Re G (care: challenge to local authority's decision)* [2003] EWHC 551 (Fam), [2003] 2 FLR 42 (at [28]–[29]). As I observed (at [55]):

> 'The fact, if fact it be, that the circumstances are such as to justify intervention by the State … does not absolve the State of its duty nonetheless to act fairly. It is not enough for the State to make a fair decision: the State must itself act fairly in the way in which it goes about arriving at its decision.'

A parent who wishes to give evidence in answer to a local authority's care application must surely be permitted to do so.

[57] Secondly, there is the right to confront one's accusers. So, a parent who wishes to cross-examine an important witness whose evidence is being relied upon by the local authority must surely be permitted to do so.

[58] I stress the word important. I am not suggesting that a parent has an absolute right to cross-examine every witness or to ask unlimited questions of a witness merely with a view to 'testing the evidence' or in the hope, Micawber-like, that something may turn up. Case management judges have to strike the balance, ensuring that there is a fair trial, recognising that a fair trial does not entitle a parent, even in a care case, to explore every by-way, but also being alert to ensure that no parent is denied the right to put the essence of their case to witnesses on those parts of their evidence that may have a significant impact on the outcome.

[59] Quite apart from the fundamentally important points of principle which are here in play, there is great danger in jumping too quickly to the view that nothing is likely to be achieved by hearing evidence or allowing cross-examination, in concluding that the outcome is obvious. My Lord has referred to what Megarry J said in *John v Rees*. The forensic context there was far removed from the one with which are here concerned, but the point is equally apposite. As I said in *Re TG* [2013] 1 FCR 229, [2013] 1 FLR 1250 at [72]: 'Most family judges will have had the experience of watching a seemingly solid care case brought by a local authority being demolished, crumbling away, at the hands of skilled and determined counsel.'

[60] I agree with my Lady that there can, in principle, be care cases where the final order is made at the case management hearing. But, unless the decision goes by concession or consent, it will only be exceptionally, in unusual circumstances and on rare occasions, that this can ever be appropriate. *Re H (children)* (B4/2014/2033) (unreported), to which my Lady has referred, was such a case, but the particular and unusual facts which there justified a summary process need to be borne in mind. *Re H* is not and must not be treated as justification for any general principle, let alone for proceeding as the judge did in the present case.

[61] Quite apart from the fact that such a ruthlessly truncated process as the judge adopted here was fundamentally unprincipled and unfair, it also prevented both the children's guardian and the court doing what the law demanded of them in terms of complying with the requirements of

the Children Act 1989 and PD12A. I agree with my Lady's analysis, in particular in relation to care plans and the meaning and effect of the various provisions in ss 31 and 31A of the Act to which she has referred.

See also *VBC v AGM and others* [2019] EWFC 64 [Appendix 2], [15]–[17], [24]–[42] (Sir Mark Hedley) addressing the same point (concluding that the Court has jurisdiction to bring proceedings to an end at any time before the conclusion of a final hearing)

See also *Re H-L (children: summary dismissal of care proceedings)* [2019] EWCA Civ 704, [2019] 2 FCR 844, [3]–[10], [46] (Peter Jackson LJ) providing an overview of the law on this point (suggesting that FPR[2] Pt 12 is likely to contain all necessary procedural provisions)

See also *Re BB (care proceedings) (mid-trial dismissal and withdrawal of allegations)* [2021] EWFC 20, [32]–[37] (Darren Howe QC sitting as a judge of the High Court) considering *VBC v AGM and others* [2019] EWFC 64 (addressing whether *VBC v AGM and others* [2019] EWFC 64 survives *Re H-L (children: summary dismissal of care proceedings)* [2019] EWCA Civ 704, [2019] 2 FCR 844)

See also *A Local Authority v W and others* [2020] EWFC 40, [2020] 4 WLR 83, [44]–[58] (MacDonald J) considering *Re H-L (children: summary dismissal of care proceedings)* [2019] EWCA Civ 704, [2019] 2 FCR 844, addressing a related point (determining the approach which applies to the case management powers for summarily determining disputed findings of fact)

See also *Re N (a child)* [2012] EWCA Civ 1563, [2013] 1 FLR 1244, [3]–[11] (McFarlane LJ) addressing a related point (summarily determining cases at IRHs[3])

See also *RE v North Yorkshire County Council and others* [2015] EWCA Civ 1169, [2016] 1 WLR 512, [32]–[40], [49]–[50] (Hayden J) addressing a related point (summarily determining cases at IRHs)

See also *Re F (a child)* [2007] EWCA Civ 810, [44] (Wall LJ) addressing a related point (the irrelevance of 'no case to answer')

5.1.4 Case management: active case management: delay: 26-week time limit: generally

Re S (a child) (care proceedings: residential assessment) [2014] EWCC B44 (Fam), [2015] 2 FCR 287 [24]–[34] (Sir James Munby P)

[24] Section 32(1)(a)(ii) does not describe some mere aspiration or target, nor does it prescribe an average. It defines, subject only to the qualification in s 32(5) and compliance with the requirements of s 32(6) and (7), a

2 Family Procedure Rules 2010, SI 2010/2955.
3 Issue resolution hearing.

mandatory limit which applies to all cases. It follows that there will be many cases that can, and therefore should, be concluded well within the 26-week limit. I repeat what I said in my first 'View from the President's Chambers: The process of reform' [2013] Fam Law 548:

> 'My message is clear and uncompromising: this deadline can be met, it must be met, it will be met. And remember, 26 weeks is a deadline, not a target; it is a maximum, not an average or a mean. So many cases will need to be finished in less than 26 weeks.'

[25] What then of the qualification in s 32(5)?

[26] In *Re B-S (children) (adoption: leave to oppose)* [2013] EWCA Civ 1146, [2013] 3 FCR 481, [2014] 1 WLR 563 (at [32]–[46]), the Court of Appeal spelt out the essentials which the law and good practice demand in all cases when the court is being asked to approve a care plan for adoption or being asked to make a non-consensual placement order or adoption order. Giving the judgment of the court, I said this (at [49]):

> 'We do not envisage that proper compliance with what we are demanding, which may well impose a more onerous burden on practitioners and judges, will conflict with the requirement, soon to be imposed by statute, that care cases are to be concluded within a maximum of 26 weeks. Critical to the success of the reforms is robust judicial case management from the outset of every care case. Case management judges must be astute to ensure that the directions they give are apt to the task and also to ensure that their directions are complied with. Never is this more important than in cases where the local authority's plan envisages adoption.'

I continued:

> 'If, despite all, the court does not have the kind of evidence we have identified, and is therefore not properly equipped to decide these issues, then an adjournment must be directed, even if this takes the case over 26 weeks. Where the proposal before the court is for non-consensual adoption, the issues are too grave, the stakes for all are too high, for the outcome to be determined by rigorous adherence to an inflexible timetable and justice thereby potentially denied.'

[27] That approach, which is entirely compatible with the requirements of s 32, applies not just in the particular context under consideration in *Re B-S* but more generally.

[28] In my seventh 'View' [2013] Fam Law 1394, I described the remarkable work being done by the Family Drug and Alcohol Court (FDAC) under the inspirational leadership of District Judge (Magistrates' Court) Nicholas Crichton. I touched on the question of how the FDAC model was to meet the challenge of the 26-week time limit and fit with the PLO. I said:

> '... we must see how best the PLO can accommodate the FDAC model (I put it this way, rather than the other way round). We must

always remember that the PLO is a means of achieving justice and the best outcomes for children and, wherever possible, their families. It is not, and must never be allowed to become, a straightjacket, least of all if rigorous adherence to an inflexible timetable risks putting justice in jeopardy.'

[29] More recently, in *Re NL (a child) (appeal: interim care order: facts and reasons)* [2014] EWHC 270 (Fam), [2014] 3 FCR 464, [2014] 1 WLR 2795 (at [40]), Pauffley J has expressed the point in words which I cannot improve upon and which I wholeheartedly endorse: 'Justice must never be sacrificed upon the altar of speed.'

[30] So despite the imperative demand of s 32(1)(a)(ii), there can be exceptions. But before going further it is vital to recall the equally imperative language of ss 32(5) and 32(7). An extension beyond 26 weeks is to be permitted only if it is 'necessary to enable the court to resolve the proceedings justly'. This is precisely the same language as appears in s 38(7A) of the 1989 Act and s 13(6) of the 2014 Act, so it must mean the same. Specifically, the learning in *Re TG* and in *Re H-L* must, in my judgment, apply as much to s 32(5) of the 1989 Act as it does to s 38(7A) of the 1989 Act and s 13(6) of the 2014 Act. Moreover, extensions are 'not to be granted routinely' and require 'specific justification'.

[31] In what circumstances may the qualification in s 32(5) apply?

[32] This is not the occasion for any elaborate discussion of a question which, in the final analysis, can be determined only on a case by case basis. But some preliminary and necessarily tentative observations are appropriate.

[33] There will, as it seems to me, be three different forensic contexts in which an extension of the 26-week time limit in accordance with s 32(5) may be 'necessary':

(i) The first is where the case can be identified from the outset, or at least very early on, as one which it may not be possible to resolve justly within 26 weeks. Experience will no doubt identify the kind of cases that may fall within this category. Four examples which readily spring to mind (no doubt others will emerge) are (a) very heavy cases involving the most complex medical evidence where a separate fact finding hearing is directed in accordance with *Re S (a child) (care proceedings: challenge to findings of fact)* [2014] EWCA Civ 25, [2014] 1 FCR 477, [2014] 1 FLR 1421 (at [29]), (b) FDAC type cases (see further below), (c) cases with an international element where investigations or assessments have to be carried out abroad and (d) cases where the parent's disabilities require recourse to special assessments or measures (as to which see *Re C (a child) (care proceedings: deaf parent)* [2014] EWCA Civ 128, [2014] 3 FCR 627, [2014] 1 WLR 2495 (at [34])).

(ii) The second is where, despite appropriately robust and vigorous judicial case management, something unexpectedly emerges to change the nature of the proceedings too late in the day to enable the case to be concluded justly within 26 weeks. Examples which come to mind are (a) cases proceeding on allegations of neglect or emotional harm where allegations of sexual abuse subsequently surface, (b) cases which are unexpectedly 'derailed' because of the death, serious illness or imprisonment of the proposed carer, and (c) cases where a realistic alternative family carer emerges late in the day.

(iii) The third is where litigation failure on the part of one or more of the parties makes it impossible to complete the case justly within 26 weeks (the type of situation addressed in *Re B-S* (para [49])).

[34] I repeat, because the point is so important, that in no case can an extension beyond 26 weeks be authorised unless it is 'necessary' to enable the court to resolve the proceedings 'justly'. Only the imperative demands of justice—fair process—or of the child's welfare will suffice.

See also *Re M-F (children)* [2014] EWCA Civ 991, [2015] 1 WLR 909, [25]–[28], [57]–[58] (Sir James Munby P) considering *Re S (a child) (care proceedings: residential assessment)* [2014] EWCC B44 (Fam), [2015] 2 FCR 287 (disparaging use of the phrase 'planned and purposeful delay', [57], [58])

See also *Re S-L (children: adjournment)* [2019] EWCA Civ 1571, [2020] 1 FCR 206, [12]–[13] (Peter Jackson LJ) addressing a related point (adjourning final hearings)

See also *Re P-S (children)* [2018] EWCA Civ 1407, [2018] 4 WLR 99, [60]–[69] (Sir James Munby P) considering Re S *(a child) (care proceedings: residential assessment)* [2014] EWCC B44 (Fam), [2015] 2 FCR 287 (and delaying for SGO[4] assessments)

See also *Re T (children)* [2015] EWCA Civ 606, [2016] 1 WLR 14, [31]–[36] (McFarlane LJ) addressing a related point (judgments are part of timetables for cases and the implication of that)

5.1.5 Case management: active case management: delay: justice determines delay, not welfare

Re F (a child: adjournment) [2021] EWCA Civ 469, [2021] 2 FCR 341, [14]–[15] (Peter Jackson LJ)

[14] The decision not to adjourn the trial was a case management decision. In *Re A (children) (remote hearing: care and placement orders)* [2020] EWCA Civ 583, [2020] 2 FCR 245, [2020] 1 WLR 4931 at [3], this court emphasised, in the context of remote hearings, that:

> 'The decision whether to conduct a remote hearing, and the means by which each individual case may be heard, are a matter for the judge or magistrate who is to conduct the hearing. It is a case management decision over which the first instance court will have a wide discretion, based on the ordinary principles of fairness, justice and the need to

4 Special guardianship order.

promote the welfare of the subject child or children. An appeal is only likely to succeed where a particular decision falls outside the range of reasonable ways of proceeding that were open to the court and is, therefore, held to be wrong.'

[15] Applying that standard, the Judge's decision was in my view wrong, for the following reasons:

(1) The court's first task was to get its legal bearings. The welfare paramountcy principle under subsection 1(1) of the Children Act 1989 applies when a court determines any question with respect to the upbringing of a child. It does not apply to case management decisions. The touchstone for case management decisions is justice, not welfare, though in a family case welfare plays an important part in the assessment. That is made clear by the terms of the overriding objective in r 1 of the Family Procedure Rules 2010, which requires the court to deal with a case *justly, having regard to any welfare issues involved.* That includes *ensuring that it is dealt with expeditiously and fairly*. (The delay principle under s 1(2) Children Act 1989 does apply to case management decisions, as of course does the 26-week timetable set by s 32 for disposing of an application for a care order.) In the present case, it is unclear whether the Judge was influenced by incorrect submissions about the welfare principle, but he did not state that he was applying a test of fairness, or indeed what test he was applying.

(2) The Equal Treatment Bench Book, whose most recent edition was published in February 2021, is the product of serious thought about fairness in the conduct of legal proceedings. It is written by judges for judges. Its guidance should be taken into account wherever it is applicable. It was applicable here, and the Judge was squarely referred to it, but he did not mention it. It advises the court to achieve *sensitive listing*. It advises that a woman in the last month of pregnancy *should not be expected to attend a court or tribunal unless she feels able to do so*. Whether that refers to physical attendance or to participation, the Judge should have addressed the fact that his order was not in accordance with the guidance. Instead, he adopted a 'try it and see' approach of the kind that the guidance clearly aims to avoid. It is also there to protect women from the argument, made in this case, that there is no medical evidence of any particular risk to the pregnancy. It was not for the mother to put forward additional medical reasons to justify her request for postponement; if such evidence exists it may add to the picture, but its absence does not weaken the guidance.

(3) The final hearing will be of very considerable importance for this family. It will determine J's future and will very likely influence the future of the unborn child, for whom proceedings are also contemplated. A hearing in these circumstances is bound to be exceptionally stressful for a person in this young mother's position, and her experience of her first pregnancy can only exacerbate

matters. Her evidence will doubtless be significant, and she will face cross-examination. The Local Authority has suggested that she need not attend court in person and that she could give evidence by video link and attend the rest of the hearing 'from the comfort of her own home'. This overlooks the important fact that a party participating in a court hearing remotely is still attending court and should be able to engage fully with the process. The mother is in any event entitled to expect that she could attend for the whole of the hearing in person if she wants, and certainly that she should be able to choose to attend court to give evidence: indeed we are told that the court was willing to accommodate that.

(4) The Judge did not sufficiently grapple with these matters. The difficulty began when the court imposed a date, despite being told of the mother's situation and that of her advocate. At the hearing itself, the starting point was to identify the likely practical arrangements for the hearing, but that did not happen. A general intention to allow breaks in proceedings, whatever their format, does not remedy the position if the hearing should not be taking place at all. Then, no adequate consideration was given to the mother's anxiety, expressed with moderation, at the prospect of having to participate in such a heavy hearing during her last month of pregnancy. Rather than engaging with her concerns, the Judge told her that it would be better for her if the hearing went ahead, and he did not refer to the fact that she would be doing so without her advocate of choice in a case with a long history. The approach taken was that a person in her position could accommodate the court process, provided allowances were made. Ground 1 is made out ...

5.1.6 Case management: active case management: delay: criminal proceedings are not usually good reason

Re H (children) [2006] EWCA Civ 1875, [14]–[15] (Ward LJ)

14. ... In answering the question which trial should come first the judge reminded himself of the case of *Re TB (Care Proceedings: Criminal Trial)* [1995] FLR 801. I need not cite at great length from that case. He did so in his judgment drawing particularly upon the observations of Butler Sloss LJ at page 804:

> 'Each case has to be seen on its own facts and considered on its own merits, and the welfare of the child has to take priority over the detriment to the family coming up for trial. The detriment to the family of having to face criminal proceedings and care proceedings and to have a trial run, as they might see it, in the care court, is not in itself a reason for delaying care proceedings. There will be cases where it is right, in the interests of the children, that the care proceedings are delayed for the outcome of the criminal proceedings. It is a relevant but not determining factor in considering the welfare

> of children that they should have parents whose case is properly tried and who would not have been put at risk in the criminal trial for some particular reason that may come out in the care proceedings. But the issue of delay is all important.'

The general rule was stated by my lady to be this at page 805:

> 'One starts with the fact that the criminal proceedings of themselves are not a reason to adjourn the care proceedings. There must be some detriment to the children in the broadest terms for not bringing on the care proceedings because delay is detrimental generally to the children.'

She added that:

> 'I think we do have to hold the line that in the majority of cases, unless there are circumstances which warrant taking a different course, that the care proceedings should come on, even if they are to be heard before the criminal proceedings.'

15. That general approach has been consistently applied as the judge pointed out more recently in the case of *R v L* [2006] EWCA 1902 (Crim), [2006] 1 WLR 3092, where in the Criminal Division of this court the President of the Queen's Bench Division, Sir Igor Judge, sitting unusually with the President of the Family Division, endorsed the general rule that ordinarily care proceedings should come first. HHJ Cryan did not follow that general rule. …

5.1.7 Case management: active case management: experts

See Chapter 8.1 Experts: obtaining evidence

5.1.8 Case management: active case management: fact-finding

See Chapter 3.3 Threshold criteria: fact-finding: case management

5.1.9 Case management: pandemic restrictions

Lancashire County Council v M and others [2020] EWFC 43, [2021] 1 FLR 138, [1], [28]–[46] (MacDonald J) *quotation limited to* [1], [30], [45]–[46]

1. The COVID-19 pandemic has resulted in a temporary but fundamental shift in the manner in which the Family Court and the Family Division of the High Court hear and determine family cases. Namely, a very marked increase in the use of remote hearings conducted by means of electronic communications platforms. That temporary shift has resulted in the court having to consider, in each case, whether that case is suitable for a remote or, increasingly commonly, a hybrid hearing (whereby certain parties and / or their lawyers attend the court building while others attend the hearing

by remote means) or whether the case should be adjourned for what may be an extended period until a fully face to face hearing can be achieved. That, to an extent, is the question in this case.

…

30. With respect to the authorities and guidance dealing with the application of these cardinal statutory and procedural principles in the context of the COVID-19 pandemic, the approach taken has evolved over time as the courts have gained experience and understanding of the suitability or otherwise of remote hearings in particular cases and of the nature and likely duration of the ongoing impact of the public health emergency on the family justice system has become clearer. In particular, I am satisfied that the factors to be taken into account today when considering whether to adjourn for a face to face hearing or to hold a remote or hybrid hearing have further developed when compared to the approach taken the very beginning of the public health crisis in March and April of this year. Within this context, it is important to summarise briefly the evolution of the principles applicable to the determination of the question now before the court.

…

45. As Mr Storey articulated during the course of his submissions, since March the relevant principles and guidance applicable to determining the question of whether to hold a remote or, now more commonly, a hybrid hearing or to adjourn to await a fully face to face hearing have necessarily evolved as the understanding of the nature, extent and likely future impact of the COVID-19 pandemic has evolved, as acknowledged in the President's document *The Family Court and COVID-19: The Road Ahead*. Within this context, having regard to the statutory provisions, procedural rules, case law and guidance summarised above, I am satisfied that the following factors inform the question of whether, in a given case, a hearing should be conducted by way of a remote hearing or a hybrid hearing or adjourned for a fully face to face hearing at a later date:
    i) The welfare of the subject child or children;
    ii) The statutory duty to have regard to the general principle that delay in determining the question is likely to prejudice the welfare of the child;
    iii) The requirement to deal with cases justly, having regard to the welfare issues involved;
    iv) The extent to which a remote or hybrid hearing will provide the judge with a proper basis upon which to make a full judgment;
    v) The steps that can be taken to reduce the potential for unfairness by enabling the cases to proceed fairly when previously it may have been adjourned, having regard in particular to the need to make every effort to accommodate and enhance the ability of lay parties to engage fully in the remote or hybrid process, including the extent to which it is possible to arrange for a lay party to engage with that process from a location other than their home where they can be

supported by at least one member of their legal team and, where appropriate, any interpreter or intermediary;

vi) The impact of the COVID-19 pandemic on the likely timescales for a fully face to face hearing in preference to a remote or hybrid hearing and the need to evaluate any potential unfairness against that timescale;

vii) The statutory requirement that all public law children cases are to be completed within 26 weeks and that any extension to the 26 week timetable must be necessary to enable the court to resolve the proceedings justly;

viii) The requirement, so far as is practicable, to allot to the case an appropriate share of the court's resources, while taking into account the need to allot resources to other cases, evaluated in the context of the limitations placed by the COVID-19 pandemic on the resources currently available to give effect to fully face to face hearings; and

ix) The individual circumstances of the particular case and the parties, including but not limited to:

- a) Whether the parties consent to or oppose a remote or hybrid hearing;
- b) The importance and nature of the issue to be determined bearing in mind that parties appearing before the court should expect the issues to be limited only to those which it is necessary to determine to dispose of the case, and for oral evidence or oral submissions to be limited to that which it is necessary for the court to hear;
- c) Whether there is a special need for urgency, or whether the decision could await a later hearing without causing significant disadvantage to the child or the other parties;
- d) Whether the parties are legally represented;
- e) The ability, or otherwise, of any lay party (particularly a parent or person with parental responsibility) to engage with and follow remote proceedings meaningfully, including access to and familiarity with the necessary technology, funding, intelligence/personality issues, language, ability to instruct their lawyers (both before and during the hearing) and other matters;
- f) Whether evidence is to be heard or whether the case will proceed on the basis of submissions only;
- g) The source of any evidence that is to be adduced and assimilated by the court. For example, whether the evidence is written or oral, given by a professional or lay witness, contested or uncontested, or factual or expert evidence;
- h) The scope and scale of the proposed hearing;
- i) The available technology. A telephone hearing is likely to be a less effective medium than using video;
- j) The experience and confidence of the court and those appearing before the court in the conduct of remote hearings using the proposed technology;

k) Any 'Covid-safe' alternatives that may be available for some or all of the participants to take part in the court hearing by physical attendance in a courtroom before the judge;

l) Any other factors idiosyncratic to the particular case.

46. Whilst each decision will be fact specific and will fall to be determined having regard to these and possibly other factors, it is clear from the signposts set out in *The Family Court and COVID-19: The Road Ahead* that adjourning cases indefinitely or for a period of many months will not be a viable option and that adjourning a case to await a fully face to face hearing is unlikely to be a proper course where an effective and fair remote or hybrid hearing can be held with steps taken to maximise the fairness of that remote or hybrid process.

See also *Re A (children) (remote hearing: care and placement orders)* [2020] EWCA Civ 583, [2020] 2 FCR 245, [2]–[9] (Sir Andrew McFarlane P) addressing a related point (establishing the original guidance during the pandemic restrictions)

See also *Re B* (children) (remote hearing: interim care order) [2020] EWCA Civ 584, [2020] 2 FLR 330, [2]–[4] (Sir Andrew McFarlane P) considering *Re A (children) (remote hearing: care and placement orders)* [2020] EWCA Civ 583, [2020] 2 FCR 245, addressing a related point (that the principles of substantive law and procedural fairness remain unchanged by pandemic restrictions)

See also *Re C (children: Covid-19: representation)* [2020] EWCA Civ 734, [2020] 3 FCR 333, [22]–[25] (Peter Jackson LJ) addressing a related point (the physical attendance of leading counsel and its interplay with the right to a fair trial)

See also *Re B (children) (remote hearing: interim care order)* [2020] EWCA Civ 584, [2020] 2 FLR 330, [4]–[5], [35] (Sir Andrew McFarlane P) addressing a related point (the use of video link as opposed to telephone for urgent removal cases)

5.1.10 Case management: active case management: withdrawal of applications

GC v A County Council and others [2020] EWCA Civ 848, [2021] 1 FCR 561, [16]–[20] (Baker LJ)

The law

[16] Under r 29.4(2) of the Family Procedure Rules 2010, a local authority may only withdraw an application for a care order with the permission of the court. This requirement has been in force (in an earlier incarnation in the Family Proceedings Rules 1991 now repealed) since the implementation of the Children Act 1989. We were only referred to one case in which the provision has been considered by this Court, in the early days of the Act – *Re DB and CB (minors); London Borough of Southwark v B* [1993] 2 FCR 607, [1993] 2 FLR 559 in which at page 573 Waite LJ set out the following approach:

> 'The paramount consideration for any court dealing with [an application to withdraw care proceedings] is accordingly the question whether the withdrawal of the care proceedings will promote or conflict with the welfare of the child concerned. It is not to be assumed, when determining that question, that every child who is made the subject of care proceedings derives an automatic advantage from having them continued. There is no advantage to any child in being maintained as the subject of proceedings that have become redundant in purpose or ineffective in result. It is a matter of looking at each case to see whether there is some solid advantage to the child to be derived from continuing the proceedings.'

This approach is consistent with s 1(5) of the Act, which provides that:

> 'where a court is considering whether or not to make one or more orders under this Act with respect to a child, it shall not make the order or any of the orders unless it considers that doing so would be better for the child than making no order at all.'

[17] Since then, the provision has been considered by judges of the Family Division in a number of cases at first instance, in particular in *A County Council v DP and others* [2005] EWHC 1593 (Fam), [2005] 2 FLR 1031 (McFarlane J, as he then was), *Redbridge London Borough Council v B and C and A* [2011] EWHC 517 (Fam), [2011] 2 FLR 117 (Hedley J), *Re J, A, M and X (children)* [2013] EWHC 4648 (Fam) (Cobb J), and *A Local Authority v X, Y and Z (permission to withdraw)* [2017] EWHC 3741 (Fam), [2018] 2 FLR 1121 (MacDonald J). The latter three cases were decided following the implementation of the Family Procedure Rules 2010 which, unlike their predecessors, include the overriding objective in r 1.1.

[18] For my part, I would endorse the approach evolved in these first instance decisions, which can be summarised as follows.

[19] As identified by Hedley J in the *Redbridge* case, applications to withdraw care proceedings will fall into two categories. In the first, the local authority will be unable to satisfy the threshold criteria for making a care or supervision order under s 31(2) of the Act. In such cases, the application must succeed. But for cases to fall into this first category, the inability to satisfy the criteria must, in the words of Cobb J in *Re J, A, M and X (children)*, be 'obvious'.

[20] In the second category, there will be cases where on the evidence it is possible for the local authority to satisfy the threshold criteria. In those circumstances, an application to withdraw the proceedings must be determined by considering (1) whether withdrawal of the care proceedings will promote or conflict with the welfare of the child concerned, and (2) the overriding objective under the Family Procedure Rules. The relevant factors will include those identified by McFarlane J in *A County Council v DP* which, having regard to the paramountcy of the child's welfare and the overriding objective in the FPR, can be restated in these terms:

(a) the necessity of the investigation and the relevance of the potential result to the future care plans for the child;
(b) the obligation to deal with cases justly;
(c) whether the hearing would be proportionate to the nature, importance and complexity of the issues;
(d) the prospects of a fair trial of the issues and the impact of any fact-finding process on other parties;
(e) the time the investigation would take and the likely cost to public funds.

M (Children) v Wiltshire Council and others [2020] EWCA Civ 1717, [2021] 2 FCR 242, [36]–[40] (Macur LJ) *quotation limited to* [36]–[37], [40]

[36] There is common ground between all parties as to the relevant law to be applied in respect of applications for the withdrawal of care proceedings. The relevant principles to be applied have been summarised in several first instance decisions, invariably including reference to the decision of MacFarlane J (as he then was) in *A County Council v DP, RS, BS (by the children's guardian)* [2005] EWHC 1593 (Fam), [2005] 2 FLR 1031 which lists the relevant factors that the judge should consider when the s 31 Children Act 1989 threshold criteria may otherwise be established. Most recently, Baker LJ in *Re GC (a child) (withdrawal of care proceedings)* [2020] EWCA Civ 848, [2020] 4 WLR 92, [2020] 2 FLR 1151, [16]–[20], has reviewed and restated the applicable principles. If in the relevant case the threshold criteria might be established then these may be summarised to be judicial consideration of the necessity of the investigation and the relevance of the potential result to the future care plans for the child; the obligation to deal with cases justly; whether the proceedings would be proportionate to the nature, importance and complexity of the issues; the prospects of a fair trial of the issues and the impact of any fact-finding process on other parties; and, the time the investigation would take and the likely cost to public funds.

[37] I gratefully adopt Baker LJ's clear exposition of the same, which renders repetition otiose. However, additionally I would endorse the comments made by MacDonald J in *A Local Authority v X, Y and Z (permission to withdraw)* [2017] EWHC 3741 (Fam), [2018] 2 FLR 1121 @ [53], referring to the decision of Cobb J in *J, A, M and X (children)* [2013] EWHC 4648 (Fam), to the effect that the court considering such an application must adopt an objective and dispassionate approach, regardless of the 'emotive' subject matter in prospect. That is, the nature of the harm that has befallen the subject child cannot by itself be determinative of the outcome of withdrawal proceedings, however serious it may be. Likewise, evidential complexity alone should not be determinative of outcome if forensic scrutiny could reasonably establish the relevant facts upon which to determine welfare considerations, whether by reason of positive or negative 'threshold' findings.

…

[40] Equally, it should be recognised that a local authority is under a continuing duty to review the evidence in the case and to take decisions which may appear incongruent to the uninformed observer in light of the nature of the apparent significant harm that has befallen the subject child and which led to the institution of care proceedings. Whilst the application is subject to court scrutiny in accordance with FPR 29, Pt 4, it is nevertheless a difficult, important, and significant decision for a local authority to take and will not be undertaken lightly. In this case, and particularly in light of the conclusion I reach, I think it right to record that the application was obviously made in good faith after anxious, although in my view inexact, scrutiny of the evidence.

See also *A County Council v DP and others* [2005] EWHC 1593 (Fam), [2005] 2 FLR 1031, [18]–[19] (McFarlane J) addressing the same point (confirming that the Court's role is not one of a 'neutered 'rubber stamp')

5.2 CASE MANAGEMENT: COMPLIANCE

5.2.1 Case management: compliance: no amending timetables without permission

Re W (children) [2014] EWFC 22, [2015] 1 FLR 1092, [18]–[19] (Sir James Munby P)

18. I am aware that a recent amendment to CPR 3.8, inserting a new paragraph (4), permits this in civil cases:

> '(3) Where a rule, practice direction or court order –
> (a) requires a party to do something within a specified time, and
> (b) specifies the consequence of failure to comply,
>
> the time for doing the act in question may not be extended by agreement between the parties except as provided in paragraph (4).
>
> (4) In the circumstances referred to in paragraph (3) and unless the court orders otherwise, the time for doing the act in question may be extended by prior written agreement of the parties for up to a maximum of 28 days, provided always that any such extension does not put at risk any hearing date.'

There is no such provision in the Family Procedure Rules, and for good reason. Indeed, such agreements are forbidden by FPR 4.5(3):

> 'Where a rule, practice direction or court order –
> (a) requires a party to do something within a specified time; and
> (b) specifies the consequence of failure to comply,
>
> the time for doing the act in question may not be extended by agreement between the parties.'

In accordance with and deriving from the court's powers under FPR 12.24, the standard form of case management order, use of which is mandatory, spells out (as did Judge Rutherford's order in this case) the consequence of failure to comply, namely the obligation on every party to 'immediately inform the Court if any party or person fails to comply with any part of this order.'

19. I repeat what I said in *In re W*. I emphasise that the parties in cases in the Family Court are *not* permitted to amend a timetable fixed by the court without the *prior* approval of the court. I emphasise the obligation on every party, spelt out (as in this case) in the standard form of case management order, to inform the Court 'immediately' in the event of any non-compliance. That obligation is imposed for good reason, though too often, as in the present case, it also is not complied with.

See also *London Borough of Redbridge v A and others* [2016] EWHC 2627 (Fam), [11]–[12] (MacDonald J) considering *Re W (children)* [2014] EWFC 22, [2015] 1 FLR 1092, providing an overview of the law on a related point (non-compliance)

5.2.2 Case management: compliance: compliance with orders is mandatory

Re W (a child) (adoption: leave to oppose); Re H (children) (adoption: leave to oppose) [2013] EWCA Civ 1177, [2014] 1 FCR 191, [50]–[54] (Sir James Munby P)

[50] That the parents and their representatives should have been put in this position is quite deplorable. It is, unhappily, symptomatic of a deeply rooted culture in the family courts which, however long established, will no longer be tolerated. It is something of which I complained almost thirteen years ago: see *Re S (a child) (ex parte orders)* [2000] 3 FCR 706, [2001] 1 All ER 362. Perhaps what I say as President will carry more weight than what I said when the junior puisne.

[51] I refer to the slapdash, lackadaisical and on occasions almost contumelious attitude which still far too frequently characterises the response to orders made by family courts. There is simply no excuse for this. Orders, including interlocutory orders, must be obeyed and complied with *to the letter* and *on time*. Too often they are not. They are not preferences, requests or mere indications; they are orders: see *Re W (a child) (care proceedings: welfare evaluation)* [2013] EWCA Civ 1227 at [74], [2013] All ER (D) 122 (Oct) at [74].

[52] The law is clear. As Romer LJ said in *Hadkinson v Hadkinson* [1952] 2 All ER 567 at 569, [1952] P 285 at 288, in a passage endorsed by the Privy Council in *Isaacs v Robertson* [1984] 3 All ER 140 at 142, [1985] AC 97 at 101:

> 'It is the plain and unqualified obligation of every person against, or in respect of, whom an order is made by a court of competent jurisdiction, to obey it unless and until that order is discharged. The uncompromising nature of this obligation is shown by the fact that it

extends even to cases where the person affected by an order believes it to be irregular or even void.'

For present purposes that principle applies as much to orders by way of interlocutory case management directions as to any other species of order. The court is entitled to expect—and from now on family courts will demand—strict compliance with all such orders. Non-compliance with orders should be expected to have and will usually have a consequence.

[53] Let me spell it out. An order that something is to be done by 4 pm on Friday, is an order to do that thing by 4 pm on Friday, not by 4.21 pm on Friday let alone by 3.01 pm the following Monday or sometime later the following week. A person who finds himself unable to comply timeously with his obligations under an order should apply for an extension of time *before the time for compliance has expired.* It is simply not acceptable to put forward as an explanation for non-compliance with an order the burden of other work. If the time allowed for compliance with an order turns out to be inadequate the remedy is either to apply to the court for an extension of time or to pass the task to someone else who has available the time in which to do it.

[54] Non-compliance with an order, any order, by anyone is bad enough. It is a particularly serious matter if the defaulter is a public body such as a local authority. And it is also a particularly serious matter if the order goes to something as vitally important as Judge Barclay's order did in this case: the right of a parent facing the permanent loss of their child to know what case is being mounted against them by a public authority.

See also *London Borough of Redbridge v A and others* [2016] EWHC 2627 (Fam), [11]–[12] (MacDonald J) addressing the same point

See also London Borough of Bexley v V and others [2014] EWHC 2187 (Fam), [5]–[8] (Keehan J) considering *Re W (a child) (adoption: leave to oppose); Re H (children) (adoption: leave to oppose)* [2013] EWCA Civ 1177, [2014] 1 FCR 191

See also *Re H (a child) (analysis of realistic options and SGOs)* [2015] EWCA Civ 406, [2016] 1 FLR 286, [33] (Ryder LJ) addressing a related point (the possible impact of casual non-compliance)

5.2.3 Case management: compliance: repercussions for non-compliance

Re L (a child) [2015] EWFC 15, [2015] 1 FLR 1417, [8]–[25] (Sir James Munby P) *quotation limited to* [23]–[25]

23. This endemic failure of the professions to comply with PD27A must end, and it must end now. *Fifteen years* of default are enough. From now on:

    i) Defaulters can have no complaint if they are exposed, and they should expect to be exposed, to public condemnation in judgments in which they are named.

ii) Defaulters may find themselves exposed to financial penalties of the kind referred to by Mostyn J in *J v J*.

iii) Defaulters may find themselves exposed to the sanction meted out by Holman J in *Seagrove v Sullivan*.

The professions need to recognise that enough is enough. It is no use the court continuing feebly to issue empty threats. From now on delinquents can expect to find themselves subject to effective sanctions, including but not limited to those I have already mentioned. If, despite this final wake-up call, matters do not improve I may be driven to consider setting up the special delinquents' court suggested by Mostyn J.

24. I make clear that PD27A has nothing to do with judicial *amour-propre*, nor is its purpose to make the lives of the judges easier. On the contrary, as I observed in *Re X and Y*, it is simply a reflection of the ever increasing burdens being imposed upon judges at all levels in the family justice system. I continued (paras 5-6):

> '5 … The purpose of all this is to ensure that the judge can embark upon the necessary pre-reading in a structured and focused way, making the best and most efficient use of limited time, so that when the case is actually called on in court everyone can proceed immediately to the heart of the matter, without the need for any substantial opening and with everyone focusing upon the previously identified issues. The objective is to shorten the length of hearings and thereby to increase the 'throughput' of the family courts – with the ultimate objective of bringing down waiting times and reducing delay.
>
> 6 But these wholly desirable objects – wholly desirable in the public interest and in the interests of litigants generally – are imperilled whenever there is significant non-compliance with the Practice Direction …'

25. The judges of the Family Division and the Family Court have had enough. The professions have been warned.

5.3 CASE MANAGEMENT: INTERNATIONAL ISSUES

5.3.1 Case management: international issues: all issues

See Chapter 6 International issues

5.4 CASE MANAGEMENT: CHILDREN

5.4.1 Case management: children: children giving evidence: proper approach

Re W (children) (abuse: oral evidence) [2010] UKSC 12, [2010] 1 FCR 615, [22]–[28], [30]–[31] (Lady Hale)

[22] However tempting it may be to leave the issue until it has received the expert scrutiny of a multi-disciplinary committee, we are satisfied that

we cannot do so. The existing law erects a presumption against a child giving evidence which requires to be rebutted by anyone seeking to put questions to the child. That cannot be reconciled with the approach of the European Court of Human Rights, which always aims to strike a fair balance between competing Convention rights. Article 6 requires that the proceedings overall be fair and this normally entails an opportunity to challenge the evidence presented by the other side. But even in criminal proceedings account must be taken of the art 8 rights of the perceived victim (see *SN v Sweden* (2002) 39 EHRR 304). Striking that balance in care proceedings may well mean that the child should not be called to give evidence in the great majority of cases, but that is a result and not a presumption or even a starting point.

[23] The object of the proceedings is to achieve a fair trial in the determination of the rights of all the people involved. Children are harmed if they are taken away from their families for no good reason. Children are harmed if they are left in abusive families. This means that the court must admit all the evidence which bears upon the relevant questions: whether the threshold criteria justifying state intervention have been proved; if they have, what action if any will be in the best interests of the child? The court cannot ignore relevant evidence just because other evidence might have been better. It will have to do the best it can on what it has.

[24] When the court is considering whether a particular child should be called as a witness, the court will have to weigh two considerations: the advantages that that will bring to the determination of the truth and the damage it may do to the welfare of this or any other child. A fair trial is a trial which is fair in the light of the issues which have to be decided. Mr Geekie accepts that the welfare of the child is also a relevant consideration, albeit not the paramount consideration in this respect. He is right to do so, because the object of the proceedings is to promote the welfare of this and other children. The hearing cannot be fair to them unless their interests are given great weight.

[25] In weighing the advantages that calling the child to give evidence may bring to the fair and accurate determination of the case, the court will have to look at several factors. One will be the issues it has to decide in order properly to determine the case. Sometimes it may be possible to decide the case without making findings on particular allegations. Another will be the quality of the evidence it already has. Sometimes there may be enough evidence to make the findings needed whether or not the child is cross-examined. Sometimes there will be nothing useful to be gained from the child's oral evidence. The case is built upon a web of behaviour, drawings, stray remarks, injuries and the like, and not upon concrete allegations voiced by the child. The quality of any ABE interview will also be an important factor, as will be the nature of any challenge which the party may wish to make. The court is unlikely to be helped by generalised accusations of lying, or by a fishing expedition in which the child is taken slowly through the story yet again in the hope that something will turn

up, or by a cross-examination which is designed to intimidate the child and pave the way for accusations of inconsistency in a future criminal trial. On the other hand, focused questions which put forward a different explanation for certain events may help the court to do justice between the parties. Also relevant will be the age and maturity of the child and the length of time since the events in question, for these will have a bearing on whether an account now can be as reliable as a near contemporaneous account, especially if given in a well-conducted ABE interview.

[26] The age and maturity of the child, along with the length of time since the events in question, will also be relevant to the second part of the inquiry, which is the risk of harm to the child. Further specific factors may be the support which the child has from family or other sources, or the lack of it, the child's own wishes and feelings about giving evidence, and the views of the child's guardian and, where appropriate, those with parental responsibility. We indorse the view that an unwilling child should rarely, if ever, be obliged to give evidence. The risk of further delay to the proceedings is also a factor: there is a general principle that delay in determining any question about a child's upbringing is likely to prejudice his welfare (see s 1(2) of the Children Act 1989). There may also be specific risks of harm to this particular child. Where there are parallel criminal proceedings, the likelihood of the child having to give evidence twice may increase the risk of harm. The parent may be seeking to put his child through this ordeal in order to strengthen his hand in the criminal proceedings rather than to enable the family court to get at the truth. On the other hand, as the family court has to give less weight to the evidence of a child because she has not been called, then that may be damaging too. However, the court is entitled to have regard to the general evidence of the harm which giving evidence may do to children, as well as to any features which are particular to this child and this case. That risk of harm is an ever-present feature to which, on the present evidence, the court must give great weight. The risk, and therefore the weight, may vary from case to case, but the court must always take it into account and does not need expert evidence in order to do so.

[27] But on both sides of the equation, the court must factor in what steps can be taken to improve the quality of the child's evidence and at the same time to decrease the risk of harm to the child. These two aims are not in opposition to one another. The whole premise of *Achieving Best Evidence* and the special measures in criminal cases is that this will improve rather than diminish the quality of the evidence to the court. It does not assume that the most reliable account of any incident is one made from recollection months or years later in the stressful conditions of a courtroom. Nor does it assume that an 'Old Bailey style' cross-examination is the best way of testing that evidence. It may be the best way of casting doubt upon it in the eyes of a jury but that is another matter. A family court would have to be astute both to protect the child from the harmful and destructive effects of questioning and also to evaluate the answers in the light of the child's stage of development.

[28] The family court will have to be realistic in evaluating how effective it can be in maximising the advantage while minimising the harm. There are things that the court can do but they are not things that it is used to doing at present. It is not limited by the usual courtroom procedures or to applying the special measures by analogy. The important thing is that the questions which challenge the child's account are fairly put to the child so that she can answer them, not that counsel should be able to question her directly. One possibility is an early video'd cross-examination as proposed by Pigot. Another is cross-examination via video-link. But another is putting the required questions to her through an intermediary. This could be the court itself, as would be common in continental Europe and used to be much more common than it is now in the courts of this country.

...

[30] It will be seen that these considerations are simply an amplification of those outlined by Smith LJ in *Re M (a child) (care proceedings: witness summons)* [2007] 1 FCR 253 at [45], [2007] 1 FLR 1698), but without the starting point (at [44]). The essential test is whether justice can be done to all the parties without further questioning of the child. Our prediction is that, if the court is called upon to do it, the consequence of the balancing exercise will usually be that the additional benefits to the court's task in calling the child do not outweigh the additional harm that it will do to the child. A wise parent with his child's interests truly at heart will understand that too. But rarity should be a consequence of the exercise rather than a threshold test (as in *Huang v Secretary of State for the Home Dept, Kasmiri v Secretary of State for the Home Dept* [2007] UKHL 11 at [20], [2007] 4 All ER 15 at [20], [2007] 2 AC 167).

[31] Finally, we would indorse the suggestion made by Miss Branigan QC for the child's guardian, that the issue should be addressed at the case management conference in care proceedings or the earliest directions hearing in private law proceedings. It should not be left to the party to raise. This is not, however, an invitation to elaborate consideration of what will usually be a non-issue.

See also *Re R (children)* [2015] EWCA Civ 167, [11]–[15] (King LJ), [33]–[36] (Briggs LJ) considering *Re W (children) (abuse: oral evidence)* [2010] UKSC 12, [2010] 1 FCR 615

5.4.2 Case management: children: children giving evidence: meaningful engagement with *Re W*

Re E (a child) [2016] EWCA Civ 473, [2016] 3 FCR 499, [56]–[63] (McFarlane LJ)

Children giving evidence: discussion

[56] It is of note that, despite the passage of some six years since the Supreme Court decision in *Re W*, this court has been told that the previous culture

and practice of the family courts remains largely unchanged with the previous presumption against children giving evidence remaining intact. That state of affairs is plainly contrary to the binding decision of the Supreme Court which was that such a presumption is contrary to Article 6 of the European Convention on Human Rights.

[57] In any case where the issue of children giving oral evidence is raised it is necessary for the court to engage with the factors identified by Baroness Hale in *Re W*, together with any other factors that are relevant to the particular child or the individual case, before coming to a reasoned and considered conclusion on the issue.

[58] It is crucial that any issue as to a child giving evidence is raised and determined at the earliest stage, and in any event well before the planned trial date. The court will not, however, be in a position to come to a conclusion on that issue unless it has undertaken an evaluation of the evidence which is otherwise available. Where there has been an ABE interview, and the quality and/or content of that interview are to be challenged, it is likely that the judge will have to view the DVD before being in a position to decide the *Re W* issue.

[59] The court should also have regard to the *Working Party of the Family Justice Council Guidelines on the issue of Children Giving Evidence in Family Proceedings* issued in December 2011 [2012] Fam Law 79. The *Guidelines*, which were specifically developed to assist courts following the decision in *Re W*, contain a list of no less than 21 factors to which the court should have regard when determining whether a child should give oral evidence in the context of the principal objective of achieving a fair trial (paragraph 9(a) to (v)). The *Guidelines* require the court to carry out a balancing exercise 'between the following primary considerations:

i) the possible advantages that the child being called will bring to the determination of truth balanced against;
ii) the possible damage to the child's welfare from giving evidence i.e. the risk of harm to the child from giving evidence.'

[60] Whilst not all of the elements described by Baroness Hale in *Re W* or in paragraph 9 of the *Guidelines* will be relevant in every case, it is plain that the court undertaking a *Re W* determination will need to engage in a relatively full and sophisticated evaluation of the relevant factors; simply paying lip-service to *Re W* is not acceptable. By 'full' I do not wish to suggest that a lengthy judgment is required, but simply that the judge must consider each of the relevant points with that process recorded in short-form in a judgment. Such a detailed process is in my view justified given the importance of the decision for the welfare of the child and for the fairness of hearing.

[61] It is plainly good practice for the court to be furnished with a written report from the children's guardian and submissions on behalf of the child before deciding whether that child should be called as a witness. This court understands that it is, however, common-place for guardians

to advise that the child should not be called to give evidence on the basis that they will or may suffer emotional harm as a result of doing so. Where such advice is based upon the consideration of harm alone, it is unlikely to be of great assistance to the court which is required to consider not only 'harm' but also the other side of the balance described in the *Guidelines*, namely the possible advantages that the child's testimony will bring to the determination of truth.

[62] Part of any consideration of the overall welfare of a child must be that decisions as to his or her future, or the future of other children, are based, so far as is possible, upon a true understanding of important past events. Whilst the process of giving oral evidence in relation to allegations of past harmful experiences will almost always be an unwelcome one for any child, and for some that process itself may be positively harmful, those negative factors, to which full and proper weight should be given, are but one half of the balancing equation. In some cases, despite the negative factors, it may nevertheless be in accordance with the wider welfare interests of the child for him or her to be called to give evidence. Each case will be different, but even where the child may suffer some emotional harm from the process, if such harm is likely to be temporary and where the quality and potential reliability of the other evidence in the case is weak, it may (in addition to any fair trial issues) nevertheless be in the child's best interests to give oral evidence. If the ABE interview process is poor, and there is little or no other evidence, then it may be that no findings of fact in accordance with allegations made by a child can properly be made unless the child is called to give evidence. The *Re W* exercise must plainly take account of such a situation.

[63] The observations made in the previous paragraph are intended only to make the point there made; they are not intended to establish any new test or template for decision making over and above what is said in *Re W* and the *Guidelines* to which recourse should be had as a matter of routine in every case where there is a *Re W* application.

See also *Re F* [2016] EWCA Civ 546, [2016] 3 FCR 255, [40]–[41] (Sir James Munby P) addressing the same point

5.4.3 Case management: children: children giving evidence: no right to give evidence

Re P-S (children) (care proceedings: right to give evidence) [2013] EWCA Civ 223, [2013] 2 FCR 299, [22]–[39] (Sir Alan Ward) *quotation limited to* [36]

[36] Nevertheless, in my judgment, it should now be declared that the child does have the former important but limited right, that is to say, a right to be heard in the proceedings. It is apparent from the foregoing that the right to be heard does not specify how the child is to be heard, for the Convention expressly recognises that the voice of the child may be conveyed 'either directly, or through a representative or appropriate body'. Indeed the

guidance at para 43 (General Comment No 12 (2009)) prefers the child being heard under conditions of confidentiality, not in open court. It may be enough that a social worker, ie the CAFCASS officer or guardian hears the views of the child and it does not seem essential that it has to be the judge who hears directly from the child. So, whilst the child must be listened to, there is nothing in the Convention which entitles the child to give evidence to the judge. In my judgment a child has no right to give evidence.

5.4.4 Case management: children: children giving evidence: ABE[5] interviews

See Chapter 7.4 Evidence: children

5.4.5 Case management: children: children meeting judges

Re KP (a child) (abduction: judge meeting child: conduct of interview) [2014] EWCA Civ 554, [2014] 2 FCR 545, [50]–[56] (Moore-Bick LJ) *quotation limited to* [56]

[56] Despite having great respect for this judge, who is highly experienced in the conduct of proceedings where the voice of the child needs to be heard, our conclusion is that on this occasion the conduct of the judicial interview did indeed fall on the wrong side of the line. Having summarised the submissions of Mr Turner and Mr Gupta, with which we agree, we can set out the reasons supporting this conclusion in short terms as follows:

(i) During that part of any meeting between a young person and a judge in which the judge is listening to the child's point of view and hearing what they have to say, the judge's role should be largely that of a passive recipient of whatever communication the young person wishes to transmit.

(ii) The purpose of the meeting is not to obtain evidence and the judge should not, therefore, probe or seek to test whatever it is that the child wishes to say. The meeting is primarily for the benefit of the child, rather than for the benefit of the forensic process by providing additional evidence to the judge. As the *Guidelines* state, the task of gathering evidence is for the specialist CAFCASS officers who have, as Mr Gupta submits, developed an expertise in this field.

(iii) A meeting, such as in the present case, taking place prior to the judge deciding upon the central issues should be for the dual purposes of allowing the judge to hear what the young person may wish to volunteer and for the young person to hear the judge explain the nature of the court process. Whilst not wishing to be prescriptive, and whilst acknowledging that the encounter will proceed at the

5 Achieving Best Evidence in Criminal Proceedings: Guidance on interviewing victims and witnesses and guidance on using special measures (Ministry of Justice, 2011).

pace of the child, which will vary from case to case, it is difficult to envisage circumstances in which such a meeting would last for more than 20 minutes or so.

(iv) If the child volunteers evidence that would or might be relevant to the outcome of the proceedings, the judge should report back to the parties and determine whether, and if so how, that evidence should be adduced.

(v) The process adopted by the judge in the present case, in which she sought to 'probe' K's wishes and feelings, and did so over the course of more than an hour by asking some 87 questions went well beyond the passive role that we have described and, despite the judge's careful self-direction, strayed significantly over the line and into the process of gathering evidence (upon which the judge then relied in coming to her decision).

(vi) In the same manner, the judge was in error in regarding the meeting as being an opportunity for K to make representations or submissions to the judge. The purpose of any judicial meeting is not for the young person to argue their case; it is simply, but importantly, to provide an opportunity for the young person to state whatever it is that they wish to state directly to the judge who is going to decide an important issue in their lives.

See also *Re F* [2016] EWCA Civ 546, [2016] 3 FCR 255, [42]–[44] (Sir James Munby P) considering *Re KP (a child) (abduction: judge meeting child: conduct of interview)* [2014] EWCA Civ 554, [2014] 2 FCR 545

See also *Re P-S (children) (care proceedings: right to give evidence)* [2013] EWCA Civ 223, [2013] 2 FCR 299, [42] (Sir Alan Ward) addressing a related point (urging judges to be 'very cautious' when seeing children in the absence of the other parties)

See also *London Borough of Brent v D and others* [2017] EWHC 2452 (Fam), [2017] 4 WLR 193, [49]–[51] (MacDonald J) addressing a related point (ordinarily, the question of children seeing judges should be raised and determined at IRHs)

5.4.6 Case management: children: children attending courts

Re K (a child) [2011] EWHC 1082 (Fam), [2011] 2 FLR 803, [2]–[21], [33]–[35], [38]–[40] (Peter Jackson J) *quotation limited to* [33]–[36]

33. In the generation that has passed since the decision in Re W, thinking about these issues has undoubtedly evolved. It does not greatly matter whether the evolution has been driven by the Human Rights Act 1998, or whether, as I believe, the two processes have taken place in sympathetic parallel. In either case, in considering child welfare and children's rights we would, I think, give more weight to the potential benefits of greater involvement by children who want to be present when important decisions about their future are made. It can no longer be presumed that attendance in court is likely to be harmful: if this is so, thought must surely first be given to

adapting court procedures to meet children's needs before deciding to exclude them. Nor should children have to prove that their attendance at proceedings about them is in their interests. The starting point should be an open evaluation of the consequences of attendance or non-attendance in terms of the welfare of the child and the court's ability to manage its proceedings fairly.

34. Each case will depend on its own circumstances, but the following factors will generally be relevant:

(1) The age and level of understanding of the child. The claims of children of secondary school age will be stronger than those of primary school age, but what matters is whether the child has a sufficient level of understanding of the decision that the court has to make, and the way it will go about making it.

(2) The nature and strength of the child's wishes. The court will need to consider whether a refusal to allow attendance will create or increase a sense of alienation in the child. A decision made in the child's presence may be one that he or she will find easier to understand, and where necessary respect and obey.

(3) The child's emotional and psychological state. If there is clear evidence, probably in the form of expert advice, that attendance is likely to lead to harmful or unpredictable consequences for the child's emotional condition, the child's wishes may have to be overruled.

(4) The effect of influence from others. The court will be on its guard against signs of manipulation of the child. Special pressure from any quarter may be magnified by attendance and make it inappropriate.

(5) The matters to be discussed. Rule 12.14 requires the court to have regard to these. In proceedings concerning separation from family or placement in secure accommodation, the matters for discussion are of such high importance to the child that an expectation of involvement may be no more than a natural response.

(6) The evidence to be given. Again, the rule also requires the court to have regard to this. In cases where the evidence is likely to be particularly difficult or distressing, or where it concerns matters that the child should be protected from hearing, attendance can be denied on the basis that it will be harmful. In other cases, the evidence will be no more than a rehearsal of what the child already knows.

(7) The child's behaviour. In secure accommodation cases, the risk of fight or flight may be so high as to make attendance unwise. On the other hand, the fact that children in secure accommodation will inevitably have to be guarded cannot in itself be a reason for proceeding in their absence. As to the chance of disruption in court, the safety of other court users must be considered. Children who are in secure accommodation often find their way there after violence at home or at school, and in the secure unit itself. The fact that trouble at court cannot be ruled out will be a factor, but may not be a conclusive reason for refusing attendance. Criminal courts

routinely accommodate people who pose a risk to the public, and family courts are used to dealing with situations of high emotion.

(8) Practical and logistical considerations. These will particularly come into play in secure accommodation cases. There are secure units throughout the country, and a child may be placed a great distance from the relevant court. The length of the journey, the amount of time the child will be out of placement, and the cost of attendance where supervision is required may also inform the decision. However, the court will be slow to refuse to allow a child to attend for such reasons alone, unless it has exhausted possible alternatives. The availability of a video link in or near the placement should at least be considered, consistent with the Public Law Proceedings Guide to Case Management (paragraph 24) which encourages the court to make full use of technology.

(9) The integrity of the proceedings. The court always retains the power to manage proceedings in a way that achieves overall fairness. Other considerations, such as the interests of other parties, may influence decisions about a child's attendance.

35. The above evaluation may well lead to the conclusion that a child of sufficient understanding who wants to attend an important hearing about his or her future should be allowed to do so for at least part of the time, unless there are clear reasons justifying refusal. This situation will most often be found in, but is not limited to, public law proceedings. In cases where attendance at the hearing itself is not thought appropriate, a meeting with the judge is a possible alternative.

36. Secure accommodation applications self-evidently involve deprivation of liberty, and the reasons for refusing a child's request to attend the hearing (which may be found in a high risk of psychological harm to the child) will need to be particularly cogent.

5.4.7 Case management: children: children giving instructions

Re W (a child) [2016] EWCA Civ 1051, [2016] 3 FCR 630, [27], [31]–[36] (Black LJ) *quotation limited to* [27], [36]

[27] The question of whether a child is able, having regard to his or her understanding, to instruct a solicitor must be approached having in mind this acknowledgment of the autonomy of children and of the fact that it can at times be in their interests to play some direct part in the litigation about them. What is sufficient understanding in any given case will depend upon all the facts …

…

[36] Sometimes there will be a clear answer to the question whether the child is able, having regard to his or her understanding, to give their own instructions to a solicitor. In cases of more difficulty, the court will have to take a down to earth approach to determining the issue, avoiding

too sophisticated an examination of the position and recognising that it is unlikely to be desirable (or even possible) to attempt to assemble definitive evidence about the matter at this stage of the proceedings. All will depend upon the individual circumstances of the case and it is impossible to provide a route map to the solution. However, it is worth noting particularly that, given the public funding problems, the judge will have to be sure to take whatever steps are possible to ensure that the child's point of view in relation to separate representation is sufficiently before the court. The judge will expect to be guided by the guardian and by those solicitors who have formed a view as to whether they could accept instructions from the child. Then it will be for the judge to form his or her own view on the material available at that stage in the proceedings, sometimes (but certainly not always) including expert opinion on the question of understanding (see *Re H (a minor) (care proceedings: child's wishes)* (supra) at page 450). Understanding can be affected by all sorts of things, including the age of the child, his or her intelligence, his or her emotional and/or psychological and/or psychiatric and/or physical state, language ability, influence etc. The child will obviously need to comprehend enough of what the case is about (without being expected to display too sophisticated an understanding) and must have the capacity to give his or her own coherent instructions, without being more than usually inconsistent. If the judge requires an expert report to assist in determining the question of understanding, the child should be under no illusions about the importance of keeping the appointment with the expert concerned. It is an opportunity for the child to demonstrate that he or she does have the necessary understanding and there is always a risk that a failure to attend will be taken to show a failure to understand.

Re Z (interim care order) (rev 1) [2020] EWCA Civ 1755, [2021] 2 FCR 689, [45], [47]–[48] (Baker LJ)

[45] The first procedural irregularity concerns Z's competence to give instructions. The laws and rules governing the representation of children in family proceedings are set out in s 41 of the Children Act and Pt 16 of the Family Procedure Rules, including Practice Direction 16A. This is not the place for a lengthy exegesis of the rules which are far from straightforward. For present purposes, the relevant provisions can be summarised as follows.

(1) The law distinguishes between (a) certain types of proceedings ('specified proceedings' under the Children Act and proceedings relating to adoption) in which, under s 41(1) and FPR r 16.3 it is mandatory for the court to appoint a Cafcass officer (or a Welsh family proceedings officer) to act as guardian for a child and (b) other proceedings where (under r 16.4) the court has the power to appoint a guardian if the circumstances require it. Examples of cases which may justify such an appointment are provided in paragraph 7.2 of PD 16A.

(2) Proceedings under s 31 of the Children Act fall into the category of specified proceedings. Proceedings under s 8 of the Act do not.

(3) Although there is considerable overlap between the rules relating to the representation of children in specified and non-specified proceedings, the rules are discrete. Appointment of a guardian in specified proceedings is governed by r 16.3, appointment in non-specified proceedings by r 16.4. Rule 16.6 sets out circumstances in which a child may conduct proceedings without a guardian but those rules do not apply where the child is the subject of and party to specified proceedings: r 16.6(2).

(4) Under s 41(3), in specified proceedings 'where (a) the child concerned is not represented by a solicitor and (b) any of the conditions mentioned in subsection (4) is satisfied, the court may appoint a solicitor to represent him.' The conditions in s 41(4) are that '(a) no officer of [Cafcass] or Welsh family proceedings officer has been appointed for the child; (b) the child has sufficient understanding to instruct a solicitor and wishes to do so; (c) it appears to the court that it would be in the child's best interests for him to be represented by a solicitor.'

(5) In addition, under the rules, in both specified and non-specified proceedings, the child's guardian must appoint a solicitor for the child unless one has already been appointed: PD 16A paragraphs 6.2 and 7.7.

(6) Under r 16.29(2) and (3), a solicitor appointed under s 41(3) or by the guardian under PD16A must represent the child in accordance with instructions from the guardian unless the solicitor considers, having taken into account the guardian's views and any direction given by the court, that the child (a) wishes to give instructions which conflict with those of the guardian and (b) is able, having regard to the child's understanding, to give instructions on the child's own behalf.

(7) Attitudes to the direct participation of children in proceedings have evolved in recent years – see for example the decisions of this Court in *Mabon v Mabon* [2005] EWCA Civ 634, [2005] Fam 366, [2005] 2 FCR 354, *Re F (children)* [2016] EWCA Civ 546, [2016] 3 FCR 255 and *Re W (a child)* [2016] EWCA Civ 1051, [2016] 3 FCR 630, [2017] 1 WLR 1027. In the latter case, Black LJ observed (paragraph [27]) …

(8) At paragraph [36], Black LJ expanded upon the approach to the assessment of the child's understanding in these terms …

(9) It is also important to note the observation of this Court in *Re S (a minor) (independent representation)* [1993] Fam 263, [1993] 2 FCR 1 that 'understanding is not an absolute. It has to be assessed relatively to the issues in the proceedings'

…

[47] There is a further reason for concern in this case to which I alluded during the hearing. Z has a diagnosis of autistic spectrum disorder. In

those circumstances, he falls within the protection of the UN Convention on the Rights of Persons with Disabilities 2006. Under art 13 (1) of the Convention:

> 'States Parties shall ensure effective access to justice for persons with disabilities on an equal basis with others, including through the provision of procedural and age-appropriate accommodations, in order to facilitate their effective role as direct and indirect participants, including as witnesses, in all legal proceedings, including at investigative and other preliminary stages.'

[48] The application of this provision in the context of rules relating to representation in care proceedings was not considered in submissions before us. But it seems to me that there are strong arguments for saying that, in a case where a 15-year-old boy without disabilities would be able to participate directly in court proceedings, it is incumbent on the court and professionals working with a disabled 15-year-old boy to take such steps as may be necessary to facilitate his participation in the proceedings, particularly where the proceedings involve a fundamental question such as his removal from the family home.

See also *CS v SBH* [2019] EWHC 634 (Fam), [2019] 2 FCR 610, [56]–[65] (Williams J) considering *Re W (a child)* [2016] EWCA Civ 1051 (in the context of an appeal)

5.5 CASE MANAGEMENT: NOTICE

5.5.1 Case management: notice: withholding notice to fathers with PR[6]

M v F and others [2011] EWCA Civ 273, [2011] 1 FCR 533, [25] (Longmore LJ), [30]–[45] (Black LJ) *quotation limited to* [25], [30]–[31], [37], [43]–[45]

[25] I agree with Thorpe LJ that this appeal, for which I agree permission should be granted, must be dismissed. I also agree that it would be better for the court not to put itself into any straightjacket such as that suggested at [43] of the judge's judgment, that 'a significant physical risk … must clearly be demonstrated'. It is sufficient to say, as the judge did, that 'a very high degree of exceptionality is required' and that such high degree was not demonstrated in this case.

…

[30] The declarations M sought were wide ranging. Her objective was to ensure that the local authority did not consult F about the child whilst he was looked after by them, to ensure that he was not notified of care and adoption proceedings relating to the child or joined as a party to them, and to ensure that the local authority did not make enquiries of

6 Parental responsibility.

family members when seeking prospective adopters. She also sought a prospective determination (also by way of declaration) that the child's welfare required F's consent to any adoption to be dispensed with.

[31] The decided authorities similarly arise in the context of care and adoption. My Lord, Thorpe LJ, has referred to two of those to which we were taken, namely *Re H (a child) (adoption: disclosure), Re G (a child) (adoption: disclosure)* [2001] 1 FCR 726, [2001] 1 FLR 646 (a decision of the then President of the Family Division, Dame Elizabeth Butler-Sloss P) and *Re B (a child) (parentage: knowledge of proceedings)* [2003] EWCA Civ 1842, [2004] 1 FCR 473, sub nom *Re AB (care proceedings: service on husband ignorant of child's existence)* [2004] 1 FLR 527 (*Re B*) (a decision of the Court of Appeal). We were also referred to *Re X (Care: Notice of Proceedings)* [1996] 3 FCR 91, [1996] 1 FLR 186 (a decision of Stuart White J), *Re C (Care: Consultation with Parents; Not in Child's Best Interests)* [2005] EWHC 3390 (Fam), [2006] 2 FLR 787 and *Bury Metropolitan BC v D, Re D (unborn baby) (birth plan: future harm)* [2009] EWHC 446 (Fam), [2009] 2 FCR 93, [2009] 2 FLR 313. Mostyn J mentions additional authorities in his judgment and there are yet more in the law reports. I will mention only one of them, the Court of Appeal authority of *Re C (a child) (adoption: duty of local authority)* [2007] EWCA Civ 1206, [2007] 3 FCR 659, [2008] Fam 54.

...

[37] The thrust of these cases is, therefore, that the court will not be persuaded to sanction the withholding of information about the existence of a child from that child's parent or to dispense with service on him of proceedings in relation to the child in anything other than exceptional circumstances where there are, as the President put it in *Re H, Re G*, 'strong countervailing factors'.

...

[43] Mr Anelay and Mr Squire accept that 'the starting point is that [F] should know of the existence of his son and should be able to participate in future care and adoption proceedings' and that 'only in an exceptional case should that general rule be overridden'. This realistic position accords with the authorities as I see them. I would observe, in passing, that this approach is also consistent with another strand of authority which includes, notably, the House of Lords decision in *Re D (Minors) (Adoption Reports: Confidentiality)* [1996] AC 593. That case was concerned with whether particular evidence (part of a report of the guardian ad litem) should be disclosed to the mother in contested adoption proceedings but the five principles which Lord Mustill identified as governing that decision are illuminating when considering the more fundamental prior question of whether a parent should be informed of the very existence of the proceedings or even that they have a child. The principles are set out at p 615 of the report. All repay consideration. They culminate in the following:

'5. Non-disclosure should be the exception and not the rule. The court should be rigorous in its examination of the risk and gravity of the feared harm to the child, and should order non-disclosure only when the case for doing so is compelling.'

In *Re X (children) (adoption: confidentiality)* [2002] EWCA Civ 828, [2002] 3 FCR 648, [2002] 2 FLR 476 the Court of Appeal added that the interests of the adult parties may also support non-disclosure in an appropriate case.

[44] The appellant's complaint is that the judge did not just look for exceptional circumstances but proceeded on the basis that only a significant physical risk would do and this was to set the test too high.

[45] I agree that the authorities do not impose a requirement of significant physical risk. Harm and risk come in many guises and, like Thorpe LJ, I would be anxious about attempting to define what may make a case exceptional enough to justify departing from normal principles ...

A Local Authority v M and others [2020] EWHC 2741 (Fam), [2020] 4 WLR 157, [2]–[3], [21]–[32] (MacDonald J) *quotation limited to* [32]

32. Drawing these threads together, in determining the local authority's application for an order dispensing with service of these proceedings on the father, I am satisfied that I should apply the following legal principles in deciding whether to exercise my power to dispense with service of proceedings for an order under the inherent jurisdiction on a father with parental responsibility:

i) The starting point is that a father should be able to participate (in a wide sense) in proceedings concerning his child. The court should start with full participation then consider partial participation and then, only as a device of last resort, the father's exclusion from the proceedings.

ii) The court's task is to identify the nature and extent of the harm in contemplation. The court should be rigorous in its examination of the risk and gravity of the feared harm.

iii) There is no requirement that a significant *physical* risk be demonstrated. Harm and risk comes in many guises.

iv) When evaluating the risk of future harm, there is no minimum requirement. The court must be alert both to the risk and to the magnitude of the consequences should the risk eventuate, and must also consider whether and to what extent that risk can be managed by the court's control of its own processes. The greater the harm the smaller need be the risk.

v) The court is not determining a question with respect to the upbringing of the child so the welfare of the child, whilst an important consideration, is not paramount.

vi) Authorities in the Strasbourg jurisprudence put a high bar on excluding a parent with parental responsibility. In this context, where a parent has parental responsibility or a right to respect for family life under Art 8, a high degree of exceptionality must be demonstrated by strong countervailing factors to justify their exclusion from participation in the proceedings.

vii) It must be remembered that exceptionality is not, in itself, a test or a short cut and a fair balance must be struck between the factors that are present in the individual case.

The Mother v Northumberland County Council and another [2021] EWCA Civ 1221, [12]–[21] (Macur LJ) *quotation limited to* [18]–[21]

18. In *Re A local authority v B (Dispensing with Service)* [2020] EWHC 274, MacDonald J when dealing with an application by the Local Authority to dispense with service of the proceedings seeking a declaration authorising deprivation of his liberty on the father of 17-year-old B helpfully listed the seven legal principles which he said he derived from the authorities and applied in the exercise of his discretion. He listed them in [32] of his judgment. I do not repeat them in their entirety here for they are uncontroversial and readily accessible. As an aside, they appear to me to be equally applicable to a non-party's participation in child care or matrimonial proceedings, but I draw attention to the final two to highlight the point of 'exceptionality'. That is, he said:

> 'vi) Authorities in the Strasbourg jurisprudence put a high bar on excluding a parent with parental responsibility. In this context, where a parent has parental responsibility or a right to respect for family life under Art 8, a high degree of exceptionality must be demonstrated by strong countervailing factors to justify their exclusion from participation in the proceedings.
>
> vii) It must be remembered that exceptionality is not, in itself, a test or a short cut and a fair balance must be struck between the factors that are present in the individual case.'

19. These two last principles are undoubtedly rightly drawn, but I would venture to suggest that unless (vi) is read as necessarily subject to (vii) and the two are seen to ride in tandem, that the question of what is exceptional as opposed to highly exceptional will detract from the essential task of balancing fact specific features in every case. It will become 'the test' or 'the short cut'.

20. The balancing exercise will inevitably reveal that some features are heavily weighted against dispensation of service, for example in the case of a parent with parental responsibility who has established strong family ties with the subject child. But this will not be determinative, for there could be a feature, or accumulation of features, of greater weight to dislodge what should be the default position in all cases where party status would otherwise be assured or a form C6A served. These features may not necessarily relate to physical or psychological harm, and as

the authorities make clear the list of factors is non exhaustive. Different combinations of factors will apply in every case. Different weighting will be merited by the circumstances. It will not be sensible to attempt a comparison of the seriousness of harm by extraction from other cases save in the most general of senses. That which appears objectively minor in comparison to other cases of harm may have greater impact because of other features in the case.

21. I think the judgment *in re X (a Child) (Care Proceedings: Notice to Father without Parental Responsibility)* [2017] 4 WLR 110 which involved a father without parental responsibility and without protection of Article 8 encapsulates the overall position very well. HHJ Bellamy sitting as a High Court Judge said at [46]:

> '46. Each year local authorities issue care proceedings in the Family Court in which the fathers of the children concerned do not have parental responsibility and who, though not parties, are nonetheless entitled to receive a copy of Form C6A. Until they receive Form C6A some fathers are in a state of ignorance about the existence of their child. Others are aware of the existence of the child and of the fact that they are the child's biological father but have thus far shown no interest in the child's life. For the children involved it is important that attempts are made to engage with their birth father and perhaps also his wider family. The starting point must be two-fold. First, that it will normally be in the interests of the child that her birth father should receive a copy of Form C6A thereby enabling him to apply for party status so that he can participate in the proceedings. Second, that the child and her mother should not be put at risk of harm as a result of seeking to engage the father in the proceedings. It is a matter of balance and that is the case whether or not the father is entitled to the protection of Article 8 and Article 6.'

See also *Re B (a child) (parentage: knowledge of proceedings)* [2003] EWCA Civ 1842, [2004] 1 FCR 473, [3], [14], [19] (Thorpe LJ) addressing the same point (in the context of concealing a pregnancy from a husband following an alleged stranger rape)

See also *Re A, B and C (adoption: notification of fathers and relatives)* [2020] EWCA Civ 41, [2020] 2 FCR 567 [45]–[89] (Peter Jackson LJ) providing an overview of the law on this point (in the context of adoption cases), see Chapter 5.5.3 Case management: notice: withholding notice to fathers: adoption case: putative fathers

See also *Re CD (notice of care proceedings to father without parental responsibility)* [2017] EWFC 34, [2017] 4 WLR 110, [21]–[40], [42]–[46] (HHJ Clifford Bellamy sitting as a judge of the High Court) addressing a related point (providing notice to a father without PR, including considering the ECHR[7])

7 Convention for the Protection of Human Rights and Fundamental Freedoms (1950) CETS 5.

5.5.2 Case management: notice: withholding notice to fathers: not formally governed by s 1[8]

Re A, B and C (adoption: notification of fathers and relatives) [2020] EWCA Civ 41, [2020] 2 FCR 567, [82]–[84] (Peter Jackson LJ) *quotation limited to* [82], [84]

Welfare paramountcy?

[82] As noted above, there is uncertainty about whether what I have described as the core principles (welfare paramountcy, the prejudicial effect of delay and the welfare checklists) apply directly to a decision about notifying a father or relatives about the existence of a child or of proceedings. In a sense, not much turns on this: child welfare, prompt decision-making and a comprehensive review of all relevant factors are central to the notification decision, regardless of whether they are directly mandated by statute. Nevertheless, decision-makers are entitled to know whether their decision should place child welfare above everything else or not, and a correct formulation of the principles reduces the risk of error in decisions at the margins.

...

[84] For these reasons I conclude that while child welfare, prompt decision-making and a comprehensive review of every relevant factor, including those mentioned in the checklists, are all central to the notification decision, the decision is not one that is formally governed by the provisions of s 1 of the CA 1989 or of the ACA 2002 and the welfare of the child is not the paramount consideration of the local authority and the court in this context.

5.5.3 Case management: notice: withholding notice to fathers: adoption cases: putative fathers

Re A, B and C (adoption: notification of fathers and relatives) [2020] EWCA Civ 41, [2020] 2 FCR 567, [45]–[89] (Peter Jackson LJ) *quotation limited to* [89]

[89] The principles governing decisions (by local authorities as adoption agencies or by the court) as to whether a putative father or a relative should be informed of the existence of a child who might be adopted can be summarised in this way.

1. The law allows for 'fast-track' adoption with the consent of all those with parental responsibility, so in some cases the mother alone. Where she opposes notification being given to the child's father or relatives her right to respect for her private life is engaged and can only be infringed where it is necessary to do so to protect the interests of others.
2. The profound importance of the adoption decision for the child and potentially for other family members is clearly capable of supplying

8 Children Act 1989, s 1.

a justification for overriding the mother's request. Whether it does so will depend upon the individual circumstances of the case.

3. The decision should be prioritised and the process characterised by urgency and thoroughness.
4. The decision-maker's first task is to establish the facts as clearly as possible, mindful of the often limited and one-sided nature of the information available. The confidential relinquishment of a child for adoption is an unusual event and the reasons for it must be respectfully scrutinised so that the interests of others are protected. In fairness to those other individuals, the account that is given by the person seeking confidentiality cannot be taken at face value. All information that can be discovered without compromising confidentiality should therefore be gathered and a first-hand account from the person seeking confidentiality will normally be sought. The investigation should enable broad conclusions to be drawn about the relative weight to be given to the factors that must inform the decision.
5. Once the facts have been investigated the task is to strike a fair balance between the various interests involved. The welfare of the child is an important factor but it is not the paramount consideration.
6. There is no single test for distinguishing between cases in which notification should and should not be given but the case law shows that these factors will be relevant when reaching a decision:
   (1) *Parental responsibility.* The fact that a father has parental responsibility by marriage or otherwise entitles him to give or withhold consent to adoption and gives him automatic party status in any proceedings that might lead to adoption. Compelling reasons are therefore required before the withholding of notification can be justified.
   (2) *Article 8 rights.* Whether the father, married or unmarried, or the relative have an established or potential family life with the mother or the child, the right to a fair hearing is engaged and strong reasons are required before the withholding of notification can be justified.
   (3) *The substance of the relationships.* Aside from the presence or absence of parental responsibility and of family life rights, an assessment must be made of the substance of the relationship between the parents, the circumstances of the conception, and the significance of relatives. The purpose is to ensure that those who are necessarily silent are given a notional voice so as to identify the possible strengths and weaknesses of any argument that they might make. Put another way, with what degree of objective justification might such a person complain if they later discovered they had been excluded from the decision? The answer will differ as between a father with whom the mother has had a fleeting encounter and one with whom she has had a substantial relationship, and as between members of the extended family who are close to the parents and those who are more distant.

(4) *The likelihood of a family placement being a realistic alternative to adoption.* This is of particular importance to the child's lifelong welfare as it may determine whether or not adoption is necessary. An objective view, going beyond the say-so of the person seeking confidentiality, should be taken about whether a family member may or may not be a potential carer. Where a family placement is unlikely to be worth investigating or where notification may cause significant harm to those notified, this factor will speak in favour of maintaining confidentiality; anything less than that and it will point the other way.

(5) *The physical, psychological or social impact on the mother or on others of notification being given.* Where this would be severe, for example because of fear arising from rape or violence, or because of possible consequences such as ostracism or family breakdown, or because of significant mental health vulnerability, these must weigh heavily in the balancing exercise. On the other hand, excessive weight should not be given to short term difficulties and to less serious situations involving embarrassment or social unpleasantness, otherwise the mother's wish would always prevail at the expense of other interests.

(6) *Cultural and religious factors.* The conception and concealed pregnancy may give rise to particular difficulties in some cultural and religious contexts. These may enhance the risks of notification, but they may also mean that the possibility of maintaining the birth tie through a family placement is of particular importance for the child.

(7) *The availability and durability of the confidential information.* Notification can only take place if there is someone to notify. In cases where a mother declines to identify a father she may face persuasion, if that is thought appropriate, but she cannot be coerced. In some cases the available information may mean that the father is identifiable, and maternal relatives may also be identifiable. The extent to which identifying information is pursued is a matter of judgement. Conversely, there will be cases where it is necessary to consider whether any confidentiality is likely to endure. In the modern world secrets are increasingly difficult to keep and the consequences, particularly for the child and any prospective adopters, of the child's existence being concealed but becoming known to family members later on, sometimes as a result of disclosure by the person seeking confidentiality, should be borne in mind.

(8) *The impact of delay.* A decision to apply to court and thereafter any decision to notify will inevitably postpone to some extent the time when the child's permanent placement can be confirmed. In most cases, the importance of the issues means that the delay cannot be a predominant factor. There

may however be circumstances where delay would have particularly damaging consequences for the mother or for the child; for example, it would undoubtedly need to be taken into account if it would lead to the withdrawal of the child's established carers or to the loss of an especially suitable adoptive placement.

(9) *Any other relevant matters.* The list of relevant factors is not closed. Mothers may have many reasons for wishing to maintain confidentiality and there may be a wide range of implications for the child, the father and for other relatives. All relevant matters must be considered.

7. It has rightly been said that the maintenance of confidentiality is exceptional, and highly exceptional where a father has parental responsibility or where there is family life under art 8. However exceptionality is not in itself a test or a short cut; rather it is a reflection of the fact that the profound significance of adoption for the child and considerations of fairness to others means that the balance will often fall in favour of notification. But the decision on whether confidentiality should be maintained can only be made by striking a fair balance between the factors that are present in the individual case.

See also *Re L (adoption: identification of possible father)* [2020] EWCA Civ 577, [2020] 3 FCR 360, [1], [21]–[24] (Peter Jackson LJ) addressing a related point (the correct approach concerning 'possible fathers', as opposed to putative fathers, and DNA testing of a mothers' other children)

5.5.4 Case management: notice: no duty to consult extended family: adoption cases

Re H (care and adoption: assessment of wider family) [2019] EWFC 10, [2019] 2 FCR 443, [1], [15]–[53] (Cobb J) *quotation limited to* [1], [22], [44]–[53]

[1] In public law proceedings under Pt IV of the Children Act 1989 (CA 1989), social work assessments are commonly undertaken of members of the subject child's wider family or friends who are proposed as potential carers in the event that the child cannot be safely placed with parents. The issue which arises in this case is whether a local authority is required, by statute or otherwise, to notify wider family members of the existence of the subject child, and/or assess them, when they are *not* proposed by parents as potential alternative carers, and where the parents (or either of them) specifically do *not* wish the wider family to be involved.

...

[22] What is clear from paragraphs [17]–[21] above is that while there are strong indicators of the importance of wider family engagement in the processes contemplated by this child-centred legislation, there are no provisions of either the CA 1989 or the ACA 2002, the AAR 2005, or

associated Practice Direction, which absolutely require or place a duty on a local authority to inform, consult, assess or otherwise consider members of the wider family of a child in circumstances such as these.

…

[44] The simple but not unimportant issue raised in this case has given me cause to conduct a reasonably widely-drawn review of statute, guidance and case-law. Drawing the strands of this review together, I have reached the conclusion that I should accede to the application of the local authority. I propose to give the father an opportunity to inform his parents himself of the existence of H. He should be supported in this exercise by a social worker or by the Children's Guardian, should he ask for it. If he chooses not to notify his family himself, I shall authorise the local authority to do so. My reasons, in conclusion, are as follows.

[45] First, repeating a point made earlier (see [22]), none of the provisions of statute, regulations or rules to which I have referred, impose any absolute duty on either the local authority or the Children's Guardian, or indeed the court, to inform or consult members of the extended family about the existence of a child or the plans for the child's adoption in circumstances such as arise here. However, the ethos of the CA 1989 is plainly supportive of wider family involvement in the child's life, save where that outcome is not consistent with their welfare.

[46] Secondly, this is not a situation, given the absence of a de facto relationship between the grandparents and H, in which I can find support for the relief which the local authority seeks by reliance on art 8 ECHR (see [39] above); this is not a case in which I can point to 'the real existence in practice of close personal ties' (*Lebbink*) between H and his grandparents or wider family. H has no Convention right to assert.

[47] Thirdly, while recent appellate case-law offers clear guidance on the route by a court or adoption agency should reach a decision to place a child for adoption in the face of parental opposition ([30]–[32]), it offers no clear steer on this particular issue.

[48] Consequently, the court, and/or the local authority or adoption agency, is enabled to exercise its broad judgment on the facts of each individual case, taking into account all of the family circumstances, but attaching primacy to the welfare of the subject child.

[49] In exercising that broad discretion, I would suggest that the following be borne in mind. There will be cases (if, for instance, there is a history of domestic or family abuse) where it would be unsafe to the child or the parent for the wider family to be involved in the life of the child, or even made aware of the existence of the child. There will be cases where cultural or religious considerations may materially impact on the issue of disclosure. There will be further cases where the mental health or well-being of the parent or parents may be imperilled if disclosure were to be ordered, and this may weigh heavy in the evaluation. But in exercising

judgment – whether that be by the local authority, adoption agency or court – I am clear that the wider family should not simply be ignored on the say-so of a parent. Generally, the ability and/or willingness of the wider family to provide the child with a secure environment in which to grow (s 1(4)(f)(ii) ACA 2002) should be carefully scrutinised, and the *option itself* should be 'fully explored' (see [28]). The approach taken by Sumner J in the *Birmingham* case more than a decade ago, to the effect that 'cogent and compelling' grounds should exist before the court could endorse an arrangement for the despatch of public law proceedings while the wider family remained ignorant of the existence of the child (see [29] above), remains, in my judgment, sound. This approach is in keeping with the key principles of the CA 1989 and the ACA 2002 that children are generally best looked after within their own family, save where that outcome is not consistent with their welfare, and that a care order on a plan for adoption is appropriate only where no other course is possible in the child's interests (see *Re B (a child)* and *Re B-S*).

[50] As the DfE and FRG and associated guidance makes clear (see [25]–[27] above), good social work practice requires the early identification of family members who may be able to provide safe care to meet the child's needs, and/or contribute to the decision making in respect of the child where there are child protection or welfare concerns; the FRG rightly refers to a 'duty' on local authorities to work in partnership with parents and relatives. It was this exercise which Holman J in *Z County Council v R* [2001] described when, at p 375 ibid, he referred to the fact that 'there should normally be wide consultation with, and consideration of, the extended family; and that should only be dispensed with after due and careful consideration' (my emphasis by underlining).

[51] As I said in *Re RA*, and again above, a high level of justification is required before the court can sanction adoption as an outcome for a child particularly where this follows contested process. Even in an *un* contested process a thorough 'analysis' of the options is necessary (*Re JL & AO* at [32]); while 'analysis' is different from 'assessment' (a sufficient 'analysis' may be performed even though the natural family are unaware of the process (*Re RA* at [34])).

[52] I am not insensitive to the fact that the father feels some embarrassment and shame about his lifestyle (see [10] above), and/or the fear of possible rejection or ostracism from his family should they know about his life, and his children; I recognise that he is entitled to respect for his right to privacy. But I cannot allow his discomfort or embarrassment or the risk of rejection to dominate this decision; all that I know about his family, as a strong unit, indicates the improbability of rejection.

[53] As I have indicated above ([48]), in the final analysis, any court or statutory agency faced with this dilemma must place the child's best interests at the centre of its decision making. It must be the life-long best interests of H which determine the decision. In this case, I am influenced by the fact that it is possible that, contrary to his expectations, the father's family

> may actually be able to offer the mother and father support in caring for H ...

See also *Re F (assessment of birth family)* [2021] EWFC 31, [2021] 3 FCR 27, [1], [3], [17]–[32] (Cobb J) addressing the same point (in the context of an adopted mother's birth family)

5.6 CASE MANAGEMENT: JOINDER

5.6.1 Case management: joinder: reference to s 10(9)[9]

Re B (a child) (care proceedings: joinder) [2012] EWCA Civ 737, [2012] 2 FCR 554, [36]–[52] (Black LJ) *quotation limited to* [36]–[40], [48]–[52]

[36] There is no guidance in the 1989 Act or the Family Procedure Rules 2010, SI 2010/2955 (the 2010 Rules) which specifically assists as to the approach that should be taken to an application for joinder and the welfare of the child is not the paramount consideration in either an application for party status or an application for leave to make a substantive application because neither of these applications involves the court in determining 'any question with respect to ... the upbringing of a child', see for example (in relation to joinder/discharge of a party) *North Yorkshire CC v G* [1994] 1 FCR 737, [1993] 2 FLR 732 and *Re W (Discharge of Party to Care Proceedings)* [1997] 2 FCR 190, [1997] 1 FLR 128 and (in relation to leave to apply for a s 8 order) *JR v Merton London Borough* [1992] 2 FCR 174, sub nom *Re A (minors) (residence order)* [1992] 3 All ER 872.

[37] There is authority to the effect that although no s 8 order is actually being sought by the person who is seeking to be joined as a party, reference must be had to s 10(9), see *W v Wakefield City Council* [1994] 2 FCR 564, [1995] 1 FLR 170 in which Wall J (as he then was) also considered two other decisions by Family Division judges, *G v Kirklees Metropolitan BC* [1993] 1 FCR 357, [1993] 1 FLR 805 and *North Yorkshire CC v G* [1994] 1 FCR 737, [1993] 2 FLR 732. It was not argued before us that these authorities were wrong or that the introduction by r 1 of the 2010 Rules of an overriding objective required them to be reconsidered and I can see no reason why they should be questioned. It is logical that a judge determining an application to become a party to proceedings should have an eye to what may follow joinder. To illustrate this with an obvious example, there would be no point in joining someone as a party if they would then inevitably be refused leave to bring an application in relation to the child and would have no other legitimate role in the proceedings.

[38] Section 10 sets out when the court may make a s 8 order in relation to a child. Certain people are entitled to apply for such an order, certain people require leave to make the application, and there are also situations

9 Children Act 1989, s 10(9).

in which the court can make an order even though no application has been made. Section 10(9) is concerned with the factors that may be particularly relevant where someone other than the child is applying for leave to seek a s 8 order. It provides:

> 'Where the person applying for leave to make an application for a section 8 order is not the child concerned, the court shall, in deciding whether or not to grant leave, have particular regard to—
>
> (a) the nature of the proposed application for the section 8 order;
>
> (b) the applicant's connection with the child;
>
> (c) any risk there might be of that proposed application disrupting the child's life to such an extent that he would be harmed by it; and
>
> (d) where the child is being looked after by a local authority—
>
> (i) the authority's plans for the child's future; and
>
> (ii) the wishes and feelings of the child's parents.'

[39] It can be seen that s 10(9) does not contain anything in the nature of a test by which an application should be judged, nor even criteria which must be satisfied before leave can be given, nor is anything of the kind to be derived from the rest of s 10. Neither does the subsection circumscribe the factors that can be taken into account in determining the leave application; it leaves the court to take into account all the material features of the case and merely highlights certain matters which are of particular relevance.

[40] A feature which is not specifically picked out in s 10(9) but has been acknowledged in the authorities to be of relevance is the merit of the proposed application …

…

[48] I hope I might be forgiven for indulging myself with my own summary of the position which I hope reflects Thorpe LJ's view albeit put in slightly different terms. As I said earlier, I do not see s 10(9) as containing a test. By picking out some factors to which the court should have 'particular regard', it acknowledges by implication that there may be other factors which the court has to consider. It would be wrong, in my view, to try to list or limit these factors which will vary infinitely from case to case. One amongst them is plainly the prospects of success of the application that is proposed; leave will not be given for an application that is not arguable. I do not intend to attempt a definition of what is arguable but I would make a few observations before I leave the question of the proper approach to an application to which s 10(9) applies, whether directly or through an application to be joined as a party with a view to seeking the sort of outcome that could be the subject of a s 8 order.

[49] The first observation is that the fact that a person has an arguable case may not necessarily be sufficient to entitle him or her to leave under s 10

or to joinder as a party. I say this because s 10(9) picks out other factors as requiring particular regard and I think it must follow that there may be situations in which, when the judge exercises his or her discretion, balancing all the relevant factors, the presence of an arguable case is outweighed by those other factors or, indeed, by any other factor that carries particular weight in the individual circumstances of the case. Suppose, for example, that the applicant wishes to advance a barely arguable case with many attendant problems in relation to a child with special needs who is securely placed with an irreplaceable long-term family who will be unable to withstand the rigours of any further litigation.

[50] The second observation is that there is room, in cases concerning children, for applications or proposed applications to be checked at a very early stage and without wholesale investigation. The court has a broad discretion to conduct the case as is most appropriate given the issues involved and the evidence available, see for example *Re B (Minors) (Application for Contact)* [1994] 2 FCR 812, [1994] 2 FLR 1, *Re C (a child) (contact: conduct of hearing), Re* [2006] EWCA Civ 144, [2006] 1 FCR 447, [2006] 2 FLR 289 and *Re N, A v G* [2009] EWHC 1807 (Fam), [2010] 1 FLR 272. Accordingly, some cases can appropriately be determined on submissions alone, for example. Furthermore, it is not always necessary for findings to be made in relation to all (or sometimes any) disputed facts, perhaps because the result does not depend upon them or because there are quite sufficient undisputed facts to form the foundation of the decision that needs to be taken. What is more, there is no absolute entitlement to assessment with a view to caring for a child; *TL v Hammersmith and Fulham London BC* [2011] EWCA Civ 812, [2011] 3 FCR 343 contains observations relevant to this point.

[51] It is for the judge to ensure in each case that there is a fair determination of the claims of the parties and the issues in the case. Thorpe LJ's statement in *Re J* that judges should be careful not to dismiss the possibility of a child being cared for by grandparents 'without full inquiry' must be read in the context of the facts of the particular case he was considering. The prospects of a grandparent taking over the child's care must, of course, always be looked into carefully because it can be greatly to a child's benefit to be kept within the family by such a placement. Our attention was invited also to *Re C (Family Placement)* [2009] EWCA Civ 72, [2009] 1 FLR 1425 which exemplifies this. But there are various levels of investigation of the possibilities. At one end of the spectrum, the grandparent's proposals may need to be explored at a full hearing with reports and on oral evidence; at the other a careful but limited examination of the situation by the local authority may disclose overwhelming reasons why care by the grandparent is obviously not an option. I do not think, therefore, that what Thorpe LJ said should properly be interpreted as a requirement that any grandparent who wishes to put forward proposals should be joined as a party to existing care proceedings or given leave to issue a s 8 application or still less permitted to air their case at a full hearing on evidence. Sometimes some or all of these things will be

appropriate, sometimes none and it is for the judge to weigh the various factors and decide what the proper order is in the individual case. This court is slow to interfere with discretionary decisions of this kind.

[52] Finally, a word about delay. Section 10(9)(c) provides that the court must have particular regard to 'any risk there might be of [the] proposed application disrupting the child's life to such an extent that he would be harmed by it'. In *Re M (Minors) (Contact: Leave to Apply)* [1995] 3 FCR 550 at 560, [1995] 2 FLR 86 at 95–96, Ward LJ said that this particular provision was directed at risk to the child arising from the proposed application rather than arising from the making of any order that might result from it. Delay occasioned by or associated with the application is an obvious source of disruption and harm and must properly be considered under this heading.

See also *Re M (minors) (sexual abuse: evidence)* [1993] 1 FCR 253 (CA), 256H–257E (Butler-Sloss LJ) addressing a related point (joinder of other parties in care proceedings should be where they present a separate point of view, albeit referred to as 'intervention' and 'intervene' herein)

See also *North Yorkshire County Council v G and others* [1994] 1 FCR 737 (FD), 741B–742C (Douglas Brown J) considering *Re M (Minors) (Sexual Abuse: Evidence)* [1993] 1 FCR 253 (allowing an appeal against a sibling's joinder)

See also *Re W* [2004] EWHC 3342 (Fam), [2005] 2 FLR 468, [29]–[40] (Sumner J) considering *Re M (minors) (sexual abuse: evidence)* [1993] 1 FCR 253 (upholding a decision to refuse an aunt's joinder)

5.6.2 Case management: joinder: fathers without PR

Re P (care proceedings: father's application to be joined as party) [2001] 3 FCR 279 (FD), 286D–E (Connell J)

> I accept the general proposition relied on by counsel for the appellant and propounded by Holman J, namely, that as a general rule and unless there is some justifiable reason for not joining him, a natural father should be permitted to participate as a party in care proceedings relating to his son.

5.6.3 Case management: joinder: joinder of foster carers or prospective adopters is usually inappropriate

Re T (a child) (early permanence placement) [2015] EWCA Civ 983, [2016] 1 FCR 521, [43]–[54] (Sir James Munby P) *quotation limited to* [43], [49]–[54]

[43] From the very earliest days of the 1989 Act (which, it will be remembered, came into force in October 1991), the court has set its face against the joinder in care proceedings of foster parents or prospective adopters. Two decisions of this court explain why.

...

[49] In my judgment, there is no reason to depart from this long-established approach and, indeed, every reason to follow it. There is nothing in art 8 or in the Strasbourg jurisprudence which calls for any different approach. There is nothing in the recent case law on adoption (*Re B (a child) (care order: proportionality: criterion for review)* [2013] 2 FCR 525, [2013] 3 All ER 929, *Re B-S (children) (adoption: leave to oppose)* [2013] 3 FCR 481, [2014] 1 WLR 563, *CM v Blackburn with Darwen BC* [2015] 2 FCR 116, [2015] 1 WLR 2441and *Re R (a child) (placement: realistic options)* [2015] 2 FCR 499, [2015] 1 WLR 3273) which justifies, let alone requires, any change in approach. Nor, in particular, is there anything in the status or function of an early permanence placement foster carer which either justifies or requires any change in approach.

[50] I agree, therefore, with the essential thrust of the submissions by Mr Donnelly, Mr Tyler and Miss Anning as I have summarised them at paras [28]–[29], above. The care judge is concerned at most with consideration of adoption *in principle*, not with evaluating the merits of particular proposed adopters. There is no need for the prospective adopters to be joined, for it is the children's guardian (who will be aware of Mr and Mrs X's stance and can, if necessary, address their suitability) who has the task, indeed is under the duty, of subjecting the local authority's care plan to rigorous scrutiny and, where, appropriate, criticism. So, I agree, Mr and Mrs X's joinder to the care proceedings is inappropriate. Moreover, as was pointed out, and I agree, there is no need for Mr and Mrs X to be parties to the care proceedings to demonstrate that they are suitable prospective adopters for T, for they have already been positively assessed.

[51] The truth is, as Mr Tyler submitted, that, putting on one side Mr and Mrs X's role as early permanence placement foster carers, and, I emphasise, without in any way wishing to belittle or diminish all that they have done for T, this is a case where there has been an unexceptional period of time caring for an unexceptional child in an unexceptional case. This, in my judgment, is not an exceptional case justifying any departure from the general approach. For the reality is, as Mr Tyler correctly put it, that the 'status quo' and attachment on which Miss Scriven and Miss Fottrell placed such emphasis do not differ significantly from what is found in the many similar care cases where a child has been successfully fostered for a short period. Moreover, and to repeat, there is, in my judgment, nothing in the status or function of an early permanence placement foster carer which either justifies or requires any change in the hitherto conventional and long-established approach.

[52] To the extent I have indicated, I therefore agree with the thrust of Mr Tyler's submissions.

[53] Moreover, there is, as Miss Anning pointed out, a very real risk that if, in a case such as this, the forensic process is allowed to become in effect a dispute between the prospective adopters and the birth family, the court will be diverted into an illegitimate inquiry as to which placement will be better for the child. That, it cannot be emphasised too much, is *not* the

question before the court. I repeat, because the point is so important, what the Strasbourg court said in *YC v UK* [2013] 2 FCR 36, [2012] 2 FLR 332 (para 134):

> 'family ties may only be severed in very exceptional circumstances ... It is not enough to show that a child could be placed in a more beneficial environment for his upbringing ...'

Indeed, there are passages in Judge Troy's judgment—for example, where she refers to a 'comparative analysis of these two options', without at the same time spelling out that adoption is appropriate only as 'a last resort' and if 'nothing else will do'—which do make me wonder whether she may not in fact have fallen into precisely that error here.

[54] There is another significant matter which, in my judgment, points in the same direction. The effect of s 44(2) and (3) of the 2002 Act is to impose a period of three months' delay in a case such as this. This is an appropriate aspect of the statutory scheme in relation to private law adoptions. But it would sit most uncomfortably if, as suggested in the present case, the statutory scheme under the 2002 Act is to be run in tandem with the quite separate statutory scheme in relation to care proceedings under the 1989 Act, required, by the recently amended s 32(1)(a)(ii) of the 1989 Act, to be concluded within a total period of only 26 weeks.

See also *Re R (care proceedings: joinder of foster carers)* [2021] EWCA Civ 875, [2021] 4 WLR 104, [36]–[48], [62]–[64] (Baker LJ) providing an overview of the law on this point

5.7 CASE MANAGEMENT: INTERVENING

5.7.1 Case management: intervening: specific purposes

Re S (child case: intervener) [1997] 2 FCR 272 (CA), 276B–C (Butler-Sloss LJ)

> Therefore I would in the rather unusual circumstances of this case allow the appeal but not make Mr K a party to the proceedings. There is no need to do that. He does not wish to be an applicant; he does not wish to be a respondent. What he wishes to do is to intervene to protect himself from these serious allegations made against him and he should be therefore entitled to intervene and take part in the proceedings to the limited extent that his case is before the court and no further.

Cumbria County Council v AT and others [2020] EWFC 58, [2021] 1 FLR 1338, [31]–[38], [55] (MacDonald J)

31. It has been long established that it may be appropriate to give a person leave to intervene in proceedings for a specific purpose (see *Re S (Care: Residence: Intervener)* [1997] 1 FLR 497 CA). In the context of a case that involved allegations of sexual abuse, the Court of Appeal in *Re*

H (Care Proceedings: Sexual Abuse) [2000] 2 FLR 499 held that where specific allegations of sexual abuse are made in care proceedings against a non-party and brought before the court by the local authority for trial as a preliminary issue, it is vital that that person's evidence is before the court at that stage, even if he or she is unlikely to have party status at the substantive hearing, Lord Justice Thorpe observing:

> '[31] If there is any generalisation to be drawn from an investigation of the history of this case, it seems to me to be this. Local authorities bringing a specific allegation of sexual abuse against a named individual for trial at a preliminary issue must at the very least apply to the court to consider whether that individual should be joined, even if he is unlikely to have party status at the substantive hearing, when welfare considerations will predominate and long-term will be decisions taken as to the future of the children. This case seems to me to demonstrate a general proposition that unless the accused adult deliberately absents himself from the proceedings, thereby inviting condemnation, it is vital that his evidence should be before the court. Unless he is made a party, that is left to the discretion of the other parties marshalling their cases. Unless he is a party, he will not be sufficiently represented and protected during the forensic process. Unless he is a party, he will not be joined in the collection of essential expert evidence.'

32. However, with respect to non-parties against whom specific allegations of sexual abuse are made, it is important to note that the same year, in *Re H (Care Proceedings: Intervener)* [2000] 1 FLR 775, the Court of Appeal made clear that there is no right for non-parties against whom allegations are being made by a local authority in public law proceedings to intervene. In that case Butler-Sloss P made clear that each case has to be looked at on its own merits and that the court has to identify the particular reason why it is *necessary* for a person to intervene. Within this context, there are a number of examples in the authorities where intervener status has not been considered necessary notwithstanding allegations may be made against the person in question during the course of proceedings.

33. In *Re H (Care Proceedings: Intervener)*, the Court of Appeal allowed an appeal against a decision to accord a non-subject sibling intervener status where the proposed intervener was a witness in the proceedings against whom an allegation of perverting the course of justice was to be put, and who was at risk of being prosecuted for conspiracy. In *Re BJ (Care: Third Party Intervention)* [1999] Fam Law 613 the Court of Appeal upheld the judge's ruling refusing to allow a non-subject 12-year-old boy to intervene in care proceedings relating to his nephew where allegations of sexual misconduct had been made against that 12-year-old child and, where, accordingly, he was at risk of findings being made. In *T (Children)* [2011] EWCA Civ 1818 consideration was given by the Court of Appeal to how the evidence of a former intervenor would have to be treated if he was no longer an intervenor but his alleged conduct was nonetheless relied on by one party and disputed by another within the

context of public law proceedings. At [26] and [27] Ward LJ observed as follows with respect to the effect of hearing former intervenor, identified in the case as DH, as a witness rather than as an intervenor, pursuant to the decision of the judge under appeal:

> 'As things stand at the moment, it would be for the judge to judge the credibility of this boy. He may be able to say 'I am not satisfied by him, therefore I cannot be satisfied that the complaint against the father is made out.' That is the end of it. He can, of course, come to a conclusion that, having heard DH, he is quite satisfied that DH has in fact abused KE and N and, although he said he is not intending to make findings, he may be driven not to make findings in the care proceedings as such, but to explain his judgment by expressing his conviction in that way. In any event, he, the judge, will deal with this on the disposal. He will have seen four weeks of this case. He will know full well how much weight to place upon the various factors and how important it is in the life of these five children whether or not this boy has done what is alleged against him.'

34. Also relevant to the question of whether it is appropriate to accord a person intervener status in proceedings will be the provisions of the overriding objective in FPR 2010 r 1.1. The overriding objective requires the court, when making case management decisions, to have regard to the need to ensure that the case is dealt with expeditiously and fairly, dealt with in a way that is proportionate to the nature, importance and complexity of the issues, in a way that ensures the parties are on an equal footing, in a way that saves expense and in a way that allots to the case an appropriate share of resources, whilst taking into account the need to allot resources to other cases. In this context, I note that in *Re H (Care Proceedings: Intervener)* Butler-Sloss P observed as follows at [12]:

> 'Another element is this. These are of course … proceedings which are largely, if not entirely, funded by the state, one way or another, either through the local authority, both ratepayers and state money. Both the parents, who are separately represented for care proceedings, and if this girl is allowed to intervene, D, will no doubt be represented on legal aid. There will be, inevitably, a proliferation of documents because, although it is suggested they should be edited and she might not get all the documents in the case, since she is crucial to the case she would have to have all the documents which concerned her. I would have little doubt that they would be at least half, if not the majority of the documents in the case. Of course, her counsel would have to have the right to examine his client in chief and to cross-examine every other witness in the proceedings. No doubt he would exercise the restraint that counsel always do, but he would have the right, where relevant, to deal with these matters in some detail. This would be an increase of the expense of these proceedings which is a relevant factor, even when one is urged (as we are in this court) to uphold the judge, whose primary task was looking at the welfare of this not yet 18-year-old girl.'

35. Within this context, and having regard to the pressures currently placed on the family justice system by the COVID-19 pandemic, I must also bear in mind paragraph 46 of the President's Guidance entitled '*The Family Court and COVID 19 – The Road Ahead*', which makes clear as follows:

> '[46] Parties will not be allowed to litigate every issue and present extensive oral evidence or oral submissions; an oral hearing will encompass only that which is necessary to determine the application before the court.'

36. Finally, two further matters must be borne in mind when considering whether a person appearing as a witness in public law proceedings who will face allegations being put to him or her during the course of the hearing, but against whom findings are not sought, nonetheless requires intervenor status.

37. First, where the allegations concern conduct that is criminal, the question of self-incrimination. The privilege against self-incrimination is a common law privilege. At common law, no person is bound to answer any question in civil proceedings where the answer may tend to expose them to any criminal charge or penalty or forfeiture which the judge regards as reasonably likely to be preferred or sued for (*Blunt v Park Lane Hotel* [1942] 2 KB 253 at 257). However, this common law rule can be qualified by statute. Within the context of these public law proceedings, the common law privilege against self-incrimination is qualified by the Children Act 1989 s 98. The protection afforded by s 98 of the Children Act 1989 is not absolute as s 98 does not prevent the use of a statement or admission made in proceedings under Part IV or V of the Children Act 1989 from being used in a criminal investigation. In *Re EC (Disclosure of Material)* [1996] 2 FLR 725 the Court of Appeal held that transcripts of an admission made by the father when giving evidence could be disclosed to the police, who would then be free to use the transcript in interview. The admissibility of the contents of the interview would then be, ultimately, a matter for the trial judge in the criminal proceedings.

38. Second, in general, the answers of an opponent's witness on matters of credit or other collateral matters will be treated as conclusive and may not be contradicted by calling other evidence (see *Harris v Tippett* (1811) 2 Camp. 637 and also *Palmer v Trower* (1852) 8 Exch. 247). However, this rule is not absolute. More importantly in this case, the reliability of a witnesses' denial of sexual abuse is not a matter going simply to the credit of that witness, nor a collateral matter in circumstances where the issue to be tried is whether (i) the mother developed an unreasonable and false belief that T was sexually abused by the father, or (ii) the mother deliberately fabricated false allegations of sexual abuse and induced T to make false allegations of sexual abuse against the father. In the circumstances, the mother would not be bound simply to accept the denial of the witness and could seek to contradict the denial with other evidence, if such evidence exists.

...

55. When determining whether or not it is necessary and proportionate to determine a given finding or findings, the court applies the analytical framework set out by McFarlane J (as he then was) in A Local Authority v DP. When considering whether to accord a person intervener status on a specific issue within proceedings, each case has to be looked at on its own merits and the court has to identify the particular reason why it is necessary for a person to intervene or to remain an intervenor.

See also *Re T (children)* [2011] EWCA Civ 1818, [2013] 2 FLR 795, [24]–[28] (Ward LJ) addressing the same point (emphasising that the decision is a case management decision)

See also *Re H (children) (care proceedings: sexual abuse)* [2000] 2 FCR 499 (CA), [31] (Thorpe LJ) addressing a related point (when LAs[10] make specific allegations against named individuals they should apply to courts, albeit the discussion is in the context of applying to be 'joined' and refers to 'party status')

5.7.2 Case management: intervening: no right to intervene

Re H (care proceedings: intervener) [2000] 2 FCR 53 (CA), [9]–[12] (Dame Elizabeth Butler-Sloss P)

9. The judge, in my view, gave too broad a definition (if I may call it) of the underlying principle set out in the *Re S* case. Each of these cases clearly has to be looked at on its own merits. One has to identify, if leave to intervene is given, what is the particular reason why it is necessary for a person to intervene. It is not a run of the mill application. Clearly it is not an application that should be granted because somebody is a victim or may be, as an alleged victim, the subject of robust cross-examination in care proceedings to the effect that the allegations are a pack of lies. That would only happen with older children, since generally in care proceedings the children who are younger do not give evidence.

10. Quite clearly, as I have said, all victims cannot as such intervene and ought not to be given the right to intervene. There may be cases where victims might be given the right to intervene in care proceedings. What is clear is that they cannot intervene in criminal proceedings. In this case D clearly is at risk of being said to have set her sister up in a shocking fabrication, in which case she may be at risk. That may mean, in purely civil proceedings in the family court, that in certain circumstances she should have the protection of being allowed to intervene. But against that possibility has to be weighed in the balance a number of other factors. First, there is no right as such to intervene because you are a satellite party and allegations are made against you. I think, as I said,

10 Local authorities.

the judge expressed that too broadly. Secondly, there is no protection to this vulnerable 17-year-old in the criminal court. If, as I understand it, it is likely that an attempt would be made for the criminal proceedings to be heard before the civil proceedings (and I would have thought in this case it was highly desirable that that should be so, if it is possible) D will be giving evidence in the criminal court without any protection of any sort. She will be exposed to cross-examination, including the fact that she set her sister up. It cannot be any worse, when she then comes to give evidence in the care proceedings, because she will already have been exposed to the disagreeable state of being an unprotected witness in the criminal court.

11. I cannot at the moment see why, where there are parallel proceedings both in the criminal court and in the civil court, she needs the protection in one when she cannot have the protection in the other. That is a matter that was not raised with Judge Milligan, and indeed was not a matter which (I can understand why) he did not consider himself. It is, in my view, a highly relevant factor to put into the balance as to whether or not she should be given leave to intervene. Thorpe LJ raised it in these proceedings, and it seems to me a very important element.

12. Another element is this. These are of course, not only private proceedings, the care proceedings, but they are proceedings which are largely, if not entirely, funded by the state, one way or another, either through the local authority, both rate-payers and state money. Both the parents, who are separately represented for care proceedings, and if this girl is allowed to intervene, D, will no doubt be represented on legal aid. There will be, inevitably, a proliferation of documents because, although it is suggested they should be edited and she might not get all the documents in the case, since she is crucial to the case she would have to have all the documents which concerned her. I would have little doubt that they would be at least half, if not the majority of the documents in the case. Of course, her counsel would have to have the right to examine his client in-chief and to cross-examine every other witness in the proceedings. No doubt he would exercise the restraint that counsel always do, but he would have the right, where relevant, to deal with these matters in some detail. This would be an increase of the expense of these proceedings which is a relevant factor, even when one is urged (as we are in this court) to uphold the judge, whose primary task was looking at the welfare of this not yet 18-year-old girl.

See also *Cumbria County Council v AT and others* [2020] EWFC 58 [31]–[38] (MacDonald J), see Chapter 5.7.1 Case management: intervening: specific purposes

5.7.3 Case management: intervening: costs of intervening

See Chapter 14.1.2 Costs: principles: exonerated interveners

5.8 CASE MANAGEMENT: PROTECTED OR VULNERABLE PARTIES

5.8.1 Case management: protected or vulnerable parties: protected parties: determining capacity if unclear

Re D (children) [2015] EWCA Civ 749, [23]–[36] (King LJ)

(i) Was there a failure properly to assess and determine the capacity of the mother to litigate?

23. The issue as to whether a party has capacity can come before the court in a number of ways, although as Kennedy LJ put it in *Masterman-Lister v Brutton & Co* [2002] EWCA Civ 1889 at [30]:

> 'Normally no problem arises as to when the issue of capacity should be raised. It raises itself'

24. In the present case the mother had been represented by the Official Solicitor as her litigation friend in relation to the proceedings concerning JD and so very properly at an early stage, an updating report was commissioned from Dr Morgan.

25. The jurisdictional backdrop to this course is found in *Part 15 Family Procedure Rules 2010. (FPR 2010):*

By FPR 2010 r.15.2:

> 'A protected party must have a litigation friend to conduct proceedings on that party's behalf'

26. It should be noted that the term 'litigation friend' applies to both Applicants and Respondents, the former nomenclature of 'next friend' for an applicant and 'guardian ad litem' for the Respondent having been replaced by the single term litigation friend under the *FPR 2010.*

27. A 'protected party' is defined under *FPR 2010, r2.3(1)* as:

> 'a party, or an intended party, who lacks capacity (within the meaning of the 2005 Act) to conduct proceedings.'

The '2005 Act' is the *Mental Capacity Act 2005 (MCA 2005).* It follows therefore that the statutory test found within the MCA 2005 together with the jurisprudence which has developed in that jurisdiction, have been specifically incorporated into the Rules.

28. The starting point for determining capacity is *MCA 2005, s1(2):*

> 'A person must be assumed to have capacity unless it is established that he lacks capacity'

29. *MCA 2005, s2(1)* provides:

> '(1) For the purposes of this Act, a person lacks capacity in relation to a matter if at the material time he is unable to make a decision for himself in relation to the matter because of an impairment of, or a disturbance in the functioning of, the mind or brain.'

Two stages therefore make up the process of determining whether a person does or does not have capacity in respect of the specific issue in question; here the mother's capacity to litigate. The two questions are commonly referred to as:

i) The diagnostic threshold – namely is there an impairment of, or disturbance in the functioning of the person's mind? The disturbance may be permanent or temporary and no reference is made to the degree of impairment or disturbance necessary to reach the threshold.

ii) The functional test – is the impairment or disturbance of mind sufficient to render the person incapable of making that particular decision? It has long been recognised that the test is issue–specific; a person may for example have the capacity to consent to medical treatment but not have the capacity to litigate.

30. Evidence from a suitably qualified person will be necessary as to the diagnosis. This will usually be a person with medical qualifications, ideally a psychiatrist but where, as here, the court is concerned with a person with significant learning disabilities, a psychologist may be as, if not more, appropriate.

31. Often in care proceedings the issue of capacity is uncontroversial. Either the local authority, as part of its pre proceedings work, will have obtained a medical report dealing with the issue which report will have been annexed to the application for a care order in accordance with the *Public Law Outline(PLO): FPR Part 12: PD12A*. Alternatively, the solicitor representing the parent in question, will have raised concerns as to his client's capacity and a report will have been identified as being necessary and provided for under the PLO at the *PD 12A: Stage 2 – Case Management Hearing*.

32. If either party takes issue with the outcome of the capacity assessment then, as with any other expert evidence, it is open to that party to make an application to the court for a second report by a different expert. *Section 13 of the Children and Families Act 2014 (CFA 2014):* creates a statutory code for expert evidence in children cases supplemented by *FPR 2010, Pt25*. The introduction of *s13 CFA 2014* marked the making of a statutory restriction on the power of the courts to order expert evidence reflected in the wording of the section:

> '13. Control of expert evidence and of assessments in children proceedings (1) A person may not without the permission of the court instruct a person to provide expert evidence for use in children proceedings …
>
> (6) The court may give permission…. only if the court is of the opinion that the expert evidence is necessary to assist the court to resolve the proceedings justly.

33. *FPR 2010 Part 25* and the accompanying *Practice Directions: PD 25B and PD25C* set out in considerable detail all the requirement in relation

to the instruction of an expert from the contents of the application (*CPR 2010, r25.7 & PD25C, 3.10 & 3.11*) and of the Letter of Instruction (*PD25C,4.1*) to the structure of the Expert's Report (*PD25B,9.1*) and of Discussions between Experts (*FPR 2010, r25.16*)

34. Even where, as I will set out in detail later in this judgment, there has been a wholesale failure to comply with either the rules governing the making an application for an expert or, in relation to the consequential requirements once permission has been given, such failings are not necessarily fatal to the admission of the expert evidence as the court retains its discretion to admit expert evidence, notwithstanding the procedural defects.

35. The purpose of the somewhat prescriptive approach to the instruction of experts found in the *FPR 2010* is to ensure that the expert report put before the court deals with the relevant issues, the expert having had available all the relevant evidence necessary for him or her to form an opinion. Failure to provide an adequate letter of instruction, or all the relevant documents, can lead to an expert, particularly one who may be less experienced in the forensic process, in failing to apply the correct test or adequately to address the key issues which, in turn, can lead to delay – the enemy of children's welfare.

36. Where the report is either deficient or reveals a disagreement in view as between other experts in the case, once again *Part 25* comes to the rescue by providing for written questions to be put to the expert; *FPR 2010, r 25.10* and provision for an expert's meeting *FPR 2010, r 25.16* with a view to reaching agreement or, failing that, endeavouring to narrow the issues between them. Absent agreement between the experts the court will hear evidence and make a determination.

5.8.2 Case management: protected or vulnerable parties: vulnerable witnesses: procedure

Re N (a child) [2019] EWCA Civ 1997, [2019] 4 WLR 154, [1], [38]–[51] (King LJ) *quotation limited to* [1], [43]–[51]

1. This case concerns the challenges presented to a court when seeking to ensure that a vulnerable parent is able to give their best evidence during the course of care proceedings. Achieving this outcome is necessary in order both to protect the Article 6 rights of the parent to a fair trial and to ensure that the court has the benefit of the most reliable evidence possible with which to inform its decisions.

…

43. The Working Group's recommendations were in due course incorporated, as of 27 November 2017, into FPR 2010, Part 3A and PD3AA, which makes provision for 'Vulnerable Persons: Participation in Proceedings and Giving Evidence'.

44. By rules 3A.4 and 3A.5 respectively, the court is under the following duty:

> '(a) The court must consider whether a party's participation in the proceedings (other than by way of giving evidence) is likely to be diminished by reason of vulnerability and, if so, whether it is necessary to make one or more participation directions.
>
> (b) The court must consider whether the quality of evidence given by a party or witness is likely to be diminished by reason of vulnerability and, if so, whether it is necessary to make one or more participation directions.'

The duties established under Part 3A apply as soon as possible after the start of the proceedings, and continue until the resolution of the proceedings (r 3A.9). Those duties apply equally to the parties as to the court (PD 3AA):

> '1.3 It is the duty of the court… and of all the parties to the proceedings to identify any party or witness who is a vulnerable person at the earliest possible stage of any family proceedings'

It is also the duty of all parties to work together to assist the court in complying with the requirements of Part 3A.

45. If Part 3A.4 and rule 3A.5 apply, the court must consider whether to make 'participation directions' (r 3A.1); and, where a court has decided that a vulnerable party or witness is to give evidence, it must then hold a 'ground rules hearing' (PD3AA 5.2) prior to the substantive hearing. At the ground rules hearing, directions will be given as to the conduct of the hearing, the role of advocates, the mode in which evidence is to be given, the topics for questioning and various other matters, all of which are set out in PD3AA.5.

46. The obligation on the advocates, as set out in the Practice Direction, extends to an expectation that they are familiar with the techniques employed by 'the toolkits and the approach of the Advocacy Training Council' (PD3AA.5.7). The 'toolkits' provide advocates with good practice guidance when preparing for trial in cases involving a witness with communication needs. The use of the toolkits has been endorsed in a criminal context by the Lord Chief Justice in *R v Lubemba* [2014] EWCA Crim 2064, para 40, and should be considered on a par for these purposes.

47. Toolkit 4 sets out best practice when 'planning to question someone with a learning disability' and ties into Toolkit 16 – Intermediaries. Toolkit 4 goes far beyond mere guidance as to how to deal with the court setting and evidence and provides invaluable information and guidance as to types of learning disabilities and how learning difficulties can affect communication.

48. In considering whether the mother had a fair trial, Part 3A sits side by side with Article 6 of Convention for the Protection of Human Rights and Fundamental Freedoms ('the Convention') which embodies the right

of access to a court for determination of civil rights and obligations (see *Golder v UK 524,* para.36: (1979-1980) 1 EHRR).

> 'Article 6 – Right to fair trial
>
> In the determination of his civil rights and obligations or of any criminal charge against him, everyone is entitled to a fair and public hearing within a reasonable time by an independent and impartial tribunal established by law.'

49. In *Re L (Care: Assessment: Fair Trial)* [2002] 2 FLR 730, Munby J, as he then was, considered the issue of what amounted to a fair trial. In relation to Article 6, he said as follows:

> '[92] I return to Art 6. The starting point is the court's recognition in Golderv UK ….(paras 35–36) that what Art 6 confers is an effective right of access to a court.
>
> [93] That said, the fundamental principle is clear. As the court said in Mantovanelli v France (1997) 24 EHRR 370, at 383 (para 34):
>
> > The court has […] to ascertain whether the proceedings considered as a whole, including the way in which the evidence was taken, were fair.'

50. In *P, C and S v UK (ECHR)* [2002] 2 FLR 6, the court confirmed that Article 6 embodies the right to access to a court, and went on:

> '[91] Secondly, the key principle governing the application of Art 6 is fairness. In cases where an applicant appears in court notwithstanding lack of assistance of a lawyer and manages to conduct his or her case in the teeth of all the difficulties, the question may nonetheless arise as to whether this procedure was fair (see, for example, McVicar v UK (unreported) 7 May 2002, paras 50–51 (to be published in EHRR)). There is the importance of ensuring the appearance of the fair administration of justice and a party in civil proceedings must be able to participate effectively, inter alia, by being able to put forward the matters in support of his or her claims. Here, as in other aspects of Art 6, the seriousness of what is at stake for the applicant will be of relevance to assessing the adequacy and fairness of the procedures.'

51. In my judgment, Part 3A and its accompanying Practice Direction provide a specific structure designed to give effective access to the court, and to ensure a fair trial for those people who fall into the category of vulnerable witness. A wholesale failure to apply the Part 3 procedure to a vulnerable witness must, in my mind, make it highly likely that the resulting trial will be judged to have been unfair.

See also *Re S (vulnerable parent: intermediary)* [2020] EWCA Civ 763, [2020] 3 FCR 478, [15]–[23] (Peter Jackson LJ) considering *Re N (a child)* [2019] EWCA Civ 1997, [2019] 4 WLR 154 (particularly intermediaries)

See also *Re S (vulnerable parent: intermediary)* [2020] EWCA Civ 763, [2020] 3 FCR 478 [26]–[29] (Peter Jackson LJ) addressing a related point (emphasising the importance of accounting for any hybrid/remote hearing)

5.8.3 Case management: protected or vulnerable parties: vulnerable witnesses: hearing disabilities

Re Y (leave to oppose adoption) [2020] EWCA Civ 1287, [2020] 3 FCR 578, [2]–[3] (Baker LJ) *quotation limited to* [3]

[3] Meanwhile, I would reiterate the core aspects of the guidance given by this court in *Re C* – that it is the duty of lawyers acting for a parent who has a hearing disability to identify that as a feature of the case at the earliest opportunity, that those lawyers and the local authority should make the issue known to the court at the time that the proceedings are issued, and that the court must grapple with the issue, including the support required and the funding of that support, at the first case management hearing with the aim of giving clear and detailed directions. A similar course should be adopted in this court so that, if permission to appeal is granted, the single Lord or Lady Justice can give all necessary directions, either on paper or, if appropriate, at a preliminary hearing. In the case of remote or hybrid hearings, where the party, interpreter and/or intermediary are not together in the same room, it will be necessary to consider how they can communicate with each other separately from and alongside the platform through which the hearing is being conducted. That may or may not be a matter for a court direction but it will certainly be something to be considered and arranged by the parties' solicitors.

See also *Re C (a child) (care proceedings: deaf parent)* [2014] EWCA Civ 128, [2014] 3 FCR 627, [17]–[23] (McFarlane LJ) addressing the same point (in greater detail)

See also *A Local Authority v M and others* [2021] EWFC 10, [16]–[40] (Elizabeth Isaacs QC sitting as a deputy High Court judge) considering *Re Y (leave to oppose adoption)* [2020] EWCA Civ 1287, [2020] 3 FCR 578

See Chapter 9.3.11 The welfare stage: the welfare checklists: parents' capabilities: deaf parents

5.8.4 Case management: protected or vulnerable parties: vulnerable witnesses: costs of intermediaries

Re D (a child) (no 2) [2015] EWFC 2, [2015] 1 FLR 1247, [16]–[17] (Sir James Munby P)

16. The use of an intermediary is becoming increasingly frequent, as the court becomes ever more alert to the need for 'special measures' in appropriate cases. Ms Fottrell referred me to four cases where intermediaries have been used: *Re X (A Child)* [2011] EWHC 3401 (Fam), *Re M (A Child)*

[2012] EWCA Civ 1905, *Re A (Vulnerable Witness)* [2013] EWHC 1694 (Fam), [2013] 2 FLR 1473, and *Re A (Vulnerable Witness: Fact Finding)* [2013] EWHC 2124 (Fam), [2014] 1 FLR 146. Two more examples are *Wiltshire Council v N* [2013] EWHC 3502 (Fam), [2014] Fam Law 418, and *In re C (A Child) (Care Proceedings: Deaf Parent)* [2014] EWCA Civ 128, [2014] 1 WLR 2495.

17. The cost of funding an intermediary in court properly falls on Her Majesty's Courts and Tribunals Service because, as the LAA has correctly pointed out, an intermediary is not a form of 'representation' but a mechanism to enable the litigant to communicate effectively with the court, and thus analogous to translation, so should therefore be funded by the court: see *Re X*, para 37, and *C v Sevenoaks Youth Court* [2009] EWHC 3088 (Admin), [2010] 1 All ER 735, paras 26-27; see also *Q v Q, Re B (A Child), Re C (A Child)* [2014] EWFC 31, para 52. But where the services of an intermediary are required otherwise than during a court hearing, the cost falls on the LAA: see *Re C*, para 27. And the cost of obtaining a report from an expert as to capacity and competence and/or as to the extent of any special measures required, as opposed to the cost of providing services from an intermediary, likewise falls on the *LAA: Wiltshire Council v N*, para 79.

5.9 CASE MANAGEMENT: LIP[11]

5.9.1 Case management: LIP: procedure

Re H (a child) [2014] EWCA Civ 271, [18] (Ryder LJ)

18. For my part, I would strongly suggest that in future, in an environment in which litigants in person are now the rule rather than the exception, a judge should have each party sworn or affirmed before they make submissions so that there is formal evidence on the record from that person and also that it is explained to each litigant in person by the judge that they can ask questions if necessary through the judge who will then decide whether the question is appropriate, for example, on the grounds of relevance.

Re C (a child) [2015] EWCA Civ 539, [2016] 3 FCR 177, [14]–[16] (Ryder LJ)

[14] I shall digress for a moment to consider the means by which a fair process can be afforded to a litigant in person whose language is not English, particularly in a hearing where the other party is represented. There are professional statements of good practice which already exist to ensure that a party in this position is afforded proper access to justice. The implementation of the family justice reforms has included teaching provided by the Judicial College to judges about that good practice. Magistrates sit in the Family Court as judges of that court in accordance

11 Litigants in person.

with the Crime and Courts Act 2013. They are afforded the same teaching as professional judges. I shall simply take note of the training they have had. The practice that is recommended is that litigants in person are sworn at the outset of the hearing so that their representations can be used as evidence. They should each be asked to set out their case (preferably without interruption and in a fixed time window) and they should be encouraged by the court to answer any relevant propositions put by the other party. The court should identify the key issues for them and put the same issues to each of them at the beginning or end of the statements they are invited to make.

[15] The court should ask the applicant to reply to any matters he or she has not covered before making a decision. Questions which either party wants to ask of the other party, assuming that the representations are to be relied upon as evidence, should be asked through the judge where the questioner is a litigant in person so that inappropriate control is not exercised by one party over the other and irrelevant questions can be avoided.

[16] This was not the process used by the magistrates and their legal advisor. Given that such a process might have facilitated a fairer hearing for the father in this case, it is regrettable that it or a similar appropriate process was not used. Give the number of litigants in person in the Family Court the time may have come for this process to be formalised into practice guidance or a practice direction.

See also *Re J (children)* [2018] EWCA Civ 115, [2018] 2 FCR 527, [68]–[75] (McFarlane LJ) addressing a related point (questioning of a vulnerable accuser by a LIP-accused, albeit in a private law context)

See also *PS v BP* [2018] EWHC 1987 (Fam), [2018] 4 WLR 119, [5]–[9], [23]–[34] (Hayden J) addressing a related point (the importance of ground rules hearings when considering questioning of a vulnerable accuser by a LIP-accused, albeit in a private law context)

5.9.2 Case management: LIP: McKenzie friends

Re O (children) (representation: McKenzie friend); Re W-R (a child) (representation: McKenzie friend); Re W (children) (representation: McKenzie friend)
[2005] EWCA Civ 759, [2005] 2 FCR 563, [1]–[2], [67]–[73], [126]–[135] (Wall LJ) *quotation limited to* [1]–[2], [126]–[135]

[1] This is the judgment of the court. As it relates in part to the guidance issued by the Office of the President of the Family Division relating to McKenzie Friends, reported at [2005] 35 Fam Law 405, we have taken the opportunity to show it in draft to the President, who has authorised us to say that in so far as it amplifies that guidance, he is in full agreement with it, and in particular with [124]–[138] below.

[2] These three appeals raise two important issues of practice in relation to unrepresented litigants in the family justice system. The two issues are:

(1) the circumstances in which such litigants may invoke the assistance of what have become known as 'McKenzie friends' in family proceedings held in private; and (2) the extent to which (if at all) it is necessary for an unrepresented litigant to seek the permission of the court to disclose confidential documents and information generated by the court process both to a McKenzie friend and to other third parties.

…

[126] Our second point is that we fully endorse the guidance from the office of the President referred to in the previous paragraph. Nothing in this judgment is to be read as in any sense being in conflict with it. To the contrary, whilst some points we make may contain a different or slightly stronger emphasis than that contained in the guidance, everything in this judgment is, in our view, in conformity with it. For example, the guidance contains the following two bullet points:

- 'A litigant in person wishing to have the help of a McKenzie Friend should be allowed to do so unless the judge is satisfied that fairness and the interests of justice do not so require. The presumption in favour of permitting a McKenzie Friend is a strong one …
- The court may refuse to allow a McKenzie Friend to act or continue to act in that capacity where the judge forms the view that the assistance he has given, or may give, impedes the efficient administration of justice. However, the court should also consider whether a firm an unequivocal warning to the litigant and / or the McKenzie Friend might suffice in the first instance.'

[127] The court must plainly retain control over its own procedure. We use slightly different language in our summary at [128] below, but the underlying principles being applied are, in our view, the same.

[128] Thus dealing firstly with the manner in which applications for the appointment of a McKenzie should be treated, we have already made it clear that we accept in their entirety the submissions made to us by Mr Spon-Smith. In particular, we highlight the following points:

'1. The purpose of allowing a litigant in person the assistance of a McKenzie friend is to further the interests of justice by achieving a level playing field and ensuring a fair hearing. We endorse the proposition that the presumption in favour of allowing a litigant in person the assistance of a *McKenzie* friend is very strong, and that such a request should only be refused for compelling reasons. Furthermore, should a judge identify such reasons, (s)he must explain them carefully and fully to both the litigant in person and the would-be McKenzie friend.

2. Where a litigant in person wishes to have the assistance of a McKenzie friend in private family law proceedings relating to

children, the sooner that intention is made known to the court and the sooner the court's agreement for the use of the particular McKenzie friend is obtained, the better. In the same way that judicial continuity is important, the McKenzie friend, if he is to be involved, will be most useful to the litigant in person and to the court if he is in a position to advise the litigant throughout.

3. We do not think it good practice to exclude the proposed McKenzie friend from the courtroom or chambers whilst the application by the litigant in person for his assistance is being made. The litigant who needs the assistance of a McKenzie friend is likely to need the assistance of such a friend to make the application for his appointment in the first place. In any event, it seems to us helpful for the proposed McKenzie friend to be present so that any concerns about him can be ventilated in his presence, and so that the judge can satisfy her/himself that the McKenzie friend fully understands his role (and in particular the fact that disclosure of confidential court documents is made to him for the purposes of the proceedings only—as to which see [132] to [138] below) and that the McKenzie friend will abide by the court's procedural rules.

4. In this context it will always be helpful for the court if the proposed McKenzie friend can produce either a short curriculum vitae or a statement about himself, confirming that he has no personal interest in the case, and that he understands both the role of the McKenzie friend and the court's rules as to confidentiality.

5. We have already stated that any litigant in person who seeks the assistance of a McKenzie friend should be allowed that assistance unless there are compelling reasons for refusing it. The following, of themselves, do not, in our judgment, constitute compelling reasons:
   (1) that the litigant in person appears to the judge to be of sufficient intelligence to be able to conduct the case on his own without the assistance of a McKenzie friend;
   (2) the fact that the litigant appears to the judge to have a sufficient mastery of the facts of the case and of the documentation to enable him to conduct the case on his own without the assistance of a McKenzie friend;
   (3) the fact that the hearing at which the litigant in person seeks the assistance of a McKenzie friend is a directions appointment, or a case management appointment;
   (4) (subject to what we say below) the fact that the proceedings are confidential and that the court papers contain sensitive information relating to the family's affairs.'

[129] We do, of course, understand the point made to us by both Mr Duncan Watson and Ms Gill that a parent who is in conflict with his or her

former partner or spouse may well be wary of allowing a stranger who is not legally qualified into a private hearing in order to assist his or her estranged partner in relation to the dispute between them. But we think there are several powerful factors which properly outweigh a reliance on any such reluctance. The first is the compelling art 6 argument. In each of the cases before us, the party opposing the litigant in person was legally represented by solicitors and counsel. Even if the litigant in person is unrepresented from choice, the art 6 argument for allowing him a McKenzie friend remains powerful.

[130] Secondly, the proceedings remain confidential. The presence of the McKenzie friend does not affect the confidentiality of the proceedings. Thirdly, as Mr Spon-Smith pointed out, participation in court proceedings involves a discussion of personal matters in front of a variety of strangers, albeit that they have an official function of some kind or another. There is, of course, currently a great deal of pressure to open up the family courts. As the law currently stands, the Press is entitled to be present in the Family Proceedings Court, although it is a right rarely taken up. If journalists are to be admitted to hearings in chambers in the county court and the High Court, parties will have to become accustomed to giving evidence in their presence.

[131] Finally, and this is the point to which we now turn, the court can, in our view, ensure that the confidentiality of the proceedings is protected against unauthorised wider disclosure of information.

Disclosure of court documents to McKenzie Friends

[132] We accept the arguments addressed to us on the disclosure issue by Mr Spon-Smith. The critical question, in our judgment is whether or not the court's permission for the disclosure of court documents to a McKenzie friend is now necessary.

[133] Section 62 of the 2004 Act marks a clear relaxation of the rules relating to the disclosure of confidential information in family proceedings. It has not, however, fundamentally altered the law. It may have limited the extent to which certain types of disclosure are a contempt of court, but it has not repealed AJA 1960, s 12, or s 97 of the 1989 Act, nor has it affected the underlying confidentiality of the information generated by family proceedings. That said, it is, in our judgment, difficult to describe a court sanctioned McKenzie friend as 'the public at large or any section of the public'. We therefore see no reason in principle why a litigant in person should not disclose the court papers to his court sanctioned McKenzie friend. At the same time, however, the McKenzie friend must appreciate that disclosure is being made for the purpose of enabling the litigant in person effectively to present his case and thus to ensure a fair hearing. The documents and information disclosed to the McKenzie friend must not be used by the McKenzie friend for any other purpose. Access to the court documents thus brings with it a clear responsibility on the part of the McKenzie friend not to disclose them or publish the information they contain to any third party or outside body without the court's permission.

[134] In the context of disclosure to a McKenzie friend therefore, emphasis in our judgment needs to be placed not only on the purpose for which disclosure of the information is required, but also the use to which the person receiving the information puts it. In our judgment, the argument that it is inappropriate for a McKenzie friend to have access to confidential and in some cases sensitive family information is best met by the judge ensuring, as a matter of practice, that whenever an application is made by a litigant in person for the assistance of a McKenzie friend, both the litigant in person and the McKenzie friend express their clear understanding to the judge of the role of the McKenzie friend and in particular the responsibility which the McKenzie friend has in relation to ensuring that the documents to which he is being given access are being disclosed to him for the sole purpose of assisting the litigant in person present his case in the proceedings.

[135] We therefore entirely endorse Mr Spon-Smith's suggestion that the court should require an assurance from both the litigant in person and the McKenzie friend that the documents will be used only for the purpose of the proceedings and to enable the litigant in person to obtain advice about how to conduct his case. For the reasons we give at [137] below, we do not think a formal undertaking is required. The McKenzie friend will need to understand, however, that it will remain a contempt if he publishes that information to the public at large or a section of the public without the permission of the court.

5.9.3 Case management: LIP: McKenzie friends: very slow to grant rights of audience

Re N (a child) (McKenzie friends: rights of audience) [2008] EWHC 2042 (Fam), [2008] 3 FCR 642, [21]–[42] (Munby J) *quotation limited to* [39]–[42]

[39] The starting point is that a McKenzie friend does not, as such, have a right of audience and, as Clarke LJ put it, that the court can exercise its discretion to grant a McKenzie friend a right of audience in accordance with s 27(2)(c) of the 1990 Act 'only … for good reason' and in the light of and bearing in mind the 'general objective' set out in s 17(1) of the Act and the 'general principle' set out in s 17(3). Moreover, as Peter Gibson LJ said in *Mensah v Islington London BC* (1 December 2000, unreported) at para 56, in the passage endorsed by Brooke LJ in *Paragon Finance plc v Noueiri (Practice Note)* [2001] 1 WLR 2357, at [67], the court should be 'very slow' to grant a McKenzie friend a right of audience.

[40] But this is *not* to say that, as a general principle, such an order can be made only in 'exceptional' circumstances. As Clarke LJ pointed out in *Clarkson v Gilbert* [2000] 3 FCR 10 at 18, [2000] 2 FLR 839 at 846, that would be, in effect, to read restrictive words into a statute which confers an unfettered discretion. Moreover, both Waller and Clarke LJJ were quite clear that the judge at first instance (Eady J) had misdirected himself in law and applied the 'wrong test' in saying that such an order could be made only in exceptional circumstances.

[41] As Clarke LJ said, '[t]here is a spectrum of different circumstances which may arise so that it is difficult to lay down precise guidelines. Cases will vary greatly.' He added, '[a]ll will depend upon the circumstances.' At one end of the spectrum there will be the 'professional' McKenzie friend who acts also as an advocate, the person, as Lord Woolf CJ put it, 'setting themselves up as an unqualified advocate' or, as Clarke LJ put it, 'holding himself out as providing advocacy services, whether for reward or not.' There, as a general principle, the court will make an order only in exceptional circumstances. At the other end of the spectrum there will be the McKenzie friend who is the litigant's spouse or partner, though even there, as Clarke LJ was careful to point out, the circumstances may vary widely. In between—and Mr Holden falls somewhere between the two ends of the spectrum though as it seems to me much nearer the spouse/partner McKenzie friend end of the spectrum than the 'professional' McKenzie friend advocate end of the spectrum—there will be a very wide range of circumstances which it is futile and indeed impossible to classify or categorise. One is, after all, faced with a *spectrum* and not, as some of Mr Bogle's submissions tended to suggest, a set of pigeon holes.

[42] At the end of the day one has to remember that, as Lord Woolf CJ put it ([2000] 3 FCR 10 at 14, [2000] 2 FLR 839 at 842), '[t]he overriding objective is that the courts should do justice.' And one also has to bear in mind, as he observed, the reality that legal aid is not available as readily as it was in the past, leading, as the *President's Guidance: McKenzie Friends* [2008] 2 FCR 90, [2008] 2 FLR 110 comments, to the growth of litigants in person in all levels of family court. Moreover, as the *Guidance* reminds us, 'the attendance of a McKenzie friend will often be of advantage to the court in ensuring the litigant in person receives a fair hearing.' Similarly, in my experience, there will be occasions—sometimes; sometimes not—when the grant of rights of audience to a McKenzie friend will, to adopt the President's words, be of advantage to the court in ensuring the litigant in person receives a fair hearing. Sometimes, indeed, it will be essential if justice is to be done and, equally importantly, perceived by the litigant in person as having been done.

See also *Re J (children)* [2018] EWCA Civ 115, [2018] 2 FCR 527, [73] (McFarlane LJ) addressing the same point (in the context of it being an alternative to an accused LIP questioning a vulnerable accuser, albeit in private law proceedings)

CHAPTER 6

International issues

Chapter contents

CHAPTER 6

International issues

6.1 INTERNATIONAL ISSUES[1]: PROCEDURE

6.1.1 International issues: procedure: early consideration of international issues

Nottingham City Council v LM and others [2014] EWCA Civ 152, [2014] 2 FCR 585, [32], [47] (Ryder LJ), [58] (Sir James Munby P) *quotation limited to* [47]

[47] … Although on the facts of this case it is not appropriate to request another member state to assume jurisdiction, the central message of this case and recent similar examples such as *Re E* should not be overlooked. Jurisdiction must be considered in every children case with an international element and at the earliest opportunity ie when the proceedings are issued and at the case management hearing.

See also *Re F (a child) (care proceedings: habitual residence)* [2014] EWCA Civ 789, [2015] 1 FCR 88, [11(iv)] (Sir James Munby P) considering *Nottingham City Council v LM and others* [2014] EWCA Civ 152, [2014] 2 FCR 585

6.1.2 International issues: procedure: judges to consider jurisdiction if not raised

Re E (a child) (care proceedings: jurisdiction) [2014] EWHC 6 (Fam), [2014] 2 FCR 264, [34]–[36] (Sir James Munby P)

BIIR—future practice in care cases

[34] What of the future?

1 Council Regulation (EC) No 2201/2003 Matrimonial and parental judgments: jurisdiction, recognition and enforcement of matrimonial and parental judgments (BIIa) applied to relevant cases before the United Kingdom's withdrawal from the European Union. The transition period ended on 31 December 2020. The 1996 Convention on Jurisdiction, Applicable Law, Recognition, Enforcement and Co-operation in Respect of Parental Responsibility and Measures for the Protection of Children HCCH 34 (1996) (the 1996 Convention) applies to cases commenced thereafter. The *Compendium* focuses on the applicable law concerning cases commenced after 31 December 2020. However, several authorities concerning BIIa appear to remain relevant. It is submitted that this is so for two principal reasons. First, BIIa had several corresponding provisions to the 1996 Convention. Secondly, aspects of the BIIa-related guidance are of general application to cases with international elements. Where relevant, I will identify the provisions from both the 1996 Convention and BIIa.

[35] It is highly desirable, and from now on good practice will require, that in any care or other public law case with a European dimension the court should set out quite explicitly, both in its judgment and in its order:

(i) the basis upon which, in accordance with the relevant provisions of BIIR, it is, as the case may be, either accepting or rejecting jurisdiction; and

(ii) the basis upon which, in accordance with art 15, it either has or, as the case may be, has not decided to exercise its powers under art 15.

[36] This will both demonstrate that the court has actually addressed issues which, one fears, in the past may sometimes have gone unnoticed, and also identify, so there is no room for argument, the precise basis upon which the court has proceeded. Both points, as it seems to me, are vital. Judges must be astute to raise these points even if they have been overlooked by the parties. And where art 17 applies it is the responsibility of the judge to ensure that the appropriate declaration is made.

See also *Re F (a child) (care proceedings: habitual residence)* [2014] EWCA Civ 789, [2015] 1 FCR 88, [11(vi)] (Sir James Munby P) considering *Re E (a child) (care proceedings: jurisdiction)* [2014] EWHC 6 (Fam), [2014] 2 FCR 264

6.1.3 International issues: procedure: good practice to record decisions

See Chapter 6.1.2 International issues: procedure: judge to consider jurisdiction if not raised

See also *Re F (a child) (care proceedings: habitual residence)* [2014] EWCA Civ 789, [2015] 1 FCR 88, [11(v)] (Sir James Munby P) considering *Re E (a child) (care proceedings: jurisdiction)* [2014] EWHC 6 (Fam), [2014] 2 FCR 264

6.1.4 International issues: procedure: Vienna Convention[2]: duty to inform foreign authorities

Re E (a child) (care proceedings: jurisdiction) [2014] EWHC 6 (Fam), [2014] 2 FCR 264, [38]–[48] (Sir James Munby P) *quotation limited to* [38], [41], [43]–[48]

The Vienna Convention

[38] Articles 36 and 37 of the Vienna Convention on Consular Relations 1963 are probably not very familiar to most family lawyers. So I set them out at length.

…

[41] This is not the occasion for any elaborate discussion of the effect of these provisions as a matter of either public international law or English domestic law (as to which see the Consular Relations Act 1968 and the

2 Vienna Convention on Consular Relations (1963) 596 UNTS 261.

Diplomatic and Consular Premises Act 1987). I am concerned only with what they suggest as good practice in care cases. But in that context there are, as it seems to me, three points to be borne in mind.

(i) First, art 36 enshrines the principle that consular officers of foreign states shall be free to communicate with and have access to their nationals, just as nationals of foreign states shall be free to communicate with and have access to their consular officers.

(ii) Second, the various obligations and rights referred to in paras (b) and (c) of art 36(1) apply whenever a foreign national is 'detained'; and where a foreign national is detained the 'competent authorities' in this country have the obligations referred to in para (b).

(iii) Third, art 37(b) applies whenever a 'guardian' is to be appointed for a minor or other foreign national who lacks full capacity. And art 37(b) imposes a particular 'duty' on the 'competent authorities' in such a case.

...

The Vienna Convention—future practice in care cases

[43] What of the future?

[44] I express no views as to the effect of arts 36 and 37 of the Convention as a matter of either public international law or English domestic law. There is no need for me to do so and it is probably better that I do not. Nor do I take it upon myself to proffer guidance to local authorities, health trusts and other public bodies as to how they should interpret whatever obligations they may have under the Convention. That is a matter for others. What I do, however, need to do is suggest how as a matter of good practice family judges, when hearing care and other public law cases, should from now on approach these provisions.

[45] In considering the possible implications of arts 36 and 37 of the Convention, family judges should assume that, in appropriate circumstances, the court may itself be a 'competent authority'. They should also assume that there is a 'detention' within the meaning of art 36 whenever someone, whether the child or a parent, is being deprived of their liberty within the meaning of art 5 of the European Convention for the Protection of Human Rights and Fundamental Freedoms 1950 (as set out in Sch 1 to the Human Rights Act 1998), for example, in accordance with ss 2 or 3 of the Mental Health Act 1984 or, in the case of a child, in accordance with s 25 of the Children Act 1989.

[46] In cases involving foreign nationals there must be transparency and openness as between the English family courts and the consular and other authorities of the relevant foreign state. This is vitally important, both as a matter of principle and, not least, in order to maintain the confidence of foreign nationals and foreign states in our family justice system. To seek to shelter in this context behind our normal practice of sitting in private and treating s 12 of the Administration of Justice Act 1960 as limiting the permissible flow of information to outsiders, is not merely unprincipled; it is likely to be counter-productive and, potentially, extremely damaging.

If anyone thinks this an unduly radical approach, they might pause to think how we would react if roles were reversed and the boot was on the other foot.

[47] Given this, it is highly desirable, and from now on good practice will require, that in any care or other public law case:

(i) The court should not in general impose or permit any obstacle to free communication and access between a party who is a foreign national and the consular authorities of the relevant foreign state. In particular, no injunctive or other order should be made which might interfere with such communication and access, nor should s 12 of the Administration of Justice Act 1960 be permitted to have this effect.

(ii) Whenever the court is sitting in private it should normally accede to any request, whether from the foreign national or from the consular authorities of the relevant foreign state, for

(a) permission for an accredited consular official to be present at the hearing as an observer in a non-participatory capacity; and/or

(b) permission for an accredited consular official to obtain a transcript of the hearing, a copy of the order and copies of other relevant documents.

(iii) Whenever a party, whether an adult or the child, who is a foreign national

(a) is represented in the proceedings by a guardian, guardian ad litem or litigation friend; and/or

(b) is detained,

the court should ascertain whether that fact has been brought to the attention of the relevant consular officials and, if it has not, the court should normally do so itself without delay.

[48] If, in any particular case, the court is minded to adopt a different or more restrictive approach it is vital that the court hears submissions before coming to a decision and that it then sets out quite explicitly, both in its judgment and in its order, the reasons for its decision.

See also *Re CB (a child)* [2015] EWCA Civ 888, [2016] 2 WLR 410, [84(i)] (Sir James Munby P) addressing a related point (LAs[3] bringing cases to the attention of a relevant consulate when contemplated)

See also *Re O (a child: the Vienna Convention on Consular Relations 1963)* [2021] EWHC 908 (Fam), [2021] 2 FCR 664, [28]–[33] (Keehan J) addressing a related point (the duty under the Vienna Convention not necessarily being absolute)

See also *Re JL and AO (babies relinquished for adoption)* [2016] EWHC 440 (Fam), [2016] 4 WLR 40, [60]–[70], [92(3)] (Baker J) addressing a related point (whether the duty is absolute in the context of a child having been relinquished for adoption)

3 Local authorities.

6.2 INTERNATIONAL ISSUES: JURISDICTION

6.2.1 International issues: jurisdiction: how to approach the issue

Warrington Borough Council v T and others [2021] EWFC 68, [22] (MacDonald J)

22. In *Re K* [2015] EWCA Civ 352 at [26] the Court of Appeal laid out the analytical structure for determining the question of jurisdiction in respect of a child. Namely, the court first determines whether or not the court in England and Wales has jurisdiction. It does so, depending on the countries involved, with or without reference to various international instruments, and in particular to the jurisdictional provisions of those international instruments. If the English court finds that it has jurisdiction on one of the applicable jurisdictional bases, it may go on to decide whether the other jurisdiction nonetheless should determine the matter. Once again, depending on the countries involved, this decision falls to be taken with or without reference to various international instruments and, in particular, the provisions in those international instruments concerning the transfer of jurisdiction. Where there is no international legal instrument operating as between the two jurisdictions concerned, the latter question will ordinarily fall to be decided by reference to the principle of *forum conveniens*.

6.2.2 International issues: jurisdiction: habitual residence[4]

Proceedings brought by A (Case C-523/07), [2010] 2 WLR 527 (CJEU), [44] (Third Chamber)

44. Therefore, the answer to the second question is that the concept of 'habitual residence' under Article 8(1) of the Regulation must be interpreted as meaning that it corresponds to the place which reflects some degree of integration by the child in a social and family environment. To that end, in particular the duration, regularity, conditions and reasons for the stay on the territory of a Member State and the family's move to that State, the child's nationality, the place and conditions of attendance at school, linguistic knowledge and the family and social relationships of the child in that State must be taken into consideration. It is for the national court to establish the habitual residence of the child, taking account of all the circumstances specific to each individual case.

Re A (children) (jurisdiction: return of child) [2013] UKSC 60, [2013] 3 FCR 559, [34]–[55] (Lady Hale DP) *quotation limited to* [34]–[35], [54]–[55]

[34] Jurisdiction under art 8 depends upon where the child is habitually resident. It has hitherto been thought (see, for example, Dicey, Morris and Collins *The Conflict of Laws* (15th edn, 2012), rr 17(2) and 18(2); *Clarke Hall and Morrison on Children*, paras 234 and 236) that the concept of habitual residence, as developed by the courts of England and Wales for

4 1996 Convention, Art 5 is similar (but not identical) to BIIa, Art 8.

the purposes of both the 1986 Act and the Hague Convention on the Civil Aspects of International Child Abduction 1980 (The Hague, 25 October 1980; TS 66 (1986); Cm 33) (the Hague Child Abduction Convention), is different from the concept of habitual residence as interpreted by the Court of Justice of the European Union for the purposes of the Regulation. Very recently, in *DL v EL (Reunite International Child Abduction Centre, intervening)* [2013] EWCA Civ 865 at [48], [2013] 3 FCR 69 at [48], the Court of Appeal has expressed the view that 'there is now no distinction to be drawn' between the test adopted in each of those three contexts. As we are dealing only with habitual residence under the Regulation, it is not strictly necessary for us to resolve that debate.

[35] Nevertheless, it is highly desirable that the same test be adopted and that, if there is any difference, it is that adopted by the Court of Justice. There are several reasons for this. First, the Law Commissions recommended the adoption of 'habitual residence' in part because it had been widely used in international conventions, including the Council of Europe Convention on the Recognition and Enforcement of Decisions concerning Custody of Children and on Restoration of Custody of Children (Luxembourg, 20 May 1980 (Cmnd 8155)) and the Hague Child Abduction Convention, and was likely to be recognised abroad: see Law Com No 138, para 4.15. As Advocate General Kokott pointed out in *Proceedings brought by A* Case C-523/07 [2010] Fam 42, [2010] 2 WLR 527, various international conventions, in particular the Hague Convention of the Protection of Minors 1961, the Hague Convention on Jurisdiction, Applicable Law, Recognition, Enforcement and Co-operation in Respect of Parental Responsibility and Measures for the Protection of Children 1996 which superseded it, and the Hague Child Abduction Convention, formed part of the legislative history of the Regulation. In part, the Regulation supersedes them. In part, they operate alongside one another. The 'fields of application of the various instruments must be consistently demarcated from one another'. This presumed a 'uniform understanding of the concept of habitual residence' (para AG23). Thus it would appear that the purpose of both the 1986 Act and the Regulation was to adopt a concept which would apply across the board.

…

[54] Drawing the threads together, therefore:

(i) All are agreed that habitual residence is a question of fact and not a legal concept such as domicile. There is no legal rule akin to that whereby a child automatically takes the domicile of his parents.

(ii) It was the purpose of the 1986 Act to adopt a concept which was the same as that adopted in the Hague and European Conventions. The Regulation must also be interpreted consistently with those Conventions.

(iii) The test adopted by the European court is 'the place which reflects some degree of integration by the child in a social and family environment' in the country concerned. This depends upon numerous factors, including the reasons for the family's stay in the country in question.

(iv) It is now unlikely that that test would produce any different results from that hitherto adopted in the English courts under the 1986 Act and the Hague Child Abduction Convention.

(v) In my view, the test adopted by the European court is preferable to that earlier adopted by the English courts, being focused on the situation of the child, with the purposes and intentions of the parents being merely one of the relevant factors. The test derived from *Shah v Barnet London BC* [1983] 1 All ER 226, [1983] 2 AC 309 should be abandoned when deciding the habitual residence of a child.

(vi) The social and family environment of an infant or young child is shared with those (whether parents or others) upon whom he is dependent. Hence it is necessary to assess the integration of that person or persons in the social and family environment of the country concerned.

(vii) The essentially factual and individual nature of the inquiry should not be glossed with legal concepts which would produce a different result from that which the factual inquiry would produce.

(viii) As the Advocate General pointed out in para AG45 and the court confirmed in para 43 of *Proceedings brought by A* [2010] Fam 42, [2010] 2 WLR 527, it is possible that a child may have no country of habitual residence at a particular point in time.

[55] So which approach accords most closely with the factual situation of the child—an approach which holds that presence is a necessary pre-cursor to residence and thus to habitual residence or an approach which focuses on the relationship between the child and his primary carer? In my view, it is the former. It is one thing to say that a child's integration in the place where he is at present depends upon the degree of integration of his primary carer. It is another thing to say that he can be integrated in a place to which his primary carer has never taken him. It is one thing to say that a person can remain habitually resident in a country from which he is temporarily absent. It is another thing to say that a person can acquire a habitual residence without ever setting foot in a country. It is one thing to say that a child is integrated in the family environment of his primary carer and siblings. It is another thing to say that he is also integrated into the social environment of a country where he has never been

Re B (a child) (habitual residence: inherent jurisdiction) [2016] UKSC 4, [2016] 2 FCR 307, [27]–[49] (Lord Wilson) *quotation limited to* [27]–[28], [37]–[47]

[27] A child's habitual residence in a state is the internationally recognised threshold to the vesting in the courts of that state of jurisdiction to determine issues in relation to him (or her). Article 8 of Council Regulation 2201/2003/EC (concerning jurisdiction and the recognition and enforcement of judgments in matrimonial matters and the matters of parental responsibility, repealing Regulation 1347/2000/EC) (OJ 2003

L338 p 1) ('Regulation B2R') provides that the courts of an EU state shall have jurisdiction in matters of parental responsibility over a child habitually resident there at the time when the court is seised. By way of exception, art 12 confers jurisdiction on a state which has other links with the child but only where the parties have accepted its jurisdiction. Article 13 provides that, where a child's habitual residence cannot be established (which means where the child is not habitually resident in any EU state) and where art 12 does not apply, jurisdiction vests in the courts of the state in which the child is present. Article 14, entitled 'Residual jurisdiction' provides that, where no court of a member state has jurisdiction under the preceding articles, jurisdiction shall be determined by the laws of each state.

[28] A child's habitual residence is also the thread which unites the provisions of the Hague Convention on the Civil Aspects of International Child Abduction 1980 (The Hague, 25 October 1980; TS 66 (1986); Cm 33) ('the 1980 Convention'). This Convention applies to a child habitually resident in a contracting state immediately before his wrongful removal or retention: art 4. It is the law of that state which dictates whether his removal or retention was wrongful: art 3(a). It is that state to which, subject to exceptions, other contracting states must order the child to be returned: art 12. Under the Hague Convention on Jurisdiction, Applicable Law, Recognition, Enforcement and Co-operation in Respect of Parental Responsibility and Measures for the Protection of Children 1996, concluded on 19 October 1996 (Cm 7727) it is, again, the courts of the contracting state of the child's habitual residence which, as against other contracting states, has jurisdiction to make orders for his protection: art 5(1).

…

[37] In the *Mercredi* case the issue for determination in England and Wales was whether a baby aged two months, lawfully removed by the French mother from the UK to La Réunion, remained habitually resident here five days later when the English court became seised of the British father's application. The CJEU carefully followed its ruling in *Proceedings brought by A* but, by reference to the different facts, chose also to stress, at paras 53 and 56, that the analysis of the social and family environment of a pre-school child would differ from that of a school-age child and would include consideration of the geographic and family origins of the parent who had effected the move and of the family and social connections of that parent and the child with the state to which they had moved.

[38] In *Re A (children) (jurisdiction: return of child)* sub nom *Re A v A (children: habitual residence) (Reunite International Child Abduction Centre intervening)* ('*A v A*') [2013] UKSC 60, [2013] 3 FCR 559, [2014] 1 All ER 827, this court held that the criterion articulated in the two European authorities (some degree of integration by the child in a social and family environment), together with the non-exhaustive identification of considerations there held to be relevant to it, governed the concept of habitual residence in the law of England and Wales: para [54](iii) and (v)

of Baroness Hale DP's judgment, with which all the members of the court (including Lord Hughes at para [81]) agreed. Baroness Hale said at (v) that the European approach was preferable to the earlier English approach because it was 'focused on the situation of the child, with the purposes and intentions of the parents being merely one of the relevant factors'.

[39] It is worthwhile to note that the new criterion requires not the child's full integration in the environment of the new state but only a degree of it. It is clear that in certain circumstances the requisite degree of integration can occur quickly. For example art 9 of Regulation B2R, the detail of which is irrelevant, expressly envisages a child's acquisition of a fresh habitual residence within three months of his move. In the *J* case, cited above, Lord Brandon suggested that the passage of an 'appreciable' period of the time was required before a fresh habitual residence could be acquired. In *Marinos v Marinos* [2007] EWHC 2047 (Fam), [2008] 2 FCR 47, [2007] 2 FLR 1018 at [31], Munby J doubted whether Lord Brandon's suggestion was consonant with the modern European law; and it must now be regarded as too absolute. In *A v A*, cited above, at para [44], Baroness Hale declined to accept that it was impossible to become habitually resident in a single day.

[40] But do the two European authorities assist in identifying the object of central relevance to this appeal, namely the point at which habitual residence is *lost*?

[41] Yes, in two ways.

[42] The first is indirect. Recital (12) to Regulation B2R states:

> 'The grounds of jurisdiction in matters of parental responsibility established in the present Regulation are shaped in the light of the best interests of the child, in particular on the criterion of proximity.'

By proximity, the 'court clearly meant the practical connection between the child and the country concerned': Lord Hughes in *A v A*, cited above, at para [80](ii). In its analysis of the concept of habitual residence the CJEU, both in *Proceedings brought by A* at para 35 and in the *Mercredi* case at paras 46 and 47, stressed the significance of recital 12. Of course it does not follow that the court can construe a child's habitual residence by reference to the result which best serves his interests. The effect of the recital is more subtle and more limited yet nevertheless significant: where interpretation of the concept of habitual residence can reasonably follow each of two paths, the courts should follow the path perceived better to serve the interests of children. Or, to be more specific to the facts of the present case: if interpretation of the concept of habitual residence can reasonably yield both a conclusion that a child has an habitual residence and, alternatively, a conclusion that he lacks any habitual residence, the court should adopt the former.

[43] The second is arrestingly direct. In her opinion in *Proceedings brought by A* Advocate General Kokott said:

> '45. It is also conceivable in exceptional cases that during a transitional stage there will no longer be habitual residence in the former state while the status in the new state has not yet crystallised into habitual residence. Precisely for such a case, article 13 of [Regulation B2R] confers a residual jurisdiction on the courts of the member state in which the child is present.'

In its judgment in the same case the court said:

> '43. However, it is conceivable that at the end of [the integration] assessment it is impossible to establish the member state in which the child has his habitual residence. In such an exceptional case, and if article 12 … is not applicable, the national courts of the member state in which the child is present acquire jurisdiction … pursuant to article 13(1) …'

The court's reference to a situation in which it is 'impossible to establish' the child's habitual residence might at first sight seem ambiguous. Is it referring to a situation in which the child has an habitual residence somewhere but the evidence does not enable the court to identify the state in which he has it? The answer is clearly no. The court is referring to a situation in which a child has no habitual residence. The court is expressly endorsing para 45 of the Advocate General's opinion (note its repetition of her words 'conceivable' and 'exceptional') but is recasting her point within the slightly ambiguous language of art 13 of Regulation B2R, namely 'where a child's habitual residence cannot be established'.

[44] In *A v A*, cited above, Baroness Hale, at para [54](viii), referred to para 45 of the Advocate General's opinion and to para 43 of the court's judgment in *Proceedings brought by A* and observed that it was 'possible' for a child to have no habitual residence. Lord Hughes, at para [80](ix), endorsed the European court's conclusion by saying that the circumstances in which a child had no habitual residence would be 'exceptional'.

[45] I conclude that the modern concept of a child's habitual residence operates in such a way as to make it highly unlikely, albeit conceivable, that a child will be in the limbo in which the courts below have placed B. The concept operates in the expectation that, when a child gains a new habitual residence, he loses his old one. Simple analogies are best: consider a see-saw. As, probably quite quickly, he puts *down* those first roots which represent the requisite degree of integration in the environment of the new state, *up* will probably come the child's roots in that of the old state to the point at which he achieves the requisite de-integration (or, better, disengagement) from it.

[46] One of the well-judged submissions of Mr William Tyler QC on behalf of the respondent is that, were it minded to remove any gloss from the domestic concept of habitual residence (such as, I interpolate, Lord Brandon's third preliminary point in the *J* case), the court should strive not to introduce others. A gloss is a purported sub-rule which distorts application of the rule. The identification of a child's habitual residence

is overarchingly a question of fact. In making the following three suggestions about the point at which habitual residence might be lost and gained, I offer not sub-rules but expectations which the fact-finder may well find to be unfulfilled in the case before him:

(a) the deeper the child's integration in the old state, probably the less fast his achievement of the requisite degree of integration in the new state;

(b) the greater the amount of adult pre-planning of the move, including pre-arrangements for the child's day-to-day life in the new state, probably the faster his achievement of that requisite degree; and

(c) were all the central members of the child's life in the old state to have moved with him, probably the faster his achievement of it and, conversely, were any of them to have remained behind and thus to represent for him a continuing link with the old state, probably the less fast his achievement of it.

[47] Lord Brandon's third preliminary point in the *J* case, set out in para [34], above, should no longer be regarded as correct; and Hogg J fell into error in being guided by it. As exemplified by the terms in which Lord Brandon applied it to the facts of that case, also set out in para [34], his analysis of a child's habitual residence afforded to parental intention a dispositive effect inconsistent with the child-focused European concept now adopted in England and Wales; and the result of his analysis was to consign a large number of children to the limbo of lacking any habitual residence in circumstances in which the modern law expects such a result to be exceptional, albeit conceivable. It is nevertheless fruitless to inquire whether the conclusion of the appellate committee about the child's loss of habitual residence in Australia within three weeks of his move would remain valid today.

See also *H v R* [2021] EWHC 2024 (Fam), [16]–[19] (MacDonald J) addressing the same point (confirming that the test for habitual residence has not changed post Brexit)

See also *Re F (a child) (care proceedings: habitual residence)* [2014] EWCA Civ 789, [2015] 1 FCR 88, [10]–[11] (Sir James Munby P) providing an overview of the law on this point

See also *Re S (a child)* [2020] EWCA Civ 923, [2021] 1 FCR 291, [32]–[34] (Moylan LJ) providing an overview of the law on this point

6.2.3 International issues: jurisdiction: habitual residence: when does habitual residence change?

Re B (a child: habitual residence) [2020] EWCA Civ 1187, [2021] 1 FCR 105, [89]–[96], [129], (Moylan LJ), [133] (Baker LJ)

[89] Picking up what Black LJ said in *Re J (Finland)*, I also propose to repeat my conclusions from *M (children)*, in particular in respect of Lord Wilson's see-saw analogy:

'[61] In conclusion on this issue, while Lord Wilson's seesaw analogy can assist the court when deciding the question of habitual residence, it does not replace the core guidance given in *A v A* and other cases to the approach which should be taken to the determination of the habitual residence. This requires an analysis of the child's situation in and connections with the state or states in which he or she is said to be habitually resident for the purpose of determining in which state he or she has the requisite degree of integration to mean that their residence there is habitual.

[62] Further, the analogy needs to be used with caution because if it is applied as though it is the test for habitual residence it can, as in my view is demonstrated by the present case, result in the court's focus being disproportionately on the extent of a child's continuing roots or connections with and/or on an historical analysis of their previous roots or connections rather than focusing, as is required, on the child's *current* situation (at the relevant date). This is not to say continuing or historical connections are not relevant but they are part of, not the primary focus of, the court's analysis when deciding the critical question which is *where* is the child habitually resident and not, simply, *when* was a previous habitual residence lost.'

[90] Finally, on the issue of habitual residence, given the circumstances of this case, it is relevant to note that habitual residence can change from one state to another extremely quickly.

[91] In *A v A*, at [44], in a passage approved by Lord Wilson in *In Re B* at [39], Lady Hale made clear that she did not 'accept that it is impossible to become habitually resident in a single day. It will all depend on the circumstances'. As an issue of fact it will, clearly, 'all depend on the circumstances' but, to use Lord Wilson's see-saw analogy, there is nothing which prevents 'deeper roots' coming up very quickly and being replaced by another habitual residence which will frequently have shallower roots. Those latter roots can still provide a sufficient, 'some', degree of integration to establish habitual residence.

[92] It sometimes appears, as referred to further below, that Lord Wilson's observations in *In Re B* have been interpreted as meaning that deep roots will invariably take time to come up. This is not the case in part because, if it was, it could result in a child continuing to be habitually resident in a country with which they had no substantive continuing practical connection.

[93] Indeed, in my view, it was in part his concern to make clear that the loss of a previous and the acquisition of a new habitual residence could *both* happen equally quickly that led Lord Wilson to conclude, at [47], that Lord Brandon's third preliminary point 'should no longer be regarded as correct' because, at [39], it was 'too absolute'. The point which had been proposed by Lord Brandon, as set out in *In Re B*, at [34], was that 'there is a significant difference between a person ceasing to be habitually resident in country A, and his subsequently becoming habitually resident in country B'.

[94] It is also relevant to note the terms of two of Lord Wilson's three 'expectations', at [46], which were as follows:

> '(b) the greater the amount of adult pre-planning of the move, including pre-arrangements for the child's day-to-day life in the new state, probably the faster his achievement of that requisite degree; and (c) were all the central members of the child's life in the old state to have moved with him, probably the faster his achievement of it and, conversely, were any of them to have remained behind and thus to represent for him a continuing link with the old state, probably the less fast his achievement of it.'

It sometimes appears that these two elements have been overshadowed by the third, namely '(a) the deeper the child's integration in the old state, probably the less fast his achievement of the requisite degree of integration in the new state'.

[95] I would emphasise that Lord Wilson's graphic analogy of the see-saw does *not* mean that habitual residence cannot change very quickly. This, as I have endeavoured to explain, is, in my view, clear from what he said in *In Re B* itself. However, it can also be seen from what Lady Hale said in *In Re LC*:

> '[63] The quality of a child's stay in a new environment, in which he has only recently arrived, cannot be assessed without reference to the past. Some habitual residences may be harder to lose than others and others may be harder to gain. If a person leaves his home country with the intention of emigrating and having made all the necessary plans to do so, he may lose one habitual residence immediately and acquire a new one very quickly. If a person leaves his home country for a temporary purpose or in ambiguous circumstances, he may not lose his habitual residence there for some time, if at all, and correspondingly he will not acquire a new habitual residence until then or even later. Of course, there are many permutations in between, where a person may lose one habitual residence without gaining another.'

[96] I need also, briefly, to deal with the jurisdictional issues raised by Ms Renton. I make clear that this is only a very limited review. Under both BIIa and the 1996 Convention, the habitual residence of the child is the primary basis on which the courts of a state will have substantive jurisdiction to determine welfare issues. Accordingly, when a child is habitually resident in an EU Member State or a 1996 Convention Contracting state, that state will have substantive jurisdiction.

...

[129] What degree of integration and what degree of disengagement will be sufficient to mean that a child is habitually resident in the state to which the family has moved will obviously vary from case to case. However, adopting what Black LJ said in *Re J (Finland)*, in my view the judge has

not demonstrated sufficiently that she had in mind the relevant factors in B's old and new lives. She did not carry out a sufficient comparative or balancing exercise of the factors connecting B with France and with Australia.

...

[133] Like my Lord, I consider that the judge erred in focusing on the position of the mother rather than the family unit as a whole. Furthermore, although the judge warned herself that there should not be 'any sort of equivalence' between the family's situation in France and Australia, it is clear reading her judgment as a whole that, when assessing the degree of current integration in France, she used the degree of historic integration Australia as a comparator. To my mind, this is a further illustration of the need for caution, identified by Moylan LJ in his judgment in the recent decision in *M (children) (habitual residence: 1980 Hague Child Abduction Convention)* [2020] EWCA Civ 1105, when applying the 'see-saw' analogy suggested by Lord Wilson in *In Re B (a child) (Reunite International Child Abduction Centre and others intervening)* [2016] UKSC 4. There is a danger that the analogy may lead judges to think that, when a family moves from one country to another, there needs to be an equivalent degree of integration in the second country to that enjoyed in the first before habitual residence in the second country can be acquired.

See also *Re B (a child) (habitual residence: inherent jurisdiction)* [2016] UKSC 4, [2016] 2 FCR 307, [40]–[47] (Lord Wilson), see Chapter 6.2.2 International issues: jurisdiction: habitual residence

See also *AC v NC* [2021] EWHC 946 (Fam), [2021] 3 FCR 205, [25]–[29] (Mostyn J) addressing the same point (including considering that the 'limbo' situation would be 'vanishingly unlikely' or 'near impossible' in light of the 'punctum temporis' where habitual residence changes, albeit in the context of a return order case under the Hague Convention[5])

See also *Re M (children: habitual residence: 1980 Hague Child Abduction Convention)* [2020] EWCA Civ 1105, [2021] 1 FCR 155, [61]–[62] (Moylan LJ) addressing the same point (albeit in a return order case under the Hague Convention)

6.2.4 International issues: jurisdiction: habitual residence: no habitual residence[6]

Warrington Borough Council v T and others [2021] EWFC 68, [31]–[34] (MacDonald J)

31. As noted, Brussels IIa has ceased to have effect in cases commenced after the conclusion of the transition period governing the departure of

5 1980 Convention on the Civil Aspects of International Child Abduction (1980) HCCH 28.
6 1996 Convention, art 6(2) is similar (but not identical) to BIIa, art 13.

the United Kingdom from the European Union, which came to an end on 31 December 2020 at 11pm. Art 5 and Art 6 of the 1996 Hague Convention provides as follows with respect to jurisdiction to take measures directed to the protection of the person or property of the child:

> 'Article 5
>
> (1) The judicial or administrative authorities of the Contracting State of the habitual residence of the child have jurisdiction to take measures directed to the protection of the child's person or property.
>
> (2) Subject to Article 7, in case of a change of the child's habitual residence to another Contracting State, the authorities of the State of the new habitual residence have jurisdiction.
>
> Article 6
>
> (1) For refugee children and children who, due to disturbances occurring in their country, are internationally displaced, the authorities of the Contracting State on the territory of which these children are present as a result of their displacement have the jurisdiction provided for in paragraph 1 of Article 5.
>
> (2) The provisions of the preceding paragraph also apply to children whose habitual residence cannot be established.'

32. With respect to the provisions of Art 6(2), having regard to the Explanatory Report for the 1996 Convention at [45], it would appear that the words 'whose habitual residence cannot be established' encompass a child who does not, as a matter of fact, have a habitual residence. It has been said that the modern concept of habitual residence operates so that it is highly unlikely that a child will be left without a habitual residence (see *Re B (A Child)(Habitual Residence: Inherent Jurisdiction)* [2016] 1 FLR 561 at [45]), although there have been cases where that has been the outcome (see for example, *Re F (Habitual Residence: Peripatetic Existence)* [2015] 1 FLR 1303 per Peter Jackson J (as he then was) and *CL v AL* [2017] EWHC 2154 (Fam) per Keehan J). Within this context, I also note that the Lagarde Explanatory Report on the 1996 Convention notes as follows at [41]:

> 'The change of habitual residence implies both the loss of the former habitual residence and the acquisition of a new habitual residence. It may be that a certain lapse of time exists between these two elements, but the acquisition of this new habitual residence may also be instantaneous in the simple hypothesis of a move of a family from one country to another. This is then a question of fact which is for the authorities called upon to make a decision to assess…'

And paragraph [4.17] of the Practical Handbook on the operation of the 1996 Hague Convention states that:

> 'However, there are circumstances where it might not be possible to establish the habitual residence of a child. Such circumstances could

include, for example: (1) when a child moves frequently between two or more States, (2) where a child is unaccompanied or abandoned and it is difficult to find evidence to establish his / her habitual residence or (3) where a child's previous habitual residence has been lost and there is insufficient evidence to support the acquisition of a new habitual residence'

33. In a situation where the child does not have a habitual residence, Art 6(2) of the 1996 Hague Convention will apply and the court of a Contracting State to the Convention will have a jurisdiction of necessity based on the presence of the child in its jurisdiction. As to the extent of that jurisdiction, the Lagarde Explanatory Report notes at [45] that:

> 'The text does not specify whether the court of the Contracting State, on the territory of which the child who has no habitual residence is present, is to retain the jurisdiction attributed to it by Article 6, paragraph 2, where measures of protection for the child have been taken in a non-Contracting State, for example in the State of the child's nationality. It seems reasonable to think that the Convention does not limit the jurisdiction of a court based on presence, but rather leaves it free to determine according to its law whether it should recognise and give effect to the measures taken in this third State.'

34. Finally with respect to the jurisdictional framework, and within the foregoing context, the United Kingdom is party to the 1996 Hague Convention and it came into force in this jurisdiction on 1 November 2012. Gabon is not a party to the 1996 Hague Convention. However, in circumstances where this court is the court currently seised of the issue of jurisdiction, and this jurisdiction is a signatory to the 1996 Hague Convention, I am satisfied that the question of whether this court has jurisdiction in respect of K falls to be determined by reference, *inter alia*, to the jurisdictional provisions that apply under Arts 5 and 6 of the 1996 Hague Convention, notwithstanding that Gabon is not a Contracting State to that Convention (see *Re A (Jurisdiction: Return of Child)* [2014] AC 1).

See also *Re B (a child) (habitual residence: inherent jurisdiction)* [2016] UKSC 4, [2016] 2 FCR 307, [45] (Lord Wilson) addressing the same point, see Chapter 6.2.2 International issues: jurisdiction: habitual residence

6.2.5 International issues: jurisdiction: habitual residence is the test: at what time?

Re NH [2015] EWHC 2299 (Fam), [2016] 1 FCR 16, [24] (Cobb J)

[24] Although like BIIa, the 1996 Child Protection Convention founds primary jurisdiction on the country of the child's habitual residence, unlike BIIa, the 1996 Child Protection Convention does not specify the time at which habitual residence is to be determined; in BIIa it is specifically said to be 'at the time the court is seised', words which are absent from the equivalent provision of the 1996 Convention. Ms Lucey and Mr Barda

presented their respective submissions as if the words 'at the time the court is seised' were imported into art 5. It is not on the facts material for a determination of the issues in this case for me to identify specifically the date at which habitual residence is to be assessed; whether the evidence were to be evaluated as at 12 May 2015 (the date on which the proceedings were issued) or 21 July 2015 (the date of the hearing), the test would be unlikely to produce a different result. But as the principle of perpetuatio fori does *not* apply under the 1996 Child Protection Convention as it does under BIIa (see in this context art 13 of the 1996 Child Protection Convention) it seems to me that the phrase should be applied as at the date of the *hearing* (see generally, paras 38–43 of the *Explanatory Report* of Paul Lagarde, 1997).

6.2.6 International issues: jurisdiction: transfer between contracting states[7]: test

Re D (care proceedings: 1996 Hague Convention: Article 9 request)
[2021] EWHC 1970 (Fam), [5], [36], [41]–[44], [58] (Knowles J)

5. Mr Setright QC informed me that this case may be one of the first occasions in which the courts of England and Wales have been invited to consider the provisions of Articles 8 and 9 of the 1996 Convention in the context of public law proceedings. Given that these provisions are likely to take on a greater degree of prominence as the United Kingdom has exited the transitional arrangements with the European Union, it is possible that this decision may assist future decision-makers.

...

The 1996 Convention

36. The formal title of the 1996 Convention is the '*Convention on Jurisdiction, Applicable Law, Recognition, Enforcement and Cooperation in respect of Parental Responsibility and Measures for the Protection of Children'*. The Preamble sets out broad statements of principle which inform the provisions of the 1996 Convention, namely the importance of international cooperation for the protection of children and the confirmation that the best interests of the child are a primary consideration in matters related to the protection of the child. The principle of *'best interests of the child'* is referenced several times elsewhere in the body of the 1996 Convention. The United Kingdom and Switzerland are both signatories to the 1996 Convention.

...

7 1996 Convention, arts 8 and 9 are similar (but not identical) to BIIa, art 15. Please note that there are material differences between the articles of the two treaties and these differences would demand careful consideration before applying any BIIa art 15 authority to a case concerning the 1996 Convention.

41. In Child and Family Agency v D (R intervening) (ECJ) [2017] 2 WLR 949, the Court of Justice of the European Union held that, with respect to applications for transfer pursuant to Article 15 of BIIA, the court having jurisdiction must determine whether the transfer of the case to that other court is such as to provide genuine and specific added value, with respect to the decision to be taken in relation to the child, as compared with the possibility of the case remaining before that court. In that context, the court having jurisdiction may take into account, among other factors, the rules of procedure in the other member state, such as those applicable to the taking of evidence required for dealing with the case. The court having jurisdiction should not, however, take into consideration within such an assessment, the substantive law of that other member state which might be applicable by the court of that other member state, if the case were transferred to it (paragraph 57).

42. Domestically, the procedural rules governing transfers under the 1996 Convention apply equally to the hitherto more familiar provisions of Article 15 of BIIA (Council Regulation (EC) No 2201/2003). The procedure for considering the making of requests pursuant to Article 9 of the 1996 Convention is set out at rule 12.65 of the Family Procedure Rules 2010:

> '(1) An application for the court to request transfer of jurisdiction in a matter concerning a child from another Member State or another Contracting State under Article 15 of the Council Regulation, or Article 9 of the 1996 Hague Convention (as the case may be) must be made to the principal registry and heard in the High Court.
>
> (2) An application must be made without notice to any other person and the court may give directions about joining any other party to the application.
>
> (3) Where there is agreement between the court and the court or competent authority to which the request under paragraph (1) is made to transfer the matter to the courts of England and Wales, the court will consider with that other court or competent authority the specific timing and conditions for the transfer.
>
> (4) Upon receipt of agreement to transfer jurisdiction from the court or other competent authority in the Member State or Contracting State to which the request has been made, the court officer will serve on the applicant a notice that jurisdiction has been accepted by the courts of England and Wales.
>
> (5) The applicant must attach the notice referred to in paragraph (3) to any subsequent application in relation to the child.
>
> (6) Nothing in this rule requires an application with respect to a child commenced following a transfer of jurisdiction to be made to or heard in the High Court.

(7) Upon allocation, the court to which the proceedings are allocated must immediately fix a directions hearing to consider the future conduct of the case.'

By way of clarification, paragraph (5) refers to a notice '*referred to in paragraph (3)*'. This is incorrect as it is paragraph (4) which contains the provision with respect to a notice that jurisdiction has been accepted by the courts in this jurisdiction.

43. Rule 12.66 sets out the procedure following receipt of a request to assume jurisdiction:

'(1) Where any court other than the High Court receives a request to assume jurisdiction in a matter concerning a child from a court or other authority which has jurisdiction in another Member States or Contracting State, that court must immediately refer the request to a Judge of the High Court for a decision regarding acceptance of jurisdiction to be made.

(2) Upon the High Court agreeing to the request under paragraph (1), the court officer will notify the parties to the proceedings before the other Member State or Contracting State of that decision, and the case must be allocated as if the application had been made in England and Wales.

(3) Upon allocation, the court to which the proceedings are allocated must immediately fix a directions hearing to consider the future conduct of the case.

(4) The court officer will serve notice of the directions hearing on all parties to the proceedings in the other Member State or Contracting State no later than 5 days before the date of that hearing.'

44. The decision of Baker J (as he then was) in Re M & L (Children) [2016] EWHC 2535 (Fam) was the first domestic decision concerning the making of a request under Article 9 of the 1996 Convention. Baker J adopted, in respect of the Convention, the approach to comity applied to cases concerning BIIA:

> '33. In my judgment, the English and Norwegian courts are equally competent in general terms to determine issues about children. Each court operates in a sophisticated and advanced legal system manned by experienced judges who are manifestly capable of making decisions in this type of case. Although there are some differences in the respective processes, and each court has advantages which the other does not, overall there is no substantial difference. Comparisons are odious. As Mostyn J observed in Re T [2013] EWHC 521 (Fam) at paragraph 37, the court
>
> > 'should not descend to some kind of divisive value judgment about the laws and procedures of our European neighbours'

and as Sir James Munby P added in Re E (supra) at paragraph 20,

> 'beneath all the apparent differences in language and legal system, family judges around the world are daily engaged on very much the same task, using very much the same tools and apply the same insights and approaches as those we are familiar with'.'

The approach to comity adopted by Baker J finds expression in the Supreme Court's decision in *In the matter of N (Children)* [2016] UKSC 15 where, at paragraph 4, Baroness Hale stated as follows:

> 'It goes without saying that the provisions of the Regulation are based upon mutual respect and trust between the member states. It is not for the courts of this or any other country to question the 'competence, diligence, resources or efficacy of either the child protection services or the courts' of another state: see *In Re M (Brussels II Revised: Article 15)* [2014] 2 FLR 1372, para. 54(v), per Sir James Munby P. As the Practice Guide for the application of the Brussels IIa Regulation puts it, at p 35, para 3.3.3, the assessment of whether a transfer would be in the best interests of the child 'should be based on the principle of mutual trust and on the assumption that the courts of all member states are in principle competent to deal with a case'. This principle goes both ways. Just as we must respect and trust the competence of other member states, so must they respect and trust ours.'

...

The Article 9 Request: Qualifying Criteria

58. There are three criteria to be considered before requests can be made pursuant to Article 9 of the 1996 Convention. First, the requesting State must fall within the terms of Article 8(2) which provide specific criteria at subparagraphs (a) to (c) and a broader catch-all at sub-paragraph (d) that the child has a '*substantial connection*' with the requesting State. Second, the purpose underlying a transfer request must not engage any of the provisions of Article 4, being issues which lie outside the scope of the 1996 Convention. Third, in accordance with Article 9(1), the authorities of the requesting State must '*consider they are better placed in the particular case to assess the child's best interests*'.

See also *Re N (children) (adoption: jurisdiction)* [2016] UKSC 15, [2016] 3 FCR 394, [36]–[58] (Lady Hale DP) providing an overview of the law on a related point (BIIa, Art 15)

See also *Nottingham City Council v LM and others* [2014] EWCA Civ 152, [2014] 2 FCR 585, [20] (Ryder LJ), [54] (Sir James Munby P) providing an overview of the law on a related point (BIIa, Art 15)

See also *Child and Family Agency v JD* (Case C-2016/819) [2017] 1 FCR 320 (CJEU), 331D–333E (Third Chamber) providing an overview of the law on a related point (BIIa, Art 15)

See also *Re D (care proceedings: 1996 Hague Convention: Article 9 request)* [2021] EWHC 1970 (Fam), [45]–[48] (Knowles J) addressing a related point (withdrawal of applications to transfer under the 1996 Convention)

6.2.7 International issues: jurisdiction: transfer between contracting states: evidence of genuine and specific added value

A Local Authority v MM [2020] EWFC 65, [2021] 1 FCR 211, [1], [25]–[29] (Mostyn J)

[1] This is an application by the fourth respondent under art 15 of Council Regulation (EC) No 2201/2003 (Brussels IIa) for the welfare stage of these care proceedings to be transferred to Romania. Although this may be one of the last applications of its type to be heard given the United Kingdom's impending abandonment of the European Union, the issue will remain relevant as art 8 of the 1996 Hague Convention on Jurisdiction, Applicable Law, Recognition, Enforcement and Cooperation in Respect of Parental Responsibility and Measures for the Protection of Children contains a similar (but not identical) provision.

...

[25] Under the second question this court has to be satisfied that the relevant court in Romania would be 'better placed' to hear the welfare phase of these care proceedings. The phrase 'better placed' is ambiguous. Does it mean merely that the other court is merely better situated geographically to deal with that part of the case? Or does it mean that the other court is more suitable, that is to say better adapted, for reasons wider than mere geography, to hear the case? It is interesting that the French translation of art 15 uses the same ambiguous phrase: '*mieux placée*'. The Spanish translation, however, uses a phrase consistent with the narrow interpretation: '*mejor situado*'. In contrast, the Italian translation uses a phrase consistent with the wider interpretation: '*più adatta*'.

[26] Our domestic authorities, and the teaching of the Court of Justice, clearly favour the wider interpretation of 'better placed'. In *Re M (a child)* [2014] EWCA Civ 152, [2014] 2 FCR 585, [2014] 2 FLR 1372 Ryder LJ held at [20]:

> 'It is entirely proper to enquire into questions of fact that might inform the court's evaluation of whether a court is better placed to hear a case. Without wishing to prescribe an exhaustive list, those facts might include the availability of witnesses of fact, whether assessments can be conducted and if so by whom (ie not a comparative analysis of welfare perceptions and principles but, for example, whether an assessor will have to travel to another jurisdiction to undertake an assessment and whether that is a lawful and/or professionally appropriate course), and whether one court's knowledge of the case provides an advantage, for example by judicial continuity between fact finding and evaluation and so on.'

[27] In *Child and Family Agency v D (RPD intervening)* [2016] EUECJ C-428/15 (27 October 2016), [2017] Fam 248, [2017] 1 FCR 320, [2017] 2 WLR 949 the Court of Justice held:

> '56. Consequently, it remains the task of the court having jurisdiction to determine, secondly, whether there is, in the Member State with which the child has a particular connection, a court that is better placed to hear the case.
>
> 57. To that end, the court having jurisdiction must determine whether the transfer of the case to that other court is such as to provide genuine and specific added value, with respect to the decision to be taken in relation to the child, as compared with the possibility of the case remaining before that court. In that context, the court having jurisdiction may take into account, among other factors, the rules of procedure in the other Member State, such as those applicable to the taking of evidence required for dealing with the case. However, the court having jurisdiction should not take into consideration, within such an assessment, the substantive law of that other Member State which might be applicable by the court of that other Member State, if the case were transferred to it. If the court were to take that into consideration, doing so would be in breach of the principles of mutual trust between Member States and mutual recognition of judgments that are the basis of Regulation No 2201/2003 (see, to that effect, judgments of 23 December 2009, *Deticek*, C-403/09 PPU, EU:C:2009:810, paragraph 45, and of 15 July 2010, *Purrucker*, C-256/09, EU:C:2010:437, paragraphs 70 and 71).'

[28] Therefore, in determining whether the other court is 'better placed' to hear the case, or part of it, the court with jurisdiction is not confined to identification of advantages which merely derive from geographical location. It can look wider than that, specifically at the rules of procedure of the other court, for example (and this is the only example given by the Court of Justice) at the procedural method for taking evidence in that court.

[29] However, the burden is on the applicant to show that the other court provides genuine and specific added value. When considering this I must remember that a transfer is an exception to the general rule that the court first validly seised will be the court of trial. Here I cite Lewison LJ in *Re M* at [50]:

> 'It is clear, therefore, that the power to transfer a case (or part of a case) to the courts of another Member State is an exception to the general principle, as the opening words of article 15 (1) themselves make clear. One of the fundamental principles of community law is that of legal certainty. It is for that reason that the ECJ (now the CJEU) has consistently held that exceptions to general principles should be narrowly interpreted: see *Case 33/78 Etablissements Somafer SA v Saar-Ferngas AG* [1979] 1 CMLR 490 at [7] (concerning jurisdiction in civil and commercial matters) and *Case 348/87 Stichting Uitvoering*

Financiële Acties v Staatssecretaris van Financiën [1989] ECR 1737 (concerning exceptions to VAT liability).'

The exceptionality of the article 15 procedure is emphasised by para 3.3.1 of the Brussels IIa Practice Guide.

6.2.8 International issues: jurisdiction: transfer between contracting states: comity

Re D (care proceedings: 1996 Hague Convention: Article 9 Request) [2021] EWHC 1970 (Fam), [72] (Knowles J)

72. Attractively put though these submissions were, I found myself ultimately unpersuaded by them. First, merely because the 1996 Convention contains a mechanism for transfer requests to be made between Contracting States does not mean that consideration of comity is satisfied thereby. Comity within the context of the 1996 Convention requires this court, when considering making a transfer request, to apply both the principle of mutual trust and the assumption that the authorities of the other Contracting State are, in principle, competent to deal with all aspects of a case.

Re M & L [2016] EWHC 2535 (Fam), [2017] 1 FCR 33, [33] (Baker J)

[33] In my judgment, the English and Norwegian courts are equally competent in general terms to determine issues about children. Each court operates in a sophisticated and advanced legal system manned by experienced judges who are manifestly capable of making decisions in this type of case. Although there are some differences in the respective processes, and each court has advantages which the other does not, overall there is no substantial difference. Comparisons are odious. As Mostyn J observed in *Re T* [2013] EWHC 521 (Fam) at paragraph [37], the court

> 'should not descend to some kind of divisive value judgment about the laws and procedures of our European neighbours'

and as Sir James Munby P added in *Re E* (supra), at paragraph [20]:

> 'beneath all the apparent differences in language and legal system, family judges around the world are daily engaged on very much the same task, using very much the same tools and apply the same insights and approaches as those we are familiar with.'

Re N (children) (adoption: jurisdiction) [2016] UKSC 15, [2016] 3 FCR 394, [4] (Lady Hale DP)

[4] It goes without saying that the provisions of the Regulation are based upon mutual respect and trust between the member states. It is not for the courts of this or any other country to question the competence, diligence, resources or efficacy of either the child protection services or the courts' of another state (see *In re M (Brussels II Revised: Article 15)*

[2014] EWCA Civ 152, [2014] 2 FCR 585, [2014] 2 FLR 1372, para [54] (v), per Munby P). As the *Practice Guide for the application of the Brussels IIa Regulation* puts it, the assessment of whether a transfer would be in the best interests of the child should be based on the principle of mutual trust and on the assumption that the courts of all member states are in principle competent to deal with a case' (p 35, para 3.3.3). This principle goes both ways. Just as we must respect and trust the competence of other member states, so must they respect and trust ours.

See also *Nottingham City Council v LM and others* [2014] EWCA Civ 152, [2014] 2 FCR 585, [19] (Ryder LJ) addressing the same point

6.3 INTERNATIONAL ISSUES: OTHER

6.3.1 International issues: other: diplomatic immunity

A Local Authority v AG and others [2020] EWFC 18, [2020] 3 WLR 133, [22]–[48] (Mostyn J) *quotation limited to* [46]–[48]

46. My conclusion is that by virtue of diplomatic immunity these proceedings cannot proceed and must be stayed. They will not be dismissed because there is outstanding a request by the Guardian that the foreign government waives the diplomatic immunity enjoyed by this family so the children can be properly protected in proceedings under Part IV of the Children Act 1989. If that waiver is granted the stay can be lifted and the proceedings can revive. The order granting the stay will record the agreements made by the mother and father to which I have referred above.

47. The fact that proceedings cannot take place does not mean that there is nothing that the organs of the British state can do to discharge its duty under articles 1 and 3 of the European Convention on Human Rights. There are diplomatic and other steps which may be taken.

48. First, it is open in a case such as this for a Local Authority to write to the Foreign & Commonwealth Office drawing the facts to the attention of the Secretary of State and inviting him to take such diplomatic steps as may be necessary. Second, it is open to the Secretary of State for Foreign & Commonwealth Affairs, on receipt of that information, to seek to persuade the foreign government to waive diplomatic immunity in respect of the diplomat and his family so that the necessary protective measures can be taken. Third, as a last resort, it is open to the British government to expel the diplomat and his family so that on their return to their homeland protective measures can be taken in respect of the children there.

See also *London Borough of Barnet v AG and others* [2021] EWHC 1253 (Fam), [83]–[119] (Sir Andrew McFarlane P and Sir Duncan Ouseley) addressing a related point (the absence of any conflict between diplomatic immunity and the ECHR[8])

8 Convention for the Protection of Human Rights and Fundamental Freedoms (1950) CETS 5.

See also *A Local Authority v X and others* [2018] EWHC 874 (Fam), [2018] 3 FCR 509, [43]–[49] (Knowles J) addressing a related point (the timing of diplomatic rights and privileges terminating)

6.3.2 International issues: other: foreign assessments: guidance when seeking a foreign authority's assistance

Re V–Z (children) [2016] EWCA Civ 475, [18], [42] (Black LJ) *quotation limited to* [42]

42. Before leaving the case, I would add that what happened here in relation to the involvement of the Slovak authorities underlines how important it is, when seeking the assistance of foreign authorities, to:

   i) Inform them clearly and comprehensively what questions they are requested to answer as part of their assessment;
   ii) Provide them with all the information that they need in order to carry out the enquiry/assessment asked of them;
   iii) Document carefully and comprehensively what material has been sent to them;
   iv) Answer any queries posed by them in the course of their assessment;
   v) Follow up assiduously any matters which require further exploration by them, or in respect of which they may be able to provide material information, such as details of local resources to assist in or supervise the care of the children;
   vi) Consider creatively how progress might be made in the event that obstacles are encountered, bearing in mind that it may be possible to communicate directly with those who are responsible for carrying out the assessment in the foreign state, although it would be prudent first to consult our Central Authority for advice as to whether that would be acceptable to the foreign state in question.

CHAPTER 7

Evidence

Chapter contents

CHAPTER 7

Evidence

7.1 EVIDENCE: RULES OF EVIDENCE

7.1.1 Evidence: rules of evidence: burden and standard of proof

See Chapter 3.1 Threshold criteria: burden and standard of proof

7.1.2 Evidence: rules of evidence: hearsay

Re W (minors) (wardship: evidence) [1990] FCR 286 (CA), 322H–323B (Neill LJ)

> In my judgment, the correct approach to the matter is to recognise that in wardship proceedings, which are of a special kind and which involve to some extent the exercise by the court of a parental or administrative jurisdiction, hearsay evidence is admissible as a matter of law, but that this evidence and the use to which it is put has to be handled with the greatest care and in such a way that, unless the interests of the child make it necessary, the rules of natural justice and the rights of the parents are fully and properly observed.

See also *Carmarthenshire County Council v Y and others* [2017] EWFC 36, [2017] 4 WLR 136 (Mostyn J), [7]–[17] addressing a related point (the general rule if a fact needs proof at final hearing is that proof is by oral evidence)

See also *Re W (children) (fact finding: hearsay evidence)* [2013] EWCA Civ 1374, [2014] 1 FCR 303, [7]–[8] (Black LJ) providing an overview of the law on this point

See also *Re A (a child)* [2015] EWFC 11, [2016] 1 FLR 1, [7]–[12] (Sir James Munby P) addressing a related point (the consequences for LAs[1] if unwilling or unable to produce first-hand evidence), see Chapter 3.2.4 Threshold criteria: general approach to threshold: formulating threshold allegations

7.1.3 Evidence: rules of evidence: lies: Lucas directions

Re H-C (children) [2016] EWCA Civ 136, [2016] 4 WLR 85, [97]–[102] (McFarlane LJ)

97. Within that list of factors, although the judge does not expressly prioritise them, the finding that Mr C lied about the quietness in his flat that night

1 Local authorities.

is given the greatest prominence in this section of the judge's analysis. A family court, in common with a criminal court, can rely upon a finding that a witness has lied as evidence in support of a primary positive allegation. The well-known authority is the case of *R v Lucas (R)* [1981] QB 720 in which the Court of Appeal Criminal Division, after stressing that people sometimes tell lies for reasons other than a belief that the lie is necessary to conceal guilt, held that four conditions must be satisfied before a defendant's lie could be seen as supporting the prosecution case as explained in the judgment of the court given by Lord Lane CJ:

> 'To be capable of amounting to corroboration the lie told out of court must first of all be deliberate. Secondly it must relate to a material issue. Thirdly the motive for the lie must be a realisation of guilt and a fear of the truth. The jury should in appropriate cases be reminded that people sometimes lie, for example, in an attempt to bolster up a just cause, or out of shame or out of a wish to conceal disgraceful behaviour from their family. Fourthly the statement must be clearly shown to be a lie by evidence other than that of the accomplice who is to be corroborated, that is to say by admission or by evidence from an independent witness.'

98. The decision in *R v Lucas* has been the subject of a number of further decisions of the Court of Appeal Criminal Division over the years, however the core conditions set out by Lord Lane remain authoritative. The approach in *R v Lucas* is not confined, as it was on the facts of *Lucas* itself, to a statement made out of court and can apply to a 'lie' made in the course of the court proceedings and the approach is not limited solely to evidence concerning accomplices.

99. In the Family Court in an appropriate case a judge will not infrequently directly refer to the authority of *R v Lucas* in giving a judicial self-direction as to the approach to be taken to an apparent lie. Where the 'lie' has a prominent or central relevance to the case such a self-direction is plainly sensible and good practice.

100. One highly important aspect of the *Lucas* decision, and indeed the approach to lies generally in the criminal jurisdiction, needs to be borne fully in mind by family judges. It is this: in the criminal jurisdiction the 'lie' is never taken, of itself, as direct proof of guilt. As is plain from the passage quoted from Lord Lane's judgment in *Lucas*, where the relevant conditions are satisfied the lie is 'capable of amounting to a corroboration'. In recent times the point has been most clearly made in the Court of Appeal Criminal Division in the case of *R v Middleton* [2001] Crim.L.R. 251.

In my view there should be no distinction between the approach taken by the criminal court on the issue of lies to that adopted in the family court. Judges should therefore take care to ensure that they do not rely upon a conclusion that an individual has lied on a material issue as direct proof of guilt.

101. In the present case Newton J did not directly refer to *R v Lucas* or to the conditions set out within that authority. By implication he held that Mr C's account of a quiet night was given deliberately, and secondly he held, rightly, that that account related to a material issue in the case. In stating that he had 'stepped back to consider whether that is because of shame or panic, or because of some dreadful accident' the judge was, again by implication, considering the general thrust of *R v Lucas* and, in stating that 'overall I reject any notion that his lies masque some dreadful accident or mistake', he seemingly rejected an innocent explanation for the 'lie'. There is, however, ground for concern that the judge may have overstepped the line and adopted an approach which, in the criminal context, would not be permitted by his statement in paragraph 79 of the judgment as follows:

> 'The only independent evidence comes from the neighbours. On the face of the evidence, the accounts are damning and in particular paint the lie to Mr C's assertion that he and the boys had a quiet, unbroken night, the context needs careful consideration.'

102. I have taken the opportunity to refer to *R v Lucas* in the hope that a reminder of the relevant approach taken in the criminal jurisdiction will be of assistance generally in family cases. In the context of this appeal I am left unclear as to whether the judge fell into error in his approach to the lie.

See also *Re A, B and C (children)* [2021] EWCA Civ 451, [54]–[58] (Macur LJ) addressing the same point (and outlining good practice), see Chapter 7.1.4 Evidence: rules of evidence: lies: Lucas directions: good practice

See also *H v City and County of Swansea and others* [2011] EWCA Civ 195, [2011] 1 FCR 550, [27]–[28] (Black LJ) addressing a related point (the need to weigh lies against other evidence)

7.1.4 Evidence: rules of evidence: lies: Lucas directions: good practice

Re A, B and C (children) [2021] EWCA Civ 451, [54]–[58] (Macur LJ) *quotation limited to* [57]–[58]

57. To be clear, and as I indicate above, a 'Lucas direction' will not be called for in every family case in which a party or intervenor is challenging the factual case alleged against them and, in my opinion, should not be included in the judgment as a tick box exercise. If the issue for the tribunal to decide is whether to believe A or B on the central issue/s, and the evidence is clearly one way then there will be no need to address credibility in general. However, if the tribunal looks to find support for their view, it must caution itself against treating what it finds to be an established propensity to dishonesty as determinative of guilt for the reasons the Recorder gave in [40]. Conversely, an established propensity to honesty will not always equate with the witness's reliability of recall on a particular issue.

58. That a tribunal's Lucas self-direction is formulaic, and incomplete is unlikely to determine an appeal, but the danger lies in its potential to distract from the proper application of its principles. In these circumstances, I venture to suggest that it would be good practice when the tribunal is invited to proceed on the basis, or itself determines, that such a direction is called for, to seek Counsel's submissions to identify: (i) the deliberate lie(s) upon which they seek to rely; (ii) the significant issue to which it/they relate(s), and (iii) on what basis it can be determined that the only explanation for the lie(s) is guilt. The principles of the direction will remain the same, but they must be tailored to the facts and circumstances of the witness before the court.

See also *Wakefield Metropolitan District Council v R and others* [2019] EWHC 3581 (Fam), [105]–[109] (Lieven J) considering *Re H-C (children)* [2016] EWCA Civ 136, [2016] 4 WLR 85

7.1.5 Evidence: rules of evidence: lies: relevance to welfare

See Chapter 9.3.12 The welfare stage: the welfare checklists: impact of lies on welfare

7.1.6 Evidence: rules of evidence: similar fact

R v P (Children: Similar Fact Evidence) [2020] EWCA Civ 1088, [2020] 3 FCR 542, [23]–[28] (Peter Jackson LJ)

Similar fact evidence in civil and family cases

[23] In *O'Brien v Chief Constable of South Wales Police* [2005] UKHL 26, [2005] 2 AC 534 the House of Lords considered the issue of similar fact evidence in civil cases, where it is contended that an individual's behaviour in other circumstances makes it more likely that he will have behaved in the manner now alleged because it is evidence of a propensity to behave in that way. Lord Bingham stated the position in this way:

> '[3] Any evidence, to be admissible, must be relevant. Contested trials last long enough as it is without spending time on evidence which is irrelevant and cannot affect the outcome. Relevance must, and can only, be judged by reference to the issue which the court (whether judge or jury) is called upon to decide. As Lord Simon of Glaisdale observed in *Director of Public Prosecutions v Kilbourne* [1973] AC 729, 756, 'Evidence is relevant if it is logically probative or disprobative of some matter which requires proof … relevant (ie. logically probative or disprobative) evidence is evidence which makes the matter which requires proof more or less probable'.
>
> [4] That evidence of what happened on an earlier occasion may make the occurrence of what happened on the occasion in question more or less probable can scarcely be denied … To regard evidence of such earlier events as potentially probative is a process of thought

which an entirely rational, objective and fair-minded person might, depending on the facts, follow. If such a person would, or might, attach importance to evidence such as this, it would require good reasons to deny a judicial decision-maker the opportunity to consider it. For while there is a need for some special rules to protect the integrity of judicial decision-making on matters of fact, such as the burden and standard of proof, it is on the whole undesirable that the process of judicial decision-making on issues of fact should diverge more than it need from the process followed by rational, objective and fair-minded people called upon to decide questions of fact in other contexts where reaching the right answer matters. Thus in a civil case such as this the question of admissibility turns, and turns only, on whether the evidence which it is sought to adduce, assuming it (provisionally) to be true, is in Lord Simon's sense probative. If so, the evidence is legally admissible. That is the first stage of the enquiry.

[5] The second stage of the enquiry requires the case management judge or the trial judge to make what will often be a very difficult and sometimes a finely balanced judgment: whether evidence or some of it (and if so which parts of it), which ex hypothesi is legally admissible, should be admitted. For the party seeking admission, the argument will always be that justice requires the evidence to be admitted; if it is excluded, a wrong result may be reached. In some cases, as in the present, the argument will be fortified by reference to wider considerations: the public interest in exposing official misfeasance and protecting the integrity of the criminal trial process; vindication of reputation; the public righting of public wrongs. These are important considerations to which weight must be given. But even without them, the importance of doing justice in the particular case is a factor the judge will always respect. The strength of the argument for admitting the evidence will always depend primarily on the judge's assessment of the potential significance of the evidence, assuming it to be true, in the context of the case as a whole.

[6] While the argument against admitting evidence found to be legally admissible will necessarily depend on the particular case, some objections are likely to recur. First, it is likely to be said that admission of the evidence will distort the trial and distract the attention of the decision-maker by focusing attention on issues collateral to the issue to be decided. This … is often a potent argument, particularly where trial is by jury. Secondly, and again particularly when the trial is by jury, it will be necessary to weigh the potential probative value of the evidence against its potential for causing unfair prejudice: unless the former is judged to outweigh the latter by a considerable margin, the evidence is likely to be excluded. Thirdly, stress will be laid on the burden which admission would lay on the resisting party: the burden in time, cost and personnel resources, very considerable in a case such as this, of giving disclosure; the lengthening of the trial, with the increased cost and stress inevitably involved; the potential prejudice

to witnesses called upon to recall matters long closed, or thought to be closed; the loss of documentation; the fading of recollections. … In deciding whether evidence in a given case should be admitted the judge's overriding purpose will be to promote the ends of justice. But the judge must always bear in mind that justice requires not only that the right answer be given but also that it be achieved by a trial process which is fair to all parties.'

[24] This analysis, given in a civil case, applies also to family proceedings. There are two questions that the judge must address in a case where there is a dispute about the admission of evidence of this kind. Firstly, is the evidence relevant, as potentially making the matter requiring proof more or less probable? If so, it will be admissible. Secondly, is it in the interests of justice for the evidence to be admitted? This calls for a balancing of factors of the kind that Lord Bingham identifies at paragraphs [5] and [6] of *O'Brien*.

[25] Where the similar fact evidence comprises an alleged pattern of behaviour, the assertion is that the core allegation is more likely to be true because of the character of the person accused, as shown by conduct on other occasions. To what extent do the facts relating to the other occasions have to be proved for propensity to be established? That question was considered by the Supreme Court in the criminal case of *R v Mitchell* [2016] UKSC 55, [2017] AC 571, where it was said that the defendant, who was charged with murder by stabbing, had used knives on a number of other occasions, none of which had led to a conviction but which on the prosecution's case showed propensity. Lord Kerr addressed this issue in the following way:

'Propensity – the correct question/what requires to be proved?

[39] A distinction must be recognised between, on the one hand, proof of a propensity and, on the other, the individual underlying facts said to establish that a propensity exists. In a case where there are several incidents which are relied on by the prosecution to show a propensity on the part of the defendant, is it necessary to prove beyond reasonable doubt that each incident happened in precisely the way that it is alleged to have occurred? Must the facts of each individual incident be considered by the jury in isolation from each other? In my view, the answer to both these questions is "No".

[43] The proper issue for the jury on the question of propensity … is whether they are sure that the propensity has been proved … That does not mean that in cases where there are several instances of misconduct, all tending to show a propensity, the jury has to be convinced of the truth and accuracy of all aspects of each of those. The jury is entitled to – and should – consider the evidence about propensity in the round. There are two interrelated reasons for this. First the improbability of a number of similar incidents alleged against a defendant being false is a consideration which should

naturally inform a jury's deliberations on whether propensity has been proved. Secondly, obvious similarities in various incidents may constitute mutual corroboration of those incidents. Each incident may thus inform another. The question … is whether, overall, propensity has been proved.

[44] The jury should be directed that, if they are to take propensity into account, they should be sure that it has been proved. This does not require that each individual item of evidence said to show propensity must be proved beyond reasonable doubt. It means that all the material touching on the issue should be considered with a view to reaching a conclusion as to whether they are sure that the existence of a propensity has been established.'

[26] Again, this analysis is applicable to civil and family cases, with appropriate adjustment to the standard of proof. In summary, the court must be satisfied on the basis of proven facts that propensity has been proven, in each case to the civil standard. The proven facts must form a sufficient basis to sustain a finding of propensity but each individual item of evidence does not have to be proved.

[27] The issue of similar fact evidence was considered by this court in the family case of *Re S (a child)* [2017] EWCA Civ 44, [2017] 2 FCR 184. A mother appealed against the dismissal of allegations of domestic abuse, including sexual assaults, by a father. One of the grounds of appeal was that the judge had erred in excluding similar fact evidence in relation to the father's alleged rape of a previous partner. That argument did not succeed for reasons given by Black LJ at [63] and summarised at [58]: the judge had excluded the evidence because the material had only very recently surfaced as part of the mother's case, that the previous partner was not being called, and that it would be unfair to the father to explore the allegation with him on the basis of the paper evidence alone. In other words, the evidence was potentially relevant but it would have been unfair to have allowed the mother to have relied upon the alleged rape of a previous partner.

[28] I mention this decision because it touched on the question of similar fact evidence, but there are significant differences between that case and the present one, both as to the underlying facts and the procedural history. In particular, in the present case, the father had been aware of the allegations for well over a year and the allegations were contained in professional reports that the court itself had directed should be gathered

7.1.7 Evidence: rules of evidence: corroboration

Re P (sexual abuse: finding of fact hearing) [2019] EWFC 27 (Fam), [267]–[269] (MacDonald J)

267. In a case in which the testimony of children, with its limitations as discussed above, is central, it is also important to note the following

further points with respect to the question of corroboration. In *Lillie and others v Newcastle CC* at [363] Eady J noted, in the context of a case in which he was required to determine allegations of sexual abuse made by multiple children in the context of a libel action, that where there is credible evidence of abuse with respect to one child, the court can look to any comparably credible evidence relating to another child for corroboration of the former. However, Eady J was also careful to make clear at [367] that with respect to the question of corroboration:

> 'I must focus upon the essential principle. Evidence about what A has done to B may be admissible and probative of what A has done to C. The value of such evidence, however, depends upon its independence. If there is a significant risk of contamination undermining that independence, the relevance and value may be correspondingly diminished. It is necessary to be wary in cases where a risk of contamination arises (which is real, as opposed to fanciful) because of the investigation process itself.'

268. Within this context, when considering whether there is evidence that corroborates the allegations made by a given subject child, the court will look to see whether that evidence has the *character* of corroborating evidence, before considering the extent to which that evidence corroborates that which it is said to. In the context of a case of alleged child sexual abuse by multiple children, in *Lillie and others v Newcastle CC* from [368] to [370] Eady J gave the following example of the application of this approach:

> '[368] For example, where a social services department investigates allegations of sexual abuse, whether from the recent or distant past, its inquiries may prompt complainants who would not have come forward of their own accord. It was made clear in *Ananthanarayanan* that a jury may well need to be given a specific direction in such cases to meet the problem. It would not suffice merely to direct the jury that they need to be sure that there has been no conspiracy to give false evidence; they would need to be sure also that there had been no influence from hearing of the allegations made by other people or by suggestions from some other person. In this case, the Claimants contend that there was a substantial risk of contamination throughout the investigation. Indeed, the Review Team were expressly warned by Constable Helen Foster of the specific risks in this case. Miss Page submits that it was pervasive.
>
> [369] She did not submit that this rendered the evidence inadmissible but asks me to bear it very much in mind wherever it may be suggested that the evidence of one child or parent should be treated as corroborative of another's. Here there are various "pervasive" problems. There was a risk of contamination through social services asking questions or suggesting that questions be asked; through parents speaking to children or to other parents; through children speaking

to other children; through police or social services interviewers suggesting concepts or events to children; through Dr San Lazaro suggesting that questions be asked, or passing on between parents or children negative messages about the Claimants, or about behaviours or phobias to watch out for.

[370] It is also important to remember that if a witness's evidence is incredible it should be rejected. It cannot be given credibility through corroboration: see the remarks of Lord Hailsham in *Kilbourne* [1975] AC 746. The principle is one of common sense and therefore just as significant in the context of civil litigation.

[371] Thus, if I am doubtful about an allegation in relation to Child X, because of a risk of contamination or for any other reason, I should assess it on its own merits. If I find Child X's evidence persuasive, then I can take into account corroborative evidence from Child Y provided I keep a sharp lookout for risks of contamination of the kinds I have identified.'

269. Finally, in relation to corroboration, as a general rule of evidence, the court may act on the testimony of a single witness even where there is no other evidence which corroborates it (see Phipson on Evidence at [14-01]). Where, in a civil case, such testimony is unimpeached the court should act on it (see *Morrow v Morrow* [1914] 2 IR 183). Within this context, whilst not directly applicable in these proceedings (and again ever mindful of the observation of McFarlane LJ (as he then was) in *Re R (Children)* that it is fundamentally wrong for the Family Court to be drawn into an analysis of factual evidence in proceedings relating to the welfare of children based upon criminal law principles and concepts), I also note that s 34(2) of the Criminal Justice Act 1988 abrogated the rule that required the court to give a jury a warning about convicting the accused on the uncorroborated evidence of a child, and that s 32 of the Criminal Justice and Public Order Act 1994 abrogated the rule which previously required juries to be given a warning (and magistrates to warn themselves) about the dangers of relying on uncorroborated evidence in a case of alleged sexual offences. The court does however, retain a discretion in such cases to give warnings in respect of witnesses (see *R v Makanjuola* [1995] 1 WLR 1348). A warning will be given where there is an evidential basis for suggesting that the evidence of the witness may be unreliable, for example an admission by a witness of a previous lie or the giving by a witness of other evidence that is clearly unreliable (see *R v Makanjuola*). The focus is on the individual witness, avoiding invoking stereotypes or broad generalisations.

See also *Re K (children)* [2019] EWCA Civ 184, [2019] 2 FCR 344, [33(6)] (Peter Jackson LJ) addressing a related point (what matters is quality not quantity of evidence)

7.1.8 Evidence: rules of evidence: identification

EH v Greenwich London Borough Council and others; Re A (children) (non-accidental injury) [2010] EWCA Civ 344, [2010] 2 FCR 106, [41] (Baron J), [79]–[83] (Wall LJ), [117] (Smith LJ) *quotation limited to* [41], [79], [81]–[82]

[41] The judge did not give himself a *Turnbull* direction in relation to identification evidence. In all cases such as this, I consider that it is incumbent upon a judge to remind himself in judgment of the precise terms of the passages in *R v Turnbull* [1976] 3 All ER 549 at 551–552, [1977] QB 224 at 228 in which Widgery CJ stated:

> 'First, whenever the case against an accused depends wholly or substantially on the correctness of one or more identifications of the accused which the defence alleges to be mistaken, the judge should warn the jury of the special need for caution before convicting the accused in reliance on the correctness of the identification or identifications. In addition he should instruct them as to the reason for the need for such a warning and should make some reference to the possibility that a mistaken witness can be a convincing one and that a number of such witnesses can all be mistaken. Provided this is done in clear terms the judge need not use any particular form of words.
>
> Secondly, the judge should direct the jury to examine closely the circumstances in which the identification by each witness came to be made. How long did the witness have the accused under observation? At what distance? In what light? Was the observation impeded in any way, as for example by passing traffic or a press of people? Had the witness ever seen the accused before? How often? If only occasionally, had he any special reason for remembering the accused? How long elapsed between the original observation and the subsequent identification to the police? Was there any material discrepancy between the description of the accused given to the police by the witness when first seen by them and his actual appearance? If in any case, whether it is being dealt with summarily or on indictment, the prosecution have reason to believe that there is such a material discrepancy they should supply the accused or his legal advisers with particulars of the description the police were first given. In all cases if the accused asks to be given particulars of such descriptions, the prosecution should supply them. Finally, he should remind the jury of any specific weakness which has appeared in the identification evidence. Recognition may be more reliable then identification of a stranger; but, even then when the witness is purporting to recognise someone whom he knows, the jury should be reminded that mistakes in recognition of close relatives and friends are sometimes made.'

…

[79] This case, in my judgment, is no exception to that rule, although it highlights a series of traps for the unwary which, in my view, judges would do well to avoid. I will identify some of these in a moment.

...

[81] I propose to identify only a few of the traps. They relate largely to identification evidence. The first concerns the *Turnbull* direction (see *R v Turnbull* [1976] 3 All ER 549, [1977] QB 224). In this regard, what the judge said was:

> 'If I were directing a jury in a criminal case, I would give them a *Turnbull* direction, warning them that they must be careful on such uncorroborated evidence of identification. As against that, the standard of proof in this case is different from that in a criminal case. I do not have to be sure. I have to decide on the balance of probability.'

[82] With great respect to the judge, this will not do. The judge *is* the jury for this purpose, and in my judgment it is imperative that where judges in care proceedings are dealing with highly controversial identification evidence, it is imperative that they give *themselves* a *Turnbul* direction. This is not a tiresome mantra which a judge must recite in order to tick a box for this court: judges need to remind *themselves* of the dangers of identification evidence.

7.1.9 Evidence: rules of evidence: adverse inferences from failure to testify

Re T and J (children) [2020] EWCA Civ 1344, [2021] 1 FCR 189, [46]–[51] (Baker LJ)

[46] It is convenient to deal with the next two grounds of appeal together, namely that the judge was wrong not to draw adverse inferences from KF's refusal to give evidence and that his assessment of KF's evidence was inadequate. In the course of oral submissions, it became clear that these two grounds overlapped and to a considerable extent amounted to the same point.

[47] Mr Peddie submitted that Judge Vavrecka wrongly failed to draw an adverse inference from KF's refusal to answer questions at the hearing. It is the role of the court to consider the totality of the evidence, which should include an adverse inference where the law requires that inference to be drawn. Here, there was no indication why the judge did not draw an adverse inference, notwithstanding his assertion that he had been significantly hampered by KF's refusal to give evidence. The consequences of failing to draw an adverse inference were significant. The local authority was alleging that the physical injuries sustained by J were inflicted either by KF or by the mother. If the judge had drawn adverse inferences against KF on the basis that he had something to hide, he would or should have proceeded to conclude that KF caused all the injuries, including the serious injuries to the genital area. He would thereby reach the decision arrived at by the jury in the later criminal trial. Furthermore, an adverse inference against KF would have had an impact upon the judge's analysis of the mother's credibility on which he relied

heavily in reaching his conclusion that there was a real possibility that she was the perpetrator of the injuries.

[48] In support of these submissions, Mr Peddie relied on the dicta of Johnson J in *Re O (care proceedings: evidence)* [2003] EWHC 2011 (Fam), [2004] 1 FLR 161. In that case, which concerned allegations of violence by a mother against a child, the mother had filed a statement denying the allegations but, as she did not give oral evidence, the district judge attached no weight to her statements and proceeded to make findings that she had injured the child. In dismissing the appeal, Johnson J observed:

> '[13] This decision, simply to attach no weight to the mother's statements, was in my view wrong. The judge could, and in my view should, have gone further. As a general rule, and clearly every case will depend on its own particular facts, where a person declines to answer questions or, as here, give evidence, the court ought usually to draw the inference that the allegations are true.
>
> ...
>
> [16] In the present case the district judge went on to consider a number of considerations supporting or discrediting what [the child] had said and eventually concluded that what she had said was true. However, in my view, unless there was some sensible reasons to the contrary, the mother's failure to give evidence should have been determinative of the allegations.'

[49] In *Re U (care proceedings: criminal conviction: refusal to give evidence)* [2006] EWHC 372 (Fam), [2006] 2 FLR 690 (a case not cited to us by counsel), Holman J was faced with a similar situation to that which arose in the present case. In *Re U*, which concerned care proceedings in respect of a baby, the father, who was in the process of appealing a conviction for murder of another child, refused to file a statement or give oral evidence on the grounds that he had been advised not to do so by his criminal lawyer. Holman J declined to draw an adverse inference against the father, notwithstanding the fact that his failure to file a statement and answer questions was plainly a contempt of court. He referred to the observations of Lord Lowry in the House of Lords decision of *R v IRC and another, ex p TC Coombs and Co* [1991] 2 AC 283 at p 300 F–H:

> 'In our legal system generally, the silence of one party in face of the other party's evidence may convert that evidence into proof in relation to matters which are, or are likely to be, within the knowledge of the silent party and about which that party could be expected to give evidence. Thus, depending on the circumstances, a prima facie case may become a strong or even an overwhelming case. But, if the silent party's failure to give evidence (or to give the necessary evidence) can be credibly explained, even if not entirely justified, the effect of his silence in favour of the other party may be either reduced or nullified.'

As Holman J observed in *Re U* (at paragraph [30]) Lord Lowry's observation does:

> 'no more than describe and illustrate the very broad discretion of the court to draw adverse inferences, which must be exercised in a very fact-specific context.'

He added that Johnson J's observation in *Re O*, cited above, which he described as obiter, was 'again very fact-specific'.

[50] In my judgment, Holman J's approach is unquestionably right. The decision whether or not to draw an adverse inference from refusal to answer questions will depend on the circumstances of the case. The fact that KF was advised by his criminal lawyer not to answer questions is a relevant consideration. It is, of course, the case that s 98 of the Children Act provides:

> '(1) In any proceedings in which a court is hearing an application for an order under Part IV or V [ie including care proceedings] no person shall be excused from
>
> (a) giving evidence on any matter; or
>
> (b) answering any question put to him in the course of his giving evidence,
>
> on the ground that doing so might incriminate him or his spouse or civil partner of an offence.
>
> (2) A statement or admission made in such proceedings shall not be admissible in evidence against the person making it or his spouse or civil partner in proceedings for an offence other than perjury.'

In *Re EC (disclosure of material)* [1997] Fam 76, [1996] 3 FCR 521, [1997] 2 WLR 322, however, this Court held that s 98(2) only gives protection against statements being admissible in evidence in criminal proceedings. It does not protect against their use in a police enquiry into the commission of an offence.

[51] It follows that His Honour Judge Vavrecka was not obliged as a matter of law to draw an adverse inference against KF from his refusal to answer questions. He plainly considered the submission that he should draw such an inference and, in my judgment, cannot be criticised for rejecting it. Furthermore, although he declined to infer from his refusal to answer questions that KF was the perpetrator of the injuries, he took his failure to give evidence into account in his overall analysis, and the fact that he was as a result left with important questions unanswered was a material factor in his conclusion that KF could not be excluded from the pool of perpetrators of the injuries. His careful and considered balancing of this aspect, alongside his detailed analysis of the mother's credibility and the lies she had told during the investigation, was plainly within his discretion as the trial judge.

Re K (threshold: cocaine ingestion: failure to give evidence) **[2020] EWHC 2502 (Fam), [2021] 2 FLR 349, [39]–[43] (Williams J)**

39. In *Re O (Care Proceedings: Evidence)* [2003] EWHC 2011 (Fam). Johnson J was very clear. He said, that '*As a general rule, and clearly every case will depend on its own particular facts, where a parent declines to answer questions or, as here, give evidence, the court ought usually to draw the inference that the allegations are true.*' The power of the court to draw adverse inferences is found elsewhere, for instance in relation to failures to participate in or comply with other directions of the court designed to assist the court in determining a case justly; for instance a failure to participate in an expert assessment can also allow the court to draw inferences against an individual: see *Re C (A Child) (Procedural Requirements of a Part 25 application)* [2015] EWCA 539 at #34. However, as the closing submissions of the Mother and the Guardian argue (and indeed the general rule proposed by Johnson J is subject to 'particular facts') the statutory framework and the jurisprudence suggest a more nuanced approach which takes account of the circumstances of the refusal or failure to give evidence and the nature of the issue and the evidence which is given by other parties.

40. Although the general approach is that any fact which needs to be proved by the evidence of witnesses is generally to be proved by their oral evidence (r22.2(1)(a) FPR 2010) facts may also be proved by hearsay evidence. The effect of Children Act 1989 s.96(3), Children (Admissibility of Hearsay Evidence) Order 1993 is to make all evidence given in connection with the welfare of a child admissible notwithstanding its hearsay nature. This would commonly include Local Authority case records or social work chronologies which are very often hearsay, often second- or third-hand hearsay but also extends to witness statements. The court should give it the weight it considers appropriate: *Re W (Fact Finding: Hearsay Evidence)* [2014] 2 FLR 703 and where hearsay goes to a central issue the court may well require the maker of the hearsay statement to attend to give oral evidence.

41. The provisions of section 1 and 4 of the Civil Evidence Act 1995 also make provision for the court to admit and rely on hearsay evidence and set out a range of factors that the court should consider in assessing the weight to be given to and the reliability of hearsay evidence. These include matters such as the circumstances in which the statement was made and whether the circumstances suggest an attempt to prevent proper evaluation of its weight.

42. Cases from other fields such as *T C Coombs v IRC* [1991] 2 AC 283 and *Wisniewski v. Central Manchester Health Authority* [1998] PIQR P324 support a more nuanced approach. Brooke LJ said in the latter case.

> From this line of authority, I derive the following principles in the context of the present case:
>
> (1) In certain circumstances a court may be entitled to draw adverse inferences from the absence or silence of a witness

who might be expected to have material evidence to give on an issue in an action.

(2) If a court is willing to draw such inferences they may go to strengthen the evidence adduced on that issue by the other party or to weaken the evidence, if any, adduced by the party who might reasonably have been expected to call the witness.

(3) There must, however, have been some evidence, however weak, adduced by the former on the matter in question before the court is entitled to draw the desired inference: in other words, there must be a case to answer on that issue.

(4) If the reason for the witness's absence or silence satisfies the court then no such adverse inference may be drawn. If, on the other hand, there is some credible explanation given, even if it is not wholly satisfactory, the potentially detrimental effect of his/her absence or silence may be reduced or nullified.

43. I consider that the approach outlined by Brooke LJ more fully reflects the proper approach. These are inquisitorial proceedings rather than adversarial, where the welfare of the children is at stake and where the authorities on fact-finding require the court to survey all the evidence and to avoid compartmentalisation. The legislative framework allows for the admission of hearsay evidence. The approach to lies in *Lucas* requires a more measured approach. At one end of the spectrum, there will no doubt be cases where the court is satisfied that a person has deliberately refused to come to court to support their written statement and where there is no excuse or explanation. In that scenario, the court might take a bright line approach and refuse to place any weight on any of their evidence and draw inferences against them that any allegations are true. In other cases, the court will need to consider the circumstances of their failure to give evidence, any explanations offered or which present themselves and the evidence itself and the issues it goes to. Where there is compelling evidence explaining an inability to attend full weight might be given and no inferences drawn. In between will be cases where the court might determine it is appropriate to rely on and give weight (even full weight) to some evidence but not to other evidence and to draw some but not necessarily all possible inferences.

See also *Re M (children)* [2019] EWCA Civ 1364, [2019] 3 FCR 141, [11]–[31] (Sir Andrew McFarlane P) addressing a related point ('privilege against self-incrimination' and 'right to silence')

See also *Re A (children)* [2020] EWCA Civ 448, [2021] 1 FCR 1, [17]–[19] (King LJ) considering *Re M (children)* [2019] EWCA Civ 1364, [2019] 3 FCR 141

7.1.10 Evidence: rules of evidence: convictions

Re Q (a child) (fact-finding rehearing) [2019] EWFC 60, [43]–[45] (Baker LJ)

Section 11 of the Civil Evidence Act 1968

43. Under the Civil Evidence Act 1968, Section 11(1) and (2):

> '(1) In civil proceedings the fact that a person has been convicted of an offence by or before any court in the United Kingdom or by a court martial, there or elsewhere, shall, subject to (3) below [not relevant to this case], be admissible in evidence for the purpose of proving, where to do so is relevant to an issue in those proceedings, that he committed that offence, whether he was so convicted upon a plea of guilty or otherwise and whether or not he is party to the civil proceedings; but no conviction other than a subsisting one shall be admissible in evidence by virtue of this section.
>
> '(2) In any civil proceedings in which by virtue of this section a person is proved to have been convicted of an offence by or before any court in the United Kingdom or by a court martial there or elsewhere: (a) he shall be taken to have committed that offence unless the contrary is proved; and (b) without prejudice to the reception of any other admissible evidence for the purpose of identifying the facts on which the conviction was based, the contents of any document which is admissible as evidence of the conviction, and the contents of the information, complaint, indictment or charge-sheet on which the person in question was convicted shall be admissible in evidence for that purpose.'

44. The scope and interpretation of section 11 was addressed by Lord Diplock in *Hunter v the Chief Constable of West Midlands Police* [1982] AC 529 at page 544D in these terms:

> 'Section 11 makes the conviction *prima facie* evidence that the person convicted did commit the offence on which he was found guilty. That does not make it conclusive evidence. The defendant is permitted by the statute to prove the contrary if he can. The section covers a wide variety of circumstances. The relevant conviction may be of someone who has not been made a defendant to the civil action and the action defendant may have had no opportunity of determining what evidence should be called on the occasion of the criminal trial. The conviction particularly of a traffic offence may have been entered upon a plea of guilty accompanied by a written explanation in mitigation. Fresh evidence not called on the occasion of his conviction may have been obtained by the defendant's insurers who were not responsible for the conduct of his defence at the criminal trial or may only have become available to the defendant himself since the criminal trial. This wide variety of circumstances in which section 11 may be applicable includes some in which justice would require that no fetters should be imposed upon the means by which a defendant may rebut a statutory presumption that the person committed the offence on which he has been convicted by a court of competent jurisdiction. In particular I respectfully find myself unable to agree with Lord Denning, Master

of the Rolls, that the only way in which a defendant can do so is by showing that the conviction was obtained by fraud or collusion, or by adducing fresh evidence (which he could not have obtained by reasonable diligence before) which is conclusive of his innocence. The burden of proof of 'the contrary' that lies upon the defendant under section 11 is the ordinary burden in a civil action: proof on a balance of probabilities; although in the face of a conviction after a full hearing, this is likely to be an uphill task.'

45. From this I note the following points are relevant to this case:
(1) the conviction is prima facie evidence that the convicted person committed the offence;
(2) the conviction is not conclusive and the convicted person is permitted to seek to prove the contrary;
(3) the standard of proof on the convicted person in those circumstances is the balance of probabilities;
(4) in practice, however, a person who has been convicted after a full hearing is likely to face an uphill task in proving he did not commit the offence;
(5) the section covers a wide variety of circumstances;
(6) no fetters should be imposed on a convicted person as to the means by which the statutory presumption may be rebutted.

See also *A Local Authority v C* [2019] EWHC 1782 (Fam), [12]–[14] (Lieven J) addressing the same point

See also *Re T and J (children)* [2020] EWCA Civ 1344, [2021] 1 FCR 189, [35]–[38] (Baker LJ) addressing a related point (subsequent criminal convictions or acquittals and reopening fact-finding), see Chapter 3.11.5 Threshold criteria: the court's findings: reopening findings: subsequent criminal convictions or acquittals

7.1.11 Evidence: rules of evidence: estoppel

A Local Authority v C [2019] EWHC 1782 (Fam), [15]–[21] (Lieven J)

15. In terms of issue estoppel, there are again two issues: firstly, whether issue estoppel has any place in Children Act proceedings; and secondly, to the degree to which it has, what matters are covered by the principle of issue estoppel here. It is important to start by being clear that issue estoppel is a rule founded on public policy which if applied means that a party cannot prove certain facts or matters; in other words, this court is bound by the earlier ruling. This was explained by Diplock LJ in Thoday v Thoday [1964] 2 WLR 371 in 1964;

'Estoppel' merely means that, under the rules of the adversary system of procedure upon which the common law of England is based, a party is not allowed, in certain circumstances, to prove in litigation particular facts or matters which, if proved, would assist him to succeed as plaintiff or defendant in an action. If the court is required to exercise an inquisitorial function and may inquire into

> facts which the parties do not choose to prove, or would under the rules of the adversary system be prevented from proving, this is a function to which the common law concept of estoppel is alien. It may well be a rational rule to apply in the exercise of such an inquisitorial function to say that if a court having jurisdiction to do so has once inquired into the truth of a particular allegation of fact and reached a decision thereon, another court of coordinate jurisdiction in the exercise of its own discretion should not re-embark upon the same inquiry, but should accept the decision of the first court. But this is a different concept from estoppel as hitherto known in English law.

16. One of the principles of issue estoppel is that the parties to the relevant actions need to be the same, *Re S, S & A (Care Proceedings: Issue Estoppel)* [1995] 2 FLR 244, Wilson J, as he then was, considered this specific issue and broadened the principle of issue estoppel, saying, at page 248:

> 'It suffices to say that, where the case against a father or stepfather is that he has perpetrated acts of abuse on children of a former family, and where the issue as to his perpetration of those acts has been directly relevant in earlier proceedings relating to that family to which he was a party, has been fully investigated and has been the subject of an express finding, in accordance with the appropriate standard of proof, that he did so perpetrate them, I would hold that he could not challenge the finding in the later proceedings. It seems overwhelmingly convenient that the issue should be taken to have been adjudicated nearer the relevant time, i.e. in the earlier proceedings, in proceedings in which the children themselves and their mother were almost certainly active participants and in which the central focus was upon those children.
>
> To that limited extent I would import the doctrine of issue estoppel into children cases. Indeed, emboldened by the words of Butler-Sloss LJ which I have already quoted, and the observation of Balcombe LJ in the Ealing case (above) at p 793H to the effect that: 'this is not ordinary civil litigation: it concerns children', I would thereby necessarily be extending the doctrine of issue estoppel in its application that the parties in both proceedings should be the same.'

17. In *Re B (Minors) (Care Proceedings: Issue Estoppel)* [1997] 3 WLR 1, Hale J, as she then was, considered the case law on whether or not the rule of issue estoppel applied in Children Act proceedings. That case concerned care proceedings in relation to two children, where there had been earlier care proceedings relating to different children in which the Judge had made specific findings that the same father had abused those other children. The Local Authority in that case argued that the father could not challenge the findings. The Guardian's counsel argued that the principle of issue estoppel did not arise in cases concerning children. The father's case was much more case-specific. Hale J reviewed the case law

on issue estoppel both generally and specifically in family law cases, and she reached the following conclusion:

> 'It seems to me that the weight of Court of Appeal authority is against the existence of any strict rule of issue estoppel which is binding upon any of the parties in children's cases. At the same time, the court undoubtedly has a discretion as to how the inquiry before it is to be conducted. This means that it may on occasions decline to allow a full hearing of the evidence on certain matters even if the strict rules of issue estoppel would not cover them. Although some might consider this approach to be a typical example of the lack of rigour which some critics discern in the family jurisdiction, it seems to me to encompass both the flexibility which is essential in children's cases and the increased control exercised by the court rather than the parties which is already a feature of the court's more inquisitorial role in children's cases (and beginning to gain ground in other litigation as shown in the Woolf Report on Access to Justice)'

18. The case law on issue estoppel distinguishes between where the factual issue upon which the estoppel is relied was actually decided and the issues were identical from those where the findings were not critical to the conclusion, see *Spencer Bower on Res Judicata*, who describes this as the determination having to be fundamental and not collateral. At paragraph 8.08 in *Spencer Bower*, the authors say:

> 'The judgement of Coleridge J in R v Hartington Middle Quarter Inhabitants contains the classic statement of principle. 'The judgement' relied upon a res judicata 'concludes, not merely as to the point actually decided, but as to a matter which it was necessary to decide, and which was actually decided, as the groundwork of the decision itself, though not then directly the point in issue.' It is 'conclusive evidence, not merely of the fact directly decided, but of those facts also which are… necessary steps to the decision, … [and] so cardinal to it that without them it cannot stand. Unless they are necessary steps, the rule fails and they are collateral facts only. He rejected the proposition that 'the judgement can only be evidence of the very fact actually decided. Where the decision necessarily involves a judicial determination of some issue of law or fact, because it could not have been legitimately or rationally pronounced without determining or assuming a particular answer, that determination, though not expressed, is an integral part of the decision. There is otherwise no such thing as an issue estoppel by implication.'

19. The problem in this regard with a criminal verdict is that there are no findings of fact and it is not known what matters asserted by the prosecution were accepted by the jury. The other complicating factor in a criminal verdict is the approach I should take to the Judge's sentencing remarks given that the Judge is not the decision maker, and his/her remarks are certainly not findings of fact by the jury. My analysis of this case law in the context of this case is as follows: firstly, having accepted the criminal

conviction pursuant to Section 11 of the Civil Evidence Act, it seems to me that I am bound by the principle of issue estoppel to find that the father intended to kill or cause serious harm to the mother. Although Hale J (as she then was) doubted the application of the principle of issue estoppel in a Children Act case, that was in the context of previous findings in civil litigation. In my view, issue estoppel must apply to the fundamental elements of the criminal conviction, once I have decided to accept the conviction. Although a normal requirement of issue estoppel is that the parties must be the same – and they are not the same in a criminal case, where of course the State prosecutes – and a civil Children Act case, given the particular nature of the criminal prosecution, I do not consider that that distinction applies. In order for the jury to have decided that the father was guilty of murder they had to find he intended to kill or cause very serious harm to the mother. Therefore, once I have accepted – as I do – that the father murdered the mother, it follows that I also find that he intended to kill her or cause her very serious harm on the night of [date redacted]. I therefore reject any suggestion that the father did not intend to harm her.

20. Secondly, once I have accepted the father had the requisite intention, then as a matter of judgment on the facts of the particular case, it seems to me that the jury must have rejected the father's account of what happened after the children went to sleep. I will refer to this in more detail below. However, I reach this conclusion as a matter of judgment, rather than on the basis of the legal principle of issue estoppel: The Local Authority rely on the Judge's sentencing remarks, which I will set out below. Those remarks do not, in my view, give rise to an issue estoppel; in other words, they do not bind me because they are not findings by the jury, and they, the jury, did not necessarily – although they very well may have in practice – formed part of the verdict. However, they are something I give a very great deal of weight to. The Judge heard days of evidence, including forensic evidence, and of other witnesses, none of which I have heard. He is a highly experienced criminal judge who reached a view on the evidence, to which it is appropriate I should give very great weight.

21. Thirdly, however, to the degree the Local Authority rely on evidence that was presented to the jury by the prosecution about the father's controlling and jealous behaviour to the mother before [date redacted], I take a different approach. Plainly no issue estoppel arises in relation to this evidence, but also, I simply cannot tell what role, if any, it took in the conviction. At the most it was relevant background material to the father's conduct when he killed the mother. The jury may or may not have accepted it or given it any weight and I therefore take the view that I should approach that part of the findings sought based on the evidence before me, rather than on any principle that it was previously accepted.

See also *Re B (minors) (issue estoppel)* [1997] 1 FCR 477 (FD), 486G–489F (Hale J) addressing a related point (the issue of estoppel in respect of civil findings)

7.2 EVIDENCE: ORAL EVIDENCE

7.2.1 Evidence: oral evidence: the importance of parents giving evidence

Re HC (children) [2014] EWCA Civ 536, [17] (McFarlane LJ), [42]–[43] (Black LJ)

17. The time came then for the parents to give their evidence, and, as I have indicated, they did not do so. I have no recollection of any case where parents have litigation capacity and where the issue is whether the children should go home to the parents or not has proceeded without the parents giving oral evidence to the court. Parents giving evidence in these circumstances face a stressful encounter with the court, but the courts understand that, and where, as it will have been the case here, the magistrates by that stage were seriously contemplating returning the children to the parents' care, I find it inexplicable that they did not ask the parents to give at least some short evidence before the court so that the magistrates could form their own opinion of the parents.

…

42. Firstly, I want to add something on the subject of the parents not having given evidence before the justices. The justices were at a serious disadvantage by virtue of the parents not giving any oral evidence. In circumstances such as this, where a case is actively contested, it is very important that parents should give evidence. Family courts are well equipped to ensure that the experience of giving evidence is as easy as possible for parents and to make allowances for the impact of stress and emotion on the way in which the parents give their evidence, whether that stress and emotion arises simply because the process of the evidence is challenging for everyone or because the parents have particular difficulties as individuals.

43. The process of giving evidence is the parents' opportunity to put their points to the court, to explain their actions and to set out their version of disputed facts. It is the court's opportunity to gather information, which is vital in order that the court can make reliable findings of fact, gauge the soundness of professional opinions that have been offered to it and make the difficult decisions that have to be made about the future welfare of the children.

See also *Re L and M (children)* [2013] EWHC 1569 (Fam), [52] (Baker J) addressing the same point (in the context of fact-finding), see Chapter 7.3.1 Evidence: approach when fact-finding: an overview

See also *Re N (children: interim order/stay)* [2020] EWCA Civ 1070, [2020] 4 WLR 119, [28]–[31] (Peter Jackson LJ) addressing a related point (the evidential process in interim hearings), see Chapter 4.4.1 Interim care and supervision orders: procedure: format of evidence

See also *A Local Authority v PT and others (re-hearing of fact-finding)* [2018] EWHC 2670 (Fam) [21] (Williams J) addressing the same point

See also *Carmarthenshire County Council v Y* [2017] EWFC 36, [2017] 4 WLR 136 (Mostyn J), [7]–[17] addressing a related point (the general rule that oral evidence under cross-examination is the gold standard, for adult witnesses), see Chapter 7.1.2 Evidence: rules of evidence: hearsay

7.2.2 Evidence: oral evidence: witness demeanour

Re B-M (children: findings of fact) [2021] EWCA Civ 1371, [22]–[30] (Peter Jackson LJ)

22. Centrally, Mr Twomey and Mr Tughan argued that the Judge effectively based her conclusion on an assessment of B's demeanour as a witness when giving evidence and that she consequently did not adequately assess B's overall credibility. They rely on a number of passages of judicial *obiter dicta*: Lord Pearce in *Onassis and Calogeropoulos v Vergottis* [1968] 2 Lloyd's Rep 403 at [36]; Leggatt J in *Gestmin SGPS SA v Credit Suisse (UK) Ltd* [2013] EWHC 3560 (Comm) at [15-22]; Leggatt LJ in *SS (Sri Lanka) v SSHD* [2018] EWCA Civ 1391 at [33-43] and Macur LJ in *Re M (Children)* [2013] EWCA Civ 1147 at [12]. These, they assert, warn judges to a greater or lesser extent against relying upon the way a witness gives evidence as opposed to the content, consistency and probability of the evidence itself. To take one example:

> '… it has increasingly been recognised that it is usually unreliable and often dangerous to draw a conclusion from a witness's demeanour as to the likelihood that the witness is telling the truth.'
>
> 'No doubt it is impossible, and perhaps undesirable, to ignore altogether the impression created by the demeanour of a witness giving evidence. But to attach any signi?cant weight to such impressions in assessing credibility risks making judgments which at best have no rational basis and at worst re?ect conscious or unconscious biases and prejudices. One of the most important qualities expected of a judge is that they will strive to avoid being in?uenced by personal biases and prejudices in their decision-making. That requires eschewing judgments based on the appearance of a witness or on their tone, manner or other aspects of their behaviour in answering questions. Rather than attempting to assess whether testimony is truthful from the manner in which it is given, the only objective and reliable approach is to focus on the content of the testimony and to consider whether it is consistent with other evidence (including evidence of what the witness has said on other occasions) and with known or probable facts.'
>
> *SS (Sri Lanka)* at [36] and [41]

23. There is, I think, a distinct difficulty in harvesting *obiter dicta* expressed in one context and seeking to transplant them into another. *Onassis* and *Gestmin* were concerned with the reliability of recollections of business conversations. In *SS (Sri Lanka)*, a tribunal had rejected an account of

torture by an asylum seeker. This court was considering an argument (for which permission to appeal had not been given) that a delay of three months in the production of the tribunal's judgment had unfairly lessened the impact that should have been made upon the judge by the appellant's demeanour as a witness, and the above observations were made in that context.

24. Further, and as noted by this court in *Kogan v Martin* [2019] EWCA Civ 1645 at [88-89] *Gestmin* is not to be taken as laying down any general principle for the assessment of evidence. Rather, as *Kogan* states, it is one of a line of distinguished judicial observations that emphasise the fallibility of human memory and the need to assess witness evidence in its proper place alongside contemporaneous documentary evidence and evidence upon which undoubted or probable reliance can be placed. The discussion in *Gestmin* is expressly addressed to commercial cases, where documentary evidence will often be the first port of call, ahead of unaided memory.

25. No judge would consider it proper to reach a conclusion about a witness's credibility based solely on the way that he or she gives evidence, at least in any normal circumstances. The ordinary process of reasoning will draw the judge to consider a number of other matters, such as the consistency of the account with known facts, with previous accounts given by the witness, with other evidence, and with the overall probabilities. However, in a case where the facts are not likely to be primarily found in contemporaneous documents the assessment of credibility can quite properly include the impression made upon the court by the witness, with due allowance being made for the pressures that may arise from the process of giving evidence. Indeed in family cases, where the question is not only 'what happened in the past?' but also 'what may happen in the future?', a witness's demeanour may offer important information to the court about what sort of a person the witness truly is, and consequently whether an account of past events or future intentions is likely to be reliable.

26. I therefore respectfully agree with what Macur LJ said in *Re M (Children)* at [12], with emphasis on the word 'solely':

> 'It is obviously a counsel of perfection but seems to me advisable that any judge appraising witnesses in the emotionally charged atmosphere of a contested family dispute should warn themselves to guard against an assessment solely by virtue of their behaviour in the witness box and to expressly indicate that they have done so.'

That was a case where the trial judge's decision to refuse even supervised contact was based unduly on a father's manner of giving evidence.

27. The same approach was taken by this court in a family case: *Re A* [2020] EWCA Civ 1230, where a finding of unlawful killing by poisoning was based upon recollection of a very brief event years earlier. At [36], King LJ noted that in *Kogan*, the court had emphasised the need for a balanced approach to the significance of oral evidence regardless of

jurisdiction and that, although it was a copyright dispute between former partners, the judgment had wider implications. She added:

> '40. I do not seek in any way to undermine the importance of oral evidence in family cases, or the long-held view that judges at first instance have a significant advantage over the judges on appeal in having seen and heard the witnesses give evidence and be subjected to cross-examination (*Piglowska v Piglowski* [1999] WL 477307, [1999] 2 FLR 763 at 784). As Baker J said in in *Gloucestershire CC v RH and others* at [42], it is essential that the judge forms a view as to the credibility of each of the witnesses, to which end oral evidence will be of great importance in enabling the court to discover what occurred, and in assessing the reliability of the witness.
>
> 41. The court must, however, be mindful of the fallibility of memory and the pressures of giving evidence. The relative significance of oral and contemporaneous evidence will vary from case to case. What is important, as was highlighted in *Kogan,* is that the court assesses all the evidence in a manner suited to the case before it and does not inappropriately elevate one kind of evidence over another.
>
> 43. In the present case, the mother was giving evidence about an incident which had lasted only a few seconds seven years before, in circumstances where her recollection was taking place in the aftermath of unimaginably traumatic events. Those features alone would highlight the need for this critical evidence to be assessed in its proper place, alongside contemporaneous documentary evidence, and any evidence upon which undoubted, or probable, reliance could be placed.'

28. Of course in the present case, the issue concerned an alleged course of conduct spread across years. I do not accept that the Judge should have been driven by the *dicta* in the cases cited by the Appellants to exclude the impressions created by the manner in which B and C gave their evidence. In family cases at least, that would not only be unrealistic but, as I have said, may deprive a judge of valuable insights. There will be cases where the manner in which evidence is given about such personal matters will properly assume prominence. As Munby LJ said in *Re A (A Child) (No. 2)* [2011] EWCA Civ 12 said at [104] in a passage described by the Judge as of considerable assistance in the present case:

> 'Any judge who has had to conduct a fact-finding hearing such as this is likely to have had experience of a witness – as here a woman deposing to serious domestic violence and grave sexual abuse – whose evidence, although shot through with unreliability as to details, with gross exaggeration and even with lies, is nonetheless compelling and convincing as to the central core… Yet through all the lies, as experience teaches, one may nonetheless be left with a powerful conviction that on the essentials the witness is telling the truth, perhaps because of the way in which she gives her evidence, perhaps because of a number of small points which, although trivial in themselves, nonetheless suddenly illuminate the underlying realities.'

29. Still further, demeanour is likely to be of real importance when the court is assessing the recorded interviews or live evidence of children. Here, it is not only entitled but expected to consider the child's demeanour as part of the process of assessing credibility, and the accumulated experience of listening to children's accounts sensitises the decision-maker to the many indicators of sound and unsound allegations.

30. None of this will be news to specialist family judges and in future I would hope that in conventional family cases any submissions that unduly labour arguments based upon the *dicta* that I have been considering will receive appropriately short shrift.

See also *Re M (children)* [2013] EWCA Civ 1147, [2014] 2 FLR 685, [11]–[12] (Macur LJ) addressing the same point

See also *A Local Authority v Mother and others* [2020] EWHC 1086 (Fam), [23]–[24] [27] (Lieven J) addressing the same point (in the context of remote hearings)

7.2.3 Evidence: oral evidence: fallibility of memory

Re A (a child) (rev 1) [2020] EWCA Civ 1230, [2021] 1 FCR 307, [38], [40]–[42] (King LJ)

[38] The present case presents the reverse problem. Here, it is argued by Mr Tyler that the judge failed to have any proper awareness of the fallibility of memory. This, he said, coupled with a failure to properly analyse all the surrounding facts – by reference to the documentary evidence in the form of contemporary or near contemporary statements – and known or probable facts, had resulted in the judge having made a wholly unsafe finding that the father was 'leaning over' the coffee cups when the mother came onto the veranda. The judge, Mr Tyler submits, relied too heavily on the impression given by the mother in the witness box, as is demonstrated by her having found (as set out at [11] above but repeated here for convenience):

> '72. I do not accept that the mother concocted this evidence. She was thoroughly cross-examined on this evidence and it was clear to me that she was recounting an event that she recalled. She was a truthful witness and I accept her account.'

...

[40] I do not seek in any way to undermine the importance of oral evidence in family cases, or the long-held view that judges at first instance have a significant advantage over the judges on appeal in having seen and heard the witnesses give evidence and be subjected to cross-examination (*Piglowska v Piglowski* [1999] 3 All ER 632, [1999] 2 FCR 481, [1999] 1 WLR 1360). As Baker J said in in *Gloucestershire CC v RH and others* at [42], it is essential that the judge forms a view as to the credibility of each of the witnesses, to which end oral evidence will be of great importance

in enabling the court to discover what occurred, and in assessing the reliability of the witness.

[41] The court must, however, be mindful of the fallibility of memory and the pressures of giving evidence. The relative significance of oral and contemporaneous evidence will vary from case to case. What is important, as was highlighted in *Kogan*, is that the court assesses all the evidence in a manner suited to the case before it and does not inappropriately elevate one kind of evidence over another.

[42] In the present case, the mother was giving evidence about an incident which had lasted only a few seconds seven years before, in circumstances where her recollection was taking place in the aftermath of unimaginably traumatic events. Those features alone would highlight the need for this critical evidence to be assessed in its proper place, alongside contemporaneous documentary evidence, and any evidence upon which undoubted, or probable, reliance could be placed.

See also *Lancashire County Council v R and others* [2013] EWHC 3064 (Fam), (2014) 135 BMLR 153, [8] (Mostyn J) addressing the same point (within a summary of applicable principles to uncertain perpetrator cases, and highlighting that '[w] ith every day that passes the memory becomes fainter and the imagination becomes more active')

See also *Lancashire County Council v The Children and others* [2014] EWHC 3 (Fam), [9] (Peter Jackson J) addressing the same point (and the notion of 'story creep'), see Chapter 7.3.3 Evidence: approach when fact-finding: discrepancies in accounts

7.2.4 Evidence: oral evidence: parents are compellable

Re Y and another (children) (care proceedings: split hearing) [2003] EWCA Civ 669, [2003] 3 FCR 240, [27] (Thorpe LJ), [28]–[35] (Hale LJ) *quotation limited to* [35]

[35] We are glad, therefore, to have the opportunity today of clarifying the situation. Parents can be compelled to give evidence in care proceedings; they have no right to refuse to do so; they cannot even refuse to answer questions which might incriminate them. The position is no different in a split hearing from that in any other hearing in care proceedings. If the parents themselves do not wish to give evidence on their own behalf there is, of course, no property in a witness. They can nevertheless be called by another party if it is thought fit to do so, and the most appropriate person normally to do so would be the guardian acting on behalf of the child.

See also *Re L-R (children)* [2013] EWCA Civ 1129, [13] (McFarlane LJ) considering *Re Y and another (children) (care proceedings: split hearing)* [2003] EWCA Civ 669, [2003] 3 FCR 240

See also *VBC v AGM and others* [2019] EWFC 64 [Appendix 2], [52]–[59] (Sir Mark Hedley) addressing the same point (and the relationship between committal and adverse inferences)

7.2.5 Evidence: oral evidence: vulnerable witnesses

See Chapter 5.8.2 Case management: protected or vulnerable parties: vulnerable witnesses: Procedure

7.3 EVIDENCE: APPROACH WHEN FACT-FINDING

7.3.1 Evidence: approach when fact-finding: an overview

Re L and M (children) [2013] EWHC 1569 (Fam), [45]–[58] (Baker J)

THE LAW

45. In determining the issues of this fact finding hearing I apply the well-established legal principles. I have summarised those principles at length in my earlier decisions in *Re JS* [2012] EWHC 1370 (Fam) and *Devon CC v EB* [2013] EWHC 968 (Fam). All counsel have referred to one or both of those summaries. I have those principles firmly in mind and need only refer to them briefly here.

46. First, the burden of proof lies at all times with the local authority.

47. Secondly, the standard of proof is the balance of probabilities.

48. Third, findings of fact in these cases must be based on evidence, including inferences that can properly be drawn from the evidence and not on suspicion or speculation. I have borne this principle in mind throughout this hearing.

49. Fourthly, when considering cases of suspected child abuse the court must take into account all the evidence and furthermore consider each piece of evidence in the context of all the other evidence. The court invariably surveys a wide canvas. A judge in these difficult cases must have regard to the relevance of each piece of evidence to other evidence and to exercise an overview of the totality of the evidence in order to come to the conclusion whether the case put forward by the local authority has been made out to the appropriate standard of proof.

50. Fifthly, amongst the evidence received in this case, as is invariably the case in proceedings involving allegations of non-accidental head injury, is expert medical evidence from a variety of specialists. Whilst appropriate attention must be paid to the opinion of medical experts, those opinions need to be considered in the context of all the other evidence. It is important to remember that the roles of the court and the expert are distinct and it is the court that is in the position to weigh up the expert evidence against its findings on the other evidence. It is the judge who makes the final decision.

51. Sixth, cases involving an allegation of non-accidental injury often involve a multi-disciplinary analysis of the medical information conducted by a group of specialists, each bringing their own expertise to bear on the problem. The court must be careful to ensure that each expert keeps

within the bounds of their own expertise and defers, where appropriate, to the expertise of others.

52. Seventh, the evidence of the parents and any other carers is of the utmost importance. It is essential that the court forms a clear assessment of their credibility and reliability.

53. Eighth, it is common for witnesses in these cases to tell lies in the course of the investigation and the hearing. The court must be careful to bear in mind that a witness may lie for many reasons, such as shame, misplaced loyalty, panic, fear and distress, and the fact that a witness has lied about some matters does not mean that he or she has lied about everything (see *R v Lucas* [1981] QB 720).

54. Ninth, as observed by Dame Elizabeth Butler-Sloss P in an earlier case

> 'The judge in care proceedings must never forget that today's medical certainty may be discarded by the next generation of experts or that scientific research would throw a light into corners that are at present dark.'

55. This principle, inter alia, was drawn from the decision of the Court of Appeal in the criminal case of *R v Cannings* [2004] EWCA 1 Crim. In that case a mother had been convicted of the murder of her two children who had simply stopped breathing. The mother's two other children had experienced apparent life-threatening events taking a similar form. The Court of Appeal Criminal Division quashed the convictions. There was no evidence other than repeated incidents of breathing having ceased. There was serious disagreement between experts as to the cause of death. There was fresh evidence as to hereditary factors pointing to a possible genetic cause. In those circumstances, the Court of Appeal held that it could not be said that a natural cause could be excluded as a reasonable possible explanation. In the course of his judgment, Judge LJ (as he then was) observed:

> 'What may be unexplained today may be perfectly well understood tomorrow. Until then, any tendency to dogmatise should be met with an answering challenge.'

56. With regard to this latter point, recent case law has emphasised the importance of taking into account, to the extent that it is appropriate in any case, the possibility of the unknown cause. The possibility was articulated by Moses LJ in *R v Henderson-Butler and Oyediran* [2010] EWCA Crim. 126 at paragraph 1:

> 'Where the prosecution is able, by advancing an array of experts, to identify a non-accidental injury and the defence can identify no alternative cause, it is tempting to conclude that the prosecution has proved its case. Such a temptation must be resisted. In this, as in so many fields of medicine, the evidence may be insufficient to exclude, beyond reasonable doubt, an unknown cause. As *Cannings* teaches,

even where, on examination of all the evidence, every possible known cause has been excluded, the cause may still remain unknown.'

57. In *Re R, Care Proceedings Causation* [2011] EWHC 1715 (Fam), Hedley J, who had been part of the constitution of the Court of Appeal in the *Henderson* case, developed this point further. At paragraph 10, he observed,

> 'A temptation there described is ever present in Family proceedings too and, in my judgment, should be as firmly resisted there as the courts are required to resist it in criminal law. In other words, there has to be factored into every case which concerns a discrete aetiology giving rise to significant harm, a consideration as to whether the cause is unknown. That affects neither the burden nor the standard of proof. It is simply a factor to be taken into account in deciding whether the causation advanced by the one shouldering the burden of proof is established on the balance of probabilities.'

58. Finally, when seeking to identify the perpetrators of non-accidental injuries the test of whether a particular person is in the pool of possible perpetrators is whether there is a likelihood or a real possibility that he or she was the perpetrator. In order to make a finding that a particular person was the perpetrator of non-accidental injury the court must be satisfied on a balance of probabilities. It is always desirable, where possible, for the perpetrator of non-accidental injury to be identified both in the public interest and in the interest of the child, although where it is impossible for a judge to find on the balance of probabilities, for example that Parent A rather than Parent B caused the injury, then neither can be excluded from the pool and the judge should not strain to do so.

See also *A Local Authority v W and others* [2020] EWFC 40, [2020] 4 WLR 83, [37]–[38] (MacDonald J) addressing the same point (setting out a similar list of principles as 'long established legal principles that govern the fact finding exercise')

7.3.2 Evidence: approach when fact-finding: wide canvas

Re U (a child) (serious injury: standard of proof); Re B (a child) (serious injury: standard of proof) [2004] EWCA Civ 567, [2004] 2 FCR 257, [26] (Dame Elizabeth Butler-Sloss P)

[26] It is for the purpose of satisfying that threshold that the local authority seeks to prove specific facts against the parent or parents. Only if it succeeds in that task can its application for a care or supervision order proceed. Thus the preliminary issue of fact constitutes the gateway to a judicial discretion as to what steps should be taken to protect the child and to promote his welfare. In those circumstances we must robustly reject Mr Cobb's submission that the local authority should refrain from proceedings or discontinue proceedings in any case where there is a substantial disagreement amongst the medical experts. For the judge

invariably surveys a wide canvas, including a detailed history of the parents' lives, their relationship and their inter-action with professionals. There will be many contributions to this context, family members, neighbours, health records, as well as the observation of professionals such as social workers, health visitors and children's guardian.

See also *Re T (children)* [2004] EWCA Civ 558, [2004] 2 FLR 838, [33] (Dame Elizabeth Butler-Sloss P) addressing a related point (viewing the totality of evidence)

See also *Re P (a child)* [2019] EWCA Civ 1346, [2020] 1 FCR 77, [47] (King LJ) addressing a related point (taking account of all relevant evidence)

7.3.3 Evidence: approach when fact-finding: discrepancies in accounts

Lancashire County Council v The Children and others [2014] EWHC 3 (Fam), [9] (Peter Jackson J)

9. To these matters, I would only add that in cases where repeated accounts are given of events surrounding injury and death, the court must think carefully about the significance or otherwise of any reported discrepancies. They may arise for a number of reasons. One possibility is of course that they are lies designed to hide culpability. Another is that they are lies told for other reasons. Further possibilities include faulty recollection or confusion at times of stress or when the importance of accuracy is not fully appreciated, or there may be inaccuracy or mistake in the record-keeping or recollection of the person hearing and relaying the account. The possible effects of delay and repeated questioning upon memory should also be considered, as should the effect on one person of hearing accounts given by others. As memory fades, a desire to iron out wrinkles may not be unnatural – a process that might inelegantly be described as 'story-creep' may occur without any necessary inference of bad faith.

See also *Wigan Council v M and others* [2015] EWFC 6, [82] (Peter Jackson J) addressing a related point (the levels of precision expected of children), see Chapter 7.4.2 Evidence: children: children giving evidence: levels of precision

7.3.4 Evidence: approach when fact-finding: inferences based on proved fact

Re A (a child) (fact-finding: speculation) [2011] EWCA Civ 12, [2011] 1 FCR 141, [26] (Munby LJ)

[26] There are, in my judgment, two different points wrapped up in this complaint which need to be disentangled and kept quite distinct. The first, on which, as a matter of principle, Ms Crowley is obviously correct, is the elementary proposition that findings of fact must be based

on evidence (including inferences that can properly be drawn from the evidence) and not on suspicion or speculation. Whether, as she would have it, Roderic Wood J fell into error in this respect, is something to be determined when I come to consider the particular findings of which complaint is made. When I come to embark upon that exercise I will, of course, have Ms Crowley's submissions on this point very much in mind. Here I merely observe that the judge, as one would expect, was very alert to the fact that suspicion cannot be the basis of findings. Thus, referring to the father's claim for asylum, the judge said (main judgment at [47]):

> 'I have ... concluded that he is a wholly unreliable historian in relation to a very significant part of his claim for asylum. Whilst I am accordingly suspicious as to his account of his activities in Iran/Iraq as a justification for asylum, I can do no more than record that suspicion. Since it is suspicion and does not achieve the necessary standard of proof to qualify as a probability I shall put that aspect of the matter firmly out of my mind.'

See also *A Local Authority v Ms A and others* [2010] EWHC 28 (Fam), [2011] 2 FLR 137, [18]–[20] (Ryder J) addressing the same point (in the context of dismissing the drawing of an inference from the mere recurrence of events and emphasising that a judicial inference must be based on fact)

7.3.5 Evidence: approach when fact finding: multiple injuries over a short duration

Re M (a child) [2010] EWCA Civ 1467, [37] (Wilson LJ)

37. The first basis of the cross-appeal is the father's responsibility for the October event. Is it likely, asks Miss Hodgson on behalf of the mother, that, within the space of less than seven weeks, the partial suffocation of a baby is caused by one parent and yet injuries to his body are, or even just may be, perpetrated by the other? It is certainly not unknown for judges to give a negative answer to that type of question and, by reference to it, to proceed to identify the perpetrator of a second non-accidental injury. When they do so, their reasoning is – in my view – in principle valid. In the present case (says Miss Hodgson) the judge posed the question to herself at a curious stage, namely in the final paragraph of her written judgment and, in particular, *after* she had announced her conclusion that she could do no more than to consign the parents to a pool. It resembled a postscript, namely that, in relation to the December injuries, she had been invited to extrapolate from the father's responsibility for the October event that he was their perpetrator but that the matters were 'quite separate and very different' and that she was unable to accede to the invitation. Of course it was quite separate. But was it very different? Yes, says Mr McIlwain on behalf of the local authority, suffocation is very different from gripping or inflicting a blow. No, says Miss Hodgson, both are born of a sudden loss of adult control.

7.4 EVIDENCE: CHILDREN

7.4.1 Evidence: children: children giving evidence

See Chapter 5.4 Case management: children

7.4.2 Evidence: children: children giving evidence: levels of precision

Wigan Council v M and others [2015] EWFC 6, [82] (Peter Jackson J)

82. I reach these conclusions for the following reasons …

(iii) There is a core of consistency in the accounts given by the children, individually and collectively. The accounts fitted together securely, but not slickly in a way that would suggest collusion. There were some inconsistencies about important details, for example their respective body positions when they were made to engage in sexual activity with each other. On behalf of Mr C, Mr Rowley QC and Mrs Hughes rightly draw attention to this and other examples. I am not troubled by the numerous variants within the evidence. They are entirely consistent with what one would expect from children who have been chronically abused. The accounts cover a very large number of highly-charged occasions over a very long period. As B said at one point, things get blurred. Young people cannot be expected to give a photographic replay of sequences of similar but varying events and get all the distasteful details right. Assessment of such evidence cannot only focus on the level of precision with which children give descriptions, but calls for a much broader survey of all the relevant features.

7.4.3 Evidence: children: ABE[2] interviews

Re Y and E (children) (sexual abuse allegations) [2019] EWCA Civ 206, [4]–[5], [31] (Baker LJ)

4. To assist courts in reaching decisions in cases involving these issues, the government has provided expert guidance, 'Achieving Best Evidence in Criminal Proceedings: Guidance on interviewing victims and witnesses and guidance on using special measures' (Ministry of Justice, 2011). Notwithstanding its title, the guidance applies to civil as well as criminal proceedings. The guidance is, however, extremely detailed and often very challenging for police officers and social workers to follow. In many cases, the investigators fail to comply with the guidance in one way or another, and the judge (or the jury in criminal cases) has to assess the extent to which those failures undermine the reliability of the evidence.

2 Achieving Best Evidence in Criminal Proceedings: Guidance on interviewing victims and witnesses and guidance on using special measures (Ministry of Justice, 2011).

5. The challenges facing judges dealing with allegations of this sort are therefore very considerable, particularly in the context of the pressures currently experienced in the family courts. But it is of the utmost importance that these cases should receive careful and thorough scrutiny, both at first instance and, where the circumstances justify the granting of permission to appeal, by the appellate court.

...

The ABE interviews

...

31. The ABE guidance document contains a large number of detailed instructions, guidelines and points of good practice. The paragraphs which are perhaps of particular importance in family proceedings are set out in my judgment in *Re W and F*, supra, at paragraphs 33 to 42. It is unnecessary to repeat that exercise here. Equally, it is unnecessary to set out extensive citations from the earlier reported cases.

Re W; Re F (children) [2015] EWCA Civ 1300, [33]–[42] (Baker J) *quotation limited to* [33]

33. The document 'Achieving Best Evidence in Criminal Proceedings – Guidance on interviewing victims and witnesses, and guidance on using special measures' was published in March 2011 by the Ministry of Justice and other departments, superseding earlier versions of the guidance. It is accepted that its relevance is not confined to criminal proceedings but extends to proceedings in the family courts. The status of the document is described in paragraph 1.1:

> 'This document describes good practice in interviewing victims and witnesses, and in preparing them to give their best evidence in court. While it is advisory and does not constitute a legally enforceable code of conduct, practitioners should bear in mind that significant departures from the good practice advocated in it may have to be justified in the courts.'

The scope of the Guidance is described in paragraph 1.3:

> 'This document considers preparing and planning for interviews with witnesses, decisions about whether or not to conduct an interview, and decisions about whether the interview should be videoed-recorded or whether it would be more appropriate for a written statement to be taken following the interview. It covers the interviewing of witnesses both for the purposes of making a video-recorded statement and also for taking a written statement, their preparation for court and the subsequent court appearance.

AS v TH (false allegations of abuse) [2016] EWHC 532 (Fam), [2016] 3 FCR 327, [48]–[52] (MacDonald J)

Police interviews of children

[48] Police interviews with children should be conducted in accordance with the *ABE Guidelines* to which I have already referred. In this case N was interviewed by both English and Scottish police officers and S was interviewed by Scottish officers. In Scotland the *Guidance on Joint Investigative Interviewing of Child Witnesses in Scotland* (The Scottish Government 2011) takes the place of the *ABE Guidelines*.

[49] Whilst DC Glendenning stated that there is no longer a requirement in Scotland to establish in an interview whether a child understands the difference between truth and lies, it would appear that her understanding is not entirely accurate. The Scottish Guidance makes clear that, whilst the Vulnerable Witnesses (Scotland) Act 2004 abolished the competence test in respect of all witnesses, the *Vulnerable Witnesses Guidance Pack* (Scottish Executive 2006) states in chapter 11 that '*the court will still have to make a judgment of the witness's truthfulness and reliability, therefore any interview should still clarify, in age appropriate ways, the witnesses level of understanding*'.

[50] The courts have further endorsed a number of the general principles set out in the *ABE Guidelines*. It is desirable that interviews with young children should be conducted as soon as possible after any allegations are made (*Re M (minors) (sexual abuse: evidence)* [1993] 1 FCR 253, [1993] 1 FLR 822). Where a child has been interviewed on a number of occasions the court may attach diminishing weight to what is said in the later interviews (*Re D (minors) (child abuse: interviews)* [1998] 2 FCR 419, [1998] 2 FLR 10). The court will wish to see responses from the child which are neither forced nor led (*Re X (a minor) (child abuse: evidence)* [1989] 1 FLR 30). It is normally undesirable for a parent to be present during an interview with the child (*Re N (child abuse: evidence)* [1996] 2 FCR 572, [1996] 4 All ER 225, and see the Cleveland Report para 12.35). In *Re S (a child)* [2013] EWCA Civ 1254 Ryder LJ confirmed that the guidance set out in the Cleveland Report at paragraph 12.34 with respect to interviewing children remain good practice.

[51] It is of note that guidance from the Children Act Advisory Committee concerning the *Memorandum of Good Practice* which preceded the *ABE Guidelines*, made clear that:

> 'Any joint child abuse interview conducted by police and social services must follow the memorandum of good practice. Otherwise, not only is the resulting interview of no forensic value, but it may impede or contaminate any further assessment of the child ordered by the court.'

[52] Where there has, as in this case, been a failure to follow the interviewing guidelines, the court is not compelled to disregard altogether the evidence obtained in interview but may rely on it together with other independent

material to form a conclusion (*Re B (allegations of sexual abuse: child's evidence)* [2006] EWCA Civ 773, [2006] 2 FCR 386, [2006] 2 FLR 1071). However, where the court finds that no evidential weight can be attached to the interviews the court may only come to a conclusion that relies on the content of those interviews where it has comprehensively reviewed all of the other evidence (*TW v A City Council* [2011] 1 WLR 819, [2011] 1 FLR 1597).

7.4.4 Evidence: children: ABE interviews: important factors concerning ABE

Re JB (a child) (sexual abuse allegations) [2021] EWCA Civ 46, [2021] 1 FCR 574, [11] (Baker LJ)

The ABE guidance

[11] The importance of complying with the ABE guidance, which is directed at both criminal and family proceedings, has been reiterated by this court in a series of cases including *TW v A City Council* [2011] EWCA Civ 17, [2011] 1 WLR 819, [2011] 1 FLR 1597, *Re W, Re F* [2015] EWCA Civ 1300, *Re E (a child)* [2016] EWCA Civ 473, [2016] 3 FCR 499, [2016] 4 WLR 105, *Re Y and F (children) sexual abuse allegations)* [2019] EWCA Civ 206 and in the judgments of MacDonald J in *AS v TH and others* [2016] EWHC 532 (Fam), [2016] 3 FCR 327 and *Re P (sexual abuse: finding of fact hearing)* [2019] EWFC 27. It is unnecessary to repeat at any length the extensive comments set out in some of those judgments. For the purposes of this appeal, the following points are of particular relevance. (Save where indicated, the paragraphs cited are from the ABE guidance.)

(1) 'The ABE guidance is advisory rather than a legally enforceable code. However, significant departures from the good practice advocated in it will likely result in reduced (or in extreme cases no) weight being attached to the interview by the courts.' (*Re P (sexual abuse: finding of fact hearing)*, supra, paragraph [856]).

(2) Any initial questioning of the child prior to the interview should be intended to elicit a brief account of what is alleged to have taken place; a more detailed account should not be pursued at this stage but should be left until the formal interview takes place (paragraph 2.5).

(3) In these circumstances, any early discussions with the witness should, as far as possible, adhere to the following guidelines.

- (a) Listen to the witness.
- (b) Do not stop a witness who is freely recalling significant events.
- (c) Where it is necessary to ask questions, they should, as far as possible in the circumstances, be open-ended or specific-closed rather than forced-choice, leading or multiple.

(d) Ask no more questions than are necessary in the circumstances to take immediate action.

(e) Make a comprehensive note of the discussion, taking care to record the timing, setting and people present as well as what was said by the witness and anybody else present (particularly the actual questions asked of the witness).

(f) Make a note of the demeanour of the witness and anything else that might be relevant to any subsequent formal interview or the wider investigation.

(g) Fully record any comments made by the witness or events that might be relevant to the legal process up to the time of the interview (paragraph 2.6, see also *AS v TH*, supra, paragraph 42).

(4) For all witnesses, interviews should normally consist of the following four main phases: establishing rapport; initiating and supporting a free narrative account; questioning; and closure (paragraph 3.3).

(5) The rapport phase includes explaining to the child the 'ground rules' for the interview (paragraphs 3.12–14) and advising the child to give a truthful and accurate account and establishing that the child understands the difference between truth and lies (paragraphs 3.18–19). The rapport phase must be part of the recorded interview, even if there is no suggestion that the child did not know the difference between truth and lies, because 'it is, or may be, important for the court to know everything that was said between an interviewing officer and a child in any case' (per McFarlane LJ in *Re E*, supra, paragraph [38]).

(6) In the free narrative phase of the interview, the interviewer should 'initiate an uninterrupted free narrative account of the incident/ event(s) from the witness by means of an open-ended invitation' (paragraph 3.24).

(7) When asking questions following the free narrative phase, 'interviewers need fully to appreciate that there are various types of question which vary in how directive they are. Questioning should, wherever possible, commence with open-ended questions and then proceed, if necessary, to specific-closed questions. Forced-choice questions and leading questions should only be used as a last resort' (paragraph 3.44).

(8) Drawings, pictures and other props may be used for different reasons – to assess a child's language or understanding, to keep the child calm and settled, to support the child's recall of events or to enable the child to give an account. Younger children with communication difficulties may be able to provide clearer accounts when props are used but interviewers need to be aware of the risks and pitfalls of using such props. They should be used with caution and 'never combined with leading questions'. Any props used should be preserved for production at court (paragraphs 3.103 to 3.112).

(9) 'The fact that the phased approach may not be appropriate for interviewing some witnesses with the most challenging communication skills (eg those only able to respond 'yes' or 'no' to a question) should not mean that the most vulnerable of witnesses are denied access to justice'. It should not be 'regarded as a checklist to be rigidly worked through. Flexibility is the key to successful interviewing. Nevertheless, the sound legal framework it provides should not be departed from by interviewers unless they have discussed and agreed the reasons for doing so with their senior managers or an interview advisor' (paragraph 3.2).

(10) Underpinning the guidance is a recognition 'that the interviewer has to keep an open mind and that the object of the exercise is not simply to get the child to repeat on camera what she has said earlier to somebody else' (per Sir Nicholas Wall P in *TW v A City Council*, supra, at paragraph [53]).

See also *Re Y and E (children) (sexual abuse allegations)* [2019] EWCA Civ 206, [32] (Baker LJ) addressing the same point

See also *Re JB (a child) (sexual abuse allegations)* [2021] EWCA Civ 46, [2021] 1 FCR 574, [40] (Baker LJ) addressing a related point (misuse of notes as 'props')

7.4.5 Evidence: children: ABE interviews: failure to follow guidance

Re SR (a child) [2018] EWCA Civ 2738, [2019] 1 FCR 809, [30]–[41] (Baker LJ) *quotation limited to* [30], [41]

[30] The importance of adhering to the guidance has been recognised repeatedly by this court – see for example *Re B (allegation of sexual abuse: child's evidence)* [2006] EWCA Civ 773, [2006] 2 FCR 386, [2006] 2 FLR 1071, *TW v A City Council* [2011] EWCA Civ 17, [2011] 1 WLR 819, [2011] 1 FLR 1597, *Re W, Re F* [2015] EWCA Civ 1300, and *Re E (a child)* [2016] EWCA Civ 473, [2016] 3 FCR 499, [2016] 4 WLR 105. Those four cases all concerned investigations in which interviews had been conducted in ways that purported to comply with the guidance but which, in various respects, manifestly failed to do so. The principles underpinning the guidance are, however, relevant to all investigations which include interviews of alleged victims of abuse, whether or not the interviews purport to have been conducted under the guidance.

...

[41] The failure to comply with the ABE guidance will often have a decisive effect on the weight to be attached to evidence obtained as a result of the investigation. This is well illustrated by the four Court of Appeal cases cited above.

Re B and another (children) (allegation of sexual abuse: child's evidence)
[2006] EWCA Civ 773, [2006] 2 FCR 386, [34]–[35], [40]–[43] (Hughes LJ)

[34] Painful past experience has taught that the greatest care needs to be taken if the risk of obtaining unreliable evidence is to be minimised. Children are often poor historians. They are likely to view interviewers as authority figures. Many are suggestible. Many more wish to please. They do not express themselves clearly or in adult terms, so that what they say can easily be misinterpreted if the listeners are not scrupulous to avoid jumping to conclusions. They may not have understood what was said or done to them or in their presence.

[35] For these and many other reasons it is of the first importance that the child be given the maximum possible opportunity to recall freely, uninhibited by questions, what they are able to say, and equally it is vital that a careful note is taken of what they say and also of any questions which are asked. All this and many other similar propositions, most of them of simple common sense, are set out in nationally agreed guidelines entitled 'Achieving Best Evidence' ('ABE').

…

[40] There was no question of this evidence being inadmissible for failure to comply with the ABE guidelines, and that has not been suggested in argument for either parent. In a family case evidence of this kind falls to be assessed, however unsatisfactory its origin. To hold otherwise would be to invest the guidelines with the status of the law of evidence and it would invite that question: which failures have the consequence of inadmissibility? Clearly some failures to follow the guidelines will reduce but by no means eliminate the value of the evidence. Some may be purely technical and have no impact at all on value. Others may reduce the value almost to vanishing point.

[41] The question for us in this case is whether the judge was compelled to the conclusion that he must disregard this evidence altogether. Mr Anelay submits that the failures here were so wholesale that that must be the consequence, on the basis that otherwise there is no point in having the guidelines.

[42] With that submission I do not agree. The purpose of the guidelines is not disciplinary; it is to present the court and for that matter the parents with the most reliable evidence which can be obtained. In every case the judge cannot avoid the task of weighing up the evidence, warts and all, and deciding whether or not it has any value or none. Everything will depend on the facts of the case. The exercise has perhaps something in common with the one which judges are used to carrying out when confronted with hearsay evidence, often in a family case third or fourth-hand hearsay.

[43] On the other hand, I agree with Mr Anelay that the fact that one is in a family case sailing under the comforting colours of child protection is not

a reason to afford to unsatisfactory evidence a weight greater than it can properly bear. That is in nobody's interests, least of all the child's.

See also *Re JB (a child) (sexual abuse allegations)* [2021] EWCA Civ 46, [2021] 1 FCR 574, [48] (Underhill LJ) addressing the same point (even substantial failures will not necessarily mean ABE cannot be relied on)

See also *Re W; Re F (children)* [2015] EWCA Civ 1300, [79] (Baker J) addressing the same point (emphasising the 'very great care' needed by those interviewing children, and that courts require a 'high standard')

7.5 EVIDENCE: OTHER

7.5.1 Evidence: other: covert recordings

Re B (a child) [2017] EWCA Civ 1579, [2018] 1 FCR 226, [10]–[16] (Sir James Munby P)

[10] The courts have had to grapple with the legal and procedural issues generated by the stool-pigeon, the eavesdropper and the concealed observer since time immemorial. Since the second half of the nineteenth century the courts have had to grapple, and keep up, with the legal and procedural issues generated by the invention of technologies for the audio or visual recording of events. On one level there is nothing very new about this. Thus, the covert filming or video-recording of personal injury or benefits claimants suspected of fraud has been an established and acceptable practice for many years. But in the family courts the issue has become much more pressing in recent years.

[11] There are, I suspect, two reasons for this. One is the ever-increasing sophistication and miniaturisation and at the same time ever decreasing cost of modern recording equipment. For anyone possessed of a smartphone or similar piece of 'kit', surreptitious audio recording or filming of events is child's play. As Peter Jackson J sagely commented in *M v F* [2016] EWFC 29, [2016] 3 FCR 604, [2016] 4 WLR 92, para [1]:

> '... nowadays it is all too easy for individuals to record other people without their knowledge. Advances in technology empower anyone with a mobile phone or a tablet to make recordings that would be the envy of yesterday's spies.'

The other, I fear, has to do with the widespread distrust in too many quarters of the competence or even the integrity of the family justice system and of the professionals involved in it. Here, of course, it is the existence of the mindset rather than its foundation in reality which is the driving force. But it does give rise to important questions of public policy: see, for example, *Re J (reporting restriction: internet: video)* [2013] EWHC 2694 (Fam), [2014] 2 FCR 284, [2014] EMLR 7, where a father filmed social workers removing his baby.

[12] That said, it needs to be accepted, with honesty and candour, that there have been in recent years in the family courts shocking examples of professional malpractice which have been established only because of the covert recording of the relevant individual. In *Medway Council v A & Ors (learning disability; foster placement)* [2015] EWFC B66 a mother made covert recordings of the abusive and racially insensitive foster carer who she was living with along with her baby; until the recordings were played she had been disbelieved. 2 In *Re F (care proceedings: failures of expert)* [2016] EWHC 2149 (Fam), [2017] 1 FLR 1304, the lamentable shortcomings of an expert, a consultant clinical psychologist, were, in significant measure, laid bare only because the mother had covertly recorded her assessment sessions with him.

[13] It is important to distinguish between open recording and covert recording. In the nature of things, it is the latter which is more problematic. Without seeking to establish a complete taxonomy, there are at a least three categories of covert recording, each of which may raise a variety of different issues (see the careful comment of Peter Jackson J in *M v F* [2016] EWFC 29, [2016] 3 FCR 604, [2016] 4 WLR 92, para [7]): covert recording of children (for an example see *M v F* [2016] EWFC 29, [2016] 3 FCR 604, [2016] 4 WLR 92), covert recording of other family members (for an example see *Re C* [2015] EWCA Civ 1096), and covert recording of professionals (see, in addition to the Cases referred to above, the Transparency Project's *Parents recording social workers – A guidance note for parents and professionals* published in December 2015, version 2, January 2016).

[14] Whatever the nature of the recording, a number of issues are likely to arise. Again without any pretence to completeness it is obvious that questions may arise as to (i) the *lawfulness* of what has been done; (ii) *best practice* outside the court room as it were; (iii) the *admissibility* of the recording in evidence; and (iv) a variety of other *evidential and practice issues* (for example, as to how the recording is to be put in evidence, problems in relation to sound and picture quality, and, in particular, disputes as to authenticity – who are the people who can be heard or seen on the recording, has the recording been edited or 'cut and spliced'? – which may necessitate calling expert evidence).

[15] Furthermore, in relation to all this it may be important to identify *who* is doing the recording and *why*. Covert surveillance and recording by the police and other agencies, including the Security Service, which in current conditions not infrequently impinges upon the family courts, is one thing. Covert surveillance and recording by others *may* – I put the point no higher, it being a matter for another day – raise rather different issues.

[16] I draw attention to these matters to show that covert recording in the context of the family courts potentially involves a myriad of issues, very few of which, despite all the judgments to which I have referred, have, even now, been systematically considered either at first instance or in this court.

See also *Re DH (a minor) (care proceedings: evidence and orders)* [1994] 2 FCR 3 (FD), 49E–52F, 54G–55H (Wall J) addressing a related point (covert surveillance by authorities in a suspected FII[3] case)

7.5.2 Evidence: other: social work notes

Re G (children) [2003] EWHC 551 (Fam), [2003] 2 FLR 42, [38] (Munby J)

38. There is one further matter to which I drew attention in *Re L* (see at paras [153]–[155]) and which requires emphasis. Social workers should at all times keep clear, accurate, full and balanced notes of all relevant conversations and meetings between themselves and/or with parents, other family members and others involved with the family. And where important meetings are held there should be a written agenda circulated in advance to all concerned. Clear, accurate, full and balanced minutes of the meeting (identifying in particular what information has been given to the meeting and by whom) should be taken by someone nominated for that task before the meeting begins. And, as soon as possible after the meeting, the minutes should be agreed by those present as being an accurate record of the meeting and then be immediately disclosed to all parties.

7.6 EVIDENCE: EXPERTS

7.6.1 Evidence: experts: all issues

See Chapter 8 Experts

3 Fabricated or induced illness.

CHAPTER 8

Experts

Chapter contents

CHAPTER 8

Experts

8.1 EXPERTS: OBTAINING EVIDENCE

8.1.1 Experts: obtaining evidence: 'necessary'

Re H-L (a child) [2013] EWCA Civ 655, [2014] 1 WLR 1160, [1]–[3] (Sir James Munby P)

1. In this appeal we have to decide the point left open in *Re TG (Care Proceedings: Case Management: Expert Evidence)* [2013] EWCA Civ 5, [2013] 1 FLR 1250.

2. In *Re TG*, in which judgment was handed down on 22 January 2013, I drew attention to the important change to rule 25.1 of the Family Procedure Rules 2010 due to be implemented with effect from 31 January 2013. Whereas previously the test for permitting expert evidence to be adduced was whether it was 'reasonably required to resolve the proceedings', the test now is whether it is 'necessary to assist the court to resolve the proceedings.' I said (para [30]):

   > 'It is a matter for another day to determine what exactly is meant in this context by the word 'necessary', but clearly the new test is intended to be significantly more stringent than the old. The text of what is 'necessary' sets a hurdle which is, on any view, significantly higher that the old test of what is 'reasonably required'.'

   We now have to decide what is meant by 'necessary.'

3. The short answer is that 'necessary' means necessary. It is, after all, an ordinary English word. It is a familiar expression nowadays in family law, not least because of the central role it plays, for example, in Article 8 of the European Convention and the wider Strasbourg jurisprudence. If elaboration is required, what precisely does it mean? That was a question considered, albeit in a rather different context, in *Re P (Placement Orders: Parental Consent)* [2008] EWCA Civ 535, [2008] 2 FLR 625, paras [120], [125]. This court said it 'has a meaning lying somewhere between 'indispensable' on the one hand and 'useful', 'reasonable' or 'desirable' on the other hand', having 'the connotation of the imperative, what is demanded rather than what is merely optional or reasonable or desirable.' In my judgment, that is the meaning, the connotation, the word 'necessary' has in rule 25.1.

See also Re C (a child) [2015] EWCA Civ 539, [2016] 3 FCR 177, [23]–[33] (Ryder LJ) considering *Re H-L (a child)* [2013] EWCA Civ 655, [2014] 1 WLR 1160 (albeit in a private law context)

8.1.2 Experts: obtaining evidence: slow to admit irregularly obtained evidence

Re M (children) [2018] EWCA Civ 607, [27]–[29], [36]–[39] (Peter Jackson LJ) *quotation limited to* [27]–[29], [38]–[39]

27. The admission of expert evidence in children proceedings is governed by s 13 of the Children and Families 2014, which provides:

13 Control of expert evidence, and of assessments, in children proceedings

(1) A person may not without the permission of the court instruct a person to provide expert evidence for use in children proceedings.

(2) Where in contravention of subsection (1) a person is instructed to provide expert evidence, evidence resulting from the instructions is inadmissible in children proceedings unless the court rules that it is admissible.

(3) A person may not without the permission of the court cause a child to be medically or psychiatrically examined or otherwise assessed for the purposes of the provision of expert evidence in children proceedings.

(4) Where in contravention of subsection (3) a child is medically or psychiatrically examined or otherwise assessed, evidence resulting from the examination or other assessment is inadmissible in children proceedings unless the court rules that it is admissible.

(5) In children proceedings, a person may not without the permission of the court put expert evidence (in any form) before the court.

(6) The court may give permission as mentioned in subsection (1), (3) or (5) only if the court is of the opinion that the expert evidence is necessary to assist the court to resolve the proceedings justly.

(7) When deciding whether to give permission as mentioned in subsection (1), (3) or (5) the court is to have regard in particular to—

(a) any impact which giving permission would be likely to have on the welfare of the children concerned, including in the case of permission as mentioned in subsection (3) any impact which any examination or other assessment would be likely to have on the welfare of the child who would be examined or otherwise assessed,

(b) the issues to which the expert evidence would relate,

(c) the questions which the court would require the expert to answer,

(d) what other expert evidence is available (whether obtained before or after the start of proceedings),

(e) whether evidence could be given by another person on the matters on which the expert would give evidence,

(f) the impact which giving permission would be likely to have on the timetable for, and duration and conduct of, the proceedings,

(g) the cost of the expert evidence, and

(h) any matters prescribed by Family Procedure Rules.

(8)–(11) ....

28. The core of this statutory provision is that expert evidence in children proceedings may not be put before the court in any form without permission (ss.5) and that permission will only be granted if it is necessary to assist the court to resolve the proceedings justly (ss.6). Further, the instruction of an expert without permission is prohibited (ss.1) and any evidence resulting from such an instruction is inadmissible unless the court rules otherwise (ss.2). When deciding whether to give permission, the court is to have regard in particular to the matters set out in ss.7: child welfare, definition of issues, effect on timetable, availability of other expert evidence, cost, and matters arising in the Rules. Although there is no hierarchy within that list, the court will inevitably be most concerned about the implications of admission or refusal of expert evidence for the welfare of the child and for the fairness of the proceedings.

29. It is understandable that the judge dealt with the application for a rehearing on its merits. However, it is not right to describe the question of the admissibility of the evidence that underpinned that application as a technicality. This is primary legislation which, unusually in proceedings relating to children, renders evidence inadmissible unless the court considers it is necessary to admit it to assist it to resolve the proceedings justly. A court considering an application to admit expert evidence is required to have regard to the matters in ss.7, whether the application is made in proceedings in the normal way or in the unusual circumstances that arose in this case.

...

38. I agree with Ms Cheetham's submissions on this point. The court should as a matter of principle be slow to admit expert evidence that has been irregularly obtained. Plainly, it will not stand on ceremony at the expense of child welfare, but if the rules are not enforced, parties are encouraged to ignore them. A lax approach will inevitably be felt to be unfair by other parties and satellite issues of this kind cause delay and increase costs. Moreover, although it has not apparently happened in this case, there would be nothing to stop a litigant shopping around, unbeknownst to the other parties, until they alight upon a favourable opinion. A response such as that of the Guardian (see paragraph 22 above) does not in my view give adequate weight to the importance of the proper procedures, which are there to serve the interests of children and of justice.

39. I would suggest that in a case like this, where a court is faced with expert evidence that has already been obtained in breach of s.13, it should as one part of its thinking ask itself whether it would have granted permission

to seek the expert evidence with which it is now presented as a *fait accompli*. That of course is not the only consideration, but to ask the question ensures that the requirements of the statute and the rules are not forgotten. In this case, had the mother made an application at the hearing on 26 April for permission to instruct a further expert, such an application would inevitably have been refused. The fact that she chose to ignore the rules is a matter the court should take into account.

8.1.3 Experts: obtaining evidence: second experts

Re W (a child) (non-accidental injury: expert evidence) [2005] EWCA Civ 1247, [2005] 3 FCR 513, [9]–[11], [35]–[40] (Wall LJ)

[9] The purpose of this judgment, therefore, is different. It is to look, quite shortly; (1) at the advisability of the court relying on a single expert in care proceedings, when the issue that expert has to address is of central importance to the judge's findings; and (2) the propriety of permitting parents who deny abusing their child what can best be described as a second opinion.

[10] I can state my conclusion at once, because I accept a submission made in their supplementary submission by Mr Hayden QC, Mr Karl Rowley and Mr Bansa Singh Hayer acting in this court on behalf of both parents. In the course of their argument about the provision of expert evidence in family proceedings they say:

> 'In many cases (probably the majority) a clear picture will emerge from a constellation of factors (eg paediatric, radiological, parental history, medical records) which will cumulatively point the court towards certain conclusions. Though those conclusions may be resisted by parents, it would be both unrealistic and unnecessary to permit parents to obtain 'mirror reports' in every discipline. In a certain number of cases, however, eg non-accidental head injury (NAHI), or pathologically 'unascertained' infant death, certain evidence may become pivotal and by its very nature not easily receptive to a challenge in the absence of any other expert opinion. In our submission, in those cases, the court should be slow to decline an application for a second expert. Strict case management (in accordance with the protocol) should also permit such evidence to be identified within a reasonable timescale.'

[11] Before giving my reasons for agreeing with this statement, I need to set out the facts …

…

[35] We were provided with a bundle of authorities by the parties. In my judgment, the only decision which is directly on the point is the decision of this court in *Daniels v Walker (Practice Note)* [2000] 1 WLR 1382. This decision must, in my judgment, be viewed with a modicum of

caution from a family perspective, since experts in family proceedings (particularly in the field of paediatric neuroradiology) are a precious and scarce resource, whereas in civil proceedings experts in less arcane fields are not only more numerous, but also more willing to undertake forensic work.

[36] With that important proviso, the question for this court in *Daniels v Walker* was what approach judges should adopt when a single expert who has been jointly instructed makes a report, and one side or other is unhappy with the report. The context was an injury suffered by the claimant some ten years previously when he was six or seven and had been struck by a car. His injuries were very serious. There was a very substantial report by a jointly instructed occupational therapist, about which the defendant's solicitors were unhappy. However, the claimant's solicitors refused to make their client and his family available to be interviewed by an expert nominated by the defendant's solicitors. The defendant applied to the judge, who refused him permission to call any further expert evidence on the point, but allowed him to put written questions to the expert. The defendant appealed to this court, which allowed his appeal. Giving the leading judgment, the Lord Chief Justice, Lord Woolf, neatly encapsulated the point in the following two paragraphs:

> '27. Where a party sensibly agrees to a joint report and the report is obtained as a result of joint instructions in the manner which I have indicated, the fact that a party has agreed to adopt that course does not prevent that party being allowed facilities to obtain a report from another expert, or, if appropriate, to rely on the evidence of another expert.
>
> 28. In a substantial case such as this, the correct approach is to regard the instruction of an expert jointly as the first step in obtaining expert evidence on a particular issue. It is to be hoped that in the majority of cases it will not only be the first step but that the last step. If, having obtained a joint expert's report, a party, for reasons which are not fanciful, wishes to obtain further information before making a decision as to whether or not there is a particular part (or indeed the whole) of the expert's report which he or she may wish to challenge, then they should, subject to the discretion of the court, be permitted to obtain that evidence.'

[37] In my judgment, these two paragraphs, with the proviso I have identified, apply to the instant case. It is to be noted that both the Lord Chief Justice and Latham LJ in *Daniels v Walker* rejected an analysis based on art 6. It is, of course, the case that the Human Rights Act 1998 had not been enacted when *Daniels v Walker* was decided on 3 May 2000. However, the Lord Chief Justice remarked:

> 'Article 6 could not possibly have anything to add to the issue on this appeal. The provisions of the CPR, to which I have referred, make it clear that the obligation on the court is to deal with cases justly. If,

> having agreed to a joint expert's report a party subsequently wishes to call evidence, and it would be unjust having regard to the overriding objective of the CPR not to allow that party to call evidence, they must be allowed to call it.'

[38] It is in the light of these observations that I am content, speaking for myself, to rely on the overriding objective in the CPR, and not to consider the case in art 6 terms.

[39] The proviso which I have identified finds appropriate expression, in my judgment, in the submission made by counsel for the parents which I have recorded in para 10 of this judgment. They rightly recognise that it would be both unrealistic and unnecessary for the court to permit parents to obtain a second opinion in every discipline. Such a second opinion, accordingly, should in my judgment normally only be permitted where the question to be addressed by the chosen expert goes to an issue of critical importance for the judge's decision in the case. For the reasons I have already given, the instruction of experts in family cases needs to be stringently controlled by the court, but in the circumstances described by Messrs Hayden, Rowley and Hayer in the extract I have cited, they are in my judgment right to submit that the court should be slow to decline an application for a second expert.

[40] It is, I think, also important to remember that a second opinion does not necessarily mean additional litigation and substantial additional litigation costs. If the second opinion confirms the first, my experience is that the issues in the case addressed by the two experts are likely to be radically reduced if not eliminated. However, as is self-evident, any medical consensus must be a true medical consensus—that is with each medical discipline making its proper contribution. The medical consensus in the hearing before Judge Newton was only a consensus because all the other doctors, including the neurologists and neuroradiologists, deferred to Dr A.

Re S (children) [2006] EWCA Civ 981, [2007] 1 FLR 90, [13]–[19] (Wilson LJ) *quotation limited to* [17]–[19]

17. In paragraph 36 of his judgment Wall LJ quoted the following passage from the judgment of Lord Woolf MR in *Daniels v Walker* [2000] 1 WLR 1382 at 1387 E:

> 'In a substantial case such as this, the correct approach is to regard the instruction of an expert jointly by the parties as the first step in obtaining expert evidence on a particular issue. It is to be hoped that in the majority of cases it will not only be the first step but the last step. If, having obtained a joint expert's report, a party, for reasons which are not fanciful, wishes to obtain further information before making a decision as to whether or not there is a particular part (or indeed the whole) of the expert's report which he or she may wish to

challenge, then they should, subject to the discretion of the court, be permitted to obtain that evidence.'

With one proviso, Wall LJ suggested that that passage applied to the *Oldham* case. The proviso was that experts in family proceedings were a precious resource, perhaps nowadays more scarce than those able and willing to undertake forensic work in civil proceedings such as *Daniels v Walker*.

18. In my view the *Oldham* case is no authority whatever for the extravagant submissions made to the judge on behalf of the parents and now made to us by Mr Collier QC on behalf of the father. Quite apart from the attendant public expense, what was the logical argument in favour of contributions from two consultant neuroradiologists; from two consultant ophthalmologists; and from two consultant neurosurgeons? What was objectionable in the subscription of all parties to a carefully crafted letter of instruction to one top expert in each discipline, whose duty of total impartiality the joint instruction could only confirm? How could it be said at that stage before the judge that there was an expert whose evidence was not only adverse to the parents but pivotal and so justified a second opinion?

19. The only argument which runs in any way counter to the conclusion that the judge was correct – and at the very least entitled – to favour the joint instruction of single experts is the risk of delay in the event that it was only at a later stage that, in the light in particular of the *Oldham* case, the court were to favour the taking of a second opinion. In his courageous submissions to us this morning Mr Collier has stressed this point. In this case the expert evidence is due to be filed by 9 June; the court's review will take place on 16 June; and the first day of the first stage of the hearing is 19 July although, fortuitously, the break between 20 July and 7 August may allow for a little more flexibility. In paragraph 12 of his judgment the judge said:

'It may be that the opinions of these single joint experts will be accepted and if so the case will likely be speedily resolved. If they are not then the court would likely be asked at that time for permission to instruct another expert or tier of experts, and the observations of the Court of Appeal in *Oldham* would be of advantage to a dissatisfied parent.'

I take that passage as being an acknowledgment on the part of the judge, which I would endorse, that it may be that at the review on 16 June, in the light of the reports then to hand, the father and mother will be in a position to press for, and indeed perhaps to obtain, permission to collect a second expert opinion in one or more disciplines. Although it may be possible for any such second opinion or opinions to be collected between 16 June and 19 July, or at least between 16 June and 7 August, in time for the fact-finding hearing to proceed as fixed, there is no denying that a direction for such further evidence might jeopardise the holding of the fact-finding hearing on those dates. Such a risk Mr Kirk QC on behalf of the local authority recognises. The tail, however, would be wagging the dog were the court, in this case or routinely, to favour what would otherwise be the premature collection of expert evidence in order not to jeopardise a hearing in the event that it were later to prove appropriate for it to be collected.

See also *Webster and another v Norfolk County Council and others; Re Webster (children)* [2009] EWCA Civ 59, [2009] 1 FCR 673, [194]–[197] (Wall LJ) considering *Re W (a child) (non-accidental injury: expert evidence)* [2005] EWCA Civ 1247, [2005] 3 FCR 513

See also *Re O-M (children) (non-accidental injury: expert evidence)* [2009] EWCA Civ 1405, [2010] 1 FCR 305, [52]–[53] (Wall LJ) addressing the same point

8.1.4 Experts: obtaining evidence: treating clinicians used as experts

Re F (a child) (fact-finding appeal) [2019] EWCA Civ 1244, [2019] 3 FCR 435, [126], [129]–[132] (Moylan LJ)

[126] I should make clear, having regard to some of the submissions made in this case, that this is not to say that a judge cannot make a finding based on the evidence of a treating clinician in preference to that of experts instructed in proceedings. As was pointed out by Mr Gray for the guardian, one of the factors which the court must take into account when deciding whether to give permission is 'what other expert evidence is available (whether obtained before or after the start of proceedings)': s 13(7)(d).

…

[129] As mentioned at the outset of this judgment, I am hesitant about giving guidance about the manner in which s 13 and Part 25 should be applied when treating medical witnesses give expert evidence. All counsel agreed that in their experience such witnesses more frequently give expert evidence than they used to and more frequently theirs is the only expert evidence. In part this may be the result of the lack of experts available to give expert evidence for the purposes of proceedings as well as for the reason given by Ms Woolrich, namely that in some cases, particularly those involving more minor injuries, the only expert evidence required for the proper determination of the proceedings is that given by treating doctors or other professionals. Those professionals may be unwilling or unable (because, possibly, of the terms of their employment) to give what might be termed formal expert evidence.

[130] In the present case, Dr Flowers made it clear that she was not in a position to act as an expert witness. This did not, of course, mean that she was not able to give expert evidence. In such circumstances there can be good reason for the provisions of s 13(5), (6) and (7) to be applied with a light touch. This is because, although her evidence would seem to come within

the scope of 'expert evidence (in any form)', s 13(5), she was not, at least initially, engaged for the purposes of the proceedings. However, despite her having made clear that she could not act as an expert witness, her role became blurred by her involvement in the experts' meeting. She was then providing 'expert evidence for use in proceedings': r 25.2(1).

[131] In this case, it is not difficult to see why this occurred because it enabled Dr Flowers to engage with the evidence being given by the instructed experts and the questions being asked by the parties without which she would have been considerably disadvantaged when giving oral evidence at the hearing. However, I agree with Mr Stonor's submission that it raises the question of whether the different perspective she brought to the case from that of the instructed experts was not overlooked. For example, there was no expectation that she would undertake the type of research that an instructed expert would be expected to undertake for the purposes of preparing a report for proceedings. Again, this does not mean that her evidence could not be accepted in preference to that of the instructed experts but it was a feature that the judge needed to have in mind when assessing the evidence.

[132] It is, of course, important that the court and the parties recognise the difference between treating professionals and those instructed for the purposes of providing expert evidence for the purposes of proceedings. As I have said, a treating professional will self-evidently have a very different focus to an expert witness. However, as Mr Stonor submitted, it would not support the proper and expeditious determination of cases if unnecessary and/or disproportionate obstacles were placed in the way of expert medical evidence being available to the court. In that context, it seems to me that a treating professional who is also an expert will in some cases be able to give expert evidence without all or even any of the requirements of Part 25 being applied. However, again as referred to above, this is a matter which requires broader analysis than can be undertaken in a single decision. Further, Dr Flowers' situation and the manner in which she became involved in these proceedings raise wider issues which would benefit from a broader consideration such as that which can be provided by the President's Working Group.

See also *Re O-M (children) (non-accidental injury: expert evidence)* [2009] EWCA Civ 1405, [2010] 1 FCR 305, [44]–[49] (Wall LJ) addressing the same point

8.1.5 Experts: obtaining evidence: particular expertise: psychological or psychiatric assessments unlikely to assist purely factual issues

Re CB and JB (minors) (care proceedings: case conduct) [1998] 2 FCR 313 (FD), 321G–322H (Wall J)

Question 2: Is it an appropriate application of the principles laid down in *Re M and R (minors) (expert opinion: evidence)* [1996] 2 FCR 617; sub nom

Re M and R (minors) (sexual abuse: expert evidence) [1996] 4 All ER 239 for expert psychiatric or psychological evidence to be adduced as to the propensity of a parent to injure a child or as to the likelihood of a parent having done so?

In my judgment, the short answer to this question is usually No, and almost certainly No, where, as indicated in answer to question 1 above, the court is dealing with an issue of fact in a split hearing upon which the threshold criteria depend. 'Never' is a difficult word to say in the Family Division, but I do not believe it was the intention of the Court of Appeal in *Re M and R (minors) (expert opinion: evidence)* [1996] 2 FCR 617, [1996] 4 All ER 239 that evidence as to adult credibility or propensity to commit acts of physical abuse should be routinely given by psychologists or psychiatrists and be routinely admissible as probative of the factual issue as to whether or not a particular parent perpetrated a particular act of abuse.

In *Re M and R (minors) (expert opinion: evidence)* the Court of Appeal, commenting on my rejection in another case of the argument that previous decisions of the Court of Appeal on the point were per incuriam because of the terms of s 3(3) of the Civil Evidence Act 1972, said ([1996] 2 FCR 617 at 633, [1996] 4 All ER 239 at 253):

> 'But while Wall, J. was wrong in his construction of s.3, we have no reason to believe that he was wrong in holding the doctor's evidence on the credibility of two women giving evidence of abuse of them when they were children dealt with an issue that did not require his expertise. The evidence was inadmissible because irrelevant, and not because it went to the ultimate issue in the case.'

I accordingly agree with a submission made by the father at an interlocutory stage of the case in the following terms:

> 'Although *Re M and R* (*minors*) [(*expert opinion: evidence*)] ([1996] 2 FCR 617, [1996] 4 All ER 239) establishes that expert evidence may be admissible, *if relevant*, in respect of the ultimate issue, it is submitted that the underlying rationale for the use of expert evidence should be kept firmly in focus – viz to assist the court in drawing inferences and conclusions where the tribunal of fact does not possess the necessary expertise to carry out that task … ([RH]'s evidence) … is in essence evidence of credibility. It is submitted that it is inadmissible not because it goes to one of the ultimate issues in the case (viz did the mother inflict one or other of the injuries) but because it is irrelevant and unnecessary. It is irrelevant and unnecessary because the court has the expertise, experience and knowledge to assess credibility.' (Counsel's emphasis.)

In this case, I ruled most of the psychiatric and psychological evidence irrelevant and thus inadmissible on this basis. The evidence I admitted as to the propensity of the mother to perpetrate the abuse on CB (or, more accurately, to the effect that she had not shaken CB) was, as I have stated, flawed and, as I found, plainly wrong.

See also *Re S (care: care: parenting skills: personality tests)* [2004] EWCA Civ 1029, [2005] 2 FLR 658 [57] (Ward LJ), [67] (Arden LJ) addressing a related point (the limitations of personality testing)

See also *Re L (children) (care proceedings)* [2006] EWCA Civ 1282, [2006] *3 FCR 301, [68]–[70] (Wall LJ)* considering *Re CB and JB (minors) (care proceedings: case conduct)* [1998] 2 FCR 313, considering *Re S (care: care: parenting skills: personality tests)* [2004] EWCA Civ 1029, [2005] 2 FLR 658

See also *Wigan Council v M and others* [2015] EWFC 8, [2016] 1 FLR 126, [1]–[2], [9]–[12] (Peter Jackson J) addressing a related point (veracity assessments will rarely be necessary)

8.1.6 Experts: obtaining evidence: particular expertise: biomechanical evidence

Re TG (a child) (care proceedings: biomechanical engineering evidence) [2013] EWCA Civ 5, [2013] 1 FCR 229, [68] (Sir James Munby P)

[68] That leaves the more general question of whether, in other cases, biomechanical evidence might in future satisfy the 'necessary' test. I would not wish to rule out the possibility, though I suspect that in the present state of the relevant science such cases will be at best infrequent in the family courts. As of today, it remains the fact that there is no case of which we are aware where such evidence has been found to be of any significant assistance. But I emphasise the qualifying words I have just used. We can only operate on the best and most up-to-date science available to us today. But we must always bear in mind that tomorrow may bring about a transformation of scientific knowledge so that, to use Dame Elizabeth Butler-Sloss P's words, new scientific research will throw light into corners that are at present dark. Whether and if so when this will come about in relation to this particular scientific discipline we cannot say. That is why, as I have already emphasised, case-management judges must always keep an open mind when deciding whether or not to permit expert evidence particularly where, as here, the science is both complex and developing.

See also *Re S (children)* [2006] EWCA Civ 981, [2007] 1 FLR 90, [20] (Wilson LJ) addressing the same point

8.1.7 Experts: obtaining evidence: procedure: prior LAA[1] authorisation

A Local Authority v DS and others [2012] EWHC 1442 (Fam), [2012] 1 WLR 3098, [42]–[55] (Sir Nicholas Wall P) *quotation limited to* [45], [54]–[55]

45. In all the circumstances of this case, therefore, I feel able to offer the following general guidance:

i) The words 'the cost thereof is deemed to be a necessary and proper disbursement on [a named individual's] public funding certificate' (or words to equivalent effect) should no longer be used when the court orders a report from an expert. The words do not bind the LSC or, for that matter anybody else. In addition, there must be doubt about the court's power to make such an order. It is, in my judgment, far better to follow the words of the Regulations, particularly if the court is being asked to approve rates in excess of those allowed by the Funding Order. A copy of such an order is attached at the end of this judgment.

ii) The test for expert evidence will shortly import the word 'necessary'. The question which the court will have to ask itself is whether or not the report of the expert is necessary for the resolution of the case. FPR rule 25.1 will shortly be amended to insert the word 'necessary' for 'reasonably required' and there will be a new Practice Direction.

iii) It is the court which makes the order for the instruction of an expert, and this responsibility neither can nor should be delegated to the parties. It is of the essence of good case management that the court should identify the issues on which it wants the expert to report. It would thus be helpful and important for the tribunal to be able to say – if it is the case and the hard pressed Tribunal with a long list has had the time – that it has read all the (relevant) papers.

iv) If the court takes the view that an expert's report is *necessary* for the resolution of the case, it should say so, *and give its reasons.* This can be done by a preamble to the order, or by a short judgment, delivered at dictation speed or inserted by the parties with the judge's approval. I have considered this point carefully, and have come to the conclusion that this does not impose an undue burden either on the court or the profession.

v) There is no substitute for reasons. A consent order is still an order of the court: it is a judicial decision and must be supported by reasons. Equally, a decision by the LSC is a decision. It too should be supported by reasons.

vi) 'Reasons' in circumstances such as these need not be lengthy or elaborate. They must, however, explain to anyone reading them *why* the decision maker has reached the conclusion he or she has particularly if the expert is seeking to be paid at rates which are higher than those set out in the table in Schedule 6 of the Funding Order

1 Legal Aid Agency.

vii) Speed is of the essence in proceedings relating to children. An application for prior authority must be made at the earliest opportunity and, once again, must be carefully drafted and supported by reasons.

viii) By like token, it behoves the LSC to deal with such applications promptly and, particularly if the application is being refused, or only granted to a limited extent, to give its reasons for its decision. Once again, the reasons can be concise. Of course the solicitor seeking prior authority can go ahead regardless, and instruct the expert at the rates the expert demands, but such a suggestion, in reality, is unreal. The expert's contract is with the solicitor, and if he or she does not recover the expert's costs from the LSC, it is the solicitor who is liable. Given the exiguous rates of remuneration, this is a risk no solicitor is willing to take, particularly where the client is impecunious.

ix) Similar considerations to those set out above apply to any challenge to the LSC's ruling.

x) If a case is urgent, it should be so marked and the reasons for its urgency explained.

xi) Courts should familiarise themselves with Part 25 of the FPR and with Practice Direction 25A which supplements it. Specifically, they should be aware of paragraph 4.3(h) or its equivalent when amended which provides that the person wishing to instruct an expert must explain to the court why the expert evidence proposed cannot be given by Social Services undertaking a core assessment or by the Children's Guardian in accordance with their respective statutory duties. The Rule and the Practice Direction are being revised to make them (it is to be hoped) more practical and 'user friendly'. Practitioners should look out, in due course, for the amendments.

…

54. A suggested form of order, depending on the facts of the individual case, could be in the following terms: –

a) The proposed assessment and report by X (as set out in paragraph 2 of this order) are vital to the resolution of this case.

b) This case is exceptional on its facts.

c) The costs to be incurred in the preparation of such reports are wholly necessary, reasonable and proportionate disbursement on the funding certificates of the publicly funded parties in this case.

d) The court considers X's hourly rate of £y and the estimated costs of the assessment report to be reasonable in the context of (his) qualifications, experience and expertise.

e) The field in which X practises, and the particular expertise which (he) brings to bear on cases involving (subject) are highly specialised. There is no realistic prospect of finding an alternative expert with the necessary expertise at lower fee.

f) (The court considers that any further delay in order to give the LSC the (further) opportunity to consider an application for prior authority to incur the costs of the proposed amendment or report would be wholly outside the child(ren's) timescale(s).

55. Even such an order (which will need, of course, to be adapted to the facts of the individual case) should be buttressed by reasons as set out in the guidance which I have attempted to give.

8.2 EXPERTS: ASSESSING EVIDENCE

8.2.1 Experts: assessing evidence: not bound by experts

Re B (a minor) (rejection of expert evidence) [1996] 2 FCR 272 (CA), 275H–276D (Ward LJ), 280D–F (Butler-Sloss LJ)

> Another success of the Children Act has been the training, including an especially the training in related disciplines, which all Judges receive. By their special allocation to this work, they acquire a body of knowledge which, strictly speaking, cannot be substituted for the evidence received, but which can be deployed to spot any weakness in the expert evidence. That is the judicial task. The expert advises, but the Judge decides. The Judge decides on the evidence. If there is nothing before the court, no facts or no circumstances shown to the court which throw doubt on the expert evidence, then, if that is all with which the court is left, the court must accept it. There is, however, no rule that the Judge suspends judicial belief simply because the evidence is given by an expert.
>
> There is no important point of principle arising in this case. This is not a case where there was no other evidence before the Judge. The mother herself, and more importantly the health visitors who also bring their expertise to bear, and the contact supervisor, each gave evidence which was at variance on matters of fact with that given by the experts. Consequently, the Judge's findings cannot be attacked on the basis that there was no evidence to support them. The proper question in this appeal is no more and no less than that which arises in other appeals, namely, were the Judge's findings against the weight of the evidence?
>
> …
>
> I agree with the judgment of Ward, LJ. Family Judges deal with increasingly difficult child cases and are much assisted in their decision-making process by professionals from other disciplines; medical, wider mental health and social work among others. The courts pay particular attention to the valuable contribution from paediatricians and child psychiatrists as well as others, but it is important to remember that the decision is that of the Judge and not of the professional expert. Judges are well accustomed to assessing the conflicting evidence of experts. As Ward, LJ said, Judges are not expected to suspend judicial belief simply because the evidence is given by an expert. An expert is not in any special position and there is no

presumption of belief in a doctor however distinguished he or she may be. It is, however, necessary for a Judge to give reasons for disagreeing with experts' conclusions or recommendations. That, this Judge did …

See also *Re S (a child) (care proceedings: surrogacy)* [2015] EWFC 99, [124] (Baker J) addressing the same point

See also *A Local Authority v K and others* [2005] EWHC 144 (Fam), [2005] 1 FLR 851, [38]–[63] (Charles J) providing an overview of the law on this point

8.2.2 Experts: assessing evidence: courts decide on all of the evidence

A Local Authority v PT and others (re-hearing of fact-finding) [2018] EWHC 2670 (Fam), [19]–[20] (Williams J)

19. The court is not limited to considering the expert evidence alone. Rather, it must take account of a wide range of matters which include the expert evidence but also include, for example, its assessment of the credibility of the witnesses and the inferences that can properly be drawn from the evidence. The court must take into account all the evidence and furthermore consider each piece of evidence in the context of all the other evidence. The court invariably surveys a wide canvas. A judge in these difficult cases must have regard to the relevance of each piece of evidence to other evidence and to exercise an overview of the totality of the evidence in order to come to a conclusion.

20. Thus, the opinions of medical experts need to be considered in the context of all of the other evidence. While appropriate attention must be paid to the opinion of medical experts, those opinions need to be considered in the context of all the other evidence. It is important to remember that the roles of the court and the expert are distinct and it is the court that is in the position to weigh up the expert evidence against its findings on the other evidence. It is the judge who makes the final decision. Cases involving an allegation of non-accidental injury often involve a multi-disciplinary analysis of the medical information conducted by a group of specialists, each bringing their own expertise to bear on the problem. The court must be careful to ensure that each expert keeps within the bounds of their own expertise and defers, where appropriate, to the expertise of others. When considering the medical evidence in cases where there is a disputed aetiology giving rise to significant harm, the court must bear in mind, to the extent appropriate in each case, the possibility of the unknown cause [*R v Henderson and Butler and Others* [2010] EWCA Crim 126 and *Re R (Care Proceedings: Causation)* [2011] EWHC 1715 (Fam)]. Today's medical certainty may be discarded by the next generation of experts. Scientific research may throw a light into corners that are at present dark. That affects neither the burden nor the standard of proof. It is simply a factor to be taken into account in deciding whether the causation advanced by the one shouldering the burden of proof is established on the balance of probabilities.'

Re FL (a child) [2020] EWCA Civ 20, [36]–[37] (Baker LJ)

36. Of course, when carrying out his assessment, the judge must take into account all relevant evidence, including expert evidence. But it is the judge, and only the judge, that is in the position to weigh up the expert evidence against the findings on the other evidence, and it is always open to a judge to arrive at a different conclusion from that reached by experts, provided that conclusion is supported by evidence. It is the judge who makes the final decision.

37. In this case, the recorder carried out a thorough evaluation of the relevant evidence. In my judgment, he gave sufficient consideration to the professional assessments of Mrs N and, where he disagreed with their conclusions, he explained his reasons for doing so. Crucially, his decision was based on his own evaluation of the family members who gave evidence, in particular his assessment of Mrs N herself. None of the arguments advanced on behalf the guardian or the local authority in this case has persuaded me that this court should interfere with that evaluation. Given the recorder's assessment of Mrs N, his decision to make a special guardianship order in her favour cannot be described as wrong.

See also *Re D (a child) (care proceedings: expert evidence)* [2010] EWCA Civ 1000, [2010] 3 FCR 244, [24] (Hughes LJ), see Chapter 8.2.4 Experts: assessing evidence: undisputed expert evidence: sound and articulated reasons to reject

8.2.3 Experts: assessing evidence: conflicting experts

Re W and another (a child: non-accidental injury) [2002] EWCA Civ 710, [2003] 2 FCR 346, [42]–[44] (Thorpe LJ)

[42] It would of course be possible for a judge to conduct a fact-finding exercise on the medical evidence alone in what would seem to me to be extreme instances. But whether or not the forensic medical evidence is the only evidence, the predominant evidence, or simply one strand within the evidence, in its assessment the judge is not exercising any discretion. He has the ordinary judicial duty to assess the expert evidence and to find the possible and probable scientific explanation for the injury or event under investigation.

[43] If the forensic experts are agreed that they are unable to advance more than a range of possibilities, none of which is inherently more probable than any other, the judge must inevitably so find and then seek his conclusion in the other available evidence, such as the evidence of the social history of the family, or in his assessment of the individuals directly involved.

[44] But if there is a stark conflict of medical evidence, the judge cannot decline to choose. If each contention is equally persuasive, he should either invite the parties to agree some tertiary referral to a national centre of excellence, or invite either the president of the Royal College of Paediatrics and Child Health, or the chairman of its Child Protection Committee to identify such an expert. To leave the issue unresolved renders the disposal stage

problematic. How is the judge to bring into the discretionary scale the sort of suspicions that this judge voiced at the conclusion of his judgment? How are the local authority to present their case on causation? Does all then turn on the evidence of the parents?

8.2.4 Experts: assessing evidence: undisputed expert evidence: sound and articulated reasons to reject

Re D (a child) (care proceedings: expert evidence) [2010] EWCA Civ 1000, [2010] 3 FCR 244, [24] (Hughes LJ)

[24] At root the question in this appeal is whether the judge was entitled to prefer this empirical or factual evidence to Dr G's prognosis derived from her psychological profile. The answer to that is yes. I do not think that it was helpful for the judge to embark upon a comparison with the direction which is given in criminal cases to jurors when they are dealing with expert evidence. Those directions no doubt are designed to remind jurors that the ultimate decision is for them, that the expert evidence must be evaluated and that if they disagree for a reason with the expert's conclusion they must do so, but that is to say no more than is the common coin of all litigation and jurors do not give reasons; judges do. In the context of a child care case, the judge is the decision-maker, the expert is not. Where there is as here undisputed expert opinion evidence, the judge ought not to reject it without sound and articulated reason. This judge said at [171] that it was for him to weigh the evidence of Dr G and the guardian in the context of all the evidence both oral and written in the case. To the extent that he parted company with the evidence or recommendations of Dr G or the guardian, he recognised that he must give his reasons.

See also *Re B (a child)* [2008] EWCA Civ 1547, [2009] 2 FLR 14 [18] (Thorpe LJ) addressing a related point (judicial doubt should lead to questioning the expert)

8.2.5 Experts: assessing evidence: inflicted injuries: unknown aetiology

Re R (a child) [2011] EWHC 1715 (Fam), [2011] 2 FLR 1384, [9]–[10], [19] (Hedley J)

9. … Thus, it can be seen that at the heart of the case lies the question of causation of the subdural haematomas and the femoral fracture. These cases occupy substantial amounts of the time expended in exercising the jurisdiction under Part IV of the Act. These issues, however, are not confined to this jurisdiction. They occupy much time of judge and jury in the Crown Court. There too these issues cause great anxiety and difficulty. In the case of *Henderson & Ors* [2010] EWCA Crim 1269 (fully reported) the Court of Appeal Criminal Division sought to address these matters. Conspicuous effort was made to ensure that the experience of the Family Court was fed into that court's consideration. It is of course

desirable, where possible, that the law applied in the two jurisdictions should be as consistent as the substantive law permits. There is, of course, a fundamental difference between the two systems in relation to the differing standards of proof that prevail. Nevertheless, it may be worth reflecting on the words of Lord Justice Moses which introduce the judgment of the court in that case. He says this:

> 'There are few types of case which arouse greater anxiety and controversy than those in which it is alleged that a baby has died as a result of being shaken. It is of note that, when the Attorney General undertook a review of 297 cases over a 10-year period following the case of Cannings, 97 were cases of what is known as 'shaken baby syndrome'. The controversy to which such cases give rise should come as no surprise. A young baby dies whilst under the sole care of a parent or child-minder. That child can give no clue to clinicians as to what has happened. Experts, prosecuting authorities and juries must reconstruct, as best they can, what has happened. There remains a temptation to believe that it is always possible to identify the cause of injury to a child. Where the prosecution is able, by advancing an array of experts, to identify a non- accidental injury and the defence can identify no alternative cause, it istempting to conclude that the prosecution has proved its case. Such a temptation must be resisted. In this, as in so many fields of medicine, the evidence may be insufficient to exclude beyond reasonable doubt an unknown cause. As Cannings teaches, even where, on examination of all the evidence, every possible known cause has been excluded, the cause may still remain unknown.'

10. The temptation there described is ever present in family proceedings too and, in my judgment, should be as firmly resisted there as the courts are required to resist it in criminal law. In other words, there has to be factored into every case which concerns a disputed etiology giving rise to significant harm, a consideration as to whether the cause is unknown. That affects neither the burden nor the standard of proof. It is simply a factor to be taken into account in deciding whether the causation advanced by the one shouldering the burden of proof is established on the balance of probabilities. In the event, this case provides a vivid illustration of that very process. The medical evidence of the subdural haematomas and the fracture is discrete and must be considered as such. However, once that is done, an overall view will need to be taken to see if there is a unifying medical hypothesis. The medical evidence in respect of the subdural haematomas and the head falls into three parts. First, there is the evidence of the neuro- surgeons: Mr Mitchell, the treating surgeon and Mr Richards, the court-appointed expert. Secondly, there is the evidence of the neuro-radiologist, Dr Jaspan, instructed as an expert; and thirdly, the overview evidence of a consultant paediatrician, Dr Mecrow, also instructed as an expert.

…

19. That said, I found the arguments against this being a perinatal event also persuasive, particularly the absence of what might ordinarily be expected to be found. In these circumstances, I am unable to find that the subdural haematomas are attributable to a perinatal event, whilst recognising the possibility that they may be. I have been impressed over the years by the willingness of the best paediatricians and those who practise in the specialities of paediatric medicine to recognise how much we do not know about the growth patterns and what goes wrong in them, particularly in infants. Since they grow at a remarkable speed and cannot themselves give any clue as to what is happening inside them, and since research using control samples is self-evidently impossible in many areas, perhaps we should not be surprised. In my judgment, a conclusion of unknown etiology in respect of an infant represents neither professional nor forensic failure. It simply recognises that we still have much to learn and it also recognises that it is dangerous and wrong to infer non-accidental injury merely from the absence of any other understood mechanism. Maybe it simply represents a general acknowledgement that we are fearfully and wonderfully made.

See also *Re M (children)* [2012] EWCA Civ 1710, [2013] 2 FLR 322, [31] (Munby LJ) considering *Re R (a child)* [2011] EWHC 1715 (Fam), [2011] 2 FLR 1384

See also *London Borough of Southwark v A Family* [2020] EWHC 3117 (Fam), [177]–[188] (Sir Mark Hedley) addressing the same point

8.2.6 Experts: assessing evidence: hair strand testing

Re H (a child: hair strand testing) [2017] EWFC 64, [2018] 1 FCR 125, [40]–[59] (Peter Jackson J) *quotation limited to* [40]–[41], [57]–[59]

[40] In my view, the variability of findings from hair strand testing does not call into question the underlying science, but underlines the need to treat numerical data with proper caution. The extraction of chemicals from a solid matrix such as human hair is inevitably accompanied by margins of variability. No doubt our understanding will increase with developments in science but, as matters stand, the evidence in this case satisfies me that these testing organisations approach their task conscientiously. Also, as previous decisions remind us, a test result is only part of the evidence. A very high result may amount to compelling evidence, but in the lower range numerical information must be set alongside evidence of other kinds. Once this is appreciated, the significance of variability between one low figure and another falls into perspective. I therefore accept the approach of the testing experts and of Dr McKinnon in preference to that of Dr Rushton on this issue. His approach requires an exactitude that can never be achieved in practice in the present day.

[41] I must say something about the reporting of test results as being within the high/medium/low range. In fairness to the testing organisations, this practice has developed at the request of clients wishing to understand the

results more easily. The danger is that the report is too easily taken to be conclusive proof of high/medium/low use, when in fact the actual level of use may be lower or higher than the description. You cannot read back from the result to the suspected use. Two people can consume the same amount of cocaine and give quite different test results. Two people can give the same test result and have consumed quite different amounts of cocaine. This is the consequence of physiology: there are variables in relation to hair colour, race, hair condition (bleaching and straightening damages hair), pregnancy and body size. Then there are the variables inherent in the testing process. Dr McKinnon explained that there is therefore only a broad correlation between the test results and the conclusions that can be drawn about likely use and that it should be recognised that in some cases (of which this is in his opinion, one) there will be scope for reasonable disagreement between experts.

…

Report writing and reading

[57] The parties have made suggestions as to how the presentation of reports might be developed so as to be most useful to those working in the field of family justice. I will record some of these suggestions and some of my own. Before doing so, I note that each of the testing organisations already produces reports that contain much of the necessary information in one shape or another. It is also important to stress the responsibility for making proper use of scientific evidence falls both on the writer and the reader. The writer must make sure as far as possible that the true significance of the data is explained in a way that reduces the risk of it becoming lost in translation. The reader must take care to understand what is being read, and not jump to a conclusion about drug or alcohol use without understanding the significance of the data and its place in the overall evidence.

[58] Comment was made during the evidence that certain courts, and in particular Family Drug and Alcohol Courts, are very familiar with the methodology of hair strand testing and the way in which reports are laid out. The objective must be for all participants in the system, professional and non-professional, to develop a similar competence, even though they do not read as many reports as the FDAC does.

[59] There are currently nine accredited hair strand testing organisations working in the family law area. It is not for the court hearing one case to dictate the way reports are written by those who have intervened in this case or by others who have not taken part, but I include the following seven suggestions in case they are helpful.

(1) Use of high/medium/low descriptor:

This is in my view useful, provided it is accompanied by:

- A numerical description of the boundaries between high/medium/low, with an explanation of the manner in which the boundaries are set should be stated.

- A clear statement that the description is of the level of substance found and not of the level of use, though there may a broad correlation.
- A reminder that the finding from the test must always be set alongside other sources of information, particularly where the results are in the low range.

(2) Reporting of data below the cut-off range:
There is currently inconsistency as between organisations on reporting substances detected between the lower limit of detection (LLoD) and the lower limit of quantification (LLoQ), and those between the LLoQ and the cut-off point.
I would suggest that reports record all findings, so that:

- a finding below the LLoQ is described as 'detected, but so low that it is not quantifiable'
- A result falling below the cut-off level is given in numerical form

and that this data is accompanied by a clear explanation of the reason for the cut-off point and the need for particular caution in relation to data that falls below it.

(3) Terminology
Efforts to understand the significance of tests are hampered by the lack of a common vocabulary to describe results in the very low ranges, Descriptions such as 'positive', 'negative', 'indicates that' and 'not detected' can be used and understood vaguely or incorrectly. The creation of a common vocabulary across the industry could only be achieved by a body such as the SoHT. In the absence of uniformity, reporters should define their terms precisely so that they can be accurately understood.

(4) Expressions of probability:
The Family Court works on the civil standard of proof, namely the balance of probabilities. It would therefore help if opinions about testing results could be expressed in that way. For example:

> 'Taken in isolation, these findings are in my opinion more likely than not to indicate ingestion of [drug].'
>
> 'Taken in isolation, these findings are in my opinion more likely than not to indicate that [drug] has not been ingested because …'
>
> 'Taken in isolation, these findings are in my opinion more likely to indicate exposure to [drug] than ingestion.'

(5) Where there is reason to believe that environmental contamination may be an issue, this should be fully described, together with an analysis of any factors that may help the reader to distinguish between the possibilities.

(6) The FAQ sheet accompanying the report (which might better be described as 'Essential Information'), might be tailored to give information relevant to the particular report, and thereby make it easier to assimilate.

(7) When it is known that testing has been carried out by more than one organisation, the report should explain that the findings may be variable as between organisations.

See also *Richmond London Borough Council v B and others* [2010] EWHC 2903 (Fam), [2011] 1 FCR 401, [1]–[2], [8]–[22] (Moylan J) addressing a related point (hair stand testing for alcohol consumption, concluding that hair testing should only be used as part of the evidential picture; that both forms of testing should be used; and identifying uses and limitations of 'cut-off' levels)

See also *Re SB and CB (minors)* [2012] EWHC 2548 (Fam), [2013] 2 FLR 1153, [25] (Baker J) addressing a related point (hair strand testing for drug misuse, including endorsing the proposition that sequential testing should be used, and that positive identification of a drug above a cut-off level is reliable evidence of exposure)

CHAPTER 9

The welfare stage

Chapter contents

CHAPTER 9

The welfare stage

9.1 THE WELFARE STAGE: THE COURT'S APPROACH

9.1.1 The welfare stage: the court's approach: welfare determines the welfare stage

Re O and N (children) (non-accidental injury) [2003] UKHL 18, [2003] 1 FCR 673, [23]–[24] (Lord Nicholls)

The welfare stage

[23] Crossing the threshold is not a reason for making a care order. When the threshold criteria are met the court proceeds to the welfare stage. The court must decide whether it is in the best interests of the child to make a care order as asked by the local authority. As with 'private law' orders made under s 8 of the 1989 Act, so with care and supervision orders made under s 31(1), the paramount consideration in making this decision is the child's welfare: s 1(1) and (4). This involves looking at the past and also looking into the future. In considering which course is in the child's best interests, the court will have regard to all the circumstances of the case.

[24] This has long been axiomatic in this area of the law. The matters the court may take into account are bounded only by the need for them to be relevant, that is, they must be such that, to a greater or lesser extent, they will assist the court in deciding which course is in the child's best interests. I can see no reason of legal policy why, in principle, any other limitation should be placed on the matters the judge may take into account when making this decision. If authority is needed for this conclusion I need refer only to the wide, all embracing language of Lord MacDermott in *J v C* [1969] 1 All ER 788 at 820–821, [1970] AC 668 at 710–711. Section 1 of the Guardianship of Infants Act 1925 required the court, in proceedings where the upbringing of an infant was in question, to regard the welfare of the infant 'as the first and paramount consideration'. Regarding these words, Lord MacDermott said:

> 'I think they connote a process whereby, when all the relevant facts, relationships, claims and wishes of parents, risks, choices and other circumstances are taken into account and weighed, the course to be followed will be that which is most in the interests of the child's welfare as that term has now to be understood.'

In principle the same approach is equally applicable under s 1 of the 1989 Act.

See also *Lancashire County Council v A* [2000] 1 FCR 509 (HL), 519E–I (Lord Clyde) addressing the same point (in the context of the functions of s 31[1])

See also *Re M and R (minors) (expert opinion: evidence)* [1996] 2 FCR 617 (CA), 624F–G (Butler-Sloss LJ) addressing the same point

See Chapter 9.2 The welfare stage: paramountcy of welfare

See Chapter 9.3 The welfare stage: the welfare checklists

9.1.2 The welfare stage: the court's approach: least interventionist approach

Re W (a child) (care proceedings: welfare evaluation: functions of local authority) [2013] EWCA Civ 1227, [2014] 1 FCR 260, [46] (Ryder LJ)

[46] Returning then to the scheme of the 1989 Act, by s 1(3)(g) of the 1989 Act, the court is required to have regard to the range of powers available to it under the Act and must make such order as it determines is in the interest of the child at the end of the proceedings. By s 1(5) an order has to be better for the child than no order before it can be made. The scheme of the Act is that the court should begin with a preference for the less interventionist rather than the more interventionist approach. Provided procedural safeguards are maintained, for example those contained in the FPR 2010 and the associated Practice Directions of the court, it is possible to make private law orders to persons who are not parties, for example a special guardianship or residence order in respect of a child to a relative or friend and also to combine the same with public law orders, for example a residence order to a relative or friend and a care or supervision order to a local authority. Specifically, s 31(5)(a) and (b) of the 1989 Act permit a court to make a care order where the local authority has limited its application to a supervision order or vice-versa. The flexibility vested in the court by Parliament is important, it reflects the control that exists in the court once proceedings are instituted and until full orders are made and the obligation upon the court to decide what is proportionate.

See also *Re B-S (Children) (adoption: leave to oppose)* [2013] EWCA Civ 1146, [2013] 3 FCR 481, [23]–[24] (Sir James Munby P) addressing the same point (in the context of adoption cases)

See also *YC v United Kingdom* (app no 4547/10) (ECtHR) [2013] 2 FCR 36, [133]–[139] (Fourth Section) addressing a related point (proportionality and the ECHR)[2], see Chapter 9.1.5 The welfare stage: the court's approach: proportionality: ECHR art 8

See Chapter 9.1.7 The welfare stage: the court's approach: adoption cases: 'nothing else will do'

1 Children Act 1989, s 31.
2 Convention for the Protection of Human Rights and Fundamental Freedoms (1950) CETS 5.

9.1.3 The welfare stage: the court's approach: no presumption of living with birth families

Re W (a child) [2016] EWCA Civ 793, [2017] 1 WLR 889, [70]–[75] (McFarlane LJ)

Natural family presumption/right

70. With respect to them, it is clear to me that both the Children's Guardian and the ISW fell into serious error by misunderstanding the need to evaluate the question of A's future welfare by affording due weight to all of the relevant factors and without applying any automatic 'presumption' or 'right' for a child to be brought up by a member of her natural family. The extracts from the reports of both of these witnesses indicate that they determined their recommendation for A on just that basis. Mrs Fairbairn repeatedly described the child as having a 'right' to be brought up by the natural family where there is a viable placement available. The Guardian advised that adoption is not in A's best interests because the grandparents can provide her with a home. Putting the correct position in lay terms, the existence of a viable home with the grandparents should make that option 'a runner' but should not automatically make it 'a winner' in the absence of full consideration of any other factor that is relevant to her welfare; the error of the ISW and the Guardian appears to have been to hold that 'if a family placement is a 'runner', then it has to be regarded as a 'winner''.

71. The repeated reference to a 'right' for a child to be brought up by his or her natural family, or the assumption that there is a presumption to that effect, needs to be firmly and clearly laid to rest. No such 'right' or presumption exists. The only 'right' is for the arrangements for the child to be determined by affording paramount consideration to her welfare throughout her life (in an adoption case) in a manner which is proportionate and compatible with the need to respect any ECHR Art 8 rights which are engaged. In *Re H (A Child)* [2015] EWCA Civ 1284 this court clearly stated that there is no presumption in favour of parents or the natural family in public law adoption cases at paragraphs 89 to 94 of the judgment of McFarlane LJ as follows:

> '89. The situation in public law proceedings, where the State, via a local authority, seeks to intervene in the life of a child by obtaining a care order and a placement for adoption order against the consent of a parent is entirely different [from private law proceedings], but also in this context there is no authority to the effect that there is a 'presumption' in favour of a natural parent or family member. As in the private law context, at the stage when a court is considering what, if any, order to make the only principle is that set out in CA 1989, s 1 and ACA 2002, s 1 requiring paramount consideration to be afforded to the welfare of the child throughout his lifetime. There is, however, a default position in favour of the natural family in public law proceedings at the earlier stage on the question of establishing the court's jurisdiction to make any public law order. Before the court may make a care order or a placement for adoption order,

the statutory threshold criteria in CA 1989, s 31 must be satisfied (CA 1989, s 31(2) and ACA 2002, s 21(2)).

…

94. It is clear that for Russell J the outcome of this case did not turn on the deployment of the 'presumption' that she describes, and this point was not taken within the appeal. My attribution of some prominence to it is not therefore determinative of the appeal. My aim is solely to point out the need for caution in this regard. The House of Lords and Supreme Court have been at pains to avoid the attribution of any presumption where CA 1989, s 1 is being applied for the resolution of a private law dispute concerning a child's welfare; there is therefore a need for care before adopting a different approach to the welfare principle in public law cases. As the judgments in Re B , and indeed the years of case law preceding Re B , make plain, once the s 31 threshold is crossed the evaluation of a child's welfare in public law proceedings is determined on the basis of proportionality rather than by the application of presumptions. In that context it is not, in my view, apt to refer to there being a 'presumption' in favour of the natural family; each case falls to be determined on its own facts in accordance with the proportionate approach that is clearly described by the Supreme Court in Re B and in the subsequent decisions of this court.'

72. In the present appeal the point has more prominence because of the central focus afforded to the 'right' or presumption by both the ISW and the Guardian and by the fact that the judge relied upon their evidence without drawing attention to this erroneous approach.

73. It may be that some confusion leading to the idea of their being a natural family presumption has arisen from the use of the phrase 'nothing else will do'. But that phrase does not establish a presumption or right in favour of the natural family; what it does do, most importantly, is to require the welfare balance for the child to be undertaken, after considering the pros and cons of each of the realistic options, in such a manner that adoption is only chosen as the route for the child if that outcome is necessary to meet the child's welfare needs and it is proportionate to those welfare needs.

74. The total absence of any reference in the evidence of either the Guardian or the ISW to the welfare checklist in ACA 2002, s 1(4) and/or to the need to undertake a *Re B-S* compliant analysis only goes to reinforce my conclusion that both of these seasoned professionals fell into the trap that I have described and did indeed use the existence of a viable family placement as a hyperlink to the outcome of the case without taking any, in the case of the Guardian, or any proper, in the case of the ISW, regard to any other factor that might weigh to the contrary arising from A having achieved a full and secure placement with Mr and Mrs X.

75. As Mr Feehan helpfully observed in his closing submissions, it is all very well to purport to undertake a balancing exercise, but a balance has to have

a fulcrum and if the fulcrum is incorrectly placed towards one or other end of that which is to be weighed, one side of the analysis or another will be afforded undue, automatic weight. Taking that point up from where Mr Feehan left it, in proceedings at the stage prior to making a placement for adoption order the balance will rightly and necessarily reflect weight being afforded to any viable natural family placement because there is no other existing placement of the child which must be afforded weight on the other side of the scales. Where, as here, time has moved on and such a placement exists, and is indeed the total reality of the child's existence, it cannot be enough to decide the overall welfare issue simply by looking at the existence of the viable family placement and nothing else.

See also *Re G (a child) (care proceedings: welfare balancing exercise: proportionality)* [2013] EWCA Civ 965, [2013] 3 FCR 293, [56] (McFarlane LJ) addressing a related point (the importance of birth families), see Chapter 9.1.13 The welfare stage: the court's approach: adoption cases: adoption essentials: (ii) adequately reasoned judgments: non-linear approach

See also *Re P (a child) (care and placement: evidential basis of local authority case)* [2013] EWCA Civ 963, [2013] 3 FCR 159, [102] (Black LJ) addressing a related point (children's interests include being brought up by their natural families)

9.1.4 The welfare stage: the court's approach: balancing the human rights of children and parents

Yousef v Netherlands (app no 33711/96) (ECtHR), [2002] 3 FCR 577, [73] (Second Section)

73. The court reiterates that in judicial decisions where the rights under art 8 of parents and those of a child are at stake, the child's rights must be the paramount consideration. If any balancing of interests is necessary, the interests of the child must prevail (see *Elsholz v Germany* [2000] 3 FCR 385 at 397–398 (para 52) and *TP and KM v UK* [2001] 2 FCR 289 at 311 (para 72)). This applies also in cases such as the present.

See also *R and H v United Kingdom* (app no 35348/06) (ECtHR), (2012) 54 EHRR 2, [73]–[74] (Fourth Section) addressing the same point (in the context of care proceedings)

See also *YC v United Kingdom* (app no 4547/10) (ECtHR), [2013] 2 FCR 36, [134] (Fourth Section) addressing the same point (in adoption cases), see Chapter 9.1.5 The welfare stage: the court's approach: proportionality: ECHR art 8

See also *Strand Lobben and others v Norway* (app no 37283/13) (ECtHR), (2020) 70 EHRR 14, [220] (Grand Chamber) addressing the same point (emphasising the importance of balancing the interests of children and their biological families, albeit 'fully conscious of the primordial interest of the child')

See also *Johansen v Norway* (app no 17383/90) (ECtHR), (1997) 23 EHRR 33, [78] (Chamber) addressing the same point (emphasising the need for a 'fair balance' between the rights of children and parents, albeit attaching 'particular importance to the best interests of the child')

9.1.5 The welfare stage: the court's approach: proportionality: ECHR art 8

YC v United Kingdom (app no 4547/10) (ECtHR), [2013] 2 FCR 36, [133]–[139] (Fourth Section) *quotation limited to* [133]–[135]

133. The court's case law regarding care proceedings and measures taken in respect of children clearly establishes that, in assessing whether an interference was 'necessary in a democratic society', two aspects of the proceedings require consideration. First, the court must examine whether, in the light of the case as a whole, the reasons adduced to justify the measures were 'relevant and sufficient'; second it must be examined whether the decision-making process was fair and afforded due respect to the applicant's rights under art 8 of the Convention (see *K v Finland* [2001] 2 FCR 673 (para 154); *RK v UK* [2009] 1 FLR 274 (para 34); *TS v UK* App no 61540/09 (19 January 2010, unreported); *AD v UK* [2010] 2 FLR 1 (para 'fair '82); *Neulinger v Switzerland* [2011] 2 FCR 110 (para 134); and *R v UK* [2011] 2 FLR 1236 (paras 75 and 81)).

134. The court reiterates that in cases concerning the placing of a child for adoption, which entails the permanent severance of family ties, the best interests of the child are paramount (see *Johansen v Norway* (1996) 23 EHRR 33 (para 78), *Kearns v France* [2008] 2 FCR 19 (para 79), and *R v UK*, cited above, paras 73 and 81). In identifying the child's best interests in a particular case, two considerations must be borne in mind: first, is it in the child's best interests that his ties with his family be maintained except in cases where the family has proved particularly unfit; and second, is it in the child's best interests to ensure his development in a safe and secure environment (see *Neulinger v Switzerland*, cited above, para 136; and *R v UK*, cited above, paras 73–74). It is clear from the foregoing that family ties may only be severed in very exceptional circumstances and that everything must be done to preserve personal relations and, where appropriate, to 'rebuild' the family (see *Neulinger v Switzerland*, cited above, para 136; and *R v UK*, cited above, para 73). It is not enough to show that a child could be placed in a more beneficial environment for his upbringing (see *K v Finland*, cited above, para 173; and *TS v UK*, cited above). However, where the maintenance of family ties would harm the child's health and development, a parent is not entitled under art 8 to insist that such ties be maintained (see *Neulinger v Switzerland*, cited above, para 136; and *R v UK*, cited above, para 73).

135. The identification of the child's best interests and the assessment of the overall proportionality of any given measure will require courts to weigh a number of factors in the balance. The court has not previously set out an exhaustive list of such factors, which may vary depending on the circumstances of the case in question. However, it observes that the

considerations listed in s 1 of the 2002 Act (see para 103, above) broadly reflect the various elements inherent in assessing the necessity under art 8 of a measure placing a child for adoption. In particular, it considers that in seeking to identify the best interests of a child and in assessing the necessity of any proposed measure in the context of placement proceedings, the domestic court must demonstrate that it has had regard to, inter alia, the age, maturity and ascertained wishes of the child, the likely effect on the child of ceasing to be a member of his original family and the relationship the child has with relatives.

See also *Re B (children) (care: interference with family life)* [2003] EWCA Civ 786, [2004] 1 FCR 463, [34] (Thorpe LJ) addressing the same point (applying ECHR art 8 to care welfare decisions)

See also *Johansen v Norway* (app no 17383/90) (ECtHR), (1997) 23 EHRR 33, [78] (Chamber) addressing the same point (in the context of adoption)

See also *Re C and B (children) (care order: future harm)* [2000] 2 FCR 614 (CA), [33]–[34] (Hale LJ) addressing the same point

See also *P, C and S v United Kingdom* (app no 56547/00) (ECtHR), [2002] 3 FCR 1, [113]–[120] (Second Section) addressing the same point

See also *EH v Greenwich London Borough Council and others; Re A (children) (non-accidental injury)* [2010] EWCA Civ 344, [2010] 2 FCR 106, [64] (Baron J), [95]–[98] (Wall LJ) addressing the same point

See also *M v Neath Port Talbot County Borough Council and others* [2010] EWCA Civ 821, [2010] 3 FCR 100, [22] (Wilson LJ) considering *EH v Greenwich London Borough Council and others Re A (children) (non-accidental injury)* [2010] EWCA Civ 344, [2010] 2 FCR 106

9.1.6 The welfare stage: the court's approach: proportionality: a cross-check

Re M (a child) [2018] EWCA Civ 240, [2018] 2 FCR 253, [64]–[65] (King LJ)

[64] The word proportionality is much used in the context of applications for placement or adoption order. In reality it is a cross-check by the court that the seriousness of the order it is considering is a justifiable response to the seriousness of the problem that exists.

[65] In many cases this exercise can add little or nothing to the conventional welfare assessment, but there will be cases such, as the present, where the harm is not so easy to evaluate and where the cross-check is of particular importance. In my judgment, notwithstanding the judge's care in listening to the evidence and making findings of fact, he failed thereafter to step back and conduct a clear analysis, having pulled together the totality of the evidence before the court. This left the parties, in this difficult and finely balanced case, without a proper understanding how the positives enumerated by the judge at the beginning of his judgment were balanced against the risks of harm on the other.

9.1.7 The welfare stage: the court's approach: adoption cases: 'nothing else will do'

Re B (a child) (care order: proportionality: criterion for review) [2013] UKSC 33, [2013] 2 FCR 525, [33]–[34] (Lord Wilson), [73]–[77], [104]–[105] (Lord Neuberger P), [194]–[198], [215] (Lady Hale) *quotation limited to* [73]–[77], [194]–[198], [215]

The care order: the correct legal test

[73] I turn to consider the first question, which involves first identifying the correct test. The effect of s 1(1) of the 1989 Act is that, when considering whether to make a care order, the court must treat the welfare of the child as the paramount consideration, and this involves taking into account in particular the factors identified in s 1(3), which includes, in para (g), the range of powers available to the court. As Lady Hale (who knows more about this than anybody) says at [194], the 1989 Act was drafted with the Convention in mind; in any event, with the coming into force of the Human Rights Act 1998 ('the 1998 Act'), the 1989 Act must now, if possible, be construed and applied so as to comply with the Convention. So too the Adoption and Children Act 2002 ('the 2002 Act') must, if possible, be construed and applied so as to comply with the Convention. It also appears to me that the 2002 Act must be construed and applied bearing in mind the provisions of the UN Convention on the Rights of the Child 1989 (New York, 20 November 1989; TS 44 (1998); Cm 1976) ('UNCRC').

[74] A care order in a case such as this is a very extreme thing, a last resort, as it would be very likely to result in Amelia being adopted against the wishes of both her parents.

[75] As already mentioned, it is clear that a judge cannot properly decide that a care order should be made in such circumstances, unless the order is proportionate bearing in mind the requirements of art 8.

[76] It appears to me that, given that the judge concluded that the s 31(2) threshold was crossed, he should only have made a care order if he had been satisfied that it was necessary to do so in order to protect the interests of the child. By 'necessary', I mean, to use Lady Hale's phrase in para [198], 'where nothing else will do'. I consider that this conclusion is clear under the 1989 Act, interpreted in the absence of the Convention, but it is put beyond doubt by art 8. The conclusion is also consistent with UNCRC.

[77] It seems to me to be inherent in s 1(1) that a care order should be a last resort, because the interests of a child would self-evidently require her relationship with her natural parents to be maintained unless no other course was possible in her interests. That is reinforced by the requirement in s 1(3)(g) that the court must consider all options, which carries with it the clear implication that the most extreme option should only be adopted if others would not be in her interests. As to art 8, the Strasbourg court

decisions cited by Lady Hale at [195]–[198] make it clear that such an order can only be made in 'exceptional circumstances', and that it could only be justified by 'overriding requirements pertaining to the child's welfare', or, putting the same point in slightly different words, 'by the overriding necessity of the interests of the child'. I consider that this is the same as the domestic test (as is evidenced by the remarks of Hale LJ in *Re C and B (children) (care order: future harm)* [2000] 2 FCR 614 at [34], [2001] 1 FLR 611 quoted by Lady Hale at [198], below), but it is unnecessary to explore that point further.

…

Proportionality

[194] Once the threshold is crossed, s 1(1) of the 1989 Act requires that the welfare of the child be the court's paramount consideration. In deciding what will best promote that welfare, the court is required to have regard to the 'checklist' of factors in s 1(3). These include, at (g), the range of powers available to the court in the proceedings in question. By s 1(5), the court must not make any order unless it considers that doing so would be better for the child than making no order at all. The Act itself makes no mention of proportionality, but it was framed with the developing jurisprudence under art 8 of the European Convention very much in mind. Once the Human Rights Act 1998 came into force, not only the local authority, but also the courts as public authorities, came under a duty to act compatibly with the Convention rights.

[195] It is well-established in the case law of the European Court of Human Rights that 'the mutual enjoyment by parent and child of each other's company constitutes a fundamental element of family life, and … domestic measures hindering such enjoyment amount to an interference with the right protected by art 8 of the Convention' (*Johansen v Norway* (1996) 23 EHRR 33, [1996] ECHR 17383/90, among many others). However, such measures may be justified if aimed at protecting the 'health or morals' and 'the rights and freedoms' of children. But they must also be 'necessary in a democratic society'. The court has recently summed up the principles in the context of an order freeing a child for adoption, in *R v UK* [2011] 2 FLR 1236, [2011] ECHR 35348/06 at para 81:

> 'In assessing whether the freeing order was a disproportionate interference with the applicants' Art 8 rights, the court must consider whether, in the light of the case as a whole, the reasons adduced to justify that measure were relevant and sufficient for the purposes of para 2 of Art 8 of the European Convention (see, among other authorities, [*K v Finland* [2001] 2 FCR 673, [2001] 2 FLR 707 at para 154]) … The court would also recall that, while national authorities enjoy a wide margin of appreciation in deciding whether a child should be taken into care, stricter scrutiny is called for as regards any further limitations, such as restrictions placed by those authorities on parental rights of access, and as regards any legal safeguards

designed to secure the effective protection of the right of parents and children to respect for their family life. Such further limitations entail the danger that the family relations between a young child and one or both parents would be effectively curtailed (see [*Elsholz v Germany* [2000] 3 FCR 385, [2000] ECHR 25735/94 at para 49], and [*Kutzner v Germany* [2003] 1 FCR 249, (2002) 35 EHRR 653 at para 67]). For these reasons, measures which deprive biological parents of the parental responsibilities and authorise adoption should only be applied in exceptional circumstances and can only be justified if they are motivated by an overriding requirement pertaining to the child's best interests (see [*Aune v Norway* App no 52502/07 (28 October 2010, unreported) at para 66]; [*Johansen v Norway* (1996) 23 EHRR 33, [1996] ECHR 17383/90 at para 78] and, mutatis mutandis, [*P v UK* [2002] 3 FCR 1, [2002] 2 FLR 631 at para 118]).'

[196] The Strasbourg court itself has consistently applied a stricter standard of scrutiny to the national courts' decisions to restrict or curtail contact between parent and child than it has to the decision to take a child into care in the first place. This is because, as stated, for example, by the Grand Chamber in *K v Finland* [2001] 2 FCR 673, [2001] 2 FLR 707, at para 178, there is:

> '… the guiding principle whereby a care order should in principle be regarded as a temporary measure, to be discontinued as soon as circumstances permit, and that any measures implementing temporary care should be consistent with the ultimate aim of reuniting the natural parents and the child … The positive duty to take measures to facilitate family reunification as soon as reasonably feasible will begin to weigh on the responsible authorities with progressively increasing force as from the commencement of the period of care, subject always to its being balanced against the duty to consider the best interests of the child.'

[197] Thus it is not surprising that Lewison LJ was troubled by the proportionality of planning the most drastic interference possible, which is a closed adoption, in a case where the threshold had not been crossed in the most extreme way (see [174], above). However, I would not see proportionality in such a linear fashion, as if the level of interference should be in direct proportion to the level of harm to the child. There are cases where the harm suffered or feared is very severe, but it would be disproportionate to sever or curtail the family ties because the authorities can protect the child in other ways. I recall, for example, a case where the mother was slowly starving her baby to death because she could not cope with the colostomy tube through which the baby had to be fed, but solutions were found which enabled the child to stay at home. Conversely, there may be cases where the level of harm is not so great, but there is no other way in which the child can be properly protected from it.

[198] Nevertheless, it is quite clear that the test for severing the relationship between parent and child is very strict: only in exceptional circumstances

and where motivated by *overriding requirements* pertaining to the child's welfare, in short, where nothing else will do. In many cases, and particularly where the feared harm has not yet materialised and may never do so, it will be necessary to explore and attempt alternative solutions. As was said in *Re C and B (children) (care order: future harm)* [2000] 2 FCR 614 at [34], [2001] 1 FLR 611:

> 'Intervention in the family may be appropriate, but the aim should be to reunite the family when the circumstances enable that, and the effort should be devoted towards that end. Cutting off all contact and the relationship between the child or children and their family is only justified by the overriding necessity of the interests of the child.'

…

(4) Was the order proportionate?

[215] But that is not the end of the story. We all agree that an order compulsorily severing the ties between a child and her parents can only be made if 'justified by an overriding requirement pertaining to the child's best interests'. In other words, the test is one of necessity. Nothing else will do.

See also *Re B-S (children)(adoption: leave to oppose)* [2013] EWCA Civ 1146, [2013] 3 FCR 481, [22] (Sir James Munby P) considering *Re B (a child) (care order: proportionality: criterion for review)* [2013] UKSC 33, [2013] 2 FCR 525

9.1.8 The welfare stage: the court's approach: adoption cases: 'nothing else will do': proper use

Re W (A child) [2016] EWCA Civ 793, [2017] 1 WLR 889, [68]–[69] (McFarlane LJ)

'Nothing else will do'

68. Since the phrase 'nothing else will do' was first coined in the context of public law orders for the protection of children by the Supreme Court in Re B, judges in both the High Court and Court of Appeal have cautioned professionals and courts to ensure that the phrase is applied so that it is tied to the welfare of the child as described by Baroness Hale in paragraph 215 of her judgment:

> 'We all agree that an order compulsorily severing the ties between a child and her parents can only be made if 'justified by an overriding requirement pertaining to the child's best interests'. In other words, the test is one of necessity. Nothing else will do.'

The phrase is meaningless, and potentially dangerous, if it is applied as some freestanding, shortcut test divorced from, or even in place of, an overall evaluation of the child's welfare. Used properly, as Baroness Hale explained, the phrase 'nothing else will do' is no more, nor no less, than a useful distillation of the proportionality and necessity test as embodied in the ECHR and reflected in the need to afford paramount consideration to the welfare of the child throughout her lifetime (ACA 2002 s 1). The phrase 'nothing else will do' is not some sort of hyperlink providing a direct route to the outcome of a case so as to bypass the need to undertake a full, comprehensive welfare evaluation of all of the relevant pros and cons (see *Re B-S* [2013] EWCA Civ 1146, *Re R* [2014] EWCA Civ 715 and other cases).

69. Once the comprehensive, full welfare analysis has been undertaken of the pros and cons it is then, and only then, that the overall proportionality of any plan for adoption falls to be evaluated and the phrase 'nothing else will do' can properly be deployed. If the ultimate outcome of the case is to favour placement for adoption or the making of an adoption order it is that outcome that falls to be evaluated against the yardstick of necessity, proportionality and 'nothing else will do'.

See also *Re M (a child) (care proceedings: long-term foster care)* [2014] EWCA Civ 1406, [2015] 1 FCR 305, [31]–[32] (Black LJ) addressing the same point

See also *Re M-H (a child)* [2014] EWCA Civ 1396, [2015] 2 FLR 357, [8]–[11] (Macur LJ) addressing the same point

9.1.9 The welfare stage: the court's approach: adoption cases: adoption essentials: (i) proper evidence

Re B-S (children) (adoption: leave to oppose) [2013] EWCA Civ 1146, [2013] 3 FCR 481, [33]–[40] (Sir James Munby P)

Adoption—essentials

[33] Two things are essential—we use that word deliberately and advisedly—both when the court is being asked to approve a care plan for adoption and when it is being asked to make a non-consensual placement order or adoption order.

Adoption—essentials: (i) proper evidence

[34] First, there must be proper evidence both from the local authority and from the guardian. The evidence must address *all* the options which are realistically possible and must contain an analysis of the arguments for and *against* each option. As Ryder LJ said in *Re R (children) (care and placement order: paternal grandparents)* [2013] EWCA Civ 1018 at [20], [2013] All ER (D) 203 (Jul) at [20], what is required is:

> '… evidence of the lack of alternative options for the children and an analysis of the evidence that is accepted by the court sufficient to drive it to the conclusion that nothing short of adoption is appropriate for the children …'

The same judge indicated in *Re S* [2013] All ER (D) 401 (Jul) at [21] that what is needed is: 'An assessment of the benefits and detriments of each option for placement and in particular the nature and extent of the risk of harm involved in each of the options.' McFarlane LJ made the same point in *Re G (a child) (care proceedings: welfare balancing exercise: proportionality)* [2013] 3 FCR 293 at [48], when he identified: 'the need to take into account the negatives, as well as the positives, of a plan to place a child away from her natural family'. We agree with all of this.

[35] Too often this essential material is lacking. As Black LJ said in *Re V* [2013] 3 FCR 407 at [88]:

> '… I have searched without success in the papers for any written analysis by local authority witnesses or the guardian of the arguments for and against adoption and long-term fostering … It is not the first time that I have remarked on an absence of such material from the evidence, see *Plymouth City Council v G* [2010] EWCA Civ 1271, [2011] 1 FCR 282. Care should always be taken to address this question specifically in the evidence/ reports and that this was not done here will not have assisted the judge in his determination of the issue.'

In the *Plymouth* case she had said this (at [47]):

> '… In some respects the reports of the guardian and the social worker, and the social worker's statement, are very detailed, giving information about health and likes and dislikes, wishes and feelings. However there is surprisingly little detail about the central issue of the type of placement that will best meet the children's needs … In part, this may be an unfortunate by-product of the entirely proper use, by both witnesses, of the checklist of factors and, in the case of the social worker's placement report, of the required pro forma. However, the court requires not only a list of the factors that are relevant to the central decision but also a narrative account of how they fit together, including an analysis of the pros and cons of the various orders that might realistically be under consideration given the circumstances of the children, and a fully reasoned recommendation …'

[36] Black LJ has not altered the views that she expressed on these earlier occasions and the other members of the court agree with every word of them. We draw attention in particular to the need for 'analysis of the pros and cons' and a 'fully reasoned recommendation'. These are essential if the exacting test set out in *Re B* and the requirements of arts 6 and 8 of the Convention are to be met. We suggest that such an analysis is likely to be facilitated by the use—which we encourage—of the kind of 'balance sheet' first recommended by Thorpe LJ, albeit in a very different context, in *Re A (medical treatment: male sterilisation)* [2000] 1 FCR 193 at 206, [2000] 1 FLR 549 at 560.

[37] It is particularly disheartening that Black LJ's words three years ago in the *Plymouth* case seem to have had so little effect.

[38] Consider the lamentable state of affairs described by Ryder LJ in *Re S* [2013] All ER (D) 401 (Jul), where an appeal against the making of a care order with a plan for adoption was successful because neither the

evidence nor the judge's reasoning was adequate to support the order. It is a lengthy passage but it merits setting out almost in full:

> '[22] What was the evidence that was available to the judge to support her conclusion? … Sadly, there was little or no evidence about the relative merits of the placement options nor any evidence about why an adoptive placement was necessary or feasible.
>
> [23] The allocated social worker in her written statement recommended that [S] needed:
>
> > "a permanent placement where her on-going needs will be met in a safe, stable and nurturing environment. [S]'s permanent carers will need to demonstrate that they are committed to [S], her safety, welfare and wellbeing and that they ensure that she receives a high standard of care until she reaches adulthood
> >
> > Adoption will give [S] the security and permanency that she requires. The identified carers are experienced carers and have good knowledge about children and the specific needs of children that have been removed from their families …"
>
> [24] With respect to the social worker … that without more is not a sufficient rationale for a step as significant as permanent removal from the birth family for adoption. The reasoning was in the form of a conclusion that needed to be supported by evidence relating to the facts of the case and a social worker's expert analysis of the benefits and detriments of the placement options available. Fairness dictates that whatever the local authority's final position, their evidence should address the negatives and the positives relating to each of the options available. Good practice would have been to have heard evidence about the benefits and detriments of each of the permanent placement options that were available for S within and outside the family.
>
> [25] The independent social worker did not support adoption or removal but did describe the options which were before the court when the mediation opportunity was allowed:
>
> > "*Special Guardianship Order*: This is the application before the court and which would afford [S] stability, in terms of remaining with the same primary carer and the opportunity to be raised within her birth family. I do not consider that the situation within the family is suitable at present for this order to be made.
> >
> > *Adoption*: [S] could be placed with a family where she should experience stability and security without conflict. This may be the best option for [S] if current concerns cannot be resolved in a timely manner."
>
> [26] In order to choose between the options the judge needed evidence which was not provided. The judge's conclusion was a choice of one

option over another that was neither reasoned nor evidenced within the proceedings. That vitiated her evaluative judgment which was accordingly wrong.'

[39] Most experienced family judges will unhappily have had too much exposure to material as anodyne and inadequate as that described here by Ryder LJ.

[40] This sloppy practice must stop. It is simply unacceptable in a forensic context where the issues are so grave and the stakes, for both child and parent, so high.

Re A (medical treatment: male sterilisation) [2000] 1 FCR 193 (CA), 206E–H (Thorpe LJ)

> … Pending the enactment of a checklist or other statutory direction it seems to me that the first instance judge with the responsibility to make an evaluation of the best interests of a claimant lacking capacity should draw up a balance sheet. The first entry should be of any factor or factors of actual benefit. In the present case the instance would be the acquisition of foolproof contraception. Then on the other sheet the judge should write any counterbalancing dis-benefits to the applicant. An obvious instance in this case would be the apprehension, the risk and the discomfort inherent in the operation. Then the judge should enter on each sheet the potential gains and losses in each instance making some estimate of the extent of the possibility that the gain or loss might accrue. At the end of that exercise the judge should be better placed to strike a balance between the sum of the certain and possible gains against the sum of the certain and possible losses. Obviously only if the account is in relatively significant credit will the judge conclude that the application is likely to advance the best interests of the claimant.

See also *Re Y (children)* [2014] EWCA Civ 1553, [2015] 2 FLR 615, [24] (Ryder LJ) considering *Re B-S (children)(adoption: leave to oppose)* [2013] EWCA Civ 1146, [2013] 3 FCR 481

9.1.10 The welfare stage: the court's approach: adoption cases: adoption essentials: (i) proper evidence: realistic options

Re R (a child) (placement: realistic options) [2014] EWCA Civ 1625, [2015] 2 FCR 499, [56]–[65] (Sir James Munby P)

[56] *Re B-S* did not change the *law*. *Re B-S* was primarily directed to *practice*. It expressed ([2013] 3 FCR 481, [2014] 1 WLR 563, para [30]) our:

> 'real concerns, shared by other judges, about the recurrent inadequacy of the analysis and reasoning put forward in support of the case for adoption, both in the materials put before the court by local authorities and guardians and also in too many judgments.'

It continued 'This is nothing new. But it is time to call a halt.' It demanded (para [40]) that 'sloppy practice must stop'. It spelt out (see para [32]) 'what good practice, the 2002 Act and the Convention all demand'.

[57] The core requirements were identified as follows (paras [33]–[44]):

> '[33] Two things are essential—we use that word deliberately and advisedly—both when the court is being asked to approve a care plan for adoption and when it is being asked to make a non-consensual placement order or adoption order …
>
> [34] First, there must be proper evidence both from the local authority and from the guardian. The evidence must address *all* the options which are realistically possible and must contain an analysis of the arguments *for* and *against* each option …
>
> [41] The second thing that is essential, and again we emphasise that word, is an adequately reasoned judgment by the judge …
>
> [44] The judicial task is to evaluate *all* the options, undertaking a global, holistic and … multi-faceted evaluation of the child's welfare which takes into account *all* the negatives and the positives, *all* the pros and cons, of *each* option.'

[58] The nature of that exercise has been helpfully illuminated by Ryder LJ in *CM v Blackburn with Darwen BC* [2015] 2 FCR 116, para [33]. Put more shortly, by Ryder LJ himself, in *Re Y* [2014] EWCA Civ 1553, para [24]:

> 'The process of deductive reasoning involves the identification of whether there are realistic options to be compared. If there are, a welfare evaluation is required. That is an exercise which compares the benefits and detriments of each realistic option, one against the other, by reference to the s 1(3) welfare factors. The court identifies the option that is in the best interests of the children and then undertakes a proportionality evaluation to ask itself the question whether the interference in family life involved by that best interests option is justified.'

I respectfully agree with that, so long as it is always remembered that, in the final analysis, adoption is only to be ordered if the circumstances meet the demanding requirements identified by Baroness Hale in *Re B* [2013] 2 FCR 525, [2013] 3 All ER 929, paras [198], [215].

[59] I emphasise the words 'realistically' (as used in *Re B-S* in the phrase 'options which are realistically possible') and 'realistic' (as used by Ryder LJ in the phrase 'realistic options'). This is fundamental. *Re B-S* does not require the further forensic pursuit of options which, having been properly evaluated, typically at an early stage in the proceedings, can legitimately be discarded as not being realistic. *Re B-S* does not require that every conceivable option on the spectrum that runs between 'no order' and 'adoption' has to be canvassed and bottomed out with reasons in the evidence and judgment in every single case. Full consideration is required only with respect to those options which are 'realistically possible'.

[60] As Pauffley J said in *Re LRP (Care Proceedings: Placement Order)* [2013] EWHC 3974 (Fam), [2014] 2 FLR 399, [2014] All ER (D) 114 (Feb), para [40], 'the focus should be upon the sensible and practical possibilities rather than every potential outcome, however far-fetched.' And, to the same effect, Baker J in *Re HA (Capacity to Change)* [2013] EWHC 3634 (Fam), [2014] 2 FLR 540, [2014] All ER (D) 29 (Jan), para [28]:

> 'rigorous analysis and comparison of the realistic options for the child's future ... does not require a court in every case to set out in tabular format the arguments for and against every conceivable option. Such a course would tend to obscure, rather than enlighten, the reasoning process.'

'Nothing else will do' does *not* mean that 'everything else' has to be considered.

[61] What is meant by 'realistic'? I agree with what Ryder LJ said in *Re Y* [2014] EWCA Civ 1553, para [28]:

> 'Realistic is an ordinary English word. It needs no definition or analysis to be applied to the identification of options in a case.'

[62] In many, indeed probably in most, cases there will be only a relatively small number of realistic options. Occasionally, though probably only in comparatively rare cases, there will be only one realistic option. In that event, of course, there will be no need for the more elaborate processes demanded by *Re B-S* and *CM v Blackburn with Darwen BC*: see *Re S (a child)* [2013] EWCA Civ 1835, paras [45]–[46], and Re Y, paras [23], [25]. The task for the court in such a case will simply be to satisfy itself that the one realistic option is indeed in the child's best interests and that the parent's consent can properly be dispensed with in accordance with s 52(1)(b) of the 2002 Act, as explained in *Re P (children) (adoption: parental consent)* [2008] EWCA Civ 535, [2008] 2 FCR 185, [2008] 2 FLR 625.

[63] Two points require further elaboration.

[64] I have referred to the situation where, typically at an early stage in the proceedings, an option, after proper evaluation, can legitimately be discarded as not being realistic. This arises not infrequently with suggestions that various members of the wider family may be suitable carers for the child. The Public Law Outline ('PLO') (Family Procedure Rules 2010, SI 2010/2955, PD12A) stresses the vital importance of such potential carers being identified and assessed, at the latest, as soon as possible after the proceedings have begun. Not infrequently some of those putting themselves forward do not secure a sufficiently positive initial viability assessment to justify pursuing them further as potential carers. In other words, the interim processes under the PLO lead to a judicial determination, prior to the final hearing, that they do not offer a realistic option justifying further consideration. This process not infrequently

leads to a 'whittling down' of a longer list of possible options to a sometimes significantly shorter list of the realistic options which alone require consideration at the final hearing.

[65] This process of identifying options which can properly be discarded at an early stage in the proceedings itself demands an appropriate degree of rigour, in particular if there is dispute as to whether or not a particular option is or is not realistic. But *Re B-S* does not require that every stone has to be uncovered and the ground exhaustively examined before coming to a conclusion that a particular option is not realistic. Nor is there any basis for assuming that more than one negative assessment is required before a potential carer can be eliminated. On the contrary, in *Re T (a child) (residential parenting assessment)* [2011] EWCA Civ 812, [2011] 3 FCR 343, [2012] 2 FLR 308, para [93], Black LJ rejected the proposition that:

> 'a parent facing the permanent removal of their child has a right in all cases to an assessment of their choice rather than one carried out or commissioned by the local authority.'

See also *Re W-C (children)* [2017] EWCA Civ 250, [13] (McFarlane LJ) considering *Re R (a child) (placement: realistic options)* [2014] EWCA Civ 1625, [2015] 2 FCR 499

See also *Re S (a child)* [2013] EWCA Civ 1835, [45]–[47] (McFarlane LJ) addressing a related point (when there is only one realistic option)

9.1.11 The welfare stage: the court's approach: adoption cases: adoption essentials: (i) proper evidence: LAs[3] shall evidence options, possibly by alternative plans

Re W (a child) (care proceedings: welfare evaluation: functions of local authority) [2013] EWCA Civ 1227, [2014] 1 FCR 260, [100]–[102] (Ryder LJ)

[100] The local authority will set out in its evidence the range of services that are available in respect of each placement option and under each of the orders which the court can impose to best meet the harm and/or likelihood of harm identified by the court. The court undertakes the following evaluation to determine what is best for the child:
(i) What is the welfare analysis of each of the placement options that are available;
(ii) What is the welfare evaluation, that is the best option among those available; and
(iii) What orders are proportionate and necessary, if any.

[101] The local authority is required to provide the evidence to enable the judge to undertake the welfare and proportionality evaluations. That includes a description of the services that are available and practicable for each

3 Local authorities.

placement option and each order being considered by the court. It may be convenient for that to be put into the form of the s 31A care plan in the alternative so that the court may expressly undertake its statutory function to consider the same or in evidence filed in support. There should be no question of an authority declining to file its evidence or proposed plans in response to the court's evaluations. None of this strays into the impermissible territory of seeking to bind the local authority's care planning and review processes once a full order is made. If a local authority make it clear that they will not implement a care plan option about which evidence has been given and which the judge prefers on welfare and proportionality grounds, then in a rare case they can be subjected to challenge in the High Court within the proceedings. If and in so far as the local authority are of the opinion that they need to change a care plan option approved by the court once the proceedings are complete, they are entitled to do so and must do so in accordance with the processes laid out in the regulations. If they do so without good reason they will risk an appropriate challenge including on behalf of the child after a referral from an IRO to CAFCASS or a Welsh family proceedings officer

[102] Nothing in the above analysis should be taken to suggest that family courts need to be more or less protective of children in the findings, value judgments and orders that they make, nor that it is necessary to have a sequential series of hearings or a split hearing to decide the questions identified. Save in the most complex cases, it is to be expected that local authority witnesses, guardians and court appointed experts will address the issues identified by the court (whether in its practice directions or in its case based directions) on the basis or alternative bases identified so that an holistic analysis can be conducted by the court wherever possible at the same time as findings are made. Likewise, nothing in the above analysis should be taken to suggest that it is necessary to exceed the timetable for the proceedings or for the child as described in the Annex to Practice Direction 36C 'Pilot Practice Direction 12A, Care, Supervision and other Part 4 Proceedings: Guide to Case Management' (the Public Law Outline).

9.1.12 The welfare stage: the court's approach: adoption cases: adoption essentials: (ii) adequately reasoned judgments: global, holistic evaluation

Re B-S (children)(adoption: leave to oppose) [2013] EWCA Civ 1146, [2013] 3 FCR 481, [41]–[46] (Sir James Munby P)

Adoption—essentials: (ii) adequately reasoned judgments

[41] The second thing that is essential, and again we emphasise that word, is an adequately reasoned judgment by the judge. We have already referred to Ryder LJ's criticism of the judge in *Re S*. That was on 29 July 2013. The very next day, in *Re P (a child) (care and placement: evidential basis of local authority case)* [2013] 3 FCR 159, appeals against the making of

care and placement orders likewise succeeded because, as Black LJ put it (at [107]):

> '… the judge … failed to carry out a proper balancing exercise in order to determine whether it was necessary to make a care order with a care plan of adoption and then a placement order or, if she did carry out that analysis, it is not apparent from her judgments. Putting it another way, she did not carry out a proportionality analysis …'

She added (para [124]): 'there is little acknowledgment in the judge's judgments of the fact that adoption is a last resort and little consideration of what it was that justified it in this case'.

[42] The judge must grapple with the factors at play in the particular case and, to use Black LJ's phrase (para [126]), give 'proper focused attention to the specifics'.

[43] In relation to the nature of the judicial task we draw attention to what McFarlane LJ said in *Re G (a child) (care proceedings: welfare balancing exercise: proportionality)* [2013] 3 FCR 293:

> '[49] In most child care cases a choice will fall to be made between two or more options. The judicial exercise should not be a linear process whereby each option, other than the most draconian, is looked at in isolation and then rejected because of internal deficits that may be identified, with the result that, at the end of the line, the only option left standing is the most draconian and that is therefore chosen without any particular consideration of whether there are internal deficits within that option.
>
> [50] The linear approach … is not apt where the judicial task is to undertake a global, holistic evaluation of each of the options available for the child's future upbringing before deciding which of those options best meets the duty to afford paramount consideration to the child's welfare.'

We need not quote the next paragraph in McFarlane LJ's judgment, which explains in graphic and compelling terms the potential danger of adopting a linear approach.

[44] We emphasise the words 'global, holistic evaluation'. This point is crucial. The judicial task is to evaluate *all* the options, undertaking a global, holistic and (see *Re G* [2013] 3 FCR 293 at [51]) multi-faceted evaluation of the child's welfare which takes into account *all* the negatives and the positives, *all* the pros and cons, of *each* option. To quote McFarlane LJ again (para [54]):

> '… What is required is a balancing exercise in which each option is evaluated to the degree of detail necessary to analyse and weigh its own internal positives and negatives and each option is then compared, side by side, against the competing option or options.'

[45] McFarlane LJ added this important observation (para [53]) which we respectfully endorse:

> '... a process which acknowledges that long-term public care, and in particular adoption contrary to the will of a parent, is 'the most draconian option', yet does not engage with the very detail of that option which renders it 'draconian', cannot be a full or effective process of evaluation. Since the phrase was first coined some years ago, judges now routinely make reference to the 'draconian' nature of permanent separation of parent and child and they frequently do so in the context of reference to 'proportionality'. Such descriptions are, of course, appropriate and correct, but there is a danger that these phrases may inadvertently become little more than formulaic judicial window-dressing if they are not backed up with a substantive consideration of what lies behind them and the impact of that on the individual child's welfare in the particular case before the court. If there was any doubt about the importance of avoiding that danger, such doubt has been firmly swept away by the very clear emphasis in *Re B* on the duty of the court actively to evaluate proportionality in every case.'

[46] We make no apologies for having canvassed these matters in such detail and at such length. They are of crucial importance in what are amongst the most significant and difficult cases that family judges ever have to decide. Too often they are given scant attention or afforded little more than lip service. And they are important in setting the context against which we have to determine the specific question we have to decide in relation to *Re W* [2011] 1 FCR 342, [2011] 1 FLR 2153.

See also *Re FL (a child)* [2020] EWCA Civ 20, [31]–[33] (Baker LJ) addressing a related point (the risk of courts not identifying and considering realistic options)

9.1.13 The welfare stage: the court's approach: adoption cases: adoption essentials: (ii) adequately reasoned judgments: non-linear approach

Re G (a child) (care proceedings: welfare balancing exercise: proportionality) [2013] EWCA Civ 965, [2013] 3 FCR 293, [49]–[56] (McFarlane LJ)

[49] In most child care cases a choice will fall to be made between two or more options. The judicial exercise should not be a linear process whereby each option, other than the most draconian, is looked at in isolation and then rejected because of internal deficits that may be identified, with the result that, at the end of the line, the only option left standing is the most draconian and that is therefore chosen without any particular consideration of whether there are internal deficits within that option.

[50] The linear approach, in my view, is not apt where the judicial task is to undertake a global, holistic evaluation of each of the options available for the child's future upbringing before deciding which of those options best meets the duty to afford paramount consideration to the child's welfare.

[51] One only has to take an extreme example of the effect of linear consideration to see the potential danger for this approach. The linear model proceeds by evaluating and then eliminating each individual option in turn before selecting the option at the end of the line, without evaluation of its own internal merits or de-merits, simply on the basis that it is the only remaining outcome. Much therefore depends on which end of the line the selector starts the process. Conventionally those judges who deploy a linear approach start, for understandable reasons, with the option of rehabilitation to a parent and end with the option of a care or adoption order. If, however, for the purposes of observing the dangers in the process, one were to start at the other end of the line and look at long-term foster care or adoption first, and were then to rule that out on the basis that there are risks and negatives attaching to it, the linear approach would soon arrive at 'rehabilitation to a parent' as the only remaining option and select that without any consideration of whether that is in fact the best outcome for the child. All would agree that such an approach would be untenable. I hope, however, that this example demonstrates how inappropriate the linear model is for a judge who is tasked with undertaking a multi-faceted evaluation of a child's welfare at the end of which one of a range of options has to be chosen.

[52] In the present case, Mr Horsley's submission (recorded at para [22], above) to the effect that by the time the judge came to considering which order to make, she had already ruled out the prospect of J being placed in the mother's care and therefore the only viable option was to make a care order, is, with respect, a classic description of the linear approach and, for the reasons I have given, it should not be deployed by a court charged with making a choice between two or more options in relation to a child's welfare.

[53] A further concern about the linear model is that a process which acknowledges that long-term public care, and in particular adoption contrary to the will of a parent, is 'the most draconian option', yet does not engage with the very detail of that option which renders it 'draconian', cannot be a full or effective process of evaluation. Since the phrase was first coined some years ago, judges now routinely make reference to the 'draconian' nature of permanent separation of parent and child and they frequently do so in the context of reference to 'proportionality'. Such descriptions are, of course, appropriate and correct, but there is a danger that these phrases may inadvertently become little more than formulaic judicial window-dressing if they are not backed up with a substantive consideration of what lies behind them and the impact of that on the individual child's welfare in the particular case before the court. If there was any doubt about the importance of avoiding that danger, such doubt has been firmly swept away by the very clear emphasis in *Re B* on the duty of the court actively to evaluate proportionality in every case.

[54] In mounting this critique of the linear model, I am alive to the fact that, of course, a judgment is, by its very nature, a linear structure; in common with every other linear structure, it has a beginning, a middle and an end. My focus is not upon the structure of a judge's judgment but upon that

part of the judgment, indeed that part of the judicial analysis before the written or spoken judgment is in fact compiled, where the choice between options actually takes place. What is required is a balancing exercise in which each option is evaluated to the degree of detail necessary to analyse and weigh its own internal positives and negatives and each option is then compared, side by side, against the competing option or options.

[55] If authority is required to support the need for the court to place all of the countervailing factors into the scales in order to evaluate which option, on balance, best meets the welfare needs of the child, it is not necessary to look further than the House of Lords decision in *J v C* [1969] 1 All ER 788, [1970] AC 668, a decision which remains authoritative on this point, where Lord MacDermott said ([1969] 1 All ER 788 at 821, [1970] AC 668 at 710–711) that the welfare principle connotes:

> 'a process whereby, when all the relevant facts, relationships, claims and wishes of parents, risks, choices and other circumstances are taken into account and weighed, the course to be followed will be that which is most in the interests of the child's welfare as that term is now to be understood.'

[56] Finally, before turning to the first instance welfare determination in the present case, I should make reference to those occasions when judges may use a phrase such as 'first consideration' when referring to the weight that is to be given to the relationship between a child and her parents and natural family. In the light of *Re B* [2013] 2 FCR 525, [2013] 3 All ER 929, with the repeated use in their Lordships' judgments of phrases such as 'high degree of justification', 'necessary', 'required', 'a very extreme thing', 'a last resort' and 'nothing else will do', it is clear that the importance of a child either living with, or maintaining a relationship with, her parents and natural family has certainly not been reduced. In this regard I would expressly link what I have said in this part of this judgment with that of Black LJ (which is being handed down today) in *Re P (a child) (care and placement: evidential basis of local authority case)* [2013] EWCA Civ 963, [2013] 3 FCR 159.

See also *Re R (a child) (placement: realistic options)* [2014] EWCA Civ 1625, [2015] 2 FCR 499, [18] (McFarlane LJ), [69] (Sir James Munby P) addressing the same point (emphasising the danger of casting a judgment as linear simply because of its structure, focus must instead be on the judicial analysis)

See also *Re B-S (children)(adoption: leave to oppose)* [2013] EWCA Civ 1146, [2013] 3 FCR 481, [43]–[45] (Sir James Munby P), see Chapter 9.1.9 The welfare stage: the court's approach: adoption cases: adoption essentials: (i) proper evidence

See also *Re C (a child) (care and placement: long-term welfare decision)* [2013] EWCA Civ 1257, [2014] 1 FCR 173, [29]–[31] (McFarlane LJ) addressing the same point (in the context of requiring consideration of ACA 2002[4] when determining care orders in adoption cases), see Chapter 9.3.2 The welfare stage: the welfare checklists: approach to the checklists: adoption cases

4 Adoption and Children Act 2002.

9.1.14 The welfare stage: the court's approach: cases not concerning adoption: *Re B-S*[5] approach applies

Re J (children) [2019] EWCA Civ 2300, [2020] 1 FCR 572, [27]–[28] (Baker LJ)

[27] At a final hearing in care proceedings, once the court has found that the threshold criteria are satisfied, it proceeds to consider what order should be made in the light of its findings, having regard to the principles in s.1, including the paramountcy of the child's welfare and the relevant factors in the checklist in s.1(3). The relevant factors will always include, under s.1(3)(g), the range of powers available to the court. As successive decisions of this court have established, this requires the judge to identify the realistic options and analyse and compare the advantages and disadvantages of each, before setting out his decision in a fully-reasoned judgment. There is nothing in any of the cases cited by Mr Horne to contradict or undermine this requirement. Although this approach was originally prescribed in cases where the court is considering a plan for adoption, of which *Re B-S* is the most frequently-cited, it plainly applies to all proceedings under s.31 of the Children Act. Indeed, in my judgment, the discipline of identifying and articulating the realistic options and the advantages and disadvantages of each before making a final order is one which should be followed whenever the court is making a decision about the future of a child.

[28] The approach is concisely explained in the following passage from the judgment of McFarlane LJ, as he then was, in *Re G (A Child)* [2013] EWCA Civ 965:

'49. In most child care cases a choice will fall to be made between two or more options. The judicial exercise should not be a linear process whereby each option, other than the most draconian, is looked at in isolation and then rejected because of internal deficits that may be identified, with the result that, at the end of the line, the only option left standing is the most draconian and that is therefore chosen without any particular consideration of whether there are internal deficits within that option.

50. The linear approach, in my view, is not apt where the judicial task is to undertake a global, holistic evaluation of each of the options available for the child's future upbringing before deciding which of those options best meets the duty to afford paramount consideration to the child's welfare.'

See Chapter 9.1.9 The welfare stage: adoption cases: adoption essentials: (i) proper evidence

See Chapter 9.1.12 The welfare stage: adoption cases: adoption essentials: (ii) adequately reasoned judgments: global, holistic evaluation

5 *Re B-S (children) (adoption: leave to oppose)* [2013] EWCA Civ 1146, [2013] 3 FCR 481.

9.1.15 The welfare stage: the court's approach: cases not concerning adoption: 'nothing else will do' does not apply

Re DAM (children) [2018] EWCA Civ 386, [2018] 2 FLR 676, [42] (Peter Jackson LJ)

42. Dealing specifically with the criticisms of the judge's approach, set out in paragraph 33 above …

(5) I reject the argument that a court considering whether to make a care order has to be satisfied that 'nothing else will do'. A care order is a serious order that can only be made where the facts justify it, where it is in the child's interests, and where it is necessary and proportionate. But the aphorism 'nothing else will do' (which, as has been said, is not a substitute for a proper welfare evaluation and proportionality check) applies only to cases involving a plan for adoption. That is clear from the case in which it originated, *In re M (A Child) (Care Proceedings: Threshold Criteria)* [2013] UKSC 33 , which concerned an application for a care order with a care plan for adoption. It is clear, where it is not explicit, that all the justices were addressing a situation involving the severance of the parental relationship altogether, and not one involving physical separation under a care order, where the parent retains parental responsibility. That is confirmed by the summary given by the President in *Re B-S*:

> '22. The language used in *Re M* is striking. Different words and phrases are used, but the message is clear. Orders contemplating non-consensual adoption – care orders with a plan for adoption, placement orders and adoption orders – are 'a very extreme thing, a last resort', only to be made where 'nothing else will do', where 'no other course [is] possible in [the child's] interests', they are 'the most extreme option', a 'last resort – when all else fails', to be made 'only in exceptional circumstances and where motivated by overriding requirements pertaining to the child's welfare, in short, where nothing else will do': see *Re M* paras 74, 76, 77, 82, 104, 130, 135, 145, 198, 215.' …

9.2 THE WELFARE STAGE: PARAMOUNTCY OF WELFARE

9.2.1 The welfare stage: paramountcy of welfare: meaning of 'welfare'

Re O and N (children) (non-accidental injury) [2003] UKHL 18, [2003] 1 FCR 673, [23]–[25] (Lord Nicholls)

The welfare stage

[23] Crossing the threshold is not a reason for making a care order. When the threshold criteria are met the court proceeds to the welfare stage. The court must decide whether it is in the best interests of the child to make

a care order as asked by the local authority. As with 'private law' orders made under section 8 of the Act, so with care and supervision orders made under section 31(1) , the paramount consideration in making this decision is the child's welfare: section 1(1) and (4) . This involves looking at the past and also looking into the future. In considering which course is in the child's best interests, the court will have regard to all the circumstances of the case.

[24] This has long been axiomatic in this area of the law. The matters the court may take into account are bounded only by the need for them to be relevant, that is, they must be such that, to a greater or lesser extent, they will assist the court in deciding which course is in the child's best interests. I can see no reason of legal policy why, in principle, any other limitation should be placed on the matters the judge may take into account when making this decision. If authority is needed for this conclusion I need refer only to the wide, all embracing language of Lord MacDermott in *J v C* [1970] AC 668, 710–711. Section 1 of the Guardianship of Infants Act 1925 required the court, in proceedings where the upbringing of an infant was in question, to regard the welfare of the infant 'as the first and paramount consideration'. Regarding these words, Lord MacDermott said:

> 'I think they connote a process whereby, when all the relevant facts, relationships, claims and wishes of parents, risks, choices and other circumstances are taken into account and weighed, the course to be followed will be that which is most in the interests of the child's welfare as that term has now to be understood.'

In principle the same approach is equally applicable under section 1 of the Children Act 1989.

[25] The Children Act directs the court, when making a decision regarding a child's welfare, to have particular regard to the factors set out in the welfare checklist in section 1(3) …

See also *Re G (children) (religious upbringing: education)* [2012] EWCA Civ 1233, [2012] 3 FCR 524, [25]–[34] (Munby LJ) addressing the same point (providing a broad definition of the coterminous term 'best interests' as taking into account, where appropriate, 'a wide range of ethical, social, moral, religious, cultural, emotional and welfare considerations', albeit in private law proceedings)

See Chapter 9.3 The welfare stage: the welfare checklists

9.2.2 The welfare stage: paramountcy of welfare: meaning of 'paramount': child-parents

Birmingham City Council v H (a minor) [1994] 1 FCR 896 (HL), 903A–F (Lord Slynn)

> It is clear that the draftsman of the statute did not specifically provide for a situation where both parent and child are children within the meaning of the Act. Although wider arguments have been addressed on the basis of

other sections of the Act, it seems to me that the problem is resolved on an analysis of the structure of s 34 itself which deals with the special situation of children in care.

The starting point is that by subs (1) the appropriate authority must allow the child in care reasonable contact with four categories of person, a parent, a guardian, a person in whose favour a residence order was in force, or a person who has had the care of the child immediately before the care order in question was made. If there is an issue about contact, any one of those persons may apply to the court under subs (3) and the court, 'may make such order as it considers appropriate with respect to the contact which is to be allowed between the child and that person'. For this purpose, 'the child' is the child in care in respect of whom an order is sought by one of the four categories of person. That child is the subject matter of the application. The question to be determined relates to that child's upbringing and it is that child's welfare which must be the court's paramount consideration. The fact that the parent is also a child does not mean that both parent's and child's welfare is paramount and that each has to be balanced against the other. Under subs (3) the question to be determined does not relate to the applicant's upbringing even if the applicant is a child.

By subs (2):

> 'On an application made by the authority or the child, the court may make such order as it considers appropriate with respect to the contact which is to be allowed between the child and any named person.'

In this application the child in care may apply and, if that child is the applicant, it is that child's welfare which is directly involved and which is paramount even if the other 'named person' is also a child. The welfare of any other 'named person', even if a child, is not also paramount so as to require a balancing exercise to be carried out.

See also *F v Leeds City Council* [1994] 2 FCR 428 (CA), 430G–432C (Ward J) considering *Birmingham City Council v H (a minor)* [1994] 1 FCR 896

9.2.3 The welfare stage: paramountcy of welfare: meaning of 'paramount': siblings

Re S (children) (relocation: permission) [2011] EWCA Civ 454, [2011] 2 FCR 356, [55] (Sir Mark Potter)

[55] At the same time, it is important to bear in mind that, when the court is considering the welfare interests of siblings, the case of each requires careful and separate consideration pursuant to s 1 of the 1989 Act. An individual exercise is required in respect of each child and where there is a conflict between the respective best interests of each child, the court must balance the welfare of one against that of the other in coming to its decision: *Re T and E (Children's Proceedings: Conflicting Interests)* [1995] 3 FCR 260, [1995] 1 FLR 581. This means that, if the court

concludes or acts on the basis that it is in the welfare interests of siblings to stay together, and there is a dispute as to where or with whom they should live, it must be particularly astute to come to the decision which involves least risk to their collective welfare

See also *Re A (children) (conjoined twins: surgical separation)* [2000] 3 FCR 577 (CA), 621D–623H (Ward LJ) addressing the same point (in the context of conjoined twins with conflicting interests, in extremis)

9.3 THE WELFARE STAGE: THE WELFARE CHECKLISTS

9.3.1 The welfare stage: the welfare checklists: approach to the checklists

Re G (children) (residence: same-sex partner) [2006] UKHL 43, [2006] 3 FCR 1, [40] (Baroness Hale)

[40] My Lords, it is of course the case that any experienced family judge is well aware of the contents of the statutory checklist and can be assumed to have had regard to it whether or not this is spelled out in a judgment. However, in any difficult or finely balanced case, as this undoubtedly was, it is a great help to address each of the factors in the list, along with any others which may be relevant, so as to ensure that no particular feature of the case is given more weight than it should properly bear. This is perhaps particularly important in any case where the real concern is that the children's primary carer is reluctant or unwilling to acknowledge the importance of another parent in the children's lives.

Re DAM (children) [2018] EWCA Civ 386, [2018] 2 FLR 676, [42] (Peter Jackson LJ)

42. Dealing specifically with the criticisms of the judge's approach, set out in paragraph 33 above …

(3) In the almost 30 years since it was devised, the 'welfare checklist' has stood the test of time and its value to decision-makers, as described in *Re G*, cannot be overstated. It is obligatory to have regard to its contents when considering what order should be made. That obligation will be discharged if it is evident that in substance all the relevant, significant welfare factors have been taken into account. I do not accept that there is an obligation to articulate a checklist analysis *before* announcing a decision. However, to omit any reference to the substance of the checklist, or to relegate the exercise until after the court has stated its conclusion, carries risks of the kind seen in this appeal.

(4) The absence of a point in the judgment where the judge can be seen to have drawn together the welfare factors for comparative evaluation is an undoubted weakness. However, analysis of the judgment as a whole shows that the judge did evaluate all the significant welfare factors,

> although not in a methodical order that would have made his reasoning easier to appreciate …

See also *Re P (a child)* [2016] EWCA Civ 3, [2017] 1 FLR 417, [48] (Ryder SP) addressing the same point (including highlighting that there is no need for a judge to 'laboriously' rehearse the checklist as if 'a pilot conducting his pre-flight checks')

See also *Re L (children)* [2017] EWCA Civ 1137, [2017] 4 WLR 141, [28] (McFarlane LJ) addressing a related point (the danger of the checklists appearing like a list as opposed to an 'important set of preliminary signposts')

See also *Re M (a child)* [2018] EWCA Civ 240, [2018] 2 FCR 253, [63] (King LJ) considering *Re G (children) (residence: same-sex partner)* [2006] UKHL 43, [2006] 3 FCR 1

9.3.2 The welfare stage: the welfare checklists: approach to the checklists: adoption cases

Re C (a child) (care and placement: long-term welfare decision) [2013] EWCA Civ 1257, [2014] 1 FCR 173, [29]–[31] (McFarlane LJ)

[29] Further, where the court is seized of both an application for a care order and an application for a placement for adoption order, I would question the wisdom, when making a care order in the middle of the process of evaluating the ultimate question of whether or not a placement for adoption order is to be made, of 'approving a care plan for adoption' by reference only to the CA 1989, s 1 welfare provisions. In common with the practice of many family judges, that was the course taken by the judge in the present case. It is, however, a practice which may inadvertently lead the court away from engaging with a proper, holistic evaluation of the central welfare question and, where placement for adoption is an issue, doing so within the structure of ACA 2002, s 1 rather than CA 1989, s 1. Any judge, who is aware that (either at the current hearing or at a hearing shortly thereafter) he or she is going to be considering whether or not to make a placement for adoption order, would be wise only to approve a care plan for adoption where such a plan seems likely to meet the welfare requirements of ACA 2002, s1 and s 52.

[30] By way of example, it is a consequence of the linear structure in the present judgment that EB is ruled out at a stage where the judge is solely considering the welfare checklist in s 1(3) of the 1989 Act. He then goes on to make the care order and to approve the care plan for adoption (para 85). It is only after that point that the judge, for the first time, makes reference to s 1(2) of the 2002 Act and to the enhanced welfare checklist in s 1(4) of the 2002 Act with its focus upon the whole life nature of an adoption decision.

[31] The 1989 Act welfare checklist must, by reason of s 1(4)(b) of the 1989 Act, be used when the court is considering making a care order under s 31.

A linear judgment, which unnecessarily compartmentalises the decision making into discrete and separate stages ('care order' and only then 'adoption'), with the 1989 Act provisions alone being used to approve a plan for adoption, in some cases may prevent the evaluation of what is ultimately the one issue in the case, the choice between family placement or adoption, as a whole and for that evaluation to be undertaken with the tailor-made, adoption-focused, welfare checklist in s 1 of the 2002 Act at the forefront of the judicial mind.

Re R (a child) (placement: realistic options) [2014] EWCA Civ 1625, [2015] 2 FCR 499, [19]–[20] (McFarlane LJ)

[19] In the present case there were only two options for ES. The judge faced a binary decision. Either the child was to go home on some basis or another to be cared for by her mother, or, given her age, an adoptive placement was to be sought. That was the only issue in the case; that was what the case was all about. The judge had apparently heard four days of evidence followed by a day of oral submissions. The entirety of his judgment, including the analysis under ACA 2002, s 1(4) which follows the announcement of his decision to rule the mother out, is entirely engaged in analysing the positives and negatives from the point of view of the child of that option. Looked at as a whole, which is the perspective that must be applied, it is simply not possible to say that the judge compartmentalised his analysis so as to render his approach worthy of criticism on the basis described in *Re B-S*.

[20] Although it does not affect the substance of his evaluation in the present case, I would, however, question the judge's decision to analyse the issues in the case first under the welfare checklist in CA 1989, prior to making a care order endorsing the care plan for adoption, and before moving on to conduct a second analysis using the welfare checklist in ACA 2002. There was one issue in this case: should the child be returned to the mother or go forward for adoption. That is an adoption question to which the factors in ACA 2002 directly apply. In the circumstances it was necessary, and necessary only, to analyse which outcome was to be chosen, by giving the child's welfare paramount consideration throughout her lifetime through the lens of the welfare checklist in ACA 2002, s 1(4). There was no need to conduct a preliminary, lower level, analysis using the CA 1989 checklist or to make a care order in the middle of the judgment; if the adoption plan was ultimately chosen then a care order would readily be justified and made at the conclusion of the hearing.

See also *Re E (a child) (adoption: proportionate outcome)* [2013] EWCA Civ 1614, [2014] 3 FCR 240, [26] (McFarlane LJ) addressing a related point (although a judge does not have to explicitly reference the checklists it is crucial to demonstrate consideration of the relevant factors and compliance with the law)

See Chapter 15.2 Appeals: adequacy of reasons

9.3.3 The welfare stage: the welfare checklists: wishes and feelings: weight attached is case-specific

Re P (minors) (wardship: care and control) [1992] 2 FCR 681 (CA), 687C–E (Butler-Sloss LJ)

> How far the wishes of children should be a determinative factor in their future placement must of course vary on the particular facts of each case. Clearly, the Judge was aware of the children's views and feelings which he ascertained for himself and which confirmed the evidence of the court welfare officer. Those views must be considered and may, but not necessarily must, carry more weight as the children grow older. Appropriate weight must be given to their wishes. But looking at these children, a number of other important factors emerge which counter-balance their express wishes …

See also *Re P-S (children) (care proceedings: right to give evidence)* [2013] EWCA Civ 223, [2013] 2 FCR 299, [43]–[44] (Sir Alan Ward) addressing a related point (there is no rebuttable presumption to follow a mature child's wishes)

See also *London Borough of Barking and Dagenham v A and another* [2019] EWHC 2017 (Fam), [2019] 2 FLR 1102, [35] (MacDonald J) addressing a related point (children's preferences are one factor in the case and weight depends on the particular circumstances)

9.3.4 The welfare stage: the welfare checklists: 'change in his circumstances': status quo arguments

Re M'P-P (children) (adoption: status quo) [2015] EWCA Civ 584, [2015] 2 FCR 451, [46]–[51] (McFarlane LJ)

Discussion

[46] The decision called for in the present case was a difficult one, requiring a choice to be made between two potential carers, one a family member unknown to the children and the other a foster carer/prospective adopter with whom they had a strong and beneficial attachment. The determination of this appeal is, likewise, not a straightforward matter. As will become plain, I have felt driven to hold that the appeal should be allowed, not on the basis that the judge was 'wrong' in his decision, but on other grounds. It must follow that the applications must now be re-heard. I therefore intend to be careful not to express any view as to the eventual outcome of that rehearing; to do so would not only be impertinent but also extremely unwise as this court has not been made privy to all of the evidence that may be called in that hearing.

[47] At the beginning of this judgment I indicated that the appeal, in part, raises the question of the relative weight that is to be attached to the issues of 'status quo' and 'family' when they appear to be in opposition to each other in proceedings relating to a child. In recent times the importance of a local authority and the court giving full weight to the importance

of a 'family' placement, unless this is established to be so contrary to a child's welfare that a long-term placement in public care or adoption is necessary, has been stressed in a range of decisions, of which *Re B* [2013] 2 FCR 525, [2013] 3 All ER 929 and *Re B-S* [2013] 3 FCR 481, [2014] 1 WLR 563 are the most prominent. Less has been said in the recently reported cases about the weight to be afforded to the bundle of factors that family lawyers have historically referred to as 'the status quo argument'. That this is so may, in part, be a consequence of the status quo simply not being a factor in many public law cases where, at the time of the final hearing, the child is, on any view, in a home that is temporary; the dispute is normally about the home to which the child is to move (be that in the family or with strangers) with no option to stay where he is.

[48] The validity of the status quo argument is certainly well established in the pre-CA 1989 authorities. In *D v M (minor: custody appeal)* [1982] 3 All ER 897 at 902–903, [1983] Fam 33 at 41, Ormrod LJ said:

> '… it is generally accepted by those who are professionally concerned with children that, particularly in the early years, continuity of care is a most important part of a child's sense of security and that disruption of established bonds is to be avoided whenever it is possible to do so. Where, as in this case, a child of two years of age has been brought up without interruption by the mother (or a mother substitute) it should not be removed from her care unless there are strong countervailing reasons for doing so. This is not only the professional view, it is commonly accepted in all walks of life …'

Factors in any particular case relating to the status quo will fall to be considered in a case to which CA 1989, s 1 applies under s 1(3)(c) where the court must have regard to 'the likely effect on [the child] of any change in his circumstances'.

[49] In more recent times the prescient observations of Ormrod LJ, which were made at a time when the early work of John Bowlby and others on 'Attachment Theory' was available, have been borne out by the enhanced understanding of the neurological development of a young child's brain that has become available, particularly, during the past decade. As a result, the importance of a child's attachment to his or her primary care giver is now underpinned by knowledge of the underlying neurobiological processes at work in the developing brain of a baby or toddler.

[50] In the context of 'attachment theory', the wording of ACA 2002, s 1(4)(f), which places emphasis upon the 'value' of a 'relationship' that the child may have with a relevant person, is particularly important. The circumstances that may contribute to what amounts to a child's 'status quo' can include a whole range of factors, many of which will be practically based, but within that range the significance for the child of any particular relationship is likely to be a highly salient factor. The focus within CA 1989, s 1(3)(c) is upon the 'likely effect on' the child of any change. The focus in ACA 2002, s 1(4)(f)(i) is upon 'the value to the child' of any particular relationship continuing.

[51] It is not my purpose in this judgment to express a view upon the relative importance of attachment/status quo arguments as against those relating to a placement in the family. Each case must necessarily turn on its own facts and the weight to be attached to any factor in any case will inevitably be determined by the underlying evidence …

9.3.5 The welfare stage: the welfare checklist: harm or risk of harm: the same standard as s31

Re B (children) (sexual abuse: standard of proof) [2008] UKHL 35, [2008] 2 FCR 339, [70] (Baroness Hale)

[70] My Lords, for that reason I would go further and announce loud and clear that the standard of proof in finding the facts necessary to establish the threshold under s 31(2) or the welfare considerations in s 1 of the 1989 Act is the simple balance of probabilities, neither more nor less. Neither the seriousness of the allegation nor the seriousness of the consequences should make any difference to the standard of proof to be applied in determining the facts. The inherent probabilities are simply something to be taken into account, where relevant, in deciding where the truth lies.

9.3.6 The welfare stage: the welfare checklists: harm or risk of harm: risk of harm

Re F (a child: placement order: proportionality) [2018] EWCA Civ 2761, [2019] 1 FCR 432, [22]–[24] (Peter Jackson LJ)

[22] I fully endorse the submission that this court should be slow to interfere with the evaluation of a specialist judge whose conclusions emerged from the crucible of a trial. Moreover, as Mr Tyler freely acknowledged, the local authority behaved entirely properly in stepping in to protect Robbie from harm at his parents' hands. The starting point on this appeal is therefore a complete acceptance by this court of the problems with which the judge was faced. The evidence showed the mother to be a vulnerable person who has repeatedly let her own needs get in the way of her responsibilities towards her son, placing him at clear risk of significant harm. Her decisions to flout the written agreement, to continue to drink, to remain in touch with the father, and then to lie about it, were extraordinarily foolish. Her insight into her shortcomings was limited. The professionals who had been working with her in good faith were understandably deeply disappointed. Moreover, they and the judge were absolutely right to be concerned about delay for a child of this age, when the proceedings had already been on foot for eight months.

[23] However, this was not the whole picture. The relationship between mother and child is of good quality, with no complaint being made about Robbie's daily care over the 11 months he lived at home and was regularly seen by a range of professionals. The mother herself does not have serious mental

health problems or any established addiction. She is not an alcoholic. Her drinking in recent years has been described as behavioural. Until her late 20s, she was functioning normally. She therefore has a different profile to very many parents who come before the Family Court in cases of this kind.

[24] In these circumstances, close attention needed to be paid to the nature and extent of the risks. As foreshadowed at the start of this judgment, there must be (to borrow a phrase from a different context) an intense focus on the *type of risk* that is involved, *how likely* it is to happen, and what the *likely consequences* might then be. Only by carrying out this exercise is it possible to know what weight to give to the risks before setting them alongside other relevant factors. So, for example, the risk of further physical harm to a child who has been severely injured by a denying parent is likely to be a factor of predominant weight. By contrast, to borrow from the evidence in this case, where a mother who untruthfully denies drinking goes to a park at night to drink alone, leaving her baby with its grandmother, the court will view that risk with a sense of proportion.

See also *Re K (children: placement orders)* [2020] EWCA Civ 1503, [2021] 1 FCR 835, [30] (Peter Jackson LJ) considering *Re F (a child: placement order: proportionality)* [2018] EWCA Civ 2761, [2019] 1 FCR 432

9.3.7 The welfare stage: the welfare checklists: harm or risk of harm: may include long-term separation from parents

Re G (care proceedings: welfare evaluation) [2013] EWCA Civ 965, [2013] 3 FCR 293, [46]–[47] (McFarlane LJ)

[46] Where the options for the child do not include placement for adoption or adoption, the court will apply the 'welfare checklist' in s 1(3) of the 1989 Act to the welfare evaluation. The wording of certain elements of the welfare checklist must, I would suggest, involve a direct comparison of the relevant options that are being considered, for example:

'(c) the likely effect on him of any change in his circumstances …

(e) any harm which he has suffered or is at risk of suffering;

(f) how capable each of his parents, and any other person in relation to whom the court considers the question to be relevant, is of meeting his needs.'

[47] Under s 1(3)(c), consideration of the effect of any change in the child's circumstances must involve considering, in the present case, not just the prospect of returning to the mother's care but must include consideration of the effects, positive and negative, of placement in long-term foster care. Under s 1(3)(e), consideration of the risk of harm obviously will include the potential for future harm from parental care, but must also require evaluation of any risk of harm from the alternative option provided by 'any other person', namely the local authority as corporate parent, for example emotional harm as a result of long-term separation of a child

from his parent. Under s 1(3)(f), when considering how capable 'each of his parents, and any other person' are to meet the child's needs, again I would suggest that, alongside consideration of the parent's capacity, there is a need to look at the strengths and detriments in the local authority's capacity to meet his needs through long-term fostering.

9.3.8 The welfare stage: the welfare checklists: harm or risk of harm: uncertain perpetrators

See Chapter 3.8.4 Threshold criteria: 'whodunnit' cases: uncertain perpetrator findings: relevance in present cases

See Chapter 3.8.5 Threshold criteria: 'whodunnit cases': uncertain perpetrator findings: relevance in later cases

9.3.9 The welfare stage: The welfare checklists: parents' capabilities: taking account of LA support

Re B-S (children) (adoption: leave to oppose) [2013] EWCA Civ 1146, [2013] 3 FCR 481, [28] (Sir James Munby P)

[28] Third (*Re B* para 105), the court's assessment of the parents' ability to discharge their responsibilities towards the child must take into account the assistance and support which the authorities would offer. So 'before making an adoption order … the court must be satisfied that there is no practical way of the authorities (or others) providing the requisite assistance and support.' In this connection it is worth remembering what Hale LJ had said in *Re O (Supervision Order)* [2001] EWCA Civ 16, [2001] 1 FLR 923, para 28:

> 'It will be the duty of everyone to ensure that, in those cases where a supervision order is proportionate as a response to the risk presented, a supervision order can be made to work, as indeed the framers of the Children Act 1989 always hoped that it would be made to work. The local authorities must deliver the services that are needed and must secure that other agencies, including the health service, also play their part, and the parents must co-operate fully.'

That was said in the context of supervision orders but the point is of wider application.

9.3.10 The welfare stage: the welfare checklists: parents' capabilities: learning disabled parents

Re D (a child) (no 3) [2016] EWFC 1, [2017] 4 WLR 55, [25]–[29], [164] (Sir James Munby P)

25. In a case such as this it is vitally important always to bear in mind two well-established principles. The first is encapsulated in what the Strasbourg

court said in *Y v United Kingdom* (2012) 55 EHRR 33, [2012] 2 FLR 332, para 134:

> 'family ties may only be severed in very exceptional circumstances and … everything must be done to preserve personal relations and, where appropriate, to 'rebuild' the family. *It is not enough to show that a child could be placed in a more beneficial environment for his upbringing.* However, where the maintenance of family ties would harm the child's health and development, a parent is not entitled under article 8 to insist that such ties be maintained (emphasis added).'

26. The second is encapsulated in the well known passage in the judgment of Hedley J in *Re L (Care: Threshold Criteria)* [2007] 1 FLR 2050, para 50:

> 'society must be willing to tolerate very diverse standards of parenting, including the eccentric, the barely adequate and the inconsistent … it is not the provenance of the state to spare children all the consequences of defective parenting. In any event, it simply could not be done.'

27. This leads on to the profoundly important of observations of Gillen J, as he then was, sitting in the Family Division of the High Court of Justice in Northern Ireland, in *Re G and A (Care Order: Freeing Order: Parents with a Learning Disability)* [2006] NIFam 8, para 5. So far as I am aware, his decision has never been reported, but the transcript is freely available on the BAILII website.

28. Gillen J referred to a number of papers and reports, including 'Finding the Right Support', a research paper from Bristol University's Norah Fry Research Centre funded and published by the Baring Foundation in 2006. He continued:

> 'A reading of these documents leads me to set out a number of matters which I feel must be taken into account by courts when determining cases such as this involving parents with a learning disability particularly where they parent children who also have a learning disability.'

He then set those matters out in eight numbered paragraphs. Although lengthy, they are so important that they require quotation in full. Accordingly, I set them out in an Annex to this judgment. I respectfully agree with everything said by Gillen J. I commend his powerful words to every family judge, to every local authority and to every family justice professional in this jurisdiction.

29. Gillen J's words require to be read in full, but two passages set the tone:

> '(2) People with a learning disability are individuals first and foremost and each has a right to be treated as an equal citizen. Government policy emphasises the importance of people with a learning disability being supported to be fully engaged playing a role in civic society and their ability to exercise their rights and responsibilities needs to be strengthened. They are valued citizens …

(4) This court fully accepts that parents with learning difficulties can often be 'good enough' parents when provided with the ongoing emotional and practical support they need. The concept of 'parenting with support' must underpin the way in which the courts and professionals approach wherever possible parents with learning difficulties ... judges must make absolutely certain that parents with learning difficulties are not at risk of having their parental responsibilities terminated on the basis of evidence that would not hold up against normal parents. Their competences must not be judged against stricter criteria or harsher standards than other parents.'

...

Annex

164. Extract from the judgment of Gillen J in *Re G and A (Care Order: Freeing Order: Parents with a Learning Disability)* [2006] NIFam 8, para 5:

> '(1) An increasing number of adults with learning difficulties are becoming parents. The Baring Foundation report records that whilst there are no precise figures on the number of parents with learning difficulties in the population, the most recent statistics come from the First National Survey of Adults with Learning Difficulties in England, where one in fifteen of the adults interviewed had children. Whatever the figure it is generally recognised that their number is steadily rising and that they represent a sizable population whose special needs require to be adequately addressed. The Baring Foundation report refers to national policy in England and Scotland committing government to "supporting parents with learning disabilities in order to help them, wherever possible, to ensure their children gain maximum life chance benefits." Nonetheless the courts must be aware that surveys show that parents with learning disabilities are apparently more likely than other parents to have their children removed them and permanently placed outside the family home. In multidisciplinary jurisdiction such as the Family Division, it is important that the court is aware of such reports at least for the purposes of comment. It is important to appreciate these currents because the Children Order (Northern Ireland) 1995 places an emphasis on supporting the family so that children can remain with them and obligations under disability discrimination legislation make public services accessible to disabled people (including parents with learning difficulties). Moreover the advent of the Human Rights Act 1998 plays an important role in highlighting the need to ensure the rights of such parents under Articles 6 and 8 of the European Convention of Human Rights and Fundamental Freedoms ("the Convention").
>
> ...
>
> (3) It is important that a court approaches these cases with a recognition of the possible barriers to the provision of appropriate support to parents including negative or stereotypical attitudes about

parents with learning difficulties possibly on the part of staff in some Trusts or services. An extract from the Baring Foundation report provides a cautionary warning:

> "For example, it was felt that some staff in services whose primary focus was not learning difficulties (eg in children and family teams) did not fully understand the impact of having learning difficulties on individual parents' lives; had fixed ideas about what would happen to the children of parents with learning difficulties and wanted an outcome that did not involve any risks (which might mean them being placed away from their family); expected parents with learning difficulties to be 'perfect parents' and had extremely high expectations of them. Different professionals often had different concepts of parenting against which parents were assessed. Parents' disengagement with services, because they felt that staff had a negative view of them and 'wanted to take their children away' was also an issue, as were referrals to support services which were too late to be of optimum use to the family – often because workers lacked awareness of parents' learning difficulties or because parents had not previously been known to services".

…

(5) Parents must be advised by social workers about their legal rights, where to obtain advice, how to find a solicitor and what help might be available to them once a decision has been taken to pursue a care application. Too narrow a focus must not be placed exclusively on the child's welfare with an accompanying failure to address parents' needs arising from their disability which might impact adversely on their parenting capacity. Parents with learning disabilities should be advised of the possibility of using an advocate during their case eg from the Trust itself or from Mencap and clear explanations and easy to understand information about the process and the roles of the different professionals involved must be disclosed to them periodically. Written information should be provided to such parents to enable them to consider these matters at leisure and with their advocate or advisers. Moreover Trusts should give careful consideration to providing child protection training to staff working in services for adults with learning disabilities. Similarly those in children's services need training about adults with learning disabilities …

…

(7) Children of parents with learning difficulties often do not enter the child protection system as the result of abuse by their parents. More regularly the prevailing concerns centre on a perceived risk of neglect, both as the result of the parents' intellectual impairments, and the impact of the social and economic deprivation commonly faced by adults with learning difficulties. It is in this context that a shift must

be made from the old assumption that adults with learning difficulties could not parent to a process of questioning why appropriate levels of support are not provided to them so that they can parent successfully and why their children should often be taken into care. At its simplest, this means a court carefully inquiring as to what support is needed to enable parents to show whether or not they can become good enough parents rather than automatically assuming that they are destined to fail. The concept of "parenting with support" must move from the margins to the mainstream in court determinations …

9.3.11 The welfare stage: the welfare checklists: parents' capabilities: deaf parents

A Local Authority v M and others [2021] EWFC 10, [136]–[142] (Elizabeth Isaacs QC sitting as a deputy High Court judge) *quotation limited to* [142]

142. It is encouraging that the local authority has firmly stated and confirmed its intention to learn lessons from the review of its approach in this case in order to improve its service provision to deaf parents in the future. In due course I will order that a copy of this judgment in full is to be sent to the director of the local authority's Children's Services Department for full consideration in that regard. There are a number of lessons to be taken from this case, but the following points in relation to the approach to deaf parents are perhaps the most critical in importance.

Point 1

The local authority should have ensured that the social workers working with M as a deaf person were aware of their obligations under the Equality Act 2010.

Point 2

M was wrongly identified in most, if not all, of the court orders as being 'hearing impaired'. All parties should have ensured that M's disability as a deaf parent of the children was accurately recorded by the court.

Point 3

There should have been a 'joined-up' approach between Adult Services and Children's Services before A was born, to identify M's needs as a deaf parent, particularly in light of the clearly identified potential safeguarding issues and M's increased vulnerabilities as a deaf parent reporting domestic abuse, and to identify the extent of the local authority's duties to M as a parent with protected characteristics under the Equality Act 2010.

Point 4

The local authority should have ensured that the pre-birth assessment incorporated expert advice about the extent of M's needs as a deaf person, and should have been carried out by professionals with the skills suitable to understand and analyse the impact of M's deafness on her parenting.

Point 5

The deaf awareness training for Social Worker 3 was not accessed in a timely fashion. The local authority should have ensured that all social workers and contact supervisors working with M as a deaf person received adequate and timely deaf awareness training. Such training should have included information about how to provide information in a clear and appropriate way to a deaf person who also has communication difficulties.

Point 6

Using F to communicate with M was not appropriate for matters of substance.

Point 7

Using text messaging to communicate with M, whilst her preferred mode of communication and appropriate for regular contacts and discussion about everyday matters and arrangements, was not appropriate for matters of substance.

Point 8

The local authority should have ensured that a lip reader was made available to support M as a deaf person at ALL meetings as soon as the need was confirmed by Dr Austen in November 2018. Although there were attempts to engage M in face-to-face meetings for which lip speakers were booked, more efforts could have been made, particularly in respect of basic social work meetings and around the issues noted in contact.

Point 8

The local authority should have provided information to M as a deaf person in an accessible format, interpreted into simple English using a lip speaker.

Point 9

The local authority should have made information to M as a deaf person with associated cognitive difficulties written in simplified English, at a reading level that was accessible.

Point 10

The local authority should not have arranged supervised contacts without ever providing deaf awareness training for any of the contact supervisors, without ever using a lip speaker or an intermediary to assist M as a deaf person in contact, and without ever holding any review with the contact supervisors of the progress of contact.

Point 11

The local authority should have provided deaf awareness training to the children's foster carer who was involved in providing information to M at the start of contact sessions.

Point 12

> The local authority should have ensured that, in considering the issue of procedural fairness in relation to M as a deaf parent, the SWET explicitly identified *how* they fulfilled the requirement to communicate adequately with a deaf parent. It was not enough simply to state that the SWET would be made available to M's legal representatives; that did not obviate the need for the local authority to fulfil its own responsibilities to M as a deaf person.

9.3.12 The welfare stage: the welfare checklists: impact of lies on welfare

Re K (children: placement orders) [2020] EWCA Civ 1503, [2021] 1 FCR 835, [29] (Peter Jackson LJ)

[29] The next general matter concerns the significance of lies. The correct approach to lies in relation to fact-finding is well known and the judge appropriately gave himself a *Lucas* direction in that context. Here the more pertinent matter for our purpose concerns lies in the context of welfare. Lies, however disgraceful and dispiriting, must be strictly assessed for their likely effect on the child, and the same can be said for disobedience to authority. In some cases, the conclusion will simply be that the child unfortunately has dishonest or disobedient parents. In others, parental dishonesty and inability to co-operate with authority may decisively affect the welfare assessment. But in all cases the link between lies and welfare must be spelled out. That did not happen in *Re Y (a child)* [2013] EWCA Civ 1337, where Macur LJ said this at [7](4):

> 'I consider the case appears to have been hijacked by the issue of the mother's dishonesty. Much of the local authority's evidence is devoted to it. The Children's Guardian adopts much the same perspective. It cannot be the sole issue in a case devoid of context. There was very little attention given to context in this case. No analysis appears to have been made by any of the professionals as to why the mother's particular lies created the likelihood of significant harm to these children and what weight should reasonably be afforded to the fact of her deceit in the overall balance.'

See also *Re F (a child: placement order: proportionality)* [2018] EWCA Civ 2761, [2019] 1 FCR 432, [25] (Peter Jackson LJ) addressing the same point (highlighting the need to pay close attention to the true significance of dishonesty and lack of insight)

9.4 THE WELFARE STAGE: CARE PLANNING

9.4.1 The welfare stage: care planning: duty to keep plans under review

Re A (a child) [2008] EWCA Civ 650, [2008] 2 FLR 1183, [7]–[8] (Wall LJ)

7. When the Children Act 1989 (the Act) was first implemented, the local authority's care plan in proceedings under Part IV of the Act was not a statutory document; indeed, no mention of it was made in the Act. However, by amendment of what is now section 31A of the Act, the care plan is not only a statutory document, but one which the local authority is obliged to keep up to date. I read section 31A of the Act:

> '(1) Where an application is made on which a care order might be made with respect to a child, the appropriate local authority must, within such time as the court may direct, prepare a plan ("a care plan") for the future care of the child.
>
> (2) While the application is pending, the authority must keep any care plan prepared by them under review and, if they are of the opinion some change is required, revise the plan, or make a new plan, accordingly.'

8. So, in my judgment, in the instant case, the local authority was under a statutory obligation to do what in fact it did not do, which was to amend the care plan during the course of the proceedings to reflect the new evidence. In my judgment it did not require the consent or permission of the judge to do that. The judge had no jurisdiction over it whatsoever. It was the responsibility of the local authority to present the new care plan to the judge and, if the judge did not like the care plan, his only remedy was not to make a care order. That is all trite law.

See also *Re S and W (children) (care proceedings: care plan)* [2007] EWCA Civ 232, [2007] 1 FCR 721, [28] (Wall LJ) addressing the same point (in the context of explaining the significance of care plans), see Chapter 9.4.5 The welfare stage: care planning: role of the court and LAs

9.4.2 The welfare stage: care planning: no authority for 'starred care plans'

Re S (children: care plan); Re W (children: care plan) [2002] UKHL 10, [2002] 1 FCR 577, [16]–[17], [23]–[28], [34]–[44] (Lord Nicholls) *quotation limited to* [17], [43]

[17] Stated shortly, the two innovations fashioned by the Court of Appeal were these. First, the court enunciated guidelines intended to give trial judges a wider discretion to make an interim care order, rather than a final care order. The second innovation was more radical. It concerns the position after the court has made a care order. The Court of Appeal propounded a new procedure, by which at the trial the essential milestones of a care

plan would be identified and elevated to a 'starred status'. If a starred milestone was not achieved within a reasonable time after the date set at trial, the local authority was obliged to 'reactivate the interdisciplinary process that contributed to the creation of the care plan'. At the least the local authority must inform the child's guardian of the position. Either the guardian or the local authority would then have the right to apply to the court for further directions: see the judgment of Thorpe LJ ([2001] 2 FCR 450 at [29], [30]).

...

[43] In his judgment Thorpe LJ noted that the starring system 'seems to breach the fundamental boundary between the functions and responsibilities of the court and the local authority' (see [2001] 2 FCR 450 at [31]). I agree. I consider this judicial innovation passes well beyond the boundary of interpretation. I can see no provision in the 1989 Act which lends itself to the interpretation that Parliament was thereby conferring this supervisory function on the court. No such provision was identified by the Court of Appeal. On the contrary, the starring system is inconsistent in an important respect with the scheme of the 1989 Act. It would constitute amendment of the 1989 Act, not its interpretation. It would have far-reaching practical ramifications for local authorities and their care of children. The starring system would not come free from additional administrative work and expense. It would be likely to have a material effect on authorities' allocation of scarce financial and other resources. This in turn would affect authorities' discharge of their responsibilities to other children. Moreover, the need to produce a formal report whenever a care plan is significantly departed from, and then await the outcome of any subsequent court proceedings, would affect the whole manner in which authorities discharge, and are able to discharge, their parental responsibilities.

9.4.3 The welfare stage: care planning: twin-tracking

Re D and K (minors) (care plan: twin track planning) [1999] 3 FCR 109 (FD), 110H–112E (Bracewell J)

Twin track planning

This problem was addressed by the Children Act Advisory Committee in the annual report 1993–94 as follows:

> 'Care plans should be as full as the facts of the individual case allow. For example, where a permanent substitute family is to be found it is helpful if a range of possible adopters are identified and there is no reason why the adoption panel should not have become involved, so long as the child has not been directly involved, for example in meetings or placement. The crucial distinction is between planning in advance of the court's

> decision, which is to be encouraged and on the other hand pre-empting the decision of the court. Local authorities should have these matters in mind when preparing the care plan in order to avoid unnecessary delay.'

In my experience that resulted in a very limited response from local authorities generally and so it was that in the *Handbook of Best Practice in Children Act Cases* published by the Children Act Advisory Committee June 1997 there appears the following:

> '... 9 If the plan is for an adoptive placement, the court will be handicapped in assessing the plan and the timescale, unless the child concerned has already been considered and approved by the adoption and fostering panel, and potential suitable adoptive families have been identified. It is not good practice to await the making of a care order before obtaining such information, because the court is deprived of important background information and significant delay can occur in placing the child in the event of the court approving the plan.' (See *Clarke Hall & Morrison on Children*, p 1/11002–3, para 20004.)

If the local authority in this case had presented the children to the adoption panel earlier then this court might well have had a care plan which set out the anonymised details of a suitable identified family approved for adoption thereby enabling the court to balance the option of rehabilitation versus adoptive placement with an identified family in the light of full background information.

In such cases it should be made abundantly clear to the natural family at the earliest date that the local authority are considering two options; namely rehabilitation within a strictly time limited framework, or adoption outside the family and that inquiries are proceeding on a twin track so that the court can be presented with well-researched options in order to prevent delay. Such a course requires an approach from a local authority which breaks the mould of sequential planning.

Local authorities traditionally have exhausted the possibility of rehabilitation to parents or extended family before even beginning to address the possibility of permanency outside the family. I recognise that there can be a tension between on the one hand giving every opportunity for assessment of the parents and extended family, which may involve many and varied inquiries, and on the other hand seeking to prevent delay for the children by planning for permanence. However, provided the local authority make it clear to the parents and family that twin track planning in no way pre-empts outcome, then the process can only be in the interests of the child. For too long there has been a culture in which adoption has been regarded as the equivalent of failure and therefore a procedure to be considered only as a last resort when all else has been tried and has not succeeded. Such sequential planning often promotes delay with serious consequences for the welfare of the child.

Whenever care proceedings are commenced the court should be pro-active at an early directions hearing by inquiring of the local authority whether twin track planning is suitable for that case and if so giving appropriate directions. As part of their overall role designated care judges should liaise with their director or assistant director of social services with responsibility for children, with the chairmen of adoption and fostering panels, with panel managers of guardians ad litem, and with other concerned persons in order to ensure that within that area there is a general co-operation and understanding of the principles in order to provide facilities for twin track planning to be undertaken in suitable cases.

It is now well-researched that children deprived of permanent parenting grow up with unmet psychological needs and far too many children have to wait too long before permanent families are found for them when they cannot return to their natural families. The longer the delay, the more difficult it is to place children who often become progressively more disturbed in limbo, thereby rendering the task of identifying suitable adoptive families a lengthy and uncertain process. The older the child, the greater is the risk of break down in an adoptive placement. It is therefore incumbent on local authorities and guardians to seek to prevent these delays by identifying clearly the options available for the court by twin track planning as opposed to sequential planning.

9.4.4 The welfare stage: care planning: contingency planning

CM v Blackburn with Darwen Borough Council and others [2014] EWCA Civ 1479, [2015] 2 FCR 116, [22]–[26] (Ryder LJ)

[22] As I remarked at [61] of *Re W* there is no longer a requirement in the Regulations to set out a contingency plan although many local authorities do so as a matter of good practice. The concept of a contingency plan used to be described in government guidance (and in particular in guidance issued by the Secretary of State under s 7 of the Local Authority Social Services Act 1970 as LAC (99) 29), which was impliedly withdrawn when the new regulatory scheme came into being. It remains good practice to have such a plan because nothing can ever be certain. The existence of a contingency does not negate the force of a primary decision. That is to misunderstand the concepts of planning and forecasting.

[23] A care plan does not have to contain information that is not prescribed. The duty imposed on the local authority by s 31A(3) of the Children Act 1989 is to give prescribed information in a prescribed manner. If a court finds that prescribed information is missing it can and should require it to be provided but if a court identifies an issue that needs to be decided but which falls outside the prescribed information, it should direct that evidence be filed on the issue (see *Re W* above). It needs to be understood that there is a distinction to be drawn between a court requiring a defective or inadequate care plan to be re-drawn or an alternative care plan to be

provided and a court requiring evidence about an issue that will need to be decided in order to come to its ultimate determination.

[24] It is accordingly relevant to observe that the words complained of in the care plan in this case need not have been there. Neither the timetable for the adoptive placement nor any contingency in the event of the plan failing to be implemented is a requirement of the regulatory scheme (see in particular regs 9 and 11 and Sch 2 to the Regulations). Although by para 3(3)(c) of Sch 2 to the Regulations, the expected duration of a foster care placement has to be provided in a plan, that is only if the child is not in the care of the responsible (local) authority, a circumstance that is not relevant to this discussion. Furthermore, the concept of a limit on the time taken to undertake an adoption search is personal to the welfare of the child concerned ie something based on the individual welfare needs of the child derived from the facts of the case rather than a general requirement. It is not a requirement placed upon an adoption agency by the Adoption Agencies Regulations 2005, SI 2005/389, as amended, which, like the 2010 Regulations, is silent about timescales. The adoption placement plan described in Sch 5 to the 2005 Regulations which prescribes a date for placement is in the context of a child matched with identifiable prospective adopters which again is a circumstance not relevant to the facts of this case.

[25] The statutory scheme in the Adoption and Children Act 2002 has been well rehearsed in the recent decisions of this court. I need only recollect that s 22(2) of the Act requires a local authority to apply to the court for a placement order where the child is subject to a care order or an application has been made for a care order and the local authority 'are satisfied that the child ought to be placed for adoption' ie when the agency decision maker has made a decision that the child ought to be placed for adoption. At that point the court takes over. In the absence of the consent of those with parental responsibility the court has to make a decision under s 21 of the Act whether to dispense with a parent or guardian's consent and the test for dispensation is set out in s 52(1) of the Act which provides that:

> 'The court cannot dispense with the consent of any parent or guardian of a child to the child being placed for adoption or to the making of an adoption order in respect of the child unless the court is satisfied that […]
>
> (b) the welfare of the child requires the consent to be dispensed with.'

[26] A placement order is a decision relating to the adoption of a child. Accordingly, s 1 of the 2002 Act applies. Section 1(2) provides that the paramount consideration of the court must be the child's welfare throughout her life. The factors to which the court must have regard, among others, are set out in a welfare checklist at s 1(4). Delay is relevant to that decision because s 1(3) provides that in general any delay in coming to the decision is likely to prejudice the child's welfare. Once

a decision is made, however, delay is a matter for the local authority adoption agency not the court. That is because the limit of the court's jurisdiction over local authorities and their planning and review functions is clearly circumscribed by Parliament. It has been trite law since the decision of the House of Lords in *A v Liverpool City Council* [1981] 2 All ER 385, [1982] AC 363 that the courts will not interfere in the operative decisions of local authorities save in the proper exercise of its supervisory or reserved jurisdictions, for example in relation to contact.

9.4.5 The welfare stage: care planning: role of the court and LAs

Re S and W (children) (care proceedings: care plan) [2007] EWCA Civ 232, [2007] 1 FCR 721, [25]–[30] (Wall LJ)

Some basic propositions

[25] Before turning to examine the local authority's decision making processes in these proceedings, we regret to say that we think it necessary to set out what we had previously thought to be some elementary principles of family law and practice as they affect the relationship between a judge hearing proceedings under Pt IV of the 1989 Act, and the local authority which brings them.

[26] We fully endorse the statement of the law set out in para 2 of Wall LJ's reasons for listing the applications for oral hearing. The division of responsibility between the local authority and the court in care proceedings is, we think, well known, although we acknowledge that it is sometimes difficult to implement it in practice. It plainly needs, however, to be restated.

[27] Parliament has placed the responsibility for making care orders on the court, not on the local authority which brings the proceedings. Before a care order can be made, the local authority has to satisfy the court that the threshold criteria under s 31 of the 1989 Act are satisfied, and the court also has to be satisfied that a care order is in the best interests of the child concerned. To the latter end, the court is under a duty rigorously to scrutinise the care plan advanced by the local authority, and if the court does not think that it meets the needs of the child concerned, the court can refuse to make a care order. So much is elementary.

[28] The significance of local authority care plans was, we think, both recognised and reinforced by Parliament in the enactment of s 31A of the 1989 Act through the medium of s 121(2) of the 2002 Act. There is now a mandatory duty on local authorities to prepare a care plan for each child who is the subject of care proceedings, to keep that care plan under review and if some change is required, to revise the care plan or to make a new plan accordingly—see s 31A(1) and (2) of the 1989 Act. This case, it seems to us, is about both the merits of the local authority's late changes of plan on the facts, and the methodology of its decision making processes.

[29] What, however, is equally elementary is that once the court has made a final care order, responsibility for its implementation passes to the local authority, and save for the powers identified by the House of Lords in the case of *Re S (children: care plan); Re W (children: care plan)* [2002] UKHL 10, [2002] 1 FCR 577, [2002] 2 All ER 192, neither the court nor the children's guardian has any further role in the children's lives.

[30] What appears not to be understood, however, and thus needs to be clearly repeated, is that not only does the court have the duty rigorously to scrutinise the care plan and to refuse to make a care order if it does not think the plan in the child's best interests; the court also has the right to invite the local authority to reconsider the care plan if the court comes to the conclusion that the plan—or any change in the plan—involves a course of action which the court believes is contrary to the interests of the child, and which would be likely to lead the court to refuse to make a care order if the local authority were to adhere to the care plan it has proposed.

See also *Re T-S (children)* [2019] EWCA Civ 742, [2019] 3 FCR 192, [35] (Sir Andrew McFarlane P) addressing the same point

See also *Re W (a child) (care proceedings: welfare evaluation: functions of local authority)* [2013] EWCA Civ 1227, [2014] 1 FCR 260, [79]–[81] (Ryder LJ) addressing the same point, see Chapter 9.4.7 The welfare stage: care planning: court dissatisfaction with final care plans

9.4.6 The welfare stage: care planning: role of the court and LAs: courts retain control over contact

Re K [2007] EWHC 393 (Fam), [2008] 1 FLR 1, [23]–[26] (Munby J)

23. The starting point is the general principle stated by Butler-Sloss LJ in *Re B (Minors) (Care: Contact: Local Authority's Plans)* [1993] 1 FLR 543 at pages 548 and 551:

> 'once a care order has been made, the court can no longer monitor the administrative arrangements for the child and has no say in those arrangements … After the care order is made, the court has no continuing role in the future welfare of the child. The local authority has parental responsibility for the child.'

But this is subject to an important qualification in relation to matters of contact. As Butler-Sloss LJ expressed it in *Re L (Sexual Abuse: Standard of Proof)* [1996] 1 FLR 116 at page 124, explaining her earlier judgment in *Re B (Minors) (Care: Contact: Local Authority's Plans)* [1993] 1 FLR 543 :

> 'The effect of the Children Act is to set aside the former powers of the court in wardship and to remove from the court any continuing control over children after the making of a care order unless or until a further application was made to the court. On the making of a further

application, such as for residence or contact to the child, the powers of the court and the exercise of discretion under s 1 are restored for the duration of the application. If the care order remains in place, other than by control over contact by virtue of the provisions of s 34, the court has no further part to play in the future welfare of the child.'

24. It follows from this that the court, when considering issues of contact by or to a child in care, is *not* fettered by the care plan, even if the care plan is one that has previously been considered and approved by the court. Indeed, in *Re B (Minors) (Care: Contact: Local Authority's Plans)* [1993] 1 FLR 543 the court specifically rejected the local authority's submissions (see at pages 548 and 552) that the court 'ought not to make a contact order if the effect was to undermine or thwart the long-term plans of the local authority' and that the court 'cannot go behind the long-term plans of the local authority unless they were acting capriciously or were otherwise open to scrutiny by way of judicial review.' Butler-Sloss LJ explained the true principle at page 551:

> 'The proposals of the local authority, based on their appreciation of the best interests of the child, must command the greatest respect and consideration from the court, but Parliament has given to the court, and not to the local authority, the duty to decide on contact between the child and those named in s 34(1). Consequently the court may have the task of requiring the local authority to justify their long-term plans'

though, she added,

> 'to the extent only that those plans exclude contact between parent and child.'

25. That is not of course to deny the very considerable weight that the local authority's plan may carry because, as Butler-Sloss LJ had just observed:

> 'the issue of contact often depends on whether contact would frustrate long-term plans for the child in a substitute home, such as adoption where continuing contact may not be for the long-term welfare of the child. The presumption of contact, which has to be for the benefit of the child, has always to be balanced against the long-term welfare of the child and particularly where he will live in the future. Contact must not be allowed to destabilise or endanger the arrangements for the child and in many cases the plans for the child will be decisive of the contact application.'

26. Moreover, section 34 assumes that, at least in the first instance, contact is a matter for the exercise of discretion by the local authority. But the principle is clear. In the final analysis it is for the court, exercising its powers under section 34 , to determine questions of contact, whatever the care plan may or may not have to say on the subject. Furthermore the role of the court in relation to matters of contact is now enhanced in the light of its duties and powers under sections 26 and 27 of the Adoption and Children Act 2002 .

9.4.7 The welfare stage: care planning: court dissatisfaction with final care plans

Re W (a child) (care proceedings: welfare evaluation: functions of local authority) [2013] EWCA Civ 1227, [2014] 1 FCR 260, [79]–[90] (Ryder LJ) *quotation limited to* [79]–[86], [89]–[90]

[79] This brings me to that part of the welfare evaluation which is the consideration of the s 31A care plan. It is part of the case management process that a judge may require a local authority to give evidence about what services would be provided to support the strategy set out in its care plan, that is to support the placement options available to the court and meet the risk identified by the court. That may include evidence about more than one different possible resolution so the court might know the benefits and detriments of each option and what the local authority would or would not do. That may also include requiring the local authority to set out a care plan to meet a particular formulation or assessment of risk, even if the local authority does not agree with that risk.

[80] The court's powers extend to making an order other than that asked for by a local authority. The process of deciding what order is necessary involves a value judgment about the proportionality of the state's intervention to meet the risk against which the court decides there is a need for protection. In that regard, one starts with the court's findings of fact and moves on to the value judgments that are the welfare evaluation. That evaluation is the court's not the local authority's, the guardian's or indeed any other party's. It is the function of the court to come to that value judgment. It is simply not open to a local authority within proceedings to decline to accept the court's evaluation of risk, no matter how much it may disagree with the same. Furthermore, it is that evaluation which will inform the proportionality of the response which the court decides is necessary.

[81] It is likewise not open to a local authority within proceedings to decline to identify the practicable services that it is able to provide to make each of the range of placement options and orders work in order to meet the risk identified by the court. That is the purpose of a s 31A care plan. If a local authority were able to decline to join with the court in the partnership endeavour of identifying the best solution to the problem, then there would be no purpose in having a judicial decision on the question raised by the application. It might as well be an administrative act. Parliament has decided that the decision is to be a judicial act and accordingly, the care plan or care plan options filed with the court must be designed to meet the risk identified by the court. It is only by such a process that the court is able to examine the welfare implications of each of the placement options before the court and the benefits and detriments of the same and the proportionality of the orders sought.

[82] To do otherwise is to risk a disproportionate intervention into the lives of the child and the parents simply because of the financial or other priorities of different local authorities. To put it into stark terms, it cannot be right

that in one local authority a child would be placed with a parent or other kinship carer with significant support to meet the risk whereas in another local authority the same child would be placed with a view to adoption in the implementation of a plan to meet the same risk. The proportionality of placement and order are for the court. The services that are available are for the authority. In this regard, I cannot improve on the words of the court most recently in *Re B-S* (at [29]):

> 'It is the obligation of the local authority to make the order which the court has determined is proportionate work. The local authority cannot press for a more drastic form of order, least of all press for adoption, because it is unable or unwilling to support a less interventionist form of order. Judges must be alert to the point and must be rigorous in exploring and probing local authority thinking in cases where there is any reason to suspect that resource issues may be affecting the local authority's thinking.'

[83] The same point applies with equal force to a less interventionist form of order which is argued for by a local authority whether that is because the authority disagrees with the judge or is unable or unwilling to support that which is necessary. Although it may not seem as obvious, an order that fails to meet the risk may set up the child's placement for failure. That is critically important where the plan is to maintain a placement with a parent or member of the extended family by the imposition of an order of the court because, as I shall discuss, it would be a disproportionate interference in the child's family life to make an order then fail to support that which has been decided to be in the interests of the child. For the reasons that follow, this court has concluded that although it is for the local authority to decide *what* services to supply, as a matter of law they must supply sufficient services to prevent the state's intervention becoming disproportionate. The decision about the proportionality of intervention is for the court, the decision about the services which are necessary is for the local authority. Not all services will be practicable and it is for these reasons that the court needs to know what services are practicable in support of each of the placement options and orders that the court may approve and make. A local authority cannot refuse to provide lawful and reasonable services that would be necessary to support the court's decision because it disagrees with the decision or the court's evaluations upon which the decision is based. It should form no part of a local authority's case that the authority declines to consider or ignores the facts and evaluative judgments of the court. While within the process of the court, the state's agencies are bound by its decisions and must act on them.

[84] If the local authority's care plan fails to meet the court's expectations, the court may ask the local authority to reconsider. If the plan in its formulation or content is deficient on public law grounds, then once the family court has asked for that to be rectified (perhaps more than once) then the High Court may engage with the issue to decide the challenge.

In Re X; Barnet London Borough Council v Y and X [2006] 2 FLR 998 , Munby J (as he then was) concluded that a care plan was not in a child's best interests and also that the local authority's decision making process had breached the procedural safeguards guaranteed to both the child and her mother under both Articles 6 and 8 of the Convention. Furthermore, he held that although the procedural defects had been overtaken by events the local authority's care plan would breach the child's and the mother's Article 8 Convention rights. He warned of the potential consequences for the local authority if their decision had to be challenged in judicial review and he offered injunctive protection should any act be proposed that would be a precipitate abuse of their powers. In the event none was necessary. As a consequence my Lord in that case suggested that the local authority re-consider its position and have in mind the wise words of Wilson J (as he then was) in *Re C (Adoption: Religious Observance)* [2002] 1 FLR 1119 at [51]:

> 'The guardian argues that not even a judge of the Family Division has power to quash a local authority decision and that a damaging impasse can develop between a court which declines to approve their care plan and the authority which decline to amend it. The impasse is more theoretical than real: the last reported example is *Re S and D (Children: Powers of Court)* [1995] 2 FLR 456 . For good reason, there are often, as in this case, polarised views about the optimum solution for the child: in the end, however, assuming that they feel that the judicial processing of them has worked adequately, the parties will be likely to accept the court's determination and, in particular, the local authority will be likely to amend their proposals for the child so as to accord with it. The event of a failure to make amendment in such circumstances would be the proper moment for a guardian to consider taking proceedings for judicial review … In the normal case let there be – in the natural forum of the family court – argument, decision and sometimes, no doubt with hesitation, acceptance: in other words, between all of us a partnership, for the sake of the child.'

[85] As the postscript to Re X reveals, the local authority acquiesced in the judge's evaluation and changed its care plan. The circumstance in which a local authority can or indeed should be judicially reviewed on the content of a care plan should be rare indeed. With his characteristic diplomacy, Wilson J made clear that once the no doubt strong opinions of the parties and the court have been ventilated, it is for the family court to make a decision. That should be respected by the local authority. For the avoidance of doubt, I shall be more plain. If the local authority disagree with the judge's risk evaluation they must in a case where it is wrong appeal it. The appellate court will be able to consider such an appeal, where that is integral to the order or judgment of the court. If the welfare evaluation is not appealed then it stands and the local authority must respect it and work with it while the proceedings are outstanding. To do otherwise risks disproportionate, irrational or otherwise unlawful conduct on their part.

[86] There is no purpose in Parliament having decided to give the decision whether to make an order and the duty to consider the basis upon which the order is made to the judge if the local authority that makes the application can simply ignore what the judge has decided and act as if they had made the decision themselves and on a basis that they alone construe.

...

[89] Aside from any remedy available in the administrative court if such a situation arises, there is also available an application to discharge the care order if the care plan implemented by the authority is no longer proportionate or in the interests of the child and an application for relief under section 7 of the Human Rights Act 1998 where a person claims that an authority has acted or proposes to act in a way which is made unlawful by section 6(1) , that is in a way which is incompatible with a Convention right. An example of the full powers of the High Court and the family court being used where a local authority continues to act inappropriately can be found in *Re S and W (Care Proceedings)* [2007] EWCA Civ 232, [2007] 2 FLR 275 . A recent example of injunctive relief being granted under section 7 of the Human Rights Act 1998 can be found in *RCW v A Local Authority* [2013] EWHC 235 (Fam), [2013] 2 FLR 95 per Cobb J.

[90] It is important to recollect in this context that it is not appropriate to use continuing interim care orders to supervise the role of the local authority and subject only to intended legislation and existing Rules and Practice Directions relating to timetabling, Lord Nicholls approach in *Re S; Re W* remains good:

> '[90] From a reading of s 38 as a whole, it is abundantly clear that the purpose of an interim care order, so far as is presently material, is to enable the court to safeguard the welfare of a child until such time as the court is in a position to decide whether or not it is in the best interests of the child to make a care order. When that time arrives depends on the circumstances of the case and is a matter for the judgment of the trial judge. That is the general, guiding principle. The corollary to this principle is that an interim care order is not intended to be used as a means by which the court may continue to exercise a supervisory role over the local authority in cases where it is in the best interests of a child that a care order should be made.'

Re T-S (children) [2019] EWCA Civ 742, [2019] 3 FCR 192, [35]–[48] (Sir Andrew McFarlane P) *quotation limited to* [36], [48]

[36] In almost all cases there is, at least by the conclusion of the court process, unanimity of view as between the local authority and the court over the care plan that is to be followed if a particular order is made. Where, as is currently the position in the present case, the view of the court and that of the local authority diverge on a central element of the plan for the child's future welfare, previous authority holds that a process of mutual respect

and reconsideration should be undertaken with the expectation that, by the end of that process, sufficient common ground may be achieved to enable the court to make an order on the basis of a care plan that accords with an accepted view of the child's welfare needs. Where, however, an impasse remains, the court may have to choose between the 'lesser of two evils' or, where the circumstances merit it, contemplate formal challenge to the local authority's decision by judicial review.

…

[48] Firstly, the approach of a court to a potential impasse with a local authority on an important element in the care plan for a child has been well established for over 20 years. Insofar as there has been movement, it has been in the direction of emphasising the role of the court *during* proceedings (see Ryder LJ in *Re W*), but, in like manner to the approach taken by Peter Jackson LJ in *Re T* (with whom I agreed in that case), I consider that when, as here, the focus is upon the care plan after the proceedings are concluded, there is a need for mutual respect and engagement between the court and a local authority.

Re T (a child) [2018] EWCA Civ 650, [2018] 3 FCR 61, [39]–[44] (Peter Jackson LJ) *quotation limited to* [42]–[44]

[42] Although they touch upon the same subject, the decision of the Court of Appeal in *Re CH* (above) does not appear to have been cited in *Re W*. For my part, I would view the two decisions as seeking to make essentially the same point, though the tone in *Re W* is markedly more imperative. I particularly refer to the observations that it is not open to a local authority within proceedings to decline to accept the court's evaluation of risk [81] and that a local authority cannot refuse to provide lawful and reasonable services that would be necessary to support the court's decision [83]. I would agree with these propositions to the extent that the court's assessment of risk is sovereign *within proceedings* and that a local authority cannot refuse to provide a service if by doing so it would unlawfully breach the rights of the family concerned or if its decision-making process is unlawful on public law grounds. However, the family court cannot dictate to the local authority what its care plan is to be, any more than it can dictate to any other party what their case should be. What the court can, however, expect from a local authority is a high level of respect for its assessments of risk and welfare, leading in almost every case to those assessments being put into effect. For, as has been said before, any local authority that refused to act upon the court's assessments would face an obvious risk of its underlying decisions being declared to be unlawful through judicial review. That must particularly be so where decisions fail to take account of the court's assessments. Or where, as in this case, there is an impasse, there may have to be an appeal. But in the end, experience shows that the process of mutual respect spoken of by Thorpe LJ will almost inevitably lead to an acceptable outcome.

[43] It is clear from these decisions that the court has both a power and a duty to assert its view of risk and welfare by whatever is the most effective means. I cannot agree with the submission made on the behalf of the guardian – 'some judges might have pursued the matter further with the agency decision maker, but this judge cannot be said to have been wrong not to do so'. As Lord Justice McFarlane remarked during argument, that amounts to a lottery, depending upon the inclinations of one judge as against another. The obligation upon the court is not merely to make its assessment, but to see it through. That is a matter of principle, and not one of individual judicial inclination.

[44] The present case is somewhat more complicated than *Re CH* or *Re W*. Here, as Ms Fottrell notes, the judge's preferred plan was dependent upon a separate step being taken by the local authority within a different statutory framework. Without the grandmother being approved as a foster carer, it would not be lawful to place Alan with her under a care order. I therefore examine the law as it applies to the approval of connected persons as foster carers.

See also *Re S and W (children) (care proceedings: care plan)* [2007] EWCA Civ 232, [2007] 1 FCR 721, [34]–[35] (Wall LJ) addressing the same point

See also *Re S and D* [1995] 1 FCR 626 (CA), 634A–635C (Balcombe LJ) addressing the same point (identifying the 'lesser of two evils' choice)

9.4.8 The welfare stage: care planning: court dissatisfaction with final care plans: cogent reasons needed to force more draconian orders

Oxfordshire County Council v B [1998] 3 FCR 521 (FD), 525C–E (Hale J)

Following on from that preliminary point, s 31(5) of the 1989 Act does, of course, allow the court to make an order other than that for which the local authority ask. If the local authority ask for a supervision order, the court may make a care order: if the local authority ask for a care order, the court may make a supervision order. It is accepted, however, by the guardian ad litem that there must in general be cogent and strong reasons to force upon the local authority a more draconian order than that for which they have asked. I shall therefore look at this case in that light.

See also *Re T (a child) (care order)* [2009] EWCA Civ 121, [2009] 2 FCR 367, [64] (Sir Mark Potter P) considering *Oxfordshire CC v B* [1998] 3 FCR 521

9.4.9 The welfare stage: care planning: court dissatisfaction with final care plans: courts not bound by parties' agreements

Re T (a child) (care order) [2009] EWCA Civ 121, [2009] 2 FCR 367, [40]–[49] (Sir Mark Potter P)

Was the judge obliged to give effect to the parties' agreement?

[40] Mr Chisholm has submitted (and speaking for myself, I needed no persuasion) that, on being presented with a proposed agreed order of this

kind, the court retains a discretion, and indeed is under a duty, to consider the appropriateness of the order before approving the care plan put forward by the local authority. One only has to consider the requirement set out in s 1(1) of the 1989 Act that, when a court determines any question with respect to the upbringing of a child, the child's welfare shall be the court's paramount consideration, to appreciate that must be so. Furthermore, by s 1(5), where the court is considering whether or not to make one or more orders under the Act with respect to a child, it shall not make that order or any of the orders unless it considers that doing so would be better for the child than making no order at all. Accordingly the court is bound to submit to critical scrutiny the terms of any care plan or order proposed to it by way of a final disposal of care proceedings.

[41] In *Devon CC v S* [1992] 1 FCR 550, [1992] 3 All ER 793, the court was concerned with an appeal by a local authority against the decision of justices who, on an application to convert an interim care order into a full care order, the terms of which were agreed between all the parties concerned, had insisted on hearing oral evidence at length and, without prior warning, to the parties of their intention, made an order providing for contact which was substantially different from that which had been agreed. Thorpe LJ recognised ([1992] 1 FCR 550 at 553, [1992] 3 All ER 793 at 796) that:

> '… there is an overriding duty in the court to investigate the proposals advanced by the parties, even when those proposals are fully agreed'

but went on to state that:

> '… the profundity of that investigation must reflect the reality that there is consensus amongst the parties to the litigation, particularly when the parties include a public authority with statutory duties and a guardian ad litem on behalf of the child.'

[42] In *Hackney London BC v G* [1994] 2 FCR 216, sub nom *Re G (a minor) (care order: threshold conditions)* [1995] Fam 16, in relation to the duty of the court to satisfy itself that the existence of the threshold criteria for a s 31 order have been established, Wall LJ referred to the passage from *Devon CC v S* which I have just quoted and stated ([1994] 2 FCR 216 at 223, [1995] Fam 16 at 22):

> '… I respectfully agree with and adopt this sentence in Thorpe J's judgment. There is a plain and overriding duty in the court to investigate the material placed before it for the making of a care order under s 31. The court is no rubber stamp'.

[43] Wall LJ held that the nature of the investigation to be carried out by the court depended on the facts of the individual case. He made the further observation that, if the parties are agreed that a care order is appropriate and are agreed upon the factual substrata underlying the fulfilment of the threshold criteria, then the court's investigation may properly be limited to perusal of documentation and approval of an agreed order.

[44] There appears to be no reported case in which the court has made a care order despite the unanimous agreement of the parties to the making of a supervision order. The authorities directly concerned with the question whether or not, in given circumstances, a care order is to be preferred have all involved adjudication of opposing cases advanced by the parties. Nonetheless, it seems to me clear that, even when that is not so, the power in s 31(5) to make a care order on an application for a supervision order cannot be neutered by an agreement reached between the parties outside the court, particularly where, as here, the proceedings have originated in an application for a care order which has become 'diluted' by the time of the final hearing. The decision to end proceedings and to make the appropriate statutory order is and remains the responsibility of the court. Indeed, the duty of the court to treat the welfare of the child as the paramount consideration requires the court to make an appropriate judicial investigation. While it may well be proper, as observed by Wall J in *Hackney London BC v G*, to limit that investigation to perusal of the documentation where there is unanimity between the local authority the guardian and the parents upon the appropriate order, it may nonetheless be the case, by reason of the history of the proceedings and reservations which have developed in the judge's mind in relation to the conduct of the parties or the welfare of the child, that a more elaborate investigation, including the hearing of oral evidence, is appropriate.

[45] In different, but comparable, circumstances, where a judge is contemplating consensual withdrawal of proceedings:

> '... a court is [not] bound to allow the withdrawal of proceedings where all of the parties agree that that should occur. Family Proceedings Rules 1991, SI 1991/1247 r 4.5(4) expressly provides that a precondition of withdrawal is that the "the court thinks fit". There is thus a judicial discretion and it does not, therefore, follow as night follows day that the court's discretion of proceedings would end simply because the parties all agree that then proceeding should be withdrawn. The withdrawal provisions (and indeed the guardian system in public law itself) came into existence as a result of childcare tragedies in the 1970s and 1980s. The court's role in such matters is not to be that of a neutered rubber stamp for the parties' requests.'

See per McFarlane J in *A County Council v DP, RS, PS (by the Children's Guardian)* [2005] EWHC 1593 (Fam) at [19], [2005] 2 FLR 1031 at [19].

[46] Similarly, in private law proceedings, the President's *Practice Direction (residence and contact orders: domestic violence and harm)* [2008] 2 FCR 273 of 9 May 2008, which applies to any family proceedings in which an application is made for a residence order or contact order in respect of a child under the 1989 Act or the Adoption and Children Act 2002 or in which any question arises about residence or contact, provides ([2008] 2 FCR 273 at 274) that:

> '4 ... any proposed residence or contact order, whether to be made by agreement between the parties or otherwise must be scrutinised

by the court accordingly. The court shall not make a consent order for residence or contact or give permission for an application for a residence or contact order to be withdrawn, unless the parties are present in court, except where it is satisfied that there is no risk of harm to the child in so doing.'

[47] Finally, and in any event, s 31(5) of the 1989 Act provides that:

'The court may—

(a) on an application for a care order, make a supervision order;

(b) on an application for a supervision order, make a care order.'

[48] This provision expressly confers upon the judge discretion on an application for either type of order to refuse one and substitute the other. There is no suggestion that the court is fettered in its powers under this section by reason of any agreement which the parties may have reached as to which is the more appropriate. What is important when the court addresses this question whether or not to reflect the agreement of the parties in its order or to take some different course, is that the court should examine the background facts as well as the reasoning underlying the agreement and come to a measured conclusion, taking the relevant considerations into account. I would add that Human Rights considerations dictate that, when faced with a choice between the making of a care order and the less draconian provisions of a supervision order supported by the agreement of all the parties, the court should, so far as is consistent with the paramountcy of the child's welfare, favour the making of a supervision order, as the sufficient and proportionate response to any risk presented to the child, in preference to the protection afforded by a care order, given the potentially greater inroad into the parents' (and indeed the child's) rights to respect for their family and private life which the latter represents.

[49] Additionally, as a broad proposition, where the decision which the judge is disposed to make would result in rejecting the unanimous approach of the parties, it is important that the judge should justify with some precision the reasoning for taking his proposed course, involving as it will a departure from professional assessment and guidance, often from a number of sources, such as the guardian, council social workers and, in this case, an independent social worker.

CHAPTER 10

Care and supervision orders

Chapter contents

CHAPTER 10

Care and supervision orders

10.1 CARE AND SUPERVISION ORDERS: DESIGNATED LOCAL AUTHORITY

10.1.1 Care and supervision orders: designated LA[1]: correct interpretation

Re Y (a child) [2019] EWCA Civ 2209, [2020] 1 FCR 296, [34]–[36], [39]–[41] (King LJ)

Designation of local authorities

[34] Section 31(8) Children Act 1989 provides:

> '8. The local authority designated in a care order must be—
>
> (a) the authority within whose area the child is ordinarily resident; or
>
> (b) where the child does not reside in the area of a local authority, the authority within whose area any circumstances arose in consequence of which the order is being made.'

[35] The starting point for consideration as to which local authority should be designated is s 31(8)(a). If a child is found to be ordinarily resident in an area, then that is the end of the matter and the local authority in that area will be the designated authority. In *Re B (a child) (habitual residence: inherent jurisdiction)* [2016] UKSC 4, [2016] AC 606, [2016] 2 FCR 307, the Supreme Court said that the question to be posed is: 'in what place had Y achieved a degree of social and family integration at the time that the interim care order was granted'.

[36] The judge applying that criterion found that Y has no ordinary place of residence ([23]).

…

[39] In those circumstance, the court must turn to s 31(8)(b) and determine 'the authority within whose area any circumstances arose in consequence of which the order is being made'. In *Northampton CC v Islington Council* [2001] Fam 364, [1999] 3 FCR 385 (*Northampton*), Thorpe LJ reviewed the various conflicting authorities in relation to the interpretation of s 31(8)(b). He said:

1 Local authority.

'I am convinced that section 31(8) was never intended to be a gateway to extensive judicial investigation of a number of relevant facts and circumstances as the prelude to the exercise of some discretionary choice. It was surely intended to be a simple test to enable the court to make a rapid designation of the authority upon which is to fall the administrative, professional and financial responsibility for implementing the care order and the care plan. Where the child has connections with more than one area ordinary residence determines on the basis that almost every child will have an ordinary residence, if not a presence, in some local authority area. In the rare case where a child lacks an ordinary residence in a local authority area the court designates the area in which occurred the events that carried the application over the section 31 threshold.'

'The circumstances to which the judge should have regard are the primary circumstances that carry the case over the section 31 threshold. That may be a positive act or series of acts, such as sexual or physical abuse. If there has been extensive abuse there will usually be an ultimate or an outstanding episode that triggered local authority intervention. The judge will have no difficulty in locating that event. In other cases the foundation for the care order may be negative conduct such as neglect, consistently poor parenting or a failure to provide emotional support. Even in chronic cases without any acute episode it will usually be simple enough for the judge to discern the place or, if more than one, the principal place at which the failure occurred. In my opinion the judge's function is to carry out a rapid and not over sophisticated review of the history to make a purely factual determination. It is a question of fact and not of discretion.'

[40] More recently, in *Re D (a child)* [2012] EWCA Civ 627, [2013] Fam 34, [2012] 2 FCR 153 Ward LJ said:

'[19] If one asks which local authority is to bear the burden of responsibility for implementing the care order and care plan, it seems to me that the answer is fairly obvious. For the s 31 threshold to be crossed the child must be suffering, or be likely to suffer, significant harm at the time the local authority initiated the procedure for the protection of the child concerned. Where the child is ordinarily living, or where the relevant threshold events take place, is the relevant locus which provides the best identification of a practical, temporal and physical connection between local authority and child. The burden of the eventual responsibility for implementing the care order should then fall on the local authority having that connection. The designation of the appropriate local authority under s 31(8) seeks to do just that.

[20] As I see it, ss 31(8)(a) and (b) are in harmony. Take s 31(8)(b) first. When the child – and this must mean the child who is the subject of the care order – does not reside (perhaps does not *ordinarily* reside per Northamptonshire CC) in the area of a local authority, the

authority to be designated in the order is the authority within whose area any circumstance arose in consequence of which the order is being made. The temporal focus is on the time leading up to the issue of the proceedings. The factual focus is on the primary circumstances that carry the case over the section 31 threshold. The local authority where these events happen has the responsibility to take action and should be charged with the responsibility of providing the care that follows.'

[41] Since *Northamptonshire* and *Re D (a child)*, where there has been a dispute between two local authorities as to which is to be the designated local authority, the 'circumstances (which) arose in consequence of which the order is being made' under CA 1989, s 31(8)(b) has been informed by reference to 'the primary circumstances that carry the case over the s 31 threshold'. Although perhaps more apposite on the facts of this case would be, also per Thorpe LJ, a consideration of the 'ultimate or an outstanding episode that triggered local authority intervention'.

Northamptonshire County Council v Islington London Borough Council [1999] 3 FCR 385 (CA), 393B–397B (Thorpe LJ) *quotation limited to* 393B–D, 393F–397B

... However I conclude that this case does require a decision on the following difficult issues.

(a) What is the proper construction of paras (a) and (b) of s 31(8) in conjunction? Is it legitimate to construe the opening phrase of para (b) as though it read 'where the child does not ordinarily reside ...'?

(b) What is the proper construction of the disregard section? Is the judgment of Wilson J to be preferred to that of Bracewell J?

(c) Where the case falls for decision under s 31(8)(b) what is the ambit of the judicial task? Has the judge the wide discretion which emerges from the decisions in the reported cases?

...

Let me begin with the proper construction of s 38(8)(b). Wilson J demonstrated why he concluded that Parliament did not mean what it appeared to have said. Unless the court inserted the word 'ordinarily' into the first phrase of s 31(8)(b) there would be cases in which the child in question fell into neither para (a) nor para (b). As he put it ([1996] 3 FCR 582 at 586, [1996] Fam 55 at 59):

'Take L himself. He is ordinarily resident nowhere. But is he resident in the area of a local authority? The disregard provided in s. 105(6) has no bearing upon this question because it relates only to ordinary residence. Incarceration does not preclude simple "residence" – indeed it secures it – and counsel do not seek to dissuade me from the view that L must be taken for the time being to be resident in the area of Birmingham City Council, where he has lived in a secure unit for almost four months.'

I agree with this logic and sympathise with the attempt to find a legitimate construction to avoid that result. But is the solution adopted by Wilson J legitimate? He first acknowledged the contrary view of Singer J expressed in *Re R (care proceedings: jurisdiction)* [1995] 3 FCR 305. He then gave three reasons for his conclusion that the omission of the word 'ordinarily' from para (b) was a Parliamentary slip. His first was drawn from the genesis of the subsection. Its legislative predecessor was s 20(2) of the Children and Young Persons Act 1969 which, in very similar language expressed the test for designation but the residence in both paras (a) and (b) was expressed to be habitual. Then cl 12(10) of the draft 'Children Bill' annexed to the Law Commission report *Family Law: Review of Child Law, Guardianship and Custody* (Law Com no 172) had 'reside' without adjectival qualification in both paras (a) and (b). In relation to this genesis he said ([1996] 3 FCR 582 at 588, [1996] Fam 55 at 61):

> 'The draft bill did not define or qualify the references to residence. It seems clear to me that, when Parliament resolved to bring the provision into line with the previous law, it inserted "ordinarily" into para. (a) but forgot to do so into para. (b).'

He then turned to s 37(5) of the 1989 Act where, as in s 31(8), in para (a) the draftsman wrote 'ordinarily resident' but in para (b) wrote 'reside'. However s 116 of the Courts and Legal Services Act 1990 amended s 37(5) to write 'ordinarily' equally into para (b). Of that Wilson J said ([1996] 3 FCR 582 at 588, [1996] Fam 55 at 61):

> 'Mr. Clough contends that it is inconceivable that, in correcting a perceived error in s.37(5), Parliament would have accidentally failed to make any necessary correction of the analogous s.31(8). I disagree …'

Having considered authorities warning judges against reading words into an Act of Parliament he concluded ([1996] 3 FCR at 588–589, [1996] Fam 55 at 62):

> 'Nevertheless for the reasons already given, I am of the firm opinion that Parliament's omission of the word "ordinarily" in s. 31(8)(b) is not only accidental but inflicts a heavy defeat upon the intention of the 1989 Act by removing children resident but not ordinarily resident in the area of an authority from what purport to be and are intended to be comprehensive provisions for the making and designation of care orders.'

This court has carried out some research into the genesis of s 31(8) and also into the subsequent amendment of s 37(5) without unearthing anything of relevance to the dilemma.

So in the end it seems to me that the principal justification for the judicial rewriting of s 31(8)(b) is to ensure that it provides a mechanism for designation in all and not just the vast majority of cases. That is a powerful consideration. Although I am doubtful of the reasoning of Wilson J I agree with him that s 31(8) must be construed to provide a test for all cases and I cannot at the moment see a better solution than that which he devised.

Turning to the second question, the attraction of the construction favoured by Bracewell J is its simplicity. The ordinary residence immediately preceding the commencement of the period of disregard is deemed to continue uninterrupted. The court is relieved from what may be a contentious and disputed investigation of what other circumstances have changed within the period of disregard. Any construction of s 105(6) can be said to produce anomalous results. We should not be over impressed by anomaly arguments where the court's function is simply to determine which authority are to be designated in the care order. I am convinced that s 31(8) was never intended to be a gateway to extensive judicial investigation of a number of relevant facts and circumstances as the prelude to the exercise of some discretionary choice. It was surely intended to be a simple test to enable the court to make a rapid designation of the authority upon which is to fall the administrative, professional and financial responsibility for implementing the care order and the care plan. Where the child has connections with more than one area ordinary residence determines on the basis that almost every child will have an ordinary residence, if not a presence, in some local authority area. In the rare case where a child lacks an ordinary residence in a local authority area the court designates the area in which occurred the events that carried the application over the s 31 threshold.

On that approach I lean towards Bracewell J's inclination to hold that the area of ordinary residence immediately prior to the commencement of the stay to be disregarded should be notionally extended throughout that stay. I would not say that developments affecting the family during the period to be disregarded cannot in any case be considered. But I would say that such cases should be exceptional.

I turn now to the third question. The Family Division judges have construed para (b) to vest in them a broad discretion to designate any local authority area that might loosely be said to be in the frame. Wilson J in *Gateshead* put it thus ([1996] 3 FCR 582 at 589, [1996] Fam 55 at 62):

> 'L does not ordinarily reside in the area of an authority and so I must designate the authority "within whose area any circumstances arose in consequence of which the order is being made". The words "any circumstances arose" are very wide. Parliament might have chosen narrower words, such as "the circumstances substantially arose", which would often have given rise to a difficult inquiry. As they stand, the words

seem to me to recognize that the circumstances which cause a care order to be made in respect of a child of L's age will often be multifarious and will have arisen at numerous different stages of his life. I consider that, in principle, where para. (b) applies, more than one local authority may well qualify for designation and that in that event the court can choose which to designate.'

Mr Munby QC in *Re P (a minor) (care order: designated local authority)* [1998] 1 FCR 653 accepted the approach of Wilson J and indeed extended the field of choice when he said (at 676–677):

'The "circumstances … in consequence of which" a care order is made, as those words are used in s 31(8)(b), are not confined to, though they will always include, the circumstances of that period of the child's own life which is relevant to the "threshold" inquiry under s 31(2) and circumstances in the child's life which "arose" in the places where he lived during that period. In an appropriate case, the "circumstances … in consequence of which" a care order is made will include any circumstances, whenever and wherever they arose, whether before or after the child was born and whether or not arising in any place at which the child has ever lived, which go to the inability of the child's parent to give him that quality of care which is referred to in s 31(2)(b)(i). Furthermore, the "circumstances … in consequence of which" a care order is made will embrace the actions of any local authority, not otherwise brought within the ambit of s 31(8)(b), which itself institutes or carries on care proceedings or which becomes in some other way sufficiently involved in care proceedings for it properly to be said that a care order has been made, wholly or in part, "in consequence of" the actions of that authority.'

I have reached the conclusion that this liberality only invites unnecessarily extensive issues. The more multifarious the circumstances, the more local authorities there will be in the frame with the opportunity for, and likelihood of, unnecessary contests. The circumstances to which the judge should have regard are the primary circumstances that carry the case over the s 31 threshold. That may be a positive act or series of acts, such as sexual or physical abuse. If there has been extensive abuse there will usually be an ultimate or an outstanding episode that triggered local authority intervention. The judge will have no difficulty in locating that event. In other cases the foundation for the care order may be negative conduct such as neglect, consistently poor parenting or a failure to provide emotional support. Even in chronic cases without any acute episode it will usually be simple enough for the judge to discern the place or, if more than one, the principal place at which the failure occurred. In my opinion the judge's function is to carry out a rapid and not over sophisticated review of the history to make a purely factual determination. It is a question of fact and not of discretion.

In summary my view of these three interacting subsections is that they should be given that construction that achieves the result for which I conclude they were designed: that is a simple mechanism to determine the question of administration. If that involves a degree of artificiality and the import of legal fiction any misgivings can be met by recognising the limited purpose and effect of the court's function. After all it must be assumed that all local authorities are equally competent, professional and committed in the discharge of responsibilities cast upon them by the making of a care order.

Over the course of years the swings and roundabouts principle is likely to even out any seeming disadvantage to an individual authority by designation in a particular case. These subsections are not about child protection or the promotion of child welfare. They are to be read as a simple test, to be operated by the court in what should be the unlikely event of dispute, to determine which local authority are to be responsible for the care plan and its implementation.

See also *Re D (a child) (care order: designated local authority)* [2012] EWCA Civ 627, [2012] 2 FCR 153, [18]–[23] (Ward LJ) considering *Northamptonshire County Council v Islington London Borough Council* [1999] 3 FCR 385

See also *Re B (a child) (designated local authority)* [2020] EWCA Civ 1673, [2021] 1 FCR 633, [11], [79] (King LJ) addressing a related point (emphasising that the process should be 'rapid and not over sophisticated')

See also *Re Y (a child)* [2019] EWCA Civ 2209, [2020] 1 FCR 296, [57]–[61] (King LJ) addressing a related point (the application of the test to circumstances where threshold would have been crossed for a period of time)

10.1.2 Care and supervision orders: designated LA: the ordinary residence of newborns

C v Plymouth City Council [2000] 2 FCR 289, [23] (Thorpe LJ)

23. But assuming for the purposes of this judgment that Mr Tyzack is right in that submission, it seems to me that it was plainly open to the judge to deal with the issue in the sensible way that he did, by holding that a newborn babe is incapable of ordinary residence apart from the mother from whose body the baby has been so recently severed. In relation to a newborn baby, the ordinary residence necessarily has to be dependent on the residence of the mother. I would, for my part, uphold the judgment without the slightest hesitation in that primary conclusion.

Re S (a child) [2017] EWCA Civ 2695, [21]–[50] (King LJ) *quotation limited to* [43]–[45], [49]–[50]

43. What is clear from *A v A*, at both the Court of Appeal and Supreme Court level and in the European jurisprudence, is that, in order to establish

habitual residence, there will be an expectation that the child will have been present in the area where it is suggested that he, or she, is habitually resident.

44. In my judgement, the requirement of physical presence must equally apply to a determination of ordinary residence. The majority of the Court of Appeal in *A v A* was robust in suggesting that presence may be an absolute requirement. The Supreme Court do not specifically deal with the issue, but favour "presence". The Advocate General in *OL v OP* addressed the matter head-on, as already quoted at paragraph [81], although the Advocate General regarded it as "not inconceivable that there may be wholly exceptional circumstances in which physical presence will not be necessary".

45. In my judgment, it is not necessary for this court to express an opinion as to whether there may be, as the Advocate General suggests, exceptional circumstances which will mean that physical presence is not required, or whether physical presence is an absolute, essential ingredient of ordinary residence. In my judgment, whichever approach is applied, LL was not ordinarily resident in the County Council area. On the more draconian (Court of Appeal) interpretation, it brooks no argument as LL has never been present in the County Council area. If there is scope for an exception to that requirement then, in my judgment, there are no exceptional circumstances which would render physical presence unnecessary on the facts of the present case. LL was not only never present at the place of the mother's ordinary residence but he had never lived with her mother; he was the subject of an interim care order with a care plan, the effect of which was that they would never actually live together.

…

49. In my judgment, this is one of those rare cases where a child has no ordinary residence. In the light of the majority view of the Supreme Court in *A v A* and confirmed by the European Court, presence, in my view, is a requisite before the child can acquire ordinary residence in a specified area. If I am wrong and presence is not an essential ingredient in order for ordinary residence to be established, I am nevertheless of the view that where circumstances arise where there has not only been no presence, but also that the baby in question has never lived with the parent through whom ordinary residence is asserted, that cannot be a basis upon which to make a finding that that baby's ordinary residence follows that of his or her mother's.

50. It follows that, in my view, the judge was wrong to conclude that the County Council should be the designated local authority. This case is one of those rare cases where the child in question, having been removed from his parents at birth, has no ordinary residence either in his or her own right, or by way of deemed ordinary residence by reference to his or her primary carer. The court must, therefore, determine the designated local

authority by reference to s.31(8)(b). It was accepted by all parties that, in those circumstances, the designated local authority would be the City Council.

10.1.3 Care and supervision orders: designated LA: procedure: agreed chronologies if disputed

Re B (a child) (designated local authority) [2020] EWCA Civ 1673, [2021] 1 FCR 633, [11]–[15] (King LJ) *quotation limited to* [13]–[15]

[13] The judge should have had the benefit of a single, agreed, objective chronology to work from, supported by statements addressing the test where appropriate. The history in this case was unusually complicated and it was clear that the decision as to designation would turn on the application of the disregard provision. In those circumstances it would have been prudent, once each of the local authorities had had an opportunity to consider each other's case notes, for they or their representatives to make a concerted attempt to agree a chronology, or failing that, to produce a single chronology highlighting areas of disagreement where relevant. Instead the court was presented with three separate chronologies. These chronologies most closely resemble a pick-and-mix of facts and opinion seemingly designed solely to assist the case of the party producing the document. Chronologies should not be interwoven with opinion, nor should it be the judge's job to cross-check them in order to establish what is, and what is not, agreed by the parties.

[14] This judge was put in an impossible position in trying to tease out the true course of events. By way of example only: the manner of J's movement from the father to the home of DB in February 2019 was a critical issue in determining whether, on the one hand, J was accommodated by Lincolnshire or, on the other, the move was a private fostering or private family arrangement as between the father and DB which had been merely facilitated by Lincolnshire. The chronologies filed by Salford and Lincolnshire contradicted each other as to who it was that made arrangements for J to move to DB's care, meaning that it became necessary for the court to go to the source material.

[15] I am only too aware of the pressure under which local authorities work. However, when chronologies like these are produced, judicial time is wasted in trying to discern precisely the facts from which the court should work. I would remind all parties that chronologies must be concise, non-partisan and purely factual. Whilst the judge reserved judgment precisely because of the volume of paper he had been given, he cannot have been expected to have read and cross referenced all the material, and in my judgment it is little wonder that errors crept in. It is just unfortunate that one, namely Lincolnshire's state of knowledge when J moved from the home of DB to that of her mother, was a matter of considerable significance.

10.2 CARE AND SUPERVISION ORDERS: CARE ORDERS

10.2.1 Care and supervision orders: care orders: placement with parents[2]

Re T (a minor) (care order) [1994] 1 FCR 663 (CA), 665G–H (Bracewell J)

> The Children Act 1989 has not, in my judgment, altered the previous law as set out in *M v Westminster City Council* [1985] FLR 325. In that case the Court of Appeal did not consider it wrong in law to make a care order where the local authority intended to leave the child in the day-to-day care of the parents. Nor in that case were the justices to be criticized for deciding in the exercise of their discretion to make a care order rather than a supervision order. The making of any order under the 1989 Act and in accordance with s 1 of that Act is an exercise by the court of its judicial discretion …

10.2.2 Care and supervision orders: care orders: placement with parents: care or supervision

Re O (a child) (supervision order: future harm) [2001] EWCA Civ 16, [2001] 1 FCR 289, [23]–[26] (Hale LJ)

[23] The point, therefore, must be the need for compulsion. Nobody should be in any doubt that a supervision order is compulsory. The parents' failure to co-operate is very cogent evidence indeed that something more stringent may be needed, or, at the very least, that there is a continuing risk of harm to the child.

[24] A care order is, however, very different from a supervision order. There are three main points. First, it gives a local authority power to remove the child without recourse even to a family proceedings court for an emergency protection order. The parents' only means of challenging that removal is by an application to discharge the care order, which usually takes some time to be heard, especially if, as in this case, it would have to be transferred to a higher court. Given the judge's findings as to the nature of risk, the slowness of any deterioration, the level of protection available from other sources including the father, it is very difficult to say that the local authority need to have this power. The care plan itself, as I have already indicated, does not suggest that they do.

[25] Secondly, it gives the local authority parental responsibility for the child coupled with the power to control the parents' exercise of that

2 Authorities concerning the principle of placing children at home with parents under a care order need to be considered in light of the *President's Public Law Working Group Report* (March, 2021), which identifies several possible concerns regarding placement at home with parents under care orders [158]–[162]. The report is not law but was endorsed by the President of the Family Division, Sir Andrew McFarlane. Available at www.judiciary.uk/publications/message-from-the-president-of-the-family-division-publication-of-the-presidents-public-law-working-group-report/, accessed 20 December 2021.

responsibility. Again, the care plan does not suggest that the local authority wish to exercise parental responsibility or control the parents' exercise of it. It expressly states, for example, 'that A's social, moral and academic education will be the responsibility of his parents'. Under 'Health' it points out that he 'continues to be in good health and he will need to receive the usual check-ups and vaccinations via the local health visitor and GP service'. This is not indicative of the suggestion that the local authority need to be in a position to arrange that for him. In any event, that could be done by inserting appropriate requirements in the supervision order.

[26] The third difference is one of timing. Mr Forbes in particular has argued that it might be difficult to achieve a further order in three years' time, but of course that difficulty would only arise if by then the risk of harm had disappeared or almost disappeared, or the need for an order had disappeared or almost disappeared. If that were not the case, the local authority would have to investigate and take any action which was thought appropriate to protect the child.

See also *Re S (J) (a minor) (care or supervision order)* [1993] 2 FCR 193 (FD), 223B–E, 226D–E (HHJ Coningsby QC sitting as a High Court judge) addressing the same point

See also *Re O (care or supervision order)* [1997] 2 FCR 17 (FD), 22C–23H (Hale J) addressing the same point

10.2.3 Care and supervision orders: care orders: placement with parents: LA subsequent removal from parents

Re E (a child) (care order: change of care plan) [2014] EWFC 6, [2015] 3 FCR 622, [28]–[50] (Baker J) *quotation limited to* [34]–[36], [48]–[51]

[34] To my mind, where a care order has been granted on the basis of a care plan providing that the child should remain at home, a local authority considering changing the plan and removing the child permanently from the family is obliged in law to follow the same approach. It must have regard to the fact that permanent placement outside the family is to be preferred only as a last resort where nothing else will do. Before making its decision, it must rigorously analyse all the realistic options, considering the arguments for and against each option. This is an essential process, not only as a matter of good practice, but also because the local authority will inevitably have to demonstrate its analysis in any court proceedings that follow the change of care plan, either on an application for the discharge of the care order or an application for placement order under the Adoption and Children Act 2002. This process of rigorous analysis of all realistic options should be an essential feature of all long-term planning for children. And, as indicated by Munby J in *Re G*, the local authority must fully involve the parents in its decision-making process.

[35] While this process is being carried out, the child should remain at home under the care order, unless his safety and welfare requires that he be removed immediately. This is the appropriate test when deciding whether the child should be removed under an interim care order, pending determination of an application under s 31 of the Children Act: *Re LA (Care: Chronic Neglect)* [2009] EWCA Civ 822, [2010] 1 FLR 80. The same test should also apply when a local authority's decision to remove a child placed at home under a care order has led to an application by the parents to discharge the order and the court has to decide whether the child should be removed pending determination of the discharge application. As set out above, under s 33(4) of the 1989 Act, the local authority may not exercise its powers under a care order to determine how a parent may exercise his or her parental responsibility for the child unless satisfied it is necessary to do so to safeguard or promote the child's welfare. For a local authority to remove a child in circumstances where its welfare did not require it would be manifestly unlawful and an unjustifiable interference with the family's art 8 rights.

[36] In submissions before the district judge, and before this court, it was argued on behalf of the local authority that its removal of D from the family home was lawful simply by reason of the care order. That submission is fundamentally misconceived. The local authority's removal of the child would only be lawful if necessary to safeguard or promote his welfare. Any other removal, or threatened removal, of the child is prima facie unlawful and an interference of the art 8 rights of the parents and child. In such circumstances, the parents are entitled to seek an injunction under s 8 of the HRA.

...

General observations and guidance

[48] On behalf of the local authority, Miss Griffiths, who did not appear before the district judge, informed the court that, as a result of the reduction in the time taken to complete care proceedings under the family justice reforms, there has been an increase in the numbers of care cases being concluded with a final care order on the basis of the child remaining at home. If so, there will inevitably be an increase in the number of cases where the local authority concludes that a child should subsequently be removed.

[49] To avoid the problems that have arisen in this case, the following measures should be taken in future cases.

(1) In every case where a care order is made on the basis of a care plan providing that a child should live at home with his or her parents, it should be a term of the care plan, and a recital in the care order, that the local authority agrees to give not less than 14 days' notice of a removal of the child, save in an emergency. I consider that 14 days is an appropriate period, on the one hand to avoid unnecessary delay

but, on the other hand, to allow the parents an opportunity to obtain legal advice.

(2) Where a care order has been granted on the basis of a care plan providing that the child should remain at home, a local authority considering changing the plan and removing the child permanently from the family must have regard to the fact that permanent placement outside the family is to be preferred only as a last resort where nothing else will do and must rigorously analyse all the realistic options, considering the arguments for and against each option. Furthermore, it must involve the parents properly in the decision-making process.

(3) In every case where a parent decides to apply to discharge a care order in circumstances where the local authority has given notice of intention to remove a child placed at home under a care order, the parent should consider whether to apply in addition for an injunction under s 8 of the HRA to prevent the local authority from removing the child pending the determination of the discharge application. If the parent decides to apply for an injunction, that application should be issued at the same time as the discharge application.

(4) When a local authority, having given notice of its intention to remove a child placed at home under a care order, is given notice of an application for discharge of the care, the local authority must consider whether the child's welfare requires his immediate removal. Furthermore, the authority must keep a written record demonstrating that it has considered this question and recording the reasons for its decision. In reaching its decision on this point, the local authority must again inter alia consult with the parents. Any removal of a child in circumstances where the child's welfare does not require immediate removal, or without proper consideration and consultation, is likely to be an unlawful interference with the art 8 rights of the parent and child.

(5) On receipt of an application to discharge a care order, where the child has been living at home, the allocation gatekeeper at the designated family centre should check whether it is accompanied by an application under s 8 HRA and, if not, whether the circumstances might give rise to such an application. This check is needed because, as discussed below, automatic legal aid is not at present available for such applications to discharge a care order, and it is therefore likely that such applications may be made by parents acting in person. In cases where the discharge application is accompanied by an application for an order under s 8 HRA, or the allocation gatekeeper considers that the circumstances might give rise to such an application, he or she should allocate the case as soon as possible to a circuit judge for case management. Any application for an injunction in these circumstances must be listed for an early hearing.

(6) On hearing an application for an injunction under s 8 HRA to restrain a local authority removing a child living at home under a care order

pending determination of an application to discharge the care order, the court should normally grant the injunction unless the child's welfare requires his immediate removal from the family home.

[50] The guidance set out in the preceding paragraph has been seen and approved by the President of the Family Division.

[51] Finally, this case has highlighted a further major problem. These parents face the prospect of losing their son permanently. If this prospect had arisen in the context of care proceedings, they would be entitled as of right to non-means tested legal aid. It is difficult to see why similar automatic public funding should not be available where the local authority proposes the removal of a child living at home under a care order and the parents apply to discharge that order and for an interim injunction under s 8 HRA. The justification for automatic public funding in care proceedings is the draconian nature of the order being claimed by the local authority. Where a local authority seeks to remove a child placed at home under a care order, the outcome of the discharge application may be equally draconian. Because this father is working, and earns a very low wage from which he has contributed to the support of his family, he, and possibly the mother, are disqualified from legal aid. Miss Fottrell and Miss Sprinz and their solicitors are at present acting pro bono. It is unfair that legal representation in these vital cases is only available if the lawyers agree to work for nothing.

See also *Re S (a child)* [2018] EWCA Civ 2512, [33]–[41], [49]–[52], [65] (King LJ) providing an overview of the law on this point

See also *Re E (a child) (care order: change of care plan)* [2014] EWFC 6, [2015] 3 FCR 622, [10]–[11], [37]–[41], [49]–[51] (Baker J) addressing a related point (the remedies available to parents are applications for discharge of care orders, and also HRA[3] injunctions)

See also *Re G (children)* [2019] EWCA Civ 1779, [2020] 1 FLR 391, [20]–[23] (Baker LJ) considering *Re E (a child) (care order: change of care plan)* [2014] EWFC 6, [2015] 3 FCR 622, addressing a related point (the remedy of HRA injunctions)

10.2.4 Care and supervision orders: care orders: placement with wider family: coming forwards at the earliest opportunity

Re G and B (children) [2007] EWCA Civ 358, [2007] 2 FLR 140, [42] (Wall LJ)

42. The moral of the case, yet again, is that the available options for a child should be teased out as early as possible, and if a family member wishes to be considered to care for a child, he or she should come forward at the earliest possible opportunity. Translated into the facts of this case, Ms B should have come forward after the death of Mr G. There would have been time to assess her between August and October. By the end of

3 Human Rights Act 1998.

October/early November it was, in my judgment (and here I agree with the judge) too late, and the judge was entitled to say so, particularly since there was objective evidence before him pointing to Ms B's unsuitability.

10.2.5 Care and supervision orders: care orders: long-term foster care or adoption

Re V (children) (long-term fostering versus adoption) [2013] EWCA Civ 913, [2013] 3 FCR 407, [95]–[96] (Black LJ)

[95] Also entering the picture is C's view. The judge thought she may have been given a rosy tinted view of adoption and not told that long-term fostering could provide the same security. My difficulty with that is that I do not think that fostering and adoption can, in fact, be equated in terms of what they offer by way of security. I do not intend to embark on a comprehensive comparison of the two arrangements, merely to highlight some of the material differences. What I say should not be taken as a substitute for professional advice to the court from social services and/or the guardian in any case in which this is a significant issue.

[96] With that caveat, I make the following observations:

(i) Adoption makes the child a permanent part of the adoptive family to which he or she fully belongs. To the child, it is likely therefore to 'feel' different from fostering. Adoptions do, of course, fail but the commitment of the adoptive family is of a different nature to that of a local authority foster carer whose circumstances may change, however devoted he or she is, and who is free to determine the caring arrangement.

(ii) Whereas the parents may apply for the discharge of a care order with a view to getting the child back to live with them, once an adoption order is made, it is made for all time.

(iii) Contact in the adoption context is also a different matter from contact in the context of a fostering arrangement. Where a child is in the care of a local authority, the starting point is that the authority is obliged to allow the child reasonable contact with his parents (s 34(1) of the Children Act 1989). The contact position can, of course, be regulated by alternative orders under s 34 but the situation still contrasts markedly with that of an adoptive child. There are open adoptions, where the child sees his or her natural parents, but I think it would be fair to say that such arrangements tend not to be seen where the adoptive parents are not in full agreement. Once the adoption order has been made, the natural parents normally need leave before they can apply for contact.

(iv) Routine life is different for the adopted child in that once he or she is adopted, the local authority have no further role in his or her life (no local authority medicals, no local authority reviews, no need to consult the social worker over school trips abroad, for example).

10.2.6 Care and supervision orders: care orders: adoption cases

See Chapter 9.1 The welfare stage: the court's approach

See Chapter 9.3.2 The welfare stage: the welfare checklists: approach to the checklists: adoption cases

10.2.7 Care and supervision orders: care orders: effect of care orders: appropriate exercise of PR[4]

Re G (children) [2003] EWHC 551 (Fam), [2003] 2 FLR 42, [43]–[45] (Munby J)

43. The fact that a local authority has parental responsibility for children pursuant to section 33(3)(a) of the Children Act 1989 does not entitle it to take decisions about those children without reference to, or over the heads of, the children's parents. A local authority, even if clothed with the authority of a care order, is not entitled to make significant changes in the care plan, or to change the arrangements under which the children are living, let alone to remove the children from home if they are living with their parents, without properly involving the parents in the decision-making process and without giving the parents a proper opportunity to make their case before a decision is made. After all, the fact that the local authority also has parental responsibility does not deprive the parents of their parental responsibility.

44. A local authority can lawfully exercise parental responsibility for a child only in a manner consistent with the substantive *and procedural* requirements of article 8. There is nothing in section 33(3)(b) of the Act that entitles a local authority to act in breach of article 8. On the contrary, section 6(1) of the 1998 Act requires a local authority to exercise its powers under both section 33(3)(a) and section 33(3)(b) of the 1989 Act in a manner consistent with both the substantive and the procedural requirements of article 8.

45. In a case such as this, a local authority, before it can properly arrive at a decision to remove children from their parents, *must* tell the parents (preferably in writing) precisely what it is proposing to do. It *must* spell out (again in writing) the reasons why it is proposing to do so. It *must* spell out precisely (in writing) the factual matters it is relying on. It *must* give the parents a proper opportunity to answer (either orally and/or in writing as the parents wish) the allegations being made against them. And it *must* give the parents a proper opportunity (orally and/or in writing as they wish) to make representations as to why the local authority should not take the threatened steps. In short, the local authority *must* involve the parents properly in the decision-making process. In particular the parents (together with their representatives if they wish to be assisted) should normally be given the opportunity to attend at, and address, any critical meeting at which crucial decisions are to be made.

4 Parental responsibility.

10.2.8 Care and supervision orders: care orders: effect of care orders: limits on LA PR

Re Y *(children in care: change of nationality)* [2020] EWCA Civ 1038, [2020] 3 FCR 292, [11]–[13] (Peter Jackson LJ)

The parental responsibility of the local authority

[11] Parental responsibility means all the rights, duties, powers, responsibilities and authority which by law a parent of a child has in relation to the child and his property: CA 1989, s 3(1).

[12] The effect of a care order is prescribed by s 33 CA 1989 …

[13] On a literal reading, this provision would allow a local authority to make profound and irreversible decisions about a child, up to and including consenting to the withdrawal of life-sustaining medical treatment. This court has however held that, for the protection of the rights of children and of other holders of parental responsibility, certain decisions are of such magnitude that they should not be determined by a local authority without all those with parental responsibility having an opportunity to express their view to a court if necessary as part of the decision-making process. It held that the use of statutory powers in such cases would be a disproportionate interference with the rights of family members. In the recent decision of *Re H (a child) (parental responsibility: vaccination)* [2020] EWCA Civ 664, [2020] 2 FCR 683, Lady Justice King put the matter in this way:

> '[26] On a strict reading of s 33(3)(b), and subject only to the exceptions already highlighted, the extent to which a local authority may exercise its parental responsibility is unlimited, provided that it is acting in order to safeguard or promote the welfare of the child in its care.
>
> [27] However, whilst that may be the case when considering the section in isolation, local authorities and the courts have for many years been acutely aware that some decisions are of such magnitude that it would be wrong for a local authority to use its power under s 33(3)(b) to override the wishes or views of a parent. Such decisions have chiefly related to serious medical treatment, although in *Re C (Children)* [2016] EWCA Civ 374, [2017] Fam 137, [2016] 3 WLR 1557 (*Re C*), the issue related to a local authority's desire to override a mother's choice of forename for her children. The category of such cases is not closed, but they will chiefly concern decisions with profound or enduring consequences for the child.'

10.2.9 Care and supervision orders: care orders: effect of care orders: LAs exercising PR: medical treatment

Re H *(a child) (parental responsibility: vaccination)* [2020] EWCA Civ 664, [2020] 2 FCR 683, [24]–[30], [57]–[68] (King LJ) *quotation limited to* [24]–[30]

[24] T is in the care of the local authority. The local authority has parental responsibility for him by virtue of s 33(3)(a) and accordingly the power

under ss (3)(b) to 'determine the extent to which the parent may meet his parental responsibility'. Whilst the local authority can 'overrule' a parent's view in relation to decisions in respect of the child, there are a number of safeguards are in place, namely:

(i) By s 22(3)(a), the exercise by the local authority of its parental responsibility under s 33 is subject to its general duty in relation to a child who it is looking after, namely to 'safeguard and promote his welfare'.
(ii) By s 22(4), before making any decision with respect to a looked-after child, the local authority must, so far as is reasonably practicable, ascertain the wishes and feelings of the child and his parents regarding the matter to be decided.
(iii) By s 33(4), the local authority may not exercise its overriding parental responsibility unless it is satisfied that it is necessary to do so in order to safeguard or promote the child's welfare.
(iv) By s 33(6)–(8), the local authority may not change a child's religion, agree to his adoption, appoint a guardian for him, change his surname without written agreement or (without going through prescribed procedures) remove him from the United Kingdom for more than a month without written agreement.

[25] It should be noted that s 33 applies equally to interim care orders as it does to final care orders: s 31(11). The approach to vaccination does not depend upon whether a child is subject to an interim care order or a final care order. Many children who are subject to interim care orders are of an age where they would be expected to be vaccinated.

[26] On a strict reading of s 33(3)(b), and subject only to the exceptions already highlighted, the extent to which a local authority may exercise its parental responsibility is unlimited, provided that it is acting in order to safeguard or promote the welfare of the child in its care.

[27] However, whilst that may be the case when considering the section in isolation, local authorities and the courts have for many years been acutely aware that some decisions are of such magnitude that it would be wrong for a local authority to use its power under s 33(3)(b) to override the wishes or views of a parent. Such decisions have chiefly related to serious medical treatment, although in *Re C (children)* [2016] EWCA Civ 374, [2017] Fam 137, [2016] 3 WLR 1557 (*Re C*), the issue related to a local authority's desire to override a mother's choice of forename for her children. The category of such cases is not closed, but they will chiefly concern decisions with profound or enduring consequences for the child.

[28] At first blush, the rather difficult terms of s 100 CA 1989, would seem to preclude a local authority from using the inherent jurisdiction of the High Court as an alternative route to its powers under s 33(3)(b) CA. Section 100 provides …

[29] The use of the inherent jurisdiction by a local authority, with permission granted under s 100, is nevertheless the route which is now approved

and adopted in certain difficult cases, although in most serious medical treatment cases the local authority with care of a child will encourage/request the relevant NHS Trust to initiate proceedings. In *Re C*, when approving the use of the inherent jurisdiction by a local authority as opposed to its powers under s 33(3) CA 1989, I said:

> '[90] Whilst I may not necessarily agree with the precise way that jurisdictional issues have been approached or expressed in these very difficult cases, what is clear is that there is a cohort of cases where the common theme is that a party (whether it be a local authority or, often, an NHS Trust) has sought to bring an issue before the court, believing it to be of too great a magnitude to be determined without the guidance of the court, and without all those with parental responsibility having an opportunity to express their view as a part of the decision making process.
>
> [91] Most commonly, examples are found in the so called "medical treatment" cases where, either an NHS Trust seeks a declaration from the court that they would not be acting unlawfully in pursuing or desisting from a form of treatment notwithstanding the parent's refusal to consent, or alternatively, a local authority seeks to invoke the inherent jurisdiction of the court and thereby to submit to the court's jurisdiction notwithstanding that care proceedings may have been open to them.
>
> [92]–[95] …
>
> [96] … the court did not specifically consider the restriction found in section 100 CA 1989, which prevents the High Court from exercising its inherent jurisdiction:
>
>> "… for the purpose of conferring on any local authority power to determine any question which has arisen, or which may arise, in connection with any aspect of parental responsibility for a child."
>
> [97] In my view it was not necessary to do so. In the medical treatment cases, where a local authority either itself applies to invoke the jurisdiction of the court in relation to a serious medical issue or, as in *Re T*, declines to consent to medical treatment and asks the NHS Trust to seek a declaration of the court, the court is not being asked to *confer* a power upon the local authority in respect of an aspect of parental responsibility. On the contrary, the local authority already has the power to consent to medical treatment under section 33(3) (b) CA 1989. Far from being asked to *confer* a power on themselves, the High Court was being asked to use its inherent jurisdiction to *limit, circumscribe* or *sanction* the use of power which the local authority already has by virtue of section 33(3)(b) CA 1989.
>
> [98] In the medical treatment cases the decisions to be made may well be a matter of life and death. In the present case, the limitation on the exercise of parental responsibility proposed by the local authority, whilst not life threatening, is life affecting. Further such a decision potentially

involves such a serious invasion of the Article 8 rights of the mother that I am satisfied that the court should invoke its inherent jurisdiction in order that it may either sanction the local authority's proposed course of action as in the interests of the children or, alternatively, to refuse to sanction it as for example being in breach of Article 8.

[99] In reaching that conclusion I have not overlooked section 100(4) & (5) CA 1989:

> "(4) The court may only grant leave if it is satisfied that—
>
> (a) the result which the authority wish to achieve could not be achieved through the making of any order of a kind to which subsection (5) applies; and
>
> (b) there is reasonable cause to believe that if the court's inherent jurisdiction is not exercised with respect to the child he is likely to suffer significant harm.
>
> (5) This subsection applies to any order—
>
> (a) made otherwise than in the exercise of the court's inherent jurisdiction; and
>
> (b) which the local authority is entitled to apply for (assuming, in the case of any application which may only be made with leave, that leave is granted)."

[100] I am satisfied that the result which the local authority wish to achieve cannot be achieved either:

> (i) through the making of an order to which section 100(5) CA 1989 applies in the absence of a provision (or requirement) in section 33 CA 1989 for the local authority to make an application in relation to the giving or changing of a forename of a child or
>
> (ii) by way of a prohibited steps order or a specific issue order.

[101] That leaves the question of "whether there is reasonable cause to believe that if the court's inherent jurisdiction is not exercised with respect to the child he is likely to suffer significant harm"?

[102] The judge reached the conclusion that section 100(4)(b) CA 1989 was not satisfied; in his judgment, the giving to the babies of the names contemplated by the mother did not give the court 'reasonable cause to believe that if the court's inherent jurisdiction is not exercised' they would suffer significant harm. Further, the judge appeared to be of the view that a single issue relating to the naming of a child, is not, without more, capable of satisfying the section 31 CA 1989 threshold criteria. With respect I disagree; in my judgment, although it will only rarely be the case, the giving of a particular name to a child can give a court reasonable cause to believe that, absent its intervention, the child in question is likely to suffer

significant emotional harm. In my judgment this is one such case and there is every reason to believe that if the court's inherent jurisdiction is not invoked in order to prevent the girl child from being named "Cyanide", she is likely to suffer significant harm.

[103] In my judgment, the local authority took the correct procedural route when they made an application under section 100 CA 1989 seeking "the intervention of the High Court in order to exercise its powers pursuant to section 100 Children Act (CA) 1989 and/or its Inherent Jurisdiction" (sic).'

[30] In *Re C* therefore it was held that:

(i) Certain decisions are of such magnitude that they should not be determined by a local authority without all those with parental responsibility having an opportunity to express their view to a court as part of the decision-making process;

(ii) Section 100 CA 1989 is available to a local authority in *serious medical treatment* cases because it is not seeking to *confer* a power on itself; the High Court is instead being asked to use its inherent jurisdiction to *limit, circumscribe* or *sanction* the use of power which the local authority already has by virtue of s 33(3)(b);

(iii) As the section provides, leave to apply can only be granted where the court has reasonable cause to believe that, if the inherent jurisdiction was not exercised with respect to the children, they would be likely to suffer significant harm.

See also *Re AB (a child)* [2018] EWFC 3, [2018] 1 FCR 601, [24(iii)] (Sir James Munby P) addressing the same point (albeit in the context of LAs seeking to clothe itself with PR for treatment)

See also *Re H (a child) (parental responsibility: vaccination)* [2020] EWCA Civ 664, [2020] 2 FCR 683, [23]–[30], [55]–[56], [104] (King LJ) addressing a related point (LAs with PR can arrange for and consent to routine vaccinations, notwithstanding parental objection, albeit parental views must be taken into account)

See also *Re P (circumcision: child in care)* [2021] EWHC 1616 (Fam), [2021] 3 FRC 235, [22]–[30] (Cobb J) addressing a related point (disputed male circumcision, albeit in the context of an ICO[5])

10.2.10 Care and supervision orders: care orders: effect of care orders: LAs exercising PR: disputed forenames

Re C (children) [2016] EWCA Civ 374, [2016] 3 WLR 1557 [2]–[3], [48]–[51], [78]–[81], [90]–[105] (King LJ) *quotation limited to* [48]–[51], [104]–[105]

Forenames

48. In contrast to surnames, 'given' names or 'forenames' have not, until relatively recently, been regarded as carrying the same level of importance

5 Interim care order.

to a child as his or her surname. In *In re H (A Child) (First Name) [2002] 1 FLR 973* Thorpe LJ said:

'13. There are a number of points which should be made. The first is that none of the authorities that guide the court in determining disputes as to the surname by which a child should be known seems to be of any application to a dispute of this sort. The surname by which a child is registered and known is of particular significance in so far as it denotes the family to which the child belongs.

'14. Given names have a much less concrete character. It is commonplace for a child to receive statutory registration with one or more given names and, subsequently, to receive different given names, maybe at baptism or, maybe, by custom and adoption. During the course of family life, as a child develops personality and individuality, parents or other members of the family, may be attracted to some nickname or some alternative given name which will then adhere, possibly for the rest of the child's life, or possibly only until the child's individuality and maturity allow it to make a choice for itself as to the name by which he or she wishes to be known.

'18. If issues such as this arise, it seems to me that judges must look in a worldly, common-sense way at what is likely to be best for the child and must not place too much emphasis upon the statutory process of registration.'

49. In *In re D (Children) (Care: Change of Forename)* [2003] 1 FLR 339, a case heard several months later, Butler-Sloss LJ took a somewhat different view. Butler-Sloss LJ said that the principles to be applied are the same regardless of whether a proposed name change relates to a forename or a surname; she said, at p 346:

> 'To change a child's name is to take a significant step in a child's life. Forename or surname, it seems to me, the principles are the same, in general. A child has roots. A child has names given to him or her by parents. The child has a right to those names and retains that right, as indeed, the parents have rights to retention of the name of the child which they chose. Those rights should not be set to one side, other than for good reasons. It may be that foster parents do not appreciate the underlying importance for the child of a name, and it is significant. You would not, for instance, be likely to change the forename of a child of 7, 8 or 9, I suggest even, 5, 6 or 7, because by that time the child has made that name part of his or her identity and very young children know what their names are. You ask a very young child "what's your name?", and they will certainly be able to give you the name he or she is called by. To change that is to affect the child's identity. The right of the child and both parents to respect for that part of family life still exists, even though the child has gone into a foster placement. It may be that foster carers have not yet been sufficiently made aware that this is not a technical point. There is an

underlying importance to the principle that the name should not be changed.'

And, at p 347:

'So, the first rule, in my judgment, is that no foster parent or carer, under whatever Regulations, should unilaterally change the name of a child. If, for any reason, the foster parents or other such carers think the name should be changed, they should go straight away to the social worker in charge of the case or the adoption placement officer, whoever it may be, and ask for the change and explain why. That should then be a matter of careful consideration by the local authority, who does, of course, have shared parental responsibility. The parents, who remain with parental responsibility in all foster placements, though not, of course, in placements after freeing for adoption, should be consulted in foster placements, to be allowed to express their views, if they are capable of being found or able to express a view, and if it is a matter that cannot be achieved by consent, it may be necessary, and one would hope it would be rare that such a situation would arise, but it may be necessary to invoke the inherent jurisdiction of the court and ask the High Court to rule on whether the name should be changed. That has happened in a number of cases in surnames and I see no reason why it should not happen in, what I hope will be the rare case, for forenames.'

50. I would, with respect to Thorpe LJ, endorse the view of Butler-Sloss LJ. By 2002, when Thorpe LJ decided *In re H (A Child) (Child's Name: First Name)* [2002] 1 FLR 973 custom had already moved a long way from the days when the formal combination of a person's title together with their surname was the almost universal way in which a person would be addressed, with the use of the forename being reserved for only the closest friends and family. But, even by 2002, convention had nowhere near relaxed to the stage where, as now, forenames are used almost exclusively for all purposes, social and business, often, it would seem, entirely in the absence of surnames. Further the increase in blended families means that it is by no longer the universal norm for a family living together all to share the same surname.

51. Whilst Butler Sloss LJ in *In re D (Children) (Care: Change of Forename)* [2003] 1 FLR 339 was focusing on the effect on a child of changing its forename once it is sentient, in my judgement given the fact that in the 21st century a child will predominantly use his or her forenames for most purposes throughout his or her life, that forename is now every bit as important to that child, and his or her identity, as is his or her surname.

…

Discussion

[104] I have reached the conclusion that there is a small category of cases where, notwithstanding the local authority's powers under *section 33(3)(b)*

CA 1989, the consequences of the exercise of a particular act of parental responsibility are so profound and have such an impact on either the child his or herself, and/or the *Article 8* rights of those other parties who share parental responsibility with a local authority, that the matter must come before the court for its consideration and determination.

[105] It follows that I am also satisfied that there may be rare cases, where a local authority believes that the forename chosen by a parent, and by which he or she intends to register a child, goes beyond the unusual, bizarre, extreme or plain foolish, and instead gives the local authority reasonable cause to believe that by calling him or her that name he or she is likely to be caused significant harm. In those highly unusual circumstances, the proper route by which the local authority seek to ensure that the course it proposes is necessary and in the child's interests is (as was held by Butler-Sloss LJ in *Re D, L, and LA* supra) by putting the matter before the High Court by way of an application to invoke its inherent jurisdiction.

See also *Re M, T, P, K, and B (care: change of name)* [2000] 2 FLR 645 (FD), 649–651 (HHJ Wilkinson sitting as a judge of the High Court) addressing a related point (the child's welfare is paramount in the context of a change of surname and the approach should be similar to private law cases)

See also *Dawson v Wearmouth* [1999] 1 FCR 625 (HL), 629D–E, 631I–632A (Lord Mackay), 635E–F (Lord Jauncy) addressing a related point (the test in respect of surnames in private law applications is the child's welfare)

See also *Re S (a minor) (change of name)* [1999] 1 FCR 304 (CA), 306F–307F (Thorpe LJ) addressing a related point (concerning a Gillick competent child in care seeking a change of surname)

10.2.11 Care and supervision orders: care orders: effect of care orders: LAs exercising PR: nationality

Re Y (children in care: change of nationality) [2020] EWCA Civ 1038, [2020] 3 FCR 292, [18]–[24] (Peter Jackson LJ)

Conclusion

[18] Every local authority will encounter situations where action is needed to secure the immigration position of a child in its care. In some cases an application will be made for leave to remain. In others it may be possible for a child to have dual citizenship. These cases, where the child is gaining a benefit and losing nothing, are to be contrasted with cases where a child may lose his or her original nationality. In those cases the issue is of a magnitude that cannot in my view be resolved by a local authority acting in reliance upon its general statutory powers. In the absence of parental consent, it requires a decision of the High Court under its inherent jurisdiction. That is so whether the issue arises within or outside proceedings.

[19] Although these children had been in the care of the local authority for several years, no steps had been taken to regularise their immigration position. That is a matter of justified concern, even though there is no immediate threat of removal. The children would clearly benefit emotionally from their position being regularised and from being able to travel in and out of the country, for example if opportunities for school trips or holidays were to arise.

[20] The children's immigration status, as opposed to the question of nationality, could and should have been addressed within the existing proceedings. The judge is not to be criticised for not doing so: she was dealing with more immediate issues in difficult circumstances, but it is clear that this important question did not receive the attention it required. Even so, the court would surely have approved steps being taken to regularise the children's immigration position, short of an application for citizenship, and such steps can now be taken by the local authority under its s 33 powers. The integrity of the care orders is unaffected by this appeal.

[21] As to citizenship, the local authority had sought some advice, but there was no evidence about the options for securing the children's position in the UK through applications short of an application for citizenship. There was a general understanding that the granting of British citizenship to the children would lead to the loss of their Indian citizenship, but there was no formal evidence to this effect. There was no acknowledgement of the intrinsic gravity of a change of nationality, to the extent that the issue did not feature in the care plans or in the judgment. No consideration was given by any of the agencies to any disadvantages that might flow to the children from the loss of their nationality of birth. Nor was any consideration given to whether it was appropriate to apply now, or whether it would be more appropriate to defer an application to a time when they could express a more informed view, as the Guardian at one point seems to have contemplated.

[22] In these circumstances the judge should have made clear that the question of a change of citizenship could not be decided within the proceedings that were before her. If the local authority wished to pursue a change of citizenship at this stage, they could make an application under the inherent jurisdiction which should then have been referred to a judge of the Family Division or a judge sitting as a deputy judge of the High Court under s 9 Senior Courts Act 1981. Meantime, it was open to the judge to give directions for the necessary evidence of UK and Indian law to be gathered.

[23] I do not accept the contrary arguments presented by the local authority:

(1) The characterisation of a change of citizenship as akin to routine vaccination is misplaced. Changing a child's citizenship is a momentous step with profound and enduring consequences that requires the most careful consideration. Recognising that fact does not have far-reaching consequences for the conduct of care proceedings, as claimed, and it is not asking too much of a local

authority to put its case before the court for scrutiny. This case, in which local authority has arrived at a settled position without any of the necessary data, provides a good example of why such scrutiny is needed.

(2) It is no answer to say that the remedy for dissenting parents is to take legal action against the local authority. The difficulties with this course were touched upon in *Re C* at [76]. Further, for many parents, and particularly those whose immigration status is insecure, that will not be an effective remedy. They will only have legal representation within care proceedings, and they may have neither the knowledge nor the means to seek an injunction under the Human Rights Act or to bring judicial review proceedings. It is conceded that an application to discharge the care order would be disproportionate. Similarly, the children themselves have a central interest in the matter and in the absence of proceedings they will not have a Children's Guardian and will not be legally represented.

(3) The suggestion that the local authority would be prevented from seeking a judicial ruling by the terms of s 100 CA 1989 is not persuasive. The very existence of s 100 (3) and (4) demonstrates that there will be residual cases where the local authority's statutory powers under s 33 are inadequate. In the present case the local authority would require leave to apply for the court to exercise its inherent jurisdiction (ss (3)) and the court could only grant leave if the result sought could not be achieved by other means (ss (4)(a)) and where there is reasonable cause to believe that the children would be likely to suffer significant harm if the inherent jurisdiction was not exercised (ss 4(b)). The court would in my view be likely to find that these conditions were met in this case. Condition (a) is met as a matter of law. Condition (b) would be met by the court finding that, if it was in the children's interests for them to become British citizens, there is reasonable cause to believe that they would be likely to be significantly harmed by that course not being pursued; the nature of the harm being their liability to removal from their lifelong home country on reaching adulthood.

(4) Once it is concluded that the question of a change of citizenship is one that should be judicially decided at High Court level by reason of its importance and potential complexity, one matter that should not be overlooked is the question of the timing of any application. Depending upon expert advice, it may not need to be made as a matter of urgency, and consideration might be given to whether it should be taken at a time when the children would be more able to express their own views. That of course does not prevent an application being made now as it would be open to the court to approve an application being made at a later date.

[24] As to the outcome, the care orders remain undisturbed and I would dismiss the appeals. However, reflecting the appellants' success on the issue of law that led to permission to appeal being granted, I would

declare that s 33 CA 1989 does not entitle the local authority to apply for British citizenship for these children, in the face of parental opposition and where that may lead to a loss of their existing citizenship, without first obtaining approval from the High Court. The local authority should now indicate whether it wishes to progress the matter, in which case we will give appropriate directions.

10.2.12 Care and supervision orders: care orders: effect of care orders: LAs exercising PR: disputes regarding education

Re SW (a child) [2005] EWHC 162 (Fam), [2005] 2 FLR 508, [11]–[13] (Munby J)

11. I need not rehearse all the learning to be found in these judgments. I can take it as read. For present purposes the key principles can be summarised very shortly as follows.

12. (1) Deciding where a child should go to school is an aspect of parental responsibility: *In re Z (A Minor) (Identification: Restrictions on Publication)* [1997] Fam 1 at p 26.

13. (2) Where the court has made either an interim or a final care order parental responsibility is shared with the local authority: sections 33(3)(a) and 31(11) of the Children Act 1989. Subject to the limitations in sections 33(4) and 33(6), section 33(3)(b) confers on the local authority the 'power ... to determine the extent to which a parent ... of the child may meet his parental responsibility for him.' Accordingly it is, in the final analysis, for the local authority and not for the parent to decide where a child in care should go to school. Section 33(3)(b) does not, however, prevent the parents of a child in care exercising their right of appeal to SENDIST under section 326 of the Education Act 1996: see *Fairpo v Humberside County Council* [1997] ELR 12 at p 18.

10.2.13 Care and supervision orders: care orders: effect of care orders: not discharging SGOs[6]

See Chapter 12.3.2 SGOs: variation or discharge: care orders do not automatically discharge SGOs

10.2.14 Care and supervision orders: care orders: effect of care orders: no short-term final care orders

Re P-S (Children) [2018] EWCA Civ 1407, [2018] 4 WLR 99, [33] (Sir Ernest Ryder SP)

33. The concept of a short term care order within which the placements could be tested was raised by the judge as a justification for making full

6 Special guardianship orders.

care orders. Aside from the welfare merits of the orders, which were not adequately reasoned, the concept of a short term order is flawed. There is no mechanism for a care order to be discharged on the happening of a fixed event or otherwise to be limited in time. The exercise of parental responsibility by a local authority cannot be constrained once a full care order is made other than on public law principles of unlawfulness, unreasonableness and irrationality. The judge should have reflected on the fact that if the local authority did not in due course apply to discharge the care orders themselves it would have been incumbent on the proposed special guardians to do so and to satisfy the test for leave to make that application without the benefit of legal aid, given that in the circumstance of a disagreement with the local authority it would be highly unlikely that the special guardians would be in receipt of funding from them.

10.2.15 Care and supervision orders: care orders: withdrawal

See Chapter 5.1.10 Case management: active case management: withdrawal

10.2.16 Care and supervision orders: care orders: discharge

Re TT (children: discharge of care order) [2021] EWCA Civ 742, [4], [18]–[49] (Peter Jackson LJ) *quotation limited to* [4], [18]–[25], [31]

4. The mother sought permission to appeal, which I granted in part on 25 March 2021. In doing so, I noted that it was doubtful that any of the grounds of appeal had a real prospect of success, but that there was a compelling reason for the appeal to be heard as it offered an opportunity for this court to consider the correctness of the decision in *GM v Carmarthenshire County Council* [2018] EWFC 36, also reported as *M v Carmarthenshire County Council* [2018] 3 WLR 1126 ('*GM v Carmarthenshire*'). In that decision it was stated that on an application to discharge a care order, while there is no formal requirement on the local authority to demonstrate the continued existence of the statutory threshold under s. 31 of the Act for the making of a care order, something close to a formal threshold requirement applies. It was further stated that a discharge application should not be refused unless it can be shown that the circumstances are exceptional and that the outcome is motivated by an overriding requirement pertaining to the child's best interests. For the reasons given later in this judgment, these statements are not correct and should not be followed.

...

Applications to discharge care orders

18. The first two grounds of appeal arise from the Judge's self-direction on the law relating to an application to discharge a care order, which I will set out below. It might be thought that this was a quite straightforward matter but the Judge was presented with detailed submissions about it.

19. Section 39, which is situated in Part IV of the Act, relevantly provides:

> '39 Discharge and variation etc. of care orders and supervision orders.
>
> (1) A care order may be discharged by the court on the application of—
>
> (a) any person who has parental responsibility for the child;
>
> (b) the child himself; or
>
> (c) the local authority designated by the order.
>
> (2)–(3B) …
>
> (4) Where a care order is in force with respect to a child the court may, on the application of any person entitled to apply for the order to be discharged, substitute a supervision order for the care order.
>
> (5) When a court is considering whether to substitute one order for another under subsection (4) any provision of this Act which would otherwise require section 31(2) to be satisfied at the time when the proposed order is substituted or made shall be disregarded.'

20. Section 1 of the Act relevantly provides …

21. The combined effect of these provisions is that on the application of an entitled applicant the court may discharge a care order. Or it may replace it with a supervision order, in which case there is no requirement for the s. 31(2) threshold to be crossed. As the decision concerns a question of upbringing, the child's welfare shall be the court's paramount consideration. As the court is considering whether to vary or discharge an order under Part IV, the court shall have particular regard to the factors in the welfare checklist. As the court is considering whether to make an order under the Act, it shall not make the order unless to do so would be better for the child than making no order at all.

22. Section 3 of the Human Rights Act 1998 provides that so far as it is possible to do so, these provisions must be read and given effect in a way which is compatible with the Convention rights. Section 6 provides that it is unlawful for the court, as a public authority, to act in a way which is incompatible with a Convention right. The salient rights in this context are the Article 8 right to respect for family life and (in the context of the obligation on the state to protect children from severe abuse) the Article 3 right not to be subject to inhuman or degrading treatment. In particular, it is an aspect of Article 8 that the public care of a child should in principle be regarded as a temporary measure, to be discontinued as soon as circumstances permit, and the positive duty to take measures to facilitate family reunification must be balanced against the duty to consider the best interests of the child: *K and T v Finland* (2001) 36 EHRR 18; [2001] 2 FLR 707.

23. Although the Children Act came into effect before the Human Rights Act, it was drafted with the Convention in mind; in any event, since the

Human Rights Act the Act must if possible be construed and applied so as to comply with the Convention, and the court must consider any Convention rights before deciding whether to make a substantive order: *In re B (A Child) (Care Proceedings: Threshold Criteria)* [2013] 1 WLR 1911 at paragraphs 62, 73 and 194. A proper application of the welfare test will normally produce an outcome that is compatible with Convention rights, by having particular regard to the child's background (checklist factor d), his emotional needs (factor b) and any risk of harm (factor e). And, of course, consideration of the position of the child's parents is mandatory (factor f). But on top of this, once the welfare evaluation has been carried out, the court will cross-check the outcome to satisfy itself that it is exercising its powers in such a way that any resulting interference with Convention rights is necessary and proportionate. This cross-check does not alter the fact that the decision turns on welfare and not on rights or presumptions: see *Re W (A Child)* [2016] EWCA Civ 793; [2017] 1 WLR 889, per McFarlane LJ at 70-71. In judicial decisions where the Article 8 rights of parents and those of a child are at stake, the child's rights must be the paramount consideration; if any balancing of interests is necessary, the interests of the child must prevail: *Yousef v The Netherlands* (2003) 36 EHRR 20; [2003] 1 FLR 210.

24. The proper approach to an application to discharge a care order has been considered by this court in two cases, one before and one since the Human Rights Act. In *Re S (Discharge of Care Order)* [1995] 2 FLR 639, Waite LJ said this at 643:

> "Section 39 of the Act allows the court to discharge a care order on the application of (inter alios) a parent. Here the jurisdiction is discretionary from the outset (there being no obligation on the parent to satisfy the court that the threshold requirements no longer apply). The issue has to be determined by the court in accordance with s 1 of the Act, which (by s 1(1)) makes the child's welfare the court's paramount consideration, and (by s 1(3) and (4)) makes it mandatory for the court to have particular regard to the child's wishes and needs, the likely effect on him of any change of circumstances, the capability of his parents to meet his needs,
>
> '(3) …
>
> (e) any harm which he has suffered or is at risk of suffering; …'"

25. *Re C (Care: Discharge of Care Order)* [2009] EWCA Civ 955, [2010] 1 FLR 774 was an unusual case in which a local authority had successfully applied for the discharge of a care order and a parent appealed on the basis that the care order should have continued so as to give the child the benefit of the 'leaving care' provisions. The judgment of Hughes LJ included this passage:

'[17] The test upon an application for discharge is clearly set out by this court as long ago as 1995 in *Re S (Discharge of Care Order)* [1995] 2 FLR 639 at 643. As Waite LJ put it:

> "Section 39 of the Act allows the court to discharge a care order on the application of (inter alios) a parent. Here the jurisdiction is discretionary from the outset (there being no obligation on the parent to satisfy the court that the threshold requirements no longer apply). The issue has to be determined by the court in accordance with s 1 of the Act, which (by s 1(1)) makes the child's welfare the court's paramount consideration ..."

I need not read the remainder.

[18] I entirely agree that the applicant for such an order must make out his case. It does not follow from that that the test is simply a matter of listing potential benefits. Welfare is a more complicated and rounded consideration than that. I am quite satisfied that the judge is entitled to take into account the continuing effect, or in this case lack of effect, of the care order.'

In referring to the obligation on an applicant to make out his case, Hughes LJ was responding to a submission that before a care order could be discharged, a positive benefit to the child must be demonstrated.

...

31. In summary, when a court is considering an application to discharge a care order the legal principles are clear:
(1) The decision must be made in accordance with s. 1 of the Act, by which the child's welfare is the court's paramount consideration. The welfare evaluation is at large and the relevant factors in the welfare checklist must be considered and given appropriate weight.
(2) Once the welfare evaluation has been carried out, the court will cross-check the outcome to ensure that it will be exercising its powers in such a way that any interference with Convention rights is necessary and proportionate.
(3) The applicant must make out a case for the discharge of the care order by bringing forward evidence to show that this would be in the interests of the child. The findings of fact that underpinned the making of the care order will be relevant to the court's assessment but the weight to be given to them will vary from case to case.
(4) The welfare evaluation is made at the time of the decision. The s. 31(2) threshold, applicable to the making of a care order, is of no relevance to an application for its discharge. The local authority does not have to re-prove the threshold and the applicant does not have to prove that it no longer applies. Any questions of harm and risk of harm form part of the overall welfare evaluation.

10.3 CARE AND SUPERVISION ORDERS: CONTACT WITH CHILDREN IN CARE

10.3.1 Care and supervision orders: contact with children in care: the test under s 34[7]

Re D-S (contact with children in care: Covid-19) [2020] EWCA Civ 1031, [2020] 3 FCR 518, [11]–[14] (Peter Jackson LJ)

[11] The statutory framework surrounding parental contact with a child in care is straightforward:

(1) The local authority is under a duty to allow the child reasonable contact with his parents: CA 1989, s 34(1). It must also endeavour to promote contact between the child and his parents unless it is not reasonably practicable or consistent with his welfare: CA 1989 Sched 2 para 15(1).

(2) Where an application is made to the court, it may make such an order for contact as it considers appropriate: s 34(3). When doing so, the child's welfare is its paramount consideration. It must have regard to the welfare checklist and it must not make any order unless it would be better for the child than making no order at all: CA 1989, s 1(1), (3) and (5).

[12] In the first case, the decision about contact is one for the local authority. In the second case, it is one for the court. The fact that there will be mutual respect between the authority and the court cannot mask this distinction. A parent applying for contact is entitled to expect that the court will form its own view of what contact is appropriate in all the circumstances, however influential the professional view of the local authority may turn out to be.

[13] Once the court has formed its own view, it has a broad discretion as to whether or not to make a contact order. It may well decide, applying the 'no order' principle, not to make an order because its conclusion about what contact is appropriate is broadly equivalent to be contact that is being offered, or, for example, because the making of an order may lead to a loss of flexibility, or because practical considerations make an ideal level of contact unachievable. But the essential point is that the court must reach its own conclusion and ensure that it has the information it needs to do that. It does not defer to the local authority, and the local authority is no more entitled than any other party to the benefit of any doubt.

[14] I therefore would not accept Mr Abberley's argument in support of the judge's analysis. The question for the court was not whether the local authority's position was reasonable, but what contact was appropriate, giving paramount consideration to the children's best interests and taking account of all the circumstances, including the reality of the pressures on services at the present time.

7 Children Act 1989, s 34.

Re A and D (minors) [2010] EWHC 2503 (Fam), [2011] 1 FLR 615, [46]–[47] (Baker J)

46. Section 34(3) entitles a parent to apply without leave to the court for an order for contact and upon such application the court may make such order as it deems it appropriate with respect to contact between the child and that parent. The court, of course, also has the power under section 34(4), on application by the local authority or the child, to make an order authorising the local authority to refuse to allow contact between the child and the parent. No such application is made here. These powers give to the court an important exception to the general principle underpinning the Children Act, namely that the court may not interfere with, or give directions to, a local authority in the exercise of its powers to exercise parental responsibility in respect of the child and to determine the extent to which others with parental responsibility may exercise that responsibility.

47. In determining an application for conduct under section 34(3), the court must apply the provisions of section 1. The child's welfare is the paramount consideration. The factors in section 1(3) must be given their due weight and the court under section 1(5) must not make the order unless it considers that doing so would be better for the child than making no order at all. Guidance as to the exercise of its discretionary powers was given by Butler-Sloss LJ, as she then was, in *Re B (Minors) (Contact: Local Authority's Plans)* [1993] 1FLR 543. Although that authority is now nearly twenty years old, the guidelines remain important:

> 'Contact applications generally fall into two main categories – those which ask for contact as such and those which are attempts to set aside the care order itself. In the first category there is no suggestion that the applicant wishes to take over the care of the child and the issue of contact often depends on whether the contact would frustrate the long term plans for the child in a substitute home such as adoption where continuing contact may not be for the long term welfare of the child. The presumption of contact which has to be for the benefit of the child has always to be balanced against the long term welfare of the child particularly where he will live in the future. Contact must not be allowed to de-stabilise or endanger the arrangements for the child and in many cases the plans for the child will be decisive on the contact application. There may also be cases where the parent is having satisfactory contact with the child and there are no long term plans or those plans do not appear to the court to preclude some future contact. The proposals of the local authority based on their appreciation of the best interests of the child must command the greatest respect and consideration from the court but Parliament has given to the court, and not the local authority, the duty to decide on contact between the child and those named in section 34(1)'.

See also *Re E (children in care: contact)* [1994] 1 FCR 584 (CA), 590F–G, 592G–593B (Sir Stephen Brown P) addressing the same point (considering that there is a presumption of continuing parental contact)

See also *Re P (minors) (contact with children in care)* [1993] 2 FLR 156 (FD), 161 (Ewbank J) addressing a related point (reasonable access differing from contact at the discretion of a LA)

10.3.2 Care and supervision orders: contact with children in care: newborns

Re M (care proceedings: judicial review) [2003] EWHC 850 (Admin), [2004] 1 FCR 302, [44] (Munby J)

Concluding thoughts

[44] It will be for the family proceedings court (or, if the case is transferred up, the Family Division) to hear and determine whatever application the local authority may decide to make. It is for that court, not for me, to decide M's future. There are, however, a number of things I can properly say in the circumstances and think I ought to say …

(iv) If a baby is to be removed from his mother one would normally expect arrangements to be made by the local authority to facilitate contact on a regular and generous basis. It is a dreadful thing to take a baby away from his mother: dreadful for mother, dreadful for father and dreadful for the baby. If the state, in the guise of a local authority, seeks to intervene so drastically in a family's life—and at a time when, ex hypothesi, its case against the parents has not yet even been established—then the very least the state can do is to make generous arrangements for contact. And those arrangements must be driven by the needs of the family, not stunted by lack of resources. Typically, if this is what the parents want, one will be looking to contact most days of the week and for lengthy periods. And local authorities must be sensitive to the wishes of a mother who wants to breast-feed and must make suitable arrangements to enable her to do so—and when I say breast-feed I mean just that, I do not mean merely bottle-feeding expressed breast milk. Nothing less will meet the imperative demands of the Convention. Contact two or three times a week for a couple of hours a time is simply not enough if parents reasonably want more …

See also *A Local Authority v S (a child) (care proceedings: contact)* [2005] EWHC 3494 (Fam), [2006] 1 FLR 333, [27]–[35] (Bodey J) considering *Re M (care proceedings: judicial review)* [2003] EWHC 850 (Admin), [2004] 1 FCR 302 (emphasising that Munby J's comments were obiter and although not dissenting from Munby J's views, Bodey J commented daily contact was 'exceptionally unusual')

See also *Re K* [2008] EWHC 540 (Fam), [24]–[31] (Munby J) addressing a related point (s 34(4) orders relating to newborns, on an interim basis)

10.3.3 Care and supervision orders: contact with children in care: procedure: if leave is required

Re M (minors) (contact: leave to apply) [1995] 3 FCR 550 (CA), 558E–561F (Ward LJ) *quotation limited to* 559B–561F

Section 34(3) gives the court a wide and unfettered discretion in dealing with such applications. It reads:

> 'On an application made by –
>
> (a) any person mentioned in paras.(a) to (d) of subs.(1); or
>
> (b) any person who has obtained the leave of the court to make the application,
>
> the court may make such order as it considers appropriate with respect to the contact which is to be allowed between the child and that person.'

This can be contrasted with s 10(9) which deals with leave to apply for section 8 orders:

> 'Where the person applying for leave to make an application for a section 8 order is not the child concerned, the court shall, in deciding whether or not to grant leave, have particular regard to:
>
> (a) the nature of the proposed application for the section 8 order;
>
> (b) the applicant's connexion with the child;
>
> (c) any risk there might be of that proposed application disrupting the child's life to such an extent that he would be harmed by it; and
>
> (d) where the child is being looked after by the local authority–
>
> (i) the authority's plans for the child's future; and
>
> (ii) the wishes and feeling of the child's parents.'

It is quite clear that s 10(9) does not govern applications for contact to a child in care because s 9(1) provides that:

> 'No court shall make any section 8 order, other than a residence order, with respect to a child who is in the care of a local authority.'

It is equally clear, however, from s 10(9)(d) that children in care may be the object of section 10(9) applications and that must include an application for a residence order. If the court were faced with an application by a grandparent for leave to apply for a residence order, alternatively a contact order, it would be anomalous, in my judgment, were the court not to take into account for the exercise of the section 34(3) discretion the criteria specifically laid out for consideration in s 10(9). Those particular factors seem to me to be also apposite for s 34(3). The court must, of course, have regard to all the circumstances of the case, for each case is different, but in my judgment the court should always have particular regard at least to the following:

(a) *The nature of the contact which is being sought.* Contact to children in care varies infinitely from that which is frequent to that which takes place two, three or four times a year to keep memory alive. It varies from contact which is face to face to contact which is indirectly maintained through the exchange of letters, cards, photographs, and gifts.

(b) *The connexion of the applicant to the child.* The more meaningful and important the connexion is to the child, the greater is the weight to be given to this factor. Grandparents ought to have a special place in any child's affection worthy of being maintained by contact but it is easy to envisage family circumstances, very much like those before us in this case where, however loving the grandparent may be, life's wheel of misfortune has diminished the importance to the child of that blood tie and may, for example, have strengthened the claims for contact by former foster-parents who have forged close attachment to the child. The fact is that Parliament has refused to place grandparents in a special category or to accord them special treatment. Nevertheless, by virtue of para 15 of Sch 2, contact between a child and his or her family will be assumed to be beneficial and the local authority will need to file evidence to justify why they have considered that it is not reasonably practicable or consistent with the child's welfare to promote that contact.

(c) *Disruption.* This seems to me to be the factor of crucial significance, *a fortiori* when the child is in care. The child will only have come into care if life had already been so thoroughly disrupted that such intervention was judged to be necessary. The need then for stability and security is usually vital. The breakdown of the foster placement may be so harmful that it should not be placed at risk. All that is obvious. It is, nonetheless, significant and appropriate that the risk of disruption which is primarily contemplated in s 10(9)(c) is the risk "there might be of that *proposed application* [for a section 8 order] disrupting the child's life to such an extent that he would be *harmed* by it". I add the emphasis to make two points. The harm envisaged is harm which, through s 105(1), is defined by s 31(9) to mean impairment of health or development as those words are there defined. A child's upset, unhappiness, confusion or anxiety, needs to be sufficiently severe before it can amount to an impairment of emotional, social, or behavioural development. Secondly, the risk must arise from the proposed application. The very knowledge that litigation is pending can be sufficiently unsettling to be harmful; if leave is given, the process of investigating the merits of the application can be sufficiently disruptive if it involves the children in more interviews, psychiatric investigations and so forth. The stressfulness of litigation may impair the ability of those who have care of the child properly to discharge their responsibility to the child's detriment. Questions of that sort are the narrow focus of the court's attention in weighing this factor. That is not to say that the court shuts its eyes to what prospects of eventual success the application has and if the making of a contact order would be so manifestly disruptive as to be totally inimical to the child's welfare, then such an obviously unsustainable claim will not be permitted to get off the starting blocks. Except in the most obvious case, it is incumbent on the respondent to the application to produce some evidence to establish disruption.

(d) *The wishes of the parents and the local authority.* They are very material, though not determinative. That the parents' wishes are relevant is consistent with the whole underlying philosophy of the Act, a cornerstone of which is the protection of the integrity and independence of the family. When a care order is made, the local authority acquires parental responsibility. Their exercise of that responsibility commands equal protection from unwarranted interference. Their duty imposed by s 22(3) is to "safeguard and promote (the child's) welfare". Accordingly, *per* Balcombe, LJ in *JR v Merton London Borough* [1992] 2 FCR 174 at p 194G; *sub nom Re A and Others (Minors Residence Orders: Leave to Apply)* [1992] Fam 182 at p 193D:

> '… the court should approach the application for leave on the basis that the authority's plans for the child's future are designed to safeguard and promote the child's welfare and that any departure from those plans might well disrupt "the child's life to such an extent that he would be harmed by it".'

I would adopt Butler-Sloss, LJ's words in *Re B (Children in Care: Contact)* [1993] 1 FCR 363 at p 380:

> 'Contact applications generally fall into two main categories, those which ask for contact as such, and those which are attempts to set aside the care order itself. In the first category, there is no suggestion that the applicant wishes to take over the care of the child and the issue of contact often depends on whether contact would frustrate long-term plans for the child in a substitute home, such as adoption where continuing contact may not be for the long-term welfare of the child and particularly where he will live in the future. Contact must not be allowed to destabilize or endanger the arrangements for the child and in many cases the plans for the child will be decisive of the contact application. There may also be cases where a parent is having satisfactory contact with the child and there are no long-term plans or those plans do not appear to the court to preclude some future contacts. The proposals of the local authority, based on their appreciation of the best interest of the child, must command the greatest respect and consideration from court, but Parliament has given to the court, and not to the local authority, the duty to decide on contact between the child and those named in s.34(1). Consequently the court may have the task of requiring the local authority to justify their long-term plans to the extent only that those plans exclude contact between parent and child.'

Mutatis mutandis, those words seem to me equally apt to applications for leave under s 34(3).

10.3.4 Care and supervision orders: contact with a children in care: ICO-contact decisions should not pre-determine issues

Re H-T (children); Re T-H (children) [2012] EWCA Civ 1215, [2013] 1 FLR 705, [39]–[42] (McFarlane LJ) *quotation limited to* [39]–[40]

39. In summary, in my view the judge, understandably struck and coloured in his view as he was by the serious nature of the injuries to Ke, fell into the trap of predetermining issues in the case which more properly should be left for the final hearing. In making that observation I am reminded of the decision now nearly 20 years ago of Ewbank J in the case of *A v M v Walsall MBC* [1993] 2 FLR 244. In a judgment which no doubt was characteristic both of the judge and of the time, which is therefore very short, Ewbank J dealt with a similar issue on appeal from magistrates and observed that it was not the function of the first instance court to determine matters which effectively decided the case. It was for the first instance court at an interim hearing to decide whether or not there should be contact pending the final hearing of the case and for the court only at the final hearing to determine issues such as whether rehabilitation should or should not be ruled out.

40. Family cases are organic. Cases of this sort where something appalling has apparently happened need the parents to have some limited space to understand and come to terms with what has happened and the court should at least entertain the hope, if not expectation, that the parents may change their position and move forward in a way that allows the prospect of rehabilitation to be open for the best interests of the children at a later stage in the proceedings. In my view, the judge was led into predetermining issues which were not before him. All he was to determine was whether or not there should be some form of interim contact between 2 July and when the court could look at the issue again, either following receipt of the expert's report or at a later stage.

10.3.5 Care and supervision orders: contact with children in care: during national pandemic restrictions

Re D-S (contact with children in care: Covid-19) [2020] EWCA Civ 1031, [2020] 3 FCR 518, [10] (Peter Jackson LJ)

[10] As the judge eloquently wrote, the present emergency has caused sad losses for many people and real challenges for the professional services. For many children in care and for their families, the loss of contact will have been particularly difficult. Where it is unavoidable, it is an occasion for sympathy, but where it can to some extent be remedied, that should be attempted where possible. This is underscored by the prevailing guidance from the Department of Education, entitled *Coronavirus (Covid-19): Guidance For Children's Social Care Services*:

> 'What about court orders related to contact for children in care?

> We expect that contact between children in care and their birth relatives will continue. It is essential for children and families to remain in touch at this difficult time, and for many children, the consequences of not seeing relatives would be traumatising.
>
> Contact arrangements should, therefore, be assessed on a case by case basis taking into account a range of factors, including the government's current social distancing guidance and the needs of the child. However, we expect the spirit of any court ordered contact in relation to children in care to be maintained.
>
> Where it may not be possible, or appropriate, for the usual face-to-face contact to happen at this time, keeping in touch will, for the most part, need to take place virtually. In these circumstances, we would encourage social workers and other professionals to reassure children that this position is temporary. We would also expect foster parents and other carers to be consulted on how best to meet the needs of the children in their care and to be supported to facilitate that contact, particularly if those carers are shielding or medically vulnerable.
>
> We recognise that some young children may not be able to benefit from virtual contact with their family, because of their age or other communication challenges. In these circumstances, local authorities should work with families to identify ways to have safe face-to-face interactions, whilst still adhering to social distancing guidance.
>
> When considering the most appropriate ways for children to stay in touch with their families, social workers and carers should seek the views of children who may welcome different forms of contact, including less formal and more flexible virtual contact with their birth families.'

The key point is that contact arrangements should be assessed on a case-by-case basis.

10.3.6 Care and supervision orders: contact with children in care: s 34(4) orders: merely permits LA prohibition of contact

Re W (a child) (parental contact: prohibition) [2000] 1 FCR 752 (CA), 757B–758E (Thorpe LJ)

> That summary is intended to set the scene. Against that background Miss Hyde repeatedly submitted that since the court is under a duty to promote the welfare of the child therefore the court must have jurisdiction to prohibit contact to a child in care. That seems to us a non sequitur. Of course in so far as the court has jurisdiction, in the exercise of that jurisdiction it must put welfare paramount. But the paramount principle does not help to determine the jurisdictional boundaries. In our judgment the strongest point for Miss Hyde is the width of the statutory language: see sub-s (2), 'the court may make such order as it considers appropriate' and sub-s (5), 'the court may make an order under this section' and sub-s (7), 'an order under this section may impose such conditions as the court considers appropriate'.

On the other hand it is in our judgment important to construe s 34 in the context of the statute as a whole and in recognition of the statutory objectives. Perhaps the most striking reform introduced by Pt IV of the statute was to shift the power from the court to the local authority on and after the making of the care order. As Butler-Sloss LJ lucidly expressed it in *Re L (minors) (care proceedings: appeal)* [1996] 2 FCR 352 at 361:

> 'The effect of the Children Act is to set aside the former powers of the court in wardship and to remove from the court any continuing control over children after the making of a care order unless or until a further application was made to the court. On the making of a further application, such as for residence or contact to the child, the powers of the court and the exercise of discretion under s.1 are restored for the duration of the application. If the care order remains in place, other than by control over contact by virtue of the provisions of s.34, the court has no further part to play in the future welfare of the child, see *Re B (children in care: contact)* ([1993] 1 FCR 363 at 377). This interchange between the judicial control of children, the subject of applications, and the local authority responsibility for children placed in care under the Children Act, is a difficult and sensitive area. The point at which the court withdraws from further control over the child and passes the responsibility to the local authority is a matter of the exercise of discretion by the court and will vary with each set of circumstances. But at some point, if a care order is made by the court, it must hand over the future arrangements for the child to the local authority. That is not abdication of responsibility by the court; it is acting in accordance with the intention of the legislation. The Children Act provides for many of the most important decisions, including whether to place a child for adoption to be made by the local authority and therefore there is nothing untoward in the Judge leaving the ultimate decision in the hands of the local authority with whom the child is placed.'

Another legislative objective was to impose upon local authorities a clearer and a higher duty to promote contact between children in care and parents and others having a significant place in their lives. Taking these two cornerstones of the Pt IV provisions in conjunction we are of the opinion that the primary purpose of s 34 is to impose obligations and restraints on local authorities with children in care. The obligation is the duty to promote contact. The restraint is upon their discretion to refuse contact unless they have first persuaded a judge that such a refusal is necessary. The power of the judge to supervise and control is the power to require the local authority to go further in the promotion of contact than the authority themselves consider appropriate. The other power is to monitor the local authority's proposal to refuse contact in order to ensure that their proposal is not excessive. We do not believe that the legislation ever intended the jurisdiction of the judge under s 34 to be deployed so as to inhibit the local authority in the performance of their statutory duty by preventing contact which the local authority considers advantageous to welfare. Although we recognise the width of the statutory language we are of the opinion that the construction for which Miss Hyde contends invades unduly and unnecessarily what Butler-Sloss LJ described as a difficult and sensitive area.

See also *Re H (termination of contact)* [2005] EWCA Civ 318, [2005] 1 FCR 658, [11] (Thorpe LJ) addressing a related point (granting s 34(4) orders stringently)

See also *A v M and Walsall Metropolitan Borough Council* [1994] 1 FCR 606 (FD), 607G–608F (Ewbank J) addressing a related point (interim s 34(4) orders permitted if risk is so severe that contact should be stopped)

10.3.7 Care and supervision orders: contact with children in care: s 34(4) orders: only if s34(4) is foreseeably needed

Re L (minors) (care proceedings: appeal) [1996] 2 FCR 352 (CA), 363F–364C (Butler-Sloss LJ)

Contact

The guardian ad litem asked for an order to be made under s 34(4), authorizing the local authority to refuse to allow contact between the children and the family, although the local authority did not seek such an order. The Judge said:

> 'It seems to me on balance I ought to accede to Mr Tolson's submission because, as I see it, it can do no harm if the county council do not wish to terminate contact and on the other hand if there should arise an occasion where, for whatever reason, whether it be the destructive behaviour of the children or whatever, their professionals come to the conclusion that contact ought to be refused then it can be done without further application to the court, because I cannot foresee that there would be any evidence before the court on that occasion which the guardian has not put forward today, so I am prepared to make that order.'

The order giving leave to terminate contact was contrary to the local authority's present intentions and to the indications made by the Judge as to the possibility of rehabilitation. Section 34(1) requires a local authority to allow the child in care reasonable contact with his parents unless by subs (4) the court authorizes termination of such contact. A section 34(4) order in our view is appropriate where there is no likelihood of rehabilitation and the child is, for instance, to be placed for adoption or with foster-parents without continuing contact with the natural family. In the context of this case it was surprising that a section 34(4) order should be made and to do so to save a further application to the court if the circumstances should change had the effect of handing over to the local authority the residual responsibility still vested in the court. It was premature to make an order which was not to be implemented in the foreseeable future.

See also *Re T (children in care: contact)* [1997] 3 FCR 73 (CA), 79C–81G (Simon Brown LJ) considering *Re L (minors) (care proceedings: appeal)* [1996] 2 FCR 352

10.3.8 Care and supervision orders: contact with children in care: s 34(4) orders: discharge of s 34(4) orders

Re T (children in care: contact) [1997] 3 FCR 73 (CA), 81H–84C (Simon Brown LJ) *quotation limited to* 82H–84C

With those considerations in mind, I turn now to consider what should be the court's general approach to a section 34(9) application for the discharge of a section 34(4) order.

Clearly such an application must be considered by the court, and considered indeed with the child's welfare in mind as the paramount consideration – save only in the very limited circumstances provided for by s 91(17) when the court's leave is required.

That said, it is plain that there must be demonstrable some material change of circumstance between the making of the section 34(4) order and the application to discharge it: the courts are obviously entitled to screen out what are essentially no more than disguised appeals against the original orders.

How much help, then, is to be derived from the passage which I have already cited from Butler-Sloss, LJ's judgment in *Re B* [1993] 1 FCR 363: the passage relied upon by the Judge below? To my mind, in this context very little. In the first place one must bear in mind the very different situation which the court was there considering: a particular category of care case in which a parent applies for contact with a view to rehabilitation. Butler-Sloss, LJ was not speaking in the context of an existing section 34(4) order, let alone an application to discharge such an order. Secondly, the formulation in any event appears, perhaps unavoidably, to beg more questions than it raises: '... such a change of circumstances as to require further investigation and reconsideration ...' How much change is 'such a change', and what precisely is encompassed within a requirement for 'further investigation and reconsideration' (in that case, of the local authority plan, in this case the desirability of the local authority retaining their section 34(4) authorization to terminate contact)? This second question seems to me of equal importance to the first. As Butler-Sloss, LJ said in *Re B (Minors) (Application for Contact)* [1994] 2 FCR 812 at p 817D:

> '[Counsel] argued that ... a Judge is obliged to hold a full hearing, permitting the parties to call oral evidence and cross-examine any witness they may choose. In my view a Judge in family cases has a much broader discretion both under the Children Act 1989 and previously to conduct the case as is most appropriate for the issues involved and the evidence available (see the judgment of Sir Stephen Brown, P. in *Re W* [1993] 2 F.C.R. 427). There is a spectrum of procedure for family cases from the *ex parte* application on minimal evidence to the full and detailed investigations on oral evidence which may be prolonged. Where on that spectrum a Judge decides a particular application should be placed is a matter for his discretion. Applications for residence orders

> or for committal to the care of a local authority or revocation of a care order are likely to be decided on full oral evidence, but not invariably. Such is not the case on contact applications which may be and are heard sometimes with and sometimes without oral evidence or with a limited amount of oral evidence.'

The judgment in *Re W* had cited a *dictum* of Balcombe, LJ – '… this is not ordinary civil litigation: it concerns children' – and continued thus:

> 'In our judgment that is a salutary observation and it would be unwise in this jurisdiction to seek to restrict the discretion of the court by imposing a rigid formula on the conduct of proceedings.'

Applying these considerations to an application to discharge a section 34(4) order, I conclude that the court should initially have two main interlocking considerations in mind: first, the extent to which circumstances have changed from when the order was originally made; and second, bearing those changes in mind, the extent to which it now seems appropriate to reinvestigate the central question. The court should ask itself: where on the 'spectrum of procedure' should this particular application be placed? Clearly the greater the apparent change in circumstances, the more intensively will the court be prepared to reconsider the desirability of leaving the section 34(4) order in place.

I would not myself speak in terms of the onus being on the applicant. But it should certainly be borne in mind that there are clear implications in all this not merely for the best use of court time but more importantly for the welfare of the children themselves. Children are often aware of the court's processes and troubled by the uncertainty and disruption engendered. Nor should the courts be expected to welcome applications which essentially seek to reopen already decided questions.

10.3.9 Care and supervision orders: contact with children in care: enforcement: LAs can be subject of committal

A Local Authority v HP and another; Re P-B (children) (contact order: penal notice) [2009] EWCA Civ 143, [2009] 2 FCR 105, [45]–[52] (Wall LJ)

[45] We start from the premise that the contact ordered by the judge was in the best interests of the child, and that it was being frustrated—or, at the lowest, it was in danger of being frustrated by the local authority foster father. On any view it was in AB's interests to see Mr B and his half-brother, and the order for Sunday contact was one which the judge was plainly entitled to make in the exercise of her discretion. It must follow, we think, that the order was properly enforceable against the local authority, to which it was—correctly—addressed: see s 34(1) of the 1989 Act. In short, the order was enforceable by committal.

[46] Furthermore, the local authority not only had parental responsibility for AB, it also had the power, given to it under s 33(3)(b) of the 1989

Act to 'determine the extent to which' others might meet their parental responsibility for AB. With that power comes the responsibility to obey contact orders made by the court under s 34. Above all, it is plain that Parliament has left the question of contact between individuals and children in care to judges, not to the discretion of local authorities. For present purposes, perhaps, it is sufficient to note that there is no appeal against the contact order.

[47] There is, we think, no dispute that the county court in ordinary civil proceedings not only has the power to make orders and injunctions against local authorities, but also has the power to enforce them by committal. Such orders are, no doubt rare because local authorities are not only creatures of statute, but, in the main, law abiding. In any event, Mr Main Thompson properly conceded that the court had jurisdiction to attach a penal notice to injunctive or directive orders (for example for the service of documents). He submitted, however, that an order for contact was not in this league, particularly when the local authority had given assurances that contact pursuant to the order of the court would be facilitated.

[48] We note in passing that in *Re S* (supra) Ward and Wall LJJ, plainly incensed at a local authority's failure to honour an undertaking, imposed a penal notice directed to the Head of Children's Services on the order made by this court. We have, however, already made the point that the local authority in that case did not argue that the court's order was not enforceable at first instance by committal, and it is plain from the report that no authority was cited to the court either for or against the proposition that a penal notice could not be attached to the order.

[49] It would, in our judgment, be an extraordinary state of affairs if a circuit judge was unable to enforce an order made under s 34 of the 1989 Act. Since at the date of the hearing before Judge Pearce the only means of enforcement of her contact order was by way of committal (however unusual such an order might be) the jurisdiction to order committal must, in our judgment, exist, as must the power to warn the local authority in advance by way of penal notice of the consequence of its disobedience of an order directed to it.

[50] We agree with Miss Hyde that Parliament has entrusted the carefully constructed contact regime relating to children in care in the hands of the court. In our judgment it follows that FPR 1991 4.21A, which is directed to private law proceedings, is not exhaustive, but that since, on its face, it is not expressed to apply to orders under s 34 of the 1989 Act, CCR Ord 29, r 1 is available to fill the gap.

Question 2: Did the judge have power to impose a penal notice?

[51] If, as we think, the court had power to enforce its order by committal, it also had power to attach to the order a penal notice.

[52] We are therefore of the view that the judge had jurisdiction, sitting as a circuit judge in the county court, to impose a penal notice on a contact order made under s 34 of the 1989 Act.

See also *Re F (a minor) (contact: child in care)* [1994] 2 FCR 1354 (FD), 1358A–D (Wilson J) addressing a related point (the absence of power to force would-be attendees)

See also *Birmingham City Council v H (a minor)* [1994] 1 FCR 896 (HL), 903F (Lord Slynn) addressing a related point (the absence of power to force would-be attendees)

10.4 CARE AND SUPERVISION ORDERS: SUPERVISION ORDERS

10.4.1 Care and supervision orders: supervision orders: nature and purpose

Re T (a minor) (care order) [1994] 1 FCR 663 (CA), 666F–667B (Bracewell J)

> The nature of a supervision order is to help and assist a child where the parents have full responsibility for the care and upbringing. It does not involve any statutory level of monitoring and it does not give the local authority parental responsibility. Any conditions attached to a supervision order cannot in themselves be enforced by the court. That was made clear in the case of *Croydon London Borough v A and B* [1992] 2 FCR 481, breaches can only be evidence in further proceedings.
>
> The essence of a supervision order is to advise, assist and befriend the supervised child. The directions which may be attached under Sch 3 to the Children Act 1989 are restricted to requiring a responsible person, that is the parent in this case, to take reasonable steps to ensure the child lives at a specified place, presents to a specified person, participates in specified activities and submits to various examinations where appropriate. The limits of such requirements do not, in my judgment, begin to address the problems of these parents who continue, to date, to exercise their parental responsibilities in a way which still merits some criticism.
>
> The contract drawn up between the parents and the local authority cannot be enforced without further court proceedings, whereas a care order places on the local authority a positive duty to ensure the welfare of the child and protect her from inadequate parenting. That is the framework and essence of the Act.

See also *Re T (a child) (supervision order: duration)* [2008] EWCA Civ 199, [2008] 3 FCR 319, [2] (Thorpe LJ) addressing a related point (supervision orders are usually made where there is 'real risk' that carers will fail unless supported)

See Chapter 10.2.2 Care and supervision orders: care orders: placement with parents: care or supervision

10.4.2 Care and supervision orders: supervision orders: 'requirements' and 'conditions'

Re V (a minor) (care or supervision order) [1996] 2 FCR 555 (CA), 563D–565G (Waite LJ) *quotation limited to* 563H–565F

Having, for those reasons, declined to grant a care order, the Judge proceeded to consider the merits of making a supervision order. He clearly regarded the making of a supervision order as being more in S's interests than making no order at all, although his reasons for that view were not expressly stated. He simply said, immediately after the passage I have just quoted:

> 'Consequently, I do not think that the risk of that fracture is in [S's] best interests and therefore, whilst I am absolutely satisfied that an order is necessary in this case, I think that a care order would be a step too far, and it is appropriate that I should make a supervision order with conditions.'

He then proceeded to state the conditions which, as set out in his formal order, read as follows. The order is made in the standard form CHA 20 headed: 'Order for the supervision of a child'. It omits to state who the child's supervisor is to be, but it must necessarily be implicit that the order was intended to be made in favour of the local authority. After naming the child the order continues at para 2:

> 'The court orders that this child shall:
>
> 1. Attend Hollybank School as a weekly boarder and take part in all school activities as arranged.
> 2. [S] should only not attend school if he is certified unfit by a medical practitioner.
> 3. Each Monday [S] should take £20 from his State allowances for use in activities arranged by the school.
> 4. [S] should attend meetings at PHAB at Dewsbury when they have been arranged.'

Miss Hamilton has argued on behalf of the guardian ad litem, with the support of the local authority (which in the interests of saving costs has not been represented on this appeal), that the Judge's approach to the making of a supervision order was misconceived. In the first place, he spoke of conditions attached to his proposed supervision order. That is something, Miss Hamilton points out, for which the Act makes no provision at all. Schedule 3 is confined to dealing with directions to be given by the supervisor and requirements to be imposed with consent by the court. Those requirements, moreover, are dependent upon the consent of any 'responsible person'. Such an individual is defined in para 1 of Sch 3 as meaning in relation to a supervised child:

> '... any person who has parental responsibility for the child ...'

Accordingly, if the conditions imposed by the Judge are to be viewed as Schedule 3 requirements, they needed the consent of the mother and the father. In fact, at the stage of the hearing before the Judge, no such consent had been forthcoming from either of them.

Miss Hamilton further points out, and this is accepted by counsel for the mother and the father, that the so-called conditions 2 and 3 are provisions which the Judge would in any event have had no jurisdiction to introduce into a supervision order under any guise whatsoever.

Despite the brave efforts made by Mrs Pope, for the mother, and Miss Trimmer, for the father, to defend the form of order chosen by the Judge, the criticisms made of it by Miss Hamilton are, in my view, well-founded. The concept of a supervision order subject to conditions simply cannot be fitted into the framework of the Children Act legislation. The Judge may have been misled by the suggestions in the statement of the social worker that such an option was available. The fact that Sch 3 to the Act was not cited to him may have added to his difficulties. Nevertheless, there is no escaping from the inference that the Judge had misconceived the nature and the purpose of a supervision order.

Mrs Pope has told the court today that she had instructions on the mother's behalf to consent to whatever changes in the order were necessary to bring it into compliance with the Act and the terms of Sch 3. That would involve rewriting the surviving 'conditions' 1 and 4 as 'requirements' under para 3 to which the mother would be willing to give the necessary consent.

Miss Trimmer was given similar instructions on behalf of the father.

Even if the supervision order were to be so corrected however, and thus given validity as a matter of form, that would still fail to eliminate the essential difficulty arising from the fact that a supervision order rests primarily upon the consent of the parent affected by it. Any provisions incorporated into a supervision order, either by direction of the supervisor or by requirements directly stated by the Judge, are incapable of being enforced directly through any of the ordinary processes by which courts of law enforce obedience to their directions. The only sanction, when any infringement of the terms of a supervision order, or of directions given under it, occurs is a return by the supervisor to court. There the ultimate sanction will be the making of a care order under which the local authority will be given the necessary legal powers to enforce its will.

The whole tenor of the judgment of the Judge suggests to me that this is something which he had failed to appreciate. He was attracted to the option of a supervision order, subject to conditions, as something which he saw as a middle road; that is to say, he saw it as a means to the achievement of the same ends as a care order, but in a way that would be less obviously invasive of the parents' freedom and potentially less disruptive of their marriage. The fallacy underlying that view was in thinking that a supervision order was capable of achieving the same ends as a care order. If the mother failed to comply with the 'requirements' imposed on her by the supervision order

> by refusing to allow S to attend Hollybank, the only recourse to procure his attendance would be, if it depended solely upon the making of a supervision order, a fresh application to the court -this time for a care order to replace the frustrated provisions of the supervision order. Give the imminence of S's 17th birthday, that would be a wholly empty sanction.

See also *Re S (a minor) (care or supervision order)* [1996] 2 FCR 719 (CA), 726E–727G (Beldam LJ) considering *Re V (a minor) (care or supervision order)* [1996] 2 FCR 555

10.4.3 Care and supervision orders: supervision orders: duration: initial orders can be shorter than one year

M v Warwickshire County Council [1994] 2 FCR 121 (FD), 124B–D (Thorpe J)

> It seems to me very important that in construing the Act the court should, wherever possible, favour construction that is likely to make for practical advantage. It is obviously advantageous to those who have the management of difficult cases, such as this, that there should be a flexible range of powers. This case well illustrates the advantages of and need for a discretion that is not confined to a choice between 12 months or no supervision order at all.
>
> The language of para 6(1) of Sch 3 does not, in my judgment, preclude the construction that it provides only a maximum and not a minimum. Accordingly, I conclude that the court has jurisdiction to make a supervision order for an initial duration of less than 12 months.

See also *Re T (a child) (supervision order: duration)* [2008] EWCA Civ 199, [2008] 3 FCR 319, [11]–[19] (Thorpe LJ) addressing a related point (supervision orders cannot be for more than 1 year, initially)

10.4.4 Care and supervision orders: supervision orders: duration: guidance regarding seeking extensions

Re T (a child) (supervision order: duration) [2008] EWCA Civ 199, [2008] 3 FCR 319, [20]–[23] (Thorpe LJ)

> [20] I would fill the void in para 6 by suggesting a like practice in relation to supervision orders. Clearly before any extension is sought the need for and the acceptance of extension will be canvassed in correspondence. That exploration will reveal whether the extension is consensual and, if not, the extent of the dispute. The issue of any necessary application should not be delayed so as to imperil the local authority's imperative need for a determination before the expiration of the current order. I say imperative because once the order has expired the applicant would be compelled to prove and the court to determine the s 31 threshold since the application would have become not an application for extension but an application for a new order.

[21] In the great majority of cases the listing and determination of an extension application will not much burden the court. The determination will be discretionary and the factors relevant to the exercise of that discretion are unlikely to be either extensive or complex.

[22] In summary I would doubt the need for any application to extend a supervision order of twelve months' duration before the last quarter of its first life. How well within that quarter the application should sensibly be issued depends upon the facts of each case, that is to say the extent of the issues raised by the application, and the ascertainable capacity of the relevant court.

[23] I accept that the practice that I suggest lacks the pragmatic appeal of that adopted by Judge Hunt. But that appeal derives in part from the fact that in this case, the risk to be safeguarded lies outside the parental home. The order is not to be seen as intrusive or threatening. In the commoner case where the parent's shortcomings require the imposition of a supervision order the legislative requirement for the court to review the continuing need for the order becomes apparent.

10.4.5 Care and supervision orders: supervision orders: duration: test for extensions

Re A (a minor) (supervision order: extension) [1995] 2 FCR 114 (CA), 117A–D (Butler-Sloss LJ)

> There is no direct guidance in the Act on the criteria to be applied on the hearing of an extension application. One has to stand back and look at the purpose of the extension of the supervision order. In previous legislation the supervision order might run for a period up to three years. Paragraph 6(1) in part II of Sch 3now brings a supervision order to an end after one year but by subpara (3) on application by the supervisor the court may extend it for such period as it may specify. The order may not however by para 6(4) be extended beyond three years. There is no bar however upon a local authority making a fresh application under s 31 for a supervision order in which case the threshold criteria would have to be proved to trigger the jurisdiction of the court to consider whether to make an order.
>
> If s 31 was to be imported into an application to extend an existing supervision order there would be no purpose to the specific provision in para 6 in Part II of Sch 3. At the expiry of the one-year period the local authority or other supervisor would be required to make a fresh application under s 31. Looking at the framework of the Act the s 31 application was clearly not intended to be invoked on extension applications and, bearing in mind the earlier provision for a three-year period, the purpose of the alteration is in my view clear. It allows the local authority to keep in place a supervision order for three years as before but under the greater control of the courts, part of the philosophy of the Act at the application stage. After

> a year the local authority has to justify to the court that the welfare of the child requires the supervision order to continue and there is an opportunity for the application to extend to be opposed.

See also *Re A (a minor) (supervision order: extension)* [1995] 2 FCR 114 (CA), 117E–G (Butler-Sloss LJ) addressing a related point (no power to substitute care orders on extension applications)

10.4.6 Care and supervision orders: supervision orders: supervision orders alongside SGOs

See Chapter 12.2.6 SGOs: general principles: SGOs alongside public law orders

CHAPTER 11

Placement and adoption orders

Chapter contents

CHAPTER 11

Placement and adoption orders

11.1 PLACEMENT AND ADOPTION ORDERS: PLACEMENT ORDERS: GENERALLY

11.1.1 Placement and adoption orders: placement orders: generally: approach in care cases

See Chapter 9.1 The welfare stage: the court's approach

See Chapter 9.2 The welfare stage: paramountcy of welfare

See Chapter 9.3.2 The welfare stage: the welfare checklists: approach to the checklists: adoption cases

See also *Surrey County Council v S* [2014] EWCA Civ 601, [2014] 3 FCR 453, [27]–[30] (Ryder LJ) addressing a related point (that care and placement order applications should be heard concurrently, and LAs[1] should be astute to the timetabling of ADM[2] decision making so that all matters can be heard together)

11.1.2 Placement and adoption orders: placement orders: generally: ADM decisions

Re P-B (a child) (placement order) [2006] EWCA Civ 1016, [2007] 3 FCR 308, [17]–[20] (Thorpe LJ)

[17] Mr O'Brien stresses that he local authority essentially has two quite separate functions in this field. Its first and, perhaps for us, most familiar function is in the protection, support and assistance of children under Pts (iii) and (iv) of the Children Act 1989. However, it is, under the terms of the Adoption and Children Act 2002, also an adoption agency and its function as an adoption service is distinct under s 3 of the 2002 Act. Thus, says Mr O'Brien, there are these interlinked duties. Thus the local authority in pursuance of its responsibilities and duties under the 1989 Act may reach a decision that adoption is the right future for the child and so declare in the care plan. The case must then be presented to the panel, which must reach its recommendation under the terms of the regulation. If the decision of the panel supports the provisional decision of the local authority acting under Pt 4 of the 1989 Act, then the decision of the panel must be considered independently by the local authority as an adoption agency under the

1 Local authorities.
2 Agency decision maker.

provisions of reg 19. Effectively, that means that a senior officer in the local authority must take a decision to endorse the positive recommendation of the panel to complete the statutory process. Once that is done, says Mr O'Brien, the way is clear for the issue of an application for a placement order. Prior thereto, the issue of an application would be plainly premature.

[18] So, in the very shortest summary, the dispute is as to what is meant by the requirement in s 22 that a local authority is to apply for a placement order if they are satisfied that the child ought to be placed for adoption; is the local authority acting under the provisions of Pts 3 and 4 of the Children Act 1989, or is the local authority acting as an adoption agency under the terms of the 2002 Act?

[19] I am in no doubt in my mind that Mr O'Brien is right in his construction. It is in its role as an adoption agency that the local authority must be satisfied, and that process cannot be achieved until there has been complete compliance with the requirements of the regulations, namely that the appointed officer has taken the positive decision to endorse the recommendation of the panel.

[20] Accordingly, on the facts of this case it was not open to the local authority to issue the placement order application any earlier than it did, and the question for the judge then was whether to permit the consolidation and contemporaneous conclusion of the two applications. Mr Keehan has not made any specific criticism of the short judgment given by Judge Connor, which was noted but not transcribed, and the question must be: was his discretionary conclusion within the wide ambit of his discretion? I am in no doubt that it was.

See also *Re B (placement order)* [2008] EWCA Civ 835, [2008] 2 FCR 570, [69]–[74], [81]–[86] (Wall LJ) addressing a related point (the approach to flawed panels is to adjourn and require reconsideration, the court process does not rectify material failings)

11.1.3 Placement and adoption orders: placement orders: generally: uncertainty regarding finding adopters: not necessarily reason to refuse orders

Re T (children: placement order) [2008] EWCA Civ 248, [2008] 1 FCR 633, [17]–[18] (Hughes LJ)

[17] Insofar as Mr Keehan submits that there should be no placement order if there is anticipated real difficulty in placing the child—and I am not sure that he does—I for my part emphatically disagree. Certain it is that to make a placement order the judge making of any decision relating to adoption, including the making of a placement order, the court must make the child's welfare its paramount consideration: see s 1(1), (2) and (7). But even if there is a real possibility that an adoptive placement will not be found, it by no means follows that adoption is not in the best interests of the child. Since a child cannot usually be placed without a placement

order, to say otherwise would be to deprive the child of the chance of what has been determined to be the best possible outcome for him. Mere uncertainty as to whether adoption will actually follow is not a reason for not making a placement order. Indeed, s 22(2)(a), referred to above, clearly contemplates that a placement order may be applied for before it is known whether there will be a care order or not. Plainly a placement order can be, and perhaps usually should be, made at the same time as a care order is made on a plan for adoption which the judge approves, even though at that stage a good deal of investigation and preparation is needed before the child can actually be placed, and it is not known whether a suitable family will be found or not …

[18] But the difference in this unusual case is that it was not simply a matter of potential difficulty of placement. The boys were, at present, not suitable for placement for adoption. It would not be known whether they ever would be until a particular exercise had been carried out, in the form of the specialised foster placement over several months. And as the guardian in particular explained, it might well turn out that adoption was not simply not achievable, but was not in the boys' best interests, because their needs could better be met by the kind of substitute family found only in long term fostering. The generalised consideration that adoption would ideally be best does not, on these unusual facts, lead automatically to the conclusion that it was yet possible to say whether it was in the best interests of these boys. In those circumstances I am persuaded that the finding that adoption was in their best interests, and thus that a placement order should follow, was premature.

Re S-H (a child) [2008] EWCA Civ 493, [2008] 2 FLR 918, [28] (Wilson LJ)

28. … For it is an insufficient foundation for a placement order that the long-term aim of the court is that the child should be adopted. The necessary foundation is that – broadly speaking – the child is presently in a condition to be adopted and is ready to be adopted, even though in some cases the court has to countenance the possibility of substantial difficulty and thus delay in finding a suitable adoptive placement or even of failure to find one at all.

11.1.4 Placement and adoption orders: placement orders: generally: uncertainty regarding finding adopters: not necessarily reason to refuse orders: dual planning

Re P (children) (adoption: parental consent) [2008] EWCA Civ 535, [2008] 2 FCR 185, [135]–[140] (Wall LJ) *quotation limited to* [137]

[137] In our judgment, a local authority can be 'satisfied that the child ought to be placed for adoption' within the meaning of s 22(1)(d) of the 2002 Act even though it recognises the reality that a search for adoptive parents may be unsuccessful and that, if it is, the alternative plan will have to be

for long-term fostering. The wording, after all, is 'ought to be' not 'will be'. That being so there can be no objection in principle to dual planning in appropriate cases.

11.1.5 Placement and adoption orders: placement orders: generally: evidence concerning likelihood of finding adopters

Re M (a child) [2018] EWCA Civ 240, [2018] 2 FCR 253, [59]–[61] (King LJ)

[59] I quite accept that in these days of strained resources, it cannot be expected that an adoption social worker should routinely attend court. I also understand that there can be no specific 'family finding' until such time as a placement order has been made. Notwithstanding this, with respect to the judge, I do not agree that the enquiries made described by the judge as 'limited but appropriate' were adequate in the circumstances of this case.

[60] This court is aware from its combined experience, that considerable information can be gleaned as to the likely availability at any one time of prospective adopters over the country together with a prospective timescale, without the necessity of revealing the identity of the child. On the face of it E could well be a challenging child to place: she is reaching the higher end for placement even for a little girl. She has significant cultural needs as a black Zimbabwean child, she has physical problems which, whilst not of the most serious, cannot be ignored, together with speech and developmental delay. She has potential attachment difficulties, the latter surely a feature likely to impact upon the ease of finding her a permanent substitute family away from her mother.

[61] In a case of this kind, the court will need the best available evidence about the likelihood of identifying suitable adopters and the length of time that should be devoted to the search before alternatives are considered. More often than not, the allocated social worker will be able to give this evidence after careful discussion with the social worker who would be responsible for the family finding, but there may still be cases where direct evidence from the family finder will be required. Regardless of whether this was such a case, as I say above, I do not consider the evidence before the judge to have been sufficient to allow him securely to undertake his balancing of the options.

11.1.6 Placement and adoption orders: placement orders: generally: placing twins separately

Prospective adopters for BT and another v County of Herefordshire District Council and others [2018] EWFC 76, [1]–[2] (Keehan J)

1. I am concerned with two children, BT and GT who are twins who were born in 2010. It is almost impossible to imagine the circumstances in

which it would be considered appropriate to separate twins and place them for adoption by different prospective adopters. This is, however, what occurred in this case and I have before me an application by a couple, whom I shall refer to as A and B, to adopt BT and an application by a single carer whom I shall refer to as C, to adopt GT.

2. As I shall set out in some detail, I am satisfied and find that the court is in the position of considering applications to adopt the twins in two separate homes because of the incompetence and serial failings of the local authority, Herefordshire Council, and the egregious behaviour of some of its former staff.

11.1.7 Placement and adoption orders: placement orders: generally: dispensing with parental consent: welfare 'requires' it

Re B-S (children) (adoption: leave to oppose) [2013] EWCA Civ 1146, [2013] 3 FCR 481, [6], [17]–[29] (Sir James Munby P) *quotation limited to* [6], [17]–[24]

[6] The court cannot make a placement order unless either the parent has consented or the court is satisfied that the parent's consent should be dispensed with: s 21(3). The court cannot dispense with a parent's consent unless either the parent cannot be found, or lacks capacity to give consent, or the welfare of the child 'requires' the consent to be dispensed with: s 52(1). In deciding whether or not to make a placement order the paramount consideration of the court must be the child's welfare 'throughout his life': s 1(2). The court must have regard to the 'welfare checklist' in s 1(4). So far as material for present purposes a placement order continues in force until it is revoked under s 24 or an adoption order is made: s 21(4).

...

Adoption—fundamental principles

[17] Before proceeding any further, it is necessary for us to go back to first principles and to emphasise a number of essential considerations that judges *must* always have in mind, and we emphasise this, at *every* stage of the process. Regrettably, the continuing lack of attention to what has been said in previous judgments necessitates our use of plain, even strong, language.

[18] We start with art 8 of the European Convention for the Protection of Human Rights and Fundamental Freedoms 1950 (as set out in Pt I of Sch 1 to the Human Rights Act 1998) (the Convention). There is no need for us to go through the jurisprudence of the Strasbourg court. The relevant passages from three key decisions: *K v Finland* [2001] 2 FCR 673, (2001) 36 EHRR 255, *R v UK* (2011) 54 EHRR 28, [2011] 2 FLR 1236[1], and *YC v UK* [2013] 2 FCR 36, (2012) 55 EHRR 967, are set out by the Supreme Court in *Re B* [2013] 2 FCR 525, [2013] 3 All ER 929. The overarching principle remains as explained by Hale LJ, as she then was,

in *Re C and B (children) (care order: future harm)* [2000] 2 FCR 614 at 625, [2001] 1 FLR 611 at 621 (para 34):

> '... Intervention in the family may be appropriate, but the aim should be to reunite the family when the circumstances enable that, and the effort should be devoted towards that end. Cutting off all contact and the relationship between the child or children and their family is only justified by the overriding necessity of the interests of the child.'

To this we need only add what the Strasbourg court said in *YC v UK* [2013] 2 FCR 36, (2012) 55 EHRR 967 (para 134):

> '... family ties may only be severed in very exceptional circumstances and ... everything must be done to preserve personal relations and, where appropriate, to "rebuild" the family ... It is not enough to show that a child could be placed in a more beneficial environment for his upbringing ...'

[19] In this connection it is to be remembered, as Baroness Hale of Richmond pointed out in *Down Lisburn Health and Social Services Trust v H* at [34], that the United Kingdom is unusual in Europe in permitting the total severance of family ties without parental consent.

[20] Section 52(1)(b) of the 2002 Act provides, as we have seen, that the consent of a parent with capacity can be dispensed with only if the welfare of the child 'requires' this. 'Require' here has the Strasbourg meaning of necessary, 'the connotation of the imperative, what is demanded rather than what is merely optional or reasonable or desirable': *Re P (children) (adoption: parental consent)* [2008] EWCA Civ 535 at [120], [125], [2008] 2 FCR 185 at [120], [125], [2008] 2 FLR 625. This is a stringent and demanding test.

[21] Just how stringent and demanding has been spelled out very recently by the Supreme Court in *Re B* [2013] 2 FCR 525, [2013] 3 All ER 929. The significance of *Re B* was rightly emphasised in two judgments of this court handed down on 30 July 2013: *Re P (a child) (care and placement: evidential basis of local authority case)* [2013] EWCA Civ 963 at [102], [2013] 3 FCR 159 at [102] (per Black LJ), and *Re G (a child) (care proceedings: welfare balancing exercise: proportionality)* [2013] EWCA Civ 965 at [29]–[31], [2013] 3 FCR 293 at [29]–[31] (per McFarlane LJ). As Black LJ put it in *Re P*, *Re B* is a forceful reminder of just what is required.

[22] The language used in *Re B* is striking. Different words and phrases are used, but the message is clear. Orders contemplating non-consensual adoption—care orders with a plan for adoption, placement orders and adoption orders—are 'a very extreme thing, a last resort', only to be made where 'nothing else will do', where 'no other course [is] possible in [the child's] interests', they are 'the most extreme option', a 'last resort—when all else fails', to be made 'only in exceptional circumstances and where motivated by *overriding requirements* pertaining to the child's welfare, in

short, where nothing else will do': see *Re B* [2013] 2 FCR 525 at [74], [76], [77], [82], [104], [130], [135], [145], [198], [215], [2013] 3 All ER 929.

[23] Behind all this there lies the well-established principle, derived from s 1(5) of the 1989 Act, read in conjunction with s 1(3)(g), and now similarly embodied in s 1(6) of the 2002 Act, that the court should adopt the 'least interventionist' approach. As Hale J, as she then was, said in *Re O (care or supervision order)* [1997] 2 FCR 17 at 22, [1996] 2 FLR 755 at 760:

> '... the court should begin with a preference for the less interventionist rather than the more interventionist approach. This should be considered to be in the better interests of the children ... unless there are cogent reasons to the contrary.'

[24] Linked with this is the vitally important point made by Wall LJ in *Re P (children) (adoption: parental consent)* [2008] 2 FCR 185 at [126], [2008] 2 FLR 625:

> '... Section 52(1) is concerned with adoption—the making of either a placement order or an adoption order—and what therefore has to be shown is that the child's welfare "requires" *adoption* as opposed to something short of adoption. A child's circumstances may "require" statutory intervention, perhaps may even "require" the indefinite or long-term removal of the child from the family and his or her placement with strangers, but that is not to say that the same circumstances will necessarily "require" that the child be adopted. They may or they may not. The question, at the end of the day, is whether what is "required" is adoption.'

Re P (children) (adoption: parental consent) [2008] EWCA Civ 535, [2008] 2 FCR 185, [113]–[132] (Wall LJ) *quotation limited to* [113]–[128]

Discussion

[113] We welcome the opportunity afforded by this case to revisit s 52(1)(b) of the 2002 Act, and with it, in particular, the phrase 'the welfare of the child requires the consent to be dispensed with'. We propose, accordingly, to address firstly Mr Geekie's question: what is meant by welfare in s 52(1)(b)?

[114] In our judgment, the answer to this question is self-evident, and is to be found in s 1 of the 2002 Act, which we have set out in full at para [37] of this judgment. Section 1(1) plainly applies when the court is deciding whether or not to dispense with parental consent to a placement order. Such a decision is manifestly 'a decision relating to the adoption of a child'. In these circumstances, s 1(2) of the 2002 Act requires the court (the word is the mandatory 'must') in these circumstances to treat 'the child's welfare throughout his life' as its 'paramount consideration'. 'Paramount consideration' as Lord MacDermott classically held in *J v C* [1969] 1 All ER 788 at 821, [1970] AC 668 at 711 means a consideration which 'rules upon and determines the course to be followed'.

[115] In this context, in our judgment, 'welfare throughout (the child's) life' plainly means welfare as determined by the court or adoption agency, having regard to the matter set out in s 1(4) of the 2002 Act. Section 1(4) of the 2002 Act provides a checklist far wider than that provided in s 1(3) of the 1989 Act. If and insofar, therefore, as *Re S* gives the impression that the items which have to be taken into account when 'welfare' in s 1 of the 2002 Act are equivalent to the so-called welfare checklist in s 1(3) of the 1989 Act, that impression is, plainly, erroneous. However, even a cursory examination of *Re S* demonstrates, I think, that this is not the case. Since special guardianship orders, which were the focus of the discussion in *Re S* are made under the 1989 Act, the debate on the appropriateness in any given case of an adoption order as opposed to a special guardianship order required consideration of both s 1(3) of the 1989 Act and s 1(4) of the 2002 Act—see *Re S* at [48](i) and (ii):

> '[48] The special nature of the jurisdiction also has implications for the approach of the courts:
>
> (i) In view of the importance of such cases to the parties and the children concerned, it is incumbent on judges to give full reasons and to explain their decisions with care. Short cuts are to be avoided. It is not of course necessary to go through the welfare check-list line by line, but the parties must be able to follow the judge's reasoning and to satisfy themselves that he or she has duly considered it and has taken every aspect of it relevant to the particular case properly into account.
>
> (ii) Provided the judge has carefully examined the facts, made appropriate findings in relation to them and applied the welfare check-lists contained in s 1(3) of the 1989 Act and s 1 of the 2002 Act, it is unlikely that this court will be able properly to interfere with the exercise of judicial discretion, particularly in a finely balanced case. (We think it no co-incidence that all three of the appeals with which these judgments are concerned fall to be dismissed, although each reaches a different result.)'

[116] In our judgment, similar considerations apply to applications under s 52(1)(b) of the 2002 Act. The guidance is, we think, simple enough. The judge must, of course, be aware of the importance to the child of the decision being taken. There is, perhaps, no more important or far-reaching decision for a child than to be adopted by strangers. However, the word 'requires' in s 52(1)(b) is a perfectly ordinary English word. Judges approaching the question of dispensation under the section must, it seems to us, ask themselves the question to which s 52(1)(b) of the 2002 gives rise, and answer it by reference to s 1 of the same Act, and in particular by a careful consideration of all the matters identified in s 1(4).

[117] In summary, therefore, the best guidance which in our judgment this court can give is to advise judges to apply the statutory language with care to the facts of the particular case. The message is, no doubt, prosaic, but

the best guidance, we think, is as simple and as straightforward as that. Moreover, it very much echoes what this court said in *Re S* in relation to special guardianship orders.

[118] Without wishing to qualify in any way the clarity and simplicity of what we have just said, but in deference to Mr Geekie's careful argument, we think we should add a few words about the Strasbourg jurisprudence to which he referred us.

[119] Plainly art 8 is engaged; and it is elementary that, if art 8 is not to be breached, any intervention under Pt IV or Pt V of the 1989 Act, and any placement or adoption order made without parental consent in accordance with s 52(1)(b) of the 2002 Act, must be proportionate to the legitimate aim of protecting the welfare and interests of the child. As Hale LJ (as she then was) said in *Re C and B (children) (care order: future harm)* [2000] 2 FCR 614 at [33]:

> '… under art 8 of the Convention both the children and the parents have the right to respect for their family and private life. If the state is to interfere with that there are three requirements: first, that it be in accordance with the law; secondly, that it be for a legitimate aim (in this case the protection of the welfare and interests of the children); and thirdly, that it be 'necessary in a democratic society'.'

[120] 'Necessary' takes its colour from the context but in the Strasbourg jurisprudence has a meaning lying somewhere between 'indispensable' on the one hand and 'useful', 'reasonable' or 'desirable' on the other hand. It implies the existence of what the Strasbourg jurisprudence calls a 'pressing social need'. Hale LJ continued at para [34]:

> 'There is a long line of European Court of Human Rights jurisprudence on that third requirement, which emphasises that the intervention has to be proportionate to the legitimate aim. Intervention in the family may be appropriate, but the aim should be to reunite the family when the circumstances enable that, and the effort should be devoted towards that end. Cutting off all contact and the relationship between the child or children and their family is only justified by the overriding necessity of the interests of the child.'

[121] She reiterated that in *Re O (a child) (supervision order: future harm)* [2001] EWCA Civ 16, [2001] 1 FCR 289, adding at para [28] that 'Proportionality, therefore, is the key'. There is no need to refer in detail to the Strasbourg case law. A recent statement of the principle can be found in *Hasse v Germany* [2005] 3 FCR 666 at para 93.

[122] To the same effect is the judgment of Thorpe LJ in *Re B (children) (care: interference with family life)* [2003] EWCA Civ 786 at [34], [2004] 1 FCR 463 at [34]:

> '… where the application is for a care order empowering the local authority to remove a child or children from the family, the judge in modern times may not make such an order without considering

> the European Convention for the Protection of Human Rights and Fundamental Freedoms 1950 art 8 rights of the adult members of the family and of the children of the family. Accordingly he must not sanction such an interference with family life unless he is satisfied that that is both necessary and proportionate and that no other less radical form of order would achieve the essential end of promoting the welfare of the children.'

[123] That last observation reflects the well-established principle, derived from s 1(5) of the 1989 Act, read in conjunction with s 1(3)(g), and now similarly embodied in s 1(6) of the 2002 Act, that, particularly in the context of public law proceedings, the court should adopt the 'least interventionist' approach. As Hale J (as she then was) said in *Re O (minors) (care or supervision order)* [1997] 2 FCR 17 at 22:

> 'the court should begin with a preference for the less interventionist rather than the more interventionist approach. This should be considered to be in the better interests of the children ... unless there are cogent reasons to the contrary.'

[124] In assessing what is proportionate, the court has, of course, always to bear in mind that adoption without parental consent is an extreme—indeed the most extreme—interference with family life. Cogent justification must therefore exist if parental consent is to be dispensed with in accordance with s 52(1)(b). Hence the observations of the Strasbourg court in *Johansen v Norway* (1996) 23 EHRR 33 upon which Mr Geekie in particular relied. That was a case where the court had to consider a permanent placement with a view to adoption. At para 78 it said:

> 'These measures were particularly far-reaching in that they totally deprived the applicant of her family life with the child and were inconsistent with the aim of reuniting them. Such measures should only be applied in exceptional circumstances and could only be justified if they were motivated by an overriding requirement pertaining to the child's best interests.'

[125] This is the context in which the critical word 'requires' is used in s 52(1)(b). It is a word which was plainly chosen as best conveying, as in our judgment it does, the essence of the Strasbourg jurisprudence. And viewed from that perspective 'requires' does indeed have the connotation of the imperative, what is demanded rather than what is merely optional or reasonable or desirable.

[126] What is also important to appreciate is the statutory context in which the word 'requires' is here being used, for, like all words, it will take its colour from the particular context. Section 52(1) is concerned with adoption—the making of either a placement order or an adoption order—and what therefore has to be shown is that the child's welfare 'requires' *adoption* as opposed to something short of adoption. A child's circumstances may 'require' statutory intervention, perhaps may even 'require' the indefinite or long-term removal of the child from the family and his or her placement

with strangers, but that is not to say that the same circumstances will necessarily 'require' that the child be adopted. They may or they may not. The question, at the end of the day, is whether what is 'required' is adoption.

[127] In our judgment, however, this does not mean that there is some enhanced welfare test to be applied in cases of adoption, in contrast to what Mr Geekie called a simple welfare test. The difference, and it is an important, indeed vital, difference, is simply that between s 1 of the 1989 Act and s 1 of the 2002 Act.

[128] In the first place, s 1(2) of the 2002 Act, in contrast to s 1(1) of the 1989 Act, requires a judge considering dispensing with parental consent in accordance with s 52(1)(b) to focus on the child's welfare 'throughout his life'. This emphasises that adoption, unlike other forms of order made under the 1989 Act, is something with lifelong implications. In other words, a judge exercising his powers under s 52(1)(b) has to be satisfied that the child's welfare now, throughout the rest of his childhood, into adulthood and indeed throughout his life, requires that he or she be adopted. Secondly, and reinforcing this point, it is important to bear in mind the more extensive 'welfare checklist' to be found in s 1(4) of the 2002 Act as compared with the 'welfare checklist' in s 1(3) of the 1989 Act; in particular, the provisions of s 1(4)(c)—which specifically directs attention to the consequences for the child 'throughout his life'—and s 1(4)(f). This all feeds into the ultimate question under s 52(1)(b): does the child's welfare *throughout his life* require adoption as opposed to something short of adoption?

See also *Re B (a child) (care order: proportionality: criterion for review)* [2013] UKSC 33, [2013] 2 FCR 525, [33]–[34] (Lord Wilson), [73]–[77], [104]–[105] (Lord Neuberger P), [194]–[198], [215] (Lady Hale), see Chapter 9.1.7 The welfare stage: the court's approach: adoption cases: 'nothing else will do'

11.2 PLACEMENT AND ADOPTION ORDERS: PLACEMENT ORDERS: REVOCATION

11.2.1 Placement and adoption orders: placement orders: revocation: applications for leave to apply to revoke: test

Re T (application to revoke placement order: change if circumstances)
[2014] EWCA Civ 1369, [2015] 1 FCR 238, [41]–[45], [60] (Russell J)

Law

[41] The revocation of placement orders is governed by s 24 of the Adoption and Children Act 2002 which provides (s 24(1)) that the court may revoke a placement order on the application of any person. Permission to apply for revocation has to be given when the application is made by anyone other than the child or the local authority (s 24(2)); permission or leave cannot be given unless the court is satisfied that there has been a change in circumstances since the order was made. Thus there are two stages, the

first being has there been a change in circumstances? The second, if so should leave be granted? While the first is primarily a factual question for the judge to decide the second is subject to judicial discretion when the court has to decide whether there is a real prospect of success. In this case the judge decided that there was no change in circumstances.

[42] There is limited authority for the approach which should be taken in measuring whether there has been a change in circumstances, a phrase that appears throughout the Adoption and Children Act 2002. In *Re P (a child) (adoption order: leave to oppose making of adoption order)* [2007] EWCA Civ 616, [2007] 2 FCR 407, [2007] 1 WLR 2556 the meaning of 'a change in circumstances' in respect of s 47(5) and s 47(7) was considered and the approach of Wall LJ, as he then was, was endorsed and followed in *Re B-S (children)* [2013] 3 FCR 481, [2014] 1 WLR 563. In his judgment Wall LJ considered the meaning of change in circumstances;

> '[26] In our judgment, analysis of the statutory language in ss 1 and 47 of the 2002 Act leads to the conclusion that an application for leave to defend adoption proceedings under s 47(5) of the 2002 Act involves a two-stage process. First of all, the court has to be satisfied, on the facts of the case, that there has been a change in circumstances within s 47(7). If there has been no change in circumstances, that is the end of the matter, and the application fails. If, however, there has been a change in circumstances within s 47(7) then the door to the exercise of a judicial discretion to permit the parents to defend the adoption proceedings is opened, and the decision whether or not to grant leave is governed by s 1 of the 2002 Act. In other words, "the paramount consideration of the court must be the child's welfare throughout his life."
>
> The meaning of "a change in circumstances"
>
> [27] Before examining in greater detail how the discretion, if it arises, falls to be exercised, it is, we think, necessary to decide what is meant by the phrase "a change in circumstances since the placement order was made" in s 47(7) of the Act.
>
> [28] For the father, Miss Platt accepted that not every change in circumstances would suffice to open the door to the exercise of the judicial discretion identified in [26] above. She accepted that the change in circumstances had to be relevant or material to the question of whether or not leave should be granted. She invited us, however, to decline to put any further gloss on the statute. Parliament, she argued, could have attached an adjective such as "significant" to the phrase "change in circumstances", as indeed it had done in s 14D(5) of the 1989 Act in relation to the variation or discharge of a special guardianship order.
>
> [29] Miss Platt submitted that in making a change in circumstances the pre-requisite for the exercise of the discretion under s 47(7), Parliament

had chosen not to qualify the change in circumstances in any way. What was required was, simply, "a change in circumstances". Miss Platt was, moreover, able to argue that the point was reinforced by the fact that the special guardianship provisions in the 1989 Act referred to in [28] above were themselves contained within and introduced through the mechanism of the 2002 Act. The word "significant" which Mr Pressdee invited us to attach to the phrase was simply not there, and had crept in, she argued, only through Hansard, to which the judge had been referred, and, at best, represented the relevant ministers' view. This was not, she argued, a satisfactory aid to statutory construction.

[30] We agree with Miss Platt's submissions on this point. We do not think it permissible to put any gloss on the statute, or to read into it words which are not there. The change in circumstances since the placement order was made must, self-evidently and as a matter of statutory construction, relate to the grant of leave. It must equally be of a nature and degree sufficient, on the facts of the particular case, to open the door to the exercise of the judicial discretion to permit the parents to defend the adoption proceedings. In our judgment, however, the phrase "a change in circumstances" is not ambiguous, and resort to Hansard is both unnecessary and inappropriate.

[31] Furthermore, in our judgment, the importation of the word "significant" puts the test too high. Self-evidently, a change in circumstances can embrace a wide range of different factual situations. Section 47(7) does not relate the change to the circumstances of the parents. The only limiting factor is that it must be a change in circumstances "since the placement order was made". Against this background, we do not think that any further definition of the change in circumstances involved is either possible or sensible.

[32] We do, however, take the view that the test should not be set too high, because, as this case demonstrates, parents in the position of S's parents should not be discouraged either from bettering themselves or from seeking to prevent the adoption of their child by the imposition of a test which is unachievable. We therefore take the view that whether or not there has been a relevant change in circumstances must be a matter of fact to be decided by the good sense and sound judgment of the tribunal hearing the application.'

[43] In *Re P* the Court of Appeal did not consider whether there had been a relevant change in circumstances. While the court in *Re B-S* was considering leave to oppose the making of an adoption order and not the revocation of a placement order the court urged judges to bear in mind the wise and humane words of Wall LJ and later at para [84] said the *Re B* approach must apply to applications to revoke placement orders in accordance with s 24 of the Act.

[44] The change has to be *relevant* to the circumstances of the case; s 24(3) does not relate the change to the circumstances of the parent or parents

and it would be unacceptable on any level to exclude any change in circumstance to the children who are the subject of the orders. As set out in para [31] in *Re P* 'Section 47(7) does not relate change to the circumstances of the parents. The only limiting factor is that it must be a change in circumstances 'since the placement order was made'.' This must apply to s 24.

[45] The approach of the appellate court has not changed following the Supreme Court decision of *Re B* when considering the appeals from fact-finding determinations: as considered in several cases and summarised by McFarlane LJ in *Re G (a child) (care proceedings: welfare balancing exercise: proportionality)* [2013] EWCA Civ 965, [2013] 3 FCR 293, [2014] 1 FLR 670 (paras [32]–[33]) and approved by the President in *Re B-S* [2013] 3 FCR 481, [2014] 1 WLR 563 (at [78]). The approach to fact finding remains the same: *Re A (children) (fact-finding appeal)* [2013] EWCA Civ 1026, [2014] 1 FCR 24 (at [34]). It follows that the finding that was made by the judge with regards to the Appellant's meeting with the mother on Christmas Eve cannot be said to be plainly wrong; indeed it is now accepted by the Appellant. Similarly the judge's finding based on that meeting that in December the Appellant still had a relationship with the mother of some kind cannot be said to be plainly wrong.

…

Conclusion

[60] The judge was wrong to find that there had been no relevant change of circumstances. The judge should have considered any change of circumstance within the context of the case as a whole. In any case the relevance of any change should be set against the finding or threshold upon which the original orders were made so that the test is not set too high. This will vary from case to case but in this case the threshold was at the lower end of the scale and the test should reflect that; it should be proportionate to the facts of this case.

M v Warwickshire (children) (placement order) [2007] EWCA Civ 1084, [2007] 3 FCR 681, [22] (Wilson LJ)

[22] It is as clear that s 1 of the Act *does not apply* to an application for leave to apply to revoke a placement order under s 24(2) as it is that it *does apply* to an application for leave to oppose the making of an adoption order under s 47(5). In the end such was agreed between both sides before the judge in the present case; and he accepted it. The reason lies, of course, in the wording of s 1(7). To determine an application for leave to apply under s 24(2) is to come to a decision about granting leave for the 'initiation' of proceedings by an individual under the Act; and so it does not fall within s 1(7)(b). Nor does it fall within s 1(7)(a) because, as was also held in *Re P*, at [22], the determination of an application for leave is not a decision whether to make the substantive order which the

applicant aspires ultimately to secure or to prevent. So the determination of an application for leave under s 24(2) is not 'included' in either limb of s 1(7). But the matter is put beyond doubt by the final 15 words of s 1(7) which, importantly, are not part of the second limb, at (b), but qualify the whole subsection. Their effect is not only that the determination of an application under s 24(3) for leave to initiate revocation proceedings is not specifically included under s 1(7)(a) or (b) in the phrase 'coming to a decision relating to the adoption of a child' but also that it is positively excluded from it. In *Re P*, at [23], this court suggested that the final words of s 1(7) might refer to applications for leave under different statutes, such as an application for leave to apply for a special guardianship order under s 14A(3)(b) of the 1989 Act. To the charge that such may be far-fetched, the court's response might be that, had the requirement for leave to apply for revocation under s 24(2)(a) been brought to its attention, it might have identified that more obvious example of a situation to which the words apply.

See also *Re C (revocation of placement orders)* [2020] EWCA Civ 1598, [2021] 2 FCR 303, [13]–[14] (Baker LJ) addressing the same point

See also *Re B-S (children) (adoption: leave to oppose)* [2013] EWCA Civ 1146, [2013] 3 FCR 481, [7]–[9] (Sir James Munby P) addressing the same point

See also *Re S-H (a child)* [2008] EWCA Civ 493, [2008] 2 FLR 918, [22] (Wilson LJ) addressing a related point (prospects of success are weighed but it was 'not written in stone' that they had to be real)

11.2.2 Placement and adoption orders: placement orders: revocation: applications for leave to apply to revoke: not an embargo to placement: good practice

M v Warwickshire (children) (placement order) [2007] EWCA Civ 1084, [2007] 3 FCR 681, [14] (Wilson LJ)

[14] Section 24(5) of the Act provides that, where an application for the revocation of a placement order has been made and has not been disposed of, the child may not be placed for adoption without the court's leave. Notwithstanding submissions on behalf of the mother to the contrary, the judge held that there was nothing, whether in that subsection or elsewhere, which precluded a placement without leave while an application for *leave* to apply for revocation was pending. I agree with the judge; and in this court the mother does not argue to the contrary. The judge went on to observe, however, that, were an application for leave to have been issued but not to have been disposed of, it would normally be good practice for a local authority either to agree not to place the child until its disposal or at least to agree to give notice, say of 14 days, to the applicant of any proposed placement. In this regard I also agree with him. Given such notice, the applicant might perhaps be able either to take steps to challenge the lawfulness of the decision to place at that juncture or, probably more

easily, to seek an expedited hearing of the application for leave, from which might flow, in the fine, developing tradition of collaboration between local authorities and courts, a short further agreed moratorium on placement until the hearing. In the present case Warwickshire issued a precautionary application for leave to place in order to guard against the possible rejection of their submission that leave was unnecessary; and, very properly, they have continued to refrain from placing the children until the determination of this appeal. Indeed they add that, were it to be dismissed, they would not propose to apply for the leave to place which would then be required but, rather, would await the outcome of the hearing of the applications for revocation, fixed to begin on 17 December 2007. The present stance of the proposed adopters, so Warwickshire tell us, is that, were the mother's applications for revocation to continue to be allowed to proceed, they would also await the outcome of the hearing in December in the hope that the applications would be dismissed and thus that the children would again become free swiftly to be placed with them.

Re F (a child) (placement order) [2008] EWCA Civ 439, [2008] 2 FCR 93, [37]–[45], [78]–[102] (Wall LJ), [115] (Wilson LJ) *quotation limited to* [97]–[102]

What should have happened in the instant case

[97] In my judgment, one of two things should have happened. Firstly, although this is not intended as a criticism, the letter from the father's solicitors on dated 17 January should have contained an additional paragraph along the following lines:

> 'We invite you to give an undertaking that you will take no steps to place (*the child*) with prospective adopters pending the hearing of our client's application. If that undertaking is not received by 10.00am on 18 January, we shall apply without notice in the first instance to the county court for an order in those terms.'

[98] At the hearing of this appeal, we had some debate about the jurisdiction of the court to grant such an injunction. This is not a subject on which I, like Wilson LJ, whose judgment I have also read in draft, entertain any doubts. I am satisfied that the county court has such jurisdiction and would, moreover, have exercised it as a temporary, holding measure, until both sides could be before the court. The judge would either then have given directions for a swift hearing, or resolved the matter summarily. But even if there had been a summary adjudication against the father, he would have been heard.

[99] What should have happened in the alternative is; (1) that the agency should have replied promptly to the letter of 17 January; and (2) that it should have explained that its plans were at an advanced stage of preparation and, indeed, about to be implemented. It could then itself have applied to the court, on short notice, for leave to place the child for adoption under s 24(5) of the 2002 Act.

[100] Either way, there would have been a hearing on the merits. It might have been very short. Mr Cobb realistically accepted that the judge would have had a very broad discretion to deal with the matter summarily if necessary—see *Re B* to which reference was made earlier in this judgment. If the case had gone against him, the father would have lost. But he would have been heard. The court would have made the decision, and justice would have both been done and been seen to be done.

[101] Local authorities and adoption agencies must understand that it is the court which is in control, and which has been given by Parliament the responsibility for making these decisions. The courts are not a rubber stamp for local authority/agency actions, however, reprehensible.

[102] In para 14 of his judgment in the *Warwickshire* case, Wilson LJ emphasised the need for good practice to supplement the 2002 Act. I wholeheartedly agree with him. I hope that this judgment makes crystal clear not only what that good practice should be in relation to s 24(5) of the 2002 Act but *why* good practice is so important. It is for this reason that I propose widespread dissemination of our judgments in this case. Any local authority falling below the standards of good practice, and indulging in the shoddy behaviour demonstrated by the East Sussex County Council in the instant case can expect not only severe judicial displeasure, and applications for judicial review: it is also likely that any repetition of the disgraceful behaviour identified in this case will be visited by orders for costs.

11.2.3 Placement and adoption orders: placement orders: revocation: applications for leave to apply to revoke: when are children 'placed'?

Coventry City Council v PGO and others [2011] EWCA Civ 729, [2011] 3 FCR 38, [43]–[45] (Lord Wilson) *quotation limited to* [44]

[44] I hold that a child is not 'placed' for adoption until he begins to live with the proposed adopters or, if he is already living with them in their capacity as foster carers, when the adoption agency formally allows him to continue to live with them in their fresh capacity as prospective adopters. In my view such is the natural construction of the verb 'place', which the *Shorter Oxford English Dictionary* defines as 'put or set in a particular place, position or situation'. It is thus a construction which, in the usual case in which the child is not already living with the proposed adopters, requires straightforward reference to a readily discernible fact, namely whether he has begun to live with them. The construction of Coulson J seems to me, by contrast, to make identification of the date of placement more difficult; and to the first meeting between the adopters and the child he attaches a significance which I find hard to justify in logic. Regulation 35(2) of the Adoption Agencies Regulations 2005, SI 2005/389, requires an adoption agency to send to a prospective adopter with whom it has decided to place a child an 'adoption placement plan', which, by para 3 of Sch 5, must identify the '[d]ate on which it is proposed to place the

child for adoption with the prospective adopter'. On the plan sent to the adopters in the present case Coventry duly identified 23 February 2011 as 'PLACEMENT DAY' and I consider that they were correct to do so.

11.2.4 Placement and adoption orders: placement orders: revocation: test for revocation

Re C (revocation of placement orders) [2020] EWCA Civ 1598, [2020] 2 FCR 303, [14]–[24] (Baker LJ)

[14] … Applications for leave to apply to revoke a placement order are not infrequently made, but rarely succeed, no doubt because in most cases the child will be placed for adoption within a few months of the placement order being made and it will be very difficult for a birth parent in such a short period of time to demonstrate sufficient change of circumstances to open the door to revocation. As a result, substantive applications for revocation of a placement order rarely come before the court and, as stated above, counsel have been unable to find any reported case in which such an application has been determined. It follows that there is no case law providing guidance on how a court should approach an application to revoke a placement order once leave has been granted.

[15] This does not give rise to any difficulty, however, because the law is relatively straightforward and uncontroversial. Before the judge, and before this court, there has been consensus amongst the legal representatives as to the applicable principles. In his judgment, the judge began by adopting a 'note on the applicable legal framework' drafted by Ms Celestine Greenwood and approved by all parties. He appended that document to his judgment and included in the body of the judgment a passage which he described as a 'short summation' of the law.

[16] The starting point is s 1 of the 2002 Act which provides (so far as relevant to this appeal) …

[17] Under art 8 of ECHR, any interference with the exercise of the right to respect for family life should be proportionate to its legitimate aim. There can be no greater interference than the permanent removal of a child. A court making a decision relating to the adoption of a child must therefore consider whether that outcome is proportionate to the aim of securing the child's welfare. In *YC v United Kingdom (App no 4547/10)* [2013] 2 FCR 36. [2012] 2 FLR 332, (2012) 55 EHRR 33, the ECtHR said (at paragraph 134):

> 'The Court reiterates that in cases concerning the placing of a child for adoption, which entails the permanent severance of family ties, the best interests of the child are paramount. In identifying the child's best interests in a particular case, two considerations must be borne in mind: first, it is in the child's best interests that his ties with his family be maintained except in cases where the family has proved particularly unfit; and secondly, it is in the child's best interests to ensure his

development in a safe and secure environment. It is clear from the foregoing that family ties may only be severed in very exceptional circumstances and that everything must be done to preserve personal relations and, where appropriate, to 'rebuild' the family.'

[18] Following this and other decisions of the European Court, the Supreme Court addressed the question of the proportionality of an adoption order in *Re B (care proceedings: appeal)* [2013] UKSC 13, [2013] 2 FCR 525, [2013] 2 FLR 1075. In the Supreme Court's judgment, Lord Neuberger, at paragraph [104] endorsed:

> 'the principle that adoption of the child against her parents' wishes should only be contemplated as a last resort – when all else fails. Although the child's interests in an adoption case are 'paramount' … the court must never lose sight of the fact that those interests include being brought up by her natural family, ideally her natural parents or at least one of them.'

At paragraph [198], Baroness Hale of Richmond, having reviewed the case law of the European Court, concluded:

> 'It is quite clear that the test for severing the relationship between parent and children is very strict: only in exceptional circumstances and where motivated by overriding requirements pertaining to the child's welfare, in short where nothing else will do.'

[19] Following the decision of the Supreme Court in *Re B*, the Court of Appeal addressed the approach to proportionality in adoption cases in a series of reported decisions, notably *Re G* [2013] EWCA Civ 965, [2013] 3 FCR 293, [2014] 1 FLR 670 and *Re B-S* [2013] EWCA Civ 1146, [2013] 3 FCR 481, [2014] 1 WLR 563. In *Re G*, McFarlane LJ (as he then was) observed:

> '[49] In most child care cases a choice will fall to be made between two or more options. The judicial exercise should not be a linear process whereby each option, other than the most draconian, is looked at in isolation and then rejected because of internal deficits that may be identified, with the result that, at the end of the line, the only option left standing is the most draconian and that is therefore chosen without any particular consideration of whether there are internal deficits within that option.
>
> [50] The linear approach, in my view, is not apt where the judicial task is to undertake a global, holistic evaluation of each of the options available for the child's future upbringing before deciding which of those options best meets the duty to afford paramount consideration to the child's welfare.
>
> …
>
> [54] In mounting this critique of the linear model, I am alive to the fact that, of course, a judgment is, by its very nature, a linear structure; in

common with every other linear structure, it has a beginning, a middle and an end. My focus is not upon the structure of a judge's judgment but upon that part of the judgment, indeed that part of the judicial analysis before the written or spoken judgment is in fact compiled, where the choice between options actually takes place. What is required is a balancing exercise in which each option is evaluated to the degree of detail necessary to analyse and weigh its own internal positives and negatives and each option is then compared, side by side, against the competing option or options.'

[20] In *Re B-S,* the court identified the fact that non-consensual adoption is unusual in the European context, that under ECtHR law family ties are only to be severed in very exceptional circumstances and that, as a result, everything must be done where possible to rebuild a family. The court stressed that it is incumbent on (a) the local authority that applies for care and placement orders, (b) the children's guardian entrusted with representing the children in the proceedings, and (c) the court to carry out a robust and rigorous analysis of the advantages and the disadvantages of all realistic options for the child and, in the case of the court, set out that analysis and its ultimate decisions in a reasoned judgment.

[21] In *Re F (a child) (placement order: proportionality)* [2018] EWCA Civ 2761, [2019] 1 FCR 432, [2019] 1 FLR 779, Peter Jackson LJ (at paragraph [2]) identified the following factors to be considered when analysing the risks likely to arise if a child is, on the one hand, rehabilitated with the birth family or, on the other hand, placed for adoption:

'(1) The type of harm that might arise.

(2) The likelihood of it arising.

…

(3) The consequences: what would be the likely severity of the harm to [the child] if it did come to pass?

(4) Risk reduction/mitigation: would the chances of harm happening be reduced or mitigated by the support services that are or could be made available?

(5) The comparative evaluation: in the light of the above, how do the welfare advantages and disadvantages of [the child] growing up with his mother compare with those of adoption?

(6) Proportionality: ultimately, is adoption necessary and proportionate in this case?'

[22] Although these statements of principle have been expressed in judgments concerning the making of care and placement orders, they plainly have a bearing on applications to revoke a placement order.

[23] In the 'short summation' of the law included in his judgment in this case, His Honour Judge Sharpe summarised the principles in these terms.

Having summarised s 1 of the 2002 Act, and set out in full the welfare checklist in s 1(4), he continued:

> '16. In addition to those specific legislative matters the following principles can be drawn from the extensive case law which has developed, but in particular from the landmark decision of *Re B (a child)* [2013] UKSC 33, [2013] 2 FCR 525, [2013] 2 FLR 1075:
>
> (a) the paramount consideration for a court when considering an outcome for a child is that child's welfare;
>
> (b) it is a principle of the law that the welfare of a child is best met by maintaining the connection with birth parents to as full an extent as possible;
>
> (c) that principle is underpinned by application of the least interventionist principle enshrined in s 1(6);
>
> (d) adherence to those principles reflects and respects both the importance of the right to family life set out in art 8(1) of ECHR and the limited scope for interference with that right as set out in the exceptions in art 8(2);
>
> (e) interference in the right to family life, which is the right both of the parent and of the child, is parametered by necessity, proportionality and legality.
>
> (f) As a consequence, the permanent severing of ties between a child and her birth parents is an outcome only to be ordered in exceptional circumstances and where motivated by overriding requirements pertaining to the child's welfare.
>
> (g) To arrive at that conclusion the possibility of parental care or, in the alternative, care by members of the wider birth family must be shown to be options which are not realistic either by reason of unavailability (ie they do not exist) or because such care cannot meet the welfare needs of the child.
>
> (h) That option of parental or family care should not be rejected if identified deficits could be remedied through appropriate and proportionate support provided by the Local Authority, even if such support would be necessary for an extended period of time.
>
> (i) In order to arrive at a valid conclusion that a child's welfare requires their permanent removal from parental/family care it is necessary to consider individually all of the competing options for care, to assess their respective strengths and weaknesses and then to look at those options against each other to ensure that every option is fully considered against every other option.
>
> (j) Having done so and identified the outcome most able to meet the welfare needs of the child it is necessary to consider

> whether that outcome is itself a proportionate interference in the rights of the child.'

[24] It seems to me that this distillation of the principles is clear and comprehensive. I am happy to endorse it.

11.3 PLACEMENT AND ADOPTION ORDERS: ADOPTION ORDERS

11.3.1 Placement and adoption orders: adoption orders: adoption versus long-term foster care

See Chapter 10.2.5 Care and supervision orders: care orders: long-term foster care or adoption

11.3.2 Placement and adoption orders: adoption orders: cannot be subject to a condition precedent

Re W (adoption: procedure: conditions) [2015] EWCA Civ 403, [2015] 3 FCR 99, [54]–[58] (Sir James Munby P)

[54] I have already set out Judge Watson's order in full. So far as relevant to this point, the key parts of the order are these:

> 'upon the court indicating that the Adoption Order for M will be made upon written confirmation to the court that he has undertaken a procedure for circumcision
>
> THE COURT ORDERS THAT:
>
> …
>
> 2. The Court makes an Adoption Order in respect of B to the Applicants to be made 7 days from todays date.
>
> 3. The court has approved an Adoption Order in respect of M such order to be made upon notification of the procedure as set out above.
>
> …
>
> 5. Permission for a Stay of the Orders made today is refused save that the orders will be made in accordance with the timescales set out above.'

[55] Ms Bazley and Ms McGrath make two complaints about this.

[56] The first relates to M's circumcision. It is tolerably clear from the order, though the language of the judgment (whichever version one takes) is unclear and, to my mind ambiguous, that Judge Watson did not on 29 September 2014 make an immediately effective adoption order in relation to M. According to the language of the order it 'will be made' and is 'to be made' upon the happening of the specified event. In other words, perfection of an adoption order in relation to M was expressed to

be subject to what as a matter of law is properly described as a condition precedent, namely that M be circumcised. Ms Bazley and Ms McGrath submit that the court cannot properly make an adoption order effective only on satisfaction of a condition precedent. As they ask rhetorically, what is to happen if the condition precedent cannot be satisfied? Does one treat the condition precedent as determinative, with the consequence that the child is not adopted—and if so, what is to happen? Or does one treat the decision for adoption as determinative and, in effect, ignore the condition precedent? They pose the questions not for the purpose of inviting answers but in order to demonstrate that such an order is not merely unworkable in practice but also wrong as a matter of principle. How, after all, does an adoption order subject to such a condition precedent meet the 'adoption as a last resort' principle spelt out in the authorities?

[57] In the event the issue has arisen in a very practical way because Ms McGrath told us on instructions that the local authority has been unable to identify any NHS hospital or private clinic willing to perform a circumcision on a child of M's age, absent medical reasons for doing so—a position, we were told, that is unlike to change.

[58] I agree with Ms Bazley and Ms McGrath. Paragraph 3 of the order is irretrievably flawed. It is in a form which is wrong as a matter of substance. No adoption order can be made expressed to be subject to satisfaction of a condition precedent. Accordingly, in relation to para 3 of the order the appeal must be allowed on this ground also.

11.3.3 Placement and adoption orders: adoption orders: post-adoption contact opposed by prospective adopters

Re B (a child: post-adoption contact) [2019] EWCA Civ 29, [2019] 2 FCR 569, [18]–[26], [52]–[62] (Sir Andrew McFarlane P) *quotation limited to* [52]–[62]

Discussion

[52] The starting point for any consideration of this issue must be the settled position in law reached by the decision in *Re R*, which was confirmed by this court in the *Oxfordshire* case and in *Re T*. The judgment in *Re R* was, itself, on all fours, so far as imposing contact on unwilling adopters, with the position described by Lord Ackner in *Re C*.

[53] As stated by Wall LJ in *Re R*, prior to the introduction of ACA 2002, s 51A, the position in law was, therefore, that 'the imposition on prospective adopters of orders for contact with which they are not in agreement is extremely, and remains extremely, unusual'.

[54] Although s 51A has introduced a bespoke statutory regime for the regulation of post-adoption contact following placement for adoption by an adoption agency, there is nothing to be found in the wording of s 51A or of s 51B which indicates any variation in the approach to be taken to the imposition of an order for contact upon adopters who are unwilling

to accept it. Indeed, as Mr Goodwin's submissions, in my view, establish, both the Explanatory Note and the fact that Parliament only afforded the court power to make orders of its own motion if such orders are to *prohibit* contact, Parliament's intention in enacting s 51A was aimed at enhancing the position of adopters rather than the contrary.

[55] Although Miss Meachin's submissions were based upon the assertion that the new provisions were intended to increase the number of adoption cases where an order is made for direct contact, she was unable to point to any material either within the new statutory provisions or elsewhere to support this assertion. In concluding she adopted the submissions of Mr Goodwin which were to the contrary and she did not submit that the judge made any error of law in the manner in which she approached the issue of contact.

[56] The judge in the present case, having referred to *Re R*, noted the parents' submission that s 51A must be given a purposive interpretation in order to reflect 'the changing view about the benefits of greater openness in adoption' before stating that she accepted recent research findings with the result that 'what was once a closed door is now very much an open one'. The judge went on to conduct a conspicuously fair, balanced and thorough welfare analysis. In so doing, it might have been argued that the judge had fallen into error by moving away from the need to afford priority in the welfare evaluation to the views of the adopters. In the event, as paragraphs 29 to 31 of the judgment demonstrate, the judge did afford very substantial weight to the adopters' position:

> 'An order would shackle [the adopters] but not offer a corresponding benefit to B.'
>
> 'It is neither necessary, nor appropriate to fetter or seek to control [the adopters'] child focused and sensitive approach.'

[57] Looked at through the prism of *Re R*, the judge's order, which entirely accords with the views of the adopters, is entirely impregnable to challenge on appeal. There are no 'unusual', let alone 'extremely unusual', circumstances in the present case and there is therefore no basis upon which a court would have been justified in overriding the views of the adopters who are, as the judge rightly observed, to have exclusive parental responsibility for B and, by law, to be trusted to make all the decisions necessary to promote her security and to meet all her emotional, psychological and physical needs. In the event, Her Honour Judge Watson went further and undertook a full and balanced welfare evaluation which entirely supported the stance taken by the adopters. The quality of this judgment, which, again, is not open to any arguable challenge on appeal, in turn bolsters the soundness of the order for no direct contact.

[58] What I have said thus far is sufficient to determine this appeal, which must, as a consequence, be dismissed. It would, however, be wrong, or at least unhelpful, to leave matters there without offering some further guidance as we have been requested to do.

[59] ACA 2002, s 51A has been brought into force at a time when there is research and debate amongst social work and adoption professionals which may be moving towards the concept of greater 'openness' in terms of post-adoption contact arrangements, both between an adopted child and natural parents and, more particularly, between siblings. For the reasons that I have given, the juxtaposition in timing between the new provisions and the wider debate does not indicate that the two are linked. The impact of new research and the debate is likely to be reflected in evidence adduced in court in particular cases. It may also surface in terms of advice and counselling to prospective adopters and birth families when considering what arrangements for contact may be the best in any particular case. But any development or change from previous practice and expectations as to post-adoption contact that may arise from these current initiatives will be a matter that may be reflected in welfare decisions that are made by adopters, or by a court, on a case-by-case basis. These are matters of 'welfare' and not of 'law'. The law remains, as I have stated it, namely that it will only be in an extremely unusual case that a court will make an order stipulating contact arrangement to which the adopters do not agree.

[60] Although, for my part, I would not challenge the soundness of each of the suggested requirements that Mr Goodwin has helpfully set out in his skeleton argument, and which are listed at paragraph [50] above, these are very largely matters of social work practice, rather than law; I do not consider that it is appropriate for this court to raise any of the listed matters to the status of being something which the Court of Appeal has stated should now be required in every case. That said, it must be a given that any social worker, children's guardian or expert who is required to advise the court on the issue of contact, will ensure that they are fully aware of any current research and its potential impact upon the welfare issues in each particular case. Equally, it is already a requirement that courts should give adequate and clear reasons for any orders that are made following contested proceedings.

[61] Post-adoption contact is an important issue which should be given full consideration in every case [ACA 2002, s 46(6)]. Whilst there may not have been a change in the law insofar as the imposition of a contact regime against the wishes of prospective adopters is concerned, there is now a joined-up regime contained within the ACA 2002 for the consideration of contact both at the placement for adoption stage and later at the hearing of an adoption application. Further, and in contrast to the situation prior to 2014 where the issue of contact on adoption was determined under s 8 by applying the CA 1989, s 1 welfare provisions, issues under both s 26 and s 51A of the ACA 2002 will be determined by applying the bespoke adoption welfare provisions in ACA 2002, s 1, where the focus is not just upon the welfare of the subject of the application during childhood but throughout their life.

[62] A placement for adoption hearing has the potential for having an important influence upon the development of any subsequent long-term

contact arrangements. As required by ACA 2002, s 27(4), the court must consider the issue of contact and any plans for contact before making a placement for adoption order. The court's order may well, therefore, set the tone for future contact, but the court must be plain that, as the law stands, whilst there may be justification in considering some form of direct contact, the ultimate decision as to what contact is to take place is for the adopters and that it will be 'extremely unusual' for the court to impose a contrary arrangement against the wishes of adopters. Although Mr Recorder Norton was plainly most careful in his choice of words when speaking of contact at the time of the placement order in the present case, and I would not criticise him for anything that he said on that occasion, it is of note that his words were interpreted by the adopters as, in some way, flagging up that direct contact would be ordered at the final adoption hearing and that, as a result, the final adoption process has been delayed for a year and the adopters have felt less than fully settled in taking up the care of B as a result. At the placement order stage courts should therefore be careful to stress that, if there is any future issue as to contact, the law, as stated in *Re R*, will apply and, save for there being extremely unusual circumstances, no order will be made to compel adopters to accept contact arrangements with which they do not agree.

11.3.4 Placement and adoption orders: adoption orders: leave to oppose adoption orders: two-stage test

Re B-S (children) (adoption: leave to oppose) [2013] EWCA Civ 1146, [2013] 3 FCR 481, [51]–[74] (Sir James Munby P) *quotation limited to* [72]–[74]

Section 47(5) of the 2002 Act—the proper approach

[72] Subject only to one point which does not affect the substance, the law, in our judgment, was correctly set out by Wall LJ in *Re P (a child) (adoption order: leave to oppose making of adoption order)* [2007] 2 FCR 407, [2007] 1 WLR 2556, though we fear it may on occasions have been applied too narrowly and indeed too harshly. The only qualification is that the exercise at the second stage is more appropriately described as one of judicial *evaluation* rather than as one involving mere *discretion*.

[73] There is a two-stage process. The court has to ask itself two questions: Has there been a change in circumstances? If so, should leave to oppose be given? In relation to the first question we think it unnecessary and undesirable to add anything to what Wall LJ said.

[74] In relation to the second question—If there has been a change in circumstances, should leave to oppose be given?—the court will, of course, need to consider all the circumstances. The court will in particular have to consider two inter-related questions: one, the parent's ultimate prospect of success if given leave to oppose; the other, the impact on the

child if the parent is, or is not, given leave to oppose, always remembering, of course, that at this stage the child's welfare is paramount. In relation to the evaluation, the weighing and balancing, of these factors we make the following points:

(i) Prospect of success here relates to the prospect of resisting the making of an adoption order, *not*, we emphasise, the prospect of ultimately having the child restored to the parent's care.

(ii) For purposes of exposition and analysis we treat as two separate issues the questions of whether there has been a change in circumstances and whether the parent has solid grounds for seeking leave. Almost invariably, however, they will be intertwined; in many cases the one may very well follow from the other.

(iii) Once he or she has got to the point of concluding that there has been a change of circumstances and that the parent has solid grounds for seeking leave, the judge must consider very carefully indeed whether the child's welfare really does necessitate the refusal of leave. The judge must keep at the forefront of his mind the teaching of *Re B*, in particular that adoption is the 'last resort' and only permissible if 'nothing else will do' and that, as Lord Neuberger emphasised, the child's interests include being brought up by the parents or wider family unless the overriding requirements of the child's welfare make that not possible. That said, the child's welfare is paramount.

(iv) At this, as at all other stages in the adoption process, the judicial evaluation of the child's welfare must take into account *all* the negatives and the positives, *all* the pros and cons, of *each* of the two options, that is, either giving or refusing the parent leave to oppose. Here again, as elsewhere, the use of Thorpe LJ's 'balance sheet' is to be encouraged.

(v) This close focus on the circumstances requires that the court has proper evidence. But this does not mean that judges will always need to hear oral evidence and cross-examination before coming to a conclusion. Sometimes, though we suspect not very often, the judge will be assisted by oral evidence. Typically, however, an application for leave under s 47(5) can fairly and should appropriately be dealt with on the basis of written evidence and submissions: see *Re P (a child) (adoption order: leave to oppose making of adoption order)* at [53]–[54].

(vi) As a general proposition, the greater the change in circumstances (assuming, of course, that the change is positive) and the more solid the parent's grounds for seeking leave to oppose, the more cogent and compelling the arguments based on the child's welfare must be if leave to oppose is to be refused.

(vii) The mere fact that the child has been placed with prospective adopters cannot be determinative, nor can the mere passage of time. On the other hand, the older the child and the longer the child has been placed the greater the adverse impacts of disturbing the arrangements are likely to be.

(viii) The judge must always bear in mind that what is paramount in every adoption case is the welfare of the child 'throughout his life'. Given modern expectation of life, this means that, with a young child, one is looking far ahead into a very distant future—upwards of 80 or even 90 years. Against this perspective, judges must be careful not to attach undue weight to the short term consequences for the child if leave to oppose is given. In this as in other contexts, judges should be guided by what Sir Thomas Bingham MR said in *Re O (a minor) (contact: imposition of conditions)* [1996] 1 FCR 317 at 324, [1995] 2 FLR 124 at 129, that 'the court should take a medium-term and long-term view of the child's development and not accord excessive weight to what appear likely to be short-term or transient problems'. That was said in the context of contact but it has a much wider resonance: *Re G (children) (education: religious upbringing)* [2012] EWCA Civ 1233 at [26], [2012] 3 FCR 524 at [26], [2013] 1 FLR 677.

(ix) Almost invariably the judge will be pressed with the argument that leave to oppose should be refused, amongst other reasons, because of the adverse impact on the prospective adopters, and thus on the child, of their having to pursue a contested adoption application. We do not seek to trivialise an argument which may in some cases have considerable force, particularly perhaps in a case where the child is old enough to have some awareness of what is going on. But judges must be careful not to attach undue weight to the argument. After all, what from the perspective of the proposed adopters was the smoothness of the process which they no doubt anticipated when issuing their application with the assurance of a placement order, will already have been disturbed by the unwelcome making of the application for leave to oppose. And the disruptive effects of an order giving a parent leave to oppose can be minimised by firm judicial case management *before* the hearing of the application for leave. If appropriate directions are given, in particular in relation to the expert and other evidence to be adduced on behalf of the parent, *as soon as* the application for leave is issued and *before* the question of leave has been determined, it ought to be possible to direct either that the application for leave is to be listed with the substantive adoption application to follow immediately, whether or not leave is given, or, if that is not feasible, to direct that the substantive application is to be listed, whether or not leave has been given, very shortly after the leave hearing.

(x) We urge judges always to bear in mind the wise and humane words of Wall LJ in *Re P (a child) (adoption order: leave to oppose making of adoption order)* at [32]. We have already quoted them but they bear repetition: 'the test should not be set too high, because … parents … should not be discouraged either from bettering themselves or from seeking to prevent the adoption of their child by the imposition of a test which is unachievable'.

Re W (a child: leave to oppose adoption) [2020] EWCA Civ 16, [2020] 2 FCR 342, [8]–[13], [40]–[42] (Peter Jackson LJ) *quotation limited to* [40]–[42]

Analysis and decision

[40] The guiding principles for the exercise of the court's power to grant leave to oppose an adoption application are clearly set out in the authorities to which I have referred. The essence of the court's task when considering an application for leave to oppose is to decide whether in all the circumstances it is in the child's interests for fresh and up-to-date consideration to be given to the question of whether parental consent to adoption should be dispensed with: see *Re B-S* at [13]. The statutory scheme is designed to ensure that when the court hears an adoption application it does not have to return to issues that were determined when the placement order was made, thereby causing delay and hindering the finalisation of plans for the child's future. Leave to oppose can therefore only be granted on welfare grounds if two hurdles have first been cleared: change of circumstances and prospects of success. Where there has been no sufficient change, the statutory answer to the welfare question is a clear 'no'. Where there is no solid prospect of anything other than an adoption order being made, the answer will similarly be 'no'. There may then be other reasons connected to the child's welfare that might lead the court to refuse leave: for example, where the existence of contested proceedings would have a harmfully destabilising effect upon the child or the placement. However, there will be cases where there has been sufficient positive change, where there are solid grounds for opposing adoption, and where there are no overriding welfare considerations to prevent leave being granted. It is for those cases, however few, that s 47(5) exists.

[41] A decision about whether to grant leave under s 47(5) should be taken promptly once the adoption application has been issued and the parents have indicated a wish to oppose. It requires 'proper evidence' (*Re B-S* at [74](iv)–(v))), but that should be gathered with a degree of determination that reflects the fact that critical time is passing for a young child awaiting a final decision about his or her future. The decision can usually be made on the basis of written evidence. Even allowing for factors beyond the court's control (particularly the need for a change of Guardian), the six months that it took to decide this application was on any view far too long, particularly when set alongside previous proceedings that had lasted for a year in B's case and two years in the case of his siblings.

[42] It is well-established that where substantial change has taken place, the likelihood of the parents being able to show a solid case for opposing adoption will be the greater. To be solid the case must have substance: see *Re B-S* at [57]–[59]. It must be a case that needs to be fully considered before a decision can be taken about adoption. This calls for a broad and practical balancing up of the welfare advantages and disadvantages of granting leave. I would not expect expert evidence or oral evidence to feature: indeed, if the court is seriously thinking that either might be necessary, it may be an indication that leave should be granted. At all

events, the decision on the grant of leave under s 47(5) should not be allowed to develop into a trial of the adoption application on incomplete evidence.

See also *Re Y (leave to oppose adoption)* [2020] EWCA Civ 1287, [2020] 3 FCR 578, [34]–[42] (Baker LJ) considering *Re W (a child: leave to oppose adoption)* [2020] EWCA Civ 16, [2020] 2 FCR 342

See also *Re S (a child)* [2021] EWCA Civ 605, [2021] 3 FCR 191, [9]–[16], [29] (Macur LJ) providing an overview of the law on this point, see Chapter 11.3.6 Placement and adoption orders: adoption orders: leave to oppose adoption orders: two-stage test: stage 2: judicial evaluation

11.3.5 Placement and adoption orders: adoption orders: leave to oppose adoption orders: two-stage test: stage 1: 'change of circumstances'

Re P (a child) (adoption order: leave to oppose making of adoption order) [2007] EWCA Civ 616, [2007] 2 FCR 407, [27]–[32] (Wall LJ)

THE MEANING OF 'A CHANGE IN CIRCUMSTANCES'

[27] Before examining in greater detail how the discretion, if it arises, falls to be exercised, it is, we think, necessary to decide what is meant by the phrase 'a change in circumstances since the placement order was made' in s 47(7) of the Act.

[28] For the father, Miss Platt accepted that not every change in circumstances would suffice to open the door to the exercise of the judicial discretion identified in [26] above. She accepted that the change in circumstances had to be relevant or material to the question of whether or not leave should be granted. She invited us, however, to decline to put any further gloss on the statute. Parliament, she argued, could have attached an adjective such as 'significant' to the phrase 'change in circumstances', as indeed it had done in s 14D(5) of the 1989 Act in relation to the variation or discharge of a special guardianship order.

[29] Miss Platt submitted that in making a change in circumstances the pre-requisite for the exercise of the discretion under s 47(7), Parliament had chosen not to qualify the change in circumstances in any way. What was required was, simply, 'a change in circumstances'. Miss Platt was, moreover, able to argue that the point was reinforced by the fact that the special guardianship provisions in the 1989 Act referred to in [28] above were themselves contained within and introduced through the mechanism of the 2002 Act. The word 'significant' which Mr Pressdee invited us to attach to the phrase was simply not there, and had crept in, she argued, only through Hansard, to which the judge had been referred, and, at best, represented the relevant ministers' view. This was not, she argued, a satisfactory aid to statutory construction.

[30] We agree with Miss Platt's submissions on this point. We do not think it permissible to put any gloss on the statute, or to read into it words which are not there. The change in circumstances since the placement order was made must, self-evidently and as a matter of statutory construction, relate to the grant of leave. It must equally be of a nature and degree sufficient, on the facts of the particular case, to open the door to the exercise of the judicial discretion to permit the parents to defend the adoption proceedings. In our judgment, however, the phrase 'a change in circumstances' is not ambiguous, and resort to Hansard is both unnecessary and inappropriate.

[31] Furthermore, in our judgment, the importation of the word 'significant' puts the test too high. Self-evidently, a change in circumstances can embrace a wide range of different factual situations. Section 47(7) does not relate the change to the circumstances of the parents. The only limiting factor is that it must be a change in circumstances 'since the placement order was made'. Against this background, we do not think that any further definition of the change in circumstances involved is either possible or sensible.

[32] We do, however, take the view that the test should not be set too high, because, as this case demonstrates, parents in the position of S's parents should not be discouraged either from bettering themselves or from seeking to prevent the adoption of their child by the imposition of a test which is unachievable. We therefore take the view that whether or not there has been a relevant change in circumstances must be a matter of fact to be decided by the good sense and sound judgment of the tribunal hearing the application.

See also *Prospective Adopters v Tower Hamlets LBC* [2020] EWFC 26, [2020] 2 FLR 174 [5] (Mostyn J) addressing the same point (identifying that the relevant change must have been outside 'the realisation of expectation')

See also *Re Y (leave to oppose adoption)* [2020] EWCA Civ 1287, [2020] 3 FCR 578 [36] (Baker LJ) addressing a related point (the need to evaluate parental assertions of change)

11.3.6 Placement and adoption orders: adoption orders: leave to oppose adoption orders: two-stage test: stage 2: judicial evaluation

Re S (a child) [2021] EWCA Civ 605, [2021] 3 FCR 191, [14], [29] (Macur LJ)

[14] The second of the two stages is a welfare analysis conducted by reference to s 1(3) and the so called 'welfare check list' contained s 1(4) of the 2002 Act.

...

[29] Finally, in September 2020 the mother applied for permission to oppose the adoption pursuant to s 47 of the 2002 Act. The relevant process is described above. The time limit for making such an application is

prescribed by the fact of placement and the issue of the application for adoption. The first stage of the process mirrors that of the application to revoke a placement order. The second stage requires the court to consider whether the parent/s have a more than fanciful prospect of successfully opposing the adoption order, which inevitably requires it to consider whether to do so would adversely affect the welfare of the child, which is paramount. The mother, as was her right, and as we have determined with good reason, appealed the refusal of her application.

See also *Re B-S (children) (adoption: leave to oppose)* [2013] EWCA Civ 1146, [2013] 3 FCR 481, [74] (Sir James Munby P), see Chapter 11.3.4 Placement and adoption orders: adoption orders: leave to oppose adoption orders: two-stage test

11.3.7 Placement and adoption orders: adoption orders: leave to oppose adoption orders: two-stage test: stage 2: judicial evaluation: exercised exceptionally?

Prospective Adopters v Tower Hamlets London Borough Council [2020] EWFC 26, [2020] 2 FLR 174, [9] (Mostyn J)

9. Is this a power which should only be exercised exceptionally? In *Re W* at [17] Thorpe LJ stated that leave to oppose would only be granted in 'exceptionally rare circumstances' and at [28] that a 'stringent approach' was necessary. It is true that in *Re B-S (Children)* at [68] the Court of Appeal disapproved of these dicta and declined to follow them, stating that their use in relation to section 47(5) should cease. This is quite problematic for a first instance judge given that it is well-established that the Court of Appeal is generally bound by its own decisions: see *Willers v Joyce (No 2)* [2016] UKSC 44 at [8]. However, I shall not apply a criterion of exceptionality and shall apply the last word of the Court of Appeal on the subject.

11.3.8 Placement and adoption orders: adoption orders: leave to oppose adoption orders: procedure: discretion to hear oral evidence

Re P (a child) (adoption order: leave to oppose making of adoption order) [2007] EWCA Civ 616, [2007] 2 FCR 407, [56] (Wall LJ)

[56] In addition, when deciding either limb, the judge has a discretion whether or not to hear oral evidence. It would be perfectly proper, for example, for the judge in an appropriate case to assume as true the facts asserted by the parents, and equally proper for him to dismiss the application on the ground that it was not in the interests of the child for the parents to be given leave to defend the proceedings. It is not necessary for the judge to conduct a full welfare hearing unless the issues which arise for decision positively require such a hearing, or require oral evidence in one of more particular respects.

11.3.9 Placement and adoption orders: adoption orders: leave to oppose adoption orders: procedure: hopeless applications

Re S (a child) [2021] EWCA Civ 605, [2021] 3 FCR 191, [30] (Macur LJ)

[30] Clearly, continuous applications seeking to overturn the placement order, or to oppose the adoption order disrupts the future planning and placement of individual children and may result in repeated hopeless applications, not least because of the potentially very short time intervals between them. Such applications may be readily disposed of at an early stage of the proceedings since, if listed before the judge who has had conduct of the case throughout, he/she may legitimately conclude on the facts found by them when making the placement order, that the degree of the change in circumstances required would be impossible to achieve in the time that has elapsed. As indicated in the authorities to which I refer above, the nature and extent of the hearing will be case specific.

11.3.10 Placement and adoption orders: adoption orders: time between hearing applications for leave and making adoption orders

Re W (a child) (adoption: leave to oppose); Re H (children) (adoption: leave to oppose) [2013] EWCA Civ 1177, [2014] 1 FCR 191, [30]–[31] (Sir James Munby P)

Future practice

[30] It is profoundly unsatisfactory that an adoption order has to be set aside in circumstances where, even though the appeal has been allowed, the end result of the process may still be that the child is adopted. The judge to whom the matter is remitted may determine that leave to oppose should be refused or, if leave to oppose is granted, may at the end of an opposed hearing decide that adoption is in the child's best interests. The problem arises, of course, because of the practice in many courts of listing the parent's application for leave to oppose and the adoption application on the same day and, if the parent's application is dismissed, proceeding then and there to make the adoption order. This practice was criticised by McFarlane LJ in *Re B (A Child)* [2013] EWCA Civ 421. In that case, as in the cases before us, the judge had made an adoption order on the same day as she had dismissed the mother's application for leave to oppose under s 47(5). McFarlane LJ said (at [10]):

> 'That is not a step that should have been undertaken on that day. The judge should have postponed making the adoption order so that the mother had limited time to come to this court, if she wished to, to seek permission to appeal. I would therefore criticise the court in Chelmsford for not allowing a window of time between refusing permission to oppose and granting the adoption order.'

He added (at [11]), 'That is a lesson for the future for other cases'.

[31] I agree with all of that. I can understand the pragmatic and very human (and humane) grounds on which judges have come to adopt the current practice, and I can see no reason why the *hearing* of the adoption application, if the judge thinks this appropriate, should not immediately follow the dismissal of the parent's application (see *Re B-S*, para [74] (ix)). Nor do I see any problem if the judge then and there announces his decision that there should be an adoption order. The problem arises if the judge proceeds then and there to *make* the formal adoption order. For the future, judges should postpone *both* the making of the formal adoption order and the holding of the celebratory event until after the parent's time for applying to this court for permission to appeal has expired. (This will necessitate some adjustment to para 12 of *President's Guidance: Listing Final Hearings in Adoption Cases,* 3 October 2008 ([2008] All ER (D) 134 (Oct), set out in the 2013 Family Court Practice, 2958. Until new guidance is issued, para 12 of the existing guidance should be applied in a manner consistent with this judgment.) It would also be prudent for judges, when dismissing an application under s 47(5), to ask the parent whether an appeal is proposed and, even if told that an appeal is not in mind, to make clear to the parent that the time for doing so is strictly limited.

See also *Re W (children) (adoption orders: leave to oppose)* [2015] EWCA Civ 403, [2015] 3 FCR 99, [29]–[32], [59] (Sir James Munby P) considering *Re W (a child) (adoption: leave to oppose); Re H (children) (adoption: leave to oppose)* [2013] EWCA Civ 1177, [2014] 1 FCR 191

11.3.11 Placement and adoption orders: adoption orders: revocation or set aside of adoption orders

CD v Blackburn with Darwen Borough Council and others [2020] EWHC 3411 (Fam), [21]–[23] (Peel J)

The Law

21. The advocates have cited numerous authorities to me. It seems to me that the relevant principles are neatly encapsulated in the judgment of Sir James Munby P in *In re O (A Child) (Human Fertilisation and Embryology Act: Adoption Revocation)* [2016] EWHC 2273 at paras 26–28:

> '26. I have been taken to the authorities: see *In re F(R) (An Infant)* [1970] 1 QB 385, *Re RA (Minors)* (1974) 4 Fam Law 182, *In re F (Infants) (Adoption Order: Validity)* [1977] Fam 165, *Re M (Minors) (Adoption)* [1991] 1 FLR 458, *In re B (Adoption: Jurisdiction to Set Aside)* [1995] Fam 239 (affirming *Re B (Adoption: Setting Aside)* [1995] 1 FLR 1), *Re K (Adoption and Wardship)* [1997] 2 FLR 221, *Webster v Norfolk County Council and the Children (by their Children's Guardian)* [2009] EWCA Civ 59, [2009] 1 FLR 1378, *Re W (Adoption Order: Set Aside and Leave to Oppose)* [2010] EWCA Civ 1535, [2011] 1 FLR 2153, *Re PW*

(Adoption) [2013] 1 FLR 96, *Re W (Inherent Jurisdiction: Permission Application: Revocation and Adoption Order)* [2013] EWHC 1957 (Fam), [2013] 2 FLR 1609, *Re C (Adoption Proceedings: Change of Circumstances)* [2013] EWCA Civ 431, [2013] 2 FLR 1393, and *PK v Mr and Mrs K* [2015] EWHC 2316 (Fam). See also, in relation to the revocation of a parental order made under section 54 of the 2008 Act, *G v G (Parental Order: Revocation)* [2012] EWHC 1979 (Fam), [2013] 1 FLR 286.

27. There is no need for me to embark upon any detailed analysis of the case-law. For present purposes it is enough to draw attention to a few key propositions:

i) Under the inherent jurisdiction, the High Court can, in an appropriate case, revoke an adoption order. In relation to this jurisdictional issue I unhesitatingly prefer the view shared by Bodey J in *Re W (Inherent Jurisdiction: Permission Application: Revocation and Adoption Order)* [2013] EWHC 1957 (Fam), [2013] 2 FLR 1609, para 6, and Pauffley J in *PK v Mr and Mrs K* [2015] EWHC 2316 (Fam), para 4, to the contrary view of Parker J in *Re PW (Adoption)* [2013] 1 FLR 96, para 1.

ii) The effect of revoking an adoption order is to restore the status quo ante: see *Re W (Adoption Order: Set Aside and Leave to Oppose)* [2010] EWCA Civ 1535, [2011] 1 FLR 2153, paras 11–12.

iii) However, 'The law sets a very high bar against any challenge to an adoption order. An adoption order once lawfully and properly made can be set aside "only in highly exceptional and very particular circumstances": "*Re C (Adoption Proceedings: Change of Circumstances)* [2013] EWCA Civ 431, [2013] 2 FLR 1393, para 44, quoting *Webster v Norfolk County Council and the Children (by their Children's Guardian)* [2009] EWCA Civ 59, [2009] 1 FLR 1378, para 149. As Pauffley J said in *PK v Mr and Mrs K* [2015] EWHC 2316 (Fam), para 14, "public policy considerations ordinarily militate against revoking properly made adoption orders and rightly so."

iv) An adoption order regularly made, that is, an adoption order made in circumstances where there was no procedural irregularity, no breach of natural justice and no fraud, cannot be set aside either on the ground of mere mistake (*In re B (Adoption: Jurisdiction to Set Aside)* [1995] Fam 239) or even if there has been a miscarriage of justice (*Webster v Norfolk County Council and the Children (by their Children's Guardian)* [2009] EWCA Civ 59, [2009] 1 FLR 1378).

v) The fact that the circumstances are highly exceptional does not of itself justify revoking an adoption order. After all, one would hope that the kind of miscarriage of justice exemplified by *Webster v Norfolk County Council and the Children (by their Children's Guardian)* [2009] EWCA Civ 59, [2009] 1 FLR 1378, is highly exceptional, yet the attempt to have the adoption order set aside in that case failed.

28. I bear in mind, also, two important observations that appear in the authorities. The first is the observation of Sir Thomas Bingham MR in *In re B (Adoption: Jurisdiction to Set Aside)* [1995] Fam 239, page 251:

"The act of adoption has always been regarded in this country as possessing a peculiar finality. This is partly because it affects the status of the person adopted, and indeed adoption modifies the most fundamental of human relationships, that of parent and child. It effects a change intended to be permanent and concerning three parties. The first of these are the natural parents of the adopted person, who by adoption divest themselves of all rights and responsibilities in relation to that person. The second party is the adoptive parents, who assume the rights and responsibilities of parents in relation to the adopted person. And the third party is the subject of the adoption, who ceases in law to be the child of his or her natural parents and becomes the child of the adoptive parents."

The other is that of Hedley J in *G v G (Parental Order: Revocation)* [2012] EWHC 1979 (Fam), [2013] 1 FLR 286, para 33:

"the adoption authorities show that the feelings of an injured party are not germane necessarily to consideration of an application to set aside. The hurt of the applicants in both *In re B (Adoption: Jurisdiction to Set Aside)* [1995] Fam 239 … and *Webster v Norfolk County Council and the Children (by their Children's Guardian)* [2009] EWCA Civ 59, [2009] 1 FLR 1378, was immeasurably greater than here and it availed them nothing."'

22. At para 43 of *ZH v HS and Others (Application to revoke adoption order)* [2020] 1 FLR 96 at para 43 Theis J stated that:

'In the context where the authorities have repeatedly made clear that it is only in exceptional and very particular circumstances that the court will permit the order to be revoked the critical considerations for the court are:

(1) Was the adoption order lawfully and properly made?

(2) The effect of revocation on the affected child.'

23. Initially, the Mother argued before me that a different test applies on an application made by her for the grant of permission to apply for an order under the inherent jurisdiction, which presupposes that she needs

permission to apply. She submitted that I need only be satisfied that she has an arguable case. She did not point to any procedural rule or case law justifying this assertion. I reject the submission. This is not a filter stage for the Mother's application, akin for example to requiring permission to appeal. She does not need permission to apply. This is the final hearing of the Mother's substantive application to revoke the care and adoption orders. The test is clearly as set out in the authorities cited above. By the end of the hearing, the Mother accepted this analysis and I approach the case accordingly.

Webster and another v Norfolk County Council and others; Re Webster (children) [2009] EWCA Civ 59, [2009] 1 FCR 673, [145]–[165] (Wall LJ) *quotation limited to* [149]

[149] This is a case in which the court has to go back to first principles. Adoption is a statutory process. The law relating to it is very clear. The scope for the exercise of judicial discretion is severely curtailed. Once orders for adoption have been lawfully and properly made, it is only in highly exceptional and very particular circumstances that the court will permit them to be set aside.

AX and another v SX and others [2021] EWHC 1121 (Fam), [2021] 4 WLR 80, [34]–[42] (Theis J)

Relevant legal framework

34. The only statutory ground for revocation of an adoption order under s 55 of the Adoption and Children act 2002 (ACA 2002) is not applicable in this case.

35. It is well established that the High Court has, by way of its inherent jurisdiction, power to revoke an adoption order. The circumstances in which a court may revoke a lawfully granted adoption order under the inherent jurisdiction is set out in a number of well-known authorities, both on appeal and at first instance. The authorities disclose no preference as between the use of the inherent jurisdiction or on appeal, save that Cobb J in *Re J (Adoption: Appeal) [2018] 2 FLR 519* at paragraph 20 suggested an appeal may be the preferred route where procedural irregularity is the ground for revocation.

36. In *Re B (Adoption: Jurisdiction to Set Aside)* [1995] Fam 239 the Court of Appeal noted that the act of adoption is final, effecting a permanent change in the status of the child and the parties. At p. 245 Swinton Thomas LJ set out the following:

> 'An adoption order has a quite different standing to almost every other order made by a court. It provides the status of the adopted child and of the adoptive parents. The effect of an adoption order is to extinguish any parental responsibility of the natural parents. Once

> an adoption order has been made, the adoptive parents stand to one another and the child in precisely the same relationship as if they were his legitimate parents, and the child stands in the same relationship to them as to legitimate parents. Once an adoption order has been made the adopted child ceases to be the child of his previous parent and becomes the child for all purposes of the adopters as though he were their legitimate child.'

And Lord Bingham MR (as he then was) observed at p. 251 that:

> 'The act of adoption has always been regarded in this country as possessing a peculiar finality. This is partly because it affects the status of the person adopted, and indeed adoption modifies the most fundamental of human relationships, that of parent and child. It effects a change intended to be permanent and concerning three parties. The first of these are the natural parents of the adopted person, who by adoption divest themselves of all rights and responsibilities in relation to that person. The second party is the adoptive parents, who assume the rights and responsibilities of parents in relation to the adopted person. And the third party is the subject of the adoption, who ceases in law to be the child of his or her natural parents and becomes the child of the adoptive parents.'

37. Whilst these observations were made in the context of the provisions of the Adoption Act 1976, the coming into force of the Adoption and Children Act 2002, whilst introducing a number of reforms, did not change the fundamental characteristics of adoption or the legal effect of an adoption order. Within this context it also remained the position under the Adoption and Children Act 2002 that, as observed by Lord Bingham in *Re B* at p. 253:

> 'An adoption order is not immune from any challenge. A party to the proceedings can appeal against the order in the usual way. The authorities show, I am sure correctly, that where there has been a failure of natural justice, and a party with a right to be heard on the application for the adoption order has not been notified of the hearing or has not for some other reason been heard, the court has jurisdiction to set aside the order and so make good the failure of natural justice. I would also have little hesitation in holding that the court could set aside an adoption order which was shown to have been obtained by fraud.'

38. Lord Bingham observed in *Re B* that the courts have been *very* strict in their refusal to allow adoption orders to be challenged, otherwise than by way of appeal. In giving examples of the types of failure in natural justice that might justify the revocation of an adoption order, at pp. 245-246 in *Re B* Swinton Thomas LJ gave the following examples:

> 'There are cases where an adoption order has been set aside by reason of what is known as a procedural irregularity: see *In re F.(R.) (An Infant)* [1970] 1 Q.B. 385, *In re R.A. (Minors)* (1974) 4 Fam.

Law 182 and *In re F. (Infants)(Adoption Order: Validity)* [1977] Fam. 165. Those cases concern a failure to effect proper service of the adoption proceedings on a natural parent or ignorance of the parent of the existence of the adoption proceedings. In each case the application to set aside the order was made reasonably expeditiously. It is fundamental to the making of an adoption order that the natural parent should be informed of the application so that she can give or withhold her consent. If she has no knowledge at all of the application then, obviously, a fundamental injustice is perpetrated. I would prefer myself to regard those cases not as cases where the order has been set aside by reason of a procedural irregularity, although that has certainly occurred, but as cases where natural justice has been denied because the natural parent who may wish to challenge the adoption has never been told that it is going to happen. Whether an adoption order can be set aside by reason of fraud which is unrelated to a natural parent's ignorance of the proceedings was not a subject which was relevant to the present appeal...As the case law stood, certainly in 1976, the powers of the court to set aside an adoption order as known to Parliament would, in my view, have been limited to the power to set aside such an order on the basis of a breach of natural justice such as I have described above, and not an inherent power to set aside an adoption order by reason of a mistake or misrepresentation.'

And at p. 248

'There is no case which has been brought to our attention in which it has been held that the court has an inherent power to set aside an adoption order by reason of a misapprehension or mistake. To allow considerations such as those put forward in this case to invalidate an otherwise properly made adoption order would, in my view, undermine the whole basis on which adoption orders are made, namely that they are final and for life as regards the adopters, the natural parents, and the child. In my judgment Mr. Holman, who appeared as *amicus curiae*, is right when he submits that it would gravely damage the lifelong commitment of adopters to their adoptive children if there is a possibility of the child, or indeed the parents, subsequently challenging the validity of the order.'

39. More recently in *Re Webster v Norfolk County Council* [2009] 2 All ER 1156 the Court of Appeal noted under the Adoption and Children Act 2002 that adoption is the process whereby a child becomes a permanent and full member of a new family, and is treated for all purposes as if born to the adopters. Wall LJ (as he then was) set out the position at [149] as follows:

'This is a case in which the court has to go back to first principles. Adoption is a statutory process. The law relating to it is very clear. The scope for the exercise of judicial discretion is severely curtailed. Once orders for adoption have been lawfully and properly made, it is only in highly exceptional and very particular circumstances that the court will permit them to be set aside.'

And at [163] that:

> '[163] The question, therefore, is whether or not a substantial miscarriage of justice, assuming that this is what has occurred, is or can be sufficient to enable the adoption orders in the present case to be set aside.'

40. With respect to what might be a substantial miscarriage of justice sufficient to justify the revocation of an adoption order, in *Webster* Wall LJ indicated that, given the public policy considerations relating to adoption and the authorities to which he referred, even a serious injustice suffered by a natural parent will not justify the revocation of an adoption order. As he set out at paragraph 149, Wall LJ was clear that only highly exceptional and very particular circumstances could lead to such an outcome. Thus, in *Webster*, the fact that the children in that case had been denied the opportunity to argue that they should grow up together with their parents as a family in breach of the Article 8 rights *and* the fact that the parents had been wrongly accused of physically abusing one of their children and three of their children had been removed wrongly and permanently from their care, did *not* amount to sufficient justification to revoke the adoption orders in that case.

41. The relevant key principles applicable to an application for the revocation of an adoption order were summarised by Sir James Munby P, as he then was, in *Re O (A Child) (Human Fertilisation and Embryology: Adoption Revocation) [2016] 4 WLR 148* at paragraph 26–28 as follows: …

42. No one has sought to suggest that is not a helpful distillation of the relevant key principles. I agree.

CHAPTER 12

Special guardianship orders

Chapter contents

CHAPTER 12

Special guardianship orders

12.1 SPECIAL GUARDIANSHIP ORDERS[1]: PROCEDURE

12.1.1 SGOs[2]: procedure: two routes to make SGOs

Re A (a child) [2018] EWCA Civ 2240, [2019] 1 FCR 105, [28]–[29] (Peter Jackson LJ)

[28] Although it did not feature in the proceedings below, we invited the parties to address us on the statutory framework within which the court was considering the competing proposals for SGOs. Section 14A of the Act provides two routes by which an SGO can be made:

- The first is under ss (3), where an order can be made on the application of an individual (a) who is entitled to make it, or (b) has obtained the leave of the court to make it.
- The second route is under ss (6) where an order can also be made in any family proceedings following (a) an application made via ss (3), or (b) where the court considers that an order should be made even though no application has been made.

In this case, no application having been made, the court was following the second route and its order was made under ss (6)(b).

[29] It is worth noting the provisions that govern the entitlement to apply for an SGO. These appear in ss (5), which includes two subparagraphs relevant to the present case.

- Subparagraph (c) entitles a person to apply if they come within s 10(5)(b) or (c). Section 10(5)(c)(ii) refers to a person who has the consent of the local authority where the child is in the care of a local authority. The definitions in sections 105 and 31(11) provide that a child is in the care of a local authority if subject to care order or, as here, an interim care order.
- Subparagraph (d) entitles a local authority foster carer to apply if the child has been living with them for at least one year immediately preceding the application.

1 It is submitted that any authorities pre-dating March 2021 may need to be read in light of the President's Public Law Working Group report *Recommendations to achieve best practice in the child protection and family justice systems* (March, 2021), which includes *Best practice guidance: Special guardianship orders*. The report is not law but was endorsed by the President of the Family Division, Sir Andrew McFarlane, available at www.judiciary.uk/publications/message-from-the-president-of-the-family-division-publication-of-the-presidents-public-law-working-group-report/, accessed 22 December 2021.

2 Special guardianship orders.

Consequently, the H's would have been entitled to apply for an SGO with the consent of the local authority, while the foster carer would have required the court's permission under s 14A(3)(b). Given the support of the Guardian, that permission would surely have been granted if it had been requested. It is nonetheless the case that the Act contains specific provisions for relatives on the one hand and for foster carers on the other, including under s 22C, which sets out the priorities for local authorities when seeking placements for children in their care.

12.1.2 SGOs: procedure: route 1: on application: test for leave: s 10(9)[3]

See Chapter 5.6.1 Case management: joinder: reference to s 10(9)

12.1.3 SGOs: procedure: route 1: on application: leave precedes notice periods

Re R (a child) (special guardianship order) [2006] EWCA Civ 1748, [2007] 1 FCR 121, [89]–[95] (Wall LJ)

[89] The decision whether or not to make a special guardianship order is, of course, for the court. In the instant case, we are not concerned with the court making an order of its own motion under s 14A(6)(b). In the instant case, the court could only make such a special guardianship order in favour of the grandparents once they had obtained the leave of the court to make an application for special guardianship (s 14A(3)b)). Furthermore, as the guardian points out, notice has to be given to the local authority three months before the date of the application.

[90] On 3 August the grandparents had not obtained leave. They plainly could not, therefore, at that point make an application for a special guardianship order. All they could do was to apply for permission to make an application for an order. The court order is plainly in error in recording their undertaking to make an application for a special guardianship order within seven days.

[91] The second pre-condition for the making of the order is notice. The grandparents are required by s 14A(7) to give notice to the local authority of their intention to make the application for a special guardianship order three months before the application itself is made. Receipt of the notice triggers the local authority's report.

[92] In our judgment, it simply was not open to the grandparents on 3 August to give notice of their intention to make an application for a special guardianship order. The reason for this is simple: they did not have the capacity on that date to make such an application. In order to give the notice required by s 14A(7), it seems to us that they must first have

3 Children Act 1989, s 10(9).

obtained permission to make the application. Only once they had obtained permission to make the application, could they give the local authority notice of their intention to do so.

[93] In our judgment the judge on 3 August confused two quite distinct concepts. The first is an actual application for a special guardianship order. The second is an application for permission to apply for such an order. Persons who have the right to make an application for special guardianship must give the local authority three months notice of their intention to make it. Persons who do not have the right to make an application for special guardianship, and who require the court's permission to make the application cannot, for the reasons we have given and as we read the statute, give notice of their intention to apply for a special guardianship unless and until they have got permission.

[94] It follows, in our judgment, that Mr Harrison is entitled to succeed on the first of the points identified in para 2 of this judgment. Neither an undertaking by the grandparents to apply for permission to make an application for special guardianship (mistakenly referred to in the order as the application itself) nor notice to the local authority of their intention to apply for permission to make an application for a special guardianship order was capable on 3 August 2006 of triggering s 14A(8).

[95] We agree with Mr Harrison's submission that it cannot have been the intention of parliament that any announcement by anybody of an intention to apply for a special guardianship order should trigger s 14A(8). Such a conclusion would, in our judgment, be absurd. If the argument is correct, a relative who had not even met the child and who had had no connection with her or her parents since her birth could give notice of an intention to apply for a special guardianship order, and the local authority would be obliged to implement the procedure identified in s 14A(8) which, it is common ground, there is no discretion to vary. Section 14A(8) is, in our judgment, only triggered either when a person who is entitled to apply gives notice of an intention to do so, or when a person who needs the court's permission to apply, obtains that permission and then gives notice.

12.1.4 SGOs: procedure: route 2: no application: generally

Re P-S (children) [2018] EWCA Civ 1407, [2018] 4 WLR 99, [52]–[56] (Sir Ernest Ryder SP)

The position of the paternal grandparents and procedural fairness:

52. The statutory scheme that applies to special guardianship orders has previously been considered by this court in *Re H (A Child) (Analysis of realistic options and SGOs)* [2015] EWCA Civ 406, [2016] 1 FLR 286 CA. Given that the judge cited that authority it was clearly in his contemplation. The paternal grandparents were able to make applications for special guardianship orders because sections 14A(3)

and 14(5)(c) when read together with section 10(5)(c)(ii) of the 1989 Act provide that they are entitled to do so if they have the consent of the local authority where the child is in the care of that local authority. That would have been so in this case had anyone directed their minds to the situation.

53. In the absence of the local authority's consent, the grandparents would have been able to apply for leave to make an application under section 10(9) of the 1989 Act where the factors to be considered by the court are specified. In a case where the local authority does not consent the leave application is an important protection for the child and the child's parents. It is not a rubber stamp. Where leave is granted, an appropriate balance is struck between the applicants, the child, the child's parents and the local authority. It is relatively common to find that local authorities who give consent to an application being made, that is who support the application on the merits, will help fund the applicant by providing representation. That happened in this case when the matter came on appeal and after a case management indication to that effect was given by this court. It ought to have happened earlier.

54. The residual power in the court to consider making a special guardianship order of its own motion in section 14A(6)(b) of the Act should not be the normal or default process because it avoids the protections that I have just referred to. That is not to say that circumstances will not arise where that residual process is in the interests of the child and the court is able to have regard to the protections in sections 14 and 10 in its decision making, but it should not be the normal process. Not only does it tend to avoid the protections in the statutory scheme but it tends to avoid good planning by the local authority and the court which will include identifying the status of the prospective special guardians, how they will achieve effective access to justice and such case management directions as will provide fairness to all parties by notice of the proceedings, the disclosure of evidence and the ability to take advice. In so far as the judge indicates that the Central Family Court and local authorities appearing in it had yet to come to terms with the need to follow this court's guidance in Re H, that time has now arrived.

55. It is difficult to understand why steps were not taken on 3 February 2017 to consider effective access to justice for the grandparents. It was clear from the recordings in the order made that the key issues in the case included whether each of the children should *"reside in a family placement under an SGO"*. It may be that the apparent consensus between the local authority, the children's guardian and the grandparents on the ultimate order they all sought obscured the immediate procedural issue before the court. Given the procedural unfairness that undoubtedly was the consequence, I have no hesitation in coming to the conclusion that it was wrong not to have made appropriate provision for the grandparents to obtain effective access to justice at the final hearing. To leave them on the sidelines without party status, without documents and without advice and without any mechanism being identified for the parents of

S to cross examine them on their proposals was unfair in more than one respect. From the children's perspective, it meant that part of their case was assumed to be incomplete when it could have been tested.

56. The solution would have been either to direct that an application for an SGO be made so that case management directions on that application relating to party status, disclosure and time for advice could be made or for case management directions to be made that otherwise secured the same procedural protections. At the Issue Resolution Hearing on 3 February 2017 the facts were such that the grandparents were a realistic option for the care of the children. The direction for an SGO assessment which is a mandatory pre-condition to the making of an order had been made and the reports were complete. I am accordingly at a loss to understand why directions were neither asked for nor made that dealt with how that application would be considered by the court. The consequence is stark even from the judge's own judgment. The grandparents did not know what was happening, did not have the evidence upon which the court was making a decision, were unable to take advice and in the event, in my judgment, did not have effective access to justice. That was not in the interests of the children. The procedure was accordingly unfair.

See also *Re H (a child) (analysis of realistic options and SGOs)* [2015] EWCA Civ 406, [2016] 1 FLR 286, [26]–[27] (Ryder LJ) addressing the same point (finding that the use of the Court's residual powers 'should not be the default position')

12.1.5 SGOs: procedure: reports: necessity[4]

Re H (a child) (analysis of realistic options and SGOs) [2015] EWCA Civ 406, [2016] 1 FLR 286, [27]–[28] (Ryder LJ)

27. In accordance with section 14A(8) CA 1989 the local authority must prepare an SGO report and by section 14A(11) the court cannot make a SGO without such a report. The statutory purpose is a very real protection. The contents of such a report are set out in a regulatory scheme which is to be found in the schedule to the Special Guardianship Regulations 2005, which is designed to ensure that necessary questions are addressed before controlling parental responsibility for a child is vested in a person other than a local authority. Such a report was never directed to be prepared in this case because no SGO application was ever made.

28. In her judgment the judge accepts that a report, a support plan and an addendum report which she identifies are sufficient for the statutory purpose. It is only because there is a concession before this court that the content of an earlier 'connected person's assessment' of A fulfil

4 Please note that the relevant regulations applicable in Wales and England differ. The Special Guardianship (Wales) Regulations 2005, SI 2005/1513 apply in Wales. The Special Guardianship Regulations 2005, SI 2005/1109 apply in England. Sch 1 to each regulation addresses the matters prescribed for reports under Children Act 1989, s 14A(8)(b)).

those requirements that this court has not moved on to question whether the assessment was sufficient for its purpose. During case management, the court should have addressed the question directly. On identifying that one of the realistic options that the court was being asked to consider was special guardianship, it should have made directions in the prospective application including for the SGO report and any relevant evidence. If a report which is being or has been prepared is to be deemed to satisfy the regulatory and statutory requirements, then the case management judge should say so: allowing anyone who disagrees to be heard given the statutory importance that is attached to the report. In other words, the assertion must be scrutinised. By section 14C(1) CA 1989 the holder of a SGO shares parental responsibility with the parents of a child but has the right to override the responsibilities of the parents. Such an order is a significant step in a child's life that is intended to have long term consequences and the protections that surround it should be respected.

Re S (a child) (adoption order or special guardianship order) (No 2)
[2007] EWCA Civ 90, [2007] 1 FCR 340, [10]–[18] (Wall LJ)

[10] The wording of Miss Shelley's submissions as recorded in [3] and [4] above gives the impression that the point was considered by the parties. There is, however, nothing in the judge's judgment to indicate that she had addressed her mind to the point, and whilst we have some sympathy with the thrust of Miss Shelley's submissions, s 14A(11) is, in our judgment, unequivocal: 'The court may not make a special guardianship order unless it has received a report dealing with the matters referred to in subsection (8).'

[11] It follows that the need for a report dealing with the matters identified in s 14A(8) as a pre-requisite for a special guardianship order being made is not limited to the receipt by the local authority of written notice under s 14A(7) by an individual who intends to make an application for such an order. It also plainly applies in relation to an order made under s 14A(6)(b) where the court (as in the instant case) considers that an order should be made, even though no application for such an order has in fact been made by any of the parties.

[12] In practice, therefore, what in our judgment should happen in a case to which s 14A(6)(b) applies, and where there is no report under s 14A(8), is that the judge should exercise his or her powers under s 14A(9) and request the local authority to conduct the investigation and to produce a report dealing with the matters contained in s 14A(8)(a) to (c) of the 1989 Act. Until that report has been received by the judge, the court cannot make a special guardianship order.

[13] It further follows, in our judgment, that in the instant case, the judge did not have the power to make a special guardianship order on 13 July 2006, and should not have done so.

[14] That said, however, we agree with Miss Shelley that on the facts of this case, the court can properly adopt a pragmatic approach to the report. In para [46] of its decision in *Re R* (*a child*) (*special guardianship order*) [2006] EWCA Civ 1748, [2007] 1 FCR 121, this court accepted the submission made by the local authority in that case that it was not possible for the court to define (and thereby limit) the requirements of a local authority to investigate and report under s 14A(8) where the court acts under s 14A(9). We agree with that proposition. However, in a case to which s 14A(6)(b) applies, and in which the bulk of the information required for the report under s 14A(8) is already before the court in a different form, it would seem to us to be unduly burdensome for the local authority to be required, as it were, to start again from scratch, and produce a fresh report, much of which would simply reproduce and duplicate the information already before the court. Such an approach is not, we think, required by the statute.

[15] We therefore accept Miss Shelley's submission that the local authority should not be required to complete an entirely new report. What we think should happen is that the local authority should be asked by the court to file a report, which will fulfil the terms of s 14A(8); (i) by providing the missing information; and (ii) by setting out the remaining information in the form of cross-references to the information already before the court in other reports.

[16] None of this is in any way to diminish the importance of the report under s 14A(8) as explained in *Re R*. Furthermore, we are clearly of the view that in every case in which the court is minded to invoke s 14A(6)(b), the court should carefully consider the manner in which its powers under s 14A(9) will fall to be exercised. In some cases, the information required by the report will already be before it in a different form. In such cases (for example, applications under the 2002 Act) we agree with Miss Shelley that it would be unduly burdensome on a local authority to have to start again from scratch, and to produce an entirely fresh report, much of which would be duplication.

[17] Miss Shelley also acknowledged, however, that in some cases, the information required by s 14A(8)(a)and (b) will simply not be before the court. In such cases, the local authority may well be required by the court to conduct a fresh investigation and prepare a fresh report. For example, in a private law case, the local authority may not be a party to the proceedings in which considerations involving s 14A(6)(b) arise. In such a case, the judge will undoubtedly need to request a full investigation and report under s 14A(9) before a special guardianship order can be made.

[18] In our view, the court should adopt a common sense approach to these matters. If the material is already before the court, it can be cross-referenced, and need not be duplicated in a different format. Where, however, a fresh investigation and report is required, the local authority must undertake both without preconceptions.

12.1.6 SGOs: procedure: reports: courts cannot limit investigations

Re R (a child) (special guardianship order) [2006] EWCA Civ 1748, [2007] 1 FCR 121, [76]–[78] (Wall LJ)

[76] We start with the third of the points identified in [2] above which, for ease of reference, we repeat:

> 'Where the court makes a request under s 14A(9) is it at the same time open to the court to define (and thereby limit) the scope of the local authority's obligation to investigate and report under s 14A(8) and the regulations?'

[77] In this regard, we accept the virtually unanimous submissions of all three counsel that the answer to this question must be No. We need not, we think, repeat the arguments already rehearsed from in particular the guardian on this point. We agree that there is no provision either in the statute or the regulations for any restriction, reduction or alteration in the information which the local authority is required to cover.

[78] We do, however, think it important to pause to reflect why this is so. In our judgment it is because special guardianship is an issue of very great importance to everyone concerned with it, not least, of course, the child who is its subject. It is plainly not something to be embarked upon lightly or capriciously, not least because the status it gives the special guardian effectively prevents the exercise of parental responsibility on the part of the child's natural parents, and terminates the parental authority given to a local authority under a care order (whether interim or final). In this respect, it is substantially different from a residence order which, whilst it also brings a previously subsisting care order in relation to the same child to an end, does not confer on any person who holds the order the exclusivity in the exercise of parental responsibility which accompanies a special guardianship order.

12.2 SPECIAL GUARDIANSHIP ORDERS: GENERAL PRINCIPLES

12.2.1 SGOs: general principles: test

Re A (a child) [2018] EWCA Civ 2240, [2019] 1 FCR 105, [14]–[17] (Peter Jackson LJ)

[14] At the risk of stating the obvious, where a court is considering whether to make an order such as an SGO it 'shall have regard in particular' to the matters that appear at s 1(3) Children Act 1989. The provision is therefore obligatory, flexible and open-ended, providing the decision-maker with a workbench and tools with which to devise a proper welfare outcome.

[15] The welfare checklist can be helpful in several ways. In the first place, paying attention to it tends to ensure that all important considerations

are taken into account. As Baroness Hale put it in *Re G (children)* [2006] UKHL 43, [2006] 3 FCR 1, [2006] 1 WLR 2305 at [40]:

> 'My Lords, it is of course the case that any experienced family judge is well aware of the contents of the statutory checklist and can be assumed to have had regard to it, whether or not this is spelled out in a judgment. However, in any difficult or finely balanced case, as this undoubtedly was, it is a great help to address each of the factors in the list, along with any others which may be relevant, so as to ensure that no particular feature of the case is given more weight than it should properly bear …'

[16] Next, its neutral content is a reminder that the assessment of welfare is not driven by presumptions. As McFarlane LJ said in *Re W (a child)* [2016] EWCA Civ 793, [2017] 1 WLR 889, [2017] 2 FLR 31 at [71]:

> 'The repeated reference to a "right" for a child to be brought up by his or her natural family, or the assumption that there is a presumption to that effect, needs to be firmly and clearly laid to rest. No such "right" or presumption exists. The only "right" is for the arrangements for the child to be determined by affording paramount consideration to her welfare throughout her life (in an adoption case) in a manner which is proportionate and compatible with the need to respect any ECHR Art 8 rights which are engaged.'

[17] Then, the open-ended nature of the checklist allows the court to take account of other matters that may bear upon the individual decision. For example, although the present case is not concerned with adoption, the lifelong significance of the decision might reasonably prompt the court to have regard to the matters appearing in the checklist in the Adoption and Children Act 2002 at s 1(4)(f).

See also *Re C (a child) (special guardianship order)* [2019] EWCA Civ 2281, [2020] 2 FCR 149, [72] (Moylan LJ) addressing a related point (the importance of welfare)

See also *Re S (a child) (adoption order or special guardianship order)* [2007] EWCA Civ 54, [2007] 1 FCR 271 [26] (Wall LJ) addressing the same point

See also *Re R (a child) (special guardianship order)* [2006] EWCA Civ 1748, [2007] 1 FCR 121 [85] (Wall LJ) addressing a related point (in the majority of cases, the type of order is subservient to the question as to where the child should live, and with whom)

12.2.2 SGOs: general principles: general comments

Re S (a child) (adoption order or special guardianship order) [2007] EWCA Civ 54, [2007] 1 FCR 271, [40]–[77] (Wall LJ) *quotation limited to* [41]–[51]

[41] The White Paper ([11] above) contains a helpful summary of the main features of the special guardianship regime, as being to:

- give the carer clear responsibility for all aspects of caring for the child or young person, and for making the decisions to do with their upbringing.
- provide a firm foundation on which to build a lifelong permanent relationship between the carer and the child or young person;
- preserve the legal link between the child or young person and their birth family;
- allow proper access to a full range of support services including, where appropriate, financial support.

[42] It also gives some helpful illustrations of some circumstances in which guardianship may be appropriate:

(i) Older children who do not wish to be legally separated from their birth families.
(ii) Children being cared for on a permanent basis by members of their wider birth family.
(iii) Children in some minority ethnic communities, who have religious and cultural difficulties with adoption as it is set out in law.
(iv) Unaccompanied asylum-seeking children who need secure, permanent homes, but have strong attachments to their families abroad.

[43] It is important to emphasise that these are only illustrations. There can be no routine solutions. We repeat what this court said in the *Re R* case (cited at [18] above) as to the importance of the issues raised by special guardianship (at [78]):

> '… special guardianship is an issue of very great importance to everyone concerned with it, not least, of course, the child who is its subject. It is plainly not something to be embarked upon lightly or capriciously, not least because the status it gives the special guardian effectively prevents the exercise of parental responsibility on the part of the child's natural parents, and terminates the parental authority given to a local authority under a care order (whether interim or final). In this respect, it is substantially different from a residence order which, whilst it also brings a previously subsisting care order in relation to the same child to an end, does not confer on any person who holds the order the exclusivity in the exercise of parental responsibility which accompanies a special guardianship order.'

[44] It is important to note also that the statutory provisions draw strong and clear distinctions between the status of children who are adopted, and those who are subject to lesser orders, including special guardianship. As we have already pointed out, the considerations in relation to adoption in the expanded check-list contained in s 1 of the 2002 Act require the court to address the question of the child's welfare throughout his life. We do not think this point needs any further explanation or emphasis. Its consequences are, however, significant.

[45] Thus, although s 14C(1) of the 1989 Act gives special guardians exclusive parental authority, this entitlement is subject of a number of limitations. Attached to the skeleton argument prepared in the case of *Re AJ* by Miss Lorna Meyer QC, Mr David Crowley, (the solicitor advocate for the child) and Mr Graham Jones (the solicitor advocate for the prospective adopters) was a helpful document entitled *Schedule of Main Differences between Special Guardianship Orders and Adoption* which set out those differences in tabular form.

[46] For ease of reference we have attached that document to the judgment of the court in that case. It is not necessary, for the purposes of any of the appeals under consideration, for us to consider, for example, whether parental consent would be required were there to be a dispute over immunisations or sterilisation. We reproduce the document because, in our judgment, it demonstrates that, in addition to the fundamental difference in status between adopted children and those subject to special guardianship orders, there are equally fundamental differences between the status and powers of adopters and special guardians. These, we think, need to be borne in mind when the court is applying the welfare checklist under both s 1(3) of the 1989 Act and s 1 of the 2002 Act.

[47] Certain other points arise from the statutory scheme:

(i) The carefully constructed statutory regime (notice to the local authority, leave requirements in certain cases, the role of the court, and the report from the local authority—even where the order is made by the court of its own motion) demonstrates the care which is required before making a special guardianship order, and that it is only appropriate if, in the particular circumstances of the particular case, it is best fitted to meet the needs of the child or children concerned.

(ii) There is nothing in the statutory provisions themselves which limits the making of a special guardianship order or an adoption order to any given set of circumstances. The statute itself is silent on the circumstances in which a special guardianship order is likely to be appropriate, and there is no presumption contained within the statute that a special guardianship order is preferable to an adoption order in any particular category of case. Each case must be decided on its particular facts; and each case will involve the careful application of a judicial discretion to those facts.

(iii) The key question which the court will be obliged to ask itself in every case in which the question of adoption as opposed to special guardianship arises will be: which order will better serve the welfare of this particular child?

[48] The special nature of the jurisdiction also has implications for the approach of the courts:

(i) In view of the importance of such cases to the parties and the children concerned, it is incumbent on judges to give full reasons and to explain their decisions with care. Short cuts are to be avoided.

It is not of course necessary to go through the welfare check-list line by line, but the parties must be able to follow the judge's reasoning and to satisfy themselves that he or she has duly considered it and has taken every aspect of it relevant to the particular case properly into account

(ii) Provided the judge has carefully examined the facts, made appropriate findings in relation to them and applied the welfare check-lists contained in s 1(3) of the 1989 Act and s 1 of the 2002 Act, it is unlikely that this court will be able properly to interfere with the exercise of judicial discretion, particularly in a finely balanced case. (We think it no co-incidence that all three of the appeals with which these judgments are concerned fall to be dismissed, although each reaches a different result.)

(iii) In most cases (as in these three appeals) the issue will be, not the actual placement of the child, but the form of order which should govern the future welfare of the child: in other words, the status of the child within the particular household. It is unlikely that the court need be concerned with the alternative of making 'no order' under s 1(5) of the 1989 Act and s 1(6) of the 2002 Act.

(iv) For the same reason, the risk of prejudice caused by delay (to which s 1(2) of the 1989 Act rightly draws attention) may be of less pivotal importance. Indeed, in many cases, it may be appropriate to pause and give time for reflection, particularly in those cases where the order in being made of the court's own motion. This is a point to which we will return specifically when considering the first appeal.

[49] We would add, however, that, although the 'no order' principle as such is unlikely to be relevant, it is a material feature of the special guardianship regime that it is 'less intrusive' than adoption. In other words, it involves a less fundamental interference with existing legal relationships. The court will need to bear art 8 of the European Convention for the Protection of Human Rights and Fundamental Freedoms 1950 (as set out in Sch 1 to the Human Rights Act 1998) in mind, and to be satisfied that its order is a proportionate response to the problem, having regard to the interference with family life which is involved. In choosing between adoption and special guardianship, in most cases art 8 is unlikely to add anything to the considerations contained in the respective welfare checklists. Under both statutes the welfare of the child is the court's paramount consideration, and the balancing exercise required by the statutes will be no different to that required by art 8. However, in some cases, the fact that the welfare objective can be achieved with less disruption of existing family relationships can properly be regarded as helping to tip the balance.

SPECIAL GUARDIANSHIP ORDERS WITHIN PRE-EXISTING FAMILY RELATIONSHIPS

[50] It is clear from the White Paper that special guardianship was introduced at least in part to deal with the potential problems arising from the use

of adoption in the case of placements within the wider family. We have referred to the *Houghton Report* concerns in this respect (see [6] above).

[51] A particular concern is that an adoption order has, as a matter of law, the effect of making the adopted child the child of the adopters for all purposes. Accordingly, where a child is adopted by a member of his wider family, the familial relationships are inevitably changed. This is frequently referred to as the 'skewing' or 'distorting' effect of adoption, and is a factor which the court must take into account when considering whether or not to make an adoption order in such a case. This is not least because the checklist under s 1 of the 2002 Act requires it to do so: see s 1(4)(f) ('the relationship which the child has with relatives'). However, the weight to be given to this factor will inevitably depend on the facts of the particular case, and it will be only one factor in the overall welfare equation.

12.2.3 SGOs: general principles: key differences to adoption

Re P-S (children) [2018] EWCA Civ 1407, [2018] 4 WLR 99, [35]–[36] (Sir Ernest Ryder SP)

35. It is trite law that whatever the degree of permanence a special guardianship order provides for a child, the order does not have the same characteristics as an adoption order. It is not intended to have. Special guardianship was introduced to provide permanence in the care of children who cannot return to their birth families but where adoption is not appropriate. The legislative framework is different. It does not extinguish the parental responsibility of a child's parents or terminate their legal relationship with the child, it can be varied or discharged (but not by a parent without the court's leave) and it comes to an end when the child reaches the age of 18. There is no direct equivalence with an adoption order and the protections around it are accordingly different. If the judge intended to suggest that the statutory schemes are the same or very similar then that was inappropriate.

36. In particular, adoption orders cannot be made unless a child has had his or her home with an adoptive applicant for a prescribed period and an adoption order may not be made unless the court is satisfied that sufficient opportunities to see the child with the applicants have been given (see section 42 of the Adoption and Children Act 2002). There are no similar residence requirements in the statutory scheme that governs special guardianship orders. The scheme for approval of potential adopters and their matching with children is also completely different from the assessment provisions relating to special guardians where the assessment is child specific.

See also *Re DF and GF (children) (placement order or special guardianship order)* [2013] EWHC 2607 (Fam) [51]–[54] (Pauffley J) providing an overview of the law on this point

12.2.4 SGOs: general principles: out of area placements

Suffolk County Council v Nottinghamshire County Council [2012] EWCA Civ 1640, [2013] 2 FLR 106, [28]–[31] (Hedley J)

28. As has already been intimated, out of area placements in prospective special guardianship cases may very well become much more common. A number of matters have arisen in this case which may well arise elsewhere. A few reflections may therefore not be out of place. It was for this reason that we decided to put our judgment in writing.

29. The law both prescribes the incidence of responsibility and provides for a high degree of flexibility. If a child is a looked after child then responsibility lies with that authority; if not, it lies with the authority in whose area the child resides. It is therefore of critical importance when a child is placed out of area to have regard as to whether a child should or will remain looked after (i.e. under an interim care order or accommodated) or not (i.e. under a residence order). At the same time the local authorities involved should co-operate from the earliest stage in deciding who will in fact execute the statutory duties that arise and who will fund that work. Local authorities have powers to make sensible arrangements between themselves wherever primary legal responsibility may in fact lie.

30. The role of the court should also be carefully considered. Section 14F imposes duties on a local authority but it does not empower the family court to direct how or (in some aspects) even whether such duties are to be performed. Moreover the statute gives the court no power to make directions as to payment of money or provision of services. Of course judges may properly express views to local authorities and are entitled no doubt to expect that they will receive serious consideration (just as judges can and do express views about adoption and care plans) and of course it is only the judge who in the end can make the special guardianship order.

31. Special guardianship is potentially a very effective way of securing kinship care without on the one hand distorting family structures by adoption and without on the other leaving the child as a child in care with all the consequences so often resented by a growing child who feels stigmatised. It is essential both that local authorities in 'out of area' placements should co-operate with each other as early in the process as is practicable in the particular case and also that the court is clear about its role and powers. They may not be as extensive as is thought or as a judge may wish but I have no reason to think that the judge cannot make a valuable contribution to the process as is often done in both adoption and care cases where the court has the confidence of the parties involved.

12.2.5 SGOs: general principles: imposition on unwilling parties

Re S (a child) (adoption order or special guardianship order) [2007] EWCA Civ 54, [2007] 1 FCR 271, [73]–[77] (Wall LJ) *quotation limited to* [73], [77]

IN WHAT CIRCUMSTANCES (IF ANY) SHOULD THE COURT IMPOSE A SPECIAL GUARDIANSHIP ORDER ON UNWILLING PARTIES?

[73] There is no doubt, as s 14A(6)(b) of the 1989 Act makes clear, that the court has power to make a special guardianship order of its own motion, where the welfare of the child is in issue in any family proceedings, although as already noted (under s 14A(11)) it must first receive a report dealing with the matters referred to in s 14A(8). If no application for a special guardianship order has been made by any of the parties to family proceedings, a common reason will be that no party wants such an order. The statute therefore implicitly envisages an order being made against the wishes of the parties, and in a case in which the party seeking a different order (for example adoption) does not want to be appointed the child's special guardian. Indeed, this is the case in all three of the current appeals.

...

[77] Whilst *Re M* highlights the intense difficulties of factual situations thrown up by the provisions of ss 6 and 16 of the 1976 Act, we do not find it of any particular assistance in addressing the two questions we have posed. The jurisdictional position is very clear: the court has the power to impose a special guardianship order on an unwilling party to the proceedings. Whether or not it should do so will depend upon the facts of the individual case, including the nature of the refuser's case and its inter-relationship with the welfare of the particular child. What seems to us clear is that if the court comes to the view on all the facts and applying the welfare checklist under the 1989 Act (including the potential consequences to the child of the refuser implementing the threat to refuse to be appointed a special guardian) that a special guardianship order will be serve the welfare interests of the child in question, that is the order which the court should make.

12.2.6 SGOs: general principles: SGOs alongside public law orders

Re F and G (discharge of special guardianship order) [2021] EWCA Civ 622, [50]–[51] (Baker LJ)

50. The view of the Public Law Working Group and the Family Justice Council is that the cases where it will be appropriate or necessary to make a supervision order alongside an SGO are likely to be very small in number. Similarly, the circumstances in which a court concludes that a care order should be made alongside an SGO are likely to be rare. The most straightforward solution will normally be to make care orders on the basis of a plan that they will be replaced by an SGO at a later date if all

goes well. I am, however, not inclined to say that an SGO can never be made alongside a care order. Given the complexity and gravity of cases that come before the family courts, it would not be right to deprive judges of an option which Parliament has made available through its carefully drafted provisions. In any event, as I have already noted, we are not concerned with an appeal against the *making* of the special guardianship order in April 2020 but rather the refusal to discharge it in February 2021.

51. It follows that I reject the first ground of appeal. A judge sitting in the family court does have jurisdiction to allow care orders and SGOs to coexist, although the circumstances in which this is will arise are likely to be rare. The more difficult question in this case is whether the judge was wrong to refuse to discharge the order in the circumstances of this case.

See Chapter 12.3.2 SGOs: variation or discharge: care orders do not automatically discharge SGOs

12.3 SPECIAL GUARDIANSHIP ORDERS: VARIATION OR DISCHARGE

12.3.1 SGOs: variation or discharge: leave to apply to discharge: test

Re M (special guardianship order: leave to apply to discharge) (rev 1) [2021] EWCA Civ 442, [2021] 3 FCR 165, [22]–[34] (Peter Jackson LJ)

Variation and discharge of SGOs

[22] Section 14D of the 1989 Act concerns the manner in which SGOs, unlike adoption orders, can be varied or discharged …

Accordingly, a parent seeking to discharge an SGO requires the leave of the court under ss (3)(b), which can only be given if the court is satisfied under ss (5) that there has been a significant change in circumstances since the making of the order. Subsection (2) also allows the court hearing family proceedings about a child to vary or discharge an SGO on its own initiative.

[23] The condition in s 14D(5) (introduced into the 1989 Act by the 2002 Act) calls to mind the somewhat analogous leave provisions in the later Act in relation to applications to revoke a placement order (s 24(3)) or to oppose the making of an adoption order (s 47(5)), both of which require 'a change in circumstances'. In *Re G (special guardianship order)* [2010] EWCA Civ 300, [2010] 2 FLR 696 at [13]), it was said that, when considering an application for leave to apply to discharge an SGO, the court should follow the two-stage approach applicable to applications for leave to revoke a placement order set out in *M v Warwickshire County Council* [2007] EWCA Civ 1084, [2007] 3 FCR 681, [2008] 1 FLR 1093 at [29]. That case established that a change in circumstances is necessary but not sufficient for leave to be granted and that, if there has been a change in circumstances, the court has to make an evaluation in which the welfare of the child and the prospects of success should both be weighed.

[24] A question arises as to correct interpretation of s 14D(5), which provides that leave may not be granted to a parent unless there has been a *significant* change of circumstances since the making of the SGO. That was considered by Ward LJ and Wilson LJ in *Re G* (above) in a somewhat unusual situation. A judge had refused to grant leave to apply to discharge a SGO. He accepted that there had been change, but not that it had been significant change, and he applied the checklist of factors in s 10(9) of the 1989 Act, which ostensibly relates only to an application for leave to apply for a s 8 order. Before the appeal was heard, the parties agreed that leave should be granted and the appeal was allowed by consent. Because of the legal issues, Wilson LJ gave a judgment, with which Ward LJ agreed. It was prefaced in this way:

> '[1]... The remarks which I will make in this short judgment must be considered in the light of the absence of adversarial argument; but possibly they will be of some use to family judges and practitioners on an interim basis pending a more satisfactory examination, at whatever level of court, of the issues raised.'

and later:

> '[14] I suggest that, until the emergence of more robust jurisprudence in relation to the proper approach to the determination of applications for leave to apply for the discharge (or variation) of special guardianship orders, the approach should be that commended in the *Warwickshire* case.'

[25] I agree that the two-stage approach taken in *Warwickshire* is the appropriate structure for a decision about granting leave under s 14D(5).

[26] In relation to the first stage, there has been some debate about the exact nature of the change in circumstances required by s 14D(5). Wilson LJ considered this in *Re G* at [12]:

> 'In the absence of full argument I am perplexed as to why, in relation to an application for leave to apply for revocation of a placement order, Parliament should there have required that the court should be satisfied of "a change" in circumstances, whereas, in relation to an application for leave to apply for discharge of a special guardianship order, Parliament, by s 14D(5) of the Act of 1989, has required the court to be satisfied that there has been "a significant change" in circumstances. Important though it is to ascribe a value to every word favoured by Parliament, I cannot think that, by s 24(3) of the Act of 2002, it was requiring proof only of an insignificant change in circumstances, whereas, in its insertion, by s 115 of the same Act, of s 14D(5) into the Act of 1989, it was requiring something different. On a more appropriate occasion we may have to consider whether there is indeed any significance in the absence of the word "significant" in s 24(3) or whether the difference in the language is immaterial and possibly even the product of poor drafting under pressure. For the time being I proceed upon the basis that there is no relevant difference

between the reference in s 24(3) to "a change" in circumstances and the reference in s 14D(5) to "a significant change" in circumstances. If, then, we have for practical purposes identical language, my view is that we should adopt an identical approach; and thus that, to the extent that in *M v Warwickshire County Council* [2007] EWCA Civ 1084, [2008] 1 WLR 991, [2008] 1 FLR 1093, this court gave guidance as to the approach to an application for leave to apply for revocation of a placement order, it should apply similarly to an application for leave to apply for the discharge of a special guardianship order. Indeed in *Re A; Coventry County Council v CC and A* [2007] EWCA Civ 1383, [2008] 1 FLR 959, this court – again in an attempt to keep things as simple as possible – suggested, at [10], that the factors relevant to the exercise of the discretion under s 24(3) of the Act of 2002, as identified in the *Warwickshire* case, were identical to those relevant to the exercise of the discretion whether to grant leave to apply for an adoption order under s 42(6) of the Act of 2002.'

[27] In this case we have had the benefit of full and thoughtful argument from Ms Ruth Cabeza for the mother and from Ms Kotilaine on the question of whether the qualifier 'significant' adds anything. They were in broad agreement that it does, and I am sure that they are right. Rather than being an error of drafting, it is coherent with the statutory scheme for the drafter to have set out to buttress an SGO from challenge by requiring any change in circumstances to be significant. There is no reason why the test should be the same across SGOs, placement orders and adoption orders. An application relating to an SGO is an attempt to disturb what is intended to be a long-term status, while the other applications concern impermanent situations where a child has not yet been placed or adopted, as the case may be. Moreover, the drafting of the two Acts shows that the word 'significant' has real meaning in this area of the law. In the welfare checklists in s 1 of both Acts, the reference is to harm, while in the threshold condition in the 1989 Act it is to significant harm. In our context, the fact that change is not described as significant does not mean (pace Wilson LJ) that it is insignificant. As a matter of ordinary language, change can be described as significant or insignificant, or it can just be described as change. The absence of an adjective does not imply the presence of its opposite – a person who is not described as happy cannot be assumed to be unhappy.

[28] I therefore conclude that the requirement under s 14D(5) for a change in circumstances to be significant means what it says and, to this extent only, I would not follow the provisional reasoning in *Re G*. If more is needed, 'significant' in the context of the s 31 threshold condition means 'considerable, noteworthy or important', according to the dictionary definition cited in the Guidance when the 1989 Act first came into force (*The Children Act 1989: Guidance and Regulations (Volume 1, Court Orders)* (HMSO 1991)), as approved by Baroness Hale in *Re B (care proceedings: appeal)* [2013] UKSC 33, [2013] 2 FCR 525, [2013] 2 FLR 1075 at [185]. As Ms Cabeza says, it does not mean trivial or unimportant, and neither does it mean exceptional, immense, or insurmountable.

[29] Turning to the second stage, what has to be shown in a case under s 24(3) is broadly 'a real prospect' of success: see *Warwickshire* at [29]. In my view, the same approach should be taken in a case under s 14D(5). Likewise, echoing relevant elements of the guidance given in the adoption context in *Re B-S (adoption: application of s 47(5))* [2013] EWCA Civ 1146, [2013] 3 FCR 481, [2014] 1 FLR 1035 at [74], the degree of any change in circumstances is likely to be intertwined with the prospects of success, and the greater the prospects of success, the more cogent the welfare arguments must be if leave is to be refused.

[30] Further, following the approach taken under s 24(3) in *Warwickshire*, the welfare of the child is an important, but not paramount factor at the second stage (For no obvious good reason, the position is different under s 47(5): see *Re P (adoption: leave provisions)* [2007] EWCA Civ 616, [2007] 2 FCR 407, [2007] 2 FLR 1069 at [26] and [35].) It must be remembered that at this stage the assessment concerns the effect on the child's welfare of the application to discharge the SGO being heard or not heard: the question of whether it is in the child's interests for the SGO to be discharged only arises if leave is granted, at which point welfare is undoubtedly paramount.

[31] Lastly, I agree with Wilson LJ in *Re G* that s 10(9) of the 1989 Act does not formally apply to an application under s 14D(5), and that it is not helpful to use it by analogy. The sub-section reads:

> '(9) Where the person applying for leave to make an application for a section 8 order is not the child concerned, the court shall, in deciding whether or not to grant leave, have particular regard to—
>
> (a) the nature of the proposed application for the section 8 order;
>
> (b) the applicant's connection with the child;
>
> (c) any risk there might be of that proposed application disrupting the child's life to such an extent that he would be harmed by it; and
>
> (d) where the child is being looked after by a local authority—
>
> (i) the authority's plans for the child's future; and
>
> (ii) the wishes and feelings of the child's parents.'

This provision is not used when considering applications under s 24(3) or s 47(5) of the 2002 Act and it does not comfortably sit alongside s 14D(5) either. Factor (a) is irrelevant unless it includes taking a view of the prospects of success, which must be done anyway. Factor (d) is by definition inapplicable where there is an SGO. Factors (b) and (c) are obviously matters that would be considered, but even then there is a danger that the requirement for disruption to be so extensive as to be harmful may skew what ought to be a broad evaluation of welfare and prospects of success.

[32] The power conferred by s 14D(5) is to be exercised firmly within the context of the overall statutory scheme governing SGOs. As Ms Kotilaine puts it, the door to reunification of children with their parents is not locked under an SGO, as it is when an adoption order is made, but the intention of the legislation is that the door will remain closed unless the court allows it to be opened to the extent of granting leave for a discharge application to be made. The parties skirmished about whether the discharge of an SGO was to be considered exceptional, but the argument goes nowhere as the concept of exceptionality commonly begs as many questions as it answers.

[33] As to the quality of the evidence, when considering applications for leave (whether under s 14D(5), s 24(3) or s 47(5)), the court is evaluating information that will usually be incomplete. It is not required to make findings of fact, but the applicant must provide credible evidence to show that there has been the necessary change and that leave should be granted. The court will seek to make a fair and realistic assessment, and where the available information is mixed or conflicting, it will no doubt be guided by undisputed facts and by corroborative evidence from independent sources. When assessing change, it will be important to establish the baseline facts that led to the making of the original order. Where there were care proceedings, there will be threshold findings, and where an SGO had been made in private law proceedings, there should similarly be a record of why that was the outcome.

[34] To sum up, when a court is considering an application for leave to apply to discharge a special guardianship order, it must first consider whether the applicant has shown, by means of credible evidence, that there has been a significant change of circumstances since the order was made. If there has not been, the application will fail. If there has, the court will decide whether leave should be granted, based on a realistic evaluation of the applicant's prospects of success in the context of the effect on the child's welfare of the application being heard or not heard. The prospects of success must be real. The child's welfare is an important factor but it is not the paramount consideration. The degree of any change in circumstances is likely to be intertwined with the prospects of success, and the greater the prospects of success, the more likely it is that leave will be granted. The provisions of s 10(9) of the 1989 Act are not applicable to an application under s 14D(5).

12.3.2 SGOs: variation or discharge: care orders do not automatically discharge SGOs

Re F and G (discharge of special guardianship order) [2021] EWCA Civ 622, [41]–[51] (Baker LJ) *quotation limited to* [41]–[49]

41. … The careful drafting of the amendments to the Children Act 1989 by which special guardianship was introduced in 2001 clearly allow for an SGO to continue after the making of a care order, be it an interim care

order under s.38 or a final care order under s.31. My reasons for reaching this conclusion are as follows.

42. First, the specific provisions of s.91 make it crystal clear that an SGO is not automatically discharged by the making of a care order. Given the care with which that section is drafted, it is obvious that, had Parliament intended that an SGO would be discharged by the making of a final care order, it would have said so in express terms.

43. Secondly, the provisions in s.33 governing the effect of a care order would make no sense if an SGO was automatically discharged by the making of a care order. Under s.33(3)(b)(i), as amended in 2002, when a care order is in force the local authority has the power to determine the extent to which 'a parent, guardian or special guardian ... may exercise his parental responsibility' for the child. The words 'special guardian' were inserted into this subsection in 2002 when the statutory provisions governing special guardianship were introduced. The fact that Parliament amended s.33(3)(b) of the Children Act so as to include the words 'special guardian' confirms that it intended that an SGO could continue after the making of a care order. This interpretation is reinforced by the terms of s.33(4) which prevents a local authority from determining the extent to which the special guardian may meet his parental responsibility for the child save where 'satisfied that it is necessary to do so in order to safeguard or promote the child's welfare'.

44. Thirdly, the provisions in s.14D governing the discharge of an SGO would make no sense if an SGO was automatically discharged by the making of a care order. Where the circumstances are appropriate, a local authority 'designated in a care order' with respect to the child may apply without leave for discharge of the SGO under s.14D(1)(f). Since a local authority is only entitled to apply for the discharge of the SGO if it is designated in a care order, and since the making of an SGO discharges any pre-existing care order, the clear implication of s.14D(1)(f) is that, where a care order comes into force, any existing SGO with respect to the child remains in force until discharged under s.14D.

45. The rationale for these provisions is plain. In some circumstances it will be appropriate for an SGO to be discharged on the making of a care order, in other circumstances not. Where an SGO has been in force for several years, the special guardians will usually have established a close relationship with the child. They may be the only persons with parental responsibility. In such circumstances, it would in all probability be wrong for the SGO to be discharged upon making a care order. Where, however, the SGO has only been in force for a short period, and the role of the special guardians in the child's life has not been established, it may be appropriate for the SGO to be discharged. Everything turns on the circumstances of the case and the welfare of the child.

46. It seems to me, however, that there is a more fundamental principle involved here. The purpose of an SGO is not merely to provide a stable

and secure home. The passage in *The Children Act 1989 Guidance and Regulations Volume 2: care planning, placement and case review* cited by Peter Jackson LJ in *Re M (Special Guardianship Order: Leave to Apply to Discharge)* defines the objective of 'permanence' in broad terms:

> 'The objective of planning for permanence is … to ensure that children have a secure, stable and loving family to support them through childhood and beyond and to give them a sense of security, continuity, commitment, identity and belonging.'

Like adoption, special guardianship is a relationship which provides long-term support for the child. There is no reason for "the sense of security, continuity, commitment, identity and belonging" to come to an end when the child moves away. On the contrary, the purpose and intention is that it will survive "through childhood and beyond". It would be contrary to the purpose of special guardianship for it to come to an end automatically upon the making of a care order.

47. I do not read any of the judicial observations cited on behalf of the mother as supporting the proposition that the two orders cannot as a matter of law coexist. The 'exclusivity' of the exercise of parental responsibility granted to a special guardian by s.14C(1)(b) referred to by Moylan J in *Re C*, supra, is expressed as being 'subject to any other order in force with respect to the child under this Act'. A pre-existing care order will not be 'in force' under the Act because under s.91(5A) it will have been automatically discharged by the making of the SGO but there is nothing in the statute to prevent a care order being made after the making of the SGO. It is important to note that the exclusivity granted by s.14C(1)(b) is as to the *exercise* of parental responsibility, not to the entitlement to parental responsibility. It is plain from other subsections in s.14C that other persons may hold parental responsibility notwithstanding the making of an SGO, even if their right to exercise it is precluded by s.14C(1)(b).

48. There is nothing in the Act to support the interpretation advanced by Ms Edmunds and Ms O'Neill that an SGO can coexist with an interim care order but not a final care order. Under s.31(11), except where express provision to the contrary is made, the phrase 'a care order' in the Act includes an interim care order. The provisions of the Act under consideration in this case contain no such express provision. It is plainly easier to envisage circumstances in which an SGO will be in existence alongside an interim care order than circumstances in which an SGO will continue after the making of a final care order. Where care proceedings are started in respect of a child who is subject to an SGO, particularly where the SGO has been in existence for some time, it is unlikely that the SGO will be discharged at the outset of the proceedings. Instead it is more likely that it will continue alongside an interim care order until the proceedings reach or move closer to a conclusion. At that point, if a final care order is made, the SGO will in some cases be discharged. But there is nothing in the wording of the Act to *require* it to be discharged. The range of circumstances that arise in proceedings under the Act is so wide

that it would be wholly wrong to adopt an interpretation of the statute that deprives the court of a flexibility that the circumstances may require. S.1(3)(g) and (4)(b) require any court considering whether to make, vary or discharge an SGO or a care order to have regard to 'the range of powers available to the court under the Act in the proceedings in question'. It is not for this Court to impose a restriction on the range of powers provided by Parliament.

49. I do not accept the submission that the making of the SGO on 20 April automatically brought the whole proceedings to an end and that there was no lawful basis to 're-enter the public arena' by making the care order. In any event, if that submission was correct, it would follow that the care order was nugatory, not the SGO. The submission provides no support for the appeal against the judge's refusal to discharge the SGO in February 2021.

CHAPTER 13

Restricting liberty

Chapter contents

CHAPTER 13

Restricting liberty

13.1 RESTRICTING LIBERTY: SECURE ACCOMMODATION[1]

13.1.1 Restricting liberty: secure accommodation: test under s 25[2]

Re B (secure accommodation order) [2019] EWCA Civ 2025, [2020] 1 FCR 507, [74]–[100] (Baker LJ) *quotation limited to* [93], [95]–[100]

[93] I therefore conclude that proportionality is one of the 'relevant criteria' which s 25(3) obliges the court to consider when hearing an application for a secure accommodation under the section.

...

[95] In the light of my conclusions about proportionality, I return to the evaluation of welfare.

[96] In *Re W (care proceedings: functions of court and local authority)* [2013] EWCA Civ 1227, [2014] 1 FCR 260, [2014] 1 WLR 1611 this court held that, in deciding what order to make at the conclusion of care proceedings, a court is required to carry out an evaluation of the proportionality of the local authority's care plan. In his judgment (with which the other members of the court, including Sir James Munby P agreed), Ryder LJ, as he then was, at paragraph [76], expressed the principle in these terms:

> 'The welfare evaluation and the question what, if any, orders are to be made engages Article 8 of the Convention and the proportionality of that intervention must be justified.'

1 In England, secure accommodation is provided under the Children Act 1989, s 25. The relevant regulations are the Children (Secure Accommodation) Regulations 1991, SI 1991/1505. In Wales, the equivalent statutory provision is s 119 of the Social Services and Well-being (Wales) Act 2014 (in operation since 2016). The Welsh statute effectively provides an identical statutory test. Perhaps readers will be less familiar with the supporting Welsh regulations, namely the Children (Secure Accommodation) (Wales) Regulations 2015, SI 2015/1988 (W298). Applicable law depends upon whether the accommodation is in England or in Wales. It is advised that care is needed concerning the applicable regulations: their details differ. Please also remember that a Welsh local authority seeking placement outside Wales must also comply with its duties under the Welsh regulations, see reg 8, and see *Re T (a child)* [2021] UKSC 35, [39], [48] (Lady Black). Her Ladyship also addresses the interrelationship between England and Wales in respect of social care in *Re T (a child)* [24]–[27]. It is submitted that authorities are generally applicable to either Act, unless indicated otherwise.

2 Children Act 1989, s 25.

At paragraph [80], he continued:

> 'The process of deciding what order is necessary involves a value judgment about the proportionality of the State's intervention to meet the risk against which the court decides there is a need for protection. In that regard, one starts with the court's findings of fact and moves on to the value judgments that are the welfare evaluation. That evaluation is the court's not the local authority's, the guardian's or indeed any other party's. It is the function of the court to come to that value judgment. It is simply not open to a local authority within proceedings to decline to accept the court's evaluation of risk, no matter how much it may disagree with the same. Furthermore, it is that evaluation which will inform the proportionality of the response which the court decides is necessary.'

[97] It follows from Ryder LJ's analysis that the evaluation of welfare and the assessment of proportionality are two sides of the same coin. The assessment of proportionality which the court is obliged to carry out as a public authority will inevitably involve an evaluation of welfare. In my judgment, this analysis applies equally to applications under s 25. Accordingly, the interpretation of s 25 proposed by Hoffmann LJ in *Re M* – that the function of the court is to control the exercise of power by the local authority rather than to exercise an independent jurisdiction in the best interests of the child – and the approach suggested by Charles J in *S v Knowsley* – that the court should assess welfare issues under s 25 on the basis that the local authority is the decision maker – are, in my view, incompatible with the court's duty under s 6 of the Human Rights Act. On an application under s 25, the court must carry out its own evaluation of whether the order would safeguard and promote the child's welfare. The intensity of that evaluation will depend on the facts of each case. In most cases, it is unlikely to involve a wide-ranging inquiry. The question for the court is whether, in all the circumstances, including the need to protect the public, the proposed order would safeguard and promote the child's welfare.

Relevant criteria revisited

[98] Having analysed the roles played by welfare and proportionality in the decision-making process under s 25, I conclude that, in determining whether the 'relevant criteria' under s 25(3) and (4) are satisfied, a court must ask the following questions.

(1) Is the child being 'looked after' by a local authority, or, alternatively, does he or she fall within one of the other categories specified in regulation 7?

(2) Is the accommodation where the local authority proposes to place the child 'secure accommodation', ie is it designed for or have as its primary purpose the restriction of liberty?

(3) Is the court satisfied (a) that (i) the child has a history of absconding and is likely to abscond from any other description

of accommodation, and (ii) if he/she absconds, he/she is likely to suffer significant harm or (b) that if kept in any other description of accommodation, he/she is likely to injure himself or other persons?

(4) If the local authority is proposing to place the child in a secure children's home in England, has the accommodation been approved by the Secretary of State for use as secure accommodation? If the local authority is proposing to place the child in a children's home in Scotland, is the accommodation provided by a service which has been approved by the Scottish Ministers?

(5) Does the proposed order safeguard and promote the child's welfare?

(6) Is the order proportionate, i.e. do the benefits of the proposed placement outweigh the infringement of rights?

(In the rare circumstances of the child being aged under 13, reg 4 of the 1991 Regulations require that the placement must also be approved by the Secretary of State.)

[99] If the relevant criteria are satisfied, s 25(4) obliges the court to make an order under the section authorising the child to be kept in secure accommodation and specifying the maximum period for which he or she may be so kept. In its submissions to this court, the ALC was rightly anxious to preserve the use of what it called 'imaginative arrangements' – the arrangements characterised by Hayden J in *Re SS* as 'the creative alternative packages of support' – and was concerned they would be squeezed out by too wide a definition of 'secure accommodation'. The recasting of the interpretation of the relevant criteria under s 25 suggested in this judgment preserves the flexible approach advocated by the ALC. If the court determining an application under s 25 is obliged to conduct an evaluation of welfare and an assessment of proportionality, and in doing so applies the principle that a secure accommodation order should always be a last resort, the court will be under an obligation to consider alternative arrangements.

[100] In my view, the date at which the relevant criteria must be satisfied is the date of the hearing. I reject Mr Feehan's submission that the time for assessment as to whether the relevant criteria are satisfied is immediately before emergency protective measures are taken. That interpretation would have the consequence that, once a court was satisfied that the criteria had been met at the point where the application under s 25 was filed, the court would be obliged at a subsequent hearing to make an order under s 25 even if the likelihood of absconding and/or significant harm had abated. Such an interpretation would be plainly contrary to the terms of s 25 itself which prohibits a child being kept in secure accommodation unless the statutory criteria are satisfied.

See also *Lancashire CC v G* [2020] EWHC 2828 (Fam), [2021] 2 FLR 34, [29]–[30] (MacDonald J) considering *Re B (secure accommodation order)* [2019] EWCA Civ 2025, [2020] 1 FCR 507

13.1.2 Restricting liberty: secure accommodation: test under s 25: 'provided for the purpose of restricting liberty': designed for or having as its primary purpose restricting liberty

Re D (a child) [2019] UKSC 42, [2019] 3 FCR 631, [91]–[93], [100]–[115] (Lady Black) *quotation limited to* [91]–[93], [100]–[103], [110]–[115]

[91] Where it applies, s 25 of the Children Act 1989 regulates the circumstances in which children can be placed and kept 'in accommodation … provided for the purpose of restricting liberty' and dictates that, save for very short periods, the court's authorisation of the arrangements is required. If the section applies to living arrangements like D's, making court authorisation obligatory, the debate as to whether it falls within the scope of parental responsibility to authorise a child's confinement would be of far less practical significance. In order to set that debate in its proper context, the scope of s 25 was therefore explored. In the light of this exploration, it appears likely that a significant number of children living in confined circumstances will be outside the ambit of the section, although clearly each case will depend upon its own facts. Accordingly, the parental responsibility issue has a real practical importance. The reasons for this provisional conclusion are set out below. They deal with the law as it applies to accommodation in England; there is a separate statutory and regulatory regime where the accommodation is in Wales, albeit in similar terms.

[92] Section 25 provides as follows …

[93] Where applicable, the section operates to prevent a child being placed or kept in secure accommodation unless one of the two conditions set out in s 25(1)(a) and (b) is satisfied. The initial placement need not involve the court, but regulations made under s 25(2) provide that a child may not be kept in secure accommodation without court authority for more than 72 hours in any period of 28 consecutive days (reg 10, Children (Secure Accommodation) Regulations 1991 (SI 1991/1505), hereafter 'the 1991 Regulations'). There are limits on the period that can be authorised by the court, being three months in the first instance, and a further period of up to six months thereafter (regs 11 and 12).

…

[100] The parties rightly stress the need to interpret the section with an eye to the whole scheme in which it takes its place. Local authorities have far-reaching welfare obligations towards children. Notably, under s 20 of the Children Act 1989, they have a duty to provide accommodation for children in need, and they must also address the accommodation and other needs of children in relation to whom care orders have been made. The children who require help will present with all sorts of different problems, and there will be those whose care needs cannot be met unless their liberty is restricted in some way. But by no means all of these children will fall within the criteria set out in s 25(1)(a) and (b), which are the gateway to the authorisation of secure accommodation. It seems unlikely that the legislation was intended to operate in such a way as to prevent a local

authority from providing such a child with the care that he or she needs, but an unduly wide interpretation of 'secure accommodation' would potentially have this effect. It is possible to imagine a child who has no history, so far, of absconding, and who is not likely actually to injure himself or anyone else, so does not satisfy s 25(1)(a) or (b), but who, for other good reasons to do with his own welfare, needs to be kept in confined circumstances. If s 25 applies whenever a child's liberty is restricted, local authorities will not be able to meet the welfare needs of children such as this. And, of course, it is similarly possible to envisage children in hospitals and care homes who need a degree of confinement, but do not satisfy either of the limbs of s 25(1). Putting it another way, the criteria set for the placing or keeping of a child in secure accommodation might be taken to reveal something of the problems which it was anticipated that children in secure accommodation would present. This, in turn, could be taken as a pointer towards the characteristics that one could expect to find in secure accommodation being used to meet those problems.

[101] It is also worth noting, when considering how s 25 fits into the statutory scheme, that a court determining an application under the section does not have the child's welfare as its paramount consideration, as would normally be the case when the court determines any question with respect to the upbringing of a child (s 1 of the Children Act 1989). If any of the relevant criteria for keeping a child in secure accommodation are satisfied, the court is obliged to make the order authorising the child to be kept in secure accommodation (s 25(4)). It would be surprising if s 25 were intended to be interpreted in such a way as to extend this displacement of the court's welfare role beyond a relatively circumscribed group of children whose circumstances make this unavoidable. Underlining this, it is worth noting that where the position of a child of 16 or 17 is being considered in the Court of Protection under the Mental Capacity Act 2005, welfare is the touchstone, as deprivation of liberty will only be endorsed where it is in the best interests of the child.

[102] So, the challenge is to interpret s 25 in such a way as to provide the protection intended by the legislature, without getting in the way of meeting the varied needs of the children for whom hospitals, care homes, and local authorities (in the exercise of their social services and education functions) have responsibility. We are grateful to the parties for the valuable detailed written submissions they have all made to assist with this process; as, for the most part, they traverse similar ground, it is unnecessary to attribute submissions in what follows. It is unnecessary also to address all the arguments advanced, given that we are not making a definitive decision as to the operation of s 25.

[103] It is submitted that the focus should be on the accommodation and the purpose for which it is provided, rather than upon the regime within the accommodation. This would be consistent with s 25(1)(a) and (b) which, in setting the criteria for the use of secure accommodation, stipulate that the child may not be placed/kept in secure accommodation unless it appears

that he is likely to abscond from 'any other description of accommodation' or to injure himself or others if he is kept in 'any other description of accommodation'. This contrast of 'secure accommodation' with 'any other description of accommodation' can be read as supporting the notion that 'secure accommodation' is a 'description of accommodation', rather than a description of a regime of care.

…

[110] Coming closer to home, we are invited to endorse the approach that Wall J took to the phrase 'accommodation … provided for the purpose of restricting liberty' in *In re C (detention: medical treatment)* ([1997] 3 FCR 49 at 63, [1997] 2 FLR 180 at 193). The case concerned a 16-year old girl suffering from anorexia nervosa. The local authority made an application for an order under the inherent jurisdiction authorising her detention in a clinic for medical treatment. Wall J was faced with the question whether the court's powers under the inherent jurisdiction were ousted by the scheme laid down by Parliament in s 25, and in addressing that issue, he needed to determine whether the clinic was, in fact, 'secure accommodation' within s 25. Having reviewed three earlier authorities (*R v Northampton Juvenile Court, Ex p London Borough of Hammersmith and Fulham* [1985] FLR 193, *South Glamorgan County Council v W and B* [1993] 1 FCR 626, [1993] 1 FLR 574, and *A Metropolitan Borough Council v DB* [1997] 1 FCR 618, [1997] 1 FLR 767) he said ([1997] 3 FCR 49 at 63, [1997] 2 FLR 180 at 193):

> 'Whilst I respectfully agree … that premises which are not designed as secure accommodation may become secure accommodation because of the use to which they are put in the particular circumstances of individual cases, it does seem to me that the more natural meaning of the words "provided for the purpose of restricting liberty" is "designed for, or having as its primary purpose" the restriction of liberty. The circumstances in which s 25 operates are based on the premise that the child has a history of absconding and is likely to abscond from any other description of accommodation. The alternative premise, "that if he is kept in any other description of accommodation he is likely to injure himself or others" once again envisages a secure regime designed to prevent self-harm. I therefore prefer to look at the clinic, and ask myself: "is it accommodation provided for the purpose of restricting liberty"? This is, of course, as Cazalet J indicates, a question of fact.'

[111] Having said that, he went on to examine the regime operated by the particular clinic, before finding that it was not secure accommodation. In his view, the 'purpose of placement of a child in the clinic is to achieve treatment: the accommodation provides a structure for that treatment'. The fact that there was a degree of restriction on the patient's liberty was an incident of the treatment programme, and the fact that steps could be taken to prevent the child from leaving the premises did not, of itself, render the clinic secure accommodation.

[112] Section 25 has played no direct role in the proceedings in the present case, and the bulk of the argument about it has occurred in writing after the conclusion of the hearing in this court. Nothing that we say about it will conclusively resolve the difficult questions that arise as to its scope and operation, and that is as it should be, because it would be undesirable that final views should be formed, without there having been an opportunity for oral argument. Furthermore, it would be better that such issues as there are about the scope of s 25 should be resolved in a case where the relevant facts have been found, so that the section can be interpreted with reference to a real factual situation. Because the issue was not under consideration at all before the appeal arrived in this court, factual findings have not been made in relation to all the matters relevant to the application of s 25 in D's case. As, by virtue of his age, D is now no longer within the scope of the Children Act, there would be absolutely no point in remitting the case for evidence to be heard, particularly as none of the parties contends that this is a s 25 case.

[113] The exercise in which we have engaged has, however, been sufficient to persuade us that s 25 is not intended to be widely interpreted, so as to catch all children whose care needs are being met in accommodation where there is a degree of restriction of their liberty, even amounting to a deprivation of liberty. There is much force in the argument that it is upon the accommodation itself that the spotlight should be turned, when determining whether particular accommodation is secure accommodation, rather than upon the attributes of the care of the child in question. This fits with the language used in s 25(1), when read as a whole. It is also consistent with the objective of ensuring that the section is not so widely drawn as to prejudice the local authority's ability to offer children the care that they need, and it ought to make it more straightforward to apply than would be the case if the issue were dependent upon the features of a child's individual care regime, so that the child might be found to be in secure accommodation in all manner of settings.

[114] A restrained construction of the section is also justified by the fact that, far from being concerned with the routine sort of problems that might require a child's freedom to be curtailed, the section has a 'last resort' quality about it. It is concerned with accommodation which has the features necessary to safeguard a child with a history of absconding who is likely to abscond from *any* other description of accommodation or to prevent injury where the child in question would be likely to injure himself or others if kept in *any* other description of accommodation.

[115] Of course, training the spotlight on the accommodation itself does not provide a complete answer to the question as to what falls within the definition of secure accommodation. Some secure accommodation will be readily recognisable from the fact that it is approved as such by the Secretary of State, but that is by no means a universal hallmark, as that approval is not needed for all types of secure accommodation. Moreover, given that it is contemplated that secure accommodation might be provided in places such as hospitals, it seems likely that there will not infrequently

be more than one purpose of the child being in the accommodation, and there is much to commend Wall J's approach to such a situation, that is to count within the definition of secure accommodation 'designed for or having as its primary purpose' the restriction of liberty. Equally, the section will have to be interpreted in such a way as to allow for situations where only a part of the premises is made over to restricting liberty.

Re T (a child) [2021] UKSC 35, [2021] 3 WLR 643, [122]–[138] (Lady Black) *quotation limited to* [130]–[138]

130. As for the question of whether the accommodation here was 'secure accommodation', again it is not possible to make findings at this late stage about T's specific placements. However, the question of what accommodation falls within the definition of secure accommodation for the purposes of section 25 does merit consideration in more general terms here. I do not propose to go over, again, the territory that I explored in *In re D* (supra), commencing at para 91 of that case. However, the issue has benefitted from further consideration during the course of this hearing, and it is possible to build upon that to develop the ideas that I set out there.

131. The concern of section 25(1) is a child who is "placed … in accommodation in England or Scotland provided for the purpose of restricting liberty ('secure accommodation')". I expressed caution in *In re D* (para 100) about an unduly wide interpretation of "secure accommodation" which might prevent a local authority from providing the appropriate care for a child whose needs can only be met if their liberty is restricted, but who does not fall within the terms of section 25(1)(a) or (b). I observed, also, that the criteria set for placing or keeping children in secure accommodation might be taken to reveal something of the problems which it was anticipated such children would present, which, in turn, could be taken as a pointer towards the characteristics that one would expect to find in "secure accommodation".

132. The court now has available to it considerably more information about the varied difficulties suffered by the group of children in relation to whom a local authority might have to consider deprivation of liberty in some shape or form. By deprivation of liberty, I do not, of course, mean the imposition of the sort of restrictions that are part of normal parenting for a child of that age, which would not amount to deprivation of liberty within article 5 (see, for example, Baroness Hale of Richmond's judgment in *In re D* at para 39). We also have further information as to the nature of approved secure accommodation units, and the alternative bespoke arrangements that local authorities make to meet the needs of children. All of this helps in interpreting the concept of secure accommodation in section 25(1). It does not deflect me from my inclination that section 25 should not be too widely interpreted, and that care has to be taken to ensure that it provides the protection intended by the legislature but without getting in the way of meeting the varied needs of the children for whom hospitals, care homes, and local authorities have responsibility.

133. I am confirmed in my view that the focus should be on the accommodation itself and the purpose for which it is provided, rather than the regime in the accommodation. I also remain of the view that there is much to commend Wall J's approach to the issue in *In re C (Detention: Medical Treatment)* [1997] 2 FLR 180, 193, that is that the words "provided for the purpose of restricting liberty" mean "designed for, or having as its primary purpose" the restriction of liberty.

134. Building on the two limbs of Wall J's interpretation, the Secretary of State submits that the only accommodation that is "designed for" the restriction of liberty is a secure children's home approved by the Secretary of State. It is difficult to consider this entirely in the abstract, as we are required to do in the present case, as the determination of whether a particular arrangement constitutes secure accommodation within the meaning of section 25 will depend very much on the specific facts. However, I can see the force in the submission that this category will be made up of secure children's homes, designed and developed as such. As to whether all will be approved by the Secretary of State, it is to be hoped that no such homes would be in use without such approval of the Secretary of State, but I suppose that it would, at least in theory, be possible for that to happen.

135. It is worth reflecting on the characteristics of approved secure children's homes, which can be gleaned from the materials before the court, because it seems to me that this insight should shape the scope of the second limb of Wall J's interpretation (that is to say, premises having as their primary purpose the restriction of liberty). Secure children's homes are said to be "a locked setting". Some of the children in them come through the youth justice system, rather than for welfare reasons. Hayden J, in In re SS (Secure Accommodation Order) [2015] 2 FLR 1358, provides a useful insight into the regime that might be expected to operate in a secure children's home. He had been told about the regime in one particular unit, but said he had no reason to believe that this was different from any other of the welfarebased units. This is what he said about it at para 18 of his judgment: "… this unit has what is referred to as an 'air-locked security system'; that is to say that only one room can be left open at any stage. There is no computer access. There is a reward system by which privileges are both earned, and taken away. It is difficult not to see, from the eyes of the young people concerned, a custodial complexion to this environment."

136. The Association of Lawyers for Children say in their written intervention in the present case that, in their experience, the sort of restrictions described by Hayden J are a common feature of approved secure children's homes, and that other restrictions that operate in such homes (varying from home to home) include "CCTV, monitoring a child in their bedroom such as audio monitoring, high fencing or walls with limited views, locked windows". This ties in with what is said on behalf of the Secretary of State about the features that tend to be present in accommodation he approves as secure children's homes, namely: a secure vehicle lock on

arrival, a secure perimeter fence forming the boundary of the home, air-lock controlled access, security doors which are specially reinforced and constantly locked, reinforced secure windows and walls, and high quality digital CCTV save for bedrooms, bathrooms and medical rooms. The specialist design is said to limit hazards such as ligature points and stairs. Education and health services are said to be provided on site.

137. There can be no doubt that the characteristics of approved secure children's homes have been developed to respond to the needs of the children who can be expected to be placed there under section 25. Those children will, of necessity, already have a history of absconding and have demonstrated that they are likely to abscond again from any other description or accommodation (section 25(1)(a)) or have demonstrated that if they are kept in any other description of accommodation they are likely to injure themselves or some other person (section 25(1)(b)). During the hearing of the appeal, Lord Stephens put the suggestion that the criteria in section 25(1) give an indication of the type of accommodation that would satisfy the definition of "secure accommodation" and should be fed into the definition. The Secretary of State agrees with that proposition and submits that secure accommodation should contain features that reduce the risk of absconding and that would substantially reduce the risk of the child injuring him or herself or another person. This is supported by the Welsh Government/Cafcass Cymru, but not by the appellant who considers that this would be likely to be unhelpful, introducing uncertainty.

138. I am prepared to accept the Secretary of State's assertion that the only form of accommodation which will properly be said to be designed for the purpose of restricting liberty is likely to be secure accommodation units of the sort approved by the Secretary of State as secure children's homes. The Secretary of State submits that only very rarely will there be accommodation which is properly termed 'secure accommodation' on the basis that, whilst it cannot be said to have been designed for the purpose of restricting liberty, it nonetheless has the restriction of liberty as its primary purpose. I would agree with this view. In so doing, I am influenced by the fact that this second category of secure accommodation should take its colour from the purpose-designed category. I am also influenced by the fact that it seems to me that the Secretary of State is correct in saying that accommodation outside a purposebuilt unit, which may well be part of a highly specialised therapeutic care package specifically designed for the individual child, will usually have as its primary purpose the provision of care and/or treatment for the child, rather than preventing the child absconding or causing harm to him or herself or others. This will therefore limit the class of placements that can properly be termed 'secure accommodation' within section 25. And where the placement is not 'secure accommodation', there can be no question of the use of the inherent jurisdiction cutting across the statutory scheme in section 25.

See also *Re B (secure accommodation order)* [2019] EWCA Civ 2025, [2020] 1 FCR 507, [52]–[59] (Baker LJ) addressing the same point

13.1.3 Restricting liberty: secure accommodation: test under s 25: welfare is relevant, not paramount

Re B (secure accommodation order) [2019] EWCA Civ 2025, [2020] 1 FCR 507, [64]–[73] (Baker LJ) *quotation limited to* [64]–[69], [72]–[73]

Does an assessment of welfare play any part in the court's decision?

[64] For over a hundred years, the law of England and Wales has recognised that the child's welfare is the paramount consideration when a court is determining any question about his or her upbringing. The principle is now enshrined in s 1(1) of the Children Act 1989. Section 1(3) contains a checklist of factors related to welfare to be taken into account in certain proceedings under the Act, but proceedings under Part III are not included. Part III is not, however, expressly excluded from the ambit of s 1(1). As a decision whether or not to place a child in secure accommodation would appear to involve a question with respect to her upbringing, it might be thought that the paramountcy principle applies to applications under s 25.

[65] For nearly 25 years, however, since the decision of this court in *Re M (secure accommodation order)* [1995] Fam 108, [1995] 2 FCR 373, [1995] 2 WLR 302, it has been accepted that the child's welfare is not paramount when deciding an application under s 25. There remains, however, some uncertainty as to the extent of the evaluation of welfare which the court is required to undertake.

[66] In *Re M*, the Court of Appeal (Butler-Sloss and Hoffmann LJJ and Sir Tasker Watkins) upheld a decision of Ward J who had dismissed an appeal from the family proceedings court authorising the local authority to keep a boy in secure accommodation. Giving the first judgment of the court, Butler-Sloss LJ (at [1995] Fam 108, 115–116, [1995] 2 FCR 373, 379–380) said:

> 'The framework of Part III of the Act is structured to cast upon the local authority duties and responsibilities for children in its area and being looked after. The general duty of a local authority to safeguard and promote the child's welfare is not the same as that imposed upon the court in s 1(1) placing welfare as the paramount consideration. I agree with Ward J as to the reasons for that distinction. Among those duties and powers is the right of a local authority to hold a child in secure accommodation for up to 72 hours without a court order. To be enabled to do so the local authority has to surmount the hurdle of the requirements of s 25(1). Only if subs (1)(a)(i) and (ii) or (b) are fulfilled may the local authority place or keep a child in secure accommodation. In coming to the decision to restrict the liberty of a child the local authority will also have regard to their duty to safeguard and promote the welfare of a child who is looked after by them (s 22(3)). The welfare principle is rightly to be considered by the local authority in coming to so serious and draconian a decision as the restriction upon the liberty of the child. They have the power, however, to place him in secure accommodation if he is likely to

injure others rather than himself (s 25(1)(b)). This power may be inconsistent with the concept of the child's welfare being paramount.

The jurisdiction of the court is to be found in the same section and the court applies the same criteria in s 25(1) as the local authority. To require the court to have regard to other criteria than those imposed upon the local authority within the same section would, in my view, be inconsistent with the purpose of the section which gives the court the power to authorise the local authority to keep the child in secure accommodation. It is the same power as that exercisable by the local authority in the same way albeit for a much shorter period. By s 25(3) the court has the specific duty to determine whether any relevant criteria are satisfied for keeping a child who may or may not already have been placed by the local authority, in secure accommodation for a period longer than 72 hours. In considering "any relevant criteria" the court has a similar duty to the local authority to include the welfare of the child concerned. Whether it is a reviewing power, as Ward J suggested, or a general duty to consider the welfare of the child, is a matter of words. No one can doubt that the restriction upon the liberty of a child, generally for his own good (subject to s 25(1)(b)) is a serious step which must be taken only when there is no genuine alternative which would be appropriate and, as *The Children Act 1989 Guidance and Regulations, vol 1, Court Orders*, para 5.1 sets out, as a last resort. Clearly the welfare of the child is of great importance and must take its place in the relevant criteria. But if at the end of the day the relevant criteria are satisfied there is a mandatory requirement that the court shall make an order authorising the child to be kept in secure accommodation.'

[67] Hoffmann LJ, agreed but articulated an interpretation of the section in slightly different terms. At [1995] Fam 108, 117B, [1995] 2 FCR 373, 380–381, he said:

'Section 25 of the Children Act 1989 is taken over in virtually identical terms from s 21A of the Child Care Act 1980, which was inserted into that Act by s 25 of the Criminal Justice Act 1982. This explains a feature of s 25 which might otherwise be puzzling, namely that subs (1) is expressed not as the grant of a power to keep children in secure accommodation if the conditions in paras (a) or (b) are satisfied, but as a restriction on a power which is assumed already to exist.'

He continued (at [1995] Fam 108, 118B–119B, [1995] 2 FCR 373, 381–382):

'the Child Care Act 1980, being concerned with the powers and duties of local authorities, contained no equivalent of s 1 of the Children Act 1989 and it seems to me very unlikely that s 25 of the latter Act was intended to have a different effect from s 21A of the Child Care Act 1980. The function of the court under s 25 is in my view to control the exercise of power by the local authority rather than to exercise an independent jurisdiction in the best interests of the child.

> What form should this control take? Subsection (3) says that the court's duty is to determine whether "any relevant criteria" are satisfied. What are the relevant criteria? I have already said that in my judgment they do not include the principles in s 1. .... In my judgment the criteria applied by the court must be the same as those applicable to an initial decision by the local authority. These include not only the question of whether para (a) or (b) of s 25(1) is satisfied, but also having regard to the local authority's general duty under s 22(3) to safeguard and promote the welfare of the child, subject to the important qualification in s 22(6)'.

Hoffmann LJ set out s 22(6) (recited above) and continued:

> 'This subsection is echoed in para (b) of s 25(1), which allows the condition to be satisfied if the child is likely to injure other persons. Both of these provisions are quite inconsistent with the full application of s 1.
>
> It seems to me that the question of whether a decision to keep the child in secure accommodation would be in accordance with these statutory duties imposed upon the local authority must be among the 'relevant criteria' to be considered by the court under s 25(3). It is said that the mandatory language of subs (4) – if the court determines that the criteria are satisfied, it 'shall' make an order – suggests that the criteria must involve giving a yes or no answer to a question of fact rather than a flexible application of general principles. But the mandatory element in subs (4) is to some extent illusory. True, the court shall make an order, but the maximum period for which he may be kept is a matter for the court's discretion. Since there is in practice little difference between an order for a very brief period and no order at all, the use of the word "shall" does not seem to me to carry much weight. Thus I think that the duty of the court is to put itself in the position of a reasonable local authority and to ask, first, whether the conditions in subs (1) are satisfied and secondly, whether it would be in accordance with the authority's duty to safeguard and promote the welfare of the child (but subject to the qualification in s 22(6)) for the child to be kept in secure accommodation and if so, for how long.'

[68] The decision in *Re M* clearly establishes that the paramountcy principle in s 1 of the Children Act does not apply to applications under s 25. It has been followed by all courts hearing applications under the section and is binding on this court. There is, however, less clarity as to the extent of the evaluation of welfare which the court is required to carry out. There is a small but perceptible difference between the view expressed by Butler-Sloss LJ and that of Hoffmann LJ. Both agreed that the court must apply the same criteria as the local authority and that the relevant criteria include welfare. Butler-Sloss LJ considered that the distinction between a reviewing power and a general duty to consider welfare was 'a matter of words' but that 'the court has the specific duty to determine whether any relevant criteria are satisfied' and that, in performing that duty, welfare is 'of great importance'. Hoffmann LJ, however, thought that function of the

court under s 25 is 'merely to control the exercise of power by the local authority rather than to exercise an independent jurisdiction in the best interests of the child'.

[69] Some might consider this to be a distinction without a difference. It should be noted that the third judge in the constitution, Sir Tasker Watkins, agreed with both judgments. In my view, however, there is a difference of approach in the two judgments. It is therefore unsurprising that in subsequent cases, courts have sometimes struggled with the issue of how to deal with cases where they perceive that, whilst the conditions in s 25(1) are satisfied, the placement proposed by the local authority would be contrary to the child's overall welfare.

...

[72] In my judgment, the 'displacement of the court's welfare role' as required by the decision in *Re M* extends only to the displacement of the paramountcy principle. It does not require the court to abdicate responsibility for evaluating impact of the proposed placement on the child's welfare. On the contrary, as Butler-Sloss LJ said, the child's welfare is plainly of great importance in deciding whether or not an order should be made. The local authority and the court must each consider whether the proposed placement would safeguard and promote the child's welfare. In some cases, the child's welfare needs will be served by a period in secure accommodation, particularly if supported by a comprehensive therapeutic programme. In other cases, the child's welfare will not be promoted by such a placement. However, just as s 22(6) allows the local authority to exercise its powers in a way that does not promote the child's welfare if necessary to protect the public, there may be cases where the court concludes that the child's welfare needs are outweighed by the need to protect the public from serious harm. Welfare is therefore not paramount but is plainly an important element in the court's analysis. It is one of the relevant criteria.

[73] This interpretation of s 25 is fortified by the Human Rights Act 1998, which came into force five years after *Re M* was decided in 1995.

See also *Re D (a child)* [2019] UKSC 42, [2019] 3 FCR 631, [101] (Lady Black) addressing the same point, see Chapter 13.1.2 Restricting liberty: secure accommodation: test under s 25: 'provided for the purpose of restricting liberty': designed for or having as its primary purpose restricting liberty

See also *Re M (A Minor) (Secure Accommodation Order)* [1995] 2 FCR 373 (CA), 379C–380E (Butler-Sloss LJ) addressing the same point (the original authority)

13.1.4 Restricting liberty: secure accommodation: test under s 25: the two limbs under s 25(1) are disjunctive

Re D (a minor) (secure accommodation order) (no 1) [1996] 2 FCR 452 (FD), 458D–E (Singer J)

There was, it therefore appears, both from the affidavit of the solicitor and from the consensus of opinion amongst those who are able to comment about the actual event clearly, in my view, a misunderstanding by the magistrates of the law, because it is clear, and no one argues to the contrary, that the absconding basis and the likely to injure herself or other person basis for an order under s 25 are disjunctive rather than conjunctive. …

13.1.5 Restricting liberty: secure accommodation: test under s 25: meaning of 'likely' in the two limbs

Re G (a child) (secure accommodation order) [2001] 3 FCR 47 (FD), 58B–H (Munby J)

Proceeding on this footing there are three factual questions which I have to consider: (1) Does G have 'a history of absconding'? (2) Is G 'likely to abscond' from any accommodation which is not secure accommodation? (3) If G does abscond, is she 'likely to suffer significant harm'?

On the basis of such evidence as is currently before the court (I put the matter this way because G has not yet herself been able to deploy such evidence as she might wish to rely on) the answer to each of these questions would quite plainly appear to be 'yes'.

(1) I have already set out the relevant facts. There is, on the basis of these facts, quite plainly a 'history of absconding'. To abscond, according to the Concise Oxford Dictionary, is to 'leave hurriedly and secretly to escape from custody or avoid arrest'. G has repeatedly done just that; she has removed herself, hurriedly and in order to escape, often within minutes, from the accommodation in which she has been placed by the local authority. On occasions she has done so using the fire escape. She has, as it appears to me, absconded repeatedly—more than half a dozen times in the last few months; there is a 'history' of absconding.

(2) 'Likely' in this context—that is, within the meaning of s 25 (1)(a)(i) of the 1989 Act—has the same meaning as when the word is used in s 31(2)(a) of the Act: see *Re D (Secure Accommodation Order)* [1999] Fam Law 311, a county court decision with which I agree. It thus refers to a real possibility, a possibility that cannot sensibly be ignored having regard to the nature and gravity of the feared event, even though it may fall short of something that is more likely than not (see *Newham London Borough Council v AG* [1992] 2 FCR 119, [1993] 1 FLR 281; *Re H and R (minors) (sexual abuse: standard of proof)* [1996] 1 FCR 509, [1996] AC 563). Is there, therefore, a 'real possibility' of G absconding again if she is placed in something other than secure accommodation? Given the frequency and persistence of her past absconding, the answer to this question, in my judgment, can only be 'yes'.

(3) 'Likely' in this context—that is, within the meaning of s 25(1)(a)(ii) of the 1989 Act—has the same meaning as when the word is used

> in ss 25(1)(a)(i) and 31(2)(a) of the Act. 'Significant harm', in my judgment, has the same meaning as when the words are used in s 31(2)(a): see s 105(1). Is there, therefore, a 'real possibility' of G suffering significant harm, as those words are explained by ss 31(9) and 31(10) of the 1989 Act? The answer, again, in my judgment, on the evidence I have seen is 'yes'.

See also *S (a minor) v Knowsley Borough Council and others* [2004] EWHC 491 (Fam), [2004] 2 FLR 716, [36]–[38] (Charles J) addressing the same point

13.1.6 Restricting liberty: secure accommodation: test under s 25: meaning of 'abscond' in the first limb

Re W (a child) [2016] EWCA Civ 804, [2016] 4 WLR 159, [21]–[23] (Macur LJ)

21. Miss Judd QC's arguments in relation to the judge's definition of "absconding" arose in the fact-specific circumstances of this case and did not persuade us that it is necessary to attempt to define the term beyond its ordinary meaning. Munby J (as he then was) in *Re G (Secure Accommodation Order)* [2001] FLR 884 at 895 relied on the definition of 'abscond' as found in the Concise Oxford Dictionary. This accords with the usual application of the term to connote the element of 'escape' from an imposed regime. Mr Tyler QC's reliance on the wider definition in the Shorter Oxford English Dictionary was perhaps born of the need to support his argument that Keehan J's approach to the issue was correct. However, it seems to me to add an unnecessary gloss to a term which is able to be readily understood. Although trite to say, the facts will speak for themselves. As it is, we were satisfied, as we indicate below, that the judge wrongly categorised W's absences from the unit in which she had been placed since January 2016 as constituting part of a history of absconding.

22. In determining that W had absconded, Keehan J invoked the facts that W had 'disengaged' with the unit, returning not "just a few hours later but well into the following day". I do not consider that this meant that W was 'absconding' from the unit, in terms of escaping indefinitely from an imposed regime, as opposed to deliberately absenting herself for a limited period, knowingly and disdainfully in breach of the night-time curfews imposed. However, the factual matrix of the case as determined by Keehan J quite clearly satisfied the criteria in s 25(1)(b). Placed in any accommodation other than that which could 'contain' her, she was in danger of serious harm.

23. Mr Tyler QC referred to his skeleton argument prepared for the proceedings below to support his assertion that the local authority relied upon the criteria in s 25(1)(a) and (b). We were satisfied that Keehan J's judgment mistakenly states the contrary. Miss Judd QC conceded that, subject to her other arguments, the criteria in s 25(1)(b) were met.

Re M (a child) (secure accommodation) [2018] EWCA Civ 2707, [4] (Peter Jackson LJ)

4. Absconding means something more than trivial disobedient absence. It may connote an element of escape from an imposed regime (*Re W* [2016] EWCA Civ 804 at [21]) but it is not limited by consideration of the intentions of the individual concerned. Judges can be relied upon to give the word its ordinary meaning and recognise behaviour that can be properly described as absconding in all the circumstances of the individual case.

See also *Re G (a child) (secure accommodation order)* [2001] 3 FCR 47 (FD), 58B–H (Munby J) addressing the same point, see Chapter 13.1.5 Restricting liberty: test under s 25: meaning of 'likely' in the two limbs under s 25(1)

13.1.7 Restricting liberty: secure accommodation: test under s 25: children's consent is unnecessary

Re W (a child) [2016] EWCA Civ 804, [2016] 4 WLR 159, [20] (Macur LJ)

20. A due regard to the wishes and feelings of a competent child so far as consistent with his or her welfare may dissuade a local authority from applying for a secure accommodation order. As a child approaches its majority, the factors to be weighed in the balance will undoubtedly acknowledge its looming legal independence. That said, we are satisfied that the subject child's consent is not a pre-requisite of the making of a secure accommodation order.

13.1.8 Restricting liberty: secure accommodation: test under s 25: identified placements are not required

Re A [2015] EWHC 1709 (Fam), [11] (Bodey J)

11. S.25 of the Children Act 1989 provides (and I paraphrase) that no child may be placed into secure accommodation unless it appears "… that, if she is kept in any other description of accommodation, she is likely to injure herself or other persons". I am entirely satisfied on everything which I have read that this threshold is met in respect of A. Conventionally, a specific placement is identified before a secure accommodation order is made. However, that is simply not possible here, and both the Local Authority and the Children's Guardian invite me to make the order in general terms, leaving it to the Local Authority, on consultation with the Children's Guardian, to place A at an appropriate unit as and when one is identified. Miss Bradley has mentioned her recollection of what she described as 'an old Scottish case' which says that one should not make an order without an identified unit in place. That is not a requirement of S.25, and in any event I would regard this case as exceptional, where there is great urgency, where everyone is at court today, and where a secure

accommodation is, frankly, the only way of protecting A from herself (unless circumstances change such that a psychiatric disposal becomes 'on offer').

13.1.9 Restricting liberty: secure accommodation: test under s 25: using child DoL[3] orders if secure accommodation is unavailable

See Chapter 13.2.1 Restricting liberty: child DoL orders: use when s 25-compliant secure accommodation is unavailable

13.1.10 Restricting liberty: secure accommodation: effect of orders: a permissive order

Re M (a child) (secure accommodation) [2018] EWCA Civ 2707, [1] (Peter Jackson LJ)

1. A secure accommodation order permits, but does not compel, a local authority to keep a child in secure accommodation. A court hearing an application for such an order under Section 25 of the Children Act 1989 or Section 119 of the Social Services and Well-being (Wales) Act 2014 in respect of a child who is being looked after by a local authority must determine whether the criteria for keeping a child in secure accommodation are satisfied and, if they are, shall authorise the child to be kept in secure accommodation for a stated period not exceeding the maximum period specified by regulations.

13.1.11 Restricting liberty: secure accommodation: effect of orders: duration for no longer than necessary

W v North Yorkshire County Council [1993] 1 FCR 693 (FD), 699E–700A (Booth J)

> Where a court is satisfied that the criteria set out in s 25 of the 1989 Act has been established, it is required under the provisions of s 25(4) to make an order authorizing the child to be kept in secure accommodation. At that stage the Act is mandatory in its terms and the court has no discretion in the matter. But having found the criteria proved, which compels it to make such an order, the court must then go on to specify the maximum term for which the child can be so kept. I accept the submission of Mrs Kershaw that at this stage the court must consider carefully the purpose to be achieved by the order which requires the liberty of a child to be restricted, and must assess, as best it can, the length of time which this is likely to take. I accept that on an initial application this may be a difficult task which the court may have little evidence to assist it. In such circumstances the court should adhere to the principle that the order should be for no longer than is necessary and

3 Deprivation of liberty.

unavoidable, and should bear in mind that the local authority may always apply for a further order if the criteria continue to exist, and it is thought that the child should be detained for a longer period. The responsibility for authorizing a child to be kept in a secure unit rests with the court and should not, in effect, be delegated to a local authority. So, when exercising its power to make such an order, the court has a duty to explain carefully why it does so, and must make findings of fact and give its reasons for specifying whatever is held to be the maximum period of time for which the order may take effect.

See also *Re M (a child) (secure accommodation)* [2018] EWCA Civ 2707, [5] (Peter Jackson LJ) considering *W v North Yorkshire County Council* [1993] 1 FCR 693

13.1.12 Restricting liberty: secure accommodation: procedure: interim orders only if adjourned

Birmingham City Council v M [2008] EWHC 1085 (Fam), [23] (McFarlane J)

Conclusions

23. The court has been assisted by a further distillation of the local authority's position in supplemental written submissions. Within those, the local authority (as it did orally) that a much shorter adjournment than that made would have been permissible to allow the Guardian to return to the country and carry out her statutory duties. Drawing matters together I conclude that the following matters of principle should apply when a court is faced with deciding whether or not to adjourn a secure accommodation application:

i) A free standing application cannot be made for an interim secure accommodation order. The power to make an interim order only arises under Children Act 1989, s 25(5) if the court adjourns the hearing of the local authority's application …

13.1.13 Restricting liberty: secure accommodation: procedure: representation of children

Re AS (secure accommodation order) [1999] 2 FCR 749 (FD), 751A–E (Bracewell J)

It has been made plain in various cases that the making of a secure accommodation order is deprivation of liberty for the child, and it is by reason of that consequence that there is a specific provision in s 25(6) of the Children Act 1989 whereby no court shall exercise the powers conferred by this section in respect of a child who is not legally represented in that court unless, having been informed of his right to apply for legal aid and having had the opportunity to do so, he refused or failed to apply. It is implicit in that provision that legal representation in order to be effective must involve the taking of instructions. In *J v Merthyr Tydfyl CBC* [1997] Fam Law

522, a decision of Wilson J in the Family Division on 4 June 1997, in an appeal from an order of a family proceedings court, the judge determined that it was wrong for the justices to have refused to allow the appellant's solicitor an opportunity of seeing their client prior to the hearing despite the court having of its own volition contacted the local authority and made arrangements that the appellant should not be brought to the court. In a decision of Ewbank J, *Re W (a minor) (secure accommodation)* [1994] 3 FCR 248 the judge, in exercising his discretion to refuse to allow the child concerned to attend court, explicitly dealt with the need for counsel and solicitors to be able to take instructions from the child so as to present the child's case before the court.

13.1.14 Restricting liberty: secure accommodation: procedure: attendance of children

See Chapter 5.4.6 Case management: children: children attending courts

13.2 RESTRICTING LIBERTY: CHILD DEPRIVATION OF LIBERTY ORDERS

13.2.1 Restricting liberty: child DoL orders: use when s 25-compliant secure accommodation is unavailable

Re T (a child) [2021] UKSC 35, [2021] 3 WLR 643, [17], [106]–[149] (Lady Black), [168]–[172] (Lord Stephens) *quotation limited to* [17], [140]–[148], [168], [171]–[172]

17. It is important to note that the focus of the present appeal is upon a relatively narrow group of cases. The Court of Appeal said (para 84 of the judgment of Sir Andrew McFarlane P, with whom the other two members of the court agreed) that the case did 'not concern the placement of children in other than the equivalent of secure accommodation', and that '[d]ifferent considerations will apply when an application is directed towards, and only directed towards, a deprivation of liberty'. Matters cannot, perhaps, be quite so simply stated now, given the evolution of the proceedings since the Court of Appeal hearing, but the focus of the appeal is still confined. In essence, it is concerned with children who the local authority consider require to be deprived of their liberty, and in relation to whom the statutory criteria for the making of a secure accommodation order under section 25 of the Children Act 1989 are satisfied, but who the local authority propose to place elsewhere than in a secure children's home which is approved for that purpose. There could be said to be two distinct categories of children within the group: (1) children who would be placed in a secure children's home but there is no place available for them, and (2) children whose needs would, in the local authority's assessment, be better met in an alternative placement. There will also be children who fall entirely outside the

group because they are unlikely to satisfy the statutory criteria in section 25, although they do need to be deprived of their liberty to keep them safe.

...

140. Lord Lloyd-Jones asked during the hearing what the Secretary of State said a judge could do where the child meets the section 25 criteria but there is no approved secure accommodation available. Given the serious shortage of approved placements, this is clearly a question of the greatest importance. The Secretary of State's response is that the inherent jurisdiction can be used to authorise deprivation of liberty of a child placed in a children's home, and section 100(4)(a) is satisfied given that the local authority cannot achieve the result they seek through a section 25 order, assuming of course that the court is satisfied that there is reasonable cause to believe that the child is likely to suffer significant harm if the inherent jurisdiction is not exercised, in which case section 100(4)(b) is also satisfied.

141. The Children's Commissioner expressly invites the court to consider what would be the case were the inherent jurisdiction to be unavailable. How would local authorities comply with their statutory duties towards children who require secure accommodation which is unavailable? How would they discharge their parental responsibility for these children? The Welsh Government and Cafcass Cymru ask what the court would do in the sort of situation confronting it in this case, if it could not have recourse to the inherent jurisdiction. These are questions which underlie many of the submissions made to this court, and they are questions which have caused me profound anxiety, not least in view of the fact that judges and others have been drawing attention to the dangerous inadequacy of this aspect of the child care system for years, without any effective steps having been taken to solve the problem of resources for children with exceptional needs. Cases such as those to which I have alluded earlier in this judgment demonstrate, it seems to me, that it is unthinkable that the High Court, with its long-established role in protecting children, should have no means to keep these unfortunate children (and others who may be at risk from them) safe from extreme harm, in some cases death. If the local authority cannot apply for an order under section 25 because there is no section 25 compliant secure accommodation available, I would accept that the inherent jurisdiction can, and will have to be, used to fill that gap, without clashing impermissibly with the statutory scheme.

142. This is a temporary solution, developed by the courts in extremis, but attended by regular expressions of anxiety of the kind articulated by the President in the present case in the Court of Appeal (see paras 5 and 88 of his judgment), and by Sir James Munby in 2017 when he was President of the Family Division (see para 7 above), and adopted with grave reservations of the type expressed in Lancashire v G. There have also been powerful expressions of concern in the submissions before us.

143. It has to be recognised that when the local authority applies under the inherent jurisdiction for the court to authorise a secure placement which is either not in a registered children's home or is in a children's home that has not been approved for secure accommodation, those placements will not satisfy all the requirements of the regulatory framework. If the placement is in an unregistered children's home, a criminal offence will be committed by any person who carries on or manages the home. The important safeguards that come with registration will be absent. If the placement is in an unregulated setting, it will equally escape these safeguards, and it is noted that the Children's Commissioner expresses particular concern about children being deprived of their liberty in unregulated placements, to the point of questioning whether such placements, for example in caravans and outward bound centres, could ever be classed as sufficiently appropriate for article 5 purposes.

144. The courts have put in place such safeguards as they can to overcome the shortcomings of the present arrangements, and I will come to these in due course. But whatever the courts devise cannot replicate the official safety net that the regulatory framework provides when it is applicable. To take an obvious example, the court is not able to carry out the sort of inspections and checks that Ofsted and the Care Inspectorate Wales are obliged to carry out.

145. I have been particularly concerned as to whether it is a permissible exercise of the inherent jurisdiction to authorise a local authority to place a child in an unregistered children's home in relation to which a criminal offence would be being committed. Ultimately, however, I recognise that there are cases in which there is absolutely no alternative, and where the child (or someone else) is likely to come to grave harm if the court does not act. I also have to recognise that there are other duties in play, in addition to those which prohibit carrying on or managing an unregistered children's home. I gave an idea earlier (see para 30 et seq) of the duties placed upon local authorities to protect and support children. How can a local authority fulfil these duties in the problematic cases with which we are concerned if they cannot obtain authorisation from the High Court to place the child in the only placement that is available, and with the ability to impose such restrictions as are required on the child's liberty? It is such imperative considerations of necessity that have led me to conclude that the inherent jurisdiction must be available in these cases. There is presently no alternative that will safeguard the children who require its protection.

146. I am reinforced in this by the way in which the President of the Family Division (in his Practice Guidance, see para 129 supra), Ofsted, and the Care Inspectorate Wales have each responded to the problem.

147. Rather than outlawing placement in an unregistered children's home, in the Practice Guidance, the President seeks to ensure that where the court authorises such a placement, registration is sought expeditiously, and that meanwhile, the court has information about the proposed placement, so it can satisfy itself that steps are being taken to apply for the necessary

registration and that the provider of the service has confirmed they can meet the needs of the child, and that the local authority is taking steps to assure themselves that the premises, those working there, and the care being given, are safe and suitable for the child. The Guidance obliges the court to monitor the progress of the application for registration and, if registration is not achieved, to review its continued approval of the child's placement. Time scales are set for the various steps.

148. Ofsted has an annex (Annex C) to its 'Introduction to children's homes' (2018) (a guide to registration) which also appears to recognise the acute practical difficulties that can be encountered. The annex acknowledges that there may be instances where placements are made in an unregistered children's home when it has been difficult or even impossible for the local authority to find registered accommodation that would accept the child. It explains that, in order to decide whether or not to take any regulatory action in relation to unregistered providers, it will carry out an investigation of each individual case, including assessing the permanency of the arrangement and the purpose of the provision of care and accommodation. Blending practicality with protection, however, it makes clear that an application for registration must be submitted as soon as possible, and that if a provider is refused registration and continues to operate, it would be liable to prosecution. It appears from the written submissions of the Welsh Government and Cafcass Cymru that the Care Inspectorate Wales may be taking a similarly practical approach.

...

168. As Lady Black has set out, the inherent jurisdiction of the High Court in relation to children is wide: it is the ultimate safety net (see paras 64–68 above). To my mind the central focus of this aspect of the inherent jurisdiction is on the welfare and safety of children rather than on the potential commission of a criminal offence under section 11 of the Care Standards Act 2000 by others. Obviously, that central focus requires the court to give anxious and detailed consideration to the risks to the child in respect of a placement in which such an offence may be committed. However, the High Court is not required to determine whether an offence will be committed or whether the individual has an available defence. It is sufficient for the court to be aware of the potential that such an offence may be committed by another and to examine how that impacts on the best interests of the child. It is no part of the court's function to "authorise" the commission of any criminal offence. Any order under the inherent jurisdiction does not do so. Rather, if the inherent jurisdiction is used, then the court "authorises" but does not "require" the placement by a local authority of a child in an unregistered children's home despite the potential that a person may be prosecuted for and convicted of an offence under section 11 of the Care Standards Act 2000. If a prosecution is brought, which it can be, then it is a matter for the criminal courts to determine whether an offence has been committed and if so, as to the appropriate sentence to impose.

...

171. I set out below the matters which must be considered in compliance with the Guidance and the addendum prior to a court authorising a placement in an unregistered children's home. I do so to emphasise the importance of those matters, in addition to any other matters which are relevant on the particular facts of an individual case. The information made available to the court is to be seen in the context of the parties' obligation to bring all matters of relevance to the welfare of children to the attention of the court to enable the court to decide the issues on an adversarial basis, or to direct further evidence or enquiries in accordance with its inquisitorial role. The matters in the Guidance are as follows:

(a) The applicant must make enquiries with either Ofsted or the Care Inspectorate Wales ("CIW") as to whether the home is registered. That process of enquiry means that either Ofsted or CIW are informed as to whether a home is being carried on or managed without registration.

(b) The applicant should make the court explicitly aware of the registration status of those providing or seeking to provide the care and accommodation for the child.

(c) The court should be made aware of the reasons why registration is not required or the reasons for the delay in seeking registration.

(d) The court will need to be satisfied that steps are being taken to apply for the necessary registration.

(e) The court will wish to assure itself that the provider of the service has confirmed that it can meet the needs of the child.

(f) The court will need to be informed by the local authority of the steps the local authority is taking in the meantime to assure itself that the premises, those working at the premises and the care being given are safe and suitable for the accommodated child.

(g) Where an application for registration has been submitted to Ofsted or CIW, the court should be made aware of the exact status of that application.

This is a summary of the matters contained in the Guidance. It is the Guidance to which reference should be made. At para 167 above I set out how the issues in the present case developed, such that certain factual findings were lacking. The Guidance post-dates the decisions of the High Court in this case but going forward any decision to place a child in an unregistered children's home must make factual findings in relation to these matters.

172. If a court authorises a placement in an unregistered children's home, then the addendum to the Guidance provides that the court must include in any order a requirement on the local authority that it should immediately notify Ofsted – if the placement is in England – or the CIW – if the placement is in Wales – that the child has been placed in an unregistered placement. The requirement extends to the local authority providing a copy of the order and the judgment of the court to either Ofsted or the CIW. In this way Ofsted or the CIW will be aware of the unregistered children's home so that immediate steps can be taken to register. Thereafter, the aim of the Guidance is to work expeditiously towards registration, so as to comply, as soon as possible,

> with the requirement to register under section 11 of the Care Standards Act 2000 or section 5 of the Regulation and Inspection of Social Care (Wales) Act 2016. The Guidance requires the court to monitor the progress of the application for registration and, if registration is not achieved, to review its Page 58 continued approval of the child's placement in an unregistered unit. Paragraph 21 of the Guidance provides that if registration is refused or the applications for registration are withdrawn, the local authority should advise the court as a matter of urgency. It further provides that the court will take this into account when deciding whether the placement of the child in the unregistered children's home continues to be in the child's best interests. It is unnecessary to envisage all the sorts of factual situations that might arise which would still call for an order authorising a placement where the children's home remains unregistered except to say that the test of necessity should be applied all the more strictly and that there will be a heightened level of anxious enquiry and scrutiny. In any event, the Guidance primarily envisages that the children's home will become registered so that a criminal offence is no longer being committed by others. The Guidance must be followed so that, in practice, within a short period of time the children's home is registered. This process of registration should continue to be energetically and pro-actively monitored by the courts.

See also *Derby City Council v BA and others* [2021] EWHC 2931 (Fam), [3], [39]–[45], [62]–[93] (MacDonald J) considering *Re T (a child)* [2021] UKSC 35, [2021] 3 WLR 643, addressing the same point (determining that placement in unregistered homes in breach of the President's guidance is not 'per se' unlawful but 'ordinarily' should not be countenanced)

See also *Re T (a child)* [2021] UKSC 35, [2021] 3 WLR 643, [165]–[166] (Lord Stephens) addressing a related point (the 'disgraceful and utterly shaming lack of provision for children who require approved secure accommodation')

See also *Re B (secure accommodation order)* [2019] EWCA Civ 2025, [2020] 1 FCR 507, [4]–[6] (Baker LJ) addressing a related point (problems arising from lack of provision of secure accommodation)

See also *Re Q (a child) (DOLS: lack of secure placement)* [2021] EWHC 123 (Fam), [1] (Knowles J) addressing a related point (continuing lack of provision of secure accommodation)

13.2.2 Restricting liberty: child DoL orders: use when s 25-compliant secure accommodation is unavailable: test for orders: paramountcy principle

Re C (a minor) (detention for medical treatment) [1997] 3 FCR 49 (FD), 58H–59B (Wall J)

> Is detention for the purposes of treatment in C's best interests?
>
> It is common ground that in exercising this particular aspect of the court's inherent jurisdiction over minors, s 1 of the Children Act 1989 applies and

the welfare of C is my paramount consideration. I have no doubt at all that it is in C's best interests to be treated in the clinic, and I am equally satisfied that the regime of treatment offered by the clinic is appropriate to C's needs. Since I regard detention as an essential component of the treatment, I am in no doubt that the order sought by the local authority is in C's best interests.

13.2.3 Restricting liberty: child DoL orders: use when s 25-compliant secure accommodation is unavailable: test for orders: should the s25 criteria apply?

Re T (a child) [2021] UKSC 35, [2021] 3 WLR 643, [152]–[155] (Lady Black)

152. … There is considerable case law demonstrating the basis on which the inherent jurisdiction is deployed in cases of this type. Sir Andrew McFarlane said in the present case (para 79) that the terms of section 25 should be treated as applying to the same effect when a local authority is placing a child or proposing to place a child in the equivalent of secure accommodation (and see also para 49 ibid). This accords with the approach that Wall J took in In re C (Detention: Medical Treatment) (see para 133 above), where he said that he did not consider he should make an order unless he was satisfied that the section 25 criteria were, by analogy, satisfied. The operation of section 25 was explored in depth recently by the Court of Appeal in In re B (supra para 3), the criteria for a section 25 order being gathered together at para 98 et seq of Baker LJ's judgment. It is no part of this appeal to review the approach laid down in those authorities. There are also reported first instance judgments describing and explaining particular uses of the inherent jurisdiction in what might be described as 'secure accommodation circumstances'. The law as to the exercise of the inherent jurisdiction in this area is, in my view, sufficiently accessible and foreseeable with advice. Outcomes need not be predictable with absolute certainty, and in this area of the law, it is important that flexibility is retained, in order that the courts can respond appropriately to the many different sets of circumstances that arise

153. There are appropriate procedural safeguards built into the application process, broadly mirroring those applicable to a section 25 application. There is provision for the child to be made a party to the process, for example, and for the appointment of a guardian, as well as for reviews of the continuing confinement. By requiring that the structure imposed by section 25 should also be observed in an application to place a child in the equivalent of secure accommodation, the President has ensured that proper procedural protection is built in for the child. The matter is also dealt with in considerable detail by Wall J in *In re C (Detention: Medical Treatment)* and Sir James Munby P in *In re A (Children) (Care Proceedings: Deprivation of Liberty)* [2018] EWHC 138 (Fam); [2019] Fam 45. In addition, the President's Practice Guidance (see above) makes a contribution to the procedural protection for the child.

154. I do not propose to go through all the detail here, only to mention some of the elements of the procedure that the courts have devised, in order to demonstrate why it seems to me sufficient to comply with the requirements of article 5. In so far as any adjustments are desirable, they must be the province of judges who have experience of dealing with these cases in practice and of the Court of Appeal.

155. It is, of course, correct that the court will not itself regulate the detailed operation of the authorised deprivation of liberty, when it authorises a proposed placement and the regime that it is planned will be adopted there. However, it will not give the local authority the authorisation that they seek without considerable exploration of the circumstances, to ensure that the proposal is appropriate. By way of example, in addition to procedural matters that I have already mentioned, I would pick out that the procedure prescribed in the case law requires that the court be provided with evidence describing the nature of the proposed regime and justifying why the proposed arrangements are necessary and proportionate in meeting the child's welfare needs. The court will need to know the child's views on the matter. And the order will include an express liberty to any party, including the child, to apply to the court for further directions on the shortest reasonable notice. Careful provision is also made for reviews by a judge, at intervals or if there is a significant change, which reviews will be in addition to the local authority's own reviews of the case.

13.2.4 Restricting liberty: child DoL orders: depriving children's liberty: three *Storck*[4] components

Storck v Germany (61603/00) (ECtHR), (2006) 43 EHRR 6, [74], [89] (Third Section)

74. However, the notion of deprivation of liberty within the meaning of Article 5 § 1 does not only comprise the objective element of a person's confinement in a particular restricted space for a not negligible length of time. A person can only be considered to have been deprived of his liberty if, as an additional subjective element, he has not validly consented to the confinement in question (see, mutatis mutandis, *HM v Switzerland*, cited above, § 46). The Court notes that, in the present case, it is disputed between the parties whether the applicant had consented to her stay in the clinic.

...

89. The Court reiterates that the question whether a deprivation of liberty is imputable to the State relates to the interpretation and application of Article 5 § 1 of the Convention and raises issues going to the merits of the case, which cannot be regarded merely as preliminary issues (see,

4 *Storck v Germany* (61603/00) (ECtHR), (2006) 43 EHRR 6.

mutatis mutandis, Nielsen, cited above, p. 22, § 57). It agrees with the parties that in the present case there are three aspects that could engage Germany's responsibility under the Convention for the applicant's detention in the private clinic in Bremen. Firstly, her deprivation of liberty could be imputable to the State owing to the direct involvement of public authorities in the applicant's detention. Secondly, the State could be found to have violated Article 5 § 1 in that its courts, in the compensation proceedings brought by the applicant, failed to interpret the provisions of civil law relating to her claim in the spirit of Article 5. Thirdly, the State could have breached its positive obligation to protect the applicant against interferences with her liberty by private persons.

Re A-F (children) (nos 1 and 2) [2018] EWHC 138 (Fam), [2019] 1 FCR 233, [8]–[9] (Sir James Munby P)

[8] The framework within which the issues arising in these cases fall to be considered is the analysis of art 5 set out by the Strasbourg court in *Storck v Germany* (2005) 43 EHRR 96, [2005] MHLR 211, paras 74, 89, repeated in *Stanev v Bulgaria* (2012) 55 EHRR 696, [2012] MHLR 23, paras 117, 120, and helpfully summarised in the Supreme Court by Lady Hale DPSC in *Surrey County Council v P and Ors (Equality and Human Rights Commission and Ors intervening), Cheshire West and Chester Council v P and Anor (Same intervening)* [2014] UKSC 19, [2014] AC 896, [2014] 2 FCR 71 (*Cheshire West*), para [37]:

> 'what is the essential character of a deprivation of liberty? ... three components can be derived from *Storck* ..., confirmed in *Stanev* ..., as follows: (a) the objective component of confinement in a particular restricted place for a not negligible length of time, (b) the subjective component of lack of valid consent, and (c) the attribution of responsibility to the state.'

[9] I refer, by way of shorthand, to these three components as *Storck* components (a), (b) and (c), sometimes they are referred to as *Storck* limbs (1), (2) and (3). To ensure clarity of exposition, I use the phrase 'deprivation of liberty' to describe the state of affairs where all three components of *Storck* are satisfied, that is, where there is a deprivation of liberty within the meaning of art 5(1) which therefore engages the State's obligations under arts 5(2)–(4). In contrast, I use the word 'confinement' to describe the state of affairs referred to in *Storck* component (a).

See also *Re P* [2014] UKSC 19, [2014] 2 FCR 71, [37] (Lady Hale DP), [63] (Lord Neuberger P) considering *Storck v Germany* (61603/00) (ECtHR), (2006) 43 EHRR 6

13.2.5 Restricting liberty: child DoL orders: depriving children's liberty: three *Storck* components: the 'acid test'

Re P [2014] UKSC 19, [2014] 2 FCR 71, [63] (Lord Neuberger P)

[63] In agreement with Lady Hale, I consider that the Strasbourg court decisions do indicate that the twin features of continuous supervision and control and lack of freedom to leave are the essential ingredients of deprivation of liberty (in addition to the area and period of confinement). In that connection, see *Guzzardi v Italy* (1980) 3 EHRR 333 (para 95) ('Supervision … carried out strictly and on an almost constant basis … [and] not able to leave his dwelling between 10 p.m. and 7 a.m.'), *HL v UK* (2004) 17 BHRC 418 (para 91) ('under continuous supervision and control and … not free to leave'), *Storck v Germany* (2006) 43 EHRR 96 (para 73) ('continuous supervision and control and … not free to leave'), *Kedzior v Poland* App No 45026/07 (16 October 2012, unreported) (para 57) ('constant supervision and … not free to leave'), *Stanev v Bulgaria* (2012) 55 EHRR 696 (para 128) ('constant supervision and … not free to leave'), and *Mihailovs v Latvia* App No 35939/10 (22 January 2013, unreported) (para 132) ('under constant supervision and … not free to leave').

Hertfordshire County Council v NK and another [2020] EWHC 139 (Fam), [2020] 1 FLR 951, [22]–[31] (MacDonald J) *quotation limited to* [26]–[31]

26. In *Storck v Germany* (2006) 43 EHRR 6 the European Court of Human Rights established three broad elements comprising a deprivation of liberty for the purposes of Art 5(1) of the ECHR, namely (a) an objective element of confinement to a certain limited place for a not negligible period of time, (b) a subjective element of absence of consent to that confinement and (c) the confinement imputable to the State. Only where all three components are present is there a deprivation of liberty which engages Art 5 of the ECHR. Within this context, in *Cheshire West and Chester v P* [2014] AC 896 the Supreme Court articulated an 'acid test' of whether a person who lacks capacity is deprived of their liberty, namely (a) the person is unable to consent to the deprivation of their liberty, (b) the person is subject to continuous supervision and control and (c) the person is not free to leave.

27. It is accepted the first limb of the 'acid test' does not require examination in the particular circumstances of this case. With respect to the application of the second and third limbs of the test to children and young people, in *Re RD (Deprivation or Restriction of Liberty)* [2018] EWFC 47 Cobb J, having reviewed the extensive case law, summarised the position as follows:

   i) 'Free to leave' does not mean leaving for the purpose of some trip or outing approved by those managing the institution; it means leaving in the sense of removing herself permanently in order to live where and with whom she chooses (*Re A-F* [2018] EWHC 138 (Fam) at

[14], repeating comments made in *JE v DE* [2006] EWHC 3459 (Fam) at [115], which had been cited with approval in *Re D (A Child)* [2017] EWCA Civ 1695, [22]);

ii) It is accepted wisdom that a typical fourteen or fifteen-year old is not free to leave her home (*Re A-F* at [31](i));

iii) The terms 'complete' or 'constant' define 'supervision' and 'control' as indicating something like 'total', 'unremitting', 'thorough', and/or 'unqualified' (*Re RD (Deprivation or Restriction of Liberty)* at [31]);

iv) It does not matter whether the object is to protect, treat or care in some way for the person taken into confinement (*Cheshire West and Chester v P* at [28]);

v) The comparative benevolence of living arrangements should not blind the court to their essential character if indeed those arrangements constitute a deprivation of liberty (*Cheshire West and Chester v P* at [35]);

vi) What it means to be deprived of liberty must be the same for everyone, whether or not they have physical or mental disabilities (*Cheshire West and Chester v P* at [46]);

vii) The person's compliance or lack of objection, the relative normality of the placement (whatever the comparison made) and the reason or purpose behind a particular placement are not relevant factors (*Cheshire West and Chester v P* at [50]);

viii) The distinction between deprivation and restriction is a matter of "degree or intensity" and "in the end, it is the constraints that matter" (*Cheshire West and Chester v P* at [56]);

ix) The question whether a child is restricted as a matter of fact is to be determined by comparing the extent of the child's actual freedom with someone of the child's age and station whose freedom is not limited (*Cheshire West and Chester v P* at [77]);

x) The sensible and humane comparison to be drawn is that between the situation of the child with the ordinary lives which young people of their ages might live at home with their families (*Cheshire West and Chester v P* at [47]);

xi) The 'acid test' has to be directly applied on each case to the circumstances of the individual under review. Where that individual is a child or young person, particular considerations apply (*Re A-F* at [30]).

28. In *Guzzardi v Italy* [1980] 3 EHRR 333 the ECtHR observed that to determine whether someone has been 'deprived of his liberty' within the meaning of Art 5, the starting point must be his or her concrete situation and account must be taken of a whole range of criteria such as the type, duration, effects and manner of implementation of the measure in question. Within this context I repeat the following, non-exhaustive, list of relevant factors that I set out in *Salford CC v M*:

i) The extent to which the child is actively prevented from leaving the placement and the extent to which efforts are made to return the child if they leave;

ii) The extent to which forms of restraint are utilised in respect of the child within the placement and their nature, intensity, frequency and duration;
iii) The nature and level of supervision that is in place in respect of the child within the placement;
iv) The nature and level of monitoring that is in place in respect of the child within the placement;
v) The extent to which rules and sanctions within the placement differ from other age appropriate settings for the child;
vi) The extent to which the child's access to mobile telephones and the Internet is restricted or otherwise controlled;
vii) The degree of access to the local community and neighbourhood surrounding the placement and the extent to which such access is supervised;
viii) The extent to which other periods outside the placement are regulated, for example transport to and from school.

29. With respect to the application of the 'acid test' to children and young people it will be seen that, as Cobb J made clear in *Re RD (Deprivation or Restriction of Liberty)*, the courts have utilised comparators against which to measure the elements of that test in respect of the subject child. In *Re A-F* at [33] Sir James Munby stated that:

> '… whether a state of affairs which satisfies the "acid test" amounts to a "confinement" for the *Storck* component (a) has to be determined by comparing the restrictions to which the child in question is subject with the restrictions that would apply to a child of the same "age", "station", "familial background" and "relative maturity" who is "free from disability".'

30. Within this context, in *Cheshire West and Chester v P* Lord Kerr observed that 'All children are (or should be) subject to some level of restraint. This adjusts with their maturation and change in circumstances'. Childhood is not a single, fixed and universal experience between birth and majority but rather one in which, at different stages, in their lives, children require differing degrees of protection, provision, prevention and participation. Within this context, with respect to the subject child, each case must be decided on its own facts.

31. However, with respect to the question of a comparator, in *Re A-F* Sir James Munby sought to lay down a 'rule of thumb' whereby, having observed that a child under the age of 15 years old is not 'free to leave' in the context used in *Cheshire West and Chester v P*, he noted that a child aged ten, even if under pretty constant supervision, is unlikely to be 'confined', a child aged 11, if under constant supervision, may, in contrast, be so 'confined', though the court should be astute to avoid coming too readily to such a conclusion and once a child who is under constant supervision has reached the age of 12, the court will more readily come to such a conclusion.

See also *Wigan Metropolitan Borough Council v W and others* [2021] EWHC 1982 (Fam), [34]–[35] (MacDonald J) providing an overview of the law on this point (comprehensive)

13.2.6 Restricting liberty: child DoL orders: depriving children's liberty: three *Storck* components: component (a) 'confinement'

Re A-F (children) (nos 1 and 2) [2018] EWHC 138 (Fam), [2019] 1 FCR 233, [21]–[25], [29]–[33] (Sir James Munby P)

[21] As I pointed out in *Re D (a child)* [2017] EWCA Civ 1695, para [30], a typical child say eight years old (the precise age being immaterial), subject to no physical or mental disabilities, who is, broadly speaking, at the same developmental stage as most children of the same age, and who is living with parents at home, without any local authority involvement, in the kind of circumstances in which, broadly speaking, most children of that age are accustomed to live in contemporary Britain, is 'living in circumstances which plainly satisfy the *Cheshire West* "acid test"', being 'under the complete supervision and control of those caring for her and … not free to leave the place where she lives.' I went on:

> 'But common-sense would plainly indicate that such a child is *not*, within the meaning of Article 5, deprived of his or her liberty. But – and this is the key question – why not? Is it because (*Storck* component (a)) there is, nonetheless, no confinement? Is it because (*Storck* component (b)) there is, in accordance with *Nielsen*, an effective parental consent? …'

I then (para [31]) postulated the situation where the same child was living with a local authority approved foster carer:

> 'the child is living in circumstances which plainly satisfy the *Cheshire West* "acid test". The State (*Storck* component (c)) is plainly involved. There is (*Storck* component (b)) no question of a *Nielsen* consent, because the child's parents have not consented and, as a matter of domestic law …, the foster carers lack the authority to consent. Does it follow that the child is therefore within the meaning of Article 5 deprived of his or her liberty, and, if not, why not?'

[22] Now this was *not* a question which arose for decision in *Re D (a child)* [2017] EWCA Civ 1695. Nevertheless, both Irwin LJ and I considered the point, in particular by reference to what Lord Kerr had said in *Cheshire West* (paras [77]–[79]): *Re D (a child)* [2017] EWCA Civ 1695, paras [32]–[39], [158]. David Richards LJ preferred (para [154]) to express no view on the point.

[23] What I said was this (para [39]):

> 'Without deciding a point which is not before us, I am inclined to think that the effect of this is that, in Lord Kerr's view, the situation of the "young" or "very young" as he describes it does *not* involve

a "confinement" for the purposes of *Storck* component (a), even though such a child is living in circumstances which plainly satisfy the *Cheshire West* "acid test." *If* this is so, though it is not something we need to decide for the purpose of disposing of this appeal and I express no concluded view, then the consequence, going back to my question, would be that the child living with foster-carers in their home is therefore not within the meaning of Article 5 being deprived of his or her liberty.'

[24] Irwin LJ, with whom I agreed (para [152]) said this (para [158]):

> 'Although it is not necessary for the decision in this case, I also agree with the President that the question whether there is "confinement" should be approached in the careful way analysed by Lord Kerr in *Cheshire West*, at paragraphs [77] to [79]. A three year-old child must be restrained for her own safety if walking near a busy road, or playing near a bonfire. This restraint would be unlawful if exercised over an adult. But it is lawful if exercised by any adult looking after the child. In my view, there is no need for an elaborate analysis of delegated parental responsibility to explain this. In such circumstances, restraint to keep the child safe lawfully could (and normally should) be exercised by any nearby adult. The true analysis is that explained by Lord Kerr. For all present purposes, "confinement" means not simply "confining" a young child to a playpen or by closing a door, but something more: an interruption or curtailment of the freedom of action normally to be ascribed to a child of that age and understanding. In most of the myriad instances in life where children are restrained in one way or another – by being compelled unwillingly to go to school, go to bed at a given time and so forth – there can be no question of their being "confined" so as to fulfil the first limb of the test in *Storck*.'

[25] I shall have to return in due course to this point, which is central to the issues arising in these cases.

…

[29] The important issue which Irwin LJ and I dealt with only obiter in *Re D (a child)* [2017] EWCA Civ 1695, because it did not arise for decision there, *does* arise for decision in the present cases. I therefore need to decide it. I can do so very shortly. Despite the reservations expressed by David Richards LJ, the law is, in my judgment, as Irwin LJ and I expressed it in the passages from our judgments in *Re D (a child)* [2017] EWCA Civ 1695 which I have set out above.

[30] Now at this point in the analysis a difficult question arises which has not hitherto been addressed, at least directly. At what point in the child's development, and by reference to what criteria, does one determine whether and when a state of affairs satisfying the 'acid test' in *Cheshire West* which has hitherto *not* involved a 'confinement' for the purposes of *Storck* component (a), and where art 5 has accordingly *not* been engaged, becomes a 'confinement' for that purpose, therefore engaging art 5

(unless, that is, a valid consent has been given by someone exercising parental responsibility)? This question raises a conceptual issue of some difficulty. And given what I have said in paragraphs [12]–[13] above, it also has very significant practical implications.

[31] In addressing this question there are three preliminary points to be borne in mind:

(i) First, the realities of the modern world, driven in significant part because the school-leaving age is now 16 and by consequential changes in the employment patterns of young people, mean that the typical child who is not yet 16 years old is not economically active and lives – in reality has no choice but to live – at home. So, the typical child of 15 is, in the sense in which the expression is used in the case-law, not free to leave the place where they live. If the 15-year old child runs away, wanting to live on their own, they will probably not get social housing and, if not taken into care, are likely to be returned home to live either with the parents or with other relatives.

(ii) Secondly, and another reality of the modern world, children nowadays tend to live more regulated and controlled lives than children of the same age would have been used to a generation or two back. The ubiquity of the motor vehicle in modern Britain, accompanied by changes in social attitudes as to what is or is not 'responsible parenting', mean that the street is no longer as safe (or seen as being as safe) an environment as it once was. It is no longer as safe (or seen as being as safe) as it once was for children to play in the street, to be allowed to roam or even to go to and from school under their own steam.

(iii) Thirdly, and as I have already explained (see paragraph [16] above), many aspects of the normal exercise of parental responsibility that interfere with a child's freedom of movement do *not* involve a deprivation of liberty engaging art 5.

[32] These matters, and in particular the first, bring into sharper focus that aspect of the 'acid test' encapsulated in the phrase 'complete supervision and control'. Given, as I have said, that the typical 15-year old is *not* free to leave, investigation of that aspect of the 'acid test' will not of itself answer the question whether a 15-year old or younger child is 'confined' for the purposes of *Storck* component (a). In terms of forensic reality, the answer to that crucial question will be determined by whether the child is under 'complete supervision and control'. So in cases such as these, that, and not freedom to leave, is likely to be the central issue.

[33] Crucial in this context is Lord Kerr's analysis in *Cheshire West* (paras [77]–[79]):

> '[77] The question whether one is restricted (as a matter of actuality) is determined by comparing the extent of your actual freedom with someone of your age and station whose freedom is not limited. Thus a teenager of the same age and familial background as MIG and MEG is the relevant comparator for them. If one compares their state with a

person of similar age and full capacity it is clear that their liberty is *in fact* circumscribed. They may not be conscious, much less resentful, of the constraint but, objectively, limitations on their freedom are in place.

[78] All children are (or should be) subject to some level of restraint. This adjusts with their maturation and change in circumstances. If MIG and MEG had the same freedom from constraint as would any child or young person of similar age, their liberty would not be restricted, whatever their level of disability. As a matter of objective fact, however, constraints beyond those which apply to young people of full ability are – and have to be – applied to them. There is therefore a restriction of liberty in their cases. Because the restriction of liberty is – and must remain – a constant feature of their lives, the restriction amounts to a deprivation of liberty.

[79] Very young children, of course, because of their youth and dependence on others, have – an objectively ascertainable – curtailment of their liberty but this is a condition common to all children of tender age. There is no question, therefore, of suggesting that infant children are deprived of their liberty in the normal family setting. A comparator for a young child is not a fully matured adult, or even a partly mature adolescent. While they were very young, therefore, MIG and MEG's liberty was not restricted. It is because they can – and must – now be compared to children of their own age and relative maturity who are free from disability and who have access (whether they have recourse to that or not) to a range of freedoms which MIG and MEG cannot have resort to that MIG and MEG are deprived of liberty.'

In other words, whether a state of affairs which satisfies the 'acid test' amounts to a 'confinement' for the purposes of *Storck* component (a) has to be determined by comparing the restrictions to which the child in question is subject with the restrictions which would apply to a child of the same 'age', 'station', 'familial background' and 'relative maturity' who is 'free from disability'.

13.2.7 Restricting liberty: child DoL orders: depriving children's liberty: three *Storck* components: component (a) 'confinement': ages: 'rules of thumb'

Re A-F (children) (nos 1 and 2) [2018] EWHC 138 (Fam), [2019] 1 FCR 233, [41]–[44] (Sir James Munby P) *quotation limited to* [41], [43]–[44]

[41] So much for the general principles. The question is raised as to whether it is possible to identify a minimum age below which a child is unlikely to be 'confined', and hence to be deprived of their liberty, given the expectation that a comparable child of the same age would also likely be under continuous supervision and control and not free to leave.

…

[43] Inevitably, one has to proceed on a case-by-case basis, having regard to the actual circumstances of the child and comparing them with the notional circumstances of the typical child of (to use Lord Kerr's phraseology) the same 'age', 'station', 'familial background' and 'relative maturity' who is 'free from disability'. Recognising that this does scant justice to the very thoughtful submissions I have had, in particular from Ms Heaton and Ms Burnell, the best I can do, by way, I emphasise, of little more than 'rule of thumb', is to suggest that:

(i) A child aged 10, even if under pretty constant supervision, is unlikely to be 'confined' for the purpose of *Storck* component (a).

(ii) A child aged 11, if under constant supervision, may, in contrast be so 'confined', though the court should be astute to avoid coming too readily to such a conclusion.

(iii) Once a child who is under constant supervision has reached the age of 12, the court will more readily come to that conclusion.

That said, all must depend upon the circumstances of the particular case and upon the identification by the judge in the particular case of the attributes of the relevant comparator as described by Lord Kerr.

[44] The question is also raised whether, in undertaking the comparison required by the 'acid test', the comparison should be made with a 'typical' child of the same age who is subject to a care order. The answer in my judgment is quite clearly, no. There is no support for any such proposition in any of the authorities and it is unsound as a matter of principle. Indeed, the proposition was rejected by Keehan J *In re AB (a child) (deprivation of liberty: consent)* [2015] EWHC 3125 (Fam), [2016] 1 WLR 1160, para [38](3). I agree with Keehan J.

13.2.8 Restricting liberty: child DoL orders: depriving children's liberty: three *Storck* components: component (b) 'lack of valid consent': neither LAs nor parents can provide 'valid consent' for children in care

Re A-F (children) (nos 1 and 2) [2018] EWHC 138 (Fam), [2019] 1 FCR 233, [12]–[13] (Sir James Munby P)

[12] I need not further explore this aspect of *Storck* component (b) for what is important for present purposes are two points:

(i) First, where a child is subject to a care order (whether interim or final) neither the local authority nor a parent can exercise their parental responsibility in such a way as to provide a valid consent for the purposes of *Storck* component (b): see *In re AB (a child) (deprivation of liberty: consent)* [2015] EWHC 3125 (Fam), [2016] 1 WLR 1160, [2016] 2 FLR 601, paras [26]–[29], [36], considered in *Re D (a child)* [2017] EWCA Civ 1695, paras [48], [109]–[112].

(ii) Secondly, a foster carer does not have parental responsibility enabling the carer to provide a valid consent for the purposes of *Storck* component (b): see *Re D (a child)* [2017] EWCA Civ 1695, para [31].

[13] Pausing there, it follows that, in relation to a child who is subject to a care order, the question of whether there is, in the sense in which I have defined the expressions, a 'deprivation of liberty' within the meaning of art 5(1) engaging the State's obligations under arts 5(2)–(4), will turn on whether there is a 'confinement' as referred to in *Storck* component (a). So the crux of the analysis for present purposes relates to Storck component (a).

See also *A Local Authority v D and others* [2015] EWHC 3125 (Fam), [2016] 1 WLR 1160, [25]–[27] (Keehan J) addressing a related point (parents may (or may not) be able to provide valid consent if a child is accommodated under s 20[5])

13.2.9 Restricting liberty: child DoL orders: depriving children's liberty: three *Storck* components: component (b) 'lack of valid consent': what if children consent?

Re T (a child) [2021] UKSC 35, [2021] 3 WLR 643, [157]–[162] (Lady Black)

157. Given the facts as they were, there was no basis on which the appellant could have sought, in this court, to have the orders authorising her two placements set aside on the basis that her consent rendered them unnecessary. Although much of the Court of Appeal's concentration, in its judgment, remained upon the argument that there was no jurisdiction to make an order unless consent was absent, it can be seen from the passage (para 86) set out above, that that argument had actually ceased to be part of the appellant's case before the end of the Court of Appeal hearing. It followed, inevitably, that Mostyn J had a discretion as to the orders he made, and it is no surprise that the Court of Appeal dismissed the appeal against them, especially as events had vindicated his assessment that T's apparent consent could not be relied upon to last. Nothing that T argues now could make any difference to this outcome, and I do not think it is unfair, in those circumstances, to describe her present argument on consent as entirely academic. It is right, therefore, that I should be particularly circumspect in any views that I express about it and I propose to be brief on this subject. Furthermore, I should make it quite clear that I have no intention, in what I say, of setting up new tests to be applied in cases of this type. This is an area in which it is uncommonly difficult to choose language which captures the position with precision, and that difficulty is compounded by the fact that the problem has to be addressed in the abstract.

158. The point that T wishes to make about consent is, as I understand it, that it would have been conducive to her welfare if the court had been prepared to put weight on her consenting to the restrictive placements, rather than making its own order. The importance of ascertaining and taking into account children's wishes and feelings about all aspects of

5 Children Act 1989, s 20.

their lives is well established, and there is no need to spell out here the various provisions that maintain this. T says, and I would accept, that it was of particular significance to her that her views should be respected.

159. In terms of the legal analysis deployed by the appellant in support of her position that her consent was all that was required, it appears to be along these lines: i) If valid consent is present, a person is not deprived of his or her liberty; ii) I consent, so I am not deprived of my liberty; iii) Therefore there is no need for an order under the inherent jurisdiction authorising the proposed arrangements, and no welfare/article 8 basis on which a court should make such an order.

160. As I see it, this is too simplistic an analysis of the court's role in an application of this type under the inherent jurisdiction. As the President said in the Court of Appeal, there is an important distinction between, on the one hand, determining whether, in any given set of circumstances, someone is deprived of their liberty for article 5 purposes, and, on the other hand, making an order (whether under section 25/section 119 or under the inherent jurisdiction) authorising a local authority to restrict a child's liberty. The former is a factual question, involving categorisation of a specific past or present set of circumstances. The latter is a prospective order, authorising (but not requiring) a local authority to take steps in response to events which it is anticipated are likely to occur. The focus is upon whether or not the factual circumstances justify the restriction proposed, should things transpire as the local authority predict.

161. The President was rightly anxious to stress (para 79 of the Court of Appeal judgment) the importance, for the protection of a child, of the court's involvement in authorising a deprivation of liberty, whether under section 25/section 119 or under the inherent jurisdiction. This is not the occasion for a comprehensive exploration of the complications attending consent to deprivation of liberty. For the moment, it is enough to observe that, even leaving to one side difficult issues about the pressures that circumstances may place on a child to consent to a proposed arrangement, an apparently balanced and free decision made by a child may be quickly revised and/or reversed. The facts of this case clearly demonstrate how insecure may be the child's apparent consent. Having said that, there may also be cases in which the child is expressing a carefully considered and firm view.

162. When the court considers the local authority's application, any consent on the part of the child will form part of the circumstances that it evaluates in deciding upon its order. I would not presume to forecast, still less dictate, what its implications would be for any particular case. That must depend upon the facts. The child needs to be, and is, protected by the institution of the proceedings and the consequent involvement of the court. His or her personal autonomy will be respected by being fully involved in those proceedings, and able to express views about the care that is being proposed, as ensured by the procedures stipulated by statute (for section 25) and by case law (for the inherent jurisdiction). It is worth noting that, in a case where the local authority is authorised to deprive the child of his

or her liberty but, when it comes to putting the restrictive arrangements into practice, the child is in fact consenting to them in circumstances where that consent is valid and sufficient, there would be no deprivation of liberty. In that situation, the local authority would simply be providing the child with accommodation.

See also *Re A-F (children) (nos 1 and 2)* [2018] EWHC 138 (Fam), [2019] 1 FCR 233, [53] (Sir James Munby P) addressing a related point (claims of valid consent normally require child and adolescent psychologists or psychiatrists)

13.2.10 Restricting liberty: child DoL orders: depriving children's liberty: three *Storck* components: component (c) 'imputable to the state'

Re A-F (children) (nos 1 and 2) [2018] EWHC 138 (Fam), [2019] 1 FCR 233, [10] (Sir James Munby P)

[10] I take *Storck* components (a), (b) and (c) in turn, starting with *Storck* component (c). It is so obvious that where a child is subject to a care order (whether interim or final) there is involvement and 'responsibility' by the State satisfying *Storck* component (c) – both the State in the form of the court and the State in the form of the local authority named in the care order – that the point requires neither elaboration nor citation of authority.

See also *Re D (a child)* [2019] UKSC 42, [2019] 3 FCR 631, [43] (Lady Hale P) addressing a related point (s20 accommodation in relation to component (c))

13.2.11 Restricting liberty: child DoL orders: procedure: exercised only by the High Court

Re A-F (children) (nos 1 and 2) [2018] EWHC 138 (Fam), [2019] 1 FCR 233, [26]–[27] (Sir James Munby P)

[26] A judge of the Family Court can make a secure accommodation order in accordance with s 25 of the Children Act 1989 (in Wales, in accordance with s 119 of the Social Services and Well-being (Wales) Act 2014). Where the placement of a child involves a 'confinement' for the purpose of *Storck* component (a), but is not 'secure accommodation' within the meaning of s 25 (s 119), the judicial sanction required if art 5 is to be complied with can be provided only by the High Court, in the exercise of the inherent jurisdiction, or, in some circumstances if the child has reached the age of 16, by the Court of Protection.

[27] In relation to the inherent jurisdiction, the following points are uncontroversial:

(i) The inherent jurisdiction can be exercised only by the High Court (in practice by the Family Division) and *not* by the Family Court (though it can be exercised in an appropriate case by a section 9 judge sitting in the Family Division) …

13.2.12 Restricting liberty: child DoL orders: procedure: key elements to the process

Re A-F (children) (nos 1 and 2) [2018] EWHC 138 (Fam), [2019] 1 FCR 233, [50] (Sir James Munby P)

Process

[50] The key elements of an art 5 compliant process can be summarised as follows:

(i) If a substantive order (interim or final) is to be made authorising a deprivation of liberty, there must be an oral hearing in the Family Division (though this can be before a s 9 judge). A substantive order must not be made on paper, but directions can, in an appropriate case, be given on paper without an oral hearing.

(ii) The child must be a party to the proceedings and have a guardian (if at all possible the children's guardian who is acting or who acted for the child in the care proceedings) who will no doubt wish to see the child in placement unless there is a very good child welfare reason to the contrary or that has already taken place. The child, if of an age to express wishes and feelings, should be permitted to do so to the judge *in person* if that is what the child wants.

(iii) A 'bulk application' (see the *Re X* cases) is not lawful, though in appropriate circumstances where there is significant evidential overlap there is no reason why a number of separate cases should not be heard together or in sequence on the same day before one judge.

13.2.13 Restricting liberty: child DoL orders: procedure: evidence

Re A-F (children) (nos 1 and 2) [2018] EWHC 138 (Fam), [2019] 1 FCR 233, [51]–[53] (Sir James Munby P)

Evidence

[51] The evidence in support of the substantive application (interim or final) should address the following matters and include:

(i) The nature of the regime in which it is proposed to place the child, identifying and describing, in particular, those features which it is said do or may involve 'confinement'. Identification of the salient features will suffice, minute detail is not required.

(ii) The child's circumstances, identifying and describing, in particular, those aspects of the child's situation which it is said require that the child be placed as proposed and be subjected to the proposed regime and, where possible, the future prognosis.

(iii) Why it is said that the proposed placement and regime are necessary and proportionate in meeting the child's welfare needs and that no less restrictive regime will do.

(iv) The views of the child, the child's parents and the Independent Reviewing Officer, the most recent care plan, the minutes of the most recent LAC or other statutory review and any recent reports in relation to the child's physical and/or mental health (typically the most recent documents will suffice).

[52] Whether and to what extent new evidence (eg, up-to-date reports) will need to be obtained, or whether reliance on existing evidence will suffice, must depend upon (a) the extent to which the existing evidence covers the various matters referred to above, (b) the age of the existing evidence (how up to date is it?) and (c) the extent to which there have been any significant changes since the existing evidence was prepared. The evidence from the guardian, which I envisage can often be quite short, will typically focus on the 'confinement' and 'deprivation of liberty' issues, unless there has been a very significant change in the child's circumstances, the application under the inherent jurisdiction should not be an occasion for re-opening the wider welfare issues previously determined in the care proceedings.

[53] The question has been raised whether a child's competency to consent to a 'confinement' can properly and fairly be assessed by a local authority social worker. Whilst I would not wish to exclude evidence on the point from a social worker who feels properly qualified to express an opinion, it is plainly undesirable that the only evidence on the point should come from an employee of the local authority responsible for the 'confinement'. And one would, in any event, expect that if a child whose circumstances require a regime more restricted than that of a comparator contemporary is nonetheless said to have the capacity to give a valid consent, that proposition would normally be made good by evidence from either a child and adolescent psychologist or, depending upon the nature of the child's difficulties, a child and adolescent psychiatrist. I recognise that in putting it this way I am departing somewhat from what Keehan J said in *A Local Authority v D, E and C* [2016] EWHC 3473 (Fam), para [44].

13.2.14 Restricting liberty: child DoL orders: procedure: interface with care proceedings

Re A-F (children) (nos 1 and 2) [2018] EWHC 138 (Fam), [2019] 1 FCR 233, [54] (Sir James Munby P)

Interface with care proceedings

[54] (i) If, when care proceedings are issued, there is a real likelihood that authorisation for a deprivation of liberty may be required, the proceedings should be issued in the usual way in the Family Court (*not* the High Court) but be allocated, if at all possible, to a Circuit Judge who is also a section 9 judge. Ms Heaton and Ms Burnell suggest that thought should be given to amending the C110A form to enable the issue to be highlighted. I agree.

(ii) Where care proceedings have been allocated for case management and/or final hearing to a judge who is not a section 9 judge, but it has become apparent that there is a real likelihood that authorisation for a deprivation of liberty may be required, steps should be taken if at all possible, and without delaying the hearing of the care proceedings, to reallocate the care proceedings, or at least the final hearing of the care proceedings, to a circuit judge who is also a section 9 judge.

(iii) The care proceedings will remain in the Family Court and must not be transferred to the High Court (note that a district judge or circuit judge has no power to transfer a care case to the High Court: see FPR 29.17(3) and (4) and PD 29C). The section 9 circuit judge conducting the two sets of proceedings – the care proceedings in the Family Court and the inherent jurisdiction proceedings in the High Court – can do so sitting simultaneously in both courts.

(iv) If this is not possible, steps should be taken to arrange a separate hearing in front of a section 9 judge as soon as possible (if at all possible within days at most) after the final hearing of the care proceedings. Typically, there will be no need for the judge to revisit matters already determined by the care judge, unless there are grounds for thinking that circumstances have changed, indeed, the care judge should, wherever possible and appropriate, address as many of these issues as possible in the care proceedings judgment.

(v) The evidence should include, in addition to all the other evidence required in the care proceedings, evidence on the matters referred to in paragraph [51] above. These matters should also, mutatis mutandis, be included in the s 31A care plan put before the court in the care proceedings.

(vi) Where the care proceedings have been concluded for some time, the process will be that indicated in paragraphs [50]–[51] above.

13.2.15 Restricting liberty: child DoL orders: procedure: continuing review is crucial

Re A-F (children) (nos 1 and 2) [2018] EWHC 138 (Fam), [2019] 1 FCR 233, [55]–[56] (Sir James Munby P)

Review

[55] Continuing review is crucial to the continued lawfulness of any 'confinement'. What is required are:

(i) Regular reviews by the local authority as part of its normal processes in respect of any child in care.

(ii) A review by a judge at least once every 12 months. The matter must be brought back before the judge without waiting for the next 12-monthly review if there has been any significant change (whether deterioration or improvement) in the child's condition or if it is proposed to move the child to a different placement.

(iii) The child must be a party to the review and have a guardian (if at all possible the guardian who has previously acted for the child).

(iv) If there has been no significant change of circumstances since the previous hearing/review, the review can take place on the papers, though the judge can of course direct an oral hearing. The form of the next review is a matter on which the judge can give appropriate directions at the conclusion of the previous hearing.

[56] The question has been raised whether, upon the making of a final order, the proceedings should be concluded, leaving the review to be conducted on the making of a fresh application by the local authority before the expiry of the previous order (and so on for each subsequent review), or whether the proceedings should be adjourned to a date fixed for hearing the next review (and so on thereafter). The argument against the former is that the local authority will have to pay a court issue fee for each review, the argument against the latter is that if the proceedings continue indefinitely this will cause Cafcass significant administrative problems and the legally-aided lawyers significant problems in relation to open, rather than concluded, legal aid certificates. The consensus arrived at by the parties, with which I agree, is that, generally speaking, it is preferable for the proceedings to be concluded at the end of the final hearing and thereafter at the end of each review, rather than being kept open. The local authority's stance was that, although there would be a cost implication for it in having to issue a fresh application for each review, the overall costs thus incurred were not significant and could properly be borne by the local authority.

CHAPTER 14

Costs

Chapter contents

CHAPTER 14

Costs

14.1 COSTS: PRINCIPLES

14.1.1 Costs: principles: generally

Re T (children) (costs) [2012] UKSC 36, [2012] 3 FCR 137, [1], [41]–[44] (Lord Phillips)

[1] It is rare for the Supreme Court to entertain an appeal that relates exclusively to costs, but this appeal raises an important issue of principle in relation to the liability of a local authority to pay the costs of a party to care proceedings.

...

[41] If in principle a local authority should be liable for the costs of interveners against whom allegations have been reasonably made that are held unfounded, then this liability should arise whether or not the interveners are publicly funded. In the present case, the five men who intervened and were exonerated should also have sought and been awarded costs. The burden of costs awarded against local authorities in such circumstances is likely to be considerable. When considering whether it is just to make an award of costs against a local authority in circumstances such as those of the present case it is legitimate to have regard to the competing demands on the limited funds of the local authority.

[42] In the context of care proceedings it is not right to treat a local authority as in the same position as a civil litigant who raises an issue that is ultimately determined against him. The 1989 Act imposes duties on the local authority in respect of the care of children. If the local authority receives information that a child has been subjected to or is likely to be subjected to serious harm it has a duty to investigate the report and, where there are reasonable grounds for believing that it may be well founded, to instigate care proceedings. In this respect the role of a local authority has much in common with the role of a prosecuting authority in criminal proceedings. It is for the court, and not the local authority, to decide whether the allegations are well founded. It is a serious misfortune to be the subject of unjustified allegations in relation to misconduct to a child, but where it is reasonable that these should be investigated by a court, justice does not demand that the local authority responsible for placing the allegations before the court should ultimately be responsible for the legal costs of the person against whom the allegations are made.

[43] Since the 1989 Act came into force, care proceedings have proceeded on the basis that costs will not be awarded against local authorities where no criticism can be made of the manner in which they have performed their duties under the Act. Wilson LJ in *Re J* [2010] 1 FCR 135 at [19], [2010] 1 FLR 1893 disclaimed any suggestion that it was appropriate 'in the vast run of these cases to make an order for costs in whole or in part by reference to the court's determination of issues of historical fact'. But, as I have indicated, there is no valid basis for restricting his approach in that case to findings in a split hearing. The principle that he applied would open the door to successful costs applications against local authorities in respect of many determinations of issues of historical fact. The effect on the resources of local authorities, and the uses to which those resources are put would be significant.

[44] For these reasons we have concluded that the general practice of not awarding costs against a party, including a local authority, in the absence of reprehensible behaviour or an unreasonable stance, is one that accords with the ends of justice and which should not be subject to an exception in the case of split hearings. Judge Dowse's costs order was founded on this practice. It was sound in principle and should not have been reversed by the Court of Appeal.

Re S (a child) (father's costs of appeal) [2015] UKSC 20, [2015] 1 FCR 549, [15]–[28], [30]–[33] (Lady Hale DP) *quotation limited to* [15]–[17], [20]–[28], [30]–[33]

[15] Under s 51 of the Senior Courts Act 1981, costs in the Civil Division of the Court of Appeal and in the family court are 'in the discretion of the court' but subject to the rules of court. Under the Civil Procedure Rules, the 'general rule' in civil proceedings is that the 'unsuccessful party will be ordered to pay the costs of the successful party' (CPR 44.2(2)(a)). However, this general rule does not apply to first instance proceedings about children (FPR 28.2(1) disapplies CPR 44.2(2)). Nor does the general rule apply to proceedings in the Court of Appeal in connection with proceedings in the Family Division of the High Court or from a judgment, direction, decision or order in any court in family proceedings (CPR 44.2(3)).

[16] However, CPR 44.2(4) and (5) do apply to children's proceedings both at first instance and on appeal:

> '(4) In deciding what order (if any) to make about costs, the court will have regard to all the circumstances, including—
>
> (a) the conduct of all the parties;
> (b) whether a party has succeeded on part of its case, even if that party has not been wholly successful; and
> (c) any admissible offer to settle made by a party which is drawn to the court's attention, and which is not an offer to which costs consequences under Part 36 apply.

(5) The conduct of the parties includes—

(a) conduct before, as well as during, the proceedings and in particular the extent to which the parties followed … any relevant pre-action protocol;

(b) whether it was reasonable for a party to raise, pursue or contest a particular allegation or issue;

(c) the manner in which a party has pursued or defended its case or a particular allegation or issue; and

(d) whether a claimant who has succeeded in the claim, in whole or in part, exaggerated its claim.'

[17] As was pointed out in *Re T*, CPR 44.2(4)(b) is relevant in a situation where the general rule applies but has no direct relevance where it does not (para [11]). This is not, of course, to say that success or failure is irrelevant in children's cases: no-one has suggested in this case that the successful party should have to pay the unsuccessful party's costs (although, as will be seen, there may be circumstances where this would be appropriate). Nor does CPR 44.2(4)(c) readily fit the conduct of children's cases, save as an aspect of the general desirability of the parties co-operating and negotiating to reach an agreed solution which will best serve the paramount consideration of the welfare of the child. As such, it is part of the general conduct of the proceedings, some aspects of which are listed in CPR 44.2(5).

…

[20] Whenever a court has to determine a question relating to the upbringing of a child, the welfare of the child is the court's paramount consideration: Children Act 1989, s 1(1). This applies just as much to care proceedings brought to protect a child from harm as it does to disputes between parents or other family members about the child's future. Although the proceedings are adversarial in form, they have many inquisitorial features. An application cannot be withdrawn without the court's consent (FPR 29.4). The court is not bound by the cases put forward by the parties, but may adopt an alternative solution of its own. The court is not bound by the choice of evidence put forward by the parties, but can decide for itself what evidence it wishes to hear. The court is very often assisted by the independent investigations and reports of the family court reporter (in private law cases) or the children's guardian (in care and adoption proceedings) and other experts. Even in care proceedings, there are many possible outcomes available to the court. Thus, for example, in a case such as this, the available outcomes ranged from a closed adoption with no contact (other than letterbox contact) with the birth family to the child going to live with her father with no further intervention by the local authority. In between could be, for example, an open adoption, a special guardianship order, long term fostering under a care order with only limited contact with the birth family, medium term fostering with increasing contact with a view to restoring the child to her birth family in due course, placement with the birth family under a care order, placement with the birth family under a supervision order together with a child

arrangements order, a child arrangements order or even no order at all. It can readily be seen, therefore, why in such proceedings there are no adult winners and losers—the only winner should be the child.

[21] Furthermore, it can generally be taken for granted that each of the persons appearing before the court has a role to play in helping the court to achieve the best outcome for the child. It would be difficult indeed for a court to decide how to secure that the child has a meaningful relationship with each parent without hearing from them both. It would be difficult indeed for a court to decide the best way of protecting a child from the risk of harm without hearing from her parents and those whose task it is to protect her. That is why parents are compellable witnesses in care proceedings, even when it is alleged that they have committed criminal offences. No-one should be deterred by the risk of having to pay the other side's costs from playing their part in helping the court achieve the right solution.

[22] It can also generally be assumed that all parties to the case are motivated by concern for the child's welfare. The parents who dispute with one another or with the local authority over their children's future do generally love their children dearly and want the best for them as they see it. There are of course some wicked, neglectful, selfish or merely misguided parents who are not motivated to do their best for their children, but these are not the generality of parents, even those whose children are the subject of care proceedings. Local authorities are not motivated by love, in the way that parents are motivated by love, but they do have statutory duties to investigate and take action to protect children if there is reasonable cause to suspect them to be suffering or likely to suffer significant harm: Children Act 1989, s 47. They will be severely criticised by press and public alike if they fail to take action when they should have done.

[23] Another consideration is that, in most children's cases, it is important for the parties to be able to work together in the interests of the children both during and after the proceedings. Children's lives do not stand still. Their needs change and develop as they grow up. The arrangements made to cater for those needs may also have to change. Parents need to be able to co-operate with one another after the case is over. Unless there is to be a closed adoption they also need to co-operate with the local authority and the people who are looking after their children. The local authority need to be able to co-operate with them. Stigmatising one party as the loser and adding to that the burden of having to pay the other party's costs is likely to jeopardise the chances of their co-operating in the future.

[24] There is one final consideration. In certain circumstances, having to pay the other side's costs, or even having to bear one's own costs, will reduce the resources available to look after this child or other children. Thus, for example, if a mother who is bringing up the children on modest means had not only to bear her own costs but also to pay the father's costs, when unsuccessfully resisting his application for more contact with the children, the principal sufferers might well be the children. Nor can it be ignored that, if local authorities are faced with having to pay the parents'

costs as well as their own, there will be less in their budgets for looking after the children in their care, providing services for children in need, and protecting other children who are or may be at risk of harm.

[25] On the other hand, there is one consideration which cannot be taken into account. The automatic availability of non-means-tested and non-merits-tested public funding for parents at first instance in care proceedings has masked the issue. It has only surfaced on appeal, as here, or for interveners, where public funding is means-tested. But the question of whether it is just to make an order for costs should as a matter of principle be determined irrespective of whether any of the parties are publicly funded. As Baker J put it in *G v E (Costs)* [2010] EWHC 3385 (Fam), [2011] 1 FLR 1566, para [39], 'Gone are the days when it is appropriate for a court to dismiss applications for costs on the basis that it all comes out of the same pot'. (The consequences of making a costs order for or against a publicly funded litigant are a separate matter.) Thus, as Lord Phillips pointed out in *Re T* [2012] 3 FCR 137, [2012] 4 All ER 1137 at [41], if in principle the local authority should be liable in costs to interveners against whom allegations, reasonably made, have been held to be unfounded, this liability should arise whether or not those interveners were publicly funded. The other five men who were exonerated in that case should also have got their costs. Parents, automatically publicly funded, who successfully resist care proceedings would also get their costs. It might even be said that successful local authorities should get their costs against the parents (or interveners) irrespective of public funding.

[26] All the reasons which make it inappropriate as a general rule to make costs orders in children's cases apply with equal force in care proceedings between parents and local authorities as they do in private law proceedings between parents or other family members. They lead to the conclusion that costs orders should only be made in unusual circumstances. Two of them were identified by Wilson J in *Sutton London BC v Davis (No 2)* [1994] 2 FCR 1199 at 1202, [1995] 1 All ER 65 at 67: 'where, for example, the conduct of a party has been reprehensible or the party's stance has been beyond the band of what is reasonable: *Havering LBC v S* [1986] 1 FLR 489 and [*Gojkovic v Gojkovic (No 2)* [1991] FCR 913 at 919, [1992] 1 All ER 267 at 273]'. Those were also the two circumstances identified in *Re T*, at [44].

Should this case be distinguished?

[27] Two questions arise: first, is there any reason to depart from the general approach in *Re T* in this case; and second, are there any other circumstances, beyond the two identified in *Re T*, in which a costs order might be justified?

[28] It cannot be a valid distinction that the people claiming costs in *Re T* were interveners wishing to clear their names rather than parents wishing to care for their children. All the reasons why costs orders are inappropriate in children's cases apply much more strongly to parents and local authorities than they do to such interveners. The fact that parents are resisting the claim of the state to take their children away from them is undoubtedly

relevant, but it is relevant to whether one of the exceptions should apply. As a general proposition, I would accept Dr Bainham's argument that parents are always entitled to resist the claim of the state to remove their children from them. They will usually be reasonable in doing so. They should not have to pay the local authority's costs if they lose. But it does not follow from that that if the local authority lose, they are unreasonable in seeking to protect the child: that will all depend upon the particular circumstances of the case.

…

[30] Secondly, however, are there circumstances other than reprehensible behaviour towards the child or unreasonable conduct of the proceedings which might justify a costs order in care proceedings? It is clear from the authorities cited above that there may be other such circumstances in private law proceedings between parents or family members. Should care proceedings be any different?

[31] I do not understand that Lord Phillips, giving the judgment of the court in *Re T* [2012] 3 FCR 137, [2012] 4 All ER 1137, was necessarily intending to rule out the possibility that there might be other circumstances in which an award of costs in care proceedings might be appropriate and just. That would be to ascribe to para [44] of the judgment the force of a statutory provision. Such a rigid rule was unnecessary to the decision in that case and cannot be treated as its ratio decidendi.

[32] On the other hand, it *was* necessary to the decision in that case that local authorities should not be in any *worse* position than private parties when it comes to paying the other parties' costs. There is an attraction in regarding local authorities in a different light from private parties, because of their so-called 'deep pockets'. But, as Lord Phillips observed, at para [34]—

> 'Local authorities have limited funds. Their costs in relation to care proceedings are met from their children's services budgets. There are many other claims on this budget … No evidence is needed … to support the proposition that if local authorities are to become liable to pay the costs of those [whom] they properly involve in care proceedings this is going to impact on their finances and the activities to which these are directed. The court can also take judicial notice of the fact that local authorities are financially hard pressed …'

While it is true that appeals are comparatively rare and their costs comparatively low compared with the costs of care proceedings generally, that is not by itself a good reason for making an exception in their case.

[33] But nor should local authorities be in any *better* position than private parties to children's proceedings. The object of the exercise is to achieve the best outcome for the child. If the best outcome for the child is to be brought up by her own family, there may be cases where real hardship would be caused if the family had to bear their own costs of achieving that outcome. In other words, the welfare of the child would be put at risk if the family had to bear its own costs. In those circumstances, just as it

may be appropriate to order a richer parent who has behaved reasonably in the litigation to pay the costs of the poorer parent with whom the child is to live, it may also be appropriate to order the local authority to pay the costs of the parent with whom the child is to live, if otherwise the child's welfare would be put at risk. (It may be that this is one of the reasons why parents are automatically entitled to public funding in care cases.)

See also *A and S (children) v Lancashire County Council* [2013] EWHC 851 (Fam), [2013] 2 FLR 1221, [18]–[19] (Peter Jackson J) addressing a related point ('conduct' is wider than just litigation conduct)

See also *G v E and others* [2010] EWHC 3385 (Fam), [2011] 1 FLR 1566, [39] (Baker J) addressing a related point (the relevance of public funding to awarding costs)

14.1.2 Costs: principles: exonerated interveners

See Chapter 14.1.1 Costs: principles: generally

14.1.3 Costs: principles: appeals

Re S (a child) (father's costs of appeal) [2015] UKSC 20, [2015] 1 FCR 549, [15]–[33] (Lady Hale DP) *quotation limited to* [29]

[29] Nor in my view is it a good reason to depart from the general principle that this was an appeal rather than a first instance trial. Once again, the fact that it is an appeal rather than a trial may be relevant to whether or not a party has behaved reasonably in relation to the litigation. As Wall LJ pointed out in *EM v SW, Re M (a child)* [2009] EWCA Civ 311, there are differences between trials and appeals. At first instance, 'nobody knows what the judge is going to find' (para [23]), whereas on appeal the factual findings are known. Not only that, the judge's reasons are known. Both parties have an opportunity to 'take stock' and consider whether they should proceed to advance or resist an appeal and to negotiate on the basis of what they now know. So it may well be that conduct which was reasonable at first instance is no longer reasonable on appeal. But in my view that does not alter the principles to be applied: it merely alters the application of those principles to the circumstances of the case.

See also *LR v A Local Authority and others* [2019] EWCA Civ 680, [3]–[7] (Baker LJ) considering *Re S (a child) (father's costs of appeal)* [2015] UKSC 20, [2015] 1 FCR 549

See also *MW v Hertfordshire County Council* [2014] EWCA Civ 405 [42]–[49] (Macur LJ) addressing a related point (ordering a proportion of the respondents' costs against an appellant LA[1] for an unmeritorious appeal, pre-dating *Re S (a child) (father's costs of appeal)* [2015] UKSC 20, [2015] 1 FCR 549)

See Chapter 14.1.1 Costs: principles: generally

1 Local authority.

14.1.4 Costs: principles: costs of translations

Re Z (a child) [2017] EWCA Civ 157, [2017] 2 FCR 404, [1]–[2], [13]–[14], [30]–[38] (Macur LJ) *quotation limited to* [36]–[38]

[36] There can be no criticism of any judge who determines that, bearing in mind the circumstances of a particular case, the party bearing the burden of proof shall be responsible for translation costs of a relevant document. The circumstances of other cases may reasonably inform a view that the party which requires the translation should bear the cost. Both of these views may be reasonable in the context of the case in hand, but cannot be considered as determinative of the issue across all cases.

[37] To deal with an issue of translation costs devoid of context does not connote a reasonable exercise of judicial discretion. Whilst the promulgation of a court's usual practice on the question creates certainty and may save some court time it could also lead to unfair demands upon either public (local authority and legal aid) or private financial resources.

[38] The application of Family Procedure Rules 2010, r 1.1(2) and (3) require collaboration between parties to avoid the prospect of time consuming satellite litigation on the issue of identification of which documents, or parts of the same, it is necessary to translate and in summary or full, together with a non-partisan appraisal of which party it would be reasonable to invite the judge to order to pay, or contribute towards, the costs of the same.

14.1.5 Costs: principles: indemnity costs

Re B (indemnity) (costs) [2007] EWCA Civ 921, [2008] 2 FCR 327, [12] (Wall LJ)

[12] I agree. I add a short judgment of my own not least because the judge below has relied upon a decision of this court in which I gave the judgment of the court in order to justify his decision for indemnity costs. In my view an order for indemnity costs is a wholly exceptional order to make in family proceedings and needs to be very carefully thought through and justified …

14.2 COSTS: OTHER

14.2.1 Costs: other: statement of costs: needed before determining the principle

A Local Authority v A Mother and others [2018] EWHC 1841 (Fam), [2018] 4 WLR 146, [60]–[62] (Knowles J) *quotation limited to* [60]

60. I make one final observation. Miss Kirby criticised the parents for failing to file a costs schedule prior to their application. That was a point well made because it is difficult to see how a court could come to a decision about costs in these circumstances without knowing the amount at stake.

The amount of costs sought must form part of "*all the circumstances*" referred to in Rule 44.2(4) otherwise it is difficult to see how the court can come to a decision on what is just in the circumstances of a particular case [FPR Rule 28.1]. Thus, I disagree with Miss Fottrell QC that a decision on costs in cases of this sort can be made on principle without full knowledge of the sum involved. Before coming to my decision, I directed a process whereby each parent could provide a schedule of costs after I had heard their submissions and gave an opportunity for the local authority to comment thereon.

14.2.2 Costs: other: wasted costs

Re G, S and H (care proceedings: wasted costs) [1999] 3 FCR 303 (FD), 313D–314F, 328A–E (Wall J)

Wasted costs orders in family proceedings: the role of the court

Unlike most civil proceedings, care proceedings under the Children Act 1989 are non-adversarial. Furthermore, public law care proceedings, in particular, are almost invariably conducted between parties all of whom, on one basis or another, are publicly funded. The local authority has to pay for care proceedings out of its annual budget: the parents and the child or children concerned (through their guardian ad litem) are usually both funded by the tax payer through legal aid. In cases where the Official Solicitor is involved, he too, derives his budget from public funds.

Contested care proceedings are extremely expensive. However, inter partes orders for costs are rare. I cannot recall ever making an order for costs in care proceedings against parents or a guardian ad litem in favour of a local authority. Cases in which the court orders a local authority to pay the costs of the other parties are, in my experience, also very rare and the order in such circumstances is usually a mark of disapprobation for the way the local authority has behaved in relation to the children or their parents.

Parents facing care proceedings often contest them in circumstances where the likelihood of care orders being made is very high, and where the parents' case is effectively hopeless. As *Ridehalgh v Horsefield* [1994] Ch 205 at 233, [1994] 3 All ER 848 at 863 makes clear, however, lawyers for parents in these circumstances are not to be penalised for pursuing a hopeless case. Parents in such cases are at risk of losing their children; no decision could be more important for both the children and their parents, and all parents at such risk are entitled to proper representation and to have their cases put.

In the instant proceedings, the parents' difficult and, as it proved, unmeritorious case was ably and economically presented by leading counsel. Of that I have no complaint. Indeed, counsel for the parents argue in their latest submissions that the preceding sentences are 'a pale reflection' of the '(exceedingly) complimentary remarks' I made in the substantive judgment about their conduct of the case overall.

It follows that a local authority which obtains a care order in a 'hopeless' case will be unlikely either to obtain or even seek an order for costs against impecunious parents, or the Legal Aid Board or the lawyers conducting the parents' case.

In these circumstances, in my judgment, and in clear contrast to commercial or other adversarial civil litigation, it is the court which has to be the watchdog over the proper expenditure of public funds. The 1989 Act specifically gives the court a pro-active, case management responsibility in both public and private law cases: see ss 11 and 32, and the numerous cases dealing with case management. In my judgment, therefore, in care proceedings it is frequently likely to be the court which will need to initiate proceedings relating to wasted costs orders.

The court clearly has the jurisdiction to initiate such proceedings: see *Ridehalgh v Horsefield* [1994] Ch 205 at 238, [1994] 3 All ER 848 at 867. Furthermore, since *Ridehalgh v Horsefield* was decided, the *Practice direction (family proceedings: case management)* [1995] 2 FCR 340, [1995] 1 All ER 586 (para 1), gives clear warning to practitioners about the consequences of failure to conduct cases economically:

> 'The importance of reducing the cost and delay of civil litigation makes it necessary for the court to assert greater control over the preparation for and conduct of hearings than has hitherto been customary. Failure by practitioners to conduct cases economically will be visited by appropriate orders for costs, including wasted costs orders.'

In my judgment, therefore, it is entirely appropriate in a case such as the present for the court to initiate the inquiry whether or not a wasted costs order should be made.

…

The terms 'improper, unreasonable or negligent' in this context are fully discussed in the judgment of the Court of Appeal in *Ridehalgh v Horsefield* [1994] Ch 205 at 232–233, [1994] 3 All ER 848 at 861–862. I do not think that the conduct which I have discussed above can be described as 'improper'. The question, to my mind, is whether or not it is either unreasonable or negligent.

'Unreasonable' is described in *Ridehalgh v Horsefield* as apt to describe conduct 'which is vexatious, designed to harass the other side rather than advance the resolution of the case'. It is plainly not limited to such conduct. The 'acid test' described in *Ridehalgh v Horsefield* is 'whether the conduct permits of a reasonable explanation'. Judged by that test, I find that: (1) the conduct of counsel for the local authority and the local authority solicitor in failing to ensure that Dr M had seen the bundle of medical records; (2) the failure of the advocates to address the same issue at the pre-hearing review; and (3) the conduct of all counsel in failing to ensure that Drs F and B had seen the parents' latest statements, do not permit of a reasonable explanation. In my judgment, therefore, the conduct in all three respects was unreasonable.

> It is also clear from *Ridehalgh v Horsefield* [1994] Ch 205 at 232, [1994] 3 All ER 848 at 862 that the term 'negligent' is not to be used as a term of art, but 'in an untechnical way to denote failure to act with the competence reasonably to be expected of ordinary members of the profession'.

See also *Ridehalgh v Horsefield and another* [1994] Ch 205 (CA), 231D–234F (Sir Thomas Bingham MR) addressing the same point (the original authority)

CHAPTER 15

Appeals

Chapter contents

CHAPTER 15

Appeals

15.1 APPEALS: TEST

15.1.1 Appeals: test: threshold criteria and welfare decisions: 'wrong'

Re B (a child) (care order: proportionality: criterion for review) [2013] UKSC 33, [2013] 2 FCR 525, [43]–[47] (Lord Wilson), [86]–[95] (Lord Neuberger P), [138]–[142] (Lord Clarke) *quotation limited to* [43]–[47], [90]–[95]

[43] In this appeal M challenges both Judge Cryan's determination that the threshold set by s 31(2) was crossed and, alternatively, his ultimate determination that Amelia's welfare demanded that he should make the care order. The time has come for me to address the criterion for appellate review of each of these determinations; but, whatever the criterion, the appellate court will factor into its review the trial judge's enjoyment of the advantages to which I have referred.

[44] On any view there is nothing discretionary about a determination of whether the threshold is crossed. I consider that in the Court of Appeal Black LJ was correct, at [9], to categorise it as, instead, a value judgement, particularly, but not only, when the court is surveying likelihood. Black LJ proceeded to adopt the approach of Ward LJ in the Court of Appeal in *Re MA (children) (care order: likelihood of significant harm)* [2010] 1 FCR 456 at [56], [2010] 1 FLR 431 that the question on an appeal against the refusal of a judge to hold that the threshold had been crossed was whether it exceeded the generous ambit of reasonable disagreement. In my judgment in that case, from the outcome of which I dissented, I asked, at [34], whether it had been 'open' to the judge to refuse to do so. In her judgment Hallett LJ asked, at [44], whether the judge had been 'plainly wrong' to refuse to do so. Although these are matters of little more than nuance, I consider in retrospect that in that case none of the three of us afforded sufficient weight to the evaluative, as opposed to the discretionary, nature of a determination whether the threshold is crossed. Ward LJ's reference to the generous ambit of reasonable disagreement seems apt only to the review of an exercise of discretion, as in *G v G* [1985] 2 All ER 225, [1985] 1 WLR 64. My own reference to whether the judge's determination had been 'open' to him now seems to me to have been singularly uninformative. Perhaps Hallett LJ came closest to the appropriate test in her reference to whether the determination had been 'plainly wrong'. But it is generally better to allow adjectives to speak for themselves without adverbial support. What does 'plainly' add to 'wrong'?

Either the word adds nothing or it serves to treat the determination under challenge with some slight extra level of generosity apt to one which is discretionary but not to one which is evaluative. Like all other members of the court, I consider that appellate review of a determination whether the threshold is crossed should be conducted by reference simply to whether it was wrong.

[45] I turn to the criterion for appellate review of the ultimate determination of whether to make a care order. This is an order which the court 'may' make (s 31(1) of the 1989 Act), albeit that the determination is governed by the paramountcy of the child's welfare (s 1(1)) and can be made only following regard to specified factors (s 1(3) and (4)(b)). The court's apparent discretion whether to make a care order has led family practitioners readily to assume that the criterion for appellate review is identical to that applicable to review of what are taken to be discretionary determinations relating to children in private law, namely that explained by Lord Fraser in *G v G* cited above; and it was not controversial when Sir Mark Potter P formally so ruled in *Re C (Adoption: Best Interests of Child)* [2009] EWHC 499 (Fam) at [33], [2009] 2 FLR 1293 at [33]. But, by contrast with the issue between the members of this court as to the impact of s 6(1) of the 1998 Act upon the role of the *appellate* judge, there is no issue that, since that Act came into force, the task of the *trial* judge in applications for care (or supervision) orders—and indeed in such applications for private law orders as can sensibly be said to represent a suggested interference with a person's right to respect for his or her family life—is more than to exercise a discretion. His task is to comply with an obligation under the subsection not to determine the application in a way which is incompatible with that right. It follows therefore that the review which, according to the majority, falls to be conducted by the appellate court must focus not just on the judge's exercise of a discretion but on his compliance or otherwise with an obligation. The criterion enunciated in *G v G*, in particular the concept of the generous ambit of reasonable disagreement, is in my view inapt to that review (as opposed, for example, to a review of a case management decision made within care proceedings: see *Re TG (a child) (care proceedings: biomechanical engineering evidence)* [2013] EWCA Civ 5 at [38], [2013] 1 FCR 229 at [38], [2013] 1 FLR 1250).

[46] Lord Neuberger, at [90] and [91], and Lord Clarke, at [139], suggest that the criterion for appellate review of an ultimate determination to make (or to refuse to make) a care order should, as in respect of the threshold, be whether it was wrong (or vitiated by serious irregularity). Just as in my view r 52.11(1) of the Civil Procedure Rules helps to identify the role of an appellate court in a challenge to the determination of a Convention-related issue, so, as Lord Clarke there suggests, r 52.11(3) helps to identify the criterion which it should adopt in that it provides: 'The appeal court will allow an appeal where the decision of the lower court was—(a) wrong; or (b) unjust because of a serious procedural or other irregularity …' I agree. To be driven to jettison the principles in *G v G* in this context is not to say

that the factors which often vitiate the exercise of a discretion—namely that the judge considered an irrelevant matter, failed to consider a relevant matter, erred in law or applied a wrong principle—become irrelevant. On the contrary they may well generate a conclusion that the determination was wrong and should be set aside and either that it should be reversed or that the application should be remitted for consideration afresh. By contrast a judge's failure to give adequate reasons for his determination is likely to lead to its being set aside as unjust within the meaning of r 52.11(3)(b).

[47] There is therefore an attractive symmetry between the criterion for review of a determination of whether the threshold is crossed and that for review of a determination of whether a care order should be made. In each case it is no more and no less than whether the determination is wrong. But the simplicity of the criterion should not disguise the difficulty, in some cases, of its application.

...

[90] The argument that the Convention or the 1998 Act requires the Court of Appeal to form its own view in every case where a trial judge's decision on proportionality is challenged, appears to me to be wrong in principle and potentially unfair or inconvenient. The argument is wrong in principle because, if the function of the Court of Appeal is as I have described, then, in my view, there can be no breach of the Convention or the 1998 Act, if it conducts a review of the trial judge's decision and only reverses it if satisfied that it was wrong. The only basis for challenging that view is, on analysis, circular, as it involves assuming that the Court of Appeal's primary function is to reconsider not to review. The argument is potentially unfair or inconvenient, because in cases where the appeal court could not be sure whether the trial judge was right or wrong without hearing the evidence and seeing the witnesses, it would either to have to reach a decision knowing that it was less satisfactorily based than that of the judge, or it would have to hear the evidence and see the witnesses for itself.

[91] That conclusion leaves open the standard which an appellate court should apply when determining whether the trial judge was entitled to reach his conclusion on proportionality, once the appellate court is satisfied that the conclusion was based on justifiable primary facts and assessments. In my view, an appellate court should not interfere with the trial judge's conclusion on proportionality in such a case, unless it decides that that conclusion was wrong. I do not agree with the view that the appellate court has to consider that judge's conclusion was 'plainly' wrong on the issue of proportionality before it can be varied or reversed. As Lord Wilson says at [44], either 'plainly' adds nothing, in which case it should be abandoned as it will cause confusion, or it means that an appellate court cannot vary or reverse a judge's conclusion on proportionality of it considers it to have been 'merely' wrong. Whatever view the Strasbourg court may take of such a notion, I cannot accept it, as it appears to me to undermine the role of judges in the field of human rights.

[92] I appreciate that the attachment of adverbs to 'wrong' was impliedly approved by Lord Fraser in the passage cited from *G v G* [1985] 2 All ER 225 at 229, [1985] 1 WLR 647 at 652 by Lord Wilson at [38], and has something of a pedigree—see eg per Ward LJ in *Assicurazioni Generali SpA v Arab Insurance Group (BSC)* [2003] 1 All ER (Comm) 140 at [195], [2003] 1 WLR 577 (although aspects of his approach have been disapproved—see *Datec Electronics Holdings Ltd v United Parcels Service Ltd* [2007] 4 All ER 765 at [46], [2007] 1 WLR 1325). However, at least where Convention questions such as proportionality are being considered on an appeal, I consider that, if after reviewing the trial judge's decision, an appeal court considers that he was wrong, then the appeal should be allowed. Thus, a finding that he was wrong is a sufficient condition for allowing an appeal against the trial judge's conclusion on proportionality, and, indeed, it is a necessary condition (save, conceivably, in very rare cases).

[93] There is a danger in over-analysis, but I would add this. An appellate judge may conclude that the trial judge's conclusion on proportionality was (i) the only possible view, (ii) a view which she considers was right, (iii) a view on which she has doubts, but on balance considers was right, (iv) a view which she cannot say was right or wrong, (v) a view on which she has doubts, but on balance considers was wrong, (vi) a view which she considers was wrong, or (vii) a view which is unsupportable. The appeal must be dismissed if the appellate judge's view is in category (i) to (iv) and allowed if it is in category (vi) or (vii).

[94] As to category (iv), there will be a number of cases where an appellate court may think that there is no right answer, in the sense that reasonable judges could differ in their conclusions. As with many evaluative assessments, cases raising an issue on proportionality will include those where the answer is in a grey area, as well as those where the answer is in a black or a white area. An appellate court is much less likely to conclude that category (iv) applies in cases where the trial judge's decision was not based on his assessment of the witnesses' reliability or likely future conduct. So far as category (v) is concerned, the appellate judge should think very carefully about the benefit the trial judge had in seeing the witnesses and hearing the evidence, which are factors whose significance depends on the particular case. However, if, after such anxious consideration, an appellate judge adheres to her view that the trial judge's decision was wrong, then I think that she should allow the appeal.

[95] I am conscious that the analysis at [80]–[90] appears to differ somewhat from that of Lady Hale at [204]–[205] and of Lord Kerr at [116]–[127]. However, at least in my opinion, it would, essentially for two reasons, be a very rare case where their approach would produce a different outcome from mine. First, it is only my category (iv) which gives rise to disagreement, in that they would not, as I understand it, accept that such types of case exist. However, many, probably most, cases that on my approach would fall into that category would, on their approach

(especially in the light of what they say about the weight to be given to the trial judge's assessment) be in category (iii), which would yield the same outcome. Secondly, the advantage which the trial judge has in hearing the evidence and seeing the witnesses will mainly apply to his findings of primary fact, inferences of fact, and assessment of probable outcomes, which then feed into his assessment of proportionality (and, in this case, necessity). When those factors come to be weighed on the question of proportionality (or necessity), the advantage the trial judge has will normally be of less significance, and sometimes even of very little, if any, significance.

See also Re *B-S (children) (adoption: leave to oppose)* [2013] EWCA Civ 1146, [2013] 3 FCR 481, [76]–[81] (Sir James Munby P) providing an overview of the law on this point

See also *Re H-W (children: proportionality)* [2021] EWCA Civ 1451, [65]–[68] (Elisabeth Laing LJ), [79]–[81] (Lewison LJ) addressing a related point (it is not a question of whether an appeal court would make the same decision but whether the decision was wrong)

See also *R (on the application of Z and another) v Hackney London Borough Council and others* [2020] UKSC 40, [2020] 1 WLR 4327, [56], [74] (Lord Sales), [119]–[120] (Lady Arden) addressing a related point (the proper approach to reviewing proportionality is more than an appeal court concluding it would have come to a different view, albeit in a judicial review case)

15.1.2 Appeals: test: case management decisions: the correct approach

Re TG (a child) (care proceedings: biomechanical engineering evidence) [2013] EWCA Civ 5, [2013] 1 FCR 229, [23], [35]–[38] (Sir James Munby P)

[23] As will be appreciated the appeal is against a case-management decision. Before turning to the issues specific to this particular case, it may be of assistance if I rehearse some basic principles.

...

[35] (4) Fourth, the Court of Appeal has recently re-emphasised the importance of supporting first-instance judges who make robust but fair case-management decisions: *Cherney v Deripaska* [2012] EWCA Civ 1235 at [17], [30], [2012] All ER (D) 43 (Oct) at [17], [30], and *Stokors SA v IG Markets Ltd* [2012] EWCA Civ 1706 at [25], [45], [46], [2012] All ER (D) 31 (Nov) at [25], [45], [46]. Of course, the Court of Appeal must and will intervene when it is proper to do so. However, it must be understood that in the case of appeals from case-management decisions the circumstances in which it can interfere are limited. The Court of Appeal can interfere only if satisfied that the judge erred in principle, took into account irrelevant matters, failed to take into account relevant matters, or came to a decision so plainly wrong that it must be regarded

as outside the generous ambit of the discretion entrusted to the judge: *Royal & Sun Alliance Insurance plc v T & N Ltd* [2002] EWCA Civ 1964 at [37]–[38], [47], [2003] PIQR P26 at [37]–[38], [47], *Fattal v Walbrook Trustee (Jersey) Ltd* [2008] EWCA Civ 427 at [33], and *Stokors SA v IG Markets Ltd* at [46]. This is not a question of judicial comity; there are sound pragmatic reasons for this approach. First, as Arden LJ pointed out in *Royal & Sun Alliance Insurance plc v T & N Ltd* at [47]: 'Case management should not be interrupted by interim appeals as this will lead to satellite litigation and delays in the litigation process.' Second, as she went on to observe: 'the judge dealing with case management is often better equipped to deal with case management issues.' The judge well acquainted with the proceedings because he or she has dealt with previous interlocutory applications will have a knowledge of and 'feel' for the case superior to that of the Court of Appeal.

[36] Exactly the same applies in family cases. Thus in *Re C (children) (residence order: application being dismissed at fact-finding stage)* [2012] All ER (D) 223 (Nov) Thorpe LJ and I dismissed the appeal notwithstanding what I said was the 'robust view' Judge Cliffe had formed when deciding to stop the hearing. And in *Re B (a child)* [2012] EWCA Civ 1545 I refused permission to appeal from an order of Judge Miranda Robertshaw involving what I described (para [16]) as 'appropriately vigorous and robust case management'. I said (para [17]):

> 'The circumstances in which this court can or should interfere at the interlocutory stage with case-management decisions are limited. Part of the process of family litigation in the modern era is vigorous case management by allocated judges who have responsibility for the case which they are managing. This court can intervene only if there has been serious error, if the case-management judge has gone plainly wrong; otherwise the entire purpose of case management, which is to move cases forward as quickly as possible, will be frustrated, because cases are liable to be derailed by interlocutory appeals.'

As Black LJ very recently observed in *Re B (a child) (interim residence order)* [2012] EWCA Civ 1742 at [35], [2013] All ER (D) 16 (Jan) at [35]: 'a judge making case-management decisions has a very wide discretion and anyone seeking to appeal against such a decision has an uphill task.'

[37] None of this, of course, is intended to encourage excess on the part of case-management judges or inappropriate deference on the part of the Court of Appeal. There is, as always, a balance to be struck. As Black LJ went on to observe in *Re B (a child) (interim residence order)* at [48]: 'Robust case management … very much has its place in family proceedings but it also has its limits.' I respectfully agree. The task of the case-management judge is to arrange a trial that is fair; fair, that is, judged both by domestic standards and by the standards mandated by arts 6 and 8 of the European Convention for the Protection of Human Rights and Fundamental Freedoms 1950 (as set out in Sch 1 to the Human Rights Act 1998) (the Convention). The objective is that spelt out in r 1.1 of the 2010

Rules, namely a trial conducted 'justly', 'expeditiously and fairly' and in a way which is 'proportionate to the nature, importance and complexity of the issues', but never losing sight of the need to have regard to the welfare issues involved.

[38] (5) Fifth, in evaluating whether an appellant meets the high threshold required to justify its intervention, the Court of Appeal must have regard to and must loyally apply the principles laid down by Lord Hoffmann, speaking for a unanimous House of Lords, in *Piglowska v Piglowski* [1999] 2 FCR 481 at 494–495, [1999] 3 All ER 632 at 643. In relation to appeals against the exercise of discretion it is conventional to refer to the classic authority of *G v G* [1985] 2 All ER 225, [1985] 1 WLR 647. Nowadays it is perhaps more helpful to refer to *Piglowska v Piglowski*, where Lord Hoffmann, having set out the key passages from *G v G* and from the later decision of the House in *Biogen Inc v Medeva plc* (1996) 38 BMLR 149, continued with this vitally important observation:

> 'reasons for judgment will always be capable of having been better expressed ... reasons should be read on the assumption that, unless he has demonstrated the contrary, the judge knew how he should perform his functions and which matters he should take into account. This is particularly true when the matters in question are so well known as those specified in s 25(2) [of the Matrimonial Causes Act 1973]. An appellate court should resist the temptation to subvert the principle that they should not substitute their own discretion for that of the judge by a narrow textual analysis which enables them to claim that he misdirected himself.' (See [1999] 2 FCR 481 at 495, [1999] 3 All ER 632 at 643–644.)

Re B-S (children) (adoption: leave to oppose) [2013] EWCA Civ 1146, [2013] 3 FCR 481, [76]–[77] (Sir James Munby P)

The appellate approach

[76] We can take this fairly shortly because the application of *Re B* [2013] 2 FCR 525, [2013] 3 All ER 929 in various family law contexts has been considered in a number of recent judgments in this court of Black LJ and McFarlane LJ: see *Re A (Children) (Fact finding hearing: non-accidental injury)* [2013] EWCA Civ 1026, [2013] All ER (D) 75 (Jul), *Re V* [2013] 3 FCR 407, *Re P (a child) (care and placement: evidential basis of local authority case)* [2013] 3 FCR 159, *Re G (a child) (care proceedings: welfare balancing exercise: proportionality)* [2013] 3 FCR 293 and, most recently, *Re A (a child) (intractable contact dispute)* [2013] EWCA Civ 1104, [2013] 3 FCR 257.

[77] We do not need to go through *Re B* yet again, except to note that it leaves undisturbed the approach in case management appeals set out by this court in *Re TG (a child) (care proceedings: biomechanical engineering evidence)* [2013] EWCA Civ 5, [2013] 1 FCR 229, [2013] 1 FLR 1250:

see *Re B* at [45] (per Lord Wilson). Nor does the new learning in *Re B* affect the traditional approach to appeals from fact-finding determinations: *Re A (Children) (Fact finding hearing: non-accidental injury)* [2013] EWCA Civ 1026 at [34], [2013] All ER (D) 75 (Jul).

See also *Re H-L (a child)* [2013] EWCA Civ 655, [2014] 1 WLR 1160, [5]–[6] (Sir James Munby P) considering *Re TG (a child) (care proceedings: biomechanical engineering evidence)* [2013] EWCA Civ 5, [2013] 1 FCR 229

See also *Re B (a child) (care order: proportionality: criterion for review)* [2013] UKSC 33, [2013] 2 FCR 525, [45] (Lord Wilson) addressing the same point (by way of comparison to appealing care orders), see Chapter 15.1.1 Appeals: test: threshold criteria and welfare decisions: 'wrong'

15.1.3 Appeals: test: case management decisions: seek expedition if necessary

Re L (a child) [2013] EWCA Civ 1778, [2014] 2 FLR 972, [2]–[3] (Ryder LJ)

2. The proceedings have been subjected to what I can only describe as unacceptable delay which has altered the balance of procedural justice which might otherwise have underscored any orders which the court could have made …

3. The second delay is with regard to a determination by this court. Regrettably, one of the parties should have asked for a direction for expedition and alerted the court to the fact that this was a case management appeal. Ideally, such an appeal should be dealt with in such a way as to avoid the adjournment of any substantive hearing already listed in the court below and in accordance with the timetables I have referred to. Sadly, that did not happen. The consequence for the child here is regrettable. In future, it would be advisable for the Court of Appeal office to be alerted by any party who becomes aware of the possibility of delay, and, in default of any other party, the children's guardian has an independent duty to keep the court informed.

Re P and another (children) (care proceedings: appointment of expert) [2009] EWCA Civ 610, [2009] 3 FCR 65, [6]–[17] (Wall LJ) *quotation limited to* [16]

[16] The moral of this case is that the capacity of this court to act swiftly is not limited to cases which require a stay. If there is a particular reason for expedition, or if an advocate wishes to engage this court as a matter of urgency, he or she should either speak to a deputy master on the telephone, or ask to be put through to a Lord Justice with family experience. In cases of lesser urgency, but which still require expedition, the advocate should invite the office to place the papers before such a Lord Justice as a matter of urgency. The Lord Justice concerned will then, in consultation with the listing office and with colleagues, be able to give directions designed to resolve the application swiftly. We re-emphasise that the system is not to be abused. The issue must be one which requires urgent attention.

See also *Re H-L (a child)* [2013] EWCA Civ 655, [2014] 1 WLR 1160, [9] (Sir James Munby P) addressing the same point

See also *Re W (a child) (non-accidental injury: expert evidence)* [2005] EWCA Civ 1247, [2005] 3 FCR 513, [33] (Wall LJ) addressing the same point (in the context of appealing the refusal of a second expert)

15.1.4 Appeals: test: fact-finding determinations: the correct approach

Re B (a child) (care order: proportionality: criterion for review) [2013] UKSC 33, [2013] 2 FCR 525, [52]–[53] (Lord Neuberger P), [108] (Lord Kerr), [199]–[200] (Lady Hale)

[52] There is no question of this court interfering with, or indeed being asked to interfere with, the findings of primary fact made by the judge. Bearing in mind that it is a second appeal tribunal, the Supreme Court is virtually never even asked to reconsider findings of primary fact made by the trial judge. The Court of Appeal, as a first appeal tribunal, will only rarely even contemplate reversing a trial judge's findings of primary fact.

[53] As Lady Hale and Lord Kerr explain at [200] and [108] respectively, this is traditionally and rightly explained by reference to good sense, namely that the trial judge has the benefit of assessing the witnesses and actually hearing and considering their evidence as it emerges. Consequently, where a trial judge has reached a conclusion on the primary facts, it is only in a rare case, such as where that conclusion was one (i) which there was no evidence to support, (ii) which was based on a misunderstanding of the evidence, or (iii) which no reasonable judge could have reached, that an appellate tribunal will interfere with it. This can also be justified on grounds of policy (parties should put forward their best case on the facts at trial and not regard the potential to appeal as a second chance), cost (appeals on fact can be expensive), delay (appeals on fact often take a long time to get on), and practicality (in many cases, it is very hard to ascertain the facts with confidence, so a second, different, opinion is no more likely to be right than the first).

...

[108] A conclusion by a judge at first instance on which facts have been proved, and which have not been, involves the judge sifting the evidence that has been led, assessing it and then deciding whether it has brought him or her to the necessary point of conviction of its truth and accuracy. Although an appellate court is competent to hear appeals against the findings of fact that the judge has made, of necessity, its review of those findings is constrained by the circumstance that, usually, the initial fact-finder will have been exposed to a wider range of impressions that influence a decision on factual matters than will be available to a court of appeal. This is not simply a question of assessing the demeanour of the witnesses who gave evidence on factual matters, although that can be important. It

also involves considering the initial impact of the testimony as it unfolds – did it appear frank, candid, spontaneous and persuasive or did it seem to be contrived, lacking in conviction or implausible. These reactions and experiences cannot be confidently replicated by an analysis of a transcript of the evidence. For this reason a measure of deference to the conclusions reached by the initial fact finder is appropriate. Unless the finding is insupportable on any objective analysis it will be immune from review.

…

[199] The judgments involved in care proceedings are of (at least) three different types. First are the decisions on the facts: for example, who did what to whom and in what circumstances …

[200] As to the first, the position is clear. The Court of Appeal has jurisdiction to hear appeals on questions of fact as well as law. It can and sometimes does test the judge's factual findings against the contemporaneous documentation and inherent probabilities. But where findings depend upon the reliability and credibility of the witnesses, it will generally defer to the trial judge who has had the great advantage of seeing and hearing the witnesses give their evidence. The question is whether the findings made were open to him on the evidence. As Lord Hoffmann explained in *Biogen Inc v Medeva plc* [1997] RPC 1, the need for appellate caution is 'based upon much more solid grounds than professional courtesy'. Specific findings of fact are 'inherently an incomplete statement of the impression which was made upon him by the primary evidence. His expressed findings are always surrounded by a penumbra of imprecision as to emphasis, relative weight, minor qualification and nuance …' In child cases, as Lord Wilson points out, there is the additional very important factor that the court's role is as much to make predictions about the future as it is to make findings about the past.

Re H (children: findings of fact) [2021] EWCA Civ 319, [22]–[27] (Edis LJ)

22. This court will not lightly interfere with the findings of fact of a judge, nor is a challenge based on a suggested insufficiency of reasons for reaching a factual conclusion an easy one to sustain. This approach applies across all jurisdictions.

23. The reasons for this high threshold are set out in decisions of the House of Lords and the Supreme Court and have frequently been applied on appeals to this court and on appeal from the Family Court to the Family Division of the High Court. It is not necessary to set out a full historical analysis of the respect shown by appellate courts to the factual findings of the judge who has heard the evidence.

24. In *Piglowska v Piglowski* [1999] 1 WLR 1360, 1372D, Lord Hoffmann said this about how judges work when finding facts, and how their reasoned judgments should be understood:-

'If I may quote what I said in *Biogen Inc v Medeva Pic* [1997] RPC 1, 45:

> "The need for appellate caution in reversing the trial judge's evaluation of the facts is based upon much more solid grounds than professional courtesy. It is because specific findings of fact, even by the most meticulous judge, are inherently an incomplete statement of the impression which was made upon him by the primary evidence. His expressed findings are always surrounded by a penumbra of imprecision as to emphasis, relative weight, minor qualification and nuance ... of which time and language do not permit exact expression, but which may play an important part in the judge's overall evaluation."

The second point follows from the first. The exigencies of daily court room life are such that reasons for judgment will always be capable of having been better expressed. This is particularly true of an unreserved judgment such as the judge gave in this case but also of a reserved judgment based upon notes, such as was given by the district judge. These reasons should be read on the assumption that, unless he has demonstrated the contrary, the judge knew how he should perform his functions and which matters he should take into account.'

25. In *Re B (a child) (Care Proceedings: Threshold Criteria)* [2013] UKSC 33, [2013] 1 WLR 1911, the Supreme Court adopted these observations as applying, in the words of Lord Wilson JSC at [42], 'all the more strongly to an appeal against a decision about the future of a child'. Lord Neuberger JSC at [53] explained the reasons for this approach:

> '.....this is traditionally and rightly explained by reference to good sense, namely that the trial judge has the benefit of assessing the witnesses and actually hearing and considering their evidence as it emerges. Consequently, where a trial judge has reached a conclusion on the primary facts, it is only in a rare case, such as where that conclusion was one (i) which there was no evidence to support, (ii) which was based on a misunderstanding of the evidence, or (iii) which no reasonable judge could have reached, that an appellate tribunal will interfere with it. This can also be justified on grounds of policy (parties should put forward their best case on the facts at trial and not regard the potential to appeal as a second chance), cost (appeals on fact can be expensive), delay (appeals on fact often take a long time to get on), and practicality (in many cases, it is very hard to ascertain the facts with confidence, so a second, different, opinion is no more likely to be right than the first).'

26. Lord Reed summarised the position in *Henderson v Foxworth Investments Ltd* [2014] UKSC 41, [2014] 1 WLR 2600 at [67] in this way:-

> 'It follows that, in the absence of some other identifiable error, such as (without attempting an exhaustive account) a material error of law,

or the making of a critical finding of fact which has no basis in the evidence, or a demonstrable misunderstanding of relevant evidence, or a demonstrable failure to consider relevant evidence, an appellate court will interfere with the findings of fact made by a trial judge only if it is satisfied that his decision cannot reasonably be explained or justified.'

27. This court has recently re-stated the law and practice in relation to the necessity for judgments to contain reasoned conclusions as to fact, and as to the practice concerning appeals where it is suggested that they do not, see *Re O (A Child: adequacy of reasons)* [2021] EWCA Civ 149.

See also *Re A (children) (fact-finding appeal)* [2013] EWCA Civ 1026, [2014] 1 FCR 24, [33]–[34] (McFarlane LJ) addressing the same point (including highlighting the advantages of first instance judges)

See also *Re S (a child: finding of fact)* [2020] EWCA Civ 1382, [2021] 1 FCR 39, [2] (Peter Jackson LJ) addressing the same point

See also *Re B-S (children) (adoption: leave to oppose)* [2013] EWCA Civ 1146, [2013] 3 FCR 481, [76]–[77] (Sir James Munby P), see Chapter 15.1.2 Appeals: test: case management decisions: the correct approach

See also *Re N (minors) (residence orders: sexual abuse)* [1996] 1 FCR 244 (CA), 245G–246B (Butler-Sloss LJ) addressing the same point (exhorting would-be appellants to 'consider very carefully the wisdom' of attempting appeals concerning finely balanced decisions on findings of fact or credibility)

15.1.5 Appeals: test: margin of respect to first instance courts

Re T (children) [2015] EWCA Civ 453, [2016] 1 FLR 347, [41] (McFarlane LJ)

41. Secondly, I have already described the approach of the judge and the experience of the judge. Where a judge correctly identifies the legal test, says he is applying it, and says he has the evidence which justifies that conclusion, and is able in the course of the judgment to refer to that evidence, this court should be slow to interfere and say he is wrong. There is no indication here that there was an error of principle in the judge's conclusion, and to my mind he should be given a substantial margin of respect by this court in having conducted the exercise that he said he had undertaken.

Re B (a child) (care order: proportionality: criterion for review) [2013] UKSC 33, [2013] 2 FCR 525, [41]–[42] (Lord Wilson)

[41] Into its review of a trial judge's determination of a child case an appellate court needs to factor the advantages which the judge had over it in appraising the case. *In Piglowska v Piglowski* [1999] 2 FCR 481 at 494–495, [1999] 3 All ER 632 at 643 Lord Hoffmann said:

'... the appellate court must bear in mind the advantage which the first instance judge had in seeing the parties and the other witnesses. This is well understood on questions of credibility and findings of primary fact. But it goes further than that. It applies also to the judge's evaluation of those facts. If I may quote what I said in [*Biogen Inc v Medeva plc*] [1997] RPC 1 at 45:

> "The need for appellate caution in reversing the trial judge's evaluation of the facts is based upon much more solid grounds than professional courtesy. It is because specific findings of fact, even by the most meticulous judge, are inherently an incomplete statement of the impression which was made upon him by the primary evidence. His expressed findings are always surrounded by a penumbra of imprecision as to emphasis, relative weight, minor qualification and nuance ... of which time and language do not permit exact expression, but which may play an important part in the judge's overall evaluation."'

[42] Lord Hoffmann's remarks apply all the more strongly to an appeal against a decision about the future of a child. In the *Biogen* case the issue was whether the subject of a claim to a patent was obvious and so did not amount to a patentable invention. Resolution of the issue required no regard to the future. The *Piglowska* case concerned financial remedies following divorce and the issue related to the weight which the district judge had given to the respective needs of the parties for accommodation. In his assessment of such needs there was no doubt an element of regard to the future. But it would have been as nothing in comparison with the need for a judge in a child case to look to the future. The function of the family judge in a child case transcends the need to decide issues of fact; and so his (or her) advantage over the appellate court transcends the conventional advantage of the fact-finder who has seen and heard the witnesses of fact. In a child case the judge develops a face-to-face, bench-to-witness-box, acquaintanceship with each of the candidates for the care of the child. Throughout their evidence his function is to ask himself not just 'is this true?' or 'is this sincere?' but 'what does this evidence tell me about any future parenting of the child by this witness?' and, in a public law case, when always hoping to be able to answer his question negatively, to ask 'are the local authority's concerns about the future parenting of the child by this witness justified?' The function demands a high degree of wisdom on the part of the family judge; focused training; and the allowance to him by the justice system of time to reflect and to choose the optimum expression of the reasons for his decision. But the corollary is the difficulty of mounting a successful appeal against a judge's decision about the future arrangements for a child. In *Re B (a child) (sole adoption by unmarried father)* [2001] UKHL 70, [2002] 1 FCR 150, [2002] 1 All ER 641, Lord Nicholls said:

'[16] ... There is no objectively certain answer on which of two or more possible courses is in the best interests of a child. In all save the most

> straightforward cases, there are competing factors, some pointing one way and some another. There is no means of demonstrating that one answer is clearly right and another clearly wrong. There are too many uncertainties involved in what, after all, is an attempt to peer into the future and assess the advantages and disadvantages which this or that course will or may have for the child …
>
> [19] … Cases relating to the welfare of children tend to be towards the edge of the spectrum where an appellate court is particularly reluctant to interfere with the judge's decision.'

See also *Re B (a child) (sole adoption by unmarried father)* [2001] UKHL 70, [2002] 1 FCR 150, [17]–[19] (Lord Nicholls) addressing the same point (in the context of welfare decisions)

See Chapter 15.1.1 Appeals: test: threshold criteria and welfare decisions: 'wrong'

15.2 APPEALS: ADEQUACY OF REASONS

15.2.1 Appeals: adequacy of reasons: generally

Re DAM (children) [2018] EWCA Civ 386, [2018] 2 FLR 676, [5]–[8] (Peter Jackson LJ)

The decision-making process

5. Judges hearing care cases in the Family Court are engaged in one of the most difficult of all judicial tasks. The decisions are of huge significance for children and their families. The evidence is often difficult and distressing, and the level of emotion high. Achieving good case management and timely decision-making, not just for the children in the individual case but for all the children who are awaiting decisions, is a demanding challenge for the specialist judges who undertake this work.

6. In every care case, the Children Act 1989 and the Human Rights Act 1998 require the court to address a series of questions. What are the facts? Has the threshold been crossed? If so, what order is in the child's best interests? Is that outcome necessary and proportionate to the problem? There is much authority from the appeal courts about each of these questions but at its simplest every valid decision will answer them.

7. It is in the judgment that the judge's reasoning is found. There is no one correct form of judgment. Every judge has his or her own means of expression. Different cases may call for different types of judgment. Some judgments will be given at the time and others will be reserved. What is necessary in every case is that the judgment should be adequately reasoned: *Re B-S* [2013] EWCA Civ 1146 at [46]. That is a matter of substance, not of structure or form: *Re R* [2014] EWCA Civ 1625 at [18]. The judgment must enable the reader, and above all the family itself, to know that the judge asked and answered the right questions.

8. This is not to say that the structure of a judgment is irrelevant. A judgment that lacks structure or is structured in a confusing way makes the judge's reasoning harder to follow and may raise the possibility that the process by which the decision was reached was faulty. Inevitably, that increases the possibility of an appeal.

Re F [2016] EWCA Civ 546, [2016] 3 FCR 255, [22]–[23] (Sir James Munby P)

[22] Like any judgment, the judgment of the Deputy Judge has to be read as a whole, and having regard to its context and structure. The task facing a judge is not to pass an examination, or to prepare a detailed legal or factual analysis of all the evidence and submissions he has heard. Essentially, the judicial task is twofold: to enable the parties to understand why they have won or lost; and to provide sufficient detail and analysis to enable an appellate court to decide whether or not the judgment is sustainable. The judge need not slavishly restate either the facts, the arguments or the law. To adopt the striking metaphor of Mostyn J in *SP v EB and KP* [2014] EWHC 3964 (Fam), [2016] 1 FLR 228, para [29], there is no need for the judge to 'incant mechanically' passages from the authorities, the evidence or the submissions, as if he were 'a pilot going through the pre-flight checklist.'

[23] The task of this court is to decide the appeal applying the principles set out in the classic speech of Lord Hoffmann in *Piglowska v Piglowski* [1999] 2 FCR 481, [1999] 3 All ER 632, [1999] 1 WLR 1360. I confine myself to one short passage (at 1372):

> 'The exigencies of daily court room life are such that reasons for judgment will always be capable of having been better expressed. This is particularly true of an unreserved judgment such as the judge gave in this case … These reasons should be read on the assumption that, unless he has demonstrated the contrary, the judge knew how he should perform his functions and which matters he should take into account. This is particularly true when the matters in question are so well known as those specified in section 25(2) [of the Matrimonial Causes Act 1973]. An appellate court should resist the temptation to subvert the principle that they should not substitute their own discretion for that of the judge by a narrow textual analysis which enables them to claim that he misdirected himself.'

It is not the function of an appellate court to strive by tortuous mental gymnastics to find error in the decision under review when in truth there has been none. The concern of the court ought to be substance not semantics. To adopt Lord Hoffmann's phrase, the court must be wary of becoming embroiled in 'narrow textual analysis'.

See also *Re YW (a child) (adequacy of reasons)* [2021] EWCA Civ 1174, [56]–[59] (Baker LJ) providing an overview of the law on this point

See also *Re W (a child)* [2019] EWCA Civ 1966, [2020] 1 FCR 676, [77]–[78] (King LJ) addressing the same point

See also *Re B (appeal: lack of reasons)* [2003] EWCA Civ 881, [2003] 2 FLR 1035, [11] (Thorpe LJ) addressing the same point (emphasising the need to 'sufficiently explain' findings, conclusions and reasoning)

See also *Re NL (a child) (appeal: interim care order: facts and reasons)* [2014] EWHC 270 (Fam), [2014] 3 FCR 464, [63]–[72] (Pauffley J) addressing a related point (magistrates should draft their own reasons)

15.2.2 Appeals: adequacy of reasons: inviting further reasons: principles to apply

Re O (a child: judgment: adequacy of reasons) [2021] EWCA Civ 149, [2021] 2 FCR 766, [55]–[61] (Baker LJ), [69]–[70] (Peter Jackson LJ)

[55] The principal reason underpinning the practice of inviting a judge to give further reasons for a decision was identified by Lord Phillips MR in *English v Emery Reimbold*, supra, at paragraph [24]:

> 'We are not greatly attracted by the suggestion that a Judge who has given inadequate reasons should be invited to have a second bite at the cherry. But we are much less attracted at the prospect of expensive appellate proceedings on the ground of lack of reasons. Where the Judge who has heard the evidence has based a rational decision on it, the successful party will suffer an injustice if that decision is appealed, let alone set aside, simply because the Judge has not included in his judgment adequate reasons for his decision. The appellate court will not be in as good a position to substitute its decision, should it decide that this course is viable, while an appeal followed by a re-hearing will involve a hideous waste of costs.'

The practice is well established in the family court – see the decisions of this Court cited by Mr Cleary, *Re B* and the *Re A Practice Note*, and, most recently, *Re I (children)* [2019] EWCA Civ 898, [2019] 3 FCR 128, [2019] 1 WLR 5822. In the *Practice Note*, Munby LJ emphasised two points:

> '16. First, it is the responsibility of the advocate, whether or not invited to do so by the judge, to raise with the judge and draw to his attention any material omission in the judgment, any genuine query or ambiguity which arises on the judgment, and any perceived lack of reasons or other perceived deficiency in the judge's reasoning process.
>
> 17. Second, and whether or not the advocates have raised the point with the judge, where permission is sought from the trial judge to appeal on the ground of lack of reasons, the judge should consider whether his judgment is defective for lack of reasons and, if he concludes that it is, he should set out to remedy the defect by the provision of additional reasons.'

[56] In *Re I*, King LJ (at paragraph [35]) explained the importance of this procedure in family cases, in particular public law cases involving children:

> 'Judgments in care cases are often given by a judge under immense time pressure whether extemporary or reserved. It is right that issues of the type identified in the Practice Note should be raised with the judge if appropriate and, in so doing, avoid the necessity of an appeal and therefore further delay for the child the subject of care proceedings.'

[57] The practice is now expressly authorised in Family Procedure Rules Practice Direction 30A, supplementing Part 30 of the Rules which applies to appeals in family proceedings to the High Court and the family court. Under the heading 'Material omission from a judgment of the lower court', the Practice Direction provides:

> '4.6 Where a party's advocate considers that there is a material omission from a judgment of the lower court or, where the decision is made by a lay justice or justices, the written reasons for the decision of the lower court (including inadequate reasons for the lower court's decision), the advocate should before the drawing of the order give the lower court which made the decision the opportunity of considering whether there is an omission and should not immediately use the omission as grounds for an application to appeal.
>
> 4.7 Paragraph 4.8 below applies where there is an application to the lower court for permission to appeal on the grounds of a material omission from a judgment or written reasons (where a decision is made in the family court by a lay justice or justices) of the lower court. Paragraph 4.9 below applies where there is an application for permission to appeal to the appeal court on the grounds of a material omission from a judgment or written reasons (where a decision is made in the family court by a lay justice or justices) of the lower court.
>
> 4.8 Where the application for permission to appeal is made to the lower court, the court which made the decision must –
>
> (a) consider whether there is a material omission and adjourn for that purpose if necessary, and
> (b) where the conclusion is that there has been such an omission, provide additions.
>
> 4.9 Where the application for permission is made to the appeal court, the appeal court –
>
> (a) must consider whether there is a material omission; and
> (b) where the conclusion is that there has been such an omission, may adjourn the application and remit the case to the lower court with an invitation to provide additions to the judgment.'

[58] The practice is, however, subject to two important qualifications.

[59] First, it must never be used as an opportunity to re-argue the case. As Mostyn J observed in *WM v HM* [2017] EWFC 25, [2017] 3 FCR 198, [2018] 1 FLR 313 (at paragraph [39]):

> 'I would observe that the demands by [Counsel] for correction and amplification of the draft judgment went far beyond what is permissible, and amounted to blatant attempts to reargue points which I had already rejected. This practice is becoming commonplace and should be stopped in its tracks in the interests of efficiency and the conservation of the resources of the court. Suggested corrections should be confined to typographical or plain numerical errors, or to obvious mistakes of fact. Requests for amplification should be strictly confined to claimed "material omissions" within the terms of FPR PD 30A para 4.6.'

[60] That observation was made in a financial remedies case but it applies with equal force in children's cases. Mostyn J's observations were endorsed by King LJ in *Re I* (at paragraph [40]) subject to the proviso:

> 'that the term "material omission" found in paragraph 4.6 is taken to embrace the totality of the matters included in paragraph 16 of Munby LJ's Practice Note …'

[61] Secondly, there are cases where the deficiencies in the judge's reasoning are on a scale which cannot fairly be remedied by a request for clarification. As King LJ said in *Re I* (at paragraph 41):

> 'It is neither necessary nor appropriate for this court to seek to identify any bright line or to provide guidelines as to the limits of the appropriate nature or extent of clarification which may properly be sought in either children or financial remedy cases.'

But where the omissions are on a scale that makes it impossible to discern the basis for the judge's decision, or where, in addition to omissions, the analysis in the judgment is perceived as being deficient in other respects, it will not be appropriate to seek clarification but instead to apply for permission to appeal.

…

[69] I also agree with what Baker LJ has said about the circumstances in which it will be appropriate for the parties or this court to ask for further reasoning. Before granting permission to appeal in this case in December, I considered whether the judge should be asked to give additional reasons, but rejected that course. It would not have been fair to the parties or to the judge himself to ask him to revisit a decision based on a hearing that had by then taken place four to five months earlier. The process would probably have taken some considerable time in itself and would have been unlikely to avert the appeal.

[70] It is of course the responsibility of the trial judge to give sufficient reasons. But all judgments are capable of improvement and where there

has been what the Practice Direction refers to as 'a material omission from a judgment' the court is required to 'provide additions', either on its own initiative or on request. That will be particularly suitable where an issue has escaped attention or where a part of the reasoning is not fully clear or needs amplification. Where the line is to be drawn will depend on the circumstances, but there will come a point where what would be required would not be additions but foundations. In those circumstances, the difficulties in returning to the trial judge were explained by Wall LJ in *Re M-W (care proceedings: expert evidence)* [2010] EWCA Civ 12, [2010] 2 FLR when, speaking of that case, he said:

> '[47] The difficulties about the *Emery Reimbold* solution are, in my judgment, legion. I put on one side the fact that this was a reserved judgment. What strikes me with greater force – if my analysis is correct – is that the judge has made up his mind without properly considering the evidence of Dr T, Messrs M and F and the guardian. Were we thus to invite him to reconsider, he would be bound to reject their evidence. To put the matter another way, the conclusion which he has reached would render impossible a proper judicial discussion of that evidence. Equally, were the judge to change his view and find the threshold satisfied, neither the mother nor the father would have any confidence in the judge's final conclusion.'

See also *Re I (children)* [2019] EWCA Civ 898, [2019] 3 FCR 128, [25]–[41] (King LJ) addressing the same point

Re M (children) (non-accidental injury) [2008] EWCA Civ 1261, [2009] 3 FCR 674, [36]–[39] (Wall LJ) addressing the same point (identifying counsel's obligations)

See also *Re A and another (children) (fact-finding: inadequate reasons)* [2011] EWCA Civ 1205, [2012] 1 FCR 379, [13]–[18] (Munby LJ) addressing the same point

15.2.3 Appeals: adequacy of reasons: inviting further reasons: relationship with appeal notices

Re P (a child) [2018] EWCA Civ 720, [2018] 3 FCR 9, [42]–[45] (McFarlane LJ)

[42] Whilst it is, fortunately, rare for parties to encounter a situation such as that which has arisen in the present case, such circumstances do, however, occur and we have been invited to offer some limited advice or guidance.

[43] The window in which a notice of appeal may be issued under Civil Procedure Rules 1998, r 52.12(2) is tight and is, in ordinary circumstances, limited to 21 days. It is often impossible to obtain a transcript of a judgment that has been delivered orally within the 21-day period. Unfortunately, it is also the experience of this court that not infrequently problems occur in the five or six stages in the administrative chain through which a request for transcripts must proceed and it may often be months before an approved transcript is provided. Whilst it is plainly more satisfactory for the judges

of this court to work on an approved transcript, and that will normally be a pre-requisite for any full appeal hearing, the Lord or Lady Justices of Appeal undertaking evaluation of permissions to appeal in family cases are now more willing to accept a note of judgment (if possible agreed) taken by a lawyer or lawyers present in court in order to determine an application for permission to appeal rather than await delivery of an approved transcript of the judgment. It is therefore important for advocates attending court on an occasion when judgment is given to do their best to make a full note of the judgment so that, if it is needed, that note can be provided promptly to the Court of Appeal when a notice of appeal is filed.

[44] The observation set out above requires adaptation when a party seeks clarification of the judge's judgment. In such a case, it must be reasonable for the party to await the conclusion of the process of clarification before being obliged to issue a notice of appeal, unless the clarification that is sought is limited to marginal issues which stand separately to the substantive grounds of appeal that may be relied upon.

[45] Where, as here, the process of clarification fails to achieve finality within a reasonable time, it is not in the interests of justice, let alone those of the respective parties, for time to run on without a notice of appeal being issued. What is a reasonable time for the process of post judgement clarification? The answer to that question may vary from case to case, but, for my part, I find it hard to contemplate a case where a period of more than four weeks from the delivery of the request for clarification could be justified. After that time, the notice of appeal, if an appeal is to be pursued, should be issued. The issue of a notice of appeal does not, of itself, prevent the process of clarification continuing if it has not otherwise been completed. Indeed, in some case the Court of Appeal at the final appeal hearing may itself send the case back to the judge for clarification. The benefit of issuing a notice of appeal, apart from the obvious avoidance of further delay, is that the Court of Appeal may itself directly engage with the judge in the hope of finalising any further outstanding matters.

15.2.4 Appeals: adequacy of reasons: addressing parties' submissions

Re H (children: findings of fact) [2021] EWCA Civ 319, [67]–[68] (Edis LJ)

67. … There is no harm in a judge failing to mention a submission which has struck them as so obviously unsustainable that it does not deserve an answer. The function of the reasons is to explain how the decision has been arrived at, not to list the obviously unimportant things which have not influenced the outcome. Where, however, there is a substantial point or piece of evidence which points away from the judge's finding the judgment should address it, and explain how the judge has approached it.

68. Many judges set out, to some extent at least, the submissions which have been made by the advocates as part of the judgment. Often this is useful,

but it is not mandatory, and I have not done it in this judgment. However, it is incumbent on a judge who has reached a particular conclusion to identify the best points which have been made in opposition to it, and to explain why they have not prevailed. This is part of explaining that conclusion, and explains to the losing party why they have lost. There is no doubt that the judge had the father's case firmly in mind and that she rejected it for reasons which can be found in the judgment. Tackling that case more directly would have made the judgment clearer, and therefore less susceptible to challenge. In saying this, I acknowledge the enormous burdens on the judges of the Family Court, particularly in the current circumstances, hearing these very difficult cases, one after another, and then having to prepare judgments at speed, often without being given time to do so. I think that the suggestions I make should not add to the time required to prepare a judgment.

See also *Re B-M (children: findings of fact)* [2021] EWCA Civ 1371, [39]–[41] (Peter Jackson LJ) considering *Re H (children: findings of fact)* [2021] EWCA Civ 319

15.2.5 Appeals: adequacy of reasons: addressing welfare checklists

Re M (a child) [2018] EWCA Civ 240, [2018] 2 FCR 253, [62]–[63] (King LJ)

[62] It follows that in my judgment that Ground 1 must succeed and the appeal be allowed. In my judgment the judge fell into error in that he failed to highlight and sufficiently to analyse these two key aspects of the welfare checklist in his global consideration.

[63] In this by no means easy case, one difficulty for the judge, faced with largely unanimous professional advice, was to tease out what was the real extent of the feared harm. I repeat that it is well established (for example: *Re G (children)* [2006] UKHL 43, [2006] 3 FCR 1, [2006] 1 WLR 2305) that it is neither necessary nor appropriate for a judge slavishly to rehearse every factor set out in the checklists. What is necessary is that important, critical (or even decisive) factors within those checklists are adequately identified and analysed so that it can be seen what part they have played in the overall decision-making process. This of particular importance, as noted in *Re G*, in cases that are difficult or finely balanced.

See also *Re LC (placement order)* [2020] EWCA Civ 787, [2020] 2 FLR 1184, [41] (Baker LJ) considering *Re M (a child)* [2018] EWCA Civ 240, [2018] 2 FCR 253

15.2.6 Appeals: adequacy of reasons: addressing realistic options

Re FL (a child) [2020] EWCA Civ 20, [31], [33] (Baker LJ)

31. I turn next to the criticisms of the structure of the judgment. As I have said in other cases, the discipline of identifying the realistic options and

summarising the advantages and disadvantages of each before making a final order is one which should be followed whenever the court is making a decision about the future of a child: see for example *Re J (Children)* [2019] EWCA Civ 2300 para 27. A judge who fails to adopt that approach runs the risk that his decision may be challenged on the grounds that he has failed to take into account a material advantage or disadvantage of one or other of the realistic options. It does not follow, however, that a judgment in which this approach is not adopted will inevitably be overturned. This court will only allow an appeal where persuaded that the decision below was wrong or unjust because of a serious procedural or other irregularity.

...

33. In the present case, however, the recorder, having assessed the evidence, concluded that placing F with his grandmother was viable. It followed that adoption was not an appropriate option because this was not a case when nothing else would do. Applying the principles established in the case law, in particular *Re B*, it was not open to him to make a placement order. In those circumstances, I do not think his failure to set out in detail the advantages and disadvantages of adoption is by itself sufficient reason for this court to intervene.

15.3 APPEALS: PROCEDURE

15.3.1 Appeals: procedure: permission: test

Re R (a child) [2019] EWCA Civ 895, [2019] 3 FCR 274, [29]–[31] (Peter Jackson LJ)

The test for permission to appeal

[29] I finally refer to a procedural issue. In this case, the application for permission to appeal correctly set out the relevant test under CPR r 52.6(1), namely that permission to appeal may be given only where –

a. the court considers the appeal would have a real prospect of success; or

b. there is some other compelling reason why the appeal should be heard.

[30] The same criteria govern appeals within the Family Court and commentary on the equivalent provision (FPR 30.3(7)) appears in the *Family Court Practice 2018* at p 1909. When seeking permission to appeal, Mr Lord cited that commentary, which is in these terms:

> 'Real prospect of success – There are two conflicting authorities on the meaning of a "real prospect of success". In *NLW v ARC* [2012] 2 FLR 129, FD, Mostyn J held that the "real prospect of success" meant it was more likely than not that the appeal would be allowed at the substantive hearing: 'anything less than a 50/50 threshold could only mean there was a real prospect of failure'. Moor J, however, has

held that a 'real prospect of success' is one that is realistic rather than fanciful, and does not mean a greater than 50/50 chance of success. ... The weight of current first instance authority follows the approach of Moor J.'

[31] Several years on, this divergence of approach continues to be referred to in applications for permission to appeal to this court and to the High Court. This appeal represents an opportunity to resolve any remaining doubt. The test for the grant of permission to appeal on an application to the Court of Appeal or to the High Court or Family Court under the first limb of the relevant sub-rule is that the appeal would have a real prospect of success. As stated in *Tanfern v Cameron-MacDonald (Practice Note)* [2000] 1 WLR 1311, [2000] 2 All ER 801, [2001] CP Rep 8, CA at [21], which itself follows *Swain v Hillman* [2001] 1 All ER 91, [2001] CP Rep 16, [1999] CPLR 779, CA, there must be a realistic, as opposed to fanciful, prospect of success. There is no requirement that success should be probable, or more likely than not.

15.3.2 Appeals: procedure: permission: LAs[1] responding to LIP[2] permission applications

Re B (a child) [2015] EWCA Civ 1053, [12] (King LJ)

12. Care cases decide the future of the babies and children the subject of the proceedings. Appeals, even if expedited, cause a significant delay in the implementation of those decisions. Whilst the terms of 52 CPD 19 are permissible, I would suggest that in circumstances where an appellant's notice is filed by a litigant in person at the conclusion of public law proceedings, the local authority involved should, as a matter of good practice, always file a respondent's statement for the assistance of the single Lord or Lady Justice at the oral application for permission to appeal. In that way the court, when faced with the presentation of an applicant's case in what will often be a layman's format, will be in a far better position to determine whether what they have before them is an understandably anguished parent, unable to accept a proper, although unwelcome outcome, or whether there is indeed a real prospect of succeeding in establishing that in the circumstances of this particular case the trial judge went wrong.

15.3.3 Appeals: procedure: permission: extensions of time for transcripts: particular dates

Re B-M (children: findings of fact) [2021] EWCA Civ 1371, [47] (Peter Jackson LJ)

47. This court is well aware of the difficulties that there can be in obtaining transcripts promptly and of the fact that it may not be realistic for a party

1 Local authorities.
2 Litigants in person.

to decide whether to make, or for this court to be able to determine, an application for permission to appeal on the basis only of a note of judgment, particularly in a heavy case of this kind. However, I would counsel against orders extending the time for making an application for permission to appeal by reference to the receipt of a transcript rather than by reference to a specific date. In a case involving young children, an open-ended extension is unlikely to be appropriate while a fixed date may be more effective as a means of securing a transcript within a reasonable time.

15.3.4 Appeals: procedure: admitting fresh evidence

Re T and J (children) [2020] EWCA Civ 1344, [2021] 1 FCR 189, [41] (Baker LJ)

[41] The starting point for determining whether fresh evidence should be admitted by this court is the overriding objective in the Civil Procedure Rules of doing justice. As this court noted in *Sharab v AlSaud* [2009] EWCA Civ 353, [2009] 2 Lloyd's Rep 160 however, the pre-CPR cases 'remain of relevance and indeed of powerful persuasive authority'. Foremost amongst those cases is, of course, *Ladd v Marshall* [1954] 1 WLR 1489, [1954] 3 All ER 745 although in cases relating to children the principles identified in that case are said to be less strictly applied: *Re W (children)* [2009] EWCA Civ 59, [2009] 1 FCR 673, [2009] 2 All ER 1156.

Webster and another v Norfolk County Council and others; Re Webster (children) [2009] EWCA Civ 59, [2009] 1 FCR 673, [135]–[138] (Wall LJ)

Ladd v Marshall (1)

[135] Although decided more than 50 years ago, this remains the leading case on the admissibility of fresh evidence either to support an appeal or to support an application for a re-hearing. It has survived the introduction of the CPR, and its approach is binding on us, although it is, I think, generally accepted that in cases relating to children, the rules it lays down are less strictly applied.

[136] The facts of the case are, of course, a long way from the facts of the instant case. The plaintiff in an action called the defendant's wife. She said she could not remember a particular transaction. The plaintiff and his witnesses were disbelieved, and judgment was entered for the defendant. Some time later, after she had obtained a decree nisi of divorce from her husband, the defendant's wife gave a statement to the plaintiff's solicitors, accepting, in effect, that she had lied to the judge. The plaintiff sought to appeal out of time, and also asked for a re-trial. He was unsuccessful in both applications.

[137] The principles to be applied for the introduction of fresh evidence are summarised by Denning LJ as follows ([1954] 3 All ER 745 at 748, [1954] 1 WLR 1489 at 1491):

'The principles to be applied are the same as those always applied when fresh evidence is sought to be introduced. In order to justify the reception of fresh evidence or a new trial, three conditions must be fulfilled: first, it must be shown that the evidence could not have been obtained with reasonable diligence for use at the trial: second, the evidence must be such that, if given, it would probably have an important influence on the result of the case, although it need not be decisive: third, the evidence must be such as is presumably to be believed, or in other words, it must be apparently credible, although it need not be incontrovertible.'

[138] The rationale for the relaxation of the rule in children's cases is explained by Waite LJ in *Re S (minors) (discharge of care order)* [1996] 2 FCR 838 at 846, [1995] 2 FLR 639 at 646, where he says:

'The willingness of the family jurisdiction to relax (at the appellate stage) the constraints of *Ladd v Marshall* upon the admission of new evidence, does not originate from laxity or benevolence but from recognition that where children are concerned there is liable to be an infinite variety of circumstances whose proper consideration in the best interests of the child is not to be trammelled by the arbitrary imposition of procedural rules. That is a policy whose sole purpose, however, is to preserve flexibility to deal with unusual circumstances. In the general run of cases the family courts (including the Court of Appeal when it is dealing with applications in the family jurisdiction) will be every bit as alert as courts in other jurisdictions to see to it that no one is allowed to litigate afresh issues that have already been determined.'

15.3.5 Appeals: procedure: representation

Oxfordshire County Council v X and others [2010] EWCA Civ 581, [2010] 2 FCR 355, [44]–[48] (Lord Neuberger MR)

[44] Finally, there is one other matter we should mention. The natural mother and the natural father were each represented before us by counsel, who made written and oral submissions in support of the judge's decision. In addition, the local authority and the children's guardian were each represented by, respectively, counsel and a solicitor advocate, who made written and oral submissions attacking the judge's decision. As a result, two sets of full legal costs were incurred, all funded by public money, to support the case for and against the appeal.

[45] We take this opportunity to emphasise in the strongest possible terms that it is only where it is clear that there is an unavoidable conflict of interest, as a matter of law, between two parties in the same interest that they should have separate legal representation, especially where public money is involved. The fact that the parties may have different factual points, or that one party's case may be seen as stronger than the other's, or that

the parties' legal advisers may see the legal arguments or the prospects somewhat differently, are not good reasons for their incurring the expense and the court time of separate representation.

[46] When it appears that a hearing may involve more than one set of legal representation to support the same outcome, very careful consideration should be given by legal advisers as to whether there really is a need for more than one legal representation. This case provides a good example, at least on the face of it. The fact that one natural parent may have seemed to have a stronger case on the facts than the other was no reason for separate representation. First, that does not of itself, in any event, mean that there was a conflict between the two parties. Secondly, on the facts, since provision of the photograph to one parent would quite probably have resulted in its provision to the other parent, there would have been no conflict in any event. As to the local authority and the guardian they too appear to have had no legal conflict, and, at least at first blush, it is not easy to see why they needed separate representation.

[47] In our view, this is a point which should be borne in mind not merely by the legal advisers, but also by judges when awarding costs. While any decision on costs is primarily a matter for the judge hearing the matter, we would hope and expect that a judge who takes the view that legal representation was unnecessarily duplicated will at least consider allowing only one set of costs, when making an order which will potentially impinge on the public purse in one form or another.

[48] We accept, of course, that in some circumstances, it is unavoidable that two parties who support the same outcome have to be separately represented, because the conflict between them is, as a matter of law, such that they cannot be jointly represented. However, even in such cases, very careful consideration should be given to the question of whether both parties should be represented at the hearing by separate advocates. In many such cases, it should be possible for one of the parties to limit himself or herself to written representations.

See also *MB v County Council and others* [2010] EWCA Civ 324, [2010] 2 FLR 283, [30]–[31] (Wall LJ) addressing a related point (the attendance of children's guardians at appeals)

See also *Birmingham City Council v H (a minor)* [1994] 1 FCR 896 (HL), 898D–G (Lord Keith) addressing the same point

15.3.6 Appeals: procedure: appealing placement orders

Re C (a child) (adoption: leave to oppose) [2013] EWCA Civ 431, [2014] 1 FCR 50, [48]–[49] (Sir James Munby P)

[48] What this case suggests is that in every case where an application to the Court of Appeal is made for permission to appeal against the making of a placement order (or of any order consequent upon the making of a

placement order) the following steps must be taken (and when I say must I mean must).

(i) The appellant's notice must be filed as soon as possible.
(ii) Those advising the appellant must give careful thought to including in the appellant's notice any appropriate application for a stay or other interim relief.
(iii) If a transcript of the judgment being appealed against is not then available:
   (a) the appellant's notice must be accompanied by whatever note of the judgment (even if unapproved) is available; and
   (b) the transcript must be ordered immediately.
(iv) When an application for a transcript is received, the court from which the appeal is being brought must deal with the application immediately.
(v) Respondents who are parties to any application consequential upon the placement order (eg, an application for an adoption order) must immediately inform both the appellant and the Court of Appeal of:
   (a) the fact of the making of the application; and
   (b) the date(s) of any hearing of the application.

[49] I invite the relevant supervising Lords Justices and the Master of the Rolls to consider a change to the present practice in the Court of Appeal. That practice, properly followed in the present case by those handling the papers in the CAO, is that an application for permission to appeal is normally not put before a Lord Justice until the bundle is complete, in particular until the transcript is available. As a general practice that is, no doubt, entirely appropriate, but there must be cases where the delay that it necessarily imposes cannot be afforded. In the context of family appeals, the present class of case is one; another (not least because of the very strict time limits on such cases which Parliament is shortly to impose) is where the proposed appeal is against an interim case management decision in a care case. In such cases there is a powerful argument for saying that, irrespective of the contents of whatever bundle has been lodged with the CAO, the papers should be put before a Lord Justice as soon as the appellant's notice is received so that immediate directions can be given if appropriate.

15.3.7 Appeals: procedure: short-term stays

Re N (children: interim order: stay) [2020] EWCA Civ 1070, [2021] 1 FCR 175, [36]–[37] (Peter Jackson LJ)

[36] A short-term stay to enable an application to be considered by an appeal court before an order is put into effect is to be distinguished from a stay pending a decision on permission to appeal or a stay pending appeal. Applications for stays of the latter kind will be considered in accordance with the principles set out in *Hammond Suddart Solicitors v Agrichem International Holdings Ltd* [2001] EWCA Civ 2065, [2002] CP Rep

21. By contrast, a short-term stay is a purely practical remedy, distinct from the decision about permission to appeal. The correct approach for the court to take to an application of this kind was described by Wilson LJ in *Re A* [2007] EWCA Civ 899, [2008] 1 FCR 599 at [27], where he confirmed that the judge should always give serious consideration to allowing an applicant 'a narrow opportunity' to approach this court so that the opportunity for a successful appeal is not unfairly eroded:

> '[27] When a judge considers that a significant change in the arrangements for a child needs to be made in effect forthwith and learns that there is an aspiration to appeal to this court, he should in my view always give serious consideration to making an order which affords the aspiring appellant a narrow opportunity to approach this court for further, temporary, relief before his order takes effect. No doubt the welfare of the child remains paramount; but, subject thereto, the judge needs to consider whether a refusal to afford a narrow opportunity for such an approach unfairly erodes the facility for effective appeal. If he decides to afford it, he can do so either by directing that the change in the arrangements should occur only at the end (say) of the following working day or by directing that the change should occur forthwith but that execution of his order be stayed until the end (say) of the following working day. The difference seems to me to be immaterial. When, however, a judge declines to take either of these courses, there remains the facility for the aspiring appellant to approach this court by telephone and no doubt usually on notice to the other party.'

Wilson LJ then set out the arrangements that then prevailed.

[37] The current arrangements are that this court can be contacted during working hours on civilappeals.registry@justice.gov.uk between 9.00 am and 4.15 pm and out of hours through the security officers at the Royal Courts of Justice on 020 7947 6260, who will refer the matter on to the Duty Clerk. Urgent applications should whenever possible be made within court hours. Unless already filed, the applicant or the applicant's representative will be required to give an undertaking to file the necessary application form and court fee. Instructions may then be given for the transmission of essential information by email so that the application can be considered by a judge, who may decide to grant a stay, for example until the end of the following working day, to enable further documents, such as a note of the judgment and draft grounds of appeal, to be sent to the court for consideration of the merits of a further stay.

See also *Re T (children)* [2015] EWCA Civ 453, [2016] 1 FLR 347, [14]–[20] (McFarlane LJ), [46] (Ryder LJ) addressing the same point

See also Re *S (a child)* [2007] EWCA Civ 958, [2007] 2 FLR 1044, [8]–[12] (Wall LJ) addressing the same point

See also *Re M (children: interim care order)* [2018] EWCA Civ 3038, [2019] 2 FCR 665, [18] (Peter Jackson LJ) addressing the same point

15.3.8 Appeals: procedure: interim removals: time is of the essence

Re NL (a child) (appeal: interim care order: facts and reasons) [2014] EWHC 270 (Fam), [2014] 3 FCR 464, [79]–[82] (Pauffley J)

Listing the appeal

[79] The penultimate matter for comment is as to the interval between the launch of the mother's appeal and this hearing. The notice of appeal was lodged with the court on 21 November. By 26 November it had been established that Miss Watson was available to represent the local authority on three identified dates in December. That same day, Ms Myerscough notified the mother's solicitors that the guardian would be on leave between 13 December and 7 January and asked that the court be informed, as it was the very next day. A record within the court file suggests the appeal papers reached Judge Everall on 29 November, so within an entirely acceptable timescale. His manuscript note reads as follows, 'This needs an early hearing date.'

[80] A listing on 28 January was eventually given.

[81] Three things should be emphasised. Firstly, appeals from interim care orders where separation has been sanctioned are amongst the most urgent of all public law hearings: time is of the essence and the court must do its utmost to list such appeals as a matter of urgency. By that I mean within days or at the most a very few weeks. Second, that listing for the convenience of counsel, whilst desirable, should not be a factor leading to a hearing date later than the court can accommodate. Third, that the guardian's ability to attend in person at the appeal hearing is of minor significance when weighed against the requirement for an early hearing. Ms G's leave arrangements should not have resulted in any delay in fixing a date—though it was never suggested, in fact, that they should.

[82] I remain profoundly troubled that more than two months—two thirds of NL's life—has elapsed since the mother's appeal was lodged. I would hope that nothing similar will happen again here or anywhere else.

15.3.9 Appeals: procedure: case management decisions: seek expedition if necessary

See Chapter 15.1.3 Appeals: test: case management decisions: seek expedition if necessary

Index

[All references are to heading number]

F

H